The Collected Works of

Marie-Louise von Franz

MLvF

Volume 1

Marie-Louise von Franz
1915-1998

Volume 1

Archetypal Symbols in Fairytales

The Profane and Magical Worlds

Marie-Louise von Franz

Translated by Roy Freeman and Tony Woolfson
in collaboration with Emmanuel Kennedy
Revised by Mark Kyburz

CHIRON PUBLICATIONS • ASHEVILLE, NORTH CAROLINA

Logo of the Foundation of Jungian Psychology, Küsnacht Switzerland:
Fons mercurialis from Rosarium Philosophorum 1550 (Fountain of Life).

Original title: *Symbolik des Märchens – Versuch einer Deutung*
Copyright © 1952, 1960 Bern, revised edition 2015
Verlag Stiftung für Jung'sche Psychologie, Küsnacht ZH

www.ChironPublications.com

Interior and cover design by Danijela Mijailovic
Cover Image by Martina Ott
Proofreading editing by Mathabo le Roux
Printed primarily in the United States of America.
Translated by Roy Freeman and Tony Woolfson

ISBN 978-1-63051-854-7 paperback
ISBN 978-1-63051-855-4 hardcover

“But all the story of the night told over,
And all their minds transfigur’d so together,
More witnesseth than fancy’s images
And grows to something of great constancy;
But, howsoever, strange and admirable.”

Hippolyta in Shakespeare *A Midsummer Night’s Dream*
Act V, Scene 1

Foreword

During her lifetime Marie-Louise von Franz expressed the wish that her books and essays might one day appear in the form of a Collected Works. As the main heir to her literary legacy, it became the task of the Foundation for Jungian Psychology, Küsnacht, to fulfil her wish.

As a first step, the Board of the Foundation decided to publish all of her books in German in a revised, and in some cases expanded, format by the Foundation's own publishing house. For her lectures or talks, the Foundation drew upon manuscripts, tape recordings or notes, as far as these were available.

Marie-Louise von Franz left behind a handwritten list of all her publications that she herself had both compiled and commented upon. In it, she indicated which editions in her view best reflected her work. Some were first editions in English or French. In these instances, the revised German editions were adapted to reflect the foreign language publications. The texts she wrote in German were largely adopted as they were.

Occasionally, slight alterations have been made to facilitate both the reading of the text and its understanding. In some places, footnotes have been added to refer to more recent research results, or further explanations have been added in endnotes. In line with the German editions, the Foreword of each volume of the Collected Works in English includes a description of the respective circumstances surrounding its creation and translation.

The Foundation is very grateful to Alison Kappes-Bates, Hirzel, for her adaptation of the existing older English editions to the new, revised German editions. Alison Kappes-Bates, whose mother-tongue is English, was a close companion to Marie-Louise von Franz for almost 20 years, including taking care of her in her final years. Where necessary, Alison Kappes-Bates has provided new, and sometimes first, translations of parts of the German texts. Both her experience in her field of expertise and her closeness to the author ensured a quality of work that reflects the German editions.

After several years of negotiation, the Foundation succeeded in signing a framework contract for the Collected Works with Chiron Publications in Asheville, North Carolina, United States. It is planned for the Collected Works to be published in its entirety within the next ten years. The Foundation would like to thank Len Cruz (CEO), Steve Buser (COO) and Jennifer Fitzgerald

(Editor), along with all the Chiron Publications employees who have contributed to the creation of the Collected Works. The Foundation is also grateful to the graphic designer, Martina Ott, Zürich, for her creative ideas and suggestions concerning layout and cover design. The combined efforts of all those mentioned above have made it possible to realise Marie-Louise von Franz's dream and to publish her enduring works, also for an avid English readership, in a revised and attractive form.

The origin of *Archetypal Symbols in Fairy Tales* has its own special history. A German philologist by the name of Hedwig von Beit, who had a particular interest in fairytales but was unable to interpret them, asked C. G. Jung if he might help her to interpret fairy tales in his sense. Jung referred von Beit to the young Marie-Louise von Franz, who took on the task with great enthusiasm. Over a period of eight years, she worked intensively on interpreting over 900 fairytales submitted by Hedwig von Beit. After taking on the final editing and publication of the three-volume work, and to the great disappointment of Marie-Louise von Franz, Hedwig von Beit published the work solely under her own name. The publication was received enthusiastically in scientific circles.

On Jung's advice, Marie-Louise von Franz waived taking any legal action in war-torn Germany during the period of its reconstruction.

Thanks to the long-standing efforts of Emmanuel Kennedy, Gommiswald, the successor of Francke Verlag, Tübingen, eventually transferred all publishing rights of the work to the Foundation for Jungian Psychology, Küsnacht. At last, the three volumes could be republished under the name of their rightful legal author by the Foundation's own publishing house.

Emmanuel Kennedy was responsible for the new German publication of *Symbolik des Märchens* (*Archetypal Symbols in Fairy Tales*). In the Foreword, he explains in detail the origins of the work. The English translation of the present volume was provided by Roy Freeman, Lucerne, with the assistance of Anthony Woolfson, Zürich. The Foundation is very grateful to Messrs. Kennedy, Freeman and Woolfson for their efforts. The translation was revised by Mark Kyburz in fall 2022.

On behalf of the Foundation for Jungian Psychology, Küsnacht,
November 2022

PD Dr. Hansueli F. Etter,
President

◊◊◊ Table of Contents ◊◊◊

A word of caution from Marie-Louise von Franz

Many years after working on *Archetypal Symbols in Fairytales* and having her own practice as a Jungian analyst, engaging in research, and widely lecturing on fairytales, Marie-Louise von Franz wrote:

> When people have sniffed a little whiff of Jungian psychology, they may be worse than if they knew nothing, for they take a fairytale and a few of the Jungian concepts and pin these on to the figures, e.g. the ego, the anima, the Self. This is worse than no interpretation for it is unscientific, not objective, infantile, and even dishonest, because in order to be able to pin Jungian concepts onto such a being, you are obliged to twist the story. If you are careful, you will see that these concepts of Jungian psychology cannot without restriction be used for the interpretation of fairytales. When I discovered this myself I suddenly realized that it must be so because a fairytale is not produced by the psyche of the individual and is not individual material. When we speak of the anima, we think of a man as an individual, of the anima of a certain being, or the ego is the ego of a person, and the shadow means the person's inferior side. But such terms must not be sneaked into a tale where they do not belong, and if they have been conceived in the course of the observation of many individuals it is quite questionable whether the concepts can be applied to material like fairytales – material which probably has been produced by many persons, or a group.[1]

[1] Marie-Louise von Franz, *The Psychological Meaning of Redemption Motifs in Fairytales*, pp. 10–11.

Introduction

(unchanged from the Francke edition of 1997)

1 A fairytale, a story of wondrous events, can impress the thoughtful listener like a riddle that hides a secret. The tale seems to spark a desire to comprehend more, to uncover the hidden meaning. Quite often, however, trying to discover the meaning of a tale leads to different interpretations that not only engage the imagination, but inspire the intellect to explore more. It appears that all attempts to interpret fairytales have so far failed to pay adequate respect to their idiosyncratic truths and to the consistency of psychic processes of the soul[1] that shimmer out of fables, legends, and fairytales. In the present work, therefore, the authors attempt to interpret psychologically certain fundamental processes of the soul that present themselves in a series of images in fairytales.

2 The history of fairytales and their research up to the beginning of the 20th century is comprehensively covered by Johannes Bolte and George Polívka, in their *Anmerkungen zu den Kinder und Hausmärchen der Brüder Grimm*[2] among many other sources. This five-volume work offers a general and easily understandable overview of the main theories up to that time. Prior to the 18th century, a scholarly examination of fairytales and their relation to poetry, mythology, and folklore in Europe did not exist. The 19th century ushered in an age of more intensive thought and passionate veneration that spurred research into fairytales. The works of the Romantics in particular helped research to outgrow the 18th century attitude that to a large extent denied assigning any kind of meaning to fairytales. Johann Wolfgang von Goethe's (1749–1832) literary fairytales (1795) contributed in no small way to raise the value of folktales. Around the same time, Johann Gottfried von Herder (1706–1763) had sensed something of the nature of fairytales in his attempt to view them in a unified way. He considered folkloristic legends and great myths together, considering them to be the "result of popular beliefs." He writes: "where one dreams because one does not know, believes because one does not see [but] affects with the whole, undivided, and unschooled soul. . ."[3] Even

[1] [German original: *Folgerichtigkeit seelischer Vorgänge*; the German words *Seele* and *seelische* pose special problems to translate.]

[2] Bolte and Polívka, *Anmerkungen zu den Kinder- und Hausmärchen der Brüder Grimm*, vol. 1, Dieterich'sche Verlagsbuchhandlung, Th. Weicher, Leipzig, 1913; vol. 2, 1915; vol. 3, 1918; vol. 4, 1930; vol. 5, 1932.

[3] Johann Gottfried von Herder; Bernhard Suphan (ed.), *Herders Sämmtliche Werke*, vols. 1–33, Weidmann'sche Buchhandlung, Berlin, 1877–1913, vol. 9, p. 525.

earlier, Giambattista Vico (1668–1744) had expressed similar, if not identical, thoughts in that he viewed myths – referring not only to Greek myths but also fables[4] – as catching glimpses of general concepts or images emerging from powerful fantasies and exhibiting similar ideas on the plane of whole civilizations. He considered fantasy to be "extended or pooled memory."[5]

3 The Brothers Grimm, Wilhelm and Jacob, were the next authors to take up the serious study of fairytales. From the 19th Century onwards, their insights shaped the opinions of fairytale collectors and fundamentally dominated fairytale research. Their narrative style set the standard for fairytale collection in Europe for years.[6] Wilhelm Grimm, in his general considerations at the end of the *Anmerkungen zu die Kinder- und Hausmärchen der Brüder Grimm*[7] wrote:

> 4 The correlation between fairytales of different epochs and widely separated regions, as well as cultures closely bordering each other, is based partly on underlying ideas and representations of particular characters, and partly on special interrelationship and solutions to the incidents. . ..
>
> 5 All these together are like a spring whose depths one does not know, but from which everyone can draw according to their needs.[8]

6 He also saw in fairytales "....................vestiges of beliefs reaching back to the oldest times, which speak of things beyond the senses in terms of images."[9]

7 It is not the intention of the present work to discuss the numerous theories that have evolved since the fairytale research of the Brothers Grimm. Here we will mention only a few of the most influential ideas. To explain the remarkable similarities of the motifs in fairytales of all lands, investigations

---

[4] Italien *favelle*, new Italian *favole*.

[5] Cf. Giambattista Vico, *Die neue Wissenschaft über die gemeinschaftliche Natur der Völker (Principi di Scienza Nuova)*. Nach d. Ausg. v. 1744, übers. and eingel. v. Erich Auerbach. 2. Auflage, W. de Gruyter, Berlin, 1744/2000, pp. 66–67, 79, 96, 168 [pages in the German or Italian edition; for an English edition, see Giambattista Vico, *Principi di Scienza Nuova (The New Science of Giambattista Vico)*, Cornell University Press, Ithaca, 1968; see also Giambattista Vico, *Scienza Nuova (The New Science) (edition 1725)*, Cambridge University Press, Cambridge UK, 2002, trans by Leon Pompa. Vico believed that societal life depends primarily on the power of human imagination to narrate the meaning of events through myths. Rational forms of understanding then gradually develop from these mythical commonalities.] Cf. also Adolf Thimme, *Das Märchen. Handbücher zur Volkskunde*, Verlag von Wilhelm Heims, Leipzig, 1909, vol. 2.

[6] See Werner Lincke, *Das Stiefmuttermotiv im Märchen der germanischen Völker*, Verlag Dr. Emil Ebering, Berlin, 1933, German. Studien, nos. 142 and 163.

[7] Commentaries (*Anmerkungen*) to *The Nursery and Household Tales of the Brothers Grimm* (hereafter referred to as *KHM* after the German title).

[8] Wilhelm and Jakob Grimm, eds., *Kinder- und Hausmärchen, gesammelt durch die Brüder Grimm*, (*MdW*), vol. 3, ed. by Fr. v. d. Leyen, Verlag der Dieterich'schen Buchhandlung, Göttingen, 1856, pp. 405–406.

[9] *KHM*, vol. 3, p. 409. German *übersinnlich* can also be translated as "supernatural."

focused on the search to find the "original homeland" of fairytales. Theodor Benfey (pp. 1809–1881) proposed India as the land of origin and this was largely accepted by many researchers.[10] Other scholars attempted to situate the original homeland in Egypt or Babylon,[11] mostly due to information from anthropological and ethnological research. It soon became obvious, however, that the question of a so-called original homeland was inadequately posed. Similarly untenable are the so-called natural-mythological explanations, according to which images in myths and fairytales represent either astronomical or meteorological phenomena, or organic-vegetative life.[12] Although there is no doubt that many mythological images allude to various natural phenomena, a one-sided reduction of their meaning to physical processes has been shown to be incorrect.[13]

8 Ethnological-anthropological research also provided fruitful initial hypotheses to explain myths and fairytales. It revealed links between many fairytale motifs and primitive customs, rituals, rites, and magical beliefs of the soul.[14] (The attempt, on the other hand, to explicate myths as mere copies of these rituals must be rejected as inadequate, since it does not account for the individual forms and their modifications.) On the basis of these interrelations, Adolf Bastian (1826–1905), proposed that the universal occurrence and similarities of mythological thought of different cultures be explained by principal structural similarities of human psychic life.[15] Bastian saw in the mythical representations what he called "elementary ideas," the "raw material... which, according to our present knowledge, we cannot go beyond."[16] He writes

---

[10] See Bolte and Polívka, *Anmerkungen*, vol. 4, pp. 289ff.; Ibid., vol. 5, p. 249. On the shortcomings of Benfey's theory, and for a summary of refutations, see Thimme, *Märchen*, pp. 15ff., 21–22, 69ff.

[11] See further Bolte and Polívka, *Anmerkungen*, vol. 5, p. 256.

[12] In general, see Bolte and Polívka, *Anmerkungen*, vol. 5, pp. 253ff. and the editorial group of the Mythological Library.

[13] Wundt, *Völkerpsychologie. Eine Untersuchung der Entwicklungsgesetze von Sprache, Mythus und Sitte*, pp. 5 and 53ff.; Elard Hugo Meyer, "Germanische Mythologie," in: *Lehrbücher d. Germ. Philologie*, vol. 1, Mayer & Müller, Berlin, 1891, p. 293; see further Ludwig Laistner, *Das Rätsel der Sphinx. Grundzüge einer Mythengeschichte*, Verlag Wilhelm Hertz, Berlin, 1889, vol. I, p. Vii, vols. 1–2; Otto Rank, "Der Mythus von der Geburt des Helden. Versuch einer psychologischen Mythendeutung," in: *Schriften zur angewandten Seelenkunde*, no. 5, ed. By Sigmund Freud, Franz Deuticke, Leipzig and Vienna, 1922, p. 6; Herbert Silberer, *Problems of Mysticism and Its Symbolism*, Moffat, Yard and Company, New York, 1917, Trans. Smith Ely Jelliffe, p. 207; C. G. Jung, "The Structure of the Psyche," in: Sir Herbert Read et al. (eds.), *Collected Works, Vol. 8: The Structure and Dynamics of the Psyche*, 2nd ed. Princeton University Press, Princeton, CW 8 ¶323ff.

[14] Cf. Edward B. Tylor, *Primitive Culture: Researches into the Development of Mythology, Philosophy, Religion, Art and Custom* (two volumes), John Murray, London 1871; Theodor Waitz, *Anthropologie der Naturvölker*, Parts 1 and 2, Friedrich Fleischer, Leipzig, 1859 (cf. especially vol. 1); Andrew Lang, *Custom and Myth*, 2nd edition. Longmans, Green, and Co., London, 1885; see also Andrew Lang, *Myth, Ritual, and Religion*, Longmans, Green, and Co., London, 1887. For application of these results in particular to fairytales by Saintyves, Nodermann, Naumann, Huet, see the literature in Bolte and Polívka, *Anmerkungen*, vol. 5, p. 257.

[15] [For more on Bastian's concepts of "psychic unity," see Klaus-Peter Köpping, *Adolf Bastian and the Psychic Unity of Mankind*, Lit Verlag, Münster, 2005.]

[16] Adolf Bastian, *Beiträge zur vergleichenden Psychologie. Die Seele und ihre Erscheingungsweisen in der Ethnographie*, Ferd. Dümmler's Verlagsbuchhandlung (Harrwitz und Grossmann), Berlin, 1868, p. 62; see also pp. 63, 70, 71.)

of the *elementary material (of thought) in the spirit of natural people*,[17] which one should study with statistical-natural science methods. The elemental ideas, which he also called a "mirroring reflex image" in the human soul, appear in numerous ethnic derivations, which he designated as "ethnic elementary ideas" or their different local elaborations as "folk ideas."[18] Due to his lack of knowledge of unconscious psychic processes of the soul in mankind, it was impossible for Bastian to provide further evidence for the emergence and functioning of his elementary ideas. He could go no further than asserting their existence.[19]

9 The hypothesis of fairytale motif migration cannot, in spite of everything, be tossed overboard since distant peregrinations of single motifs can indeed be substantiated. These findings have, with a certain justification, led numerous researchers to renounce fundamental questions concerning the emergence and meaning of myths and fairytales and to turn to individual literary-historical, philological, aesthetic, and folk psychological studies.[20] Here too we include the Finnish school,[21] with its commendable catalogues of motif statistics. We note, however, that their hope of thereby finding a particular primordial form and original homeland for individual fairytales is misguided.[22]

10 In contrast to those researchers who discount the question of meaning in fairytales, individual devotees have emerged from time to time. Often labelled as unscientific, these writers have aspired to prove a deep, primal, mysterious, and universal wisdom in the tales.[23] Anthroposophic attempts to interpret fairytales also follow similar assumptions and often contain perceptive interpretations.[24] Even if we can only partly agree, we grant that the incentive

---

[17] *"Elementarstoffen (des Denkens) im Geiste des Naturmenschen," ibid.*, p. 71.

[18] Cf. Adolf Bastian, *Die Verbleibs-Orte der abgeschiedenen Seele, Ein Vortrag in erweiterter Umarbeitung*, Weidmannsche Buchhandlung, Berlin, 1893, pp. 5–6, 83, 90, 94.

[19] Ibid., *Verbleibs-Orte*, Berlin, 1893, p. 30. Cf. for more about the acceptance and resistance to Bastian's ideas, see Hanns Bächtold-Stäubli, *Handwörterbuch des deutschen Aberglaubens*, W. de Gruyter & Co., vols. I–VII, Berlin and Leipzig 1927–1936. Vols. VIII–X, Berlin, 1936–1942. Hermann Güntert takes up Bastian's ideas and speaks of "mythical monads" (*Mythen-monaden*); see Güntert, *Der arische Weltkönig und Heiland. Bedeutungsgeschichtliche Untersuchun- gen zur indoiranischen Religionsgeschichte und Altertumskunde*, Max Niemeyer, Halle a. S., 1923, p. 391.

[20] Among other authors, see J. Bédier, G. Huet, W. Mannhardt, R. Köhler, P. Herrmann, Rittershaus, A. Bonus, Van Genepp, A. H. Krappe, J. de Vries, H. Hamann, P. Cassel, F. S. Krauss, L. Frobenius, H. Usener, A. Wünsche, L. F. Weber, R. Petsch, M. Grünbaum, A. Van Deursen, A. Olrik, A. von Loewis of Menar, F. Panzer, A. Wesselski, W. Lincke, E. Tegethoff, B. Schweitzer, H. de Boor, M. Lüthi. In general, see Bolte and Polívka, *Anmerkungen*, vol. 5, Leipzig, pp. 257ff.; see also Bolte and Mackensen, *Handwörterbuch des deutschen Märchens*, vols. 1–2, W. de Gruyter & Co., Berlin and Leipzig, 1930/1934. Among other entries, see *Anthropologische Märchentheorie* [anthropological theory of fairytales], *Anordnungsprinzipien* [ordering principles], *Geographisch-historische Methoden* [geographic-historical methods], *Formsinn* [sense of form], *Einfache Formen* [simple forms], *Fassung* [framework, setting].

[21] Among others, see K. Krohn, A. Aarne, St. Thompson, and Andrejev. For details and references, see J. Bolte and G. Polívka, *Anmerkungen*, vol. 5, Leipzig, 1932 pp. 263f. Cf. the still [as of 2010] active *Folklore Fellow Communications* published by the Kalevala Institute of the University of Turku, Finland.

[22] Concerning the objections of A. Wesselski, F. Panzer, and others, see Bolte and Polívka, *Anmerkungen*, vol. 5, p. 264.

[23] For examples, see Bolte and Polívka, *Anmerkungen*, vol. 5, p. 256.

[24] References worth mentioning include Rudolf Steiner, "Märchendeutungen," lecture delivered in Berlin on 26 December 1908; see also Rudolf Steiner, "Märchendichtungen im Lichte der Geistesforschung," in: *Ergebnisse der Geistesforschung*, vol. 11, ed. By Marie Steiner, Zbinden und Hügin,

for these attempts springs in and of itself from a correct feeling for the deep meaning of fairytales. It is the same feeling that many people unswervingly sense as arising from the fairytale itself, since the soul unconsciously resonates with the narrative content.

11 Bastian and the anthropological school, including the so-called animists (*Animisten*),[25] extended the horizons of fairytale research and placed the human being and the psychic-spiritual[26] structure at the center of attention. They also urged the application of empirical methods of research instead of the rationalistic-deductive analysis of their predecessors.[27] They thus paved the way for a psychological theory of fairytales based on objective facts. This was possible because the phenomenon of the unconscious[28] had now been discovered and included in the scientific horizon. Numerous observed facts that previously could not be rationally integrated into the prevailing view of conscious psychology were now open for clarification. This also resolved the difficulty that many researchers had when their relatively good interpretations of a rite or folktale did not find confirmation in the conscious minds of the traditional folk.

12 In a certain opposition to the main direction of the old "rational psychology," which was essentially limited to the investigation of sensory activities and rational processes and only conditionally accepted the hypothesis of the unconscious,[29] Arthur Schopenhauer (1788-1860) and Carl Gustav Carus (1789-1869) indicated the existence of the unconscious as a psychic form of life that is not identical to the ego. Carus stated that consciousness arises secondarily out of the unconscious. In his writings[30] one finds that he thought the spirit[31] emerged out of a plurality of persistent ideas, which he compared to cell monads.[32] From their combination, there evolves

---

Basel, 1942, pp. 4–8; Maria Brie, *Das Märchen im Lichte der Geisteswissenschaft*, Preuß and Jünger (Inh. Kropff and Weinberger), Breslau, 1922, pp. 3–12, 22ff.; Walter Ebersold, *Unsere Märchen*, Roter Reiter-Verlag, Zürich, 1946, esp. Pp. 45–47; Rudolf Meyer, *Die Weisheit der deutschen Volksmärchen*, Verlag der Christengemeinschaft, Stuttgart, 1935, esp. Pp. 13–22, 99–100, 126–128, 204; Rudolf Meyer, *Die Weisheit der Schweizer Märchen*, Columban-Verlag, Schaffhausen, 1944, esp. Pp. 9ff., 17ff., 41, 115.

[25] E. Tylor, *Primitive Culture*, London, 1871; see further Robert Ranulph Marett, *The Threshold of Religion*, London, 1909; John Murphy, *Primitive Man: his Essential Quest*, London, 1927, and to a certain degree also James Frazer, *The Golden Bough: A Study in Magic and Religion*, New York, 1922.

[26] [In German, *seelisch-geistig.*]

[27] Concerning the limited use of these theories, see Marett's attack against Tylor related to the meaning of the word "animism," *Encyclopaedia Britannica* under *Animism.*

[28] In the psychology of C.G. Jung, "the unconscious" refers to "the interior world of the psyche" (*Symbols of Transformation*, CW 5, ¶450). [The term pertains here exclusively to "the *collective* unconscious," that is, the world of the archetypes common to the human psyche in general.]

[29] Cf. C.G. Jung, "On the Nature of the Psyche," in: Sir Herbert Read et al. (eds.), *Collected Works, Vol. 8: The Structure and Dynamics of the Psyche*, 2nd edition. Princeton University Press, Princeton, CW 8 ¶343–355.

[30] Cf. Carl Gustav Carus, *Psyche, zur Entwicklungsgeschichte der Seele*, Kröners Taschenausgabe, no. 98, Leipzig, 1931, p. 106. For further examples, see pp. 72, 244, 377, 396.

[31] [*Geist*, there is no unambiguous translation of *Geist* or *geistigen*, it can mean spirit, mind, or psyche; as well as, ghost and ghostly.]

[32] [In German: *Zellenmonaden.*]

a spiritual[33] organism that is aware of the self. The unconscious is the more general – or the more connected to the world – part of the soul, and also the further basis for consciousness.[34] He writes that one can:

13 > . . . compare the life of the soul with ceaseless ever-widening circles of a greater current, which are lit only at one tiny place by sunlight, that is, from consciousness. That the unconscious is the basis of conscious life of the soul can be recognized by observing that the larger part of our conscious thoughts are time and again submerged back into unconsciousness and only partly and then singly do they appear again in consciousness.[35]

14 Since the unconscious is connected to the world, dreams contain a certain truth, which is observed by consciousness *in the form of a symbol* as it emerges from the unconscious.[36]

15 Unfortunately, Carus's insight did not bear fruit for fairytale research. In contrast, near the end of the 19th Century, Ludwig Laistner (1845-1896) undertook in his *Das Rätsel der Sphinx*[37] – notably alone and independently – the attempt to explain fairytales, local legends, and folkloristic motifs as nightmare phenomena.

16 Only after Sigmund Freud (1856-1939) scientifically and systematically researched the phenomenon of the unconscious and, in particular, its main expression in dreams, did fresh light fall on the problem of fairytales. A number of notable works emerged from Freud's school including Franz Riklin, "Wunscherfüllung und Symbolik";[38] Karl Abraham, "Traum und Mythus";[39] Otto Rank, *The Myth of the Birth of the Hero* and *Psychology and the Soul*;[40] Ernest Jones, *Der Alptraum*;[41] Dr. Aigremont, *Volkserotik and Pflanzenwelt* and *Fuss- and Schuh-Symbolik*;[42] Geza Roheim, *Spiegel-*

---

[33] [*geistiger*. Alternate translation: psychic.]
[34] C.G. Carus, *Psyche*, Leipzig, 1931, p. 216 [referring to ". . . the three developmental steps of the soul: unconsciousness, worldly consciousness (*Weltbewusstsein*), and self consciousness."]
[35] Ibid., *Psyche*, pp. 1–2.
[36] Ibid., *Psyche*, pp. 216–17.
[37] See above, fn. 36.
[38] Cf. Franz Riklin, "Wunscherfüllung und Symbolik im Märchen," in: *Schriften zur angewandten Seelenkunde*, no. 2, ed. Sigmund Freud, 1908, esp. p. 5.
[39] Cf. Karl Abraham, "Traum und Mythus," eine Studie zur Völkerpsychologie, in: *Schriften zur angewandten Seelenkunde*, no. 4, ed. Sigmund Freud, 1909, esp. pp. 4–9.
[40] Cf. Translations of Otto Rank, "Der Mythus von der Geburt des Helden. Versuch einer psychologischen Mythendeutung," in: *Schriften zur angewandten Seelenkunde*, no. 5, ed. Sigmund Freud, 1922, and Rank, *Seelenglaube und Psychologie. Eine prinzipielle Untersuchung über Ursprung, Entwicklung und Wesen des Seelischen*, 1930, esp. pp. 103–06.
[41] Cf. Ernest Jones, *Der Alptraum in seiner Beziehung zu gewissen Formen des mittelalterlichen Aberglaubens*, Psychoanalytischer Verlag, Leipzig, 1912.
[42] Dr. Aigremont, *Volkserotik und Pflanzenwelt. Eine Darstellung alter wie moderner erotischer und sexueller Gebräuche, Vergleiche, Benennungen, Sprichwörter, Redewendungen, Rätsel, Volkslieder, erotischen Zaubers und Aberglaubens, sexueller Heilkunde, die sich auf Pflanzen beziehen*, Erster Band, Hallescher Verlag für Literatur und Musik, Gebr. Trensinger, Halle a. S., 1909; see also Dr. Aigremont,

zauber;[43] and Georg Jacob, *"Märchen und Traum"*.[44] In these works, attempts were made to uncover the same psychic motifs in fairytales and legends that one finds in dreams of modern people. The predominant view that sees these motifs as erotic tendencies proves unsatisfactory, however, since the meaning of the unconscious material is not thereby exhaustively explained. Herbert Silberer tried again in his *Problems of Mysticism* to elaborate not only a reductive but also an anagogic symbol interpretation.[45]

17 The main virtue of Freudian psychology for fairytale research is that it revealed the principal affinity of dreams of modern people to the conceptual world of children and archaic peoples. Freud conjectured that there is a meaning in the images of dreams and myths that can also be expressed in conscious language. Differing from this view, Carl Gustav Jung (1875–1961) saw in these images the expression of a psychic basic structure[46] that, working unconsciously, triggers spiritual and instinctual functions of the soul.[47] The forces which underlie these images Jung called *archetypes*:[48]

> 18 These are the universal dispositions of the mind, and they are to be understood as analogous to Plato's forms (*Eidola*), with which the mind organizes its contents. One could also describe these forms as *categories* in analogy to logical categories, which are always and

---

Fuss- und Schuh-Symbolik und -Erotik: Folkloristische und sexualwissenschaftliche Untersuchungen. Mit einem Geleitwort von Dr. Friedrich S. Krauß, Deutsche Verlags-Aktien-Gesellschaft, Leipzig, 1909.

43 Cf. Géza Róheim, *Spiegelzauber,* vol. 6, Internationaler Psychoanalytischer Verlag, Leipzig and Vienna, 1919, Internat. Psychoanalytische Bibliothek.

44 Cf. Georg Jacob, "Märchen und Traum. Mit besonderer Berücksichtigung des Orients," in: *Beitr. z. Märchenforschung d. Morgenlandes,* vol. 1, ed. Georg Jacob and Theodor Menzel, 1923.

45 Cf. H. Silberer, *Problems of Mysticism,* New York, 1917, p. 216. Note the rather severe application using the example of a fairytale in *ibid,* pp. 217ff. Cf. also the general concept of symbols in Herbert Silberer, "Über die Symbolbildung," in: *Jahrbuch für psychoanalytische und psychopathologische Forschungen,* vol. 3, eds. Ernst Bleuler and Sigmund Freud,1912, pp. 662–682.

46 [*seelischen Grundstruktur*]

47 On the importance of an *auseinandersetzung* [consciously working through one's own unconscious figures, emotions, drives, etc.] as the way for modern people to experience the meaning of mythological images, see in general C.G. Jung, *Collected Works* (CW) *passim*, especially C.G. Jung, "Psychological Commentary on 'The Tibetan Book of the Dead,'" in: Sir Herbert Read et al. (eds.), *Psychology East and West*, 2nd edition. Princeton University Press, Princeton CW 11, CW11 ¶831ff.; see also C.G. Jung, "Psychologie und Religion," in: *Zur Psychologie westlicher und östlicher Religion,* GW 11, 2nd edition. Rascher Verlag, Zürich und Stuttgart, 1963, ¶106f. See further H. Zimmer: "The merit of the new depth psychology is that it unearths that which is timeless in us, in a form appropriate to our times, so that we can comprehend it and live by it. This psychology and the analytic method by which it operates constitute no more than a symbolic and visual means of obtaining knowledge about our being, it is a science born of our time and our predicament with which it will also pass away, but for that very reason it is to us more intelligible than any other set of symbols. . . It is our way of giving name and form to the intangible reality within us, it is the special form of māyā through which the reality of the soul can manifest itself in our historical moment" (Heinrich Zimmer, "On the Significance of Indian Tantric Yoga," in: *Spiritual Disciplines: Papers from the Eranos Yearbooks,* Princeton University Press, Princeton NJ, 1960, Bollingen XXX-4, pp. 28–29.) Cf. also Heinrich Zimmer, *The King and the Corpse, Tales of the Soul's Conquest of Evil,* ed. Joseph Campbell, Princeton University Press, Princeton NJ, 1972.

48 Cf. C.G. Jung; Sir Herbert Read et al. (eds.), *Psychological Types,* 2nd edition. Princeton University Press, Princeton CW 6 ¶746. Cf. further C.G. Jung, CW 11, *Tibetan* ¶845 and C.G. Jung, CW 8, *On the Nature of the Psyche* ¶397ff.

> everywhere present as the basic postulates of reason. Only, in the case of our "forms," we are not dealing with categories of reason but with categories of *imagination*. As the products of the imagination are always in essence visual, their forms must, from the outset, have the character of images and moreover of *typical* images, which is why, following St. Augustine, I call them "archetypes."[49]

19 Noteworthy here is that Meister Eckhart (ca. 1260–ca. 1328) also uses this concept and indeed he sees in these primordial images (*Urbildern*) the only possibility for the soul to realize itself. In his "Sermon on Ephesians 4:23," he wrote:

20

> Now St. Augustine says that together with the essence of the soul in her highest part, which is called *mens* in Latin or "mind", God created a power which the masters call a container or shrine of spiritual forms or formal images.[50]

21 And in another place Meister Eckhart writes:

> Whenever the power of the soul touches creatures, so do they take this and create images in the likeness of the creature and take this unto themselves. From this so do creatures know. . . And from the present images so do they approach the creatures, when the image is a thing, that the soul creates with the powers. If it is a stone, or a horse, or a human being, or whatever they call it, so do they take the image for that which they have drawn and make out of these one.[51]

22 Archetypal images can manifest spontaneously anytime and anywhere.[52] This fact makes it unnecessary to look for explanations in speculative

---

[49] C.G. Jung, CW 11, *Tibetan* ¶845. Cf. further C.G. Jung, "Concerning the Archetypes, with Special Reference to the Anima Concept," in: *The Archetypes of the Collective Unconscious*, CW 9/I, 2nd edition. Routledge and Kegan Paul, London, 1969, ¶111ff.; C.G. Jung, CW 11, "Psychology and religion," ¶88; C.G. Jung, CW 9i, *"Mother Archetype"* ¶148 f. Concerning seeing the being of things with the "eye of the soul" in the ancient mysteries, see Hans Leisegang, *Die Gnosis*, Kröners Taschenausgabe, vol. 32, Alfred Kröner Verlag, Leipzig, 1924, p. 9. In *Problems of Mysticism*, New York, 1917 p. 255, Silber mentions the so-called *initial motifs* of the *elementary types*. For information on the history of the concept of the archetype, see the clarifying study by Paul Schmitt, "Archetypisches bei Augustin und Goethe," in: *Eranos-Jahrbuch 12: Studien zum Problem des Archetypischen*, ed. Olga Fröbe-Kapteyn, 1945, pp. 95ff.

[50] Meister Eckhart (trans. Davies), *Selected Writings*, London, 1994 p. 235. [For the original German, see Meister Eckhart, *Deutsche Mystiker des vierzehnten Jahrhunderts. 2. vols.; see esp.* vol. 1, ed. by Franz Pfeiffer, Vandenhoeck & Ruprecht, Göttingen, 1906, p. 318 on Ephes, IV. 23.]

[51] For the original, see Meister Eckhart (Pfeiffer), *Predigten*, Göttingen, 1906, p. 3 on Wisdom 18:14.

[52] In contrast to *the idea*, the archetype does not lend itself to abstract rational processing: "The primordial image has one great advantage over the clarity of the idea, and that is its vitality. It is a self-activating organism 'endowed with generative power'" (C.G. Jung, CW 6, *Psychological Types* ¶754). One could also say "that it [the primordial image] seems to strive for its own realization, being sensed

hypotheses about the migration of fairytale motifs. The similarity of the motifs is related to the structural identity of the human psyche. The archetype itself is an indeterminate form, not identical with any specific mythological image; the latter is one possible form in which the underlying archetype can manifest itself. We can never know what an archetype is, *in and of itself;* we are dependent upon the multitude of individual forms that make the archetype visible. Fairytales, with their myriad and remarkable motifs and deeds that time and again group together, offer a rich source of these images. These tales are like colorful blossoms on the gigantic tree of the spiritual and psychic inner life of human beings. In the present work we cannot, unfortunately, recount the individual tales in all their diversity and beauty, but only briefly sketch their variations. We will try, however, not to obscure their abundance and riches.

23 The path taken to approach the meaning of fairytales is similar to that taken to interpret dreams. A dream image taken out of context does not lend itself to being replaced by a single, unequivocal rational concept, since it is in the nature of these images that they express facts of the soul in specific concrete forms, which can only be approximately described through a long process of conscious realization. Johann Jakob Bachofen (1815–1887) in his book, *An Essay on Mortuary Symbolism*, writes:

> 24 The symbol plucks all the strings of the human spirit at once; speech is compelled to take up a single thought at a time. The symbol strikes its roots in the most secret depths of the soul; language skims over the surface of the understanding like a soft breeze. The symbol aims inward; language outward. Only the symbol can combine the most disparate elements into a unified impression. Language deals in successive particulars; it expresses bit by bit what must be brought home to the soul at a single glance if it is to affect us profoundly.[53]

25 In order to uncover the meaning of the symbol's concise form, we amplified single fairytale motifs using a wide range of comparative material. To check the correctness of an interpretation of an image or motif we can follow the complete course of the fairytale. Only when we can apply a consistent interpretation to the whole fairytale, that is, when the meaning follows not only a single image, but fits the whole story and reflects a coherent

---

by the mind as an active determinant" (C.G. Jung, CW 6, *Psychological Types* ¶736). [Jung later preferred the term *archetype* to the terms *primordial* and *archaic image.*]

[53] Johannn Jakob Bachofen, "An Essay on Ancient Mortuary Symbolism," in: *Myth, Religion, & Mother Right, Selected Writings of J. J. Bachofen.* Transl. Ralph Manheim. Bollingen Series LXXXIV, Bollingen, Princeton University Press, Princeton, NJ, 1973, pp. 49–50.

developmental sequence,[54] and arises out of the fullness of an extended series of motifs, can we assume that we have captured the essentials.[55] Just as we must take dreams in their entirety to find their meaning, and just as a painting not only comprises a single figure, so we must consider all parts of a dream or a painting and their relationships to each other together to be the artist's intent to express something inexpressible. Similarly, it is necessary to take all their various forms into account when searching out the meaning of fairytales. As little as it is possible to study drama and only be interested in the movements of the main characters, so it is in fairytales: no single thread creates the whole fabric. All motifs in fairytales have a specific and noninterchangeable place in the total structure. It can even be that the same motif at different places in the tale must be interpreted differently.[56] A purely scholarly collection of similar motifs is only the initial step. The next step is to investigate the special functions of the images in the fairytale in relationship to the whole story. Thus one can encompass the whole and interpret the closed circle of the images within this context. A coherent meaning appears only in relation to *all* the characters of a fairytale.

26 When considering what happens in a fairytale, one notices that the sense of space, time, and causality is missing,[57] a characteristic, which also appears in the thought and behavior of primitive peoples and children, and which Lucien Lévy-Bruhl has called *pre-logical thought*.[58] It corresponds to that spiritual state when humans had not completely developed out of the unconscious into consciousness, and so confirms the view of fairytales as quasi-primeval happenings, acts of archetypal figures, the observed natural relationship of childlike peoples to the nature of fairytales.

---

[54] [*Sinneinheit*, literally "a unit of meaning."]

[55] The truth of our statements still remains contingent since: "Those who argue reveal more about their own limits and prejudices, especially when a particular meaning inspires them to think they can draw gold from those depths." Heinrich Zimmer, *Weisheit Indiens.* Märchen und Sinnbilder, L. C. Wittich Verlag, Darmstadt, 1938, p. 11. See also p. 101. Cf. further Heinrich Zimmer, *"Maya" der indische Mythos*, Deutsche Verlags-Anstalt, Stuttgart and Berlin, 1936, pp. 169–170.

[56] Cf. also Zimmer, "Each scene and object in them (myths and fairytales), in fact everything that occurs, can appear as a sign not merely for differences, but even for the diametric opposites, each in its own right, each according to the context and interrelations in which it stands, according to the place and within its series of signs, and according to its position in the bend of the curve [*Schwunge der Kurve*]." (*Maya*, Stuttgart and Berlin, 1936, p. 168.)

[57] Cf. among others, C.G. Jung, CW 8, *On the Nature of the Psyche* ¶405fn. 117, ¶471, esp. ¶440; C.G. Jung, "Mind and Earth," in: Sir Herbert Read et al. (eds.), *Civilization in Transition*, Princeton University Press, Princeton CW 10, Trans. by R. F. C. Hull, ¶49ff.; C.G. Jung; Maria Meyer-Grass Lorenz Jung (ed.), *Children's Dreams, Notes from the Seminar Given in 1936–1940*, Princeton University Press, Princeton 2008, translated by Ernst Falzeder and Tony Woolfson, 1936/37, 1938/39, 1939/40; cf. also C.G. Jung, "Über den Archetypus. Mit besonderer Berücksichtigung des Animabegriffs," in: *Zentralblatt für Psychotherapie*, vol. 9, no. 5, 1936, p. 269 [references as in the original].

[58] In Lucien Lévy-Bruhl, *The "Soul" of the Primitive*, Macmillan, New York, 1928; see also Lucien Lévy-Bruhl, *How Natives Think*, authorized translation by Lilian A. Clare (1926), Washington Square Press, Inc., New York, 1966.

27 In spite of this insight, we still do not really know in detail the process of how fairytales evolve. Max Lüthi achieved a significant step forward in that he showed local legends to be a more realistic and primary product of the soul.[59] As opposed to local legends, Lüthi identifies fairytales as being abstractions.[60] But what he calls "abstraction" aims – translated into our terminology – at a formal description of the archetypal images, which in fairytales, in contrast to local legends – as far as they work abstractly and strip everything down to bare essentials – still remind us of a primal experience. (To this *abstraction* belongs what Lüthi calls the two-dimensionality, geometrical linearity, abstractness, extremeness, and bluntness of fairytale motifs. With these, he includes their lack of feeling life, single-strandedness of the plot, rigidity of form, and isolation and interconnectedness; in general, what he calls the "abstract" style of the fairytales.)[61] Seen from the psychological viewpoint, local legends are to a large extent factual reports of magical incidents, which represent the experience of an invasion by the world of archetypes into consciousness. These build upon and keep alive an immense treasure trove of archetypal notions in peoples the world over, out of which grows, as Lüthi correctly observed, the remarkable "abstract" interrelationship of a fairytale storyline.[62] Indeed, local legends offer psychological researchers the advantage of illuminating the total human situation, in which the *numinous* experience of the archetypes takes place. Fairytales, on the other hand, have an advantage over legends in that they more purely represent the archetypes and let them become more clearly comprehensible in their "network of roots" and their dynamic functions.[63] Legends illuminate more

---

[59] Cf. Max Lüthi, *Die Gabe im Märchen und in der Sage. Ein Beitrag zur Wesenserfassung und Wesensscheidung der beiden Formen*, Inaugural-Dissertation der Philosophischen Fakultät, Universität Bern, Bern, 1943, pp. 114–15; Max Lüthi, *The European Folktale: Form and Nature* (trans. by John D. Niles), Indiana University Press, Bloomington & Indianapolis, 1982, pp. 11ff.

[60] Cf. "The gift of fairytales and thus the fairytale itself, exhibits the *last clarity of the outer and inner form*. With their blurring of contours, legends mirror the rich and, precisely because of that, incomprehensible concreteness of real things and processes." M. Lüthi, *Die Gabe*, Bern, 1943, p. 118. [English translation not found in *The European Folktale*.] Cf. also Lüthi, *Die Gabe*, p. 119.

[61] Among others, see M. Lüthi, *The European Folktale*, Bloomington and Indianapolis, 1982, pp. 15ff., 37, 51ff., 66, 77–79.

[62] "The abstract, isolating, diagrammatical style of the folktale embraces all motifs and transforms them. Objects as well as persons lose their individual characteristics and turn into weightless, transparent figures" (M. Lüthi, *The European Folktale*, Bloomington and Indianapolis, 1982, p. 66.)

[63] In *The European Folktale*, Lüthi mentions the "unrealistic rigidity" of fairytales (Bloomington and Indianapolis, 1982, p. 62). "The folktale (*Märchen*) does not confirm or explain, anything, it simply represents [p. 59] …It merely observes and portrays. And this dreamlike vision of the world, a vision that demands nothing of us, neither faith nor avowal, accepts itself so matter-of-factly and is given verbal expression so unerringly that we let ourselves be carried along away by it in a state of bliss [p. 85] … In its [i.e. the folktale's] view, things become light, weightless, transparent as the deceptive veil of apparent reality falls away. Whatever in the real world is bound in a complex net of interdependencies and reciprocal ties appears in the folktale in its ultimate isolation and capacity for universal interconnection [p. 87] …the world of the figures that folktales presents to us – from the stars and the minerals and all the various objects to flowers, animals, human beings, and spirits – is of value in itself, and what holds it together it together is not the 'justice of events' but rather the *rightness of events* in general [p. 89] …Not for a moment does its abstract portrayal leave us in doubt about the fact that it

the suspenseful relation of this life to another world or to an awareness of the unconscious. Fairytales, on the contrary, illuminate the unconscious forms and regularity[64] of the natural laws of the soul in a more stripped down (*abgelöster*) form.[65]

28 This regularity mirrors itself in fairytales, not only in the primeval[66] images, but also in whole sequences that are in themselves kinetic types and combine in different ways in different tales. The primordial images are not only images, but also psychic powers.[67] The circumstance that in fairytales not only motifs, but also complete episodes, repeat themselves, facilitates our efforts to interpret them. We refrain, therefore, from striving for completeness in listing all parallel tales or motifs in the assumption that by thoroughly handling the essential types, interpretation of other material with the same or similar content will naturally follow. Due to the fluid character of the archetypes and their overlapping of contours, our attempts to define the basic forms admittedly exhibit a certain fuzziness.

29 We focus in the following on fairytales and leave aside other genera, such as literary tales, animal tales, stories, and legends,[68] and only occasionally

---

intends to portray what is essential, not merely what is real." M. Lüthi, *The European Folktale*, Bloomington and Indianapolis, 1982, pp. 89–90.

[64] German: *Gesetzmässigkeit*]

[65] Cf. the similar results of Lüthi's research in M. Lüthi, *Die Gabe*, Bern, 1943, p. 140. See also, "Not only does the folktale (*Märchen*) lack a sense of gap separating the everyday world from the world of the supernatural. In its essence and in every sense, it lacks the dimension of depth. Its characters are figures without substance, without inner life, without an environment; they lack any relation to past and future, to time altogether" (Lüthi, *The European Folktale*, Bloomington and Indianapolis, 1982, p. 11).

[66] German: *urtümlich*]

[67] Cf. C.G. Jung, "On Psychic Energy," in: Sir Herbert Read et al. (eds.), *Collected Works, Vol 8: The Structure and Dynamics of the Psyche*, 2nd edition. Princeton University Press, Princeton CW 8 ¶26ff., and C.G. Jung, CW 6, *Psychological Types* ¶355.

[68] For reasons mentioned below, we do not consider the large collection of oriental fairytales. The collection of *A Thousand and One Nights* comprises many layers and is enriched by ingredients of varied literary character and contents from many lands (cf. J. Bolte and G. Polívka, *Anmerkungen*, vol. 4, Leipzig, 1930, pp. 397ff; see also Enno Littmann, ed., *Die Erzählungen aus den Tausendundein Nächten*, Deutsche Ausgabe in sechs Bänden. Zum ersten Mal n. d. arabischen Urtext der Calcuttaer Ausgabe vom Jahre 1839, Insel-Verlag, Leipzig, 1923, Appendix vol. VI, pp. 681ff.). It would have exceeded the framework of the present work to uncover the primary content of this opulent product of the oriental art of storytelling. Unfortunately, the volume *Arabic Fairy Tales, A Thousand and One Nights in their Original Form* (K. Dyroff) in the collection, *Folktales of World Literature* (*Märchen der Weltliteratur* in the following abbreviated as *MdW*), published by Verlag Diederichs, Jena, which we could have certainly used for our purposes, did not appear before the present book went to press [1952]. Similarly, *Thousand and One Days*, (cf. Paul Ernst (ed.), *Tausend und ein Tag / Orientalische Erzählungen*. Erster Band, ausgew. and eingel. v. Paul Ernst. Übertr. v. Felix Paul Greve, Insel-Verlag, Leipzig, 1909, Introduction, pp. 7ff.). Also the collection of Turkish tales coming by way of India, *Tuti-Nameh* or *The Parrot Book* carries so much the character of a didactic novel that it will not be considered here (cf. J. Bolte and G. Polívka, *Anmerkungen*, vol. 5, Leipzig, 1932, p. 188; see also Georg Rosen, *Tuti-Nameh. Das Papageienbuch. Eine Sammlung orientalischer Erzählungen. Nach der türkischen Fassung übersetzt von Georg Rosen*, vol. 17, Bibliothek der Romane, Insel-Verlag, Leipzig 1912; see Foreword to the 1st ed., pp. 415ff.). It is regrettable that for the present research, we could use only a few examples from the land which offers a sheer inexhaustible wealth of fairytales and which Benfley would like to denote as the original home of fairytales (i.e. India). Due to their artistic and consciously created, novel-like, Buddhistic-didactic clothing, and the heterogeneity of elements in collections such as the *Pantschatantra* and the *Kathasaritsagara* by Somadeva, it would require extensive literary and religious-historical research to

include them to extend our horizons. Also, we only discuss sources and formal criticism in a few exceptional cases.

30 As mentioned, investigating parallel behavioral patterns of fairytale figures demonstrates that some important motifs and problems could be taken together. This situation was used as a basis for the division of chapters. Furthermore, it became evident that all the fairytale images lead to one central secret, whose meaning the following attempt to interpret hopefully approaches.

31 Fairytales that we felt deserved a more extensive discussion are marked with an asterisk, for example: "Help in Need"* (China). This marking serves as a guideline throughout the first and continues in the second volume (*Archetypal Symbols in Fairytales. Antitheses and Renewal*) of this book. These more important fairytales are noted in the index volume and are all characterized in the same way. Other fairytales mentioned in the text also appear in the index, but without an asterisk. In addition to this fairytale index, there is also a bibliography of referenced literature, an author, and a subject index.

bring out the original kernel. For similar reasons, we refrain from discussing literary fairytales such as collected and/or retold by Musäs, Hauff, Bechstein, Andersen, etc.

Section 1

The Profane and Magical Worlds and their Main Figures

The Profane and Magical World and their Main Figures

32 Fantasy brings the future world to our doorstep; either in the heights or in the depths or in the transmigration [of souls]. We dream of traveling through the universe; is then the universe in us? The depths of our psyche we know not, but inwards goes the mysterious way. In us or nowhere is eternity with its worlds: the past and the future.

33 Die Phantasie setzt die künftige Welt entweder in die Höhe oder in die Tiefe oder in der Metempsychose zu uns. Wir träumen von Reisen durch das Weltall: ist denn das Weltall in uns? Die Tiefen unseres Geistes kennen wir nicht. – Nach innen geht der geheimnisvolle Weg. In uns oder nirgends ist die Ewigkeit mit ihren Welten, die Vergangenheit und Zukunft.

Novalis *Fragmente* Nr. 593.

34 The world in which the fairytale's story unfolds is not our normal everyday world. We encounter miraculous appearances, wonderful events, and surprising developments as if they were a matter of course. We meet talking animals, witches, and dwarves; characters and events that do not occur in our conscious wakeful state. In a fairytale, the laws of time and space lose their validity: the maiden in "Sleeping Beauty (Little Briar Rose)" awakens in full beauty after a hundred-year sleep, or the young spinning girl in "Mother Holle" falls into a well and arrives in a heavenly world where snow falls down to Earth. One could describe the sphere in which fairytales transpire as a *magical realm* in contrast to our *profane world*.[1] This magical realm is often located in a particular place, the most important examples being: Heaven, Earth, the depths of the Earth, the forest, a lake, the ocean, a remote island, the moon, a mountain, a cave, the northern mists. Gerardus van der Leeuw (1890-1950) summarized all these magical places as the *land of the soul* and

[1] The authors thank Dr. Armin Kietzmann, Altenhagen (Hannover), for the initial suggestion to divide fairytales into these two realms.

described its main aspects.[2] This realm can be found in the consciousness of primitive peoples as an untracked, desolate *beyond* that at the same time is paradoxically immediately next to where normal people live. It is the *gruesome* abode of the dead and can just as well be a beautiful Garden of Paradise like the *Garden of the Gods* of Euripides or the *Island of the Blessed.* Sometimes it lies in the West, sometimes in the East, North, or South; sometimes it is earthly, sometimes heavenly; but it is always *otherworldly.* At times, natural peoples imagine this realm to be simultaneously in different places without facing any conflict with the illogicality of their conception of space.[3]

35 The storylines of fairytales have preserved this character of the *land of the soul.* The enchanted kingdom into which the hero steps at the beginning, or which from the outset is present, has all the characteristics and aspects mentioned above. Strikingly, inside this *soul land* we almost always find some kind of a constructed (usually geometrically divided) center: a castle or a palace, a four-cornered house, or a round lake with a mountain or island in the middle. The important processes take place in this center; it is here that we touch the central problem of the fairytale.

36 The transition from everyday life, that is, the realm of normal consciousness, to the numinous otherworld, is particularly clearly portrayed in the account of the acts that take place in the magical arena. To illustrate this, we begin with the following examples.[4]

---

[2] Cf. G. v. d. Leeuw, *Religion in Essence*, vol. 1 p. §46, pp. 317–322.

[3] Ibid., pp. 319–320: "That in this way different localities often arose simultaneously, troubled neither primitive mentality nor thought of antiquity, as. . . in the case of Egypt; and the inhabitants of Eddystone (Mandegus) Island also seek the beyond in a distant country, but at the same time in a cave on their own island. . . Much the most preferable place, however, for this near-and-far, sought by the soul, is the underworld, or rather in the earth."

[4] Cf. also the investigation of H. Silberer, *Symbolik des Erwachens und Schwellensymbolik Überhaupt* [Symbols of Awakening and Threshold Symbolism] on the self-portrait of the transition to sleep in the dream.

Chapter 1
The Indefinite Place

37 The Chinese fairytale, "Help in Need," (*China):[1] begins:

> Some twenty miles east of Gingdschou lies the Lake of the Maidens. It is several miles square and surrounded on all sides by thick green thickets and tall forests. Its waters are clear and deep blue. Often all kinds of wondrous creatures show themselves in the lake. The people in the vicinity have erected a temple here for the Dragon Princess.[2]

> 38 During the time of the Tang Dynasty there lived in Gingdschou a mandarin by the name of Dschou Bau. While he was in office, it chanced that in the fifth month clouds suddenly swelled up in the sky, piling upon themselves like mountains among which wriggled dragons and serpents. . . Tempest and rain, thunder and lightning arose so that houses fell to pieces, trees were torn up by the roots, and much damage was done to the crops. Dschou Bau took the blame upon himself, and prayed to the heavens that his people might be pardoned.

> 39 On the fifth day of the sixth month he sat in his hall of audience and gave judgement; suddenly he felt quite weary and sleepy. He took off his hat and lay down on the cushions. *No sooner had he closed his eyes*[3] than he saw a warrior in helmet and armor, halberd in his hand, standing on the steps leading to the hall, who announced: "A lady is waiting outside who wishes to enter!" Dschou Bau asked him: "Who are you?" The answer was: *"I am your door-keeper. In the invisible world I have already been performing this duty for many years."* Meanwhile two figures clad in green came up the steps, knelt before him, and said: "Our mistress has come to visit you!" Dschou Bau rose.

---

[1] Those tales that we discuss in detail are noted with an asterisk (*). [Here and in the following the English translation refers to the titles of the collection, *Die Märchen der Weltliteratur (MdW)*, published by Eugen Diederichs, Jena, by the modern (2018) name of country in which the tale was recorded. This is not necessarily the name given in the title of the respective collection.]

[2] The Dragon Princess herself calls the home where she lives with her family as being "in the depths of the Eastern Sea."

[3] In recounting these tales, we emphasize certain passages that have crucial connections to the theme we are discussing by placing the original text in italics.

He beheld lovely clouds from which fell a fine rain, and strange fragrances enchanted him. Suddenly he saw a lady clad in simple gown, but of unsurpassed beauty, float down from on high, with a retinue of many female servants.[4]

40 The Dragon Princess had come to ask Dschou Bau for help. She was widowed soon after her marriage and her father then promised her in marriage to the dragon Tschauna. On account of her resistance to be married to Tschauna, battles were fought; she lost, and had to flee. She had come to Dschou Bau to beg him to lend her mercenaries.

41 Dschou Bau promised to help her, and the princess departed. *When he awoke* he sighed, thinking over his strange experience. On the following day he sent off fifteen hundred soldiers to stand guard by the Lake of Maidens.

42 On the seventh day of the sixth month, Dschou Bau rose early. *Darkness still lay before the windows*, yet it seemed to him as though he could glimpse a man before the curtain. He asked who it might be. The man said: "I am the princess's adviser. Yesterday you were kind enough to send soldiers to aid us in our distress. But they were all living men, and as such cannot fight against *invisible* spirits. You will have to send us soldiers of yours who have died, if you wish to aid us."

43 Now Dschou Bau wrote a command on a piece of paper and burned it, in order to place his deceased soldiers at the princess's disposal. The living soldiers were recalled.

44 When they were being reviewed in the courtyard after their return, one soldier *suddenly fell unconscious*. It was not until the following morning that he came to his senses again. He was questioned, and replied, "I saw a man clad in red who approached me and said, 'Our princess is grateful for the aid your master has so kindly given her. Yet she still has a request to make and has asked me to call you.' I followed him to the temple. The princess bade me to come forward and said, 'I thank your master from my heart for sending me the ghost soldiers, but Mong Yuan, their leader, is incapable. Yesterday the robbers came with three thousand men, and Mong Yuan was beaten by them. When you return and again see your master, say that I earnestly beg him to send me a capable general. Perhaps that will save me in my need.' Then she led me back again and I regained

[4] [The unabridged version continues, see footnote 5 for reference. Here follows a summary.]

consciousness." When Dschou Bau heard these words, which strangely fit well with what he had dreamed, he thought he would try to see if what he had heard was true. Therefore he chose his most victorious general, Dschong Tschong-Fu, to take the place of the unusable Mong Yuan. That evening he burned incense, offered wine, and handed over his general's soul to the princess.

45 On the twenty-sixth of the month, news came from general Dschong Tschong-Fu's camp that he had suddenly died *at midnight* on the thirteenth. Dschou Bau was frightened, and sent a man to bring him a report. The latter informed him that the general's heart had hardly ceased beating, and that in spite of the hot summer weather, his body was free from any trace of decay. So the order was given not to bury him. Then one night, an icy, spectral wind arose, which whirled up sand and stones, broke trees, and tore down houses. The standing corn in the fields was battered down. The storm lasted all day. Finally, the crash of a terrific thunderbolt was heard, the skies cleared, and the clouds scattered. That very hour the dead general began to breath painfully on his couch, and when his attendants came to him, he had returned to life again.

46 They questioned him and he told them, "First I saw a man in a purple gown riding a black horse, who came up with a great retinue. He dismounted before the door. In his hand he held a decree of appointment, which he gave me, saying, 'Our princess begs you most respectfully to become her general. I hope you will not refuse.'"

47 General Dschong Tschong-Fu wished to decline, but his wish was not heeded. Heaped with gifts garments, saddles, horses, helmets, and suits of mail, he was escorted to a city and passed through a dozen gates before he reached the hall of the princess. She explained her request and he promised to obey her will. Immediately thereafter, the robber Tschauna invaded the princess's land. With considerable military cunning, the general thoroughly squelched Tschauna's army. As a reward for his victory, he was loaded with benefits. He was given a month's leave to visit his family and dismissed with a splendid retinue. The general continued his report:

48 ". . . Then I rode away and when I arrived before our own gate, *a thunder-peal crashed* and I awoke." Thereupon the general wrote an account of what had happened to Dschou Bau, in which he conveyed the princess's thanks. Then he *paid no further heed to worldly matters, but set his house in order and turned it over to his wife and son. When a month had passed, he died without any sign of illness.* That same day

> one of his officers was out walking. Suddenly he saw a heavy cloud of dust rising along the highway, while flags and banners darkened the sun. A thousand knights were escorting a man who sat on his horse proudly like a hero. And when the officer looked at his face, it was his general Dschong Tschong-Fu. Hastily he stepped to the edge of the road, in order to allow the cavalcade to pass and watched as it rode by. The horsemen took *the way to the Lake of the Maidens, where they disappeared.*[5]

49 Here in a fairytale from the Orient we have a description that summarizes in compact form a range of motifs concerning the transition from the profane to the magical world. Reflecting on the uncertainty in locating the exact place of the magical happenings, we read that the princess floats[6] down from above, even though she comes from the depths of the Eastern Sea. Letters reach her, as she relates herself, in the cave of the Sea of Dungting. She receives messages in a palatial tent,[7] but the battle apparently takes place in front of a real city. So the magical realm is sometimes connected with a foreign place (the Eastern Sea) and sometimes it is continually surrounded by people in invisible form and can be approached at any time. Along with the indefiniteness of this space, the coincident relative incorporeality or subtle reality of the inhabitants in the magical realm arises from the fact that things are sent there in the form of smoke. This accords with the widespread belief that the *images* of the burned are transported into the spirit-world or world of the gods by way of smoke.[8]

50 Even more explicitly, the nature of the magical realm shows itself through the states that befall whoever comes close to it: exhaustion, sleepiness, and apparent death. Another Chinese fairytale, "How the Scholar Chastised the Sovereigns of the Caves" (*China), tells how a scholar experiences the underworld when he sinks into unconsciousness in a state of rapture.[9] A devil abducts him and only later does he discover that he has "died." The enchanted world is experienced when the eyes are closed – a motif found also in many European fairytales[10] – in sleep, in a state of intoxication, or in unconscious ness, and which can slip into apparent death and even all the way over into

---

[5] [This English translation relies heavily on R. Wilhelm, *The Chinese Fairy Book*, New York, 1921, pp. 142–151. The original German source is *MdW*. Wherever possible, as in the present case, published English translations of this collection are given here. The individual tales are identified with the name of the land and the number as in the original or, if a published translation exists, in the translated version.]

[6] [Although the actions in the fairytale are told in the past, the psychological images are alive in our imaginations right now. Thus the use of past tense in telling the stories, but the present tense when discussing the meaning of the characters and images.]

[7] About the customs concerning sending messages to the land of the dead, see in general Albert Wesselski, *Versuch einer Theorie des Märchens*, Prager Deutsche Studien, no. 45, E. Gierach and H. Cysarz, eds. Sudetendeutscher Verlag Franz Kraus, Reichenberg i. B., 1931, pp. 26–27.

[8] Cf. similar allusions in Bächtold-Stäubli under *Rauch* [*smoke*].

[9] [Can also be translated as a delirious state or a state of intoxication.]

[10] See the examples in Laistner, *Das Rätsel*, vol. 1, pp. 228–29; see also *ibid.*, vol. 2, *passim*.

actual (as told in the fairytale) death. In this way, the fairytale seems to speak about itself as if to say, "You can experience my reality when you are in an unconscious state or in a sleep-like condition." It may occur to the reader, as it did to Georg Jacob[11] and Laistner,[12] that the incidents in the magical realm of fairytales are fundamentally similar to dream experiences in that the enchanted world represents the unconscious.[13] The idea of this immanent world existing continuously and adjacent to our normal consciousness is evoked by the intuitive notion that our conscious daily life is always accompanied by an unconscious stream of images[14] that appear at night in our dreams.

51 In many fairytales, the circumstance that events in the magical world stem from the unconscious, can be seen in especially clear form where the initial meeting with this realm is occasioned by a dream. The events unfold in an apparently concrete world, but lack certain characteristics of reality and can thereupon be designated as "strange" or "magical." Then again, they seem to possess some kind of psychic reality.

52 The transition into the unconscious is sometimes portrayed in such a matter-of-fact way that it is as if there was no transition at all, as if the unconscious is the only reality. Even words from daily life find their way here without question. An example of how a tale runs in this form is given in the Nordic fairytale, "The Mountain of the Golden Queen":[15]

> 53 Once upon a time, a lad who tended his cattle near the woods was eating his midday meal in a clearing in the forest. As he was sitting there, he saw a rat run into a juniper bush. His curiosity led him to look for it; but as he bent over, he fell head over heels, and promptly dropped asleep. And he dreamed that he was going to find the princess on the Mountain of the Golden Queen, but he did not know the way.
>
> 54 On the following day, he once more pastured his cows near the same woods. He came to the same clearing and again ate his lunch at the same spot. And again he saw the rat and went to look for it, and again fell fast asleep. And again he dreamed of the princess on the Mountain of the Golden Queen, only this time he dreamed that in order to find her he would need seventy pounds of iron and a pair of iron shoes.

---

[11] Cf. Jacob, "Märchen and Traum," 1923.

[12] Cf. Laistner, *Das Rätsel*, and Leeuw, §60.3, p. 417.

[13] In *The European Folktale*, pp. 21ff., Lüthi observes that the faraway world of fairytales symbolizes another dimension of events.

[14] *[Vorstellungsablauf.]*

[15] [Based on Stroebe (ed.), *The Swedish Fairy Book*, 1921, trans. Frederick H. Martens, pp. 124–28.]

55 He awoke, it was all a dream; but by now he had made up his mind to find the Mountain of the Golden Queen, and he went home with his herd. On the third day, when he had led out his cattle, he could not reach the clearing of his happy dream too soon. Again the rat showed itself and when he went to look for it he fell asleep as he had done each preceding day. And again he dreamed of the princess of the Mountain of the Golden Queen, that she came to him and laid a letter and band of gold in his pocket. Upon awakening, to his indescribable surprise he found in his pocket both of the things of which he just dreamed: the letter and the band. Now he had no time to attend to his cattle any longer, and drove them straight home. Then he went to the stable, led out a horse, sold it and with the earnings bought seventy pounds of iron shoes. He made thole-pins out of the iron, put on his iron shoes, and set forth.

56 For a time he traveled by land, then at last he came to a lake he had to cross. He saw naught but water before him and behind him, and rowing so long and steadily, he wore out one thole pin after another. At length he reached land and a green meadow where no trees grew.

57 He then met a giant woman, nine yards long, and asked her the way to the Mountain of the Golden Queen. She said that she did not know, and directed him to her sister who was nine yards taller than she. This sister did not know either and directed him to her brother who was even nine yards taller. This brother was a veritable giant, twenty-seven yards tall. He took out a giant whistle and whistled in every direction, calling together all the animals on the Earth. He asked them about the Mountain of the Golden Queen, but they knew nothing of it. Then the giant blew his whistle in every direction again and called forth all the fishes in all the waters. They also knew nothing of the Mountain. Then he took out his whistle again and called for all the birds. This time the eagle said: "Yes, I know!" "Well, then," said the giant, "take this lad here and lead him there, but do not treat him unkindly!"

58 The cowherd rode on the back of the eagle. When they were above the ocean, the eagle flew down and dipped the lad up to his ankles in the water and asked if he was afraid. The lad replied "No" and the eagle flew on. Again he dipped the lad into the water up to his knees. Now the lad was afraid, "But the giant said you were not to treat me unkindly!" "Are you really afraid?" "Yes," answered the youth again. "The fear you now feel is the very same fear I felt when the princess thrust the letter and the golden band into your pocket." And the eagle flew on.

59 And with that they reached a large high mountain that had a great iron door on one side. They knocked and a serving maid appeared, opened the door, and invited them in. The youth remained and was well received, but the eagle said farewell and flew back to his native land. The youth asked for a drink, and he was at once handed a beaker containing a refreshing draught. When he had emptied and returned the beaker, he let the golden band drop into it. When the maid brought the beaker back to her mistress – who was the princess of the Mountain of the Golden Queen – the latter looked into the mug, and behold, there lay a golden band she recognized as her own. So she asked, "Is there someone here?" and when the maid answered in the affirmative, the princess said, "Bid him come in!" And as soon as the youth entered she asked him if he chanced to have a letter. The youth drew out the letter he had received in so strange a manner, and he gave it to the princess. And when she had read it she cried out, full of joy, "Now I am delivered!" And at that very moment the mountain turned into a most handsome castle, with all sort of precious things, servants, and every sort of convenience, each for its own purpose. (Here the story ends; we must take it for granted that a wedding ensued!)

60 In this tale, the magical world announces itself to the hero through three dreams, which are linked to the appearance of a rat. Rats, like mice, are animals that live in the dark underground and therefore embody unconscious animalistic impulses in humans. The premonition of the Mountain of the Golden Queen comes to the young herdsman from this realm. Later the relation to the magical world changes: it arises not through falling asleep but rather through a long journey over lakes and oceans. The same linking of the motifs – falling asleep, sinking, and at the same time finding oneself in a foreign realm – occurs in a Finnish fairytale, "The Ox's Son." In this tale, the hero comes to a cave and peers within:

61 In the inside of the earth, he perceived a ray of light apparently coming from another land. And as he went to follow the ray of light, he fell to the ground and awoke in a large and magnificent forest, at the edge of a bog. He did not know where he should go. Then came a great bird and spoke to him, "It is still quite a long way to your empire, but if you give me something to eat from your own flesh when I carry you on my back, then I will fly you there." And he climbed on the back of

the great bird. During the flight, he twice gave the bird some of the flesh from his own thigh. The bird flew him to the castle of the princess.[16]

[16] [Translated from the German of August von Löwis of Menar (ed.), *Finnische und estnische Volksmärchen*, (*MdW*), ed. Fr. v. d. Leyen and P. Zaunert, 1922. No published English translation of this collection has been found.

Chapter 2
The Moon

62 The roots of the idea of a distant magical realm spring from a widespread primitive belief that the soul leaves the body in sleep and in awakening returns back into the body.[1] A similar concept is found in the artificially induced states of ecstasy in shamans and medicine men. While one part of the personality remains in unconsciousness, the other part travels to distant realms. The journey of an Eskimo[2] shaman from Baffin Island forms the center of the tale, "Flight to the Moon":

63 A mighty angakoq,[3] who had a bear as his tornaq,[4] resolved to pay a visit to the *Moon*. He sat down *in the rear of his hut, turning his back toward the lamps, which had been extinguished. He had his hands tied up and a thong fastened around his knees and neck*. Thus prepared, *he summoned his tornaq*, which carried him *rapidly through the air* and brought him to the moon. He observed that the moon was a house,

---

[1] For examples, see Frazer, *Golden Bough*, p. 187.

[2] [The translators retain the authors' use of the term "Eskimo" for the native cultures of Greenland, Arctic Canada, and Alaska when this is the term used in the original German text and use the modern name for these Native American people, Inuit, which also includes Alaska's Yupik and the Iñupiat People, in footnoted additional remarks. Inuit is a plural noun; the singular is Inuk.]

[3] An angakoq is a religious shaman, a magical priest, who is required to mediate and sustain communication with the spirit-world. A trance state is a frequently used shamanistic technique. See note in Walter Krickeberg (ed.), *Indianermärchen aus Nordamerika, (MdW)*, eds. Fr. v. d. Leyen and P. Zaunert, Eugen Diederichs, Jena, 1924, p. 367 Cf. also Knud Rasmussen, *Die Gabe des Adlers, Eskimoische Märchen aus Alaska*, Societäts-Verlag, Frankfurt a. M., 1937, translated and revised by Aenne Schmücker, p. 200: "Shaman: according to Siberian terminology, an exorcist is called a shaman. His Eskimo name is Angàkoq. In Alaska, he is known as tôrnralik, that is, one who has helping spirits. Men and women can become exists when they have the capacity to enter into a state of trance, the drum being an important aid." See also A. Lang, *Myth*, London, 1887, vol. I, p. 115.

[4] Tornaq is the Inuit word for animal spirit guardian and helper, usually in the form of a polar bear. Cf. Franz Boas, "The Central Eskimo," in: *Sixth Annual Report of the Smithsonian Institution*, Smithsonian Institution, Bureau of Ethnology, Washington, D.C., 1888, pp. 583ff. In Fridtjof Nansen, *Eskimo Life*, Longmans, Green and Co., London and New York, 1893, pp. 212ff., the author remarks that the tornak is a subservient spirit of angakoq, who helps him gain supernatural power. Above him stands the tornarssuk, whose home is in the underworld, in the land of the souls. He appears like a bear or a one-armed giant or he can also be as small as a finger. See also p. 215, whereby tornak = tarnek (soul) = tarrak (shadow). Cf. further pp. 247ff. about angakoq, and also Eivind Astrup, *Unter den Nachbarn des Nordpols*, H. Haessel Verlag, Leipzig, 1905, authorized translation from the Norwegian by Margarethe Langseldt, pp. 234–235, the most important spirits that the Eskimo recognize, is the tornahuksuak or tornarssuk (literally, *huge shadow*). He can bring harm as well as good and keeps, as one appears to believe in northern Greenland according to the angekut (plural of angakoq), he has a human form but of supernatural dimension.

nicely covered in white deerskin that the man in the moon used to dry nearby. On each side of the entrance was the upper portion of an enormous walrus, which threatened to tear in pieces any bold intruder. Though it was dangerous to pass by the fierce animals, the angakoq, with the help of his tornaq, succeeded in entering the house.

64 In the passage, he saw the only dog of the man of the moon, which is called Tiriétiang and is dappled white and red. On entering the main room he perceived on the left side, a small additional building, in which a beautiful woman, the sun, was sitting before her lamp. As soon as she saw the angakoq enter, she blew on her fire and quickly hid behind the blaze. The man in the moon came to meet him kindly, stepping from the seat on the ledge and bidding the stranger welcome. Behind the lamps great heaps of venison and seal meat were piled up, but the man of the moon did not yet offer him anything. He said: "My wife, Ululiernang, will soon enter and we will perform a dance. Mind that you do not laugh, else she will split your belly with a knife, take out your intestines, and give them to my ermine which lives in yon house outside."

65 Before long, a woman entered carrying an oblong vessel containing her *ulo*.[5] She put it on the floor and stooped forwards, turning the vessel like a whirligig. Then she commenced dancing, and when she turned her back toward the angakoq, it was made manifest that she was hollow. She had no back, backbones, or entrails, but only lungs and heart.

66 The man joined her dance and their attitudes and grimaces looked so funny that the angakoq could scarcely keep from laughing. But just at the right moment he called to mind the warnings of the man in the moon and rushed out of the house. The man cried after him "Uqsureliktaleqdjuin"[6] ("Provide yourself with your large white bear tornaq.") Thus he escaped unhurt.

67 Reinvigorated, the angakoq returned for another visit and succeeded in mastering his inclination to laugh and was hospitably received by the man after the performance was finished. The man of the moon showed him all around the house and let him look into a small additional building near the entrance. There the visitor saw large herds of deer apparently roaming over vast plains. The man of the moon allowed him to choose one animal, which fell immediately

[5] [The characteristic tool of the Inuit women, a knife used for all possible tasks, like today's kitchen knife.]

[6] [*Uqsurelik* = with blubber, signifies in the language of the angakut, the white bear; *lauk* = large, *leqdjorpoq* = he provides himself with. F. Boas, "*The Central Eskimo,*" Washington, D.C., 1888, p. 599.]

through a hole down upon the earth. In another building he saw a profusion of seals *swimming in an ocean* and was allowed to pick out one of these also. At last the man in the moon sent him away, and his tornaq carried him back to his hut as quickly as he had left it.

68 During his visit to the moon, his body had lain *motionless and soulless*, but now it revived. The thongs with which his hands had been fastened, had fallen down, though they had been tied in firm knots. The angakoq felt *almost exhausted*, and when the lamps were relighted, he related his adventures during the flight to the moon to the eagerly listening men.[7]

69 Important in this tale is that the double description of that which happens partly in the normal human personage of the magician and at the same time in his "other self" is complete. The initiation rites that primitives go through in these cases have an explicit symbolic meaning. Being tied up and shackled is the complete abdication of all outward-directed activity.[8] Extinguishing the lamps means a simultaneous extinguishing of ego or normal daily consciousness. Calling animal spirits to help shows that the animalistic powers of the unconscious are activated.

70 From the remark at the end that the angakoq *awakes exhausted*, it becomes clear that his whole grand journey happened in his mind, that is, it expresses a psychic experience, which was induced through sinking into unconsciousness. In contrast to General Dschong Tschong-Fu in "Help in Need," the Inuit shaman succeeds – presumably due to his knowledge of magic – in regaining solid footing in this world. The danger with these outings is very great because a dissociation of the personality occurs, a process which is not uncommon, especially for the primitive mental state. One may not simply state, however, that this is a separation of body and spirit – the primitive would reject such a divisional description. Lévy-Bruhl presents[9] various cases of nightly sojourns of magicians and witches, often where an apparent body or a wild animal is left behind and the whole person embarks on the journey. The individual houses different forms simultaneously and still keeps his or her identity.

71 Not only in most heathen religions does this experience of descent serve as a basis for dogmatic statements,[10] but rather it still lived on in the tradition

---

[7] *Ibid.*, p. 599. Authors' emphasis.

[8] This is similar to the practice of tying up of the dead (to prevent their return from the land of the dead) that appears in many different cultures.

[9] See Lévy-Bruhl, *The "Soul" of the Primitive*, pp. 158ff.

[10] Bousset, *Himmelsreise*, Tübingen and Leipzig, 1901 [The Heavenly Journey of the Soul], G. v. d. Leeuw, *Religion in Essence*, vol. 1, § 44:2; H. Güntert, *Weltkönig*, p. 224; on "celestial wanderings," see Reitzenstein, *Hellenistic*, p. 86; see esp. the story of the Arda Viraf, who takes a journey through the heavens to renew the religion, during which his body lies there lifeless for seven days (p. 212).

of the early Christian monks, who in the desert sank into a kind of apparent death and in this state wandered through Heaven and Hell.[11]

72 Traces of such soul-journeys can be found in European legends and fairytales up to the present day. An excellent example are the stories about the legendary "Venetian,"[12] which one meets in many tales from southern Germany and Austria. According to these tales the "Venetians" abduct people up into the air and take them to a wonderful enchanted realm (of course nothing to do with the real Venice), where miraculous fairytale-like things happen. Ludwig Laistner reaches the correct key conclusion when he writes about this:

73 > It is known that the so-called Venetians of the German tale caught people up in a whirlwind and transported them in a flash to foreign Venice and later returned them to their home. When in one version instead [of the whirlwind], it says that someone *falls asleep* under a large pine tree and awakes in Venice, experiences an enjoyable day, goes to bed, and *on the next morning finds himself again under his old pine tree* so this reveals that the trip to the magical city of Venice was a *dream journey*. . . From this angle, the abduction by the whirlwind, Lady Midday,[13] by the Nereids, or by the wild horde is nothing other than the experience of sleep. . . [14]

74 From this it follows that great journeys and wanderings, which comprise the main action in many fairytales, basically mirror experiences of dissociation or dream states, even if these are no longer described as such. That the Venetians appear with whirlwinds, reminds one of the appearance of the thunderstorm accompanying the approach of the spirit-world in the tale "Help in Need" related above.

---

[11] This reflects remnants of incubation sleep of the antique Hellenic-Roman culture. Cf. here "Die Visionen des Zosimos," ¶139. Even if in the present case, and also often elsewhere, experiences of such descents are perceived concretely. Plato, for example, already interpreted them correctly as an unconscious state of the soul. Cf. *Timaeus*, "The proof that the godhead has given the gift of divination really to the unconscious part of man's soul, is given by the fact that no one in a conscious state attains to prophetic truth and inspiration; rather one accesses this aptitude in sleep or when the conscious activity of the soul is bound, or when one through illness or a kind of ecstasy, has lost consciousness." [Translated from the German translation of Plato by M.-L. von Franz. The translation by Benjamin Jowett runs, "And herein is a proof that God has given the art of divination not to the wisdom, but to the foolishness of man. No man, when in his wits, attains prophetic truth and inspiration; but when he receives the inspired word, either his intelligence is enthralled in sleep, or he is demented by some distemper or possession."] Cf. E. Rohde, *Psyche*, London, 1925, pp. 92ff [incubation-sleep of heroes] and Rohde, *Psyche*, vol. 2, Oxford, 1925, pp. 59ff.

[12] [Meaning "people from Venice (Italy)," but this is clearly only a euphemism for "exotic foreigners."]

[13] [*Pscipolnitsa* is a character of myth and tradition, common to much of Eastern Europe. She is known in English as Lady Midday, usually pictured as a young woman dressed in white that roamed the fields, assailing common folk working at noon and causing heatstrokes and aches in the neck. Sometimes she even caused madness.]

[14] Laistner, *Das Rätsel*, vol. 1, p. 35. Cf. also p. 67.

75 The Venetians of many southern European stories are relics of primitive guardian spirit and doppelgänger[15] beliefs, for which the bear in our present Inuit tale gives a beautiful example. Here, the guardian spirit plays the role of an alter ego, that doppelgänger who mediates the whole experience, and this does not just coincidentally appear in the form of a bear.[16]

76 The bear was a sacred animal in all the Northern lands and over a large area was especially worshipped as a bear goddess.[17] A clear example of this unconscious psychic factor in the human being is "Berserkism". It was imagined that certain heroes would leave their physical bodies, mostly just after exhibiting peculiar signs of exhaustion(!). While his body has sunk into a deep sleep (like the angakoq), the hero's soul, which has exchanged its form for that of a bear, performs enormous fighting deeds.[18] This can be understood as being in a state of rage and intoxication and total frenzied rapture,[19] in which the hero can wreak barbarous destruction, running "completely amok." This state is similar to a Dionysian frenzy,[20] which, however, can also be experienced as deep joy and release from the chains of the ego.[21] Going berserk also gave the hero great, albeit temporary, increase in strength. Whoever had the gift of being able to gain access to the depths of the unconscious like this, gained special honor.[22]

77 It is interesting that even just hearing fairytales whose content, according to our hypothesis, reflects a dream experience, sometimes exerts an effect on the teller and listener both, putting them into the state of a berserker - or a werewolf. This is reported in a Lithuanian tale, "*Der Märchenfreund* - The Fairy Tale Friend,"[23] wherein an older man lets a Russian, who is staying overnight with him, tell fairytales until he discovers that as they listened, they changed into a wolf and a bear. They took off "into freedom" and, out of hunger, killed and ate the old man's horse and then his wife, and had many adventures. Until one of them suddenly falls off the bench in front of the oven and realizes that it was all a dream. This shows that *changing into an animal*, *dreaming*, and *succumbing to the enchanted world of fairytales* reflect basically one and the same thing: immersion into the unconscious.

---

15 [Double personality.]

16 The bear plays an important role in Inuit and in Northern fairytales in general. See, for example, "Origin of the Ball Game," "The Origin of the Stars," "The Man from Grimsö and the Bear," "Bearskin," and "Snow-White and Rose-Red," "The Bear Story," "The Red Bear Ta-Ku-Ka."

17 Bachofen, *Der Bär*, pp. 13–15.

18 Ninck, *Wodan*, pp. 37, 42ff., 48–49, 86. Cf. also Bächtold-Stäubli under *Bärenhäuter* [Bearskins].

19 [German: *entrücken*.]

20 Cf. C.G. Jung, *Seminar über Kinderträume und ältere Literatur über Traum-Interpretation*, a. d. ETH Zürich, Red. v. Hans H. Baumann, Privatdruck, Zürich, 1936/37, p. 34.

21 Cf. Ninck, *Wodan*, p. 43. [See also Jung's dream of his mother's death connecting Wotan to a feeling of great joy: *Memories, Dreams, Reflections*, pp. 313-314.]

22 Ninck describes the condition in the following way: "It happens that being in the berserker state grants to the one so disposed a huge increase in strength, which 'come over' them, sometimes at specific times (evenings at the advent of darkness) and sometimes under the influ- ence of strong affects (rage, battle frenzy, or maddening pain)" (*Wodan*, p. 40).

23 Cf. also the short Russian tale "*Blendwerk* - Deceptions" (especially the first short tale).

78 A state of intoxication can also lead to one's being transported into the beyond, a kind of ecstatic rapture,[24] as related in the Chinese fairytale mentioned earlier, "How a Scholar Chastised the Princes of Hell."[25] A particularly beautiful portrayal of such an experience of ecstatic rapture is the tale, "The Lady of the Moon":

> 79 One night in mid-autumn, an emperor of the Tang dynasty sat *with two sorcerers drinking wine.* One of them took his bamboo staff and cast it *into the air*, where it transformed into a heavenly bridge. The three gentlemen climbed up to the moon together. There they saw a great castle on which was inscribed: *The Wide Halls of Crystal Coldness.* Beside it grew a cassia tree, which was in blossom, filling the air all around with its fragrance. A man sat in the tree trimming off the smaller boughs with an axe. One of the sorcerers said: "That is the man in the moon. The cassia tree grows so luxuriantly that in the course of time it would overshadow all the moon's radiance. Therefore, it must be cut down every thousand years." Then they entered into the wide halls. The silver stories towered one above the other. The columns and walls were all formed from *liquid crystal.* In the walls were cages and ponds where fish and birds moved as though alive. *The whole moon world seemed to be made of glass.* While they were still looking around them on all sides, the *Lady of the Moon* stepped up to them, clad in a white mantle and a rainbow-colored gown. She smiled and said to the emperor, "You are a prince of the mundane world of dust; you must have good fortune that you were able to find your way here." Then she called for her attendants. They came flying in on white birds, and sang and danced beneath the cassia tree. *Pure, crystal clear music floated through the air.* Next to the tree stood a mortar made of white marble. A rabbit made of jasper was grinding herbs. That was the dark side of the moon. When the dance had ended, the emperor returned to the Earth with the two sorcerers. He had the songs that he had heard on the moon written down and sung to the accompaniment of flutes of jasper in his pear-tree garden.

80 The imperial hero is accompanied by two sorcerers, similar to the Eskimo shaman and his guardian spirit. Like the tornaq, the sorcerers are in a certain sense parts of the emperor himself; they represent parts of him that have the inclination to make contact with the magical world. The unconscious is here again personified as the lunar realm. As the light that shines in the night, the moon encompasses all experiences that belong to this time; especially, as Jung

[24] [German: *entrücken.*]

[25] On the role of intoxication in journeys to the otherworld, see Bousset, *Himmelsreise*, pp. 162ff.

emphasizes,[26] the experience of Eros. Seen from a man's point of view, this is recognized as the receptive, feminine principle.[27] On the other hand, it is dangerous and also demonic, since,

81 > [F]or at night affect-laden and evil thoughts of power and revenge may disturb sleep. The moon is a disturber of sleep, and is also the abode of the departed souls, for at night the dead return in dreams and the phantoms of the past terrify the sleepless. Thus the moon also signifies madness ("lunacy").[28]

82 Many tales, therefore, connect the moon with human mortality. It is said by the Namaqua ethnic group of southern Africa:

83 > The moon once entrusted the rabbit to transfer a message to the humans. The message was, "Just as I die and arise again, so should you also die and rise again." The rabbit, however, changed the message into its opposite: "Just as I die and never rise again, so should you also die and never rise again." As punishment, the moon threw a stick at the rabbit and the stick split the rabbit's lips and he escaped. Just before, he scratched the moon in its face, and on a clear night you can still see the traces.[29]

84 According to ancient views, the moon also controls the "sublunary world" of ephemeral impermanence. It[30] creates the ebb and flow of the tides, controls the changing weather, is the lord of rain, and oversees women's monthly menstrual rhythm. The moon also rules the short-term rhythms of vegetative life. In India, the moon is called the "king of the plants and herbs," it is the life-giving, protecting patron of nature.[31] For these reasons, the moon is

---

[26] C.G. Jung, *The Structure of the Psyche*, CW 8, ¶330.

[27] A feminine moon appears in many myths: cf. Laiblin, *Das Urbild der Mutter* [The Original Image of the Mother], in *Zentralblatt für Psychotherapie*, 1936, vol. 9, p. 94. In Chinese, the moon is called Tai Yin, the great dark one, and is a symbol of the feminine receptive principle. Cf. *I Ching, the Book of Changes*, Wilhelm/Baynes, *I Ching*, Princeton, 1967 p. 302. For further support of this idea, see Bachofen, *Mutterrecht*, Stuttgart, 1861, p. 70, and C.G. Jung, *Symbols of Transformation*, CW 5, ¶408,¶487,¶577. The moon as a feminine principle fits with the fact that in most languages, the moon has feminine gender. [In German, the moon (*der Mond*) is masculine.]

[28] Jung, CW 5, ¶330. Cf. also Dieterich, *Eine Mithrasliturgie* [A Mithrasliturgy], pp. 201–203, and Deussen, *Sixty Upanishads*, p. 26, and *Kaushitaki-Upanishad*, vol. I, p. 2, where the Moon asks: "Who are you?" and the answer must be: "I am you," in order to pass to the worlds beyond. See also W. Ruben, *Die Philosophen*, Bern, 1947, pp. 266f [The Philosophers of the Upanishads]. As the sun's brother, the moon can be male, but is often male-female. See further: Bachofen, *Gräbersymbolik*, pp. 324ff; Bachofen, *Mutterrecht*, p. 22; Cumont, p. 57; J. Przyluski, "Mutter- Göttin," p. 44; C. Virolleaud, "Ischtar," p. 123; V. C. C. Collum, "Schöpferische Mutter-Göttin," pp. 243–244.

[29] See Wesselski, *Versuch*, p. 43. For other versions, see Wesselski, pp. 43–44.

[30] [I. e. the moon, which is masculine in German and many other languages and countries also, e.g. India (Sanskrit), ancient Egypt, Arabia, Hebrew, Slavonia, Latin, Lithuanian, Gothic, Teutonic, Swedish, Anglo-Saxon, and South America.]

[31] H. Zimmer, *Death and Rebirth*, New York, 1964 p. 329f.

connected with magic[32] and with all lowly animals living in swamps; it is a symbol of the unconscious, germinating, moist life.[33] In that the night signifies both complete unconsciousness and complete extinction of consciousness, the moon is a dim light in the darkness, and as such symbolises a kind of spiritual awareness, which is contained in the unconscious and distinguishes itself from the sharp intellect.[34] The moon embodies wisdom completely immersed in nature,[35] a *lumen naturae* [light of nature], as it is called by some philosophers of the Middle Ages.[36] This *moon consciousness* in its cool, detached, and observational attitude signifies a containment of all emotions and, in this sense, bestows impartial clarity; properties that are also symbolized in clear crystal or in the nature of glass, which appear in that realm.[37] The smoothness, solidity, and transparency of glass corresponds to the invisible and yet very present but intangible character of the magical world. This aspect of the unconscious is looked upon in eastern meditation as one of the highest states [of consciousness]. Thus it is written in, *The Secret of the Golden Flower*, on "Confirmatory Experiences During the Circulation of the Light," "The great world is like ice, a glassy jewel-world. The brilliancy of the light gradually crystallizes."[38] This relates, as Jung writes in his commentary, to the fixing of a clear detached consciousness.[39] Despite this, that world is paradoxically not dead, but rather contains the fullness of life.

---

[32] Compare in general Bächtold-Stäubli under *Mond* [Moon].

[33] Cf. Bachofen, *Gräbersymbolik*, pp. 324–325. Also in the views of the ancient Chinese, the rabbit or a three-legged rain toad. Cf. notes to "The Lady of the Moon" and "Sky O'Dawn."

[34] In Sanskrit, *manas*, the word for moon, is related to the English word for mind (in German, *Geist* = spirit, ghost.) This mind "does not participate, it contemplates cold and clear from far above down below and is a symbol for pure observing consciousness" (C.G. Jung, *Bericht über das Deutsche Seminar von Dr. C.G. Jung, 5.–10. Oktober 1931 in Küsnacht-Zürich,* zusammengestellt von Olga von Koenig-Fachsenfeld, Privatdruck, Stuttgart, 1932, p. 89.). Thus said Pan Shan, a Zen Buddhist (C.G. Jung, CW 11, *Forward to Suzik's "Zen Buddhism"* ¶884): "The moon of mind comprehends all the universe in its light." See also Rousselle, pp. 77, 83, 97f.

[35] For the Chinese text, "Hui Ming King" (The Book of Consciousness and Life), see R. Wilhelm, *Secret of the Golden Flower*, London, 1962, pp. 77–78:

> "A halo of light surrounds the world of the law,
> We forget one another, quiet and pure, altogether powerful and empty.
> The emptiness is irradiated by the light of the heart of heaven,
> The water of the sea is smooth and mirrors the moon on its surface,
> The clouds disappear in blue space; the mountains shine clear.
> Consciousness reverts to contemplation, the moon-disk reclines alone."

[36] Cf. C.G. Jung, *Psychology and Alchemy*, CW 12, ¶356,¶431,¶486f and Fig. 220.

[37] [in the fairytale, "The Lady of the Moon"] (trans.)

[38] Wilhelm, *Secret of the Golden Flower*, p. 50.

[39] C.G. Jung, "Commentary," in: *The Secret of the Golden Flower, a Chinese Book of Life*, translated by Cary F. Baynes, 2nd edition. Routledge & Kegan Paul, London, 1962, p. 122ff. The old German tribes imagined the heavens as being made of glass. See Maria Führer, *Nordgermanische Götterüberlieferung und deutsches Volksmärchen. 80 Märchen der Brüder Grimm vom Mythus her beleuchtet*, Neuer Filser-Verlag, München, 1938, p. 23. In fairytales, we often find the motif of the glass palace; see, for example, the crystal castle under water in the Chinese tale, "Notscha," where the dragon king lives. Cf. Hans Leisegang, The Mystery of the Serpent, in: *The Mysteries: Papers from the Eranos Yearbooks 2*, Routledge & Kegan Paul, London, 1955. One finds the same image in *Ezekiel* 1,22.

85 The rabbit in the moon, which also is composed of jasper, a gemstone, and represents the dark side of the moon, is a popular figure in China. The herbs that the rabbit grinds are actually the herbs of life from which the elixir of life, or the potion of immortality, is obtained.[40] Chinese alchemists concerned themselves with its production.[41] Also in India, the moon is the container in which the Indian nectar *Amrita*, the drink *deathless*, is stored.[42] Thus, the human soul's own knowledge of its immortality is concentrated in the image of the moon.

86 The emperor returns home enriched with a spiritual gain, the "clear tones" and "songs." This shows most impressively where the emperor and his two sorcerers found themselves with the "wine in the middle of an autumn night": in the realm of the soul.

87 Similar to the above fairytale is the Chinese tale, "King Mu of Dschou,"

> [King Mu revered a certain magician like a god and asked him to lodge with him in his palace. However, his palace was too humble and King Mu had yet another, larger and more sumptuous palace built for the magician and provided him with costly clothes, beautiful singing maidens, and luxuries of all kinds. The king's treasury was all but depleted. One day, the magician asked the king to go traveling with him.]

88 The King grasped the magician's sleeve, and thus they flew up through the air to the middle of the skies. When they stopped, they found they had reached the palace of the magician. It was built of gold and silver, and adorned with pearls and precious stones. It towered high over the clouds and rain; and none could say whereon it rested. To the eye it had the appearance of heaped-up clouds. All that it offered to the senses was different from the things of the world of men. It seemed to the King as though he were bodily present in the midst of the purple depths of the city of air, and of the divine harmony of the spheres where the Great God dwells. The King looked down, and his castles and pleasure house appeared to him like hills of earth and heaps of straw. And there the King remained for some decades and thought no more of his kingdom.

89 Then the magician again invited the King to go traveling with him once more. And in the place to which they came, there was to be seen

[40] Cf. Wilhelm, *The Chinese Fairy Book*, p. 55, and Frobenius, *Zeitalter*, p. 356.

[41] Cf. Wilhelm, *Secret of the Golden Flower*, pp. 52f.

[42] Cf. Zimmer, *Maya*, pp. 137f., 236; see also his *Kunstform und Yoga im indischen Kultbild*, pp. 112–113.

neither sun nor moon above, nor rivers or sea below. The king's dazzled eyes could not see the radiant shapes that displayed themselves; the king's dulled ears could not hear the sounds that played about them. It seemed as though his body was dissolving in confusion; his thoughts began to stray, and consciousness threatened to leave him. So he begged the magician to return. The magician put his spell on him and it seemed to the king as though he were falling into empty space.

90 When he regained consciousness, he was sitting at the same place where he had been sitting when the magician had asked him to travel with him for the first time. The servants waiting on him were the same, and when he looked down, his goblet was not yet empty, and his food had not yet grown cold.

91 The king asked what had happened. And the servants answered, "The king sat for a space of silence." Whereupon the king was quite bereft of reason, and it was three months before he regained his right mind. Then he questioned the magician. The magician said: "I was traveling with you in the spirit, O King! What need was there for your body to go along? And the place in which we stayed at that time was no less real than your own castle and your own gardens. But you are only used to permanent conditions, therefore, visions that dissolve so suddenly appear strange to you."

92 The king was content with that explanation. He gave no further thought to the business of government and took no more interest in his servants, but resolved to travel afar. So he had the eight famous steeds harnessed, and accompanied by a few faithful retainers, drove a thousand miles away. There he came to the country of the great hunters. The great hunters brought the king the blood of the white brandy to drink, and washed his feet in the milk of mares and cows. When the king and his followers had quenched their thirst, they drove on and camped for the night on the slope of the Kunlun Mountain, south of the Red River. The next day, they climbed to the peak of the Kunlun Mountain and gazed at the castle of the Lord of the Yellow Earth. Then they traveled on the Queen-Mother of the West. Before they got there, they had to pass the Weak River. This is a river whose waters will bear neither floats nor ships. All that attempt to float on its waters sink into its depths. When the king reached the shore, fish and turtles, crabs and salamanders came swimming and formed a bridge, so that he could drive across with his wagons.

93 It is said of the Queen-Mother of the West that she goes about with hair unkempt, with a bird's beak and tiger's teeth, and that she is

skilled in playing the flute. Yet this is not her true figure, but that of a spirit who serves her, and rules over the Western Sky. The Queen-Mother of the West gathers the immortals around her, and gives them to eat of the peaches of long life; and then they come to her with wagons of purple canopies, drawn by flying dragons. Ordinary mortals sink in the Weak River when they try to cross. But she was kindly disposed to King Wu. When he took leave of her, he also went on to the spot where the sun turns in after running three thousand miles a day. Then he returned again to his kingdom.

94 When King Wu was a hundred years old, the Queen-Mother of the West drew near his palace and led him away with her into the clouds.

95 And from that day on he was seen no more.[43]

96 The first part again shows a typical experience of ecstatic rapture into the realm of fantasy, actually a daydream that overtook the king at mealtime. He becomes so estranged from here-and-now reality that he feels that he has to go once again on a journey. But this journey is also a trip into the unconscious, where he meets supernatural, godly figures. The *Western Land* is also the land of the dead, as we will see in more detail further below.

[43] Wilhelm, *The Chinese Fairy Book*, pp. 95–99.

Chapter 3

The Hole in the Earth, the Sky-Hole, and the Cave

97 The connection between the state of sleep and a great journey, or quest, is depicted in an original way as "a journey of the eyes." A dream is in most cases a visual experience, in which we perceive a series of inner pictures, often even without being directly involved in the action. This probably prompts the primitive belief that it is the eyes themselves that "go out, travel around," and communicate wonderful experiences. A fairytale from the Khanty indigenous people (Russia), "The Man Who Remained Under the Earth," relates that:

> 98 The older of two hunters laid himself down to sleep during which time the younger busied himself skinning the winnings of the hunt. As this one was working, he noticed that the door opened a crack and two eyes rolled out. He set out in chase and saw how they rolled over hills, across a river, and up to a fallen cedar tree that blocked the trail. Then the eyes crawled under the trunk of the cedar tree. The young man stood waiting in front of the tree. The eyes slowly crept out and rolled the same way back again from whence they had come. To mark the path, the young man cut some wood chips and strewed them along the way. The eyes rolled back into the hut and into the clothes of the old man lying asleep. In the meantime, their meal, which had been cooking in a pot over the fire, was ready and the two men sat themselves down to eat. The young hunter asked the older one if he had dreamt anything. The older one said, "Indeed, I had a dream! Under the fallen trunk of a cedar tree I saw a veritable treasure!" First thing the next morning they set out and followed the trail of wood chips all the way to the big cedar. There they began to dig and found a cavern into which the old man crawled. He fell into the living room where a woman was sitting on a bed. She said, "All my life I have waited for you. Finally you have come!" She suggested that he stay with her and her treasure, and he agreed. However, he wished to have a word with his partner. She allowed him on the condition that he speak only one word. He tried to find the exit, but could not see any way. The woman said, "Just where you are standing, look up and go

> there." He looked up and saw an open door. The man and the woman went out together and found the young man almost starving from hunger. The older man asked the woman: "Whom should I notify that this young man is close to dying?" The woman brought a small flask out of her pocket and gave the young man a spoonful of the water that was in the flask. He immediately recovered and began to speak. The old man interrupted and said, "Go back to my house and tell my people that I am staying here." The young man set out, the older man went with the woman back into her underground room. "And both of them are still there, under the earth."[1]

99 The rolling eyes symbolize the wide-ranging clairvoyance of dream consciousness, in which human beings can jump over the boundaries of time and space set by the body and can perceive things far outside the reach of the senses. When the man is then caught spellbound by an underworld female figure, this means – as will be discussed in more detail below – that he is trapped in his unconscious soul which appears to him personified by this woman.

100 In Europe, similar tales were handed down. In Paulus Diaconus (ca. 725–ca. 799), for instance, we read:

> 101 The Franconian (or Burgundian) King Guntram (died 593), who once during the hunt was overtaken by exhaustion, sat down under a tree to rest. He put his staff in the lap of one of his entrusted retainers. All at once this attendant saw how a small snake-like animal crawled out of the mouth of the king, and made its way to a nearby brook and tried in vain to get across. He drew his sword from its sheath and laid it over the brook. The snake-like animal crawled over the sword-bridge and disappeared into an opening in the mountain. After a while, it came out again and crawled back over the sword-bridge and into the mouth of the king. After the king awoke, he told his attendants that he had dreamed he crossed a river on an iron bridge and had gone into a mountain. There he came upon a huge pile of gold. His trusted attendant told the king what he had observed. The king and his entourage made their way to the exact place in the mountain where he had gone in his dream. They dug down until they found an immense treasure.[2]

[1] H. Kunike, *Sibirien*, Jena, 1940, pp. 48–50. [For the original, see A. Ahlqvist, *Sprache der Nord-Ostjaken*, Helsingfors, 1880, pp. 3–6.]

[2] Cited in Wesselski, *Versuch*, pp. 172–173. For additional, similar examples, see Leeuw, *Religion in Essence*, vol. 1, pp. 269ff. Cf. also Emil Abegg, *Indische Psychologie*, pp. 10 –11 [Indian Psychology].

102 Once again, this concerns a part of the soul that can step out of the body, as in the Inuit tale, "Flight to the Moon," where it is personified as an animal. These few examples of otherworldly experiences already demonstrate certain motifs that thread their way through many tales. The "soul land" is often characterized by waters, like the Maiden's Lake and the Eastern Sea in "Help in Need," and even in "Flight to the Moon," when the shaman finds an ocean in which seals swim. The entrance is sometimes described as a hole. In the same Inuit tale, the reindeer, a gift from the Man of the Moon to the angakoq, falls through a hole to the Earth. Such a "sky-hole" or "heaven-hole" also occurs in another fairytale that we will discuss later, "The Woman Who Became a Spider," in which after being disappointed by her lover, a girl makes her way up to heaven:

103 The girl climbed upwards and upwards without knowing how. Finally she came to a roof with an opening that looked very much like a hole. But it was very difficult to reach that place and she did not know how she could go up there. Suddenly she plucked up her courage, jumped up high, and just managed to grab the rim. From here she could swing through the opening in the roof and looked around. Here there was again air and sky and land! A little to one side there was a lake. She went there and sat on the shore in the grass in order to die. She did not want to think any longer.[3]

104 After many adventures in which she is initiated into the mysteries of the other world and the spirit of the moon, the girl returns to the Earth. The image of the hole as the entrance into the magical realm depicts a state of inner restriction. This is a symbol of holding oneself captive and is equivalent to the extinction of light as described in detail in "Flight to the Moon." After performing the passage from one world into the other, the netherworld again opens up into the cosmic dimension. In the example depicted by Rasmussen, this netherworld is described as being just like our world except that it is inhabited by spirits. One sees therein the spiritual backdrop of processes that cannot be comprehended in our world.

105 Closely related to the symbol of the hole is that of the cave, also a manifestation of the other world. For example, people on Knossos (Greece) revered the cave where Zeus was said to have been born. Judging from the gifts of sanctification, the cave was regarded as having been the seat of the god as well as his grave. Sanctuaries of heroes and/or their graves that were home to oracles were often located in caves. Pythagoras' "cave journey," a kind of

---

[3] [Beginning only, summarized from the German translation (of the original Danish) by Schmücker in Rasmussen, *Gabe des Adlers*, Frankfurt a. M., 1937, pp. 107–114. This tale is interpreted at length in M.-L. von Franz, *Feminine in Fairy Tales*, New York, 2001, pp. 95ff.]

"descent into hell,"[4] is a classic journey to the otherworld.[5] Caves are often regarded as graves of the gods. A description of the afterworld as a cave is also found in the Chinese fairytale, "The Dragon-Princess":

> 106 *In the Sea of Dungting there is a hill, and in that hill there is a hole, and this hole is so deep that it has no bottom.* Once a fisherman was passing there, and he slipped and fell into the hole. He came to a country full of *winding ways* that led over hill and dale for many miles. Finally he reached a dragon-castle lying in a great plain. There grew a green slime that reached to his knees. He went to the gate of the castle. It was guarded by a dragon who spouted water that dispersed in a fine mist. Within the gate lay a small hornless dragon who raised his head, showed his claws, and would not let him in.
>
> 107 The fisherman spent several days in the cave, satisfying his hunger with the green slime, which he found edible and tasted like ricemush. He told the district mandarin what had happened to him, and the latter reported the matter to the emperor. The emperor sent for a wise man and questioned him concerning it.
>
> 108 The wise man said: "There are four paths in this cave. One path leads to the south-west shore of the Sea of Dungting, the second path leads to a valley in the land of the four rivers, the third path ends in a cave on the mountain of Lo-Fu, and the fourth in an island of the Eastern Sea. In this cave dwells the seventh daughter of the Dragon-King of the Eastern Sea, who guards his pearls and treasure. . ."[6]

109 In this fairytale, the place of the magical appears in especially multifarious forms, as a mountain and underworld landscape, a lake, a sea, a cave, and as a castle. Already in "Help in Need" (*China), there was ambiguity about the location of the magical processes. In the fairytale, "The Man Who Remained Under the Earth" (*Siberia), the scene in which the man can no longer find the exit betrays a remarkably uncertain conception of space. As mentioned, this motif is striking in the well-known Grimm's fairytale, "Mother Holle," where the heroine, by jumping into a well, lands in a "lovely green meadow," and thence to an oven, an apple tree, and finally to Mother Holle's house. When she shakes out the bedding, however, it snows down in the world. We

[4] [German *Höhlenfahrt* [cave journey] is also known as *Höllenfahrt* [descent into hell], like that of Ishtar.]

[5] Cf. E. Rohde, *Psyche*, London, 1925, pp. 128ff.

[6] This is the same Dungting Sea with the ninth daughter of the Dragon-King from the Eastern Sea that we encountered in the fairytale, "Help in Need."

experience here something astounding: by falling into the depths, one arrives in a heaven where it snows down onto the Earth.[7]

110 Ernst Tegethoff[8] gives a good collection of the fantastic spatial descriptions of the magical realm. It lies, for example, to the south of the sun, west of the moon, in the middle of the world; or south of the sun, east of the moon, west of all the winds; west of the Tower of Babylon, east of the sun, north of the world; it is the easternmost castle in the world, on the mountain of glass, the golden mountain by the glass palace, the crystal mountain in the empty field, the golden mount, the diamond castle, the city of glass; the other side of the fiery stream, the *Isola della felicita* [island of joy]; by the marble hills; where the sun sets and it is always winter. It is the golden tower at the end of the world; the end of the world kingdom; the city of the Sahara; the land of profound anxiety. In spite of all these variations, we are dealing with fundamentally one and the same motif, from which it follows that many different place names are often mixed together. It is always a world characterized by an entrance through a state of unconsciousness: through sleep, death, trance, or ecstatic rapture, where one can clearly recognize that it symbolizes the unconscious realm of the human soul. It is as if in the unconscious, the notions of space and time are relativized and the scales we apply to the outer world based on our human perspective lose their validity.[9]

---

7 "Sink then! I could also say, 'Climb!'" says Mephisto, when Faust wants to go to the Mothers. [J. W. v. Goethe, *Faust, A Tragedy*, New York, 1976/2001, Part 2, Chapter 15.]

8 E. Tegethoff, "Amor und Psyche," Bonn and Leipzig, 1922, p. 75.

9 Cf. C.G. Jung, "Man's sense of proportion, his rational conception of big and small, is distinctly anthropomorphic, and it loses its validity not only in the realm of physical phenomena, but also in those parts of the collective unconscious beyond the range of the specifically human. The atman is 'smaller than small and bigger than big,' he is 'the size of a thumb' yet he 'encompasses the earth on every side and rules over the ten-finger space'" ("Phenomenology of the Spirit," CW 9i, ¶408.)

Chapter 4
The Well

111 With its deep-lying water table, which looks like an eye in the dark,[1] the well is another recurring symbol of the magical realm or the land of the souls. It is often endowed with female and mothering qualities and is clearly connected to ideas about birth. A widely disseminated belief is that small children come out of a well. These are known in Germany as *Hollenteiche* [hell ponds] or *Hollenbrunnen* [hell wells], from which the stork fetches the children.[2] At the same time, the well is also the entrance to the land of the dead and the night. According to the Koran, the sun sinks every evening in the West into a well full of black mud, where the door to the underworld lies.[3] In the Germanic [i.e., Old Norse] underworld, two wells flow under the world ash, Yggdrasil from which Odin/Woden draws his divinatory power. He sacrificed one of his eyes that from that day on lay in the well Urd, from which life emerged at the beginning of time.[4] In many fairytales, the well houses all kinds of demons. Like the hole, it typifies a transitional state of the soul, the moment of going into the unconscious, which one often perceives as a sinking, descent, a going inside, going-into-oneself, a passageway into the other world.[5] One attains another state of mind or psychic state, namely an unconsciousness that, as seen from normal daytime consciousness is a faraway kingdom that is always all around us.[6] One tale that graphically describes the remarkably unreal dream-world whose nearness is self-evident for many primitive peoples is "Yiñeañeut and the Earth-Maker" (*Siberia - Koryak). Of most interest here

---

[1] Cf. G. Róheim, *Spiegelzauber*, Leipzig and Vienna, 1919, p. 212, fn. 7, "Children should not look into water or throw stones into a well, for therein lies the eye of God."

[2] Cf. H. Silberer, *Problems of Mysticism*, New York, 1917, p. 64. See also O. Rank, *Myth of the Birth of the Hero*, Baltimore, 2004, p. 97ff.; A. Dieterich, *Eine Mithrasliturgie*, Leipzig and Berlin, 1923, p. 144; M. Führer, *Nordgermanische*, München, 1938, p. 93.

[3] *Koran*, Sutra 18, Verse 84 and Jung's discussion in C.G. Jung, *Symbols of Transformation*, CW 5, ¶634. See further the legend of the Siute Indians (California) where, according to A. Lang, "Down deep under the ground – deep, deep under all the ground – is a great hole. At night, when he, the sun, has passed over the world, looked down on everything and finished his work, then he goes into his hole, and he crawls and creeps along it till he comes to his bed in the middle part of the earth. So then he, the sun, sleeps there in his bed all night" (*Myth*, London, 1887, vol. I, p. 131).

[4] Cf. M. Führer, *Nordgermanische*, München, 1938, pp. 15 and 17.

[5] For examples in which the well is a passage to the magical realm or the residence of the demons, see the collection of motifs in Bolte and Mackensen, *Handwörterbuch*, under *Brunnen* [well].

[6] See also the description of the dreamworld in Leeuw §60/3, §82/5.

is not the individual events, but rather the spatial transitions and the unreal overall atmosphere:[7]

112 Once Yiñeañeut, Canaiñut, Kilu, and Kidney-Woman went to pick berries and dig roots. Yiñeañeut parted from her friends. She left her bag on the ground, walked away from it, picked berries, and returned to her bag. She looked around and saw marrow from the bone of a reindeer-leg on her bag. She took the marrow. Yiñeañeut came to be with child from eating the marrow. On the following day, she said to her sisters, "Go alone after berries and roots, I am going to stay at home." The sisters left without her. During their absence, Yiñeañeut gave birth to a boy. Autumn set in. The brothers came up the river in their skin boats to get their sisters. The brothers loaded the skin boats with the berries, roots, and fly-agaric[8] gathered by the girls. The Reindeer people arrived. Big-Raven ordered the child [of Yiñeañeut] to be brought in. He said to it, "Look at the Reindeer people. Is your father among them?" The child did not point out any of them. For some time Big-Raven's family lived alone. One evening somebody drove up on a reindeer-sledge. His son, Ememqut went out to meet him, and saw that the newly arrived stranger was very young-looking, quite like a boy. His name was Earth-Maker (Tanu'ta).[9] Eme'mqut said to him, "You must have come to look for your son. "Yes," answered Earth-Maker, "I have come to see him. I was ashamed to come in human form and woo Yiñeañeut. Therefore I turned into the marrow of a reindeer-leg. She ate me, and became with child."

113 Earth-Maker entered the house, stayed overnight, and in the morning went off home with Yiñeañeut on a long train of reindeer-sledges. Big-Raven gave him a part of his own reindeer herd. When Earth-Maker drove up to his house, his relatives came out to see who had arrived, and, beholding Yiñeañeut with a child, said, "That woman gave birth without a husband." Yiñeañeut felt ashamed, and turned into stone. Earth-Maker, seeing this, thought, "Yiñeañeut is now dead. I shall go back, and return the reindeer to Big Raven." He did not even enter his house, but went back at once. He arrived at Big Raven's house, and suddenly saw Yiñeañeut there. "You are here! And I thought you were

[7] The tale has been shortened (i.e., some details have been omitted). Big-Raven is looked upon by the Koryak as the founder of the world. Yiñeañeut and Čanai-ñia'ut are his daughters, Eme'mqut is one of his sons. Yiñeañeut and Eme'mqut are shamans and constantly engaged in a struggle with malevolent beings (W. Jochelson, *The Koryak*, New York, 1975, pp. 18–22).

[8] [Fly agaric (*Amanita muscaria*) is a mushroom used as a hallucinogenic by the Siberian shamans and often given as a present when visiting friends.]

[9] [Tanu'ta literally means "he made the Earth" (Jochelson, *The Koryak*, p. 300).]

dead." "I was ashamed before your relatives," answered Yiñeañeut. "Therefore I turned into a stone, and came here alone."

114 On the following day they drove off again. As they drove up to Earth-Maker's house, they saw the stone still standing there. Yiñeañeut kicked it, and another Yiñeañeut stood there. She gave her in marriage to Frost-Man. From that time on, Yiñeañeut's health began to give way. Earth-Maker attended to her, gave up looking after the reindeer, and neglected his herds.

115 One day Earth-Maker went out and *stumbled* against a big snow-drift. He looked around, and saw the *entrance to an underground house*. He peeped in, and beheld a young man walking up and down. It was Cloud-Man. Cloud-Man shouted to him, "Earth-Maker, is that you?" "Yes, it is I," answered Earth-Maker. "Come in," said Cloud-Man. Earth-Maker descended, and saw an old man and an old woman sleeping there. The old man was Supervisor, the father of Cloud-Man. Cloud-Man asked Earth-Maker, "What do you think? Why is your wife's health giving way?" "I do not know," answered Earth-Maker. "Her health is declining," continued Cloud-Man, "because you did not kill the double-headed reindeer from your father's herd when you brought your young wife into your house. Just look at the fire on the hearth, and see how my father pushes your wife into it." He looked, and really saw his wife sitting on stones, which surrounded the hearth. There he also saw little boys with short straps on their thumbs. "Do you see those little boys?" said Cloud-Man. "They are to be your future children. They will be born, but they will not live long. Look at them, their straps are short." Later on Cloud-Man pointed out a six- fingered girl sitting on the cross-beam of the house, and said to Earth-Maker, "Wake up the old man, and ask him for that girl. She has a long strap around her neck. She will live long. Don't ask for boys."

116 Earth-Maker tried to waken Supervisor and his wife; and long did he call before Supervisor woke up. Earth-Maker asked him, "Why are you asleep? Why don't you watch over the earth?" "We went to sleep," answered Supervisor, "because you took your wife home, and would not kill the double-headed reindeer for us on that occasion. Therefore we sleep, and push your wife into the fire." Earth-Maker replied, "As soon as I reach home, I will kill the double-headed reindeer." After that, Supervisor asked Earth-Maker, "Do you wish to have a son?" "No," answered Earth-Maker. "I don't care for a son, give me a six-fingered girl." "All right," said Supervisor. Later on he added, "Now go home. On your way you will kill a wolf. Give the skin of that wolf to

your wife for bedding. Earth-Maker went *out of the house*, looked around, and, behold! *there was no snowdrift. He found himself in the sky. He looked down on the earth through an opening*, saw different settlements, and recognized his own camp. After that, he came *down to the earth*. On his way a wolf came running up to him. Earth-Maker killed him, and carried him home.

117 As soon as Earth-Maker came to his father's camp, he immediately went to his herd, picked out the double-headed reindeer, and offered it as a sacrifice to Cloud-Man. After that, Yiñeañeut recovered. Soon after, Yiñeañeut gave birth to a six-fingered daughter. Thus they lived, and called on each other. That's all.[10]

118 We see here how dreamworld[11] and reality are strangely mixed together.[12] The underground snowdrift is heaven and at the same time the beyond[13] in which past and future are still one, where even the unborn are visible. Earth-Maker gains insight into the fateful relations in his family and can thus even steer them to the good. Also, the remarkable transformations and doubling capacities of the individual human being show how much in the primitive mind dream and reality coincide.

---

[10] Jochelson, *The Koryak*, pp. 299–302. [Told by Yu'taw, a Maritime Koryak woman in Tavloka, 1900.]
[11] [*Traumjenseits, Traum* = dream; *Jenseits* = the world beyond consciousness.]
[12] [In *The Koryak*, Jochelson writes: "Not only all visible objects, but also the phenomena of nature, are regarded as animate beings," p. 115.] On the primitive frame of mind, whose reality and the dream otherworld (and also the fairytale world) are so close, see Lévy-Bruhl's *The "Soul" of the Primitive* (1928) and *How Natives Think* (1966).
[13] [*Jenseits*.]

Chapter 5
Water

119 In another Koryak fairytale, "Ememqut and the White Whale Woman" (Siberia - Koryak), the hero, Ememqut went out looking for White Whale Woman, one of his wives who had run away and encountered astonishing things.

> 120 While he was on his way, Ememqut found a brook from which he wanted to take a drink. He smelled smoke coming up from beneath. He looked down, and saw a house on the bottom. His aunt Amillu, and her servant Kihillu, were sitting side by side in the house. While he was drinking from the brook, his tears fell into the water, and dropped right through into his aunt's house, moistening the people below.
>
> 121 "Oh!" they said, "it is raining." They looked upward, and saw the man drinking. "Oh!" they said, "there is a guest." Then Kihillu said, "Shut your eyes, and come down." *He closed his eyes, and immediately found a ladder by which he could descend.* "Give him food," said Amillu. The servant picked up a tiny minnow from the floor, in the corner, all split and dried. She brought also the shell of a nut of the stone pine and a minnow's bladder not larger than a fingernail. Out of the latter, she poured some oil into the nutshell, and put it before Ememqut with the dried fish. "Shut your eyes, and fall to." He thought, "This is not enough for a meal," but he obeyed, and with the first movement dipped his hand into the fish-oil, arm and all, up to the elbow. He opened his eyes, and a big dried king-salmon lay before him, by the side of the oil-bowl. He ate of the fish, seasoning it with oil.[1]

122 In this account, everything is again strangely unreal. For instance, Aunt Amillu's house is actually visible in the water and Ememqut, the hero, can make his way to it by closing his eyes. This once again clearly involves a world of fantasy or dream from which a man obtains a new orientation for his life. It is not just fortuitous that we time and again draw on narratives of natural peoples to describe the magical realm. European fairytales have retained

[1] Jochelson, *The Koryak*, pp. 310–311 [Told in the village of Pallan].

similar motifs, but tend to radically shorten the exposition, as if the knowledge can no longer be taken for granted, or is no longer a vividly living memory. With the gypsies, who have remained relatively primitive, one still finds a rich selection of such motifs of transition and dreamlike descriptions of the magical kingdom, which they simply call the afterworld.[2] The translator and editor of the *Zigeuner Märchen* [Gypsy Fairy Tales], Walter Aichele and Martin Block, report[3] that the gypsies believe that at the end of the world there is a hole (hâu), through which one can let oneself down into the other world that is beneath the ground. This lies in the West, where the sun goes down. The journey there usually takes place by riding on two roosters fitted, like horses, with shoes. The time of sleep in the underworld is exactly when the sun is at midday, that is, at midnight in the upper world. In the underworld, two demonic pigs are resting, whose piglets the hero comes to take back, as well as the apple tree, the mountains, and the clouds. The underworld is also the realm of the dead; a human who speaks (or eats something) there must remain in that world. Darkness reigns. The hero must keep walking night and day for two months until he beholds a light and at the same time the castle of a black, man-eating emperor.

123 We have already come across water several times as an aspect of the magical realm, the motif of the Maiden Lake in "Help in Need" (*China), and in the image of the ocean on the moon in "Flight to the Moon" (*North America), and also in the last Siberian tale, " Ememqut and the White Whale Woman" (Siberia - Koryak). Water often has, mythologically speaking, a maternal quality. In the Vedas, the waters are called mâtritamâh, the most maternal.[4] This meaning emerges especially clearly in the widespread folk belief concerning children's ponds[5] and wells. In the waters live nixies, mermaids, and nymphs.[6] As the Germanic tribes believed that before birth the human soul tarries in the waters, so they also assumed that after death, it returns or is transported there.[7] Over the whole world one finds the belief that the kingdom of the dead is reached by crossing over water or a lake (for instance, in ancient Greece, the River Styx in the underworld Hades). Water, heavenly or subterranean, and that which surrounds the whole world as an ocean, is not only the original homeland and land of the dead of individual human beings, but in most creation myths, the actual primordial element out

---

[2] See, for example, "The Evil Mother" and "The Emperor's Son and the Monster (Ogre)."

[3] W. Aichele, *Zigeunermärchen*, Jena, 1926, p. 317, esp. his comments on "The Evil Mother."

[4] Cf. C.G. Jung, *Symbols of Transformation*, CW 5, ¶319. For water as a symbol of the mother, see also *Ibid.*, ¶306–311, 319, 540 f., 551; and *"Mother Archetype,"* CW 9i, ¶156.

[5] [The name is derived from the legend that when making a wish for children, one stands with one's back to the pond and tosses a coin into the water over one's head.]

[6] See Przyluski, "Ursprünge," pp. 15ff.

[7] See Ninck, Wodan, pp. 208, 210, 256–257, 279–280.

of which the whole cosmos arises.[8] For the ancient Egyptians, Greeks, and Gnostics, water was the *prima materia* of the universe,[9] and in India, immersion in the shimmering and continuously transforming element revealed the secret of Maya: the deceitful veil of formed matter.[10] So is water, under whose surface all submerged things reside and which conceals unimaginable depths, a symbol for the unconscious out of which everything real arises but which can also flood and engulf reality.[11] But in that the creative power of the soul resides in the unconscious, water often represents[12] the depths, which house the treasure, the value of life, for which the hero is searching.[13]

---

[8] According to the ancient Germanic tribes, the world arises out of a cauldron of boiling water, the spring Hvergelmir, under the roots of Yggdrasil, the world ash tree. On the cult of springs and wells, see Führer, *Nordgermanische*, München, p. 20, and Ninck, *Wodan*, p. 204.

[9] Cf. Erman, *Religion der Ägypter*, p. 61, and Bachofen, *Gräber-symbolik*, pp. 319–320, 332. See also Leisegang, *Die Gnosis*, p. 153 (on the creation beliefs of the Ophites), and Leisegang, pp. 206–207 (on orphic cosmology). The original water, from which arose the fertilizing wind, is called Oceanus, which flows in a circle from above to below and from below to above, like the River Jordan that flows upstream and downstream (see Leisegang, *Die Gnosis*, pp. 140–141). For the Naassenes, water symbolizes transitoriness and lies in the form of a sphere at the outer edge of the world (Leisegang, *Die Gnosis*, pp. 148–149.) See also the work of Angelus Silesius [Johann Scheffier] (1624–1677). In *The Cherubinic Wanderer*, trans. by Maria Shrady, he writes in a section titled "Divinity": "Divinity's a spring; all things therefrom have motion and yet again flows back as if it were ocean" (Paulist Press, New Jersey, 1986, p. 53, 3:168).

[10] See Heinrich Zimmer's *Maya* (pp. 44, 46, 363–365) and *Weisheit Indiens* (pp. 25–27). Also in Indian cosmogony, water is the original element through which the animating spirit-breath emerges and enlivens the whole world (cf. Deussen, *Geheimlehre*, p. 5 [*Rigveda* 10, 121, 7] and p. 7 [*Rigveda* 10, 82, 5, and 6]). Correlative to this is the Indian concept of the return into unconsciousness, "to return home like the rivers return to the sea," which is also the highest goal of the wise (Zimmer, *Maya*, p. 87). He reached the river "Ageless," which borders the Indian underworld (Zimmer, *Death and Rebirth*, p. 275; see also Zimmer, *Mother*, pp. 89-90.)

[11] Cf. C.G. Jung, Psychology and Alchemy, CW 12, ¶57. This is the idea that the flood symbolizes the bursting forth of all passions, in which everything sinks that was once shaped by consciousness. Cf. C.G. Jung, Symbols of Transformation, CW 5, ¶170. See also Psalms 124: 2-5, in which water is identified with evil.

[12] [*versinnbildlicht*, alternative translation: symbolizes]

[13] See also the Gilgamesh myth, where the hero attains the herb of immortality from the bottom of the ocean.

Chapter 6
The Island

124 In the dreamlike landscape of fairytales, certain images are often interwoven. For instance, there can be a lake or sea on the moon and, as in the ancient world, one might find a well topped by a mirror in the lake.[1] In the image of the island in the distant sea, two symbols of the land of the soul are threaded together: water, with its eternally undulating waves, and the distant solid land. A Latvian fairytale, "Adventure of a King's Son," exhibits the strong influence of Homer's *Odyssey* and offers a particularly beautiful description of such a magical island:

> 125 The son of a king once got lost on the ocean and after a long odyssey came to an island that was surrounded all around by high, high walls from which emanated wonderful sounds. The young man wanted to sail on, but his mariners were so confused and lost they could find neither the way to leave the island nor the route back from which they had come. They thus struggled a long time, until finally, they just managed to tow their ship past one small piece of the island. But on the other side they beheld a new wonder: an even higher bridge, higher than all the walls, stretched from this island to an even further, more distant island. As soon as the mariners secured the bridge, it was as if the scales fell from their eyes: now they knew just what to do; they knew where to sail and where not.
>
> 126 They sailed onwards to the second island and discovered a magnificent castle from which wonderful sounds emanated. The King's son entered the castle and found himself in a room that was empty, and then in another room that was full of sheep with one particularly large sheep in the middle. He went further into a third room and this one was filled wall to wall by one huge fish. Full of courage, the king's son drew his sword and gauged the fish's eyes out. The fish suddenly transformed itself into a huge iron giant who felt around, trying to grab the king's son. But the king's son crawled under

[1] According to Lucian, *Vera Historia* [True Story], mentioned in Róheim, *Spiegelzauber*, p. 247.

one of the sheep and hid in its fleece. Then he managed to escape back to his ship and with the mariners they put to sail. The giant threw stones at the escaping mariners. Each stone that fell on the ship became a clump of gold, but whoever took the gold into their hands became dumb. The ship sailed over the bridge back to the walled island.

127 As soon as they arrived there, the wonderful sounds stopped. "Hang it all," called out the king's son. "Someone should climb up the high wall and see what that wonderful sound is." With great difficulty, one of his mariners climbed up the wall, but no sooner did he gain the rim, than he began to clap his hands and, full of rapture, let out a cry of elation and jumped over to the other side. The king's son then sent another sailor up to the top. When this one reached the top, he clapped his hands like his predecessor, let out a cry of jubilation, and jumped like a butterfly over the wall. A third mariner was then sent, but on this one they tied a strong rope to hold him back. At the top, he too was struck silent by joy. Then they wanted to sail away, but could make no headway at all. The king's son knew no other way to move onwards but to sacrifice his most precious treasure, his sword, to the sea and beg for help. Thus entreating, he tossed his sword to the waves. Immediately, a dignified old man arose out of the water holding a diamond sword in his hand. He spoke: "Take this sword and throw it in the air!" The king's son grasped the sword and heaved it high in the air. In a flash the sword and the ship were covered in an impenetrable fog like a cloud. The ocean surged and the ship heaved forwards until it landed in front of the entrance to his father's castle.

128 Even stronger than its prototype, *Odyssey*, the dreamlike quality of the whole experience is prominent here. The distant island is clearly characterized as the center of a magical realm. The duality of the island indicates the double aspect of this world, its secret conflicting nature, which is expressed, on the one hand, in the delightful and tempting island, and on the other hand, in its harboring a monster. The huge fish embodies the creative potential of the unconscious, a motif that cannot be further delved into here. Through the fact that the king's son gains entrance to the innermost being of the magical realm with his sword, it then becomes threatening and overwhelms him as an overpowering being. The hero himself has at the same time broached an unconscious problem that now overwhelms his soul. As he obviously is not up to solving this problem alone, he is rescued by some magical help. Aid comes from the old sea god, who separates the island from the ship with a fog. This involves a kind of psychic escape through "fogging" over the conflict that has been stirred up. Here the island points to being split off from a central content, which alludes

to being detached, as it were, from the human element in the sea of the unconscious. The magic distant island thus points to an "isolated" content within the soul, a piece of conscious life, which is cut off from the ordinary land, that is, from daily consciousness. This split-off content has nevertheless an effect on consciousness – be it through enticement (the Siren's music), or through being disoriented or spellbound. Ego-consciousness is, however, partly enticed (by the music of the Sirens[2]), and partly disoriented (he himself is the cause of getting lost, i.e., "losing one's self"). Being on an island is like being banished; but even then one cannot escape merely by going inward.[3]

---

[2] On the Sirens as death demons, see Weicker, *Der Seelenvogel in der alten Literatur und Kunst: eine mythologisch-archaeologische Untersuchung*, Leipzig, 1902, pp. 37ff., 84 [The Soulbirds].

[3] Cf. also the motif of the *Islands of the Blessed*, where according to the view of the ancient Greeks, the heroes repair after death: "... these lie far removed from the world of men, in the Oceanus, on the edge of the earth, just where the *Odyssey* puts the Elysian plain, another meeting-place of the still-living. ... Homer never expressly calls the land of the Phaeacians an island, but the imagination of most readers will picture Scheriê as such, and so did the Greeks perhaps already at the time of the Hesiodic school of poets. In the same way a poet may have thought of the "Land of Destiny" that receives passing mention in Homer as an island, or group of islands; only an island surrounded and cut off by the sea can give the full impression of a distant asylum far from the world, inaccessible to all save those specially called thither. And accordingly the mythology of many peoples, especially those who live by the sea, has made a distant island the dwelling-place of the souls of the departed" (Rohde, *Psyche*, pp. 75–76, 416, fn. 44.

Chapter 7
The End of the World

129 Sometimes the beyond is described in a vague way as comprising water and at the same time land, as for instance in the impressive description of the other world by the [Inuit] in "Misana, Who Was Swept Away to the Land of the Beads":

> 130 There was once a young man who was called Misana. He was so young that he had just begun to get a small beard, yet he was a powerful hunter, who hunted walrus in all kinds of weather. But one day while out hunting in his canoe he was driven far out to sea away by a storm. For days he wandered between the ice floes. He bound four gut-skin covers round the manhole so that no water could pour in, and crawled down to the bottom of his big kayak, where he could lie outstretched while the waves tossed him about and swept him wherever they pleased. Suddenly he found himself in deep darkness and thought he was at the bottom of the sea. But no water came in through the hole in the kayak, and he realized that he had been washed upon a dark land. Tired to death, he lay down on the beach and slept.
>
> 131 He slept long, awakened, and slept again until at last he was quite rested. But it was still pitch dark around him. He rose and tried to accustom himself to the darkness, staring into it to see if he could discern anything. All he could distinguish was a loud roaring noise in the air, sometimes near, sometimes far. Sadly he groped his way back to his kayak, but when he reached the shore, he got his hands full of small, smooth, round particles. He put one of them into his mouth and discovered that there was a hole through it, and now he took the string from his storm jacket and strung it with the wonderful stones.
>
> 132 . . . He remembered having once heard of *Qasuilaoq*, the land of eternal darkness, which lay somewhere at the end of the world, and where there were only nights and no days. And now he understood that the noise in the air came from the motion of the earth; he was standing at the end of the world, and the roaring came from the mighty abyss that encompasses the earth. Thus Misana was saved

from the sea, but had come to a land that was no real land after all. Again he sat thinking for a long time until he decided to continue the journey, if possible. He turned his kayak so as to have land to the right, for he believed that he must go in that direction to come back to the world of men where day and night alternated.

133 He paddled on and on in the darkness, without knowing how long. Suddenly he noticed something floating in the water. The sky had begun to lighten a little, and he paddled up to the object and discovered that it was a dead seal. At the same moment the joy of living came back to him, and he knew that he would do his very best to return to men once more. He followed the coast and whenever he was tired he went ashore to rest. His strength returned more and more. Every morning the strip of dawn on the horizon grew higher and higher; the light increased, and he approached the regions where day alternates with night. At last it grew so light that he could see his surroundings, and now he discovered that his kayak, which had become strangely heavy to row, was completely overgrown with something that resembled hair. He was thirsty, and searched for fresh water. He found a little lake and started to drink when for the first time he saw his image in the water. He had to laugh aloud when he realized that his hair, beard, eyelashes, and eyebrows, nay, all the hair on his face, was gone. It had all been whizzed off at the end of the world. He examined the stones he had gathered, and only now did he discover that they were *sungaujarpait*, the famous and very costly big beads that were said to be found only at the end of the world.

134 [After many varied adventures with fish, seals, and women, Misana finally reached his homeland. He was by then an old man and walked with a cane, a man who had lived a restless life since he had sea otter fuzz on his chin. But it was told that he had learned so many songs that people flocked to him to hear him sing.][1]

135 This fairytale gives an account of a temporary submersion of consciousness in the indistinguishable darkness of the unconscious, with its dangers and highest values. The suspension of the alternation of night and day shows also the suspension of all opposites. For it is the opposites themselves that enable us to differentiate and perceive Being[2] consciously. Sometimes there follows a state in which the unconscious itself begins to lighten up and even to

[1] Some parts have been shortened. The tale was told to Rasmussen by Qalajaq, an Iñupiat from Point Hope, Alaska (Chukchi Sea); see Rasmussen, *Eagle's Gift*, New York, 1932, pp. 121–132.
[2] [*Seiende*, alternative translation: existence.]

"enlighten." In our fairytale, the gaining of light and enlightenment is not literal, but symbolized as the beads and the songs that Misana brought home.

136 The sought-after enlightenment was embodied as clear moonlight in the Chinese fairytale, "The Lady of the Moon," (*China) which in some other narratives can also be a precursor to further elucidation described as being brought by the illuminating sunlight in the other world. A journey to "the other side" described by the Algonquin Native People, "The Visit to the Manabozho," vividly shows this aspect of the land of the souls in its various transitional stages. The mythical legend tells of a journey by Ioscoda and his Ottawa companions who want to visit the great culture-bringer called by many different names: Manabozho, Nanahboozhoo, the Great Hare, or Rabbit, who now lives in repose in the other world. After three years of wandering eastwards over a great water, they heard the mysterious sound of a magic rattle. They followed the sound, coming closer and closer...

137 > . . . it sounded as if it was subterranean, and it shook the ground: they tied up their bundles and went toward the spot. They soon came to a large building, which was illuminated. As soon as they came to the door, they were met by a rather elderly man [Manabozho]. "Greetings, my grandsons!" said he. "Walk in, walk in; I am glad to see you: I knew when you started: I saw you encamp last evening. Sit down, and tell me the news of the country you left, for I feel interested in it." Ioscoda and his companions complied with his wishes, and when they had concluded, each one presented him with a piece of tobacco. He then revealed to them things that would happen on their journey, and predicted its successful accomplishment. "I do not say that all of you will successfully go through it," said he. "You have passed over three-fourths of your way, and I will tell you how to proceed after you get to the edge of the Earth. Soon after you leave this place, you will hear *a deafening sound*: it is the sky descending on the edge, but it keeps moving up and down; you will watch, and when it moves up, you will see a *vacant space* between it and the Earth. You must not be afraid. A *chasm of awful depth* is there, which separates the unknown from this Earth, and a *veil of darkness* conceals it. Fear not. You must leap through; and if you succeed, you will find yourselves on a beautiful plain, and in a *soft and mild light emitted by the moon*."[3]

138 Any further explanation of this vision threatens to diminish its splendor. All aspects of the other world are here unified: the yawning void of the abyss, the

[3] Henry R. Schoolcraft, *The Myth of Hiawatha, and Other Oral Legends, Mythologic and Allegoric, of the North American Indians*, 1856, pp. 278–302 [von Franz and von Beit's emphases.]

unknown, the ineffable, from which another objective light begins gradually to shine. The eerie clash of the opposites of Heaven and Earth produces a deafening drone. This reminds one of the peals of thunder and flashes of lightning, which in "Help in Need" accompany the approach and the course changes of the magical realm and which, in other tales, are sometimes represented by whirlwinds. It is the expression of a shaking-up, an inner emotion, which seems to belong to the first encounter with the sphere of the unconscious and its powers.[4]

139 Two of the hero's comrades are swept into the abyss; they were obviously not prepared for the panic of a terrifying encounter with the unconscious. Their descent into eternal darkness signifies that they fell into a mentally deranged state. Ioscoda and one comrade reach a beautiful land, however, where they meet the moon in the shape of an old woman. She leads them to her sun brother, who lets them partake of his daily journey. They succeed in making a transition into the impersonal life of the gods, so that the light of the unconscious enlightens them.

[4] Compare the statement about *Chên*, thunder, Hexagram 51 in the Chinese *The I Ching or Book of Changes*, Wilhelm/Baynes, *I Ching*, Princeton, p. 197, *Chên, The Arousing, Shock, Thunder*. There it is said of this image, "It is symbolized by thunder, which bursts forth from the Earth and by its shock causes fear and trembling. The Judgement:

Shock bring success.
Shock comes – oh, oh!
Laughing words – ha, ha!
The shock terrifies for a hundred miles,
And he does not let fall the sacrificial spoon and chalice.

The shock that comes from the manifestation of God within the depths of the earth makes man afraid, but this fear of God is good; for joy and merriment can follow upon it. . . Let the thunder roll and spread terror a hundred miles around; he remains so composed and reverent in spirit that the sacrificial rite is not interrupted. This is the spirit that must animate leaders and rulers of men – a profound inner seriousness from which all outer terrors glance off harmlessly. The Image:

Thunder repeated: the image of shock.
Thus in fear and trembling
The superior man sets his life in order
And examines himself."

Chapter 8
The Clashing Rocks

140 The clashing edges of Heaven and Earth, through which the comrades must dare to make their dangerous leap, belongs to the motif of the clashing (or smashing) rocks which is found in the myths of people the world over, and are particularly well known in the Greek form as the Symplegades (Cyanean Rocks). This motif is particularly well portrayed in an Inuit tale, "The Kayak Wizard's Dangerous Man Traps" that was reported by Knud Rasmussen.[1] Thus begins another adventure of the hero, Wander-Hawk, with his uncle:

> 141 Early in the morning, Wander-Hawk, as usual, ate a little of his mother's magic food and then put on his amulet shirt, for today he expected greater difficulties than usual. Then he and his uncle drifted again down the river with the current. Soon they heard a booming noise ahead of them, which increased gradually as they came nearer. Now they came in sight of two steep cliffs, which jutted out from either side of the bank of the river, opening and shutting like a big mouth that is chewing. Every time they closed, all the water of the river foamed into mighty whirlpools.
>
> 142 Wander-Hawk had to paddle to and fro all the time, keeping in uninterrupted motion so as not to be swallowed in the maelstrom; the mountain's mighty sluice gates damned up the great river-flood into a boiling cauldron. At last he said, "Uncle, shut your eyes." And he began to sing a magic song:
>
> 143 Travel will I free and scatheless
> Twixt these precipices narrow,
> Lip against each other biting!

144 Immediately, the cliffs opened, and the kayak darted through, but so quickly did the rocks shut after them that they cut off the point of the stern [i.e., some of the falcon's tail feathers].[2]

---

[1] Rasmussen, *Eagle's Gift*, pp. 212–214. [This is one episode in a series of adventures titled "Wander-Hawk, Who Went Out into the World to Uproot the Wickedness of Life and the Treachery of Man."]

[2] Rasmussen, *Eagle's Gift*, pp. 212–213.

145 A similar tale, from Polynesia, "Rata," relates:

> The boat was sailing along merrily over the ocean under a favorable wind, when one day Nganaoa called out: "O Rata! A fearful enemy is rising from the sea!" It was a giant clam, wide open. One of its shells was in front of the boat, the other behind, and the vessel lay in between! The next moment the horrible clam would have snapped shut and ground the boat and all its occupants to pulp. But Nganaoa was prepared for this possibility. Seizing his long spear, he thrust it into the creature's belly, so that instead of snapping shut, it sank instantly to the bottom of the sea.[3]

146 Jung emphasizes the maternal meaning,[4] whereby the mother signifies the unconscious as maternal fundament of all conscious life. In various fairytales, the way to the mothers goes through a slit in an opening and closing tree.[5] In general, this motif describes the enormous danger of a dissolution of consciousness by the polar nature of the unconscious.

[3] Quoted from Jung, *Symbols of Transformation*, CW 5, ¶538, fn. 85, following Frobenius, *Zeitalter*, Berlin, 1904, pp. 63ff. See further *ibid.*, ¶367 fn. 72. [For a detailed investigation of tribal rites, see John Layard, "The Making of Man in Malekula," 1949.]

[4] [The clashing rocks = devouring vulva = the mother; see Jung *ibid.*, ¶366.]

[5] For examples of different forms of the motif of clashing rocks (Symplegades), see "Kiviung" and the notes in Krickeberg, *Nordamerika*, p. 370); "The Creation of the World" and notes, *ibid.*, p. 389; "Tsetl-walakame" and notes, *ibid.*, p. 399; "Coyote Remains Coyote" and notes, *ibid.*, p. 405; "Ngeraod's Bundle," the excerpt from the story of "Malajasundari," esp. pp. 191– 192; "The Three Realms of the Dead," esp. Krickeberg, *Nordamerika*, p. 28) and notes (Krickeberg, *Azteken and Inka*, Jena, 1928, p. 327); "Petri Godchild" and "The Water of Life." To open and close the clashing rocks with a magical phrase has a similar meaning; see the Grimm's tale, "Simeli Mountain," where the mountain opens and closes when the right words are spoken; see also "The Poor Cobbler" and "Ali Baba and the Forty Thieves" in Ernst, *Tausend und ein Tag*, p. 270.

Chapter 9
The Forest (Woods)

147 A further aspect of the unconscious is represented by the forest or the woods,[1] which in many fairytales is the magical realm where wonderful events take place. Examples are found in "Hansel and Gretel," "Little Snow White," and in "Little Red-Cap." Where Hansel and Gretel find the house of the witch in the forest, Snow White flees from her stepmother into the forest and goes "over the mountains" to reach the seven dwarves where her fate changes wonderfully. An example of the forest as a place of magic is, among other tales, related in the German tale, "The Magic Horse":

148 A young man once left home with the sword of his dead father. He entered the service as a shepherd for an old man who was blind in one eye. The old man warned the young man about a particular forest out of which no servant had come alive. No sooner did the young herdsman take on his job, than he went into this very forest, admiring its magnificence. Suddenly a three-headed dragon came threateningly towards him and cried, "Child of Man, how did you come here? No little bird dares to soil my forest, do you want to pollute it with your sheep? You must either knock me down or wrestle me down, which do you prefer?" said the dragon with an evil grin. The young man tried in vain to wrestle the dragon down, and finally vanquished him with his sword. On the next day he repeated his visit to the forest and found it quieter and even more beautiful than before. Then suddenly a six-headed dragon appeared, out to revenge the death of his brother. Once again the wrestling failed, but once again the young man felled the dragon with his sword. Similarly on the third day with a nine-headed dragon and on the fourth day with a twelve-headed dragon with whom a fierce battle ensued, lasting until evening-tide. At sundown, the dragon lost all his strength but that of the young man grew and he slew the monster. On the fifth day, he found a small house in the forest in front of which stood a woman as old as the hills, the bushmother. She displayed her four dead sons and went after the young shepherd in revenge. With his sword, he slew her to the

[1] [In German, *der Wald* means both forest and woods.]

> ground. His right hand was weary, he could not seriously injure the old woman. But as he switched hands and took his sword in his left hand, she pleaded to be spared. He said she first had to show him the cure to heal the old man's eye. No sooner did she show him the remedy, then he cut off her head and took the medicine.[2]

149 With this, he returned and healed the old man's eye. The old man gave him a magic horse with which he had many adventures, won the hand of the princess, and became king.[3] The forest is similar to the lake or the sea, a dark realm full of unknown shapes, a piece of nature.[4] As nixies in water, so do forest women[5] live in the woods, like "the bushmother" in the above fairytale. The ancient Greeks, Celts, and Germanic tribes heard the voice of the gods in the rustling ("whistling up the wind") through the trees of the sacred grove,[6] and for the primitive, the forest houses the dead and other spirits.[7] "Full of whispering voices," writes Heinrich Zimmer,[8] "the forest encompasses life's adventures and the adventure of the soul with its abyss of forces and images."

---

[2] Zaunert, *Deutsche Märchen seit Grimm*, Cologne, 1964, pp. 203–212.

[3] More on this fairytale, especially the second part, follows below and in the second volume of this work.

[4] Silberer, Problems of Mysticism, pp. 45–47. See further C.G. Jung, "Belief in Spirits," CW 8, ¶241: "As at the beginning of many dreams something is said about the scene of the dream action, so the fairytale mentions the forest as the place of the magical happening. The forest, dark and impenetrable to the eye, like deep water and the sea, is the container of the unknown and mysterious. It is an appropriate synonym for the unconscious. . . Trees, like fishes in the water, represent the living contents of the unconscious."

[5] Ninck, *Wodan*, pp. 226 and 271. Forests often house a fortified castle in their midst. On "the Forest of Dean" in England, see C. Guest, *Mabinogion*, 1906/1937, p. 402, fn. to p. 220, where "Dean" is derived from Celtic *Din*, "a fortified mount, or fort."

[6] Cf. Mogk, *Germanische*, pp. 16ff.

[7] See Lévy-Bruhl, *The "Soul" of the Primitive*, pp. 31–36.

[8] Zimmer, "Merlin as wise old man," in: Goodrich and Thompson (eds.), *Merlin: A Casebook*, Routledge, New York, 2003, translated by Friedhelm Riuckert, p. 259. See also the beginning of Dante's *Divine Comedy*: "When I had journeyed half of our life's way, I found myself within a shadowed forest, for I had lost the path that does not stray" (Translation by Allen Mandelbaum, *The Divine Comedy of Dante Alighieri: Inferno*, Bantam Books, New York, 1980).

Chapter 10
The Mountain

150 A widespread symbol of the land of the soul[1] is the mountain, which understandably came to stand for the unconscious since one imagines that their tops are often covered in mist, and reach – like a transition – into heaven. The gods manifest or reveal themselves on mountain peaks.[2] In the Chinese fairytale mentioned earlier, "How a Scholar Chastised the Princes of Hell," a man who is on his way to Hell comes first "to a big mountain, where a cold wind whistles into the very marrow of his bones. . . This is the Mountain of the Dead. . . the border between the human world and the underworld. The rocks open to form a huge entranceway over which it is written 'Spirits' Gate.'" Also in the Swedish fairytale retold above, "The Mountain of the Golden Queen," the center of the magical realm on the other side of the sea was a large mountain where the hero found the golden queen of his dreams. Often this mountain is described in fairytales as an insurmountable glass mountain. In a Norwegian fairytale, "Farther South Than South and Farther North Than North and in the Great Hill of Gold,"[3] it is depicted as large golden mountain, or as in "Helge-Hal in the Blue Hill,"[4] as a "blue mountain." Mountains and cliffs,[5] with their darkness and dangers, are very clearly represented as a magical world in the fairytale, "Trunt, Trunt, and the Trolls in the Mountains":

151

> Two men once went up into the mountains to collect edible moss. One night they were sharing a tent, and one fell asleep, but the other remained awake. The one who was awake saw how the one who was asleep arose and crept out of the tent opening. He got up and followed his comrade, but no matter how hard he ran, he could not catch up to him. The man who had been asleep was heading straight up the mountain towards the glaciers, and the other man saw a huge giantess sitting up there on the spur of a glacier. What she was doing was this: she would stretch out her arms with her hands crossed and then draw them in again to her breasts, and in this way she was magically draw-

[1] [I.e. the collective unconscious, the objective psyche.]

[2] For example, Moses on Sinai and Mount Meru in India; see Zimmer, *Maya*, pp. 123ff, 320.

[3] Stroebe, *Norwegian Fairy Book*, New York, 1922.

[4] Ibid.

[5] [The German word *Fells* means "rocks, cliffs, mountains."]

ing the man towards her. The man ran straight into her arms, and then she ran off with him.

152 A year later, some people from this man's district were gathering moss at exactly the same place; he came there to meet them, but he was so short-spoken and surly that they could hardly get a word out of him. They asked him who he believed in and he said he believed in God. The following year he came to the moss-gatherers again, but by then he looked so much like a troll that he struck terror into them. However, he was again asked who he believed in, but he made no reply. This time he stayed a shorter time with them than the year before. The third year, he came again; by this time he had turned completely into a troll, and a very ugly looking one at that. Yet someone plucked up the courage to ask him who he believed in, but this time he said, "Trunt, Trunt, and the trolls in the fells" – and then he disappeared. After this he was never seen again, but for some years afterwards, no one dared to go out moss-collecting in that place.[6]

153 There could hardly be a more graphic depiction than this of how the demonic-alluring and "gripping" power of the mountain spirit (the giantess) promises to lead the captivated one into the light blue distance at the same time giving an image of her partly-animal, grotesque state. Once again, the mountain's magic is experienced during sleep and the glacial world reminds us of the "halls of crystal cold" on the moon in "The Lady of the Moon." The bewitched man disappears into the mysterious crevices and cracks in the mountain, his returning three times allows those who remained behind to realize his hopeless transformation. In lapidary narrative, the fairytale shows the outer and inner changes: the one degenerated to the mountain spirit turns his back on his previously venerated God-image and avows himself to the uncanny powers of nature.

154 Female demons are connected to the symbol of mountains, just like nixies to water (for instance, the "Lake of Maidens" in the tale, "Help in Need"). Thus in the Irish tale, "The Mountain of the Light Women," a hill that originally was called "Herb [Cabbage] Mountain,"[7] but is later called "Hill of the Women." In the heart of the mountain there is a magnificent palace where eternal young fairies of irresistible beauty live. They occasionally do good, but are known to put their own children in the beds of real children (*changelings*), and to rob children and young girls. In the latter case, through their gaze they make their victims *unconscious*, or ill. Only through magic can a spinstress

[6] [Slightly edited from Simpson and Árnason, *Icelandic Folktales*, Stroud, 2004, pp. 78–79.]

[7] See Müller-Lisowski, *Irische Volksmärchen*, Jena, 1923, p. 240, fn. 1. Also in "Trunt, Trunt, and the Trolls in the Mountains," herbs (i.e., moss) were being collected in the mountains.

gain mastery over the power of the demonesses. Spinstresses experience them only in the night and partly in deep sleep; the appearance of the fairies puts them in a kind of half-conscious comatose state. Here the mountain clearly characterizes the realm of the unconscious. The light women are of the same kind as the old Germanic valkyries or nixies, the white ancestresses, who live in the mountain and watch over the treasure or the dead.[8] With the Aztec, a legendary mountain is even called *the white woman.*[9] In many places, mountain carries the name of a female being.[10]

155 A further example of a hill inhabited by demons, and of the psychological impact of the meeting with the spirits, is given by the English fairytale "The Fairies on the Gump":

> 156 There was, once upon a time, a greedy, mean old fellow . . . who used to listen to the tales the people told of the Fairies and their riches, and their wonderful treasures, until he could scarcely bear to hear any more, he longed so to have some of those riches for himself; and at last his covetousness grew so great, he said to himself he must and would have some, or he should die of vexation. Now by St. Just, not far from Cape Cornwall and the sea, is a small hill – or a very large mound would, perhaps, be the truer description – called "The Gump," where the Small People used to hold their revels. So one night in September, when the Harvest Moon was at its fullest, the old fellow started off alone, and very stealthily, to walk to the Gump, for he did not want his neighbors to know anything at all about his plans. Although it was a very desolate spot, his greed was greater than his fear, and he made himself go forward. When he was still at some distance from the enchanted spot, strains of the most exquisite music anyone could possibly imagine reached his ear. The most wonderful part of it all, though, was that there was nothing to be seen, no person, no bird, not an animal even. The empty moor stretched away on every tide, the Gump lay bare and desolate before him. The only living being on it that night was he himself. The music, indeed, seemed to come from under the ground, and such strange music it was, too, so gentle, so touching, it made the old miser weep, in spite of himself, and then, even while the tears were still running down his cheeks, he was forced to laugh quite merrily, and even to dance, though he certainly did not

[8] Cf. Ninck, *Wodan*, p. 222. Woden is also known as the Lord of the Dead and lives in a mountain. See here *ibid.*, pp. 136f., 144, 314. He is, therefore, also called "The Old One of the Mountain"; see Mogk, *Germanische*, p. 72.

[9] See Krickeberg, *Azteken and Inka*, p. 340, for comments on *Quetzalcouatls Sündenfall und Tollans Untergang* (Quetzalcoatl's sin and Tollan's downfall) (no. 12).

[10] In Switzerland, for instance, the Rigi, the Jungfrau (Virgin), Vreneli's Gärtli (Vreneli's Garden in the Glärnish Alps), and in Austria, the Drei Schwestern (Three Sisters).

want to do either. All the time he was laughing and weeping, marching or dancing, his wicked mind was full of thoughts as to how he should get at the fairy treasure. At last, when he got close to the Gump, the music ceased, and suddenly, with a loud crashing noise which nearly scared the old man out of his senses, the whole hill seemed to open as if by magic, and in one instant every spot was lighted up. Thousands of little lights of all colors gleamed everywhere, silver stars twinkled and sparkled on every furze-bush, tiny lamps hung from every blade of grass. It was a more lovely sight than one ever sees nowadays, more lovely than any pantomime one has ever seen or ever will see. Then, out from the open hill marched troops of little Spriggans. Then came soldiers and servants carrying most lovely gold and silver vessels, goblets, too, cut out of single rubies, and diamonds, and emeralds, and every kind of precious stone. Then came others bearing rich meats and pastry, luscious fruits and preserves. Each servant placed his burden on the tables in its proper place, then silently retired. The old man beheld gentlemen and ladies of indescribable beauty and was invited to sit at a table adorned in riches he had never dreamed of.

157 Stooping down, he slowly and stealthily dragged himself nearer and nearer to the table. He felt quite sure that no one could see him. What he himself did not see was that hundreds of wicked little Spriggans had tied ropes on to him and were holding fast to the ends. He crawled and crawled so slowly and carefully that it took him some time to get over the ground, but he managed it at last, and got quite close up to the lovely little pair. Then slowly bringing up his hat, as a boy does to catch a butterfly, he was just going to bring it down on the silken platform and capture prince and princess, table, gold dishes and all, when hark! A shrill whistle sounded, the old man's hand, with the hat in it, was paralyzed in the air, so that he could not move it backwards or forwards, and in an instant every light went out, and all was pitch black. There were a whir-r-r and a buzz, and a whir-r-r, as if a swarm of bees were flying by him, and the old man felt himself fastened so securely to the ground that, do what he would, he could not move an inch, and all the time he felt himself being pinched, and pricked, and tweaked from top to toe, so that not an inch of him was free from torment. He was lying on his back at the foot of the Gump, though how he got there he could never tell. His arms were stretched out and fastened down, so that he could not do anything to drive off his tormentors, his legs were so secured that he could not even relieve himself by kicking, and his tongue was tied with cords, so that he could not call out. . .

158 Left at last to himself, the mortified old man lay for some time, thinking over all that had happened, trying to collect his senses, and wondering how he should manage to escape from his bonds, for he might lie there for a week without any human being coming near the place. Till sunrise he lay there, trying to think of some plan, and then, what do you think he saw? Why, that he had not been tied down by ropes at all, but only by thousands of gossamer webs! And there they were now, all over him, with the dew on them sparkling like the diamonds that the princess had worn the night before. And those dewdrop diamonds were all the jewels he got for his night's work.

159 When he made this discovery he turned over and groaned and wept with rage and shame, and never, to his dying day, could he bear to look at sparkling gold or gems, for the mere sight of them made him feel quite ill. At last, afraid lest he should be missed, and searchers be sent out to look for him, he got up, brushed off the dewy webs, and putting on his battered old hat, crept slowly home. He was wet through with dew, cold, full of rheumatism, and very ashamed of himself, and very good care he took to keep that night's experience to himself. No one must know his shame. Years, after, though, when he had become a changed man, and repented of his former greediness, he let out the story bit by bit to be a lesson to others, until his friends and neighbors, who loved to listen to anything about fairies, had gathered it all as I have told it to you here. And you may be quite sure it is all true, for the old man was not clever enough to invent it.[11]

160 And now follows the tale, "The Page and the Silver Goblet," which describes even more characteristics of the uncanny realm of the fairies.

161 There was once a little pageboy, who was in service in a stately castle. He was a very good-natured little fellow, and did his duties so willingly and well that everybody liked him, from the great Earl whom he served every day on bended knee, to the fat old butler whose errands he ran. On the other side of the Castle were gardens and pleasure grounds, opening on to a long stretch of heather-covered moorland, which, at last, met a distant range of hills. The little page-boy was very fond of going out on this moor when his work was done, for then he could run about as much as he liked, chasing bumble-bees, and catching butterflies, and looking for birds' nests when it was nesting time. But before the boy went out the old butler always gave him one warning: "Now, mind my words, laddie, and keep far away from the

[11] Shortened from Mabel Quiller Couch, *Cornwall's Wonderland*, 1914, p. 54.

Fairy Knowe [A paritucla "fairy hill," Fairy Knowe was also thought to be the haunt of spirits from the fairy kingdom in pre-Christian times.] for the Little Folk are not to be trusted."

162 Now, the little pageboy was an adventurous wight, and instead of being frightened of the Fairies, he was very anxious to see them, and to visit their abode, just to find out what it was like. So one night, when everyone else was asleep, he crept out of the castle by the little postern door, and stole down the stone steps, and along the sea shore, and up on to the moor, and went straight to the Fairy Knowe. To his delight he found that what everyone said was true. The top of the Knowe was tipped up, and from the opening that was thus made, rays of light came streaming out.

163 His heart was beating fast with excitement, but, gathering his courage, he stooped down and slipped inside the Knowe. He found himself in a large room lit by numberless tiny candles, and there, seated round a polished table, were scores of the Tiny Folk, Fairies, and Elves, and Gnomes, dressed in green, and yellow, and pink; blue, and lilac, and scarlet; in all the colors, in fact, that you can think of.

164 [He enters and sees a great feast in progress, at which the goblins, gnomes and fairies drink from a never empty, gold-framed silver cup. They invite him to join in and begin to deprive him of all his joy in life on earth.]

165 He desired to take the magic cup for himself and waited as long as he could and then suddenly stood up, grasped the stem of the cup tightly in his hand, and cried out, "I'll drink to you all in water," he cried, and instantly the ruby wine was turned to clear cold water. He raised the cup to his lips, but he did not drink from it. With a sudden jerk he threw the water over the candles, and instantly the room was in darkness. Then, clasping the precious cup tightly in his arms, he sprang to the opening of the Knowe, through which he could see the stars glimmering clearly.

166 He was just in time, for it fell to with a crash behind him; and soon he was speeding along the wet, dew-spangled moor, with the whole troop of Fairies at his heels. They were wild with rage, and from the shrill shouts of fury which they uttered, the page knew well that, if they overtook him, he need expect no mercy at their hands. And his heart began to sink, for, fleet of foot though he was, he was no match for the Fairy Folk, who gained on him steadily.

167 All seemed lost, when a mysterious voice sounded out of the darkness: "If thou wouldst gain the castle door, Keep to the black stones on the

shore." It was the voice of some poor mortal, who, for some reason or other, had been taken prisoner by the Fairies – who were really very malicious Little Folk – and who did not want a like fate to befall the adventurous pageboy; but the little fellow did not know this. He had once heard that if anyone walked on the wet sands, where the waves had come over them, the Fairies could not touch him, and this mysterious sentence brought the saying into his mind. So he turned, and dashed panting down to the shore. His feet sank in the dry sand, his breath came in little gasps, and he felt as if he must give up the struggle; but he persevered, and at last, just as the foremost Fairies were about to lay hands on him, he jumped across the watermark on to the firm, wet sand, from which the waves had just receded, and then he knew that he was safe.

168 For the Little Folk could go no step further, but stood on the dry sand uttering cries of rage and disappointment, while the triumphant pageboy ran safely along the shore, his precious cup in his arms, and climbed lightly up the steps in the rock and disappeared through the postern. And for many years after, long after the little pageboy had grown up and become a stately butler, who trained other little pageboys to follow in his footsteps, the beautiful cup remained in the Castle as a witness of his adventure.[12]

169 Another widespread motif is that one should not partake of victuals from the otherworld, otherwise one must remain there.[13] Since the page-boy in the above tale was aware of this rule and, therefore, of the difference between his world and the world of the elves, he succeeds in separating himself and escaping. Water instead of wine points to sobriety instead of inebriation. His hasty escape mirrors the typical experience of a nightmare.

170 The above two tales would be called local legends, according to Lüthi's differentiation of fairytales, folktales, and legends.[14] They are given here since their mood reveals the identity of the daemonic world with the land of dreams, that is, the unconscious. Just how widespread these tales of sinking into the unconscious are, is exemplified by the similarities with a Chinese legend, "The King of the Ants":

171 Once upon a time there was a scholar, who wandered away from his home and went to Emmet village. There stood a house, which was said to be haunted, yet it was beautifully situated and surrounded by a

---

[12] Elizabeth W. Grierson, *The Scottish Fairy Book*, 1910.
[13] A well-known example is the lotus-eaters (*lotophagi*) from *Odyssey* IX.
[14] See Lüthi, *The European Folktale*.

lovely garden. So the scholar rented it. One evening he was sitting over his books, when several hundred knights suddenly came galloping into the room. They were quite tiny, and their horses were about the size of flies. They had hunting falcons and dogs about as large as gnats and fleas.

172 They came to his bed in the corner of the room, and there they held a great hunt, with bows and arrows: one could see it all quite plainly. They caught a tremendous quantity of birds and game, and all this game was no larger than little grains of rice. When the hunt was over, in came a long procession with banners and standards. They wore swords at their side and bore spears in their hands, and came to a halt in the northwest corner of the room. They were followed by several hundred serving men. These brought with them curtains and covers, tents and tent-poles, pots and kettles, cups and plates, tables and chairs. And after them some hundreds of other servants carried in all sorts of fine dishes, the best that land and water had to offer. And several hundred more ran to and fro without stopping, in order to guard the roads and carry messages.

173 The scholar gradually accustomed himself to the sight. Although the men were so very small he could distinguish everything quite clearly. Before long, a bright colored banner appeared. Behind it rode a personage wearing a scarlet hat and garments of purple. He was surrounded by an escort of several thousands. Before him went runners with whips and rods to clear the way.

174 Then a man wearing an iron helmet and carrying a golden ax in his hand cried out in a loud voice: "His Highness is graciously pleased to look at the fish in the Purple Lake!" Whereupon the one who wore the scarlet hat got down from his horse, and, followed by a retinue of several hundred men, approached the saucer, which the scholar used for his writing-ink. Tents were put up on the edge of the saucer and a banquet was prepared. A great number of guests sat down at the table. Musicians and dancers stood ready. There was a bright confusion of mingled garments of purple and scarlet, crimson and green. Pipes and flutes, fiddles and cymbals sounded, and the dancers moved in the dance. The music was very faint, and yet its melodies could be clearly distinguished. All that was said, too, the table-talk and orders, questions and calls, could be quite distinctly heard.

175 After three courses, he who wore the scarlet hat said: "Quick! Make ready the nets and lines for fishing!" And at once nets were thrown out into the saucer, which held the water in which the scholar dipped his brush. And they caught hundreds of thousands of fishes. The one

with the scarlet hat contented himself with casting a line in the shallow waters of the saucer, and caught a baker's dozen of red carp.

176 Then he ordered the head cook to cook the fish, and the most varied dishes were prepared with them. The odor of roasting fat and spices filled the whole room. And then the wearer of the scarlet hat in his arrogance, decided to amuse himself at the scholar's expense. So he pointed to him and said: "I know nothing at all about the writings and customs of the saints and wise men, and still I am a king who is highly honored! Yonder scholar spends his whole life toiling over his books and yet he remains poor and gets nowhere. If he could make up his mind to serve me faithfully as one of my officials, I might allow him to partake of our meal."

177 This angered the scholar, and he took his book and struck at them. And they all scattered, wriggling and crawling out of the door. He followed them and dug up the earth in the place where they had disappeared. And there he found an ants' nest as large as a barrel, in which countless green ants were wriggling around! So he built a large fire and smoked them out.[15]

178 It is no accident that this story happens in the evening, as the scholar was sitting over his books. The whole experience with the ants is the daydream of a scholar grown sleepy. His ambitious and worldly plans, the whole outer world that he has turned his back on, appear in the fantasy. The contempt of the ant king is simultaneously an expression of the self-criticism of the scholar in his inferiority complex. Therefore, he pulls himself together and puts the whole fantasy to rout. However, he thereby destroys all possibility of further inner development.

179 The magical otherworld, about which we have learned in the symbols of water, moon, forest, mountain, etc., is not only the residence of spirits and demons, but is also the realm in which the enthralled[16] people of antiquity continued to live. Here the highest values are preserved and the mountain, in particular, serves as the abode of the great ones of the past. Here is "A Legend of Flowers," a tale recorded at the end of the 19th Century from the Euahlayi-speaking people of Australia:

---

[15] Wilhelm, *The Chinese Fairy Book*, New York, 1921; slightly edited.

[16] [The German *entrückten* can also mean "state of ecstasy" or "ecstatic withdrawal." This describes a mythological or biblical phenomenon when a person is corporeally transported from the earthly concrete world of appearances into a heavenly sphere. Akin to "enrapture" and "enthrall," it is found in both *Old* and *New Testaments*; see, for example, 1 Thessalonians 4:15-17: ". . . and the dead in Christ shall rise first: Then we which are alive and remain shall be caught up together with them in the clouds, to meet the Lord in the air." In a figurative sense the concept is also used to mean "in the other (spiritual) world" like a trance, intoxication, a drug-induced altered state, or a dream state.].

180 After Byamee[17] left the earth, having gone to dwell in Bullimah,[18] the far-away land of rest, beyond the top of the Oobi mountain, all the flowers that grew on the wogghees or plains, on the moorillahs or ridges, and all the flowers that grew on the trees withered and died. None grew again in their place. The earth looked bare and desolate with no flowers to brighten it. That there had ever been any became but a tradition, which the old people of the tribes told to the young ones. As the flowers were gone so were the bees.

181 Soon were seen white sugary specks on the leaves of the Bibbil, which the Daens[19] called Goonbean, and then came the clear wahlerh, or manna, running down the trees like honey, to pile into lumps which stiffened on the forks of the branches, or sometimes fell to the ground, whence the children gathered and ate it when they could not reach the branches.

182 The sorcerers, as responsible representatives of the tribes greatly longed to see the earth covered again with flowers, as before the going of Byamee. So great grew their longing that they determined to travel after him, and ask that the earth might again be made beautiful. Telling the tribes nothing of where they were going, they sped away to the north-east. On and on they journeyed, until they came to the foot of the great Oobi Oobi mountain, which towered high above them until they lost sight of its top in the sky. Steep and unscalable looked its sides of sheer rock as they walked along its base. But at length they espied a foothold cut in a rock, another and yet another, and looking upward they saw a pathway of steps cut as far as they could see. Up this ladder of stone they determined to climb. On they went, and when the first day's climb was ended the top of the mountain still seemed high above them, and even so at the end of the second and third day, for the route was circuitous and long; but on the fourth day they reached the summit. There they saw a stone excavation into which bubbled up a spring of fresh water, from which they drank thirstily, and found it so invigorated them as to make them lose all feeling of weariness, which had previously almost prostrated them. They saw at a little distance from the spring circles of piled up stones. They went into one of these, and almost immediately they heard the sound of a gayandy, the medium through which Wallahgooroonbooan's voice was heard. Wallahgooroonbooan was the spirit

[17] [Literally "Big man"; Byamee is the creator, the culture hero of the Euahlayi people. Note by L. K. Parker, *More Australian*, London, 1898.]
[18] [Byamee's camp, for the Euahayi, their Elysium].
[19] [*Daen* = an Australian Aborigine.]

messenger of Byamee. He asked the wirreenuns [sorcerors] what they wanted there, where the sacred lore of Byamee was told to such as came in search of knowledge. They told him how dreary the earth had looked since Byamee had left it, how the flowers had all died, and never bloomed again. And though Byamee had sent the wahlerh, or manna, to take the place of the long-missed honey, yet they longed to see again the flowers making the earth as colorful as it once had been.

183 Then Wallahgooroonbooan ordered some of the attendant spirits of the sacred mountain to lift the wirreenuns into Bullimah, where fadeless flowers never ceased to bloom. As the voice ceased the wirreenuns were lifted up through an opening in the sky, and set down in a land of beauty, flowers blooming everywhere, in such luxuriance as they had never seen before, massed together in lines of brilliant coloring, looking like hundreds of euloowirrees, rainbows, laid on the grass. So overcome were the wirreenuns that for some moments they could only cry, but their tears were tears of joy.

184 Remembering what they had come for, they stooped and gathered quickly until their hands were full of the various blossoms. The spirits then lifted them down again into the stone circle on the top of Oobi Oobi.

185 There sounded again the voice of the gayandy, and Wallahgooroonbooan said: "Tell your tribes, when you take them these flowers, that never again shall the earth be bare of them. All through the seasons a few shall be sent by the different winds, but Yarrageh Mayrah shall bring them in plenty, blossoms to every tree and shrub, blossoms to wave amidst the grasses on wogghees and moorillahs, thick as the hairs on an opossum's skin. But Yarrageh Mayrah shall not always make them thus thick, but only at times; but the earth shall never again be quite bare of blossoms. When they are few, and the sweet-breathed wind is not blowing to bring first the showers and then the flowers and the bees can only make scarce enough honey for themselves, then the wahlerh or manna shall again drop from the trees, to take the place of honey until Yarrageh Mayrah once more blows the rain down the mountain and opens the blossoms for the bees; and then there will be honey for all. Now make haste and take this promise, and the fadeless flowers which are the sign of it, to your people."

186 The voice ceased and the wirreenuns went back to their tribes; back with the blossoms from Bullimah. Down the stone ladder, which had been cut by the spirits for the coming of Byamee, they went; across the wogghees and over the moorillahs back to the camp of their tribes.

> Their people flocked round them, gazing with wondering eyes at the blossoms the wirreenuns carried. Fresh as when they left Bullimah were these flowers, filling the air with fragrance. When the tribes had gazed long at the blossoms and heard of the promise made to them by Byamee through his messenger, Wallahgooroonbooan, the wirreenuns scattered the flowers from Bullimah far and wide. Some fell on the treetops, some on the plains and ridges, and where they fell their kind have grown ever since.[20]

187 In other versions,[21] Byamee sits on a throne of pure, clear crystal in heaven. On both sides are high columns of crystal. Here appears the center of the unconscious as the seat of the deity, similar to the "columns formed of liquid crystal" in the palace of "The Lady of the Moon." Just as there the rabbit is grinding herbs to prepare the elixir of life, here from the mountain the water of life bubbles out of a stone. With Byamee's retirement, the blossoming happy age disappeared, a paradise with its wonderful flora.

188 Stepping into the magical circle calls forth the spirits, because there the powers of the unconscious are "concentrated" and active.[22] The magician approaches the domain of the deity through religious efforts and receives help from inside – the region of his soul. This deals with a typical rite of renewal through which life is strengthened by coming into contact with the spirits of the ancestors and steered into the proper channels. The magical place, in this case the mountain, is not only the unconscious as a realm enlivened by spirits, but further the creative foundation of life itself, out of which individual life over and over again renews itself.

189 One parallel that describes this aspect of the mountain very clearly is the tale, "Ngeraod's Bundle":

190

> In the south of Babeldaob Island there rises a magical mountain with two peaks called Ngeraod. People say that it belongs to heaven and one time supernatural beings, the Galid, lived here in a large, beautiful high and roomy house. In their entourage were the Tekil Malap, evil man-eating devils that made a nuisance of themselves in mountain woods and disturbed peaceful people. One time, the Tekil Malap stole the boat of a fisherman and wreaked havoc. When the owner discovered stains on his boat, he determined to surprise and catch them. Knowing that they would smell a human, he disguised himself

[20] Parker, *More Australian*, pp. 84–89; shortened and slightly edited.

[21] "The old magician Byamee, the greatest of all magicians, once lived on the Earth, but now lives alone in the thick bush on a hill near Noondoo. No one may look at him, otherwise he or she must die." See "The Borah of Byamee" in Parker, *Australian*, pp. 94–105. Young men got to know of Byamee during their initiation ceremony. Byamee is of course more of a divinity than a magician.

[22] On the meaning of bull-roarer, see A. Lang, *Custom and Myth*, London, 1885, pp. 29ff.

with coconut smoke and went out on the lagoon one night. Sure enough, the devils came around to see what that smell was. Even when he saw their terrible countenance, the fisherman's courage did not fail; he offered them some of his roasted coconut. They found it delicious and agreed to go out fishing with him. Together they made a great catch and, as was the custom, divided up the catch together. Before they left, the fisherman asked if they would accept some of his roasted coconut as a gift and invited them to his house. Once there, he picked up a few coconuts, still in their shells, and put these in his fire. After these were burned, he shelled the coconuts and scraped out the roasted meat inside and offered this to his guests. They thanked him and greedily gobbled up the roasted coconut meat. In return, they invited the man to come with them to where they lived and to taste their food. He agreed and they all made off. "You must always step exactly *in our footsteps*," they told him, because the way did not go along the earth but *in the air*. The man did exactly as he was told and so they soon arrived up on Ngeraod mountain.

191 There they came upon a large tree that split open in the middle and then closed again as one stepped through. The Tekil Malap said to the man: "When we now go into the house and meet our old mother and she offers you something as a gift, then refuse everything but that which rattles in the taro cupboard, and then take that!" Then they all went immediately inside and came to their mother, a giant woman with huge breasts. She made sure that the visitor was comfortable. After two days, the Tekil Malap wanted to give their guest his gift. The old woman handed him a tortoise shell which had the property of always refilling itself when someone turned one time around himself. The man, however, refused the gift. Thereupon the old woman asked him if he wanted a hen that laid money, the famous Malk ra Ngeraod, which had the head of a man. But again the man refused the present. Then the old woman asked him what she should give him. He answered: "Give me that which rattles there in the taro cupboard." "Okay then, that you shall have." said the old hag. When they readied the man for his return home, the Tekil Malap took a bundle out of the cupboard and gave it to him with instructions to hold on to it very firmly. It was the Tur re Ngeraod bundle, a piece of the sacred garamal tree[23] and was wrapped in the leaf of an areka palm. The devils then lead him to the great tree and bid the man farewell. The tree opened, the man went through, and the tree closed after his passage. Now he did exactly as he was told, he gripped the bundle tightly to his chest

[23] [The (*Hibiscus tiliaceus*).]

> and lay down on it. No sooner had he closed his eyes than he flew through the air and landed in front of his house. He went inside and hid the wonderful bundle carefully in his taro cupboard. The man discovered that with his bundle he could heal dying people and even bring the dead back to life. Through this he became rich and famous, but then people flocked to him, begging for money, full of envy of his healing powers. One day they even set his house on fire. The bundle remained unburnt, and the man cried out to let him continue to heal people in peace, but they did not heed his plea and continued to badger him until one day he threw the bundle into the bushes forever. Since then, people on earth must die but the hibiscus tree lives forever.[24]

192 Mount Ngeraod has twin peaks,[25] an expression for the two faces of the magical realm exemplified by the double-natured healing and demon man-eating aspects of the Tekil Malap devils.[26] The tree that opens and closes (motif of the clashing rocks) has the same meaning. In the following, we will often show how the magical kingdom as the unconscious, exhibits itself as being strangely ambivalent when standing face-to-face with human beings. It appears that the unconscious, like nature, can act destructively as well as beneficially towards human beings. Whether it works positively or negatively depends in a mysterious way on the individual's conscious attitude towards the unconscious.[27] This is expressed in "Ngeraod's Bundle" by the hero letting himself be led by the originally evil and destructive spirits into the magical world, and by his having to withstand the temptations of the ancient mother goddess in order to actually get to the healing treasure.[28] This polarity of the unconscious is seen mirrored in the double peaks of Mount Ngeraod throughout the whole fairytale. The description of the passage into the magical realm is again characterized by the conspicuous indefiniteness of all spatial perceptions. The airy yet concrete nature of the magical is expressed in the idiosyncratic sentence that one must step exactly in the footsteps of the spirits in order to follow them along the path through the air. It is significant that at the end, it is the evil fellow humans who destroy the gift from the magical kingdom. Profane consciousness annihilates the meaning-value of the symbols from the unconscious in that it rationalizes them.

---

[24] P. Hambruch, *Südsee*, Jena, 1921, pp. 170–174; slightly edited.
[25] Like Mount Parnassus in Greece.
[26] Think of the wife of the man of the moon in the Inuit tale, "Flight to the Moon," at whom the angakoq may not laugh. She had two sides: life and death, in that her back was hollow.
[27] On this double aspect of the unconscious, see C.G. Jung, *Symbols of Transformation*, CW 5, ¶89, ¶600 fn. 186; see also C.G. Jung, *Psychological Types*, CW 6, ¶446.
[28] This is a "mana-charged" bundle. On fetishism, see Leeuw, *Religion in Essence*, vol. 1, pp. 37ff.

193 In practically all primitive peoples, one finds traces of a belief that the ancestors become powerful demonic divinities after death and that their realm is transformed into a treasure house of unconscious images. In the views of the ancient Greeks, certain dead souls inhabited places in the earth and bestowed their blessing on the fields and revealed themselves in dreams. The *Tritopatores* played a special role in the ancestor cults as primal forefathers,[29] who became gods.[30] A related belief is mirrored in the impressive Aztec description, "How Motecuzhoma Sought the Seven Caves," where the unconscious is portrayed as the land of the ancestors and also as a source from whence the tribe's storehouse of knowledge can again and again renew itself:

> 194 King Motecuzhoma the First[31] wanted to know about Chicomoztoc, the Seven Caves, which his tradition had so often mentioned as the *home of his ancestors.* He summoned his prime minister Tlacaelel to prepare his best warriors. But Tlacaelel told him that this was not an ordinary place that one conquered, but rather a special place to discover and learn from. He advised Motecuzhoma to send wizards, sorcerers, and magicians to find this mysterious place. Motecuzhoma then called for the royal historian who explained: "Our forebears dwelt in that blissful happy place called Aztlan, which means '*Whiteness*.' In that place there is a great hill *in the midst of the waters*, and it is called Colhuacan because its summit is *twisted*, thus it is Colhuacan, meaning Twisted Hill.'[32] In this hill were *caves or grottoes* where our fathers and grandfathers lived for many years."
>
> 195 The ancestors lived there in happiness and riches. In other places, this Land is called the *Seven Caves* and lies to the North. "However, after they abandoned that delightful place and came to the mainland, everything turned against them. The weeds began to bite, the stones became sharp and cut, and the fields were filled with thistles and spines..." Since the royal historian corroborated the same story of his prime minister, Motecuzhoma ordered that all the wizards and magicians who could be found in all the provinces be brought before him. Laden with rich gifts and special attire, foods and plants, sixty

[29] *Urgrossväter*, alternative translation: primordial grandfathers.

[30] The *Tritopatores* are three elder gods worshipped at Athens named Amaclides, Protocles and Protocleon. Alternative names were sometimes given, including Eubuleus. Cf. E. Rohde, *Psyche*, London, 1925, pp. 246–249.

[31] [Also spelled Moctezuma, a historical personality (1440–1464), the fifth Aztec king; see Fray Diego Durán, *The History of the Indies of New Spain*, University of Oklahoma Press, Norman, 1994, translated, annotated, and with an Introduction by Doris Heyden; originally written in 1588. Motecuzhoma was later empowered through legend.]

[32] Colhuacan can mean both "Twisted Hill" and "Place of the Ancestors," from colli "grandfather or ancestor," and colhua, "he who has grandparents or ancestors" [Note by the translator, Doris Heyden; von Franz and von Beit's emphases.]

sorcerers set off to find the Seven Caves. They met with an evil spirit who changed them into their naguals,[33] or animal spirits: birds, jaguars, wildcats, who took them to the land of their forebears. Upon reaching the shores of a large lake, they turned back into their human forms. There they found people living peacefully who spoke the same language as the visitors. They explained to these people that they were looking for Coatlicue,[34] mother of Huitzilopochtli,[35] and Chicomoztoc, the Seven Caves, from which their ancestors had set forth.

196 They were led to an old man who welcomed them and asked who had sent them. When they said "Motecuzhoma and Tlacaelel," the old man asked who these people were, he did not know of them, nor of Motecuzhoma. The old man asked, "Why is it that all of us here are still alive in the place they abandoned? Why is it that none of us have died? Who are your leaders now?" The sorcerers answered and explained that they had brought gifts from the present leader Motecuzhoma for Huitzilopochtli and his mother. The old man said, "Pick up what you have brought and follow me." They put the gifts on their backs and followed the old man who climbed the hill with ease. They went behind him, their feet sinking into the soft sand, walking with great difficulty and heaviness. They called to the old man who was walking with such lightness that his feet did not seem to touch the ground. "What is wrong with you, O Aztecs?" he asked. "What has made you so heavy? What do you eat in your land?"

197 "We eat the foods that grow there and we drink chocolate."[36] The elder responded, "Such *rich food and drink, my children, have made you heavy, and that makes it difficult for you to reach the place of your ancestors*. Those foods will bring death. The wealth you have we know nothing about; we live *poorly and simply*. Give me your loads and wait here. I shall go call to the mistress of this land, the mother of Huitzilopochtli, so that you may see her." He picked up one of the bundles and carried it up the hill as if it were straw. Soon he returned for the others and carried them up with great ease.

198 When all the presents brought by the Aztecs had been taken uphill, a woman of great age appeared, the ugliest and dirtiest old hag that one could possibly imagine. Her face was so black and covered with filth

---

[33] [Or *nahual*, a person's animal epiphany or animal companion; see Heyden.]
[34] Coatlicue, "She of the Skirt of Snakes," actually the name of the old earth and moon goddess.
[35] [Nahuatl meaning "Left-Handed Hummingbird," the patron god of the seminomadic Mexica who had promised them their own land, later to be Mexico-Tenochtitlan.]
[36] [Some versions have here *pulque*, a highly alcoholic maguey brandy. This might be a later insertion, attesting to the fact that this is a living legend among the Chicanos of the Southwestern United States.]

that she looked like something straight out of hell. Weeping bitterly, she said to the visitors: "Welcome, my sons! Know that since your god, my son Huitzilopochtli, departed from this place, I have been awaiting his return, weeping and mourning. Since that day, I have not washed my face, combed my hair or changed my clothes. My sadness and mourning will last until he returns. Is it true, my children, that you have been sent here by the leaders of the seven barrios whom my son took away with him?"

199 The envoys lifted their eyes, and seeing this hideous and abominable woman, they were filled with fear. They humbled themselves before her and did reverence. "O great and powerful lady, we neither saw nor spoke to the heads of the seven groups. We were sent by your servant, Motecuzhoma and his minister Tlacaelel (Chuatcoatl), to visit you and seek out the place where our ancestors once lived. They commanded us to kiss your hands in their name. We wish you to know that Motecuzhoma now rules over the great city of Mexico-Tenochtitlan. He is not the first king, but the fifth.

...

200 When they returned to Tenochtitlan, the magicians and the sorcerers took the gifts to Motecuzhoma and told him: "Lord, we have carried out your order, and we have witnessed that which you wished to know. We have seen that land called Aztlan and Colhuacan, where our fathers and grandfathers lived and from whence they left on their migration. And we have brought the things that grow and are bred there." They then placed before the king many ears of corn, seed, and different kinds of flowers, tomatoes, and chilies – foods and plants grown in that land – and the rough fiber mantles and breechcloths, and all things that had been sent by the people [of Aztlan-Colhuacan-Chicomoztoc]. They told Motecuzhoma everything that had occurred with the mother of Huitzilopochtli and with her old servant, and how they had seen this man change his age, from youth to middle age to very old. They added that in that place all the ancestors who had stayed there were still alive. And Coatlicue had complained bitterly about her son Huitzilopochtli, for whom she had waited so long.

...

201 On speaking of such a land of happiness Motecuzhoma and Tlacaelel were moved and began crying bitterly. Remembering their ancestors, they became homesick, wistful at not being able to see the land of their origin. They wished dearly to return one day, once their human mission here would be fulfilled. After having thanked the magician envoys, and ordering fine presents to be given to them for their work,

> they requested that these same sorcerers take the maguey fiber mantles and breechcloths to the temple, where they should be placed upon Huitzilopochtli, since his mother had sent them to him.[37]

202 Once again, the mountain symbolizes the goal to be reached in the unconscious. It is white and the happy land is called Aztlan, the Whiteness. We are reminded of the snow white regions in the fairytale, "Mother Holle," and the whitish silver light of the kingdom of the moon in "The Lady of the Moon." The temporally and spatially foreign land is steeped in a strangely transfigured unnatural light representing a state of unconscious clairvoyance. In a Norwegian fairytale, "The Three Princesses of Whiteland,"[38] the magical realm is called simply *Whiteland*, and the hero reaches this kingdom in a roller-coaster ride on a boat over the ocean. In the legend of Motecuzhoma the magical kingdom is known as the place of origin of the people where their ancestors live in a timeless state. It is the land of eternal youth, for in climbing the hill Colhuacan continually renew life. Reconnecting back to the land of the ancestors means connecting to the unconscious where time and space are relativized and the primordial images are eternally alive.

203 Therefore, the reconnection and preservation of the contact with the ancestral spirits and animals is an integral part in many primitive myths. Jung writes:

> 204 The symbolism of the rites of renewal, if taken seriously, points far beyond the merely archaic and infantile to man's innate psychic disposition, which is the result and deposit of all ancestral life right down to the animal level – hence the ancestor and animal symbolism. The rites are attempts to abolish the separation between the conscious mind and the unconscious, the real source of life; and to bring about a reunion of the individual with the native soil of his inherited, instinctive make-up. . . It is true that without the qualities of autonomy and autarky there would be no consciousness at all, yet these qualities also spell danger of isolation and stagnation since, by splitting off the unconscious, they bring about an unbearable alienation of instinct. Loss of instinct is the source of endless error and confusion.[39]

205 Not only the rites of renewal, but also many other rituals of natural folk peoples appear to be built upon individual inner experiences, in particular

---

[37] [Shortened from Durán, *History of the Indies*, 1588/1994, trans. Doris Heyden, pp. 212–222.

[38] See S. Asbjørnsen and Jørgen.

[39] C.G. Jung, *Psychology and Alchemy*, CW 12, ¶174.

those of individuals such as shamans, medicine men, etc. An impressive example is the Inuit tale, "An Eagle Myth About Flying Swallows and Wolf Dance in a Clay Bank":

> 206 A young man, a skillful archer, once shot an eagle that was so huge it could be divided among the inhabitants as the spoil of the chase as if it were a sea creature. All got enough for a meal, but those who got the thigh bone were the most pleased. The young hunter, who was called Marten (Kavfiatsiak), realized that it was no common prey that he had slain, and he spared no pains to treat the skin so skillfully that the dead eagle looked exactly as if it were still living. Thereafter he made it his mascot, and every day offered oblations to it, placing meat between its claws each time he himself ate. And the charm worked. He became a still more skillful hunter than before. One day, when Marten was hunting, he unexpectedly fell in with two very peculiar men. One of them had the snout of a red fox, the other the snout of a white fox, carefully sewed to the front of their fur hoods. The two strangers appeared suddenly before him, stopped Marten, and said: "We have come to fetch you, and since we are not here of our own free will, you have no choice in the matter. You must follow us!" So they took Marten between them and led him into the country; far, far away to regions where he had never been before. The asked him questions he did not understand and then said they were not traveling fast enough.
>
> 207 *Shut your eyes!"* and they seized him by the hands and began to run with him at such a great speed that Marten thought a storm was blowing against them. They *never seemed to touch the ground at all.* This went on for some time, and then they told him to open his eyes. They felt the ground again under their feet. Marten looked about him and saw mountains he had never before been near, a strange country, but no houses. Once more one of the two mysterious strangers spoke and said: "Today you will meet one whom you have never seen before, and you must know that she will require plaited sinew string from you in exchange for what she will give you." Marten could think of nothing but plaited sinew string, yet he could not imagine how to obtain any so far from his home. They advanced further, still deeper into the country, when all at once they heard a strange throbbing, a throbbing which came steadily and loudly from somewhere far off. "What's that we hear?" asked Marten. "It is the beating of a mother's heart," answered the others. "The beating of a mother's heart!" thought Marten, but could not understand what that meant. Then one of the

two strangers spoke again and said: "Do you remember that you slew an eagle, a young and powerful he-eagle? What you hear now is the beating of its mother's heart." He was introduced to the beating heart, the slain eagle's mother. Marten's heart, too, was beating now, but to his great surprise the mother received him with much cordiality and thanked him for the way in which he had treated her son. For it is no sin to kill an animal provided one offers oblations to its soul. Animals live again in a new body. And now she wished to exchange gifts with him and asked him what he would like. "The only thing I would like is to get safely home. A good homeward journey!" said Marten. "I desire plaited sinew string," said the old eagle. Quite at a loss, Marten looked to the ground. He did not know where he was to find plaited sinew string when suddenly he bethought himself of his arrow tips, which were all lashed fast with plaited sinew string. He unfastened them and gave her the string, and the old mother eagle was gladdened and began to talk.

208 The two young men, she said, were her *kivfai*, her sacred messengers. It was she who had sent them forth to invite him to this bartering. Marten grew still more astonished, for it was the first time he had heard of this way of sending messages. It was quite a new and unknown fashion. After this he was merrily regaled with all kinds of delicious food, and when he was at length preparing to return home, the mother eagle begged him to hold a big dance in honor of her son. The festival should be arranged by his sending out messengers to invite the guests, and those who accepted the invitation should exchange wishes and gifts with himself and his neighbors.

209 [As farewell he received two "heart skins" of caribou, tiny little transparent bags, made of the outer membrane that surrounds the caribou heart. One bag was filled with lappets of caribous' ears; the other with lappets of the ears of wolverine and wolf. In addition the eagle mother gave the strange instruction, "Just take care that you don't lay these gifts down on the way. If you care to take them home yourself, you must not set them down on any chance ground." On the way home, his guides changed back into their natural forms and in his confusion, Marten placed the gifts of the eagle's mother on the ground. Suddenly they become huge sacks of hides, dried meat, and tallow. He had to leave them behind and afterwards send many young men out after them. On his return the young man grew silent and reserved and brooded deeply over all he had seen and heard. Then he remembered how the old eagle mother had shown him new customs and asked him to introduce them to his place of residence at a feast

> he was to celebrate in honour of her dead son. He obediently sent out invitations and, with great effort, organized the celebration exactly according to his experiences. Thus the first festival took place where people put on the masks of animals and portrayed the wondrous journey, with people acting out the parts of different animals and spirits.][40]

210 This story establishes a ritual festival based on an ecstatic experience of an individual member of the tribe. The experience of the hunter incorporates all the traces of an immersion into the unconscious, like the Angakoq consciously embarked upon in "Flight to the Moon." Also the journey of Motecuzhoma's sorcerers to the hill Colhuacan in "How Motecuzhoma Sought the Seven Caves" is based originally on a type of ecstatic religious experience.

211 In the symbol of the mountain lies still another special meaning that differentiates it from other symbols of the unconscious, such as water and moon: in China the mountain is a symbol of meditation, as in the yoga mediation "keeping still."[41] It means in this case "piling (filling) up" of power, "concentration," and also "elevation, enlightenment," and thereby the reaching of a higher state through effort. The mountain is, therefore, often the carrier of the highest symbol.[42] That the symbol of the mountain relates to meditation and spiritual elevation[43] is shown in a humorous manner in the above Aztec

---

[40] Shortened and slightly edited from Rasmussen, *Eagle's Gift*, p. 29; told to Rasmussen by Arnasungak from King Island. (We have omitted the unfortunate final episode that took place at the feast since it is not relevant in this context.) Cf. the simpler version: "Ermine is Carried off by the Young Eagle," Rasmussen, *Eagle's Gift*, pp. 9–16, from "The Blessed Gift of Joy is Bestowed Upon Man." See further J. G. Neihardt, *Black Elk Speaks*, Lincoln and London, 2000, where Black Elk tells of the origin of a sacred festival of the Oglala Lakota (Sioux) that was based on a dream or visionary experience.

[41] See hexagram no. 52 "Keeping Still (Mountain)" in the *I Ching* (Wilhelm/Baynes, *I Ching*, p. 200) and Wilhelm, *Secret of the Golden Flower*, p. 56f.

[42] That is, of God. Cf. C.G. Jung, *Alchemy Vol. 1 and 2: The Process of Individuation. Notes on Lectures given at the Eidgenössische Technische Hochschule, Zürich November 1940–July 1941*, zusammengestellt von Barbara Hannah, Privatdruck, Zürich, 1960, p. 41. Also Mead, *Fragments*, London, 1931, pp. 370-371, where he interprets the mountain as higher consciousness.

[43] Cf. also the first section of the Chinese fairytale, "The Lady of the Moon," which describes the origin: The prince and great archer, Hou I, was once ordered by Emperor Yao to shoot the ten suns out of the sky because they shone so brightly they were burning the people. Hou I shot nine of them, but the tenth got away. Upon his horse that was faster than the wind, Hou I set out to hunt the tenth sun but his horse took flight with him riding. "They went all the way to the Kunlun Mountain and met the Queen-Mother of the Jasper Sea and she gave him the herb of immortality. He took it home with him and hid it in his room. But his wife who was named Tschang O, once ate some of it on the sly when he was not at home. She immediately floated up to the clouds. When she reached the moon, she ran into the castle there and has lived there ever since as the Lady of the Moon."

In most cultures of all people, the gods and demons inhabit mountains. Cf. the Aztec god Tepeyollotl, "Heart of the Mountain" [see the Aztec fairytale, "The Mountain and Cave God of the Isthmus tribes" (source unknown) and Danzel, "The Psychology of Ancient Mexican Symbolism," in: *Spiritual Disciplines: Papers from the Eranos Yearbooks*, 1960, Bollingen XXX-4, pp. 225ff; see further Bolte and Mackensen, *Handwörterbuch*, under *Berg* ["mountain"]. On the mountain-mother, see Erman, *Religion der Ägypter*, p. 215; Przyluski, "Ursprünge und Entwicklung des Kultes der Mutter-Göttin," 1939, pp. 17–18; Walter F. Otto, "Der Sinn der eleusinischen Mysterien," in: *Eranos-Jahrbuch 1939: Die Symbolik der Wiedergeburt in der religiösen Vorstellung der Zeiten und Völker*, 1940, pp. 90–91. On India, see Zimmer, *Maya*, pp. 151 and 346. In the Old and New Testaments, God is often encountered on Mount Tabor or at Mount Sinai.

tale where the ascent is prevented by the fact that the sorcerers have lived too much of the good life. In this case, even rational concentration does not help, they get stuck in the sand. That the paradisiacal original home has apparently lost some of its fertility since they left, is peculiar to this saga.[44] This impedes the way back. The primitive mind, which only with great difficulty has recently wrenched itself apart from the unconscious, sees retrospectively a danger in returning to the land of origin. Sometimes, however, one must go back there to find again the mother, that is, the source of life in the unconscious. Then the land suddenly appears again as an eternal paradise.

212 Since Motecuzhoma's messengers are sorcerers, they can transform themselves and take on animal forms. In "Flight to the Moon," the shaman lets himself be led by his animal helper,[45] since the unconscious is also the realm of the instincts, which – as we will show below – is often symbolized in the form of animals. A South American fairytale, "How the Haimara Came to Have Such Fine Big Eyes," gives us an interesting connection between how *becoming blind, immersion in water*, and *becoming an animal* are all synonyms for going into the unconscious:

> 213 Returning on his way home from the bush one afternoon, a hunter met a Konoko-kuyuha making a basket. Although he did not immediately recognize it as the Spirit of the Bush, he noticed the strange appearance it presented since its entire face, body, and limbs were covered with thick hair. He asked the Spirit what it was doing, but the only word it deigned to answer was "Bako."[46] When he reached home, he related his experiences to his family and friends and advised them strongly not to go to sleep that night, because "It," whatever it was, might pay them a surprise visit after nightfall. All he could tell them was that it was covered with hair, and that it was making an eye-socket basket. His family only laughed at him and turning into their hammocks as usual, told one another stories, and soon fell off to sleep. The man who had warned them remained awake alone. Soon he recognized a low whistle in the distance.
>
> 214 He tried to arouse his friends by shaking their hammocks. All in vain; he had only just time enough to clamber up onto the roof, when "It," which he now recognized to be a Konoko-kuyuha, entered the house. Once inside, the hunter was able to watch its movements without

44 [Not described in the version given here, nor in Krickeberg, *Azteken and Inka*, 1928.]

45 Lycanthropy (the ability or power of a human being to undergo transformation into a wolf, or to gain wolf-like characteristics), that is, the belief that the shaman, medicine man, or witch can without further ado transform him or herself into an animal, is known by all natural peoples (see Lévy-Bruhl, *The "Soul" of the Primitive*, pp. 39–43).]

46 The shortened form of bako-ké, an Arawak term for an eye-socket; it is applied to a particular variety of baskets, characterized by having an oblong concavity in its base, a peculiarity which the name suggests.

being himself seen. He saw the Spirit stealthily approach each hammock and remove both eyes of the snoring occupants without waking them. It carefully placed these eyes in the now-completed basket, and then it left the house. Next morning, when all the people awoke, they discovered that they could see nothing, and they wondered what had happened. The man who had previously warned them, related all that had happened. They said they were now no longer fit to live on the land, and that he must take them to some waterside. He thereupon tied them one to the other, and led them to a stream. When they had reached the stream, he tied the last one to a tree so that they could not lose their way and knew where they were. There he left them, as he thought, in perfect safety, and promised to visit them shortly. After a time, he fulfilled his promise to return, but found that all of them had in the meantime gone into the water, and all had changed into fish. The one exception was the one who was tied to the tree who, being able to get into the water only up to his middle, had turned only halfway into a fish. So the man went away, promising to come again. He was a long time gone, so long in fact, that the Spirit took pity on the last man, and completed his transformation, giving him back his own two eyes, which "are all very fine and large," so to speak. Especially for a haimara fish,[47] which was what the Spirit had changed him into. And when their old friend did return at last, he cut the rope from the tree, thus allowing the haimara and other fish to play about with perfect freedom in the water, where they have remained since. This is how they were punished for their unbelief.

215 Assimilation to an animal has different values. Sometimes it is becoming a real animal in the negative sense, that is, reverting to a completely instinctual lifestyle, as in the fairytale, "Trunt, Trunt, and the Trolls in the Mountains," or in a positive sense, to let the instincts take over as a guiding spirit.

---

[47] This is the fish *Hoplias malabaricus*.

Chapter 11

The Upperworld and the Underworld

216 In the fairytales "A Legend of Flowers" and "How Motecuzhoma Sought the Seven Caves," the unconscious is viewed as the land of the ancestors and as the original homeland, which as the Christian concept of paradise was lost. Certain tales of natural peoples help us better to discern that aspect of the unconscious described as the original home, the place where people tarried before they were born. In a creation story of the Warao tribe of Guyana (South America) "The Legend of Okonorótè," we learn:[1]

217 All Warao are descendants of Okonorótè, the primordial hunter, an adventurous heavenly figure. This man originally dwelt in a sky world, which was inhabited by people, but was completely devoid of all animals except birds. One day while out hunting these heavenly birds, Okonorótè's arrow struck his target but then both bird and arrow disappeared. When he went to search for them he discovered a deep pit and looked in.

218 "And he, fascinated, unable to move,
Saw daylight beneath, him, as well as above!
There, far, far below, he could see forests grow;
Wide plains, and savannahs, where rivulets flow.
And he looked down for hours those new wonders to view,
Thinking, 'All is a dream, sure it cannot be true!'"

219 Okonorótè went back to his people and convinced them to make a long rope. It took months to prepare, but was at last finished and the hero mustered his courage and made the descent.

220 "Twas a perilous venture, to come from above
By a ladder so frail, which light currents could move.

[1] [The original account, by W. H. Brett, *Legends and Myths*, London, 1880, pp. 55–60, who was a zealous missionary, is in romanticized English verse. The version given here is a summary interspersed with Brett's original verse.]

And when he was down, he stood gazing around
In utter amazement at all things he found;
The fire, so abundant, he saw with surprise,
The quadrupeds strange, and their wonderful size."

221 He shot a young deer and with even greater effort than before, he climbed back up to the sky world with his catch. When he told his people of what he had found and showed them the deer, they realized what fortune, for they had no such meat.

222 "So they asked no permission, but said, 'We will go!'
And came down the rope ladder to this world
below.
Things then were young – no old people were
found;
Small children they carried, and all reached the
ground."

223 All but one made it down to the new world. An old woman who was evidently quite corpulent, became stuck in the hole after all others had passed through. There was a big discussion among those down on the earth about what to do with this woman. There was general agreement that it was not right to leave her there, but to rescue her would mean the death of their strongest men.

224 "So the woman remains (though the ladder gave way)

225 And will always remain there, our old Waraos say,
She fills up the hole; and, good friends, that is why
We never can get a fair peep through the sky!"

226 This descent of the Warao from their home in the sky[2] through a hole[3] reminds one of giving birth. The process appears to indicate a descent into everyday reality. The absence of all animals except birds most likely relates to the concept that only "airy beings" reside in heaven.[4] Presumably, all the people

[2] One finds the same motif in West Greenland: cf. "The Legend of the Wandering (Immigration) of the People" (Krickeberg, *Nordamerika*, p. 369) and "The Creation of the World" (Ibid., p. 382). [Skidi Pawnee; for the original, see George A. Dorsey, *Traditions of the Skidi Pawnee*, Houghton, Miffiin and Company, Boston and New York, 1904a, Memoires of the American Folk-Lore Society, p. 8].

[3] Cf. the hole through which the spirit of the moon sends down a reindeer as a gift in "Flight to the Moon."

[4] Certain Gnostic sects called heaven "Air-Earth" or "Air-World." See Baynes, "Der Erlösungsgedanke in der Christlichen Gnosis" [Concepts of Redemption in Christian Gnosis] Eranos Yearbook, C. Baynes, "Der Erlösungsgedanke", Zürich, 1938, p. 209.

there were bird-like beings. As we will later show, birds signify spiritual contents of the unconscious. Leaving the original homeland and the descent down to the earth signifies the beginning of human consciousness, which depicts a development out of the animal (instinctual-unconscious) state and a coming-into-being that was only anticipated in the previous life spent in a kind of dream-like state.

227 With other South American tribes, like the Munduruku and the Karaja (man's true, original homeland) is not heaven but the underworld. The idea that a fat person blocks the hole to the earth, which thereafter remains forever clogged, appears in several other North American myths of this kind.[5]

228 It appears, therefore, that heaven is not much different in its essence from the underworld and is clearly the world of the unconscious. Return into the other world, even the mere looking back, is blocked, since it is too tempting and alluring to people in the initial states of becoming conscious. The "return" to paradise lost would make becoming conscious impossible for mankind. In order to make this "going back" as repelling as possible, according to many fairytales, giants or titanic robbers guard the way. In the fairytale, "The Story of the Great Reed-Warbler"(Micronesia),[6] it is characteristic that the hero is helped to get back into heaven,[7] since "to go to heaven" means to "return" into the unconscious land of origin. It is typical that heaven is also often conceived of as an ocean or a great water.[8] Among the Aztecs, therefore, heaven was called "Fish Canyon" from the idea that the stars were fish in the sea of the night sky.[9] The birth of humans is imagined as the souls of children dropping down to the earth from heaven.[10] In the world view of the ancient Egyptians, the stars lead to a ship over the heavens, the "cool waters, or the ocean that was under the body of Nut."[11] There, the underworld is a second, mirror-image, darker sky, and it is said of the sun, it rises *to heaven above and then descends to the heaven (!) below.*[12] In Egypt, as in India, heaven is a female

[5] Koch-Grünberg, *Südamerika*, Jena, p. 313.

[6] [A common thrush-like bird, *Acrocephalus arundinaceus*. Recorded as "Die Geschichte von der Rohrdrossel" in P. Hambruch, *Südsee*, Jena, 1921, pp. 214–216.]

[7] [Summary of the fairytale: A man in heaven had stolen the wife of a man on earth and had taken her up to him in heaven with a net. The saddened husband is helped by a crab to enter the body of a warbler and thus fly to heaven. Accompanied by the crab in the body of another warbler, they manage to bring his wife back. When the man in heaven tries again to bring the woman back up into heaven, the crab cuts the net.]

[8] Cf. Krickeberg, *Nordamerika*, p. 373, notes to "Sintflut und Erdfischung [Deluge and Earthfishing]" [Original as "The Blue Belt," in Hoffman, *Menomini*, Washington, D.C., 1896, pp. 134– 135.] Cf. also Krickeberg, *Nordamerika*, p. 497, notes to "The Creation" (Zuni). See further the Maya myth of the twins "Hunahpu und Xbalanque," to be discussed in the second volume of this work.

[9] Cf. Krickeberg, *Azteken and Inka*, p. 332, notes to "The Story of Quetzalcoatl's Youth."

[10] Ibid., pp. 41f, in the summary myth, "The Golden Age,"esp. p. 47.

[11] [Nut was originally the goddess of the nighttime sky, but eventually became referred to as simply the sky goddess.] Cf. Erman, *Religion der Ägypter*, p. 16. This idea is also found with the Perates and Mandaeans (Sabians), both Gnostic sects. See Reitzenstein, *Hellenistic*, p. 307.

[12] Erman, *Religion der Ägypter*, p. 17.

figure, the mother.[13] The description given by the Warou points to a similar belief. It describes birth from the primordial mother.[14] Such upper watery regions are also known from the Bible: "And God made the firmament, and divided the waters which were under the firmament from the waters which were above the firmament."[15] Even the highest representation of the Christian Heaven, as the heavenly Jerusalem or Paradise, has kept its feminine-maternal meaning.[16] Returning to heaven after death is a reentry into the preconscious state of being.[17]

229 Often the underworld as the beyond is differentiated from heaven, in that the evil ones live below and the good ones live above, as the Christian concept of heaven and hell declares.[18] When such a differentiation is made, the upper sphere usually acquires a masculine sense in contrast to a feminine aspect for the lower sphere. In this case, the symbol of heaven embodies the more spiritual aspect of the unconscious soul in contrast to the instinctive side. Usually, however, the spatial notion in relation to the beyond or heaven is just as indefinite as all other localizations in the magical realm. About this the Chinese master Lü-tsu says: "The land that is nowhere is the true home."[19]

230 Sometimes the land beyond (consciousness) lies at a place where heaven and the underworld clash together. In the Gilgamesh epic, the hero goes to the land of immortality to meet *Utnapishtim*, the immortal survivor of the flood, who is called "the Remote One" (or just "the Faraway"),[20] or heaven is above and at the same time far away in the East or West;[21] in such cases different conceptions cross over. Even language knows such metaphorical allusions: one "strolls in the clouds" or "sinks into a dream." One experiences the loss of wakeful consciousness either as a sinking down or as a "floating away," as an inner exaltedness.[22]

231 Sometimes, the primordial home of a people is neither above in heaven, nor below in the underworld, but lies "on the other side of the ocean that

---

[13] On India, see Zimmer, *Maya*, pp. 105-106.

[14] With the Bella Coola (Bilxula) tribe of British Columbia, the goddess Qama'its ("our woman") rules in the uppermost heaven described as a treeless prairie. Behind her house is a salt-water pond in which she bathes and nearby lives a snake or fish being that sometimes descends to our world and then causes rocks to burst and slide down mountains; F. Boas, *Bella Coola*, 1898, pp. 27–28.

[15] Genesis 1:7, *English Revised Version.*

[16] See C.G. Jung, *"Mother Archetype,"* CW 9i ¶156. See also Leisegang, *Die Gnosis*, p. 75.

[17] See Baynes, "Der Erlösungsgedanke," p. 208. On Gnostic beliefs in Paradise, see Cumont, *Oriental Religions in Paganism*, pp. 114–115.

[18] See Cumont, p. 145.

[19] See Wilhelm, Secret of the Golden Flower, p. 53.

[20] [Gilgamesh, Tablet 1, line 40. Gardner, Maier/Henshaw p. 58 and Tablet IX.]

[21] See Dieterich, *Eine Mithrasliturgie*, 1923, pp. 180–82, and Lévy-Bruhl, *The "Soul" of the Primitive*, p. 313f.

[22] See also Meister Eckhart, (Pfeiffer edition), *Works of Meister Eckhart*, "Sermon on Luke 21:26: The Powers of Heaven Shall Be Moved:" *Dâ von ist diu sêle ein götlicher himel und ein geistlicher, dâ got siniu volkomeniû werc inne ruowende tougen unde heimliche volbringet.* ["The soul is then a godly heaven and a spiritual one, where God secretly brings his work to completion in unbroken stillness."]

surrounds the world." Thus, the Aztecs tell of their ancestors in "The Legend of the Wandering (Immigration) of the People":

> 232 Their tribe came over the waters by boat to the place called *Tamoanchan*, which means, "there is the house from which they descended" (that is, "Place of the Original House").[23] These people were supposed to settle down there to live, but they later continued onwards with God behind them, "carrying their bundles, and it was said that God instructed them. They continued on their wandering, looking towards the face of the sun. . . "[24]

233 This *Tamoanchan* is the land of origin and at the same time the realm of the dead. It could also signify "the house of going down" (that is, birth[25]), similar to the image in the Waroa tale "The Legend of Okonoróté."

234 An example depicting the underworld as identical to the land of origin, as the other side of heaven was for the Warao, is found in a tale from the Karajá tribe of central Brazil, "Kaboi":

> 235 Kaboi, the forefather of the Karajá, lived with his people in the underworld. The sun shone there when it was night on the earth and vice-versa. One day the cry of the Seriema bird was so loud and persistent that Kaboi decided to follow the sound with some of his people. Going on in this way, they came to a hole that led up to the surface of the earth. But only his companions could get through, Kaboi had such a large body that he got stuck and could only look out of the opening with his head. The Karajá wandered through the new land and found much fruit, bees, and honey. They also encountered many dead trees and dry wood. They brought all this to the place where Kaboi was waiting, and showed him what they had found. "The land is good and fertile," they reported, "but the rotting wood shows us that whoever lives will soon decay and die. Therefore it is better to remain in our homeland."
>
> 236 In Kaboi's realm, people are very old, they only die when they become so old they can no longer make any movements.
>
> 237 When Kaboi returned to the rest of his people and showed them the fruit, most of them wanted to go to the upper world. It was futile for

[23] [English: Graulich, p. 53]; for the German, see Krickeberg, *Azteken and Inka*, 1928, who follows Bernardino de Sahagún, *Historia General de las Cosas de Nueva España* (General History of the Things of New Spain), ed. Angel María Garibay, Porrúa, Mexico, 1956. Alternative translation: "we go down to our home."]

[24] de Sahagún, *Historia General*, vol. 3, p. 209.

[25] See note in Krickeberg, *Azteken and Inka*, p. 348.

> Kaboi to warn them: "You will find everything you need, but you will quickly die there!" In spite of his warning, many of his people went up through the hole and populated the world. The rest stayed behind with Kaboi in the underworld. There they still live, in their full power, but the people who live on the surface of the earth go more and more towards their demise.[26]

238 This tale shows not only the identity of heaven and underworld and hence the relativization of space in the unconscious, but also shows at the same time that the *concept of time* changes with the emergence of consciousness. Whilst the Warao tale closes with the immigration to the earth, the Karajá are aware of the problems that accompany gaining consciousness. Just as enticing as earthly fruits are, they are acquired at the high price of an early death. This is spared to those caught in the magical world and who are "still today in their full power." As long as humans do not become individuals through gaining consciousness, they live in complete *species consciousness* and, therefore, feel themselves immortal as part of the species. The spirits of the ancestors as primordial images of all existence embody the constituents of this *species consciousness*. As such they represent, therefore, those who remain in the other world; or, according to other versions, they embody the immortal humans that have returned into the other world and partake of the archetypal (divine) dimension. On the other hand, the development of an individual consciousness paved the way for a conception of individual[27] death to emerge for the first time.[28]

---

[26] Koch-Grünberg, *Südamerika*, pp. 196–197. [In German, originally collected and published in Paul Ehrenreich, "Beiträge zur Völkerkunde Brasiliens," in: *Veröffentlichungen aus dem Kgl. Museum für Völkerkunde*, vol. 2, Museum für Völkerkunde, Berlin, 1891.] See also the Hopi myth "The Coming of the Hopi from the Underworld" (H. R. Voth, *Hopi*, New York, 1905, pp. 10–16). In a tale from the Munduruku (central Brazil), the underworld is likewise the original homeland. An armadillo accidentally digs a hole in the ground from which humans emerged. Cf. notes to "The Beginning of the World" in Koch-Grünberg, *Südamerika*. In spite of the large cultural difference, Plato's famous "Allegory of the Cave" in *The Republic* [Book VII in Benjamin Jowett's translation and in chapter IX in Robin Waterfield's translation (514a, 520a)] is based on the same archetypal concept.

[27] [The individuated individual, one who has worked on becoming conscious in this life; see C.G. Jung, *Memories, Dreams, Reflections*.]

[28] Cf. Jung, *Symbols of Transformation*, CW 5, ¶415: "The separation of the mother from the son signifies human being's taking leave from animal unconsciousness. It was only the power of the 'incest prohibition' that created the self-conscious individual, who before had been mindlessly one with the tribe; and it was only then that the idea of the final death of the individual became possible"; see also C.G. Jung, "The meaning of psychology for modern man," CW 10, ¶288ff.

Chapter 12
The Timeless Realm

239 In the course of an individual's becoming conscious, the magical realm (as the unconscious) has become the land of eternal youth, mighty strength, and long life, in contrast to everyday reality as the place of transient life.[1] It exists before and after, and at the same time in our world, just as it exists over and under and alongside our world.[2]

240 For the native tribes of Australia, this timeless world is called the *Altjira* (also *Alcheringa*), and it is the kingdom of totem spirits.[3] It is simultaneously the era in which time did not exist, or another kind of time, which exists parallel to our daily time. That this realm signifies the unconscious is shown by the Wichita tribe, whose gods and animals, which are ancestral spirits, are spoken of as "dreams."[4] Remarkably, the Ainu of northeast Japan also claim that fairytales are dreams. They differentiate *hengi hauki* (songs about ancestors) and *chitari hauki* (dream songs).[5] The realm of the Alcheringa is for the

---

[1] The idea that certain ancestral spirits live on under the ground is found in classical Greece. Amphiaraos was an Argivian hero and seer descended from the mysterious priest and prophet Melampous. He was drawn into war against his will, for he foresaw its unhappy end. After the decisive struggle in which opposing brothers fell, slain by each other's hand, the Argivian host turned to flight, and with them fled Amphiaraos. But before Periklymenos, who was pursuing him, could drive his spear into the fugitive's back, Zeus made the earth open before him, and accompanied by a flash of lightning Amphiaraos, his horses, his chariot, and his charioteer, were swallowed up in the depths where Zeus made him immortal. Northwards, near Lebadeia, men told of a similar marvel. In a cave of the mountainous ravine, before which Lebedeia lies, lived Trophanios forever immortal. All accounts agree in the assumption that Trophonios, like Amphiaraos, was first a mortal man, a famous master builder, who while fleeing from his foes, dived underground at Lebadeia and now lives forever in the depths of the earth whence he foretells the future to those who come and question him there. On the island of Rhodes, Althaimenes was honored as the "founder" of the Greek cities on that island. He had died, but had vanished into a chasm in the ground. See Rohde, *Psyche*, pp. 89–90. On page 92ff., he mentions "subterranean translation" in contrast to "island translation," in the sense of where the spirits went, since one can contact the spirits underground, while those on the island are far away and unreachable.

[2] In Goethe's *Faust II*, Act 1, Mephisto says about the realm of the mothers: Goddesses throne here in loneliness, Around them: no place; and even less, time. See also C.G. Carus, *Psyche* (Pforzheim, 1846), p. 219, who writes: "that when the consciousness of the organism lets the individuality, and above all the personality and freedom appear, the unconscious of the organism, however, binds the individual to the daily life of the world, and at the same time *generalizes* him, and that he, therefore, as an unconscious, actually also from all rules of the world pervaded and takes part in them, yes, that in him not only near and far, and overall spatial, and he thereby encounters the past and future, and timeliness push itself through." [Translated from p. 219, Part 2 of the 1846 German edition. This is not translated into English in the 1970 version of R. Welch. The original is a challenge to translate.]

[3] Cf. Lévy-Bruhl, *The "Soul" of the Primitive*, pp. 49–50.

[4] They are divided into four groups: Dreams-that-are-Above, or, the heavenly gods; and Dreams-down-Here, the earthly gods. The latter "dreams are in turn divided into two groups: Dreams-living-in-Water, and the Dreams-closest-to-Man"; see Dorsey, *The Mythology of the Wichita*, 1904, p. 20.

[5] F. Rumpf, *Japanische Volksmärchen*, 1938, p. 16; *hauki* means "make voice" equivalent to "songs." The hauki are traditional epic legends.

native Australians something thought, something spiritual (mental), in contrast to the sensorially perceived world.[6] Time does not exist independently of consciousness; rather, only consciousness knows a here and now, and therefore, a course of events.[7] Besides all those other worlds, the timeless foundation of the soul continues to exist. A similar thought is mentioned in a tractate of the mystic Meister Eckhart, *On the nobility of the soul*: "All things flow in time, but in eternity they remain in right measure."[8] Another unnamed medieval mystic spoke thusly of eternity: "There is neither time nor space, neither past nor future, everything is presently decided in an eternally recurring now, in which a thousand years pass as quickly as an instant."[9] This concept of a thousand years passing in an instant is found in many fairytales. Here is a Danish example, "A Moment in Heaven":

> 241 Two friends promise one another that each one will attend the wedding of the other. It came to pass, however, that one of the friends died before he married. At the wedding of the other friend, the dead man appeared, but was only visible to the groom. The dead friend let the groom come up to heaven and visit the place where he tarried for "an instant of time." When the groom returned to his wedding, he found nothing around and learned that a hundred years earlier, a wedding had taken place in which the groom had inexplicably

---

[6] SSee Richard Thurnwald, "Primitive Initiations- und Wiedergeburtsriten," in: *Eranos-Jahrbuch 1939: Die Symbolik der Wiedergeburt in der religiösen Vorstellung der Zeiten und Völker*, ed. Olga Fröbe-Kapteyn, Rhein-Verlag, Zürich, 1940, p. 353. It is the sphere of the timeless archetypal ideas that apparently never completely enter into our consciousness and time and space. See C.G. Jung, , *Psychology and Alchemy*, CW 12, ¶328. Time is mythological because it can only be grasped through motion in space, the god of time is often named in conjunction with the goddess of matter, that is, in connection with the goddess of space. See Jean Przyluski, "Die Mutter-Göttin als Verbindung zwischen den Lokal-Göttern und dem Universal-Gott," in: *Eranos-Jahrbuch 1938: Gestalt und Kult der "Grossen Mutter,"* ed. Olga Fröbe-Kapteyn, Rhein-Verlag, Zürich, 1939, pp. 42–46 and 51 [The Mother Goddess as Connection, Eranos Yearbook]. This mother goddess is also the bringer of time and the one who places death in the world. Cf. Zimmer, *Maya*, pp. 424, 468-69. Cf. also C.G. Jung, *Psychologie und Religion*, CW 11, ¶126. See further the fairytale "The Legend of Okonorótè."

[7] On the timelessness of the unconscious, see C.G. Jung, "Rebirth," CW 9i, ¶249. See also Carus, *Psyche*: "Only the conscious mind arrests the flight of time and grasps eternity," p. 21; see further A. Schopenhauer, "Geistersehn," Leipzig, 1877: "The effusive, wonderful . . . absolutely unbelievable somnambulant clairvoyance. . . loses at least its absolute comprehensibility when we allow . . . that the objective world is just a brain phenomenon, because then the order and regularity (lawfulness) based on the space, time, and causality (as brain functions) is the same as that which to a certain degree is abolished in somnambulant clairvoyance… On the other hand, if time and space were absolute and real and affiliated with being of things, then the gift of seeing of somnambulists, just as all fortunetelling and prediction, would plainly be an incomprehensible wonder… Every soothsaying (*Mantik*), if it is through dreams, in somnambulant prophesying, in the second face, or whatever else it may be called, exists in discovering a way of freeing cognition from the condition of time." [Neither the original quote nor the English translation were found. The passage is not included in Payne's English translation of *Parerga*, A. Schopenhauer, *On Spirit Seeing*, Oxford, 1974.]

[8] Original: "Alliu dinc sint ûz gevlozzen in der zît mit mâze, aber in der êwikeit sint sie sunder mâze beliben," Pfeiffer's edition, p. 390.

[9] Usually attributed to Meister Eckhart; see *Schriften und Predigten*, vol. 1, p. 73. On the question of authorship, see the notes on p. 213f.

> suddenly disappeared. Thereupon he prayed to God to take him back to heaven, and his wish was immediately granted.[10]

242 A similar idea appears in the fairytale "The Beggar and Paradise," where God once appeared on earth as a beggar and was taken in by a poor man. After a while, the beggar invited his host to come visit him where he lived. The man followed the *silver* tracks of the beggar's wagon, which never changed, and after many happenings came to a secluded paradisal garden. The tale continues:

243 The poor man stood there in great wonderment, not knowing whether he was dreaming or awake, whether he was dead or alive. He looked around in all directions and went slowly forth into the garden. He always carefully followed the silver tracks. . . [When he finally returned home,] he recognized neither his hometown nor any of the people he saw around him. Everything had changed, there were other houses, other people. He asked the people he met where his little house, his children, and his stepbrother were. No one could tell him anything about the whereabouts of his house or his people. Everybody looked upon him as a foreigner with mistrust. What does this poor man want? He had no choice but to return to the silver track and the beggar and to ask what had happened to everything. When he came again to the beautiful garden, the beggar welcomed him in a most friendly manner and so there the man remained forever, with the beggar in paradise.[11]

244 Related motifs appear also in the second part of the French fairytale, "Death's Wife":

245 Once upon a time there was a woman who never married. She never found just the right man. By now she was over forty and friends often said to her jokingly: "Margarete, you will never marry!" She would then often answer: "Yes, I will; when death comes to take me home." One day in August, when Margarete was home alone and was preparing the meal for the threshers, an unknown stranger entered her house and asked: "Do you want to take me for your man?" "Who are you?" she asked, most alarmed. "Death!" answered the stranger. "Then I will take you for my husband," she said and threw her stirring spoon away and told her friends.

---

[10] Stroebe, *The Danish Fairy Book*, pp. 158–161. See the well-known story of the monk from Heisterbach.

[11] Leskien, *Balkanmärchen*, pp. 311–321 [translated from the German].

246 She prepared a banquet, as Death had required, and they were married. Death told her that she should tell her younger brother, her godchild, who was still in the cradle, that he should visit her one day when he grew up. To get there, he should follow the setting sun. Margarete did as she was advised and they made off on their journey. At last they arrive at her husband's home. It was the castle of the rising sun. Every day her husband would leave in the morning and come back in the evening. Margarete had everything she wanted, but she soon became bored in her loneliness every day. One day someone came to the castle. Margarete was most surprised since no one ever visited the castle. It was her younger brother, her godchild! They greeted each other joyfully and the young man asked where his step-brother was, he would like to ask him a favor.

247 When Margarete's husband came home that evening, he welcomed his new guest who immediately asked what he did all day, leaving his sister at home alone. "I travel around the world, my dear brother." "Jesus, brother, you must see wondrous things! May I come along with you?" "Tomorrow you can join me, but no matter what you see and hear, you may not ask me about anything. Speak no word or you have to immediately return." "I promise, I will speak no word, stepbrother!" said the young man. The first morning, there was so much wind that the young man's hat fell off and he asked if he could pick it up. But since he had spoken, he had to return home.

248 Twice he fails to come along, because he begins to speak against the prohibition of death as soon as the wind blows his hat off his head. The third time he remains silent and sees many strange things: white doves burning two black ones, lean cows in rich country, fat cows in lean country, fighting ravens and a castle with an iron gate behind which there is a scorching heat and through which the young man is not allowed to walk. Later, Death told him that the two black doves that he had seen were the man's parents, who were allowed to go through the fire to cleanse them of sins so that they could go to Paradise; the lean cows were dissatisfied kingdoms, the fat satisfied poor; and the fighting ravens were quarreling spouses.

249 "At this moment they arrived back at the castle. The young man then announced that he would like to return home. "But why?" asked his stepbrother. "To see my friends and relatives and to live with them," answered the young man. "But consider this," said his stepbrother: "Five hundred years have passed since you left, all your friends and

> relatives are long dead and where your house once was, is now an old oak tree that is rotting from age."[12]

250 Once again, we note the impressive version of the motif of the timelessness of the other side, that is, the unconscious. How this timelessness lets its effects be shown to work over many generations is told in the Welsh fairytale "The Curse of Pantannas":

> 251 Long, long ago, at the farm of Pantannas, in Glamorgan, there lived a churlish old husbandman. He hated the Fair Folk who danced on his fields to the light of the moon, and longed to discover some way of ridding his land of them. The farmer rejoiced greatly, imagining vain things, until one evening in the spring of the year, when the wheat was green in the fields. The farmer was returning home in the red light of the setting sun, when a tiny little man in a red coat came up to him, unsheathed a little sword, and directing the point towards him, said:
>
> 252 *Dial a ddaw.* Vengeance cometh,
> *Y mae gerilaw.* Fast it approacheth.
>
> 253 On the advice of a witch, a farmer made the fairy rings on his estate unusable for the elf dance by planting corn. A tiny little man dressed in a red coat appeared to him and threathened: "*Dial a ddaw.* Vengeance cometh, *Y mae gerilaw.* Fast it approacheth."
>
> 254 In the autumn, when the corn was golden in the fields and ripe for the sickle, the farmer and his family were one night going to bed. Suddenly they heard a mighty noise, which shook the house as though it would fall. As they trembled with fear, they heard a loud voice saying: "*Daw dial.* Vengeance cometh." Next morning, no ear or straw was to be seen in the cornfields, only black ashes. The fairies had burnt all the harvest. The farmer was walking through his fields, gazing ruefully at the destruction wrought by the fairies, when he was met by the same little man as before. Pointing his sword threateningly, the elf said: "*Nid yw ond dechrau.* It but beginneth." The farmer's face turned as white as milk, and he began to plead for pardon. He was quite willing, he said, to allow the fields where the fairies had been wont to dance and sing to grow again into a greensward. They could dance in their rings as often as they wished without interference, provided only they would punish him no more. After originally saying "No," the little man pitied

[12] Tegethoff, *Französische Volksmärchen*, vol. 2, Jena, 1923, pp. 141–145.

him and said he would talk to his king. Three days later he returns and reports, "The King's word," he said, "cannot be recalled, and vengeance must come. Still, since thou repentest thee of thy fault and art anxious to atone it, the curse shall not fall in thy time nor in that of thy sons, but will await thy distant posterity."

255 The farmer passed away in peaceful old age, and his sons followed him to the churchyard without feeling any effects of the curse pronounced by the King of the fairies. More than a hundred years after the first warning had been uttered, Madoc, the heir of Pantannas, was betrothed to Teleri, the daughter of the squire of Pen Craig Daf, and the wedding was to take place in a few weeks. It was Christmastide, and they made a feast at Pantannas to which Teleri and all her kin were bidden. The feast began merrily, and all were seated 'round the hearth, passing the hours with tale and song. Suddenly, above the noise of the river which flowed outside the house, they seemed to hear a voice saying: "*Daeth amser ymddial*. The time for revenge is come." A silence fell on the joyous company. They went out and listened if they could hear the voice a second time; but long though they lingered, they could make out no sound except the angry noise of the full river plunging down its rocky bed. They went back into the house; gradually their fears were chased away, and all was as before. Again, above the sounds of mirth and the noise of the waters as they boiled over the boulders was heard a clear voice: "*Daeth yr amser*. The time is come."

256 A dread noise crashed around them, and the house shook to its foundations. As they sat speechless with fear, behold, a shapeless hag appeared at the window. Then one, bolder than the rest, said, "What dost thou, ugly little thing, want here?" "I have naught to do with thee, chatterer," said the hag. "I had come to tell of the doom which awaits this house and that other which hopes to be allied with it, but as thou hast insulted me, the veil which conceals it shall not be lifted by me." With that she vanished, no one knew how or whither. When she had gone, the voice proclaimed again, more loudly than before: "*Daeth amser ymddial*. The time for vengeance is come."

257 Terror and gloom fell upon all. Before long, the guests parted and went trembling back to their homes, and Madoc took his betrothed back to Pen Craig Daf, doing all that a fond lover could do to dispel her fears; for she had been struck to the heart with nameless dread. Then he bid her farewell and turned homewards to Pantannas. The night Madoc disappeared forever, nowhere to be found although his kinsfolk searched all over. One-by-one all those who had known Madoc died, including his beloved Teleri who never gave up that she

would see him again. Alas, worn out with fruitless longing, she died before her time, and they buried her in the graveyard of the old Chapel of the Fan. Madoc's strange disappearance became only a faint tradition.

258 Teleris's undying belief that her lover was still alive was, however, true. This is what had happened to him. As he was returning home from Pen Craig Daf, the sounds of the sweetest music he had ever heard in his life came out of a cave in the Raven's Rift, and he stopped to listen. After a while, the strains seemed to recede further into the cave, and he stepped inside to hear better. The melody retreated further and further, and Madoc, forgetting everything else, followed it further and further into the recesses of the cavern. After he had been listening for an hour or two, as he thought, the music ceased, and he suddenly remembered that after the strange events of the night, his parents would be anxious for his return. He retraced his footsteps rapidly to the mouth of the cave. When he issued forth from the hollow, the sun was high in the heavens, and he realized that he had been listening to the music longer than he had at first thought. He hastened towards Pantannas, opened the door and went in. Sitting by the fire was an aged man who asked him, "Who art thou that comest in so boldly?"

259 A sense of bewilderment came over Madoc. He looked round him. The inside of the house seemed different from what he had been accustomed to. He went to the window and looked out. There appeared to him to be several curious differences in the aspect of the country also. He became dimly conscious that some great change had passed over his life, and answered faintly, "I am Madoc." "Madoc?" said the aged man. "Madoc? I know thee not. There is no Madoc living in this place, nor have I ever known any man of that name. The only Madoc I have ever heard of was one who, my grandfather said, disappeared suddenly from this place, nobody knew whither, many scores of years ago." Madoc sank on a chair and wept. The old man's heart went out to him in his grief, and he rose to comfort him. He put his hand on his shoulder, when lo! the weeping figure crumbled into thin dust.[13]

260 This tale shows particularly impressively the antithesis between our profane, time-bound existence and the timeless primordial basis of archetypal psychic images, where the processes described in fairytales and legends actually take place.[14]

---

[13] W. Jenkyn Thomas, *The Welsh Fairy Book*, 1908, pp. 18–26.

[14] Cf. also the tale "The Earth Wants to Have Hers." On the timelessness of myths in general, see also Leeuw, *Religion in Essence*, vol. 1, p. 384f, and Lüthi, *The European Folktale*, pp. 19–21.

261 The sojourn in the magical kingdom can be experienced as encompassing a very short time, but in outer reality it covers a very long time, as we saw in the last example. However, just the opposite can also be the case: the sojourn in the other world can be experienced as a very long time whereas measured in normal reality time, it was very short. An example of this is the following Greek tale, "The Fisherman's Child and the Elves":

> 262 Once upon a time there was a man who decided to go fishing and took his small son with him. On the way, he *became tired* and placed the boy up on a tree branch and said: "Wait quietly up there, my child. When I come back I will lift you down again." After the boy had sat for a while in the tree, two ravens came and begged the boy to share with them a piece of the meat that he had. The boy did this. Shortly thereafter, a group of Nereids[15] came, took the boy with them, and carried him into a cave. Then they went to their mother and said to her: "We found a boy!" "Where did you leave him?" "In a cave." "Go and bring him here," said their mother. They went and brought the boy to their mother. The fisherman's son stayed for a while with the nymphs. But then one day, one of the nymphs was struck by a bolt of lightning as she was bathing. After this tragedy, the nymph mother said to her remaining daughters: "This came upon us because of that human child we have here. Now take him back to the place where you found him, otherwise the gracious God will kill us all." Immediately the nymph girls took the boy and carried him back to the tree where they found him. When his *father returned from fishing*, he found the boy in the tree, took him down, and they went back to their house. Once back home, the boy related everything that had happened to him when his father was away.[16]

263 This example shows clearly the relativization of time in the unconscious. Fairytales often reveal their timelessness in their own closing remarks: "And when they have not died, then they are still alive today!"[17] In this regard, fairytale beginnings and endings are especially noteworthy. Bolte and Polivka

---

[15] [Female nymphs, originally helpers to sailors. In modern Greek folklore, the term "nereid" (νεράϊδα, neráïda) has come to be used for all nymphs, or fairies, not merely nymphs of the sea. These beings are the equivalent of English "elves".]

[16] J. G. v. Hahn (trans.), *Griechische Märchen*, vol. 2, Leipzig, 1864, no. 84,* cited in Laistner, *Das Rätsel*, Berlin, 1889, vol. 1, pp. 35–36.

[17] This resembles the ending of "The Tale about the Red Sea" (Finland) and "How an Orphan Unexpectedly Found his Fortune" (Finland). See also the allusion to the division of time and space at the end of the tale "Petri Godchild" (Spain): "And they remained there and sent me here, so that I could tell you this story" (H.-J. Uther, *Diederichs Märchen der Weltliteratur*, Reinbek, 1992, *passim*). The reader can find similar endings in many other tales.

have collected many examples.[18] Further examples of how the beginnings of fairytales allude to the timelessness and spacelessness of the happenings in the magical realm are: "Once upon a time when nobody existed but God. . .", or, "In olden times, when the Lord himself still used to walk about on this earth amongst men. . ." Here is the beginning of one English fairytale: "Once upon a time, and a very good time it was, though it wasn't in my time nor in your time, nor anybody else's time. . . "[19] In the Orient, tales often begin with: "Once upon a time it was, it was not. . . ," and in Hungary: "Wherever it was, wherever it wasn't. . . " Or: "Once upon a time, I do not know where, beyond the seven kingdoms, still farther, beyond the Sea of Operenz (Ocean), on the collapsed side of a broken down oven . . . beyond the glass mountain. . . on the barren Search-Not and Ask-Dog-Not Mountain where seven slender willow trees stand"[20] And a Slovakian legend begins: "In the seventy-seventh land, where the boards were devious. . ." An Ainu tale, "Poi-Yaumbe," opens with: "We three, my younger sister, my elder brother, and I, were always together. One night I was quite unable to sleep, but whether what I now relate was seen in a dream or whether it really took place, I do not know."[21]

264 The truth of fairytales is often accentuated in strangely ambiguous ways. For instance, in "The Hare and the Hedgehog" (Grimms):[22] "This story, my dear young folks, seems to be false, but it really is true, for my grandfather, from whom I have it, used to say when relating it, 'It must be true my son, or else no one could tell it to you.'"[23] And that the fairytale is a dream incident is proven most clearly by the beginning, "Something dreamed in me and this is the story,"[24] and also at the end: "Then a rooster crowed 'Kikeriki', the fairytale has been told, 'Kikeriki.'" And in French: "*Mais une nuit ... le coq chanta, il etait jour, et mon conte est fini*" ["But one night. . . the cock crowed and it was

[18] Bolte and Polívka, *Anmerkungen*, vol. 4, pp. 13ff.

[19] The beginning of another English fairytale also alludes to an unrealistic time: "Once upon a time, when pigs spoke rhyme."

[20] [Reference unknown.] Cf. also the beginning of the tale "Youth Without Age and Life Without Death": "Once upon a time something happened whose like never occurred before – if it had not happened it would not be told – as the poplar tree bore pears and the basket willow bore sweet violet, as the bears swung their tails about, and as the wolves and lambs embraced each other and kissed in brotherly love, as the flea with its one foot shod with ninety-nine pounds of iron jumped into the skies to bring fairy tales to us, as only flies on the walls were hand-painted and anyone that doesn't believe this is a concealed liar" (Mite Kremnitz, *Roumanian Fairy Tales*, 1885, adapted and arranged by J. M. Percival).

[21] J. Batchelor, *Specimens*, Yokohama, 1880, pp. 184–188. This tale is summarized on page 592, where Batchelor notes: "I have come to the conclusion that the word [Poi-Yaumbe] is most probably meant to designate the ancient Ainu."

[22] J. and T. Grimm, *Complete Grimm's*, London, 1975, p. 760.

[23] "The Stolen Daughters" ends thus: "This is a true story, but you do not need to believe it. The person who experienced it, told it to me." See also "A Head" (Finland): "They celebrated their marriage, feasted and drank, and ordered me to tell these lies to you." See also, "The Knight With the Sinister Laugh:" "They ended up on the wrong way and I came along on the right way. They died, but I have not yet landed on the bier. And if this is a bunch of lies, then they can carry away the dog in their mouths."

[24] Bolte and Polívka, *Anmerkungen*, vol. 4, p. 16.

dawn and my story is finished."][25] Similarly, the Russian fairytale "The Princess Who Could not Laugh" ends: "I mean, wasn't it just as if the servant had dreamed all this? But everyone tells it as if it really happened, and one just has to believe that."[26]

Summary: Timeless realm

265 From the above examples, it is clear that the time and space of fairytale events not only represent the unconscious, but also that this unconscious represents itself in symbolic places like in water, on the moon, on an island, and in the mountains, whereby each of these symbols illuminates different aspects of the unknown soul in closer detail. The forest, for example, characterizes the unconscious as the unknown, rooted in the physiological vegetative life. The moon describes the unconscious as the place of the experience of inner life as natural enlightenment. The earth-hole, the cave, the spring, and the heaven-hole let the unconscious appear as the mother ground of psychic life and the passageway to inner transformations. The island brings out the quality of the unconscious as far-from-consciousness, and as another *terra firma* on the inside. The symbol of the mountain indicates an experience of the unconscious in the sense of the piling up of inner forces to form a preeminent personality.

266 Of decisive importance here is, in a broader sense, the aspect of the unconscious as the land of ancestors, ancestral spirits, the primordial ground, and the abode of the dead. It can also indicate the psychic place where one is transported in a state of rapture.[27] In these representations, the unconscious is understood as that psychic foundation out of which every species consciousness and individual consciousness unfold and that foundation to which they can return..

[25] Ibid., p. 32. Cf. also "Droll Stories from the *Pas de Calais*" and "How Hans married Jacqueline" (Tegethoff, *Französische Volksmärchen*, vol. 2, p. 20, no. 5), as well as "The Three Chicks"(*ibid.*, no. 48).
[26] A. Loepfe, *Russische*, Olten, 1941, p. 56.
[27] [The authors use the German word *entrücken*. See page 32, footnote number 24].

Chapter 13
The Realm of the Dead and the Spirit-World

267 Another manifestation of the "land of the soul," which naturally follows from the aforementioned, is the land of the dead and the world of ghosts, which is how the unconscious is described in many legends, fairytales, and myths. Especially in the conceptions of native peoples one sees a complete identity of ancestral spirits, ghosts, and demons. Possibly due to this identity, many editors thought it appropriate to include stories of spooks and reports of ghosts and spirit apparitions in their collections of fairytales and the myths of native peoples. These are, precisely speaking, not always considered to be fairytales.[1] Many of the fairytales in this work, however, contain motifs of phantoms and spirits of the dead as single elements within the tale. One thinks, for example, of the helpful actions that the soul of Cinderella's dead mother performs.[2] The identity of the magical realm with the land of the dead is impressively shown in the Chinese fairytale "Sky O'Dawn," which relates the adventures of a strange boy-hero called "Morning Sky." This figure is actually the incarnate form of Jupiter, the *star of the great year*.[3]

268 Time and again, Morning Sky undertook trips to the magical kingdom. He arrived first at the *Purple Sea*, slept in the *City of the Dead*, and then he came to a swamp *where the great primordial fog lived*, an ageless man who every thousand years turned his bones inside out and washed the marrow clean. One time he fell *into a deep well*, at the bottom of which he came upon a shoe that floated on water that was otherwise so weak, that even a feather sank to the bottom. Here he found the herb of immortality. On one of his travels he visited the Fire-Mirror Mountain where the Gleaming-Stalk-Grass grows. With the light emitted by this grass one could see the insides of people and the spirit-world. He then rode on his horse to the Land of Good-Fortune-Clouds. The emperor asked Morning Sky what the Land of Good-Fortune-Clouds really was, Morning Sky answered that it was a huge

[1] [See Lüthi, *The European Folktale*, 1982, passim.]
[2] See "Cinderella," in: J. and T. Grimm, *Complete Grimm's*, London, 1975, pp. 121–127.
[3] On this tale, see Wilhelm, *The Chinese Fairy Book*, p. 94.

swamp. There, people foretell good and bad fortune from air and clouds. If a certain house will enjoy good fortune in the future, then five-colored clouds form in the room, which then condense on grass and trees and become colored dew. This dew tastes like sweet juice. The emperor asked if he could acquire some of this dew. Morning Sky rode his horse to the Land of Good-Fortune-Clouds and brought back some of this elixir. Any elderly person who drank this dew became immediately young, and anyone who suffered illness was instantly cured.

269 Here, the *City of the Dead* is one of the many features and forms that appear in Morning Sky's travels, which share many aspects with the previously described characteristics of the magical realm. Among other spirits, Lake Dongting in "Help in Need" harbors a dead soldier. In the belief of many folk cultures, the land of the dead is generally found at the bottom of the sea or in a pool, or is only reachable after crossing stygian waters.[4] By the same token, the moon is the place where the departed souls dwell,[5] the same with the mountain[6] and the forest.[7] Also the regions of Mother Holle are originally nothing other

---

[4] The Egyptians thought that the Land of the Dead was an island in the west or a place one reached after crossing a watery expanse. Cf. Erman, *Religion der Ägypter*, Berlin and Leipzig, 1934, pp. 215ff. The place where the sun journeys in the night is called *Lower Heaven*; see *ibid.*, p. 17. For the Aztecs, the land of the dead, Teotihuacan, lay on the other side of the sea. See "The Legend of the Wandering (Immigration) of the People." Also the North Germans knew of a kingdom of the dead in the ocean or on a far-away island that was only reachable by boat. Cf. Mogk, *Germanische Religionsgeschichte*, Berlin and Leipzig, 1927, p. 60. The *Mummelsee* [Lake Mummel] is not only a child's pool but also the place where the ghost immigration was wont to disappear. Cf. Ninck, *Wodan*, Jena, 1935, p. 210, Woden and under *Grab* [grave], *Höhle* [cave], *Brunnen* [well], *Teich* [pond], and *Erdloch* [earth hole] as entrance into the land of the dead (Bächtold-Stäubli under *Hölle* [Hell]. Cf. the underworld is at the bottom of the ocean in the Sedna myth ("*Sednas Reich*"); see Krickeberg, *Nordamerika*, Jena, 1924, p. 268.

[5] Cf. C.G. Jung, *Symbols of Transformation*, CW 5, ¶ 368f. See also "Flight to the Moon," where the moon woman has a hollow back, and "The Girl in the Moon" (Nauru, Micronesia). See also P. Hambruch, *Südsee*, Jena, 1921, pp. 220–226 [in German], where a blind old woman had ants and worms in her eyes.

[6] See, for example, Erman, *Religion der Ägypter*, p. 215, where the Pharaoh returns to his two mothers, vultures with hanging breasts, on the mountain of Sehseh. See also the Germanic belief that Woden rules over the dead in a mountain. To this day several Scandinavian mountains are called *Valhalla = Halls of the fallen warriors*. Cf. Mogk, *Germanische Religionsgeschichte*, p. 61. For further similarities in Ireland, see Müller-Lisowski, *Irische Volksmärchen*, Jena, 1923, p. 320, whose notes to "Connla's Sea-Journey" mention several Irish concepts of the other world including: the West, the bottom of the ocean, the land of women, the land of the living, the land under the waves, and the land of youth. See also "The Dangerous Reward" (Wilhelm, *The Chinese Fairy Book*, 1921) and Bächtold-Stäubli under *Jenseits*: The dead live in the Gods' Mountains with the gods. At first, this place is introduced as real and earthly, but then removes itself farther and farther from the earthly level of being, in that the gods distance themselves, becoming more and more a "totally-other." The same with the dead. In earlier times, one emphasized the identity of the souls of the living and the dead, later more the differences. "The soul after death is, more or less, stronger or weaker, as it was during the lifetime; this shows itself most clearly in the pyramid texts of the Egyptians" (Bächtold-Stäubli under *Jenseits*). The dead go to the gods, becoming ever more like them and the ancestors, but "the total view of the godhead (has) become more transcendent and otherworldly."

[7] Cf. Bächtold-Stäubli (vol 4, p. 642f.) under *Jenseits* [the other side] and also *Hölle* [Hell].

than the realm of Hel, the Germanic goddess of death. All the main symbols discussed above for the unconscious overlap with the symbols for the land of the dead.

270 According to Bächtold-Stäubli, originally the "other side" and "this side" formed a unity. For natural folk cultures, there is only one reality, the real environment, which was populated with creative primordial beings, ancestors and gods. They withdraw as souls of the dead to particular places that become cultural centers.

271 [In Germany] there is the idea of the cult-cave, the waterhole, or of legends about the Hörsel-Mountain-Cave (*Hörselbergloch*),[8] and Below Mountain (*Untersberg*). Mother Holle [Hel] inhabits wells, into which Gold-Marie and Pitch-Marie in the fairytale "Mother Holle" must step, and "consequently out of which children come. . . And not only wells, but also the Mountains of the Dead are concomitantly the Venus mountains, in which Frau Bertha, Perchta,[9] cares for the souls of children who died prematurely (actually unborn children). This connection is necessary, since death and rebirth correlate at this level."[10]

272 In Australia, the cult cave contains wooden objects that represent the life force of the individual and the tribe. Caves are used for rituals to renew power; however, they house the danger of bringing decay to the uncalled, who might become stuck (in the chaos of the unconscious). The treasure cave is on this side and its dangers are also of this side, but at the same time it signifies the beyond. In time, the concept emerges of a *yonder place*. The answer to the question: "Where is the land of the dead?" is:

273 Far away, on the other side of the water – spirits (ghosts) cannot cross over water – on the other side of the forests, on the other side of the sea, but *not here*. With emphasis on the "not" and "here." In general the location is indefinite so that that no one can give information to the one. [Often] in fairytales the one looking for the land of the dead is sent from one place to another.[11]

---

[8] [The name is derived from the goddess Holba, who is identical to Mother Holle and is the wife of Wotan.]

[9] [A goddess of middle Europe, probably originally Celtic in origin, similar to Bertha and Mother Holle.]

[10] Bächtold-Stäubli, vol. 4, p. 642f.

[11] Bächtold-Stäubli, vol. 4, p. 645. In general, see the various ways of locating the land of the dead in Dieterich, *Eine Mithrasliturgie*, 1923, pp. 180–183; see also his *Nekyia. Beiträge zur Erklärung der neuentdeckten Petrusapokalypse*, 2nd ed., 1893, *passim*.

274 Often, the dead are transported (enraptured),[12] as it were, to far-away realms and unspecified locations.

> 275 According to the ancient Germanic beliefs, the Island of the Souls is near Britannia, the land of mist. . . In the South lies Muspelheim, the land of the fire giants. This Muspelheim later led the way to the connection with the concept of a residence of the dead in a fiery hell and, in conjunction with this idea, at the base of a volcano. This developed into a belief in a fiery underworld populated by innumerable droves of dead and devils. A third place of the dead of this kind is the realm of the dead at the bottom of the ocean, where the Ran[13] or one of her nine daughters lured men to death by drowning. . . If the land of the dead is far away, then the journey is long and arduous. One must give, therefore, the dead things that will ease his or her difficulties on the way."[14]

276 These may be travel appurtenances, like horses and wagons; or when it concerns a sovereign, then his corpse is laid in a boat. A living or a non-human ferryman sets the dead on the other side of the river or they might have to go on foot over thorny heaths or wander along a country road overgrown with thorn bushes.

> 277 The most important equipment for this journey is a pair of solid shoes for the dead. . . The Armenians light candles or burn lamps so that the souls can light their way into the other world. . . There are public inns along the way where the dead can find refreshment. . .[15]

278 The identity of the magical realm in general with the kingdom of the dead in particular, indicates that in ancient times the rites of the mystery cults are anticipations of the death experience. Some of these rites clearly represent a descent into the unconscious. Also the initiations in the *Tibetan Book of the Dead*, which were meant to serve as guides for the dying, if viewed psychologically describe an initiation for the living to enter the unconscious and follow the way to freedom out of a state of inner darkness and unconsciousness.[16] The mythical world of the dead with its inhabitants is thus

---

[12] [German: *entrücken*.]

[13] [Norse goddess of the sea.]

[14] Bächtold-Stäubli, vol. 4, p. 646.

[15] For this description of the realm of the dead, see Bächtold-Stäubli, vol. 4, p. 646f. under *Jenseits*.

[16] See C.G. Jung, *Tibetan*, CW 11, ¶842, ¶845. In the *Brihadaranyaka Upanishads*, it is said:
Indeed, those worlds are joyless,
enveloped in blind darkness.
After death, all things go to these worlds
– all those who are unaware and ignorant.
(fourth Adhaya, fourth Brahmana, verse 11, Deussen, *Sixty Upanishads*, p. 497).

another image of the unconscious soul with all its contents. The unconscious is, after all, the repository of everything past and of the beliefs of many generations, the world of the ancestors in us.[17] This explains the strange attraction that the dead have on the living – a motif that constitutes the main content of many ghost stories. The fairytale, "A Moment in Heaven," mentioned above, in which the dead friend entices the bridegroom away from the wedding, is a further example of this psychological fact.

279 A striking description of the magical realm that is at the same time the land of the dead, or a land between the realm of the living and that of the dead, is found in the Roma[18] fairytale, "Journey to the Kingdom of the Dead":

> 280 Once upon a time there lived a poor Gypsy boy, whose father, mother, and the girl that he loved dearly all died within the same week. With a deeply troubled heart he buried them. He could not hold a funeral banquet because he was so poor that he could barely survive from one day to the next. One week after he had performed the funeral rites, he awoke in the night as if someone was shaking his tent. He asked: "Who is there?" He heard his father say: "You buried me but gave me no milk!" The following night the same shaking happened. Again he asked: "Who is there?" This time he heard his mother say: "You buried me but gave me no milk!" Then again, one night later came the voice of his girlfriend: "You buried me but gave me no milk!" Now all was very heavy in his heart. He went out in front of his tent. The night was dark, it was so black he could see nothing. But he heard his dead girlfriend speaking, "If you want to help us find peace, go up into the mountains. There you will find a cave with three eggs. Take these and open them if you can. But you will only succeed with great difficulty!" And then the dead maiden disappeared.
>
> 281 At the break of day, the young man began his journey. When he arrived *high up in the mountains* he came upon an old woman, who was laboring with a heavy sack on her back. The young man had pity on her and said: "Give me your sack, I will carry it for you!" The old hag gave him the sack and the young man heaved it up on his shoulder. He then asked the old one what she was carrying in it; for him it was very light. "The souls of stillborn children," answered the old woman. "It is my custom to carry them to the Kingdom of the Dead." No sooner had they taken a few steps than the old woman stopped before the entrance to a *cave* and said: "Here we are!" "Why," asked the young man, "so soon?" "For you it seems like an instant,"

[17] Cf. C.G. Jung, *Children's Dreams*, Princeton, 2008, p. 73.
[18] [Modern title for Gypsy (Romani) cultures in general.]

said the old mother, "even though you have now been carrying the sack for nine years on your shoulders." This shocked the young man, but the old woman continued: "*Time passes quickly in the land of the dead* and, my little friend, that is where we are! Even if we are not yet actually in the land of the dead, we have already crossed its borders. I also know why you have embarked upon this journey! Here, I give a piece of meat, a jug full of milk, a key and some rope. With these things you can continue on your way and you will soon arrive at the cave you are seeking." The old woman gave him a bag with these things and disappeared.

282 The young man set out on his way and soon reached the *mouth of a dark cave*. He entered and hardly had he taken a step forwards when it became light all around and he found himself standing in front of a large house. He opened the gate and entered the courtyard. Forthwith an angry white dog fell upon him. He pulled the piece of meat out of his sack and threw it to the dog. Then he went on and saw a well from which a woman was drawing water. She had a bucket tied to her braids that she would raise and lower again into the well. He tossed her the rope that the old woman had given him, so that she could tie it to the bucket. "For whom are you drawing the water?" he asked. "For the dead," answered the woman, "who were buried unwashed by their relatives." Thereupon he continued on and came to the entrance to the house. With the key from his sack he opened the door and entered into a room where he found three eggs. He opened one. Suddenly the room was filled with mist out of which stepped his father and said: "Oh, I am so hungry and thirsty!" "Come into the courtyard," said his son, "You will find a jug full of milk." "I thank you," answered the father, "but it is now too late; at least I have some peace and can go further into the land of the dead." With these words he disappeared. Thereupon the young man opened the second egg and now his mother stepped out of the mist and said: "Oh, I am so hungry and thirsty!" "Come into the courtyard," said the young man, "In front of the door you will find a jug full of milk." "I thank you," answered his mother, "but it is already too late. At least I have now some peace and can go further into the land of the dead." With these words she disappeared.

283 Then the young man took the third egg in his hands and went out into the courtyard. This egg he broke next to the jug of milk. Now his beloved appeared and spoke to him: "Oh, I am so hungry and thirsty!" This time the young man quickly took the jug of milk and handed it to his loved one: "Here, drink some milk, my beloved!" The girl drank

and became as beautiful as the most beautiful of all the sun king's daughters. When she had drank all the milk, she also spoke and said: "My most beloved, you have redeemed me from death, now I will return back into life and be yours."

284 And so it happened. She turned homewards from the *dreadful mountains* and they lived together in happiness and contentment until she had to cross over into the kingdom of the dead for eternity.[19]

285 In this rich description, we meet once again the relativity of space and time in the other world, depicted as a cave, a house, and then as a mountain. This boundary region, or "intermediate kingdom," which clearly signifies the unconscious, is not yet the actual land of the dead. It describes rather a psychic state that corresponds to the state of unconsciousness in a serious illness.[20] The parents of the young man can no longer return from this state, but for the girlfriend this is possible. She can return literally through the love of the bridegroom. We will here pass over the meaning of the three eggs since this is a motif we will touch upon later towards the end of the second volume of this work. In this connection, it is enough to highlight the secret identity of the magical realm with the land of the dead as disclosed in fairytales.

[19] W. Aichele, *Zigeunermärchen*, Jena, 1926, pp. 128–130, translated.

[20] On the idea of such a border state with native peoples, see "Death. . . is not a fact, but a state of transition, no hard matter of fact, but a process that can be advanced or controlled by reflection and action. He is dead who is declared dead. . . Thus the *Talmud* prescribes a thanksgiving prayer on seeing a friend again after an absence of over twelve months: "Praised be Thou, Oh Lord, King of the World, that makest the dead live again." According to Roman custom, similarly, he who had been proclaimed dead and then returned must avoid doors and must enter his house through the roof. It is possible, then, to declare someone dead, to regard him as non-existent, and this has the same effect as actual death. In the Scandinavian sagas the *niding* is actually dead, for there can be life only within the pale of the community, where the powers are operative. . . Only proper burial makes death valid; he who has not been buried is not dead" (Leeuw, *Religion in Essence*, vol. 1, p. 202). See also Bächtold-Stäubli under *Tote* [Dead].

Chapter 14
The Inhabitants of the Land of the Spirits

286 A description of the uncanny effects that the border state between the living and the dead can exert is offered by the Chané ethnic group of central South America in their tale, "The Woman who Followed her Husband to Aguarerente":

287 A young woman wanted to marry a certain man, but he died before their wedding could take place. She loved him very much. On the day after his death, when it was still dark, he stood before the hut where the girl lived with her parents and began to work on the adobe walls. The woman came by and took his mortar stick.

288 "Who are you?'" she asked.

289 "It is me," he said. He was her dead fiancé. "Will you come with me?" "Yes, I will come with you," she said, since she loved him very much.

290 He made off in the direction where the sun rises. His face was covered so that no one would recognize him. She followed him. She went through the forest. She went over the Pampas and again through a forest. During the day he slept, at night he was awake.

291 When the young woman's father noticed that his daughter was gone, he went out looking for her. He followed her tracks and noticed that always in front there were the footprints of a fox.[1] "Anya [the dead] have taken my daughter!" said the father. He came across her body, dead, along the way. He was able to bring her back to life and took her back home. As they crossed the pampas, they saw a fox roaming around. The next morning, the young woman died. The father wept. Then came Ururuti, the white condor, and consoled the wailing father

---

[1] Koch-Grünberg, the editor of this collection of South American fairytales, notes that "Aguararenta (Foxtown) is a village in which the dead (*anya*) live. It lies in the East. During the nighttime, the shapes that live there appear in human form and during the daytime they appear as foxes. . . This is the realm of the dead for the Chané. Living people have sometimes visited Aguararenta and returned to tell what they saw there. This belief is based on dreams, which were taken to be real experiences" (*Südamerika*, Jena, 1921, p. 335.)

> saying he should not complain. Ururuti took the father on his wings and flew him to Aguararenta.
>
> 292 In Aguararenta one sleeps during the day and is awake at night. When the father came there, everyone was drinking corn beer. Ururuti then brought him to the house of his son-in-law. He spoke to his daughter, but received no answer. Then he went to Ururuti who took him back to his home. Neither he nor his wife now lamented for their lost daughter. On the following day, the father died.

293 That the dead take on animal shapes is a widely held belief among some cultures. "Very often the dead," as Lévy-Bruhl explains, "especially in the first few days after their demise, appear in the shape of animals." Also the mythological ancestors are often represented as animals.[2] According to the examples that Lévy-Bruhl gives, the souls of the dead can enter into the most varied animals: alligators, turtles, birds, snakes, sharks, frogs, and termites. They can also transform into rocks and trees. In these cases, the animals or objects are not themselves dead, but due to their unusual behavior or appearance, one recognizes that the spirit or soul of the dead has entered into them. Often, the animal or object is then considered to be sacred.[3] It is noteworthy that the soul usually enters into the lower animals. The animal transformation of the sorcerers in "How Motecuzhoma Sought the Seven Caves" belongs in the same conceptual realm. All these transformations point to the same psychological fact: a symbolic representation of *becoming unconscious*.

294 Further evidence for this comes from the Ainu tale "A Hunter in Hades":

> One day a handsome and brave young man, who was skillful in the chase, pursued a large bear into the recesses of the mountains. On and on ran the bear, and still the young fellow pursued it, up heights and crags more and more dangerous, but without ever being able to get near enough to shoot it with his poisoned arrows. At last, on a bleak mountain-summit, the bear disappeared down a hole in the ground. The young man followed the bear. He found himself in an immense cavern, at the far end of which was a gleam of light. Towards this he groped his way, and on emerging, found himself in another world. Everything there was as in the world of men, but more beautiful. There were trees, houses, villages, and human beings. With these, however, the young hunter had no concern. What he wanted was his

[2] Cf. Lévy-Bruhl, *The "Soul" of the Primitive*, p. 285; see also p. 186.

[3] Ibid., pp. 27–31, 249–52, 285–300. On similar beliefs among the ancient Germans, see Mogk, *Germanische Religionsgeschichte*, p. 65.

bear that had totally disappeared. The best plan seemed to be to seek it in the remote mountain district of this new underground world. So he followed a valley upwards, and, being tired and hungry, he picked some grapes and mulberries that were hanging on the trees and ate them as he trudged along.

295 Suddenly, for some reason or other, he happened to look down upon his own body. To his horror he found himself transformed into a serpent! On making the discovery his cries and groans were turned into serpent's hisses. What was he to do? To go back like this to his native world, where snakes are hated, would be certain death. No plan presented itself to his mind. But, unconsciously, he wandered, or rather crept and glided, back to the entrance of the cavern that led home to the world of men; and there, at the foot of a pine-tree of extraordinary size and height, he fell asleep. In a dream the goddess of the pine-tree appeared to him and said, "I am sorry to see you in this state. Why did you eat of the poisonous fruits of Hades? The only thing you can do to recover your proper shape is to climb to the top of this pine-tree, and fling yourself down. Then you may, perhaps, become a human being again."

296 Upon waking from this dream, the young man, or rather the snake, was filled half with hope and half with fear. But he resolved to follow the goddess's advice. So, he slithered up the tall pine-tree, and when he reached its topmost branch, after hesitating a few moments, he flung himself down. On coming to his senses, he found himself standing at the foot of the tree. Close by was the body of an immense serpent, ripped open so as to allow somebody to crawl out of it. After offering up thanks to the pine-tree and setting up objects of reverence in her honor, he quickly retraced his steps through the long, tunnel-like cavern, through which he had originally entered Hades. After walking for a certain time, he emerged into the world of men to find himself on the mountain-top, whither he had pursued the bear which he had never seen again.

297 On reaching his home, he went to bed, and dreamt a second time. The same goddess of the pine-tree appeared before him and said, "I have come to tell you that you cannot stay long in the world of men after once eating the grapes and mulberries of Hades. There is a goddess in Hades who wishes to marry you. It was she who, assuming the form of a bear, lured you into the cavern, and thence to the underworld. You must make up your mind to come away." And so it turned out. The young man awoke; but a grave sickness overpowered him. A few

> days later he went a second time to Hades, and returned no more to the land of the living.[4]

298 Once again, the dead are obviously animals, and the goddess of this realm appears as a bear that transforms the young hunter into a snake.[5] The fairytale portrays the experience of being enraptured by another state described as a sinking into the unconscious from which the young man cannot free himself. The actual force of attraction comes from a feminine goddess who draws him lovingly onwards.[6]

299 The widespread motif that warns of the dangers of partaking of food from the underworld, made famous by the episode of the lotus eaters (*lotophagi*) in the *Odyssey*, IX, symbolizes the fascination exerted by the unconscious, which revitalizes people, but at the same time distances them from reality.[7]

300 According to primitive belief, the dead take on human form at night and they sleep or appear as animals during the day. Sometimes during the night the dead seek the living. But these must die if they glimpse the land of the dead. The dead easily attract the living to them with the effect that the living become perishable ghosts. Lévy-Bruhl writes in detail about the danger of death's contagion that is based on a deep "mystical union,"[8] that is, the unconscious participation (*participation mystique*) of the group. People from cultures that live more closely in harmony with natural rhythms often claim that it is the dead who deliberately draw their close ones to themselves, whether it be out of love or "jealousy of those who are still privileged to see the light of day."[9]

301 This is told in a particularly clear way in the tale "The Woman Who was Killed by the Ghost of her Husband":

> 302 There was once a woman who had lost her husband and was so sad that she could not give up hope that he was still alive. One night she heard the sound of a flute playing the music that her husband used to play. That night, the ghost of her husband came to her and asked how she and her children were. He lay in the hammock and said that there were a lot of fleas biting terribly on his back, she should get a light and look at his back. What she saw were worms chewing on him, not fleas. She knew then that this must be the ghost of her dead husband

---

[4] Chamberlain, *Aino Folk-Tales*, pp. 41–42. The collector notes, "Written down from memory. Told by Ishanashte, 22nd July, 1886."

[5] Cf. Karl Kerényi, "Mensch und Maske" [Humans and Masks], in: *Eranos-Jahrbuch 1948 – Der Mensch (2)*, ed. Olga Fröbe-Kapteyn, Rhein-Verlag, Zürich, 1949, pp. 183 ff.

[6] [There are also nefarious influences from such archetypal forces.]

[7] Cf. the page's behavior in "The Fairies on the Gump."

[8] Lévy-Bruhl, *The "Soul" of the Primitive*, p. 224.

[9] Ibid., p. 221; see also pages 224-29 and 243.

and not his real body. It was a sign for her that he had really died. She said, "No, there are no fleas here," but wondered to herself what she should do. Then she began to spit, always in the same place until there was a pile of sputum. Then she crept out of the hut and went to the neighboring village. Whenever the ghost asked about the fleas, the pile of sputum answered, "No, no; there are no fleas here." But soon the pile of spit dried up and could not answer any more. The ghost noticed the woman was gone and went out following the tracks of his wife. When she heard him coming behind her, she hid like an armadillo in the ground. He walked past, but soon noticed and came back and said, "I am dead, but even if I am dead, I miss you and will come and soon kill you." He disappeared into the darkness.

303 She crept out of her hiding place, went to the next village, and told her friends everything that had happened. But then what the ghost said really happened. Soon she became very ill and died.[10]

304 While from the front the demon of the dead normally looks alive, his back[11] reveals that he is actually dead. The danger for humans that come into contact with the realm of the dead is the same as that which led the Warao in "The Legend of Okonoróté," to stop up the hole through which one can look back into the magical primal land.[12] The immense threat for some people consists in falling back into the unconscious, out of which they freed themselves with much effort. In particular, in so far as the unconscious is represented as the realm of the dead, this danger exists to a large extent also for those more cultured people who cannot withstand the fascination of the unconscious. For these people, each encounter with the powers of the magical realm can give rise to a weakening of the conscious "standpoint."

305 Once we identify the magical realm with the kingdom of the dead and spirit land, and assume it is a symbol of the unconscious, it follows that the contents of the land of the spirits represent psychological facts. According to Jung's view, the primitive people's[13] belief in spirits is based on their naive perceptions of spiritual[14] processes.[15] He based his conviction concerning the

---

[10] Koch-Grünberg, *Südamerika*, Jena, 1921, pp. 34–36. The Baikiri are a small tribe from Brazil. The original fairytale is collected in Karl von den Steinen, *Die Bakairi-Sprache* [The Bakairi Language], K.F. Koehlers Antiquarium, Leipzig, 1892. According to the belief of many folk cultures, the dead often do not notice they are dead, but must first be so informed by the living. See Lévy-Bruhl, *The "Soul" of the Primitive*, pp. 225–226.

[11] Like the woman (the Sun) in the fairytale, "Flight to the Moon."

[12] In "Help in Need," General Dschong Tschong-Fu also returns to the land of the dead. With his encounter he gains a death without illness, but succumbs to the allure of the land that only needs dead soldiers.

[13] [As well as more civilized people; see C.G. Jung, "Belief in Spirits," CW 8, p. 301.]

[14] [German: *geistige*].

[15] C.G. Jung, "Belief in Spirits," CW 8, ¶573ff.

existence of spirits to a large extent on dreams, visions, and his observations of psychogenic illnesses,[16] in particular, with hallucinations and psychic phenomena related to states of possession. Spirits are in this sense not only ghosts of the dead. Jung writes, "Spirits, therefore, viewed from the psychological angle, are unconscious autonomous complexes which appear as projections because they have no direct association with the ego."[17] Also, "Spirits are complexes of the collective unconscious which appear when the individual loses his adaptation to reality, or which seek to replace the inadequate attitude of a whole people by a new one."[18] Jung writes further that:

306 It is impossible to speak of the belief in spirits without at the same time considering the belief in souls. Belief in souls is a correlate of belief in spirits. Since, according to primitive belief, a spirit is usually the ghost of one who is dead, it must once have been the soul of a living person. This is particularly the case wherever the belief is held that people have only one soul. But this assumption does not prevail everywhere; it is frequently supposed that people have two or more souls, one of which survives death and is immortal. In this case the spirit of the dead is only one of the several souls of the living. It is thus only a part of the total soul – a psychic fragment, so to speak.[19]

307 The fact that we are completely unfamiliar with these different parts of the soul, which are strange, unique, and uncanny, and which, combined with the above-mentioned attraction to the ego, are so characteristic of the other-worldly dimension, might explain the disastrous, alluring effects of the spirits and why the living seem to be "pulled" into the realm of the dead. The Chinook fairytale, "Blue-Jay Visits his Sister Io'i in the Land of the Dead," gives an impressive account of the realm of the dead:

308 The ghost people decided to marry Io'i, the older sister of Blue Jay.[20] They left a dowry, and abducted her. Blue-Jay was alone and after a

[16] Cf. C.G. Jung, *Psychic Energy* and "Belief in Spirits" (both CW 8). See also Novalis, *Fragmente*, Dresden, 1929, no. 680: "When a spirit appears to us, then we empower our own spirituality, we become inspired through ourselves and the spirit"; see also Fragment 684: "When a spirit dies, it becomes human. When a human dies, he becomes a spirit."

[17] [C.G. Jung, "Belief in Spirits," CW 8, ¶585.]

[18] [Ibid., ¶597.]

[19] C.G. Jung, "Belief in Spirits," CW 8, ¶577 and ¶582–591. See further C.G. Jung, *Complex Theory*, CW 8, ¶197ff. Schopenhauer formulated similar ideas in his *Essay on Spirit Seeing and Everything Connected Therewith*: "From what has been said, it is obvious that the immediate reality of an actually existing object is not to be imputed to a ghost that appears in this way, although indirectly a reality does underlie it. Thus what we see there is certainly not the deceased man himself, but a mere *εἴδλον* (*eidelon*), a picture of him who once existed which originates in the dream-organ of a man attuned to it and is brought about by some remnant or relic, some trace that was left behind" (Schopenhauer, *On Spirit Seeing*, p. 285).

[20] Blue Jay is the culture-bringer in the shape of an animal for many tribes in the Oregon-Washington region, similar to Raven in the Pacific Northwest, and Coyote or Hare in the Midwest. He is a healer

year had passed and she had not returned, he went in search of her. A wedge used to split wood guided Blue-Jay to the land of the ghosts.[21] There, he found Io'i but all the houses were full of bones of dead people. When it became dark, the people arose and Blue-Jay went fishing with them. Io'i advised him not to speak to those people. But Blue-Jay joined them in singing a song and they immediately turned back into piles of bones.

309 They went fishing and Blue-Jay caught only leaves and branches and became very frustrated. Back on land, however, the leaves were trout and the branches were fall salmon. Blue-Jay thought the people in the land of the dead were teasing him. He did not understand how the spirits could float in a boat full of holes. Then his sister said to him, "Are they people? Are they really people? They are ghosts!" Blue-Jay, however, continued to believe they were just teasing him and he began to tease them back.

310 Then Blue-Jay decided to return home and Io'i explained in detail exactly what he must do to safely make the journey. But he did not pay attention to her advice and was burned and died. Blue-Jay himself now as dead person went to the land of the ghosts. This time he did not see the transformations as before. He tried to shout at the (dead) people, but they laughed at him. Then he gave up and became quiet. When his sister went to look for him, she found him dancing on his head, his legs upward. "She turned back and cried. Now he had really died. He had died a second time."[22]

311 Franz Boas, who collected the above myth of Blue-Jay and Io'i, also carefully noted the beliefs in the underworld of a neighboring people, the Bella Coola. The information about the land of the ghosts complements that of the Chinook and adds a few details.

312 The world below us is the country of the ghosts (*Kolkulolemx*). It is called *Asiuta'nem*. Descriptions of the ghosts' country are principally obtained from shamans who believe they have visited that country during a trance. According to the statement of an old woman who believed that as a little girl she had visited the country of the ghosts during a trance, the entrance to the country of the ghosts is through

and trickster at the same time. See also A. v. Deursen, *Der Heilbringer*, Gröningen, 1931, pp. 270–271, and esp. p. 339.

[21] [According to reports collected by Franz Boas from the neighboring Bella Coola (*Bella Coola*, New York 1898, p. 37), a wedge created an opening between the world of the humans and the world above.]

[22] Franz Boas, *Chinook Texts*, U.S. Bureau of American Ethnology, 1894, Bulletin no. 20, pp. 161–167. [The tale has been heavily summarized.]

> region, a hole situated in each house, between the doorway and the fireplace. The country of the ghosts stretches along the sandy banks of a large river. There is a hill behind their village, the base of which is covered with sharp stones. When it is summer here, it is winter there. When it is night here, it is day there. The ghosts do not walk on their feet, but on their heads. Their language is different from the one spoken on earth. The souls, on reaching the lower world, receive new names. The village of the ghosts is said to be surrounded by a fence. They have a dancing-house, in which they perform *kusiut*. It is just below the burial-place of each village. The dancing-house is very large and long. It has four levels. The women stay on the floor of the house, while the men sit on an elevated platform. The houses have doors, but the ghosts who first reach the lower world enter the house through the smoke-hole. A rope ladder placed in the smoke-hole facilitates their entrance. Two men stand at the foot of the ladder. They are called *Anoel'axsalai'x*. For a person who has once entered the dancing-house there is no return to our earth. The souls are at liberty to return to the lower heaven, which they reach by ascending the rope ladder. Those who return to the lower heaven are sent back to our earth by the deities, to be born as children in the same family to which they belonged. Those who enjoy life in the country of the ghosts, and who do not return to heaven, die a second death, and then sink to the second lower world from which there is no return.[23]

313 Here, a new aspect of the unconscious as land of the dead and souls appears for the first time: the motif of the *upside-down, inverted, reversed world* :[24] the ghosts are standing on their heads; what is apparently dead becomes alive; what appears contemptible, incomplete, and rotten turns valuable, whole, totally fresh, and alive. This belief is widespread among some tribes. It even enters into the language of the ghosts, in that everything white is ostensibly called black,[25] and that what the living understand as "standing" is called "lying." Even in European superstitious notions, reversal is characteristic of demonic underworld beings. Therefore, one comes into contact with the other world through reversed gestures and inverted rituals: one reverses clothes, exchanges left for right, places chairs, benches, bowls on their heads, etc. The Romans offered sacrifices to the dead with the left hand.[26] Also a defense

[23] F. Boas, *Bella Coola*, New York, 1898, pp. 37–38. See also the reference to the Hopi world of the dead being a kind of "backwards world" in Krickeberg's notes to "The Coming of the Hopi from the Underworld" [in German] in his *Nordamerika*, Jena, 1924, p. 409.

[24] [German: *verkehrten Welt*].

[25] [See Lévy-Bruhl, *The "Soul" of the Primitive*, p. 303].

[26] See Bächtold-Stäubli under *Umkehrung* [reversal]: "According to some concepts, everything in the other world is reversed in relation to this world. With the Dayak indigenous people of Borneo, all words

against bewitchment and the influence of spirits involved reversing the twisting of a cord of an animal or putting on a piece of clothing in the reverse order. Likewise with rhythms and numbers. "Odd numbers and inequalities rule in the realm of the dead." When speaking of a *Schrättele*,[27] a Swabian legend literally says, "Everything uneven respects curses," that is, "better not to curse, if you do you will bring on something evil." From this comes the eminent place of odd numbers in magic and superstition. The number of eggs put under the hen for brooding must always be odd. Even in ancient times there was an old and proven requirement of magical medicine to use an odd number of instruments. The devil not only limps, but one of his arms is shorter than the other. In Sweden, to extinguish a forest fire one should have a woman wearing unpaired shoes walk three times around the fire.[28] Inuit shamans report that in the other world they saw ghosts walking on their heads.[29] According to the Batak (Sumatra), "When the dead go downstairs, they go headfirst."[30]

314 By yelling at the ghosts, who talk among themselves in whispers, Blue-Jay brings some conscious clarity into that world and thereby exposes its antithetical nature. This motif can also be found in European fairytales, for instance, "The Red, White, and Black Rooster" (Germany), where the rooster crowing at dawn banishes the evil spirits of the night by his cry, "Day, day!"[31] A German belief has persisted into modern times that dwarves and elves die when struck by a ray of sunlight and that one can overcome a ghost with candlelight.[32] This signifies deflating the unconscious content by the intervention of consciousness.

315 The motif of the reversed world of the spirits expresses a psychological fact in image form. According to Jung, it can be observed that impulses from the unconscious and their representation in dreams seem to possess their own purposefulness, which run counter to the goals and intentions of ego

---

in the city of the souls mean exactly opposite to their earthly meaning. For instance, sweet means bitter, standing means lying, etc. The Italmen [original inhabitants of the Kamchatka peninsula in Russia] believed that whoever was rich in life is poor in the other world, whoever sinned in this world is righteous in the other world. The Altay Tatars believed that all objects that appear in this world crooked or misshapen have their correct, straight form in the other world. What is here left is there right. The dressing of the corpse in ancient graves is in accordance with this custom; a sword normally worn on the right hand side is placed on the left side."

27 [A German dialect word pertaining to evil people, mostly old women, who go about in the night, enter through the keyhole, and press on the sleeping one when they lie on the left side.]

28 Bächtold-Stäubli under *Umkehrung*. See also under *verkehrt* [reversed].

29 See *ibid.*, under *verkehrt* [upside-down].

30 Lévy-Bruhl, *The "Soul" of the Primitive*, p. 304. Also daytime and nighttime activities are sometimes exchanged, as in the "The Woman who Followed her Husband to Aguarerente."

31 Original title: "Der weisse, der rote und der schwarze Hahn"; see R. Köhler, *Kleinere Schriften*, vol. 3, Berlin, 1900, p. 583, and also the Icelandic fairytale, "The Servant and the Seafolk."

32 Cf. Ninck, *Wodan*, pp. 164–165, fn. 2. Cf. also "Helge-Hal in the Blue Hill" and "The King of the Ants," where the scholar throws a book at the ants and so returns them into the form they had before they were enchanted.

consciousness.[33] One well-known example is the dream of King Nebuchadnezzar (Daniel 4:7ff), which warns him of his impending insanity if he does not begin to practice justice and righteousness. The final orientation of the unconscious often diverges from that of conscious intentions and thus seems to function in a compensatory way. The balancing function of the unconscious appears – often to the good of the individual – to the observer, however, only in the individual details. The stories of indigenous people tend to reveal more the general structure of the unconscious. In summary, these images of the things being reversed appear to point to a mirroring, or a projection, of the compensatory function of the unconscious. One seldom finds in the actual fairytale such a stark portrayal, however, sometimes one can find corresponding motifs, such as the reversal of values, erroneous designations of certain things, etc. The Chinook fairytale recounted above, "Blue-Jay Visits his Sister Io'i in the Land of the Dead," illuminates particularly clearly the background of these motifs.

316 Most tales from indigenous people concern descriptions of the spirit world, the journey of the individual there, and in stories reporting healing or disastrous encounters with beings from the land of the soul. The intensive preoccupation of natural people with this realm relates to a state of consciousness that is relatively weak, that is, not continually persisting. Therefore, relatively mild forms of possession and affects arising from autonomous unconscious contents can easily overwhelm them.[34]

317 But such narratives also exist in large numbers in the folklore materials of the so-called cultured peoples. "Primitive" means "original" (or primordial); this mental state surfaces in the simple folk in Europe as well as in the deeper layers of the soul in the more educated. Although many collectors of fairytales, among others, the Brothers Grimm and editors of the fairytale collections we used for this work, recorded numerous ghost stories, they did not discuss these in detail since they were considered rather as legends under Lüthi's criteria. In this category belong many Icelandic tales, called "revenant" or "*Wiedergänger*" stories, which tell of the soul of a dead person that returns as a ghost to the world of the living. As one example from many, we mention the tale "The Bridegroom and the Revenant."

---

[33] [On this, Jung writes: "Many people who know something, but not enough, about dreams and their meaning, and who are impressed by their subtle and apparently intentional compensation, are liable to succumb to the prejudice that the dream actually has a moral purpose, that it warns, rebukes, comforts, foretells the future, etc. If one believes that the unconscious always knows best, one can easily be betrayed into leaving dreams to take the necessary decisions, and then disappointed when the dreams become more and more trivial and meaningless"; see *Nature of Dreams*, CW 8, p. 296.]

[34] Cf. C.G. Jung, "Archetypes of the Collective Unconscious," CW 9i, ¶47; *Child*, CW 9i, ¶260 f.; *Psychology and Alchemy*, CW 12, ¶437. In particular, see Jung, "Mind and earth," CW 10, ¶55 ff.: "The free sway of instinct is not compatible with a strongly developed consciousness."

318 In the church graveyard four men dig up a grave from which an enormous upper leg bone appears. The youngest and bravest of the men invites it to his wedding as a joke. Five years later he became engaged. Shortly before the wedding, the bride-to-be dreamt three nights in a row, how a gigantic man asked her if the groom remembers what he boastfully said many years earlier. On the third night he added that he would surely come to the wedding as a table guest. That evening, the monster appeared to the groom. He was as big as a giant, and with an evil gaze, said that his coming to the wedding was now irreversible, "as far as he was concerned it was completely unnecessary, but now he [the groom] can finally experience what it is like to deal with such things." On the advice of the bride, a house was built "large enough for the man to stand up in. Each wall to be exactly as long as it was high." The room was to have a white carpet and be adorned with a table set in white with a bowl of consecrated earth, a flask of water, and three candles. Next to the table was to be placed a chair and a bed. Furthermore, she told the groom that "he must himself accompany the guest to the house but may not go in front of him nor go under the same roof. Also, he should not accept any invitation from the guest and speak with him as little as possible. He was to close the house and go away as soon as he was offered to eat what was on the table."

319 On the wedding day, after the wedding meal, the guests dispersed in the rooms and as was custom the married couple remained seated, a mighty hammering was heard on the door. Outside stood the Wiedergänger and announced himself as a wedding guest. The bride pushed the groom out the door and locked it with a devout prayer. The groom acted exactly according to the instructions of the bride, showed the ghost-guest to the house and returned to the trembling guests and his singly cheerful bride. Next morning, the groom was curious about how the latecomer was doing, but his wife did not allow it; she went herself and opened the doors of the special house. Lo! The Wiedergänger had disappeared, the flask of water was empty, and the earth strewn about the floor. "That is just what I thought," said the young woman, "if you had gone inside before me and made just one step on this earth, you would come under the power of the Wiedergänger. It can do me no harm when I go inside and I will now sweep out and clean up the place." The ghost never returned and the couple remained happy ever after.[35]

[35] H. and I. Naumann (trans.), *Isländische*, Jena, 1923, pp. 126–130. It was said that when the revenant was leaving, he spoke the words, "Only water and earth for the wedding meal, My thanks he did not deserve. Cf. the extremely dramatic ghost story, "Der starke Grettir und der Wiedergänger Glam" [The Strong Grettir and the Wiedergänger Glam] (Iceland) [see "The Fight With Glam's Ghost"]. Such tales

320 In the same category are stories found all over the world about haunting nuns, monks, and priests in churches and cloisters, for example: "The Mass of the Ghosts," a tale from Brittany (France):

321 A woman once fell asleep in church on All Soul's Night and was accidentally locked in by the sexton. She awoke around midnight. She saw a priest in his Mass garments step up to the altar, where the candles lit up by themselves. "After he had bowed before the altar, he turned towards the nave of the church and said three times, "Is there somebody here, who would like to take the mass?" The woman was so afraid, she could not utter a word and the priest turned back to the sacristy and the candles went out again by themselves. When morning came, the woman went straight away to the priest and told him what she had seen. He answered: 'When what you say is true, then you could do an exceptional service to some poor soul. Go once again in the church and take your boy with you who is not yet ten years old. He should help the priest administer the Mass, and when it is finished, the priest will ask you what he asks for his trouble, what would he like to receive for his services, you must advise him to say, "I ask for heaven!" That night, the woman let herself, this time with her son, get locked in the church. The boy helped administer the Mass and when asked what he would like in return for his services, asked for heaven, just as advised. The ghost priest answered, "In three days you will be in there." And in three days the boy died.[36]

322 In spite of the christianization that the theme of going over to "the other side" is a reward to be sought, this fairytale shows that every all-too-close contact with the otherworldly metaphysical reality takes people away from this reality.[37]

323 Also in this category are stories about people who were murdered or sinners who haunt castles,[38] and the horror stories in which the dead awake from the graveyard, due to being mocked, taunted, ridiculed, or otherwise treated inconsiderately.[39]

---

also include ghost bridegrooms such as Bürger's "Lenore" and others collected in *Die Märchen der Weltliteratur*: "The Deacon of Myrká," "The Suffering of Flax," "The Ghost Bridegroom," "The Dead Maiden." Cf. the ghost bride in Goethe's "The Bride of Corinth."

[36] Tegethoff, *Französische Volksmärchen*, vol. 2, p. 219. [This tale appears in a footnote in the German original.]

[37] See also "The Mass of the Dead" (Norway), collected in Stroebe, *Norwegian Fairy Book*, pp. 13–15, and "Julspuk" [The Haunted Christmas Mass] (Sweden), Von der Leyen.

[38] See, for example, "How the Devil Learned to Play the Violin," in: Zaunert, *Deutsche Märchen seit Grimm*, 1964, pp. 80–83; see also "The Balbiermanndl," in: Zaunert, *Deutsche Märchen aus dem Donaulande*, Jena, 1926, p. 171.

[39] One example is "The Gravedigger:" A gravedigger once bumped up against a skull with his foot and said, "Come to our house tonight for dinner!" To his astonishment, the skull answered, "Yes, that would

324 A related theme is how excessive mourning by the living for a loved one who passed away can draw him or her back from the dead, with consequences.[40] The inordinate mourning of the mother is explained by the fact that her son died young, before his natural time. There is a widespread belief among many cultures that children who die young, or are victims of a violent death, go around as destructive spirits.[41] Also in the same category are the many tales in which the dead awake from their graves as vampires to go out and eat, suck blood from the living, or pull them into death.[42]

---

be fine, what time should I come?" The gravedigger said, "Around seven o'clock." Then he went straightaway to the parish priest and full of fear, asked what he should prepare for dinner. The dead person actually did come for dinner, as a "swaying figure," enjoyed his meal, and in return he invited the gravedigger for dinner. Again the poor gravedigger sought help from the priest. He was told that he should by no means miss the invitation. Just before he went, the priest served him the holy sacrament. The gravedigger appeared at seven o'clock at the graveyard. The ghost opened the door and brought him to his wife, who was preparing dinner. As they waited for it to be ready, they looked out the window. The gravedigger saw two white dogs fighting, later two women who were arguing over a sieve, and then finally a man with a wheelbarrow full of earth. Each time he noted that an olive leaf fell to the ground. Three times an olive leaf fell. He asked the ghost who these people were. The ghost explained to the gravedigger that these were people who had fought with each other or had betrayed their neighbors. After supper with the dead man and his wife was finished, the gravedigger went to the priest. The priest, however, did not recognize him. The gravedigger told him what he had experienced. Slowly the priest remembered that he once in an old parish report read that a man disappeared from the cemetery and never returned again. That was 300 years earlier. Every olive tree leaf that the gravedigger had observed falling signified the passage of a hundred years. To him, those three hundred years passed like an hour. The gravedigger was a young man when he first went to the priest. During the time that the priest remembered and found the old report, his hair became whiter and whiter until it was white as snow. Then he fell into a heap of dust. "And now the cat is out of the bag!" (Zaunert, *Deutsche Märchen aus dem Donaulande*, p. 307.) This tale contains the motif discussed above, the timelessness of the hereafter. Parallels include "The Dinner of the Spirits [The Ghost Meal]" (France); see Tegethoff, *Französische Volksmärchen*, vol. 2, no. 4; "The Nonbeliever and the Skull"(Spain); H. Meier, *Spanische*, Jena, 1940, no. 16; and "The Spouses" (Finland), Löwis of Menar, *Finnische Volksmärchen*, Jena, 1922, no. 24.

[40] See, for example, "The Mother and her Dead Son" (Russia): Once upon a time a woman mourned a very long time over her son. "Oh, if only I could see him one more time, even if he was dead!" she cried. Her people suggested that she go one night to the church, when the dead congregated and, just in case, to take a rooster along. She went there . . . Around midnight she saw that a horde of dead from the graveyard were coming, and among them her son. He was coming along with a bucket full of tears that his mother had cried for him. As she beheld him among the dead, she ran away, aghast, back to her home. The dead son sensed the spirit of his mother and followed after her. She started to fling off her clothes, but he seized everything she threw off and tore it to pieces. When she was almost at her own front door, the rooster crowed. The dead son tumbled down, but the mother died the next day. A son feels it deeply if his mother frets for his sake, but a mother rests more peacefully if her children mourn her (according to A. v. Löwis of Menar, *Russian Folktales*, London, 1971, p. 42.)

[41] Cf. E. Bargheer, *Eingeweide*, 1931, p. 160. The tears with which a mother needlessly streams out her best energy are only a burden on the son. A theme expressed in popular belief and fairytales is that excessive mourning disturbs the sleep of the dead. See the "The Shroud"(J. and T. Grimm, *Complete Grimm's*, pp. 502-503) and the variant in Bolte and Polívka, *Anmerkungen*, vol. 2, pp. 485ff. See further the variations on Cinderella (*Complete Grimm's*, pp. 121–128) in W. Lincke, *Stiefmutter*, Berlin, 1933, p. 64f.

[42] One example among many others is "The Dead Man's Liver" (Spain): A married couple had no more to eat. So the wife went to the nearby graveyard, cut out the liver from a dead man's body, returned home, and placed it in front of her husband to eat. As she lay in bed she heard a voice say, "I want to get my liver back that you stole from me." The woman cried, "Oh woe! Dear husband, who is standing there?" Her husband answered, "Be still, dear wife, he will go away." But the voice spoke again, "I will not go away, I am just behind the door, very close to you." Now even more aghast, the wife cried out again to her husband, "Oh woe, dear husband, who is standing there?" And again her husband said to her, "Be still, dear wife, he will go away." But the voice spoke again, "I will not go away, I am now under your bed, very close to you." Now the wife gripped her husband in fear and trembling, crying out once

325 Psychologically, the spirits of the dead cannot be differentiated from autonomous complexes that can dominate a person.[43] This is exemplified in mythology where, according to the belief of many cultures, the dead enjoy a kind raise in power. They gradually become assimilated into general mythological figures. For instance, in ancient Greece they became heroes and demons, or like the *Tritopatores* (see page 79), wind spirits. In other words, they merge with primeval soul images or archetypes.[44] The Aztecs called the land of the dead literally, "the place where people become gods."[45]

326 The departure of the dead into the hereafter, or land of the gods, is sometimes impeded when a debt or the circumstance under which the dead person died "too early" bind him to the realm of the living. Franz Josef Dölger collected and summarized many examples of the restlessness of those who died young or who suffered a violent death.[46] According to the views of some cultures, these spirits of the dead still house an unbroken will to live that has, however, perverted into the negative. The dead spirits in particular became, therefore, a symbol of split-off inner contents of the unconscious that disturb the psyche's equilibrium and yearn to be assimilated by consciousness. In this connection, the entry on ghosts (*Gespenst*) in Bächtold-Stäubli is interesting:

327 From Old High German *kispanst*, actually "suggestion" (intuition, inspiration: from *suggerere*). The confession formulae that speak of devilish suggestion and seduction (from the ghost of the devil: Oberlin's *Bihtebuoch*, 36),[47] prepares the ground for a change in meaning to "a ghostly deceptive deceit" . . . In the Latinity of the Middle Ages *umbraticus* [shadow] has a similar meaning to "ghost"

---

more, "Oh woe, dear husband, who is standing there?" The husband answered, "Be still, dear wife, he will go away." The voice said, "I am not going away, I am now on top of your bed, very close to you." Hysterical with fear, the wife cried out again, "Woe, dear man, who is standing there?" Her husband answered, "Be still, dear wife, he will go away." But now the voice spoke, "I am not going away! By your hair, I will drag you with me." And the dead man grabbed the woman by her hair, pulled her out of the house, down to the graveyard where he killed her, took her liver out, and placed it in his own body. Then he climbed back into his grave and lay down again. (H. Meier, *Spanische*, Jena 1940 No. 44.) This fairytale shows that every encroachment on the world of the dead provokes calamitous consequences (cf., also the fairytale, "The Curios" (Spain). Some tales (e.g., "The Dead Maiden") state that all by itself a corpse can radiate a lethal effect.

[43] [See C.G. Jung, "Belief in Spirits," CW 8, ¶582.]

[44] Cf. Rohde, *Psyche* pp. 95–97, 103, 246f., esp. p. 118: "Hesiod's description, then, of the five Ages of Men gives us the most important information about the development of Greek belief in the soul. What he tells us of the spirits of the Silver and Golden race shows that from the earliest dawn of history down to the actual lifetime of the poet, a form of *ancestor-worship* had prevailed, based on the once living belief in the elevation of disembodied and immortal souls to the rank of powerful, consciously active spirits." See also Leeuw, *Religion in Essence*, vol. 1, ss14:4, pp. 130–131.

[45] See "The Legend of the Wandering (Immigration) of the People," esp. Krickeberg, *Azteken and Inka*, Jena, 1928, pp. 88–95, and the notes on p. 349.

[46] Cf. F. J. Dölger, "Antike Parallelen," vol. 2, 1930, pp. 1 ff., esp. pp. 11–12, 28–31; see also Rohde, *Psyche*, pp. 275–77.

[47] [A book of confessions for the holy mass from the 14th century with an introduction by Jeremias Jakob Oberlin, Strasbourg 1784.]

(old penitent formula: *item, si credidit, quod Umbratici vadant et comedant: propter quod daemones ita homines decipiunt, quod se transfigurent in hominum figuras, et caetera multa quae observantur*). According to Greek and Roman superstitions, ghosts (*Eidola, lemures, larvae*) are souls. . . who find no peace in Hades.[48]

328 In Tirol and elsewhere, every frightening apparition is called a ghost and is unredeemable. Ghosts usually appear at night, in deserted places or at crossroads. They look the same as spirits of the dead. Ghosts are often vengeful: one should not look around when one hears a ghost. An encounter with ghosts can bring illness, one should speak about seeing a ghost only after three or nine days, otherwise one risks life and limb. The apotropaic signs and symbolic images of the ancient Greeks and Romans to ward off spirits were often contemptuous or indecent. Because ghosts are timid, threats accompanied by loud noises are usually successful in routing them.

329 Jung writes:

> The psychogenesis of the spirits of the dead seems to me to be mm moo less as follows. When a person dies, the feelings and emotions that bound his relatives to him lose their application to reality and sink into the unconscious, where they activate a collective content that has a deleterious effect on consciousness. The Bataks and many other indigenous people say that when a man dies his character deteriorates, so that he is always trying to harm the living in some way. This view is obviously based on the experience that a persistent attachment to the dead makes life seem less worth living, and may even be the cause of psychic illness.[49]

---

[48] H. Bächtold-Stäubli, vol. 3, p. 766f.

[49] C.G. Jung, "Belief in Spirits," CW 8, ¶598 and "Relation between the ego and the unconscious," CW 7, ¶293f. [See also the chapter "Life after Death" in his *Memories, Dreams, Reflections*, New York 1963.] Cf. also "The Deacon of Myrká," and Carnochan und Adamson, *Empire*, New York, 1935, pp. 132–134. As a further example, we summarize the Chinese fairytale "The Naughty Boy": In the vicinity of Kiautscho there lived a learned man who tutored a talented 15-year-old boy, the son of a wealthy man, in a nearby village. The boy's father was very strict and one day gave his son the task of learning one hundred pages of calligraphy and writing twelve essays while he was away on a trip. The boy thought it would all be easy and spent his time playing outside. His father had appointed the boy's uncle to check that he did his homework. When the uncle caught wind of the boy's antics, he threatened to tell his father. Out of fear of reprisals, the boy took an overdose of opium and died. He appeared to his father as a ghost, then to his uncle, both of whom get sick. The boy was engaged to be married and one night he appeared to the bride to bid her farewell and then disappeared. From that time on, people saw the ghost of a boy going about the town and fields. Then the farmers call for a magician, who said that the ghost of the boy was about to become a spirit of drought and do terrible harm. The townspeople dug up the grave and burned the boy's corpse. Then the haunting ceases and the father recovered from his illness (summarized from "Der unartige Knabe"; see Wilhelm, *Chinesische Märchen*, 1958, p. 201).

330 Since, psychologically speaking, unconscious problems of the living often appear symbolically as figures of the dead, the power of attraction of certain ghosts often set in motion whole "chains" of fatalities, and the problems behind them continue to claim victims until these problems can be reintegrated into life by a person called to the task. A fairytale example of this idea is "The Ghost of the One Who Hung Herself":

331 The great poet, Su Dung Po, loved to tell ghost stories, but he himself had never seen one. This is one of his favorites. A colleague of his, Yüan Dschan, had written a treatise claiming that ghosts do not exist One day, a scholar came to Yüan Dschan and requested an audience. "Since ancient times," began the visitor, "true stories about ghosts and spirits have been told. How does it come about that you think these are not true?" Yüan Dschan then proceeded to expound so many rational reasons why ghosts do not exist, that an objection was impossible. Then the visiting scholar became angry. " I am just such a ghost," he said. No sooner had the words left his mouth than he transformed into a devil with a green face and red hair. He looked ghastly and was frightening to behold. Then he sank into the earth and disappeared. Not long afterwards, Yüan Dschan died.

332 The actual story of the fairytale then begins:

Now there are many kinds of ghosts. But the ghosts of people who have been hanged are the worst. These ghosts are mostly women.[50]

333 In Tsingtschoufu there once lived an old man, who passed the military entrance examination and had to go to Tsinanfu to present himself. On the way, he stayed overnight on the steps of an old dilapidated temple. "He made himself comfortable and, being slightly intoxicated, closed his eyes and welcomed sleep. Suddenly he heard a rustling noise coming from inside the temple. A cool wind swept across his face, making him shudder. Then he saw a woman come out of the temple in old dirty red clothes, her face was white as chalk, like a whitewashed wall." He recognized this apparition as the ghost of a

[50] R. Wilhelm, the collector, notes that these woman "have come from poor peasant families from the countryside. Many are simple farming wives who have been mistreated by mothers in law or who suffered from hunger and had to toil their whole life long are often unhappy with their fates. Or they got involved in disputes with their in-laws, or were abused by their husbands. Then they see no way out and in despair end their lives... most often by hanging. The ghosts of ones who hung themselves and always entice other women to also hang themselves from the rafters and in that way to find death. Only then can the way to the underground open for the ghost and the wheel of transformation begin to turn anew. The ghost of the newly died can then find a substitute. Ghosts appear in many fairytales and stories. Maybe that is just chance. I also know some ghost stories and there is one that I would now like to tell, I myself heard from very credible people" (Wilhelm, *The Chinese Fairy Book*, pp. 196–201.)

woman who had hung herself. Silently he rose up and followed her on foot.

334 She came to a house, and slipped in through a crack in the door. The soldier jumped over the wall behind her and looked in through a chink in a window. There, in a dimly lit room he saw a woman about twenty years old, sitting on a bedside, sighing deeply. She held a scarf in her hands; it was soaked in tears. Next to her lay a small child, asleep. The woman cast a glance up above at the rafters. Soon she wept again, and then stroked the child. As the soldier looked more closely, he saw the ghost of the one who hung herself on the beam above. She had tied the rope around her neck and made movements to hang herself. Then the ghost waved her hand to get the woman on the bedside to look up at her. The woman pulled a bench to the middle of the room and, determined, stepped up on it. Just when she was about to slip the rope around her neck, the soldier yelled, broke the window and stepped into the room. The woman fell to the ground and the ghost disappeared. Then the man spoke to the woman, "Look well to your child; one has only one life to lose!" Before he went, he took the rope which the ghost had hung from the beam, it looked like "a ribbon without end." On the way to the temple the ghost waited for him and demanded that he return the rope. "When I have only this one thing with me, then I do not care that I did not find a substitute." The soldier showed her the rope and laughed, "You mean this thing? But when I give it to you, then you will find someone else to hang themselves. That I cannot allow."

335 Now the ghost got angry. Her face became green-black, her hair hung wild and disheveled about her neck. Her eyes filled with blood, her tongue hung far out of her mouth. She stretched both her hands out and tried to grasp the man. With clenched fist he swung at her. By mistake he hit himself in the nose and began to bleed. He threw some of the drops of his blood at the ghost. Since spirits of the dead cannot stand the blood of living humans, she let go, drew back, and began to flee. It was quite a while before the cock crowed. Then the ghost disappeared for good. On the soldier's naked arm one could still see the rope, but now it had grown onto his arm and had become a red ring of flesh.[51]

336 New in this fairytale is the motif of substitution. This is symbolized by the rope being a "loop without end." Ghosts in general embody unconscious

---

[51] Shortened from Wilhelm, *The Chinese Fairy Book*, pp. 196–201.

contents that strive for the living, that is, conscious realization. Because of this, they seek a human being who would not simply succumb again to the problem, but would consciously realize and integrate it into his life. This is why at the end of the tale the rope grew onto the arm and became a part of the soldier. These ghosts wander around and entice new victims until the great deed is finally accomplished.[52] Some problems can be handed on from generation to generation in the unconscious and demand many victims, a real "noose without end"![53] Güntert writes of the image of the noose:

337 The image of tying a noose, ensnaring, netting is one of the most spiteful, malicious, deceitful, insidious, perfidious ways to overcome something or someone and is contained in many phrases still in use today: "sent me through a loop," "tied up in guilt," "caught in a web," "flounder in a net," etc. In India it is usually the death demons who carry a noose.[54] With his noose Yama caught the thumb-sized souls of the dying . . . Also Horace writes of the *laquei mortis* [noose of death],[55] an image that was already used in the Old Testament (2. Samuel, 22:6; Psalms, 18:5 f.) . . . Water spirits too, pull their victims into their wet realms with a magic noose.[56]

338 And

> In magic practices being bound has an even greater meaning; for instance, the knot plays a significant role. It signifies an evil sign: one must loosen the belt or hair during a sacred operation since every knot brings disaster or disturbance. [This is explained as being due to the fact that] when one tightens a noose, meaning tying a knot, one consummates a demonic kind of connection. I only need to remind

---

[52] See all the folklore motifs, where the alp, the ghost ferryman, etc., is searching for a replacement, someone living who can now take his place (and spook others), thus freeing the predecessor; Laistner, *Das Rätsel*, Berlin, 1889, pp. 166f., 198–199.

[53] Many indigenous tribes and cultures associate this system with the idea of rebirth; see L. Lévy-Bruhl, *The "Soul" of the Primitive*, pp. 333ff., "Soul."

[54] [Yama is the Hindu god of death. In the Hindu story of Markandeya, when he reached sixteen years of age, Yama came to take his life as prophesied. But Markandeya refused to go along with Yama. Yama threw his noose around Markandeya and since he was hugging the Shivalingam, the noose fell around the Shivalingam also. See http://en.wikipedia.org/wiki/Markandeya.]

[55] [*Odes and Carmen*, Book III, 24.]:

Let Necessity but drive
Her wedge of adamance into that proud head,
Vainly battling will you strive
To 'scape Death's noose, or rid your soul of dread.

[56] H. Güntert, *Weltkönig* [*Arian World King*], Halle a. S., 1923, pp. 125–126, 129. See also similar material in Bächtold-Stäubli under "Faszination" and "Schlinge," as well as Isidor Scheftelowitz, *Das Schlingen- und Netzmotiv im Glauben und Brauch der Völker* [The Snare and Net Belief among Folk Culture] (Religionsgeschichtliche Versuche und Vorarbeiten), Wünsch-Deubner, Gießen, 1912.

the reader of the well-known German superstition of "tying the codpiece" (*Nestelknüpfen*).[57]

339 The noose in itself is something labyrinthine and devouring. Psychologically, we say it is a complex, an expression for something unresolved in the unconscious.[58] The view that the ghost in the Chinese fairytale strongly resists the soldier taking the noose is psychologically explained in that the unconscious tends to avoid conscious awareness of such a problem. It is, however, more like a projection of the resistance that human consciousness has against the unconscious.

340 In "The Ghost of the One Who Hung Herself," the ghost is vanquished with human blood, that is, through human reality. The drop of blood functions like the Blue-Jay's loud cry in "Blue-Jay Visits his Sister Io'i in the Land of the Dead"; as soon as there is contact with everyday human reality the sinister quality of the problem loses its overwhelming power. But blood does not always chase ghosts away. It can, as for example in the *Odyssey*, be offered in the form of sacrifice to the spirits of the dead,[59] in order to bring them closer to real life. Thus the problem that the ghost represents of getting a "blood transfusion," signifies, as it were, being supplied with blood, that is, becoming real and visible, thereby making possible an *auseinandersetzung*, a conscious confrontation and coming to terms with what it represents.

---

[57] [In the Middle Ages, tying the codpiece was used by the bride on her wedding night to ban the act of "opening Love's door." It is also known from ancient times in symbolic form: Hera delayed the birth of Hercules for seven days by knotting her fingers. In the 8th *Eclogue*, Virgil writes:

> Now, Amaryllis, ply in triple knots
> The threefold colors; ply them fast, and say
> This is the chain of Venus that I ply.].

[58] According to the beliefs of some folk cultures, one can also trap spirits with knots or nooses, see Güntert, *Weltkönig*, pp. 131–134. This means that spirits can be attracted and also banished through a person's complexes.

[59] See, for instance, Rohde, *Psyche*, p. I, 55f.

Chapter 15
Ghosts (Spirits) as Demons

341 The identity of dead spirits with a tormenting psychic complex is illustrated in more clarity in the Icelandic fairytale "The Red Bull." At the same time, it vividly reveals the archetypal power behind the spirits that bestow the images with such violence.

342 The servant Bjarni wanted to get rid of his wife so he could marry another girl. He awakened a ghost to kill his wife. But the ghost went after Bjarni himself, haunting him until he almost lost his mind. In desperation, Bjarni asked a man adept in magic lore how he could save himself from the pursuit of the revenant.[1] The man gave Bjarni a sheet of paper with signs and said he should go one night to the church of Grenjaderstad and there take all the garments for the mass off the hangers and put them on. Thus adorned, he was to stand the whole night long behind the cubicle next to the altar and not budge once from the spot. No matter what he saw he was to pay no attention when he was spoken to. They would only try to entice him out of the closet. The magician told Bjarni that an incredibly huge red bull would come and wag his tongue between the closet and the altar. If Bjarni could manage to put the sheet of paper with the characters on the bull's tongue, he would never have to fear being affiicted by the ghost again. If he failed to do this, however, he would lose his life. Bjarni carried out the instructions, resisted the enticing of the people and succeeded in placing the piece of paper with the signs on the tongue of the bull. Instantly, the bull disappeared and from that moment on, Bjarni noticed nothing more of the church and also nothing more of the plague of that ghost.[2]

343 The ghost embodies the whole psychic system of the split off, and now independently operating, obsessive murderous drive of the farm hand, which in the end becomes a complex that continually plagues him. It is noteworthy

[1] [German *Wiederkehrer*, one who has returned from the dead as a ghost.]
[2] J. Árnason, *Icelandic Folktales*, vol. 1, Leipzig, 1862 [in Icelandic]; A. Avenstrup and E. Treitel, *Isländische*, Berlin, 1919, pp. 186–188 [in German]; H. and I. Naumann (trans.), *Isländische*, Jena, 1923, pp. 154–156 [in German].

that this figure manifests its being as a red bull and not as the ghost, reminding us not only of the above-mentioned examples of the dead appearing as animals but also showing the character of ghosts as symbolic archetypal images. In many heathen religions, the bull is a god that personifies the chthonic procreative force of nature. The red color of the ghost bull signifies in this case that the complex is strongly emotionally colored. He personifies Bjarni's overpowering feelings of lust that almost drove him to murder. Through magic, he was able to keep contact with the altar, that is, his Christian moral ethics, which helped him to avoid carrying out his misdeed.

344 That spirits of the dead as conceived by the living melt into the symbolic primordial images of the unconscious can be seen in the following ghost stories in which the ghost appears neither in human nor animal form,[3] but rather as fiery sphere, for example, in "The Fire-Ball":

345 Very long ago in the village of *Kiñ-í-gûn* [Cape Prince of Wales], there lived a poor orphan boy who had no one to care for him. He was treated badly by everyone, being made to run here and there at the bidding of all the villagers. One evening, he was sent out on a frivolous task without his skin boots. It being winter he did not wish to go, but he was driven out by the others. The people continued to send him on such errands until at last he came back and told them that he had seen a great ball of fire *like the moon* coming over the hill not far away. The people laughed at him and made him go out again. Now he saw that the fireball had come nearer until it was quite close. The orphan ran inside telling what he had seen and hid himself because he was frightened. Soon after this the people in the *kashim* saw a fiery figure dancing on the gut-skin covering over the roof hole, and directly afterwards, a human skeleton came crawling into the room through the passageway, creeping on its knees and elbows. When it came into the room, the skeleton made a motion towards the people, causing all of them to fall upon their knees and elbows in the same position taken by the skeleton. Then turning about, it crawled out as it had come this time followed by the people who were forced to go after it. Outside, the skeleton crept away from the village followed by all the men, and in a short time every one of them was dead and the skeleton had vanished.

[3] Objective statements about the fate of the soul after death are not accessible to us. How far the stories about the dead or life after death are to be taken as true is not provable, but they also cannot be rejected. We can only ascertain that a significant subjective component with unconscious elements is present in the belief in ghosts. Maybe something objective is reflected here. We do not know. For a general account, see also Schopenhauer, *On Spirit Seeing*, Oxford, 1974.

346 Some of the villagers had been absent when the skeleton, or *tunghâk*,[4] came, and when they returned they found dead people lying on the ground all about. Entering the *kashim* they found the orphan boy, who told them how the people had been killed. After this, they followed the tracks of the *tunghâk* through the snow and were led up the side of the mountain until they came to a very ancient grave, where the tracks ended.

347 A few days later, the brother of one of the men who had been killed went fishing upon the sea ice far from the village. He stayed late, and it became dark while he was still a long way from home. As he was walking along, the *tunghâk* suddenly appeared before him and began to cross back and forth in his path. The young man tried to pass by and escape, but could not. The *tunghâk* kept in front of him, do what he might. As he could not think of anything else, he suddenly took a fish out of his basket and threw it at the *tunghâk*. When he threw the fish it was frozen hard, but as it was thrown and came near the *tunghâk*, it turned suddenly back, passing over the young man's shoulders, and fell into his basket again, where it began to flap about, having become alive.

348 Then the fisherman pulled off one of his dogskin mittens and threw it at the *tunghâk*. As it fell near the spirit, the mitten suddenly changed into a dog, which ran growling and snarling around the apparition, distracting its attention. The young man was able to dart by and run as fast as he could toward the village. When he had gone part of the way he was again stopped by the *tunghâk*, and at the same time a woman's voice from overhead said: "Untie his feet; they are bound with cord!" But he was too badly frightened to obey. He then threw his other mitten, and it too changed into a dog, delaying the *tunghâk* as the first one had done.

349 The young man ran off as fast as he could, and fell exhausted near the door of his *kashim* as the *tunghâk* came up. The latter passed very near without seeing him and went into the house. Finding no one there, it came out and went away. The young man then got up and went home, but he did not dare tell his mother what he had seen. The following day he went fishing again, and on his way came to a man lying in the path whose face and hands were black. When he drew near, the black man told him to get on his back and *close his eyes*. When the young man did this, they flew together and stopped just before a house.

[4] According to R. Wells and J.W. Kelly, *English-Eskimo Vocabularies*, Washington, D.C., 1890, p. 64, *too noo'ok* = skeleton, *too noo'riok* = ghost, and *toon'rok* = devil.

> Nearby was a pretty young woman. She spoke to him, saying: "Why did you not do as I told you the other night when the *tunghâk* pursued you?" He replied that he had been afraid to do it. The woman then gave him a magic stone as an amulet to protect him from the *tunghâk* in the future. Then the black man again took him back on his back, and when he opened his eyes, he was at home. After this the young man claimed to be a shaman, but he thought continually of the beautiful young woman he had seen, so that he did not have much power. At last his father said to him, "You are no shaman; you will make me ashamed of you. Go somewhere else." The next morning the young man left the village at daybreak and was never heard of again.[5]

350 This tale depicts the approaching unconscious in two forms: first, the ghost appears as a fireball, but then this becomes a skeleton. It rises from an old grave[6] and is discovered by an abused orphan. To escape from his hard life, the boy evidently tends to daydream, which blocks him from coming into life. Thus the child remains bound to the spirit-world.[7]

351 The fireball, which rises "like the moon" is a widespread symbol of the soul.[8] Ghosts often appear as balls or spheres. Bächtold-Stäubli lists under *Kugel* [ball, sphere] an extensive report of uncanny encounters with balls:

352 A black ball rolled in the darkness out in front of the wanderer; a large golden sphere comes up out of the ground near a mountain castle and weaves its way around the feet of children at play, or a strange ball is seen, like a globe, slowly and solemnly circling the cemetery. Usually such apparitions pursue the timid with thudding rolls and crashing sounds. One can poke and strike them, but then they become larger and only when one prays do they withdraw. The last resort is to seek

---

[5] Slightly shortened from W. E. Nelson, *Eskimo – Bering Strait*, 1900, pp. 510–511. [From Sledge Island; authors' emphases.]

[6] On graves being haunts of the dead, see Bächtold-Stäubli under *Hölle* and Rohde, *Psyche*, vol. 1, pp. 159–166.

[7] Eventually, he becomes a *kivitok*. Commenting on this belief, F. Nansen writes: "The *kivitut* [plural of *kivitok*] are beings of a peculiar nature. They have at one time been ordinary men, who for some reason or other, often quite insignificant, have fallen out with their families or their companions, or have felt aggrieved by them, and have therefore turned their backs on their fellows and fled to the mountains or into the interior. Here they henceforth live alone, feeding upon animals which they kill without any ordinary weapons, simply by throwing stones. . . While the *kivitok* has only been a short time away, it is still open to him to return to his fellows; but if he does not within a certain number of days obey the voice of his homeward longing, he loses the power of resuming his place among men. . . He now acquires supernatural faculties; he becomes so swift of foot that he can leap from one mountain peak to another, he can catch reindeer without weapons. . . But he pays for all this in his inability to die" (*Eskimo Life*, London and New York, 1893, p. 266f.).

[8] See, among others, Laistner, *Das Rätsel*, vol. 1, p. 63: "According to a narration from Aargau [a Canton in Switzerland], one sees fiery balls flying through the air when a *Schrätteli* presses down on somebody." Laistner adds that the fireball is also an "apparition from a nightmare" (Ibid., p. 118).

> out a wayside shrine. Some people must pay for such a meeting with a long illness, most often when the shape appears as a glowing sphere. These ball apparitions wander about, for instance, after a rainy day in the evening around the church courtyard out over the fields. Blows do nothing, dogs slink away; whoever shoots at such a thing falls seriously ill or disappears without a trace. . . More often they are seen on mountains, where they fling out sparks and roll down to the valley with a terrible noise often in a barrel as large as an awm[9] and explode with a deafening din. Or they hover in the air, flying often around crossroads, lit up brighter than the moon, and even casting a shadow by daylight. Then they dwindle away, releasing smoke and sulfurous fumes. Sometimes they have a blazing tail and set buildings on fire. . . When one approaches such a fireball, "one is confronted with a nightmarish sight: a human shape without a head and threatening with a stick." Usually these are poor souls who appear in the shape of humans. Knights and castle residents are condemned after their death to throw golden balls at silver bowling pins. . . Border crossers, suicides, double murderers, and those executed who remain unrepentant return as large fireballs. In general, [they are] souls who strive to be redeemed by a fearless living person.[10]

353 Many natural peoples believe that the soul wanders about at night and can enter into another man in the shape of a ball of fire.[11] Certain spirits in West Greenland are called "great fire."[12] According to the *Poetic Edda*, the dead often arise from the grave accompanied by fiery apparitions.[13] In his dissertation on the epiphany of the soul in German folk tales, Otto Tobler considers the light and flames of fire to be signs of haunting souls:

354

> As a sort of abbreviation, the soul can perhaps be regarded as a fiery head. Not far from the village of Horka in the communal mountains, it was told that two brothers were murdered. Each year on Christmas Eve their *heads* appear as *fiery ghosts*. . . In Eien, a town about an hour from Koblenz, there once was a man named Knable, who was known

[9] [A barrel containing forty gallons.]

[10] Bächtold-Stäubli under *Kugel.*

[11] [In the back country of Lucerne, Switzerland, even into the 1980s one spoke of "fiery balls that roll in front of one in the night"; see J. Zihlmann, *Heilige*, Hitzkirch, 1985, p. 20.]

[12] "When the kayak-men are at sea, they believe themselves to be surrounded by the so-called *ignersuit* (plural of *ignersuak*, which means 'great fire')"; see Nansen, *Eskimo Life*, p. 259. This idea is also related to the belief that the dead dwell in volcanoes. See Layard, "Der Mythos der Totenfahrt auf Malekula" [The Myth of the Death Journey on Malekula], 1938, p. 270.

[13] See *Poetic Edda*, vol. I, cited in Felix Niedner, "Die Edda," Erster Band–Heldendichtung, in: *Thule: Altnordische Dichtung und Prosa,* vol. 1, ed. Felix Niedener, trans. Felix Genzmer, 1914, p. 202, (note to verse 5 of the *Herwörliedes*).

> to have shifted property boundaries. After his death, his ghost was seen ambling aimlessly around the fields until his children had returned all property stolen by him back to their rightful owners. "This transformation motif combines anthropomorphic and spiritualizing apperceptions: the will-o'-the-wisp[14] lures people to the swamp or lake to small black-bearded men who suffocate or drown the guileless and innocent. "The will-o'-the-wisp is a widespread epiphany of the dead."[15]
>
> 355 . . . The "fire men", who during the *Fastnacht* carnival[16] wandered from Purschwitz to Wurschen, appeared in the *fiery garb or in the form of great luminous balls*, and were considered to be *ghosts* of Russian *soldiers* who had fallen in the Napoleonic wars. . . As punishment for their impiousness, rich farmers did not find any peace in their graves, but wandered about as *fireballs* in the night, people called them simply "the lights" . . . big fiery balls, the size of heads, as large as a cobbler's glass vase, always about fist-high above the ground."[17]

356 In *Psychology and Alchemy*, Jung writes[18] of a series of visual impressions and dreams in which a dead person's head appears that gradually transforms into a red ball and then into a woman's head that emits light. Jung explains that the skull-like appearance of the soul is a result of the rejection by the conscious mind. As we have indicated above, ghosts are unconscious contents that have become autonomous due to having been split off from consciousness.

357 In the Inuit fairytale, the fireball is a ghost that moves about on all fours. For the people of the village, it is humiliating to fall under his spell just by a single movement of this ghost since going about on knees and elbows is being degraded to the level of an animal. This is a symbolic expression of becoming unconscious as a result of the fascinating power emerging from an unconscious image. Just like the people and children who follow the Pied Piper of Hamelin, the specter pulls the powerless in tow behind him.

---

[14] [A will-o'-the-wisp or *ignis fatuus* Latin, from ignis, "fire" + fatuus, "foolis"), also called will-o'-wisp, corpse candle, jack-o'-lantern, and wisp) is a folkloric depiction of a ghostly light sometimes seen at night or twilight over bogs, swamps, and marshes. It resembles a flickering lamp and is sometimes said to recede if approached.]

[15] Otto Tobler, *Die Epiphanie der Seele in deutscher Volkssage*, Christian-Albrechts-Universität zu Kiel, Kiel, 1911, Inaugural-Dissertation, pp. 83–86. See further therein on the legend from Tonder, where two antagonistic brothers on the fields of their father, who tries to mediate between them, end up killing each other. "Now you can see in the fields at night. . . *three wisps*, and the middle one is jumping between the other two, as if to keep them apart. . . The *lights* at the entrance to the hamlet of Tautewalde [about 50 km south of Dresden, Germany.] are *souls of dead soldiers* who fell in the war and are buried there. . ."

[16] [A pre-Christian Spring festival that was taken on by the Catholic Church as a celebration of the end of the Lenten period of fasting. It is still practiced in Switzerland in its archaic form.]

[17] For other examples of fiery forms, see Tobler, *Epiphanie*, under *Kegel* [bowling pins], *Rad* [wheel], and *Garbe* [haystacks].

[18] C.G. Jung, *Psychology and Alchemy*, CW 12, ¶112.

358 In the second part of the fairytale, the spirit meets a fisherman, "far away from the village," in other words, far from the ordinary human sphere of consciousness. The skeleton is not merely a dead person, but has become a sinister nature spirit. As the fisherman tries to overtake the *tunghak* on the way home, the *tunghak* behaves just like his mirror image, imitating all his movements. The *tunghak* is thus an inner counterimage or shadow of the fisherman, which contains a part of the soul, its roots reaching deep into the darkest forces of nature.

359 A similar encounter appears in a South Pacific fairytale, "The Fisherman and the Spirit." In the dusk of evening, an evil spirit, a *tamburans*, takes the form of a friend of a fisherman.

360 One day towards evening, a fisherman heaved as usual the fish that he had caught over his shoulder to his "companion." This time, however, his companion straightaway ate up the catch "behind the back of the human." When the fisherman heard the cracking of lobster shells, he became alarmed and tried to escape by a ruse. Finally he climbed up a tree; the sticky sap made it impossible for the spirit to climb after him. Frightened by threats of the fisherman above him, the spirit slipped into a small hole in the ground. When daylight came, the fisherman called to his people to come and dig into the hole. This they did and the spirit was driven out and promptly beaten to death. When carrying the dead demon into the village, all the support poles suddenly snapped. One of the support poles was made of magic wood. With this pole, the villagers managed to cut open the spirit's stomach, and out spilled all the fish and lobsters. Everything was fried up, a few pigs were also prepared, and a magnificent feast was celebrated commemorating the death of the *tamburans*.[19]

361 The Greeks called this accompanying shadow-image *synopados* [companion], "he who follows behind." On this, Jung writes: "They expressed in this way the feeling of an intangible living presence, the same feeling that leads to the belief that the souls of the departed are 'shades.'"[20] The Inuit fishermen utilizes the life and nature bound aspect of the spirit when he throws him his dog-fur gloves, which then become real dogs. This means that he protects himself with his own natural instincts which are enlivened by the spirit and thereby he keeps its unbearable aspect at a distance. In spite of the dog granting the fisherman some protection, and learning that the spirit can create things, the

---

[19] P. Hambruch, *Südsee*, Jena, 1921, pp. 77–80.

[20] C.G. Jung, "Basic Postulates of Analytical Psychology," CW 8, ¶667. On the *Kra* or the shade, the shadow, the ghost, the spirit, and angels among primitives, see also Lévy-Bruhl, *The "Soul" of the Primitive*, p. 197.

Inuit man did not trust himself to follow the female voice that advised him to free up the spirit's feet. This "inner voice" is later revealed to be that of a beautiful woman whom he came upon when he was carried on the back of a black man. She shows him that the spirit is also something bound or unresolved in the dark layers of the soul, which cries for redemption.[21] The insight that the young Inuit gained in the magical realm fulfills a prerequisite to becoming a shaman. But in spite of being given distinction and competence by the other villagers, he fails because he cannot break the bond to the magical. He remains lost and in the Arctic region being lost amounts to being dead.

362 Certain Inuit tribes believed that a mighty skull-folk lives under the earth in a special, separate realm of spirits. The same idea is also found in certain native peoples of California, including the Yana.[22] One might ask why only part of the skeleton has become the representative of the spirit of the dead. Most likely, this is connected with the fact that many cultures see the head as the seat of the soul or as the center of life. Consequently, the skull is taken for the whole being of the dead, which is why one sometimes digs up the skull and keeps it at home.[23] With some tribes that practiced head hunting it was also a matter of getting the life essence of the enemy.[24]

---

[21] See Bächtold-Säubli under *Fesseln* [bondage]: "Like any bond, to be captivated may have a dual purpose, 1) to keep the one restrained in his [or her] own sphere of power, or 2) to inhibit rash action when it could be dangerous. The more common theme seems to be the fear of divine or demonic powers, because one does not know exactly what to expect from them, and so we prefer restraint. . ." The figures of Loki, Fenrir, and Cronos belong to the more dangerous powers. Water spirits can be bound by throwing steel into the spring or pond. Even poltergeists can be tied up. "In the legend of *Wilischberge*, there is a demon in the shape of a snake with a golden chain bound to an altar that can become dangerous if the bondage is loosened. The image of the binding of Prometheus, which is closely related to the confinement of the rest of the Titans and Cronus, is retained here in symbolic form." *Aeolos* [a Greek god of the winds] catches and keeps the winds in a bag. "Evil spirits can be caught in snares." Cf. the combed and cleaned strands of wool that crisscross the *Omphalos* at Delphi, a large terra cotta vessel symbolizing the navel of the world. [The *argenon*, is Greek for the white wool netting which covered the *Omphalos*. It was made of raw wool which had been corded, but not spun or dyed.] Cords and bondage play the same role as in the death cult where they are related to the widespread custom of tying up a corpse. The Egyptian mummy wrappings can be traced back to this goal. "This very old idea still lives on in the superstitious belief that the binding with which the feet of the dead are tied together the choice of body members is here significant – can cause a deep sleep. . . Furthermore, a symbolic restraint is called upon where one has to reckon that a deity might escape. . . One can occasionally find symbolic bondage. . . consecrated in sanctuaries"; see also further material in Bächtold-Stäubli.

[22] See "Hitchinna," Curtin, *Creation Myths*, Boston, 1898, pp. 325–335 [retold and discussed in detail below on page 156]; see also "The Woman Who Became a Spider," in: Rasmussen, *Gabe des Adlers*, Frankfurt a. M., 1937, p. 121 [this tale is retold and discussed in a later volume.]

[23] See Lévy-Bruhl, *The "Soul" of the Primitive*, pp. 247 and 250.

[24] See Thurnwald, "Primitive Initiationsriten," Zürich 1940, pp. 322, 372–373; see also Bargheer, *Eingeweide*, 1931, pp. 18–19, under *Eingeweide* [viscera]. In Plato's *Timaeus*, the head houses the divine essence of the person. See further Bächtold-Stäubli under *Totenschädel* [skull]: "As the popular skull-cult and skull-magic shows, the head is considered the representative of the dead, because it contains the sense organs. Therefore the dead can still speak and think. . . The dead still live." Under *Kopf* [head], Bächtold-Stäubli observes: "In contrast to the skull cult, the folk view is that the soul that lives in the head cannot find peace if the skull is not buried. Earlier beliefs held that heads stuck on poles should be secretly buried, and, according to Salic Law, they should be expiated with 15 *solidi*. That is why to this day [1920s] North Sea fishermen bury skulls that get caught in nets in the earth, or at least take the skulls with them. This tradition may be due to the idea that the dead might be carrying some fate attached to a possible evil-doing, for instance, someone who had stolen a skull and may be still followed

363 In ancient times, the alleged head of Orpheus was venerated in this way.[25] On one hand, the value ascribed to the head could be due to the observation that brain injuries affect psychic manifestations. On the other hand – and even more importantly –, the soul is often imagined as something round and ball-like. The skull thus becomes the symbol of a part of the soul.

364 "The Moon," a ghost story from the Caxinauá (upper Amazon), illuminates the connection between the ball-soul, moon, and skulls. This is only one example among many that make up a group with a similar theme, spread over both North and South America.[26]

365 A Kutanaua insidiously murdered a Marinaua in the forest.[27] The murderer impaled the head on a stick and planted it in the middle of

---

or persecuted by the owner. . . Human and animal heads have been frequently used in magic practice. Since it holds the brain and sense organs, the head is favored as a seat of life or the soul" (H. Bächtold-Stäubli under *Totenschädel*). Cf. also G. Weicker, *Seelenvogel*, Leipzig, 1902, pp. 30–32. The Inuit fairytale, "The Skull that Saved the Girl," tells of how a girl received magical help from the skull of her dead grandmother (summarized): There was once a young Inuit woman named Neruvana from the Noatak River (Alaska). She married a stranger who came to her parent's camp one day. The new husband often went out hunting with the woman's brothers. One day he told them that he and their sister were going upriver alone to hunt caribou, it would not be long before they returned home. Then the woman and her new husband left the family camp and went hunting alone. They returned a few days later with their boat full of caribou. Again they went out hunting and returned a few days later. Yet again they went out hunting alone together. They camped up river and the man went out hunting during the day. This time he remained away many nights without telling his wife where he was. Once when he had returned, he said they had better go down river again to see how her family was doing. They rowed down to the family house, but no one came out to receive her. Neruvana went ashore and found them all, her father, mother, and brothers, lying dead: killed, murdered, and stabbed to death! Beside herself with grief, she rushed down to the river to tell her husband what she had discovered. But she saw to her astonishment that he had already pushed off from the shore and was traveling down the river. She shouted after him, and he answered that he would land immediately, yet he continued on. She ran after him along the bank, without understanding, almost out of her mind. When night fell, he lay down on the opposite side of the stream and she could not cross over to him. In this way he went on traveling, and Neruvana, who had nothing to eat, languished and became thin. At last she could run no longer. She had to walk very slowly, till the day came when she crept along the bank, feeling that her death was now near. She came to a little tributary, and as she had not the strength to cross it, she thought to herself: "I will die here, but first I will look about for a nice place. She found a place where there was high, soft grass; the sun shone, and there was shelter; here she lay down to die. While she was lying there she heard a voice. "Little grandchild, you are on the right track. Take me out of the earth, help me out of the earth!" And a little later a skull lay before her; it spoke thus: "Ah! little grandchild, you have really dug me out of the ground. Now you shall not die." The head continued to guide her. After many harrowing adventures the skull ordered the girl to throw it at the boat of her enemies. The woman did so and a storm blew up. All the folk on board perished, but the head came rolling back to the bank as if nothing had happened, and laid itself beside its grandchild. Not even the fine coat collar had become wet. The skull spoke and said: "Now we have wrought the vengeance we desired, and can remain here till you grow old. Not until you die will I again leave the earth's surface. We shall live together, as we shall one day die together." These were the words of the old grandmother. And herewith ends the story of the death's head which saved Neruvana from starving to death (Rasmussen, *Eagle's Gift*, New York, 1932, pp. 162–171.)

[25] On the Gorgon, see Weicker, *Seelenvogel*, pp. 30–32. See also C.G. Jung, *Mass*, CW 11, p. 240f., on the role of the head in certain Harranite ceremonies reported by Zosimus, and about the legend of the golden head of the Pope Sylvester II, [and also the *teraphim* in Jewish Rabbinic tradition].

[26] A related idea is found in "Fox-Fire" and an episode in "Djulek Batür." See also "The Story of Wolf" (collected in Rasmussen, *Eagle's Gift*, pp. 140–149), where not a skull spirit but a round stone represents the ghost of an eagle demon killed by the hero.

[27] See Koch-Grünberg, *Südamerika*, Jena, 1921, p. 332. In his notes to this fairytale, Koch-Grünberg writes: "Kutanaua and Marinaua are tribal names for "People of the Jacy palm" and "People of the Agouti." [In the original, this tale is told in the present tense; to be consistent, we have used the past tense.]

the road and then hid nearby. Another Marinaua came along, and saw that the head was not dead, but that the eyes were shining, the eyelashes twitched, and the mouth was open. The man became afraid. He sat down and grieved and then ran back to his village. The head was left alone, hanging there. He cried and his tears dropped down.

366 The Marinaua brought their friend's head back to the village in a basket. But the head bit through the basket and fell out: when they put him in the basket, he again bit through and fell out. They left the head lying there on the road and went away. But the head rolled along behind them, following them as they fled. It even crossed a river after them. The head saw the people eating fruit and asked for some too. To calm him down they threw him fruit, but when the head ate it, the food fell out through the hole in his neck. They threw the next piece of fruit intentionally as far away as possible and the head rolled after it. Quickly, they all got up and ran off again. When the head no longer saw his comrades, it rolled along behind them again, pleading to them to wait for him, he wanted to go home with them. But they ran into their huts and closed the doors tightly behind them. The head rolled around the hut that he used to live in, crying. Then he decided to transform himself.

367 He thought of a number of forms he could change into, like a fruit or a plant. He rejected these forms because his family would then eat him! He thought: maybe the earth? No, people would walk all over me; maybe water? No, people would drink me. Animals? No, people will kill me; a tree? No, they will cut me down.

368 What should I become? I think I will become something else. My blood I will transform into the rainbow.[28] My eyes I will transform into stars and my head shall become the moon." Then the head of the Marinaua called out to his people and spoke: "Friends, my head will become the moon. When my eyes are stars and my blood the rainbow, then all you women and girls will bleed."

369 The people looked up at the sky: "See how Marinaua's head has become the full moon; he transformed his eyes into those stars and his blood into that rainbow!" That is what the people said. Marinaua was beheaded by the Kutanaua and he transformed his head into the moon.[29]

---

[28] Literally, "the way of the enemy" or "the way of the strangers."

[29] Koch-Grünberg, *Südamerika*, pp. 232–241, "Der Mond." [This version is translated from the German. The German source was translated from Portuguese by the collector, Capistrano de Abreu, João: rã-txa hu ni-ku-í. A lingua dos Caxinauás. Rio de Janeiro, 1914, pp. 458ff.]

370 The tribe of the Tembé bring the same motif in "The Rolling Skull":

> A troop of hunters encamped in the forest. The roasting skewers were heavily laden with meat. Capuchin monkeys with outstretched arms were stuck on spikes next to rolled up howler monkey tails and limb pieces from all sorts of animals. Around the camp, heads and skins were scattered; bones and viscera were all over. The hunters had all moved out of camp and had left only one boy in charge of frying and turning the meat. Then there appeared a strange man in the camp. He walked about, peering darkly at the prey, he counted the number of hammocks, and then went away again. When the hunters returned to camp at night, the boy told of the odd visitor, but no one believed him. When the men had gone to sleep in their hammocks, the boy again told the story to an old hunter; this time the old one immediately became suspicious. He and the boy untied their hammocks and withdrew into the darkness far away from the camp back into the thicket. They were not long away when they heard voices such as owls, tigers, and other night creatures. In between there were now groans of people and the crash and crunch of breaking bones. "This is Kurupira with followers who are killing the hunters," said the old man to the boy.
>
> 371 When morning came, the two went back to the camp. There were only empty, blood-stained hammocks swinging there silently; chewed up human bones were scattered around, and in the middle of the camp there lay the head of one of the hunters. When the man and his son turned to leave, the head suddenly called out, "Take me along with you, my friends!" The man and the boy looked around in amazement. "Please take me home, mates!" repeated the head. The man sent the boy ahead to the village, while he himself bound up the skull, and dragged it on the ground behind him. But soon he became frightened, and left the head on the path. But then as he went on, the head rolled on after him like a pumpkin and cried out continually: "Godfather! Godfather! Wait a bit! Take me with you!"
>
> 372 [The man tricked the head into a pit in the forest and buried it there.]
>
> 373 When it became nighttime, in the village they heard screams coming from the forest. The screams came closer and closer. "That must be the skull, it has freed itself from the pit," said the man to his villagers.
>
> 374 The head had in the meantime grown wings and claws like a giant hawk. It hovered over the ground and threw itself at the first person who stood in its way and gobbled him up. The people of the village

> now became very terrified and called in the medicine man to help. The next evening the medicine man hid in the place where the trail came out of the forest, and waited with bow and arrow for the monster to appear. When darkness fell, again came the head screaming and crashing. It set itself down in a tree at the edge of the forest. It now looked just like a giant hawk. The medicine man shot an arrow at the hawk-head, it went through both eyes and the hawk-head immediately fell down dead from the tree limb.[30]

375 In these two fairytales, the transition is described particularly impressively. Initially, the head of the dead hunter is fully human, angered, and saddened at his own death. Gradually, it moves more and more away from human nature, and becomes something evil, dangerous, and frightening. Finally, it transforms into the moon, or a hawk; that is, into a pure, natural essence. The human contours fade and in their place steps an image that is infinitely more powerful than the dead man ever was in life. Also in Chinese folk belief there is the idea that the dead, when not banned by rituals, gradually become "drought spirits" or, even later, change into werewolves or ogres who fly up into the sky. One very strong spirit of the dead even became a golden-haired werewolf, that could only be overcome by a great saint.[31] According to eastern European werewolf traditions, some werewolves arise from dead spirits.[32] Similarly, the dead in the above tales take on increasingly demonic forms. It is as if the whole realm of the dead in the figure of the lunar sphere haunts the living, and its oppressive threat can only be banned by a medicine man.[33] In the Caxinauá tale, "The Moon," the head is not initially evil, it only wants to continue living. It sees the opportunity to stay in relationship with people only by transforming itself. This will to survive, to live on,[34] has to do with the man's untimely, early death.

---

[30] Koch-Grünberg, *Südamerika*, pp. 191–193. For the original, in Nimuendajú-Unkel, see pp. 290–291.

[31] See "Gespenstergeschichten" [Ghost Stories], Wilhelm, *The Chinese Fairy Book*, pp. 197–99. See also "Tregeagle's tasks" (England). Despite being about redeeming his evil soul, it resembles a ghost returning to perform impossible tasks.

[32] See Hertz, *Der Werwolf. Beitrag zur Sagengeschichte*, 1862, pp. 88–89, 113, 122. For many Slavic tribes and the majority of modern Greeks, the werewolf is the same as the vampire. See also Hertz, *Werwolf*, p. 124ff., on the staking of murdered people.

[33] The medicine man shoots him through the eyes. On the shooting following the sun symbol, see H. Silberer, *Problems of Mysticism*, New York, 1917, pp. 187–188. The eyes are the most dangerous parts of spirit-beings. Cf. Róheim, *Spiegelzauber*, 1919, p. 215 fn. 1, on the evil eye in Germanic countries and Ireland; see ibid., pp. 217–219 on the pernicious and dangerous glance of the dead; see ibid., pp. 219–221 on the covering of the eyes of a corpse with money, broken glass, and buttons in eastern Europe; see ibid., p. 251 on the eye as a home of the soul: "It is dangerous to look at the dead, the moon, or the sun in the eye or face; it is dangerous to get caught in their mirror images"; see further p. 252: "To look into the eye of the sun or the dead means the same as setting oneself against the father." It means great danger, and if it succeeds, great power. See also p. 262.

[34] In *The "Soul" of the Primitive*, Lévy-Bruhl comments in detail on the suffering of the dead due to their condition shortly after death, such that they hang onto the living (New York 1928 p. 225f.).

376 Ninck has written[35] on this transition of dead souls in general and their demonic nature in the beliefs of Germanic peoples. Especially beautiful is a text in the Egyptian Book of the Dead about the dead being absorbed into nature and at the same time into the godhead. The dead one says: "My hair is Nun, my face is Re, my eyes are Hathor. . . All my limbs are gods, there are no limbs on me that are not gods . . . "[36] The dead appear to the living not only as animals but also as gods.[37] One finds in the Hellenistic mysteries, under Egyptian influence, the idea that the dead or the *myste* [mystic, initiant] who is taken to be dead, "like the deity, assumes twelve different forms, the forms of animal shapes, before he obtains the divine form. . . "[38] These are the twelve signs of the zodiac. Here we see clearly how the dead dissolve or merge into various collective conceptions of the deity. The next fairytale, "Skull Acts as Food-Getter" from the Arapaho, recounts the widespread idea of the head motif.

377 There was a tipi by the river, in which a man, his wife and their daughter were living. This daughter was beautiful, charming and very skilled at quill work. "Well, daughter, I don't know how we are to get our subsistence to live on," said her father one day. "Your mother has just cooked the last supply, and I am sure we don't want to starve to death!" The daughter sat by the wall of the tipi twisting the porcupine quills into tipi pendants.

378 However, somebody else also heard the remark of the old man. Early one morning, the daughter went after water and saw a fat buffalo cow lying dead near the bank of the river. "Father, when I got to the river for this water," she exclaimed, holding up the vessel, "I saw a fat buffalo cow lying there dead," she said. "Thanks! We are now saved from starvation!" said the father. So the father and mother went and skinned the buffalo cow. They brought in the beef and hide and had a good meal again. The next morning, the daughter went again for water and found another buffalo, this time a fat steer. [This continued every day; the girl found a female antelope, a deer, a black deer, and a female elk.] The family was now well supplied with fresh meat and dry meat, and was living very happily.

379 One night when they all had gone to bed, there came a voice. One could hear it sucking in a deep breath and then saying, "I have brought you a gift!" Then came the sound of something being dropped by the

[35] Ninck, *Wodan*, p. 336.

[36] Roeder, *Urkunden*, p. 256. [The final words in the German version are *das von eine Gotte frei wäre*; alternative translation, "that are available to be gods."]

[37] Ibid., p. XV.

[38] Reitzenstein, *Hellenistic Mystery-Religions*, pp. 39–40.

door. In the morning the daughter went out and saw a fat bull lying dead. The father and mother skinned the bull and took in the meat and hide, which was a very good one for a robe.

380 [This continued again night after night, with the voice bringing a fat buffalo cow, a fat buffalo steer, a female antelope, a fat deer, and finally a fat black antelope. Each time the voice became more distinct and the burden (the dead animal) heavier. Now the father and mother became suspicious of the enormous supply of beef. The next night there came a voice at the door, saying. "I have brought you the burden," dropping something very heavy. "I wonder if the folks are getting fat; they should be by this time," said the voice. At this the father wondered and said to himself: "I am going to find out who this strange voice is that brings these animals at night; who can it be, anyhow? We are living here in a lonely place, and my daughter never speaks of a man who comes to her." So he got up and went to the door and peeped through the front pin-hole to see who this mysterious person was after all. To his surprise, he saw a whitish object jump into the woods and out of sight. "Well, daughter, after we heard the voice at the door I went and had a look. I saw an odd object going from the door to the woods. It is something strange, and I think we had better be getting away from it," said he to his daughter. So she stopped her quill work and made four pairs of moccasins. She placed these at four different spots inside the tipi; two pairs under the cover of the bed at the back of the tipi, and the other two pairs at the sides of the tipi, against the wall.

381 The father and mother prepared for escape. They did not disturb the last dead animal, a male elk, which had been left outside. The very next day they started off. The father and mother went along ahead, their daughter followed along behind. That night again came the strange object to the door and said, "I have brought you the burden," dropping it at the door. After seeing the male elk outside, untouched, he said to the people inside the tipi: "You can't get away from me; there is no possible chance of escape for any of you." Then the strange object flew around the tipi, buzzing against it, but attracting no attention. So it started off, rolling along the trail, but it had got but a short distance when one pair of moccasins cried like a person behind it. So it returned to the tipi, jumped inside, but found nobody there. "You can't get away from me, my food," said the strange object. Then it started off again on the trail after the family. [He met three more times with pairs of moccasins.]

382 The father, mother, and daughter had now reached a hill and looked back to see if they were perfectly safe. They saw a skull rolling after them, now they became really frightened. Then the daughter said, "I wish there was something to obstruct its passage!" And sure enough suddenly there appeared a thick patch of thistles between them. The daughter kept looking back to watch the skull. It would toss around from place to place until it finally managed to get through the thicket. [This happened with woods and cactus.]

383 The skull managed to get through those prickly cactus all right. And then it rolled on after the family. The father and mother ran faster. "It is coming fast," said the daughter. "I do wish there was something to obstruct that skull this time!" she said. Suddenly a deep canyon appeared behind them. The skull went back and forth, rolling up and down to find the narrowest place to leap across. Then the skull came right opposite the daughter, and she told it to leap. The skull rolled back and forth and then made the jump, but the canyon was too wide for it. It whirled down below and struck the bottom with a tremendous noise like a blast of thunder. After the noise the canyon itself closed and buried the skull in the middle.

384 When the daughter reached the hill where her father and mother had waited for her, they saw a big circle of tipis further on down the way. They went into that camp and told the people the circumstances of their arrival. They said, "We were running from a strange object, which proved finally to be a skull. But there was a deep canyon behind us, into which this object whirled down. There it was broken to pieces and buried when the sides of the canyon caved in. Now that is the way we shall be placed in the ground when we die."[39]

385 The family lived in a "lonely place," far away from settlements of the profane realm. For ordinary people, this is a dangerous place of residence although they occasionally survive using gifts from the magical kingdom as helpful resources. The loneliness causes unconscious contents to emerge that become overwhelmingly powerful; the danger of being completely swallowed up by the unconscious arises for the inhabitants of this lonely tipi. "Ču'mo," a tale from the Yukaghir of Siberia, tells of what happens to three unmarried women who also are living alone. They take a piece of rock, which reminds them of a child, and out of longing for a real child they care for it until it apparently transforms into a child. But it turns out to be a man-eating demon who threatens the women; they flee, but then fall into the hands of its demonic mother.

[39] [Told by Holding-Together, recorded by Dorsey and Kroeber, *Arapaho*, Chicago, 1903, pp. 278–282.]

386 These two tales show how solitude and not being fulfilled in real life brings an unconscious element to life as if charged with spiritual energy. When unintegrated, this aspect gradually creates the danger that consciousness will fall completely under the spell of the unconscious. In the fairytale, "Skull Acts as Food-Getter," a family living in an unusually deserted place is faced with life-threatening poverty. More and more of their life-forces are lost to the magical, which increasingly saps the strength of the family alone in their tipi. It is first the father who senses something strange in the situation. He is aware of the loneliness of the place and its dangers. But it is the daughter who knows how to banish the demon by magic. We will not now go further into the details of this story. What is important here is the fact that the skull has become a general symbol of a demon,[40] which can only ritually be banished as a god. Moreover, the ritual created by the daughter became the source model for burial rites of the whole tribe.

387 That these skull demons refer to unconscious complexes rather than dead souls is shown by an even more impressive tale from the Yana of California, "Hitchinna," in which a man is swept into the unconscious not by death, but through a dream experience, and then becomes a skull demon:

> 388 Hitchinna (wildcat) had a wife and a son a few days old. Hitchinpa (young wildcat), the little son, was sleeping, and Hitchin Marimi (wild-cat woman), the wife, was taking care of her child. Hitchinna had dreamed the night before, and his dream was a bad one.
>
> 389 "I dreamed that I climbed a big pine-tree; the tree was full of cones. I was throwing them down, and had thrown down a great many, when

---

[40] See also the subject of the flying devil's head in "Yuriwaka-Daijin"(F. Rumpf, *Japanische Volksmärchen*, Jena, 1938, p. 208). A creation story from the Blackfoot people, "The Sun Gives Earth and Heaven Room," gives an interesting variation of the emergence and banning of such a demon: The moon woman had a young son. At her request, the sun father gave the child a name and called it "God" (Apistotoki). When the boy was seven years old, the mother asked the father for another child and called it "The Old Man" (Napi). Apistotoki asked his sun-father for food and received deer, Napi received berries from his moon- mother. When Napi asked her for daylight, she tried to kill him. She had a secret relationship with a snake in a tree. The sun, however, killed this snake by his heat. The moon then wanted to take revenge on the other three. The sun snapped her head off. The sun-father determined that the two sons should rule the land, whereby he gave them four things: sand, stones, water, and the skin of a fish. It became day and the sun ordered heaven and earth to spread out. The sons inhabited the world, but beforehand the sun-father warned them about their mother: "Your mother will only remain four days under the ground, then her body will follow the sun, so that you, my sons, must in time take care of the earth. The head of the moon will follow her children. The four things that I gave you will save you." In fact, the sons were able to fend off the pursuer's head [the moon] as it ran its course. Finally, they threw the waters on the head. Then they reached the ocean. The head fell into the middle of the ocean and was killed by the seawater. "And that is the reason you do not drink the water from the sea: it is so salty that it killed the head" (A. v. Deursen, *Der Heilbringer*, Gröningen, 1931, p. 113). [The last sentence in the German version is in English. The English source is Christianus C. Uhlenbeck, "Original Blackfoot Texts from the Southern Piegans Blackfoot Reservation, Teton County, Montana," in: *Verhandelingen, Nieuwe reeks*, Verhandelingen der Koninklijke Nederlandse Akademie van Wetenschappen, Afd. Letterkunde. Nieuwe reeks, Amsterdam, 1911, p. 91.]

at last I threw down my right arm. I dreamed then that I threw down my left arm." He told her no more.

390 The family goes into the woods to collect pinecones. Hitschinna throws a lot down from the tree. Suddenly his right hand fell as well. Then his left, then one leg at a time. Hitchin Marimi was scared to death; she ran away home. She was so terrified that she left the little child behind, she forgot all about it. When she reached home, she called the people together and said, "My husband went up into a pine-tree; he threw down a great many pine-cones. Then he began to throw himself down; first he threw one arm, then the other. We must hurry and hide somewhere; he will be bad very soon; he will kill us all if he finds us." The people ran to Wamarawi, which is a round mountain; they ran the whole way and went into a cave in the mountain. When all were inside, they closed the entrance very firmly, shut it up tight. Nothing could get in through that door.

391 After his wife had run home, Hitchinna threw down his ribs one by one, and kept asking his wife if she was there. He got no answer. She was gone and he did not know it. He threw down first all the ribs of his right side, then all of his left side. Every time he threw a rib he cried, "Uh! Uh!" to his wife. At last there was nothing left of him on the tree but his head, and that came down soon after. His eyes were very big now, sticking out, staring with a wild and mad look. The head lay under the tree for a while. Hitchinna had become another kind of people. He had become a Putokya (skull or head people). He was one of the skull people, a very bad, terrible people. Each one of them is nothing but a skull.

392 [Putokya (Hitchinna now as a skull demon) could only roll on the ground like a ball. After resting and thinking a while, he set off to find his wife; he rolled on until he came to the fire. There was no woman there. He looked around, could not find her, looked again, and saw the baby. He rolled to the baby, caught it up in his mouth and ate up the baby in an instant. The head spoke and said, "I dreamed last night that I ate up my own son." Then he set out again after his wife, breaking and destroying everything on his way. He found the people in Wamarawi and tried to break in but could not get into the mountain. This made him even more furious and he tried from all sides until finally he went way up to heaven and hurled himself down on the mountain. This time he almost got through, but not knowing this, he gave up. Then he went north towards his own village, destroying everything on his way.

393 Metsi[41] had learned that Putokya was out killing people in the south; he heard the roar a great way off, and said to himself, "I hear Putokya; he is killing all the people."

394 Metsi thought over what he should do. He made buckskin rings around his arms and legs and turned himself into an old, a very old woman, all bent and wrinkled with a buckskin petticoat. He put the rusty basket on his back. Putokya came near. Metsi was ready, the basket was on his back and he had a stick in his hand. He was walking along slowly, a very old decrepit woman. The old woman began to cry pitifully, "En, en, en!" Putokya stopped on the road, he made no noise, he listened to the old woman. "Are you a dead person?" asked Metsi. Putokya was silent.

395 "I heard you came from where I was," said Metsi. "I heard you when you had that bad dream, I heard you in the south, I heard you everywhere, I heard you when you turned into a Putokya, one of the head people, and wanted to kill everybody. You used to be good, you used to be wise, but now you are sick; you will die, and be among people no longer unless you are cured. That is why I started to come south; I started south to find you, to see you. It is a good thing that you came up here; now I see you. I am your relative, your cousin. I want you to be healthy, to be as you were before; to have your arms and legs again, to feel well. I want to cure you."

396 Metsi was a great trickster, he thought of a ruse and said to Putokya, "I will fix you right here on this road, just as I fixed that other man. I made a hole in the ground; a long hole, a pretty big one. I lined it with rocks; I made a little fire of manzanita wood, and when it was nice and warm in the hole, I put plenty of pitch in, and put the man on top of the pitch. It was good and soft for him, and nice and pleasant on

---

[41] Metsi is Coyote, an animal hero who unites the properties of a savior and of a devious schemer ("trickster"). He is the prairie wolf, the *canis latrans*, the hero of most animal stories in the Rocky Mountain area and has crude comic characteristics. [In other parts of North America, this trickster figure was a hare.] On the Kootenay myth "The Hare," see W. Krickeberg, *Nordamerika* (Jena, 1924), pp. 383–384, who extracts parts of this as "How Wildcat's Sons Became the Sun and Moon." For the (German) original, see F. Boas, *Sagen*, Berlin, 1891, pp. 163–164. As the "old man," he is thought of as being human (see Krickeberg, *Nordamerika*, p. 388; see also the original notes in Kroeber, *Cheyenne Tales*, New York, 1900 p. 165: "*Vihuk* or *Vihu*, White-man, is the Ojibwa Manabozho and the Blackfoot *Nap* [Old Man, 'man-yellowish-white']. Among the Arapaho also he is called White-man. Here he appears only in his so-called degraded form: that of the trickster, corresponding to the Omaha *Ictinike*." His form and nature change according to the tribe. He is the "deceiver deceived" (see Krickeberg, *ibid.*, p. 389, note to "The Coyote and the Buffalo"). He is an antagonist of the Creator. Sometimes, he exhibits not only serious traits, but also instincts: lust, gluttony, and malice (cf. Krickeberg, *ibid.*, p. 405, note to "How Coyote Married his Daughter" (Maidu) Dixon, p. 269. But he can also free people and animals from embarrassing situations; see Russell, "How Coyote Set the Animals Free" (Pima), p. 217 [For a good introduction with a foreword by Jung, see P. Radin, *Trickster*, New York, 1956.]

the pitch. I put a flat rock over the hole. He stayed there a while and was cured."

397 Putokya believed all this; had full faith in Metsi. "That is good," said Putokya. "Fix me in that way; fix me just as you fixed him." "I will," said Metsi. "I will fix you just as I fixed that man, and you will come out just as he did; you will be in the right way and have no more trouble; you will never be sick again."

398 Metsi did everything as he had said; made a long deep hole, put in fire and a great deal of pitch, a foot thick of it. He placed Putokya on the pitch; put a wide flat stone over him, put on others; put the stones on very quickly, till there was a great pile of them. The pitch began to burn well, to grow hot, to seethe, to boil, to blaze, to burn Putokya. He struggled to get out of the pitch; the stones kept him down, the pitch stuck to him. He died a dreadful death.

399 If Putokya had gotten out of the hole there would have been hard times in this world for Metsi. When Putokya was dead under the pile of rocks, Metsi threw away his old things, his basket and buckskin petticoat, put on his nice clothes, and went along on his journey. Metsi was a great cheat, but he did a good thing that time, when he burned up Putokya.[42]

400 The terrible transformation of the man is first proclaimed in a dream, just as it later actually happens. The dream announces that a dismemberment of his being will happen, a complete destruction of his personality, even his son must fall victim to it. The human in him dissolves and there is a complete identification with the spirit-being, he is transformed into a demon. Actually, this story describes an outbreak of psychosis in symbolic form. Certain African tribes use the brain of a man who has become insane for making a magic medicine in the belief that lunatics were possessed by the spirits of the dead.[43] In the ancient Orient, crazy women called "brides of the *zar*" i.e., brides of the daemons,[44] and lunatics were considered to be holy.[45] This also shows how madness, similar to death, can be brought into connection with the contents of the unconscious.

---

[42] [Jeremiah Curtin, *Creation Myths of Primitive America: in relation to the religious history and mental development of mankind*, Boston, 1898, pp. 325–335. In the original (Curtin) text, the tale is told in the present tense.]

[43] See Carnochan und Adamson, *Empire*, p. 93f. See also Mark: 5, 1–13, where Christ heals the possessed man who had lived in the tombs and was possessed by a demon, and whose name is "'Legion', for we are many." Christ banishes the demon into a herd of swine, which then plunge into the sea.

[44] [The authors use the word "daemon" when the figure is positive *and* negative; and "demon" when the figure is purely evil/negative. The translators follow this usage.]

[45] Reitzenstein, *Hellenistic*, p. 316.

401 The dismemberment of Hitchinna takes place in the forest, in the deepest unconscious [i.e., closest to the physical, instinctual realm]. He was sitting at that very moment in a tree and had thus climbed up into the heights, in a sphere, as it were, in which he loses the connection to firm ground. His body drops away piece by piece, and only the all-controlling head is left that, when it acts alone, destroys everything.[46] Later, Hitchinna/Putokya (as "head"), madly tears along like a whirlwind, indicating a frenzied, ecstatic state. A similar mysterious change in the whole system, an outbreak of madness, or a being overpowered/overwhelmed by the demonic aspect of the spirit-world [i.e., the unconscious], is described in the Warrau fairytale, "Spearlegs, the Danger of Associating with Spirits:"

> 402 There were two brothers who lived and hunted together. During the course of one day hunting deep in the heart of the forest, they heard the sounds and revelry of a drinking party. This made the elder brother say, "Come, let us go party with those people." But the younger brother replied, "No! It cannot be a real party out here in the bush so far away from everybody; those cannot possibly be proper people who are having fun. They must be spirits of some sort." Now the elder brother insisted, and they went in the direction whence the sounds came. They reached a house where apparently real people were enjoying themselves greatly. The visitors were made to sit down and drinks were handed to them. The elder one indulged and was happy; the younger refused because he was afraid of what might happen to him. As a matter of fact, the latter's suspicions were correct, because the people at the house who were partying were really not people after all, but the spirits of the *Warekki*, or large rain-frogs who had taken on human shapes.
>
> 403 They walked on and made themselves a big fire in the evening. The elder brother got drunk and hung his legs from the hammock near the fire, but did not notice when they started burning. When he noticed what has happened, however, he sharpened his shins with a knife. Thus the next morning they went on, the younger brother took care of his brother who could impale small birds with his "spearlegs," but not much else. He, therefore, never wanted to let the younger brother out of his sight and threatened to kill him should he leave him alone. One day, the younger one managed to escape with a trick. The older brother jumped up and with his pointed bones, advanced even

[46] [It is important to note that Hitchinna does not direct these events. Rather, they *happen to him*. At first, his hand falls off by itself. Only later, when his psychosis – an identification with a daemonic force – has become completely autonomous, does the unconscious, the Self, cause things to happen.]

> faster than before with his feet. He followed his brother's footsteps, chased a deer and speared it, believing it to be his brother. Then he returned to the hammock. Meanwhile, the younger brother fetched people to kill his spearlegs brother. Since he so cleverly speared his victims with his legs from the hammock, the people lured him out first with the help of a hummingbird and then a squirrel, so that he had to stand on his legs, and then they killed him.[47]

404 Here the spirits seize and intoxicate the hunter, indicating that he had become insane. Not quite a skull demon, but he too loses parts of his body: his legs and feet, that is, his connection to the earth. He literally loses a standpoint; a striking image for the inner process that happens in an outbreak of madness.

405 All these eerie, primitive ghost stories show that ghosts and daemons represent autonomous unconscious complexes, which natural people recognize not as an inner subjective condition, but rather as an experience of the outside world. They regard this as an absolutely objective event. Schopenhauer had already called attention to the impossibility of making a real philosophical distinction between the inner psychic and external-real part of spirit/ghost apparitions. He referred to the phenomenon as an archaic identity of subject and object in human thought.[48] He pointed out that in dream life, the psychic perceptions of different people can get enmeshed.[49] He reached the conclusion that the force behind all life and all motion, is "will"

---

[47] Summarized from W. E. Roth, *Inquiry into Animism*, Washington, D.C., 1915, pp. 195–196.

[48] In *On Spirit Seeing*, Schopenhauer observes: "For the perplexity attaching to the consideration of visions and spirit apparitions springs really from the fact that, with these perceptions, the boundary between subject and object, which is the first con- dition of all knowledge, becomes doubtful, indistinct, and indeed quite blurred. . . If one man alone has just seen a ghost, it will be explained as merely subjective, even though it had at least for a moment stood before him as an objective visual or acoustic experience. If, on the other hand, two or more people saw or heard it, a corporeal reality is at once attributed to it because empirically we know only *one* cause by virtue whereof several persons must necessarily have at the same time the same representation of intuitive perception, and this where one and the same body, reflecting light in all directions, affects the eyes of them all" (Oxford, 1974, p. 298).

[49] Again, see Schopenhauer: "Just as sometimes two persons simultaneously dream the same dream, and therefore while asleep perceive the same thing through the dream-organ, so *in wakefulness* the dream-organ of two (or more) can enter the same activity, whereby a ghost, seen by them simultaneously, then objectively appears as a body. But generally speaking, the difference between subjective and objective is at bottom not absolute, but always relative. For everything objective is again subjective in so far as it is always conditioned by a subject in general, in fact exists really only in this. And so in the last resort idealism is right. We often imagine we have abolished the reality of a spirit apparition when we show that it was subjectively conditioned. But what weight can this argument have with the man who knows from Kant's doctrine how large a share the subjective conditions have in the appearance of the corporeal world? Thus that doctrine shows how this world, together with the space in which it exists, the time in which it moves, and the causality in which the essence of matter consists, and then hence in accordance with its whole form, is merely a product of the brain-functions, after these have been brought into play by a stimulus of the nerves of the organs of sense, so that here we are left only with the questions concerning the thing-in-itself" (*On Spirit Seeing*, p. 298).

that lies outside of all time and all space, which manifests both in the experiencing subject and the appearing object.[50]

[50] Once again, see Schopenhauer: "But just as in any case the thing-in-itself which manifests itself in the phenomenon of an external world is *toto genere* different therefrom, so by analogy may it be related to that which manifests itself in the spirit apparition; in fact, what reveals itself in both may perhaps be ultimately the same thing, namely "will." . . . Indeed a positive confirmation of the same view is given even by the following utterance of the most famous and carefully observed clairvoyant, namely of Prevorst (vol. 1, p. 12): 'Whether the spirits can render themselves visible only under this form, or whether my eye can see them only under this form, or my sense take them in only in this way; whether they would not be more spiritual for a more spiritual eye, I cannot assert this definitely, but almost divine it.' Is this not entirely on all fours with the Kantian doctrine: 'What things-in-themselves may be we know not, but we know only their phenomenal appearances'?" (*On Spirit Seeing*, pp. 299–300).

Section 2

The Archetypal Figures of the Magical World

The Archetypal Figures of the Magical

406 Among the many archetypal ideas in fairytales, myths, and legends, some are especially common. From this, we infer that there is a wide distribution among all humans of the corresponding emotional experiences. In the following, we will focus on the most important of these images, their nature, and their function rather than on the particular details of the fairytale plot in which they occur.

Chapter 16
The Daemonic Father

407 The two primordial images that appear in almost every fairytale – either alone or together – are those of the father and mother. These parental images do not carry human or personal traits, but from time immemorial have been granted divine attributes. The archetype of the father appears in numerous symbolic forms, indicating different and contrasting aspects of its nature. It occurs as the father, grandfather, ancestor, male totem ancestor, wise old one, teacher, old man, magician, medicine man, artisan (demiurge), old chief, old king, crippled old man, black man, forest spirit, lord of the forest and the animals, as well as all the father deities such as the sun god, sky god, god of the sea, earth god, and in a broader sense as the wind, lightning and thunder, earth-fire, seed, source of death, the law, authority, and tradition. Generally speaking, the image of the father signifies the creative spiritual principle, and the activating, life-energizing dynamis.

408 By studying the places in which the fairytale takes place, it becomes apparent that the main events of the story happen in a magical space and in a magical time, and that "magic" in this case means "unconscious." This same law also applies to the figures in the tales. Those figures that represent unconscious contents are identified as magical. The archetype of the father almost always appears in the figure of a magical old man, and to this extent its form carries the aspect of a ghost or apparition. One example of such a magical, ghostly father figure is found in the Norwegian tale, "The Isle of Utrøst":

409 There was once a very poor fisherman. He worked hard but barely caught enough fish to feed his family. One day while out fishing, he was caught in a huge storm and blown far from land. In dense fog and huge waves, he thought this was his last hour. Then he passed by three cormorants and then sailed – or was driven – on and on. "All of a sudden the boat ran up on a beach and stopped. Then the fisherman opened his eyes. The sun broke through the fog, and shone on a beautiful land. Its hills and mountains were green to their very tops, fields and meadows lay among their slopes, and he seemed to breathe a fragrance of flowers and grass sweeter than any he had ever known

> before." This must be the island of Utrøst, a legendary paradise full of fertility, he thought. He followed a path to a cottage. "On the roof of the cottage grazed a white goat with gilded horns, and an udder as large as that of the largest cow. Before the door sat a little man clad in blue, puffing away at a little pipe. He had a beard so long and so large that it hung far down upon his breast. The three cormorants were his sons, who "cannot bear the smell of a Christian." The little man invited the fisherman to eat, and no matter how much he ate, the table was filled with all kinds of delicious food. Later, the three sons helped the fisherman to load his boat with fish. After a while, the fisherman began to get homesick and, richly gifted by the little man and his sons, was led home again. "Since that time fortune was his friend. And well he knew why this was so, and never forgot to prepare something good for whoever held the winter watch, when the schooner was drawn up on land in the fall. And every Christmas night there was the glow and shimmer of light, the sound of fiddles and music, of laughter and merriment, and of dancing on the deserted schooner."[1]

410 Here, the bright aspect of the ghostly old man appears in the little man, clad all in blue. His dark aspect is depicted in the three cormorants. In Nordic sagas and fairytales blue is the typical color of spirits (as in "Helge-Hal in the Blue Hill"). Trolls such as in "Lucky Andrew," are described as being blue, therefore the ghostly helper in "Kari Woodencoat"[2] first appears as a blue bull, which then later became an old man in the rock cliff. In "The Blue Belt," the hero reaches the trolls whom he ties up with a magical blue garter that he found on the road.

411 According to Germanic tradition, Odin/Woden wanders over the Earth as a stranger in a dark blue coat.[3] In India, Shiva in his terrifying aspect and the god of death, Yama, are portrayed in blue-black colors.[4] As the color of the sky and the air, blue points to something spiritual and, as the color of the sea, and generally of water, the unconscious.[5] Goethe says of the color blue, "Blue gives us an impression of cold, and thus, again, reminds us of shade."[6]

412 Accordingly, blue is the color appropriate for a spirit-being or a haunted creature that dwells in the depths of the unconscious. The three black cormorants emphasize the deathly side of that sphere, while the kindly, giving

---

[1] Stroebe, *Norwegian Fairy Book*, pp. 9–15.
[2] [Told and interpreted in detail in Book 2.]
[3] Ninck, *Wodan*, pp. 13, 69, 70, 133.
[4] Zimmer, *Maya*, pp. 311, 417.
[5] On the color blue in folk belief, see Bächtold-Stäubli under "Blau."
[6] Johann Wolfgang von Goethe, *Goethe's Theory of Colors*, trans. Charles Lock Eastlake, London, 1840, Didactic parts 6, Dept. No. 782.

aspect is expressed in the golden-horned goat, which is more of a mother symbol.

413 The divine manifestation of the magical old man occurs even more clearly in many tales of primitive peoples, such as in "A Legend of Flowers." Such a ghostly primordial father can also be the model for the tribe, to whom all the customs and rites are attributed. One example is the Tsimshian (British Columbia) fairytale, "Tseremsaaks":

> 414 Tseremsaaks went out hunting seals with his three brothers-in-law. After three days they still had not caught anything. In the evening, at the foot of a steep mountain, they dropped a stone on a rope as an anchor and fell asleep. The stone fell through the water down onto the roof of the home of Nagunaks, the whale chief, who lived there at the bottom of the sea. The noise woke Nagunaks and he sent his servant, a codfish, up to the four men to tell them to remove the anchor. But they caught the codfish and threw her far away. Again Nagunaks sent the codfish up with a message but this time the fishermen ripped her fins off. The codfish, crying in pain, told her master what had happened. Then Nagunaks pulled the boat to the bottom of the sea right at his front door. When the sleepers awake, they were very surprised and afraid. But Nagunaks invited the men into his house, had fire made, and received them hospitably. "When they entered, they saw that the house had many steps. They cried with fear, for they noticed that it was painted entirely with fish and that many terrible beings lived there." But Nagunaks invited them kindly to approach, and said to Tseremsaaks, "Thou shalt be my brother." They exchanged gifts and from those of Tseremsaaks Nagunaks made many more. Then he gave a great feast, and all the sea chieftains appeared in fish form. Nagunaks gave each chieftain one of the gifts from Tseremsaaks. The Nagunaks began to Tseremsaaks: "Now pay attention to what is happening here." Water entered the house and all the fish, utensils, and the even the boat, began to dance in the water. When the dance was over, the water ran out, Tseremsaaks received more presents and then also the order that he should repeat everything seen there with his people in the upper world. As soon as the four men went to sleep in the boat that evening, Nagunaks brought it back up to the surface. The fisherman woke up in the morning, and "as they looked around, they became aware that seaweed had grown on their bodies, clothes, and boat itself. They went back to the house, but no one recognized them. They had been mourned for dead, for they had not been at the bottom of the sea for two days, but for two years! Then Tseremsaak built a great house and decorated it like that of Nagunaks. Now, all the descendants

> of his sister still carry out ritual dances with the songs and ornaments that Tseremsaaks brought up from the bottom of the sea."[7]

415 This story constitutes part of tribal traditions and describes the original encounter of the ancestors with the totem spirit of the clan.[8] Significantly, the first contact takes place in the evening, as the men lie down to sleep. Lost at the foot of a steep mountain, that is, near the border to the magical realm, they throw out the anchor stone, which builds the bridge to the living god on the ocean floor. This divinity responds, despite the terror of the men, with goodness. Generally, in mythology the whale is often portrayed as being a dangerous, devouring monster. In this North American tale, the dangerous aspect of the god appears in the form of his servant (the shark), which he first sends to contact the men. But the men remain undaunted and must be drawn down by the god of the depths. The festivities that then occur heighten the experience and bring the men, through the various characters, the influx of waters, and the all-encompassing dance, into a state of ecstasy.

416 Such hunting experiences, which lead to encounters with the spirit of a totem animal, are found not only in fairytales from native people but also, for instance, in the English folk tale, "The Seal Catcher and the Merman":

417 It chanced one day in northern Scotland, that an experienced seal catcher "stabbed a larger-than-usual seal with his hunting-knife, and whether the stroke had not been sure enough or not, I cannot say, but with a loud cry of pain the creature slipped off the rock into the sea, and disappeared under the water, carrying the knife along with it. . . On his way he met a horseman, who was so tall and so strange-looking and who rode on such a gigantic horse, that he stopped and looked at him in astonishment, wondering who he was, and from what country he came." After a short negotiation, the rider took the seal-catcher on his giant horse and after a furious ride threw him over a rocky reef into the sea. Instead of drowning, the seal-catcher and the horseman – who had dove into the sea with him – entered a huge hall crowded with living seals. Even the catcher himself had taken the form of a seal! The seals were evidently in mourning. Then his guide

[7] F. Boas, *Indianische*, Berlin, 1895, pp. 291–292. Boas notes that the tale is "Told by an old man from Meqtlak'qa'tla, and a woman from Port Essington." Translated by Roy Freeman from the German. In *Tsimshian* (Washington D.C., 1916, p. 846), Boas provides comparative notes on similar tales from the Tsimshian in English.

[8] See Krickeberg, *Nordamerika*, p. 401: "This is one of many stories which tell of the origin of clan insignia and kinship customs by going back to the meeting of the legendary ancestor with a mythical animal. Many of the native tribes of the US-Canadian Northwest coast [Tsimshian, Kwakiutl, Tlingit, and Haidu among others] are made up of a number of such families (clans) each with their own heraldic animals. For instance, with the Tsimshian, one of the families of the Eagle clan has the whale on its crest."

> showed him the lost hunting knife and then led him to an adjoining room where the seal he wounded in the morning lay dying. "That is my father," said his guide, "whom thou wounded this morning, thinking that he was one of the common seals who live in the sea, instead of a Merman who hath speech, and understanding, as you mortals have. I brought thee hither to bind up his wounds, for no other hand than thine can heal him." The seal-catcher said he was no healer, but feeling great remorse for what he had done, he did his best. Magically, the wound healed at his touch and the hunter was released under the condition of an oath never to kill a seal again. His guide brought him back up to the land in the same way as they had come. Before the hunter arrived at the door of his home, his guide gave him a bag saying, "Thou hast done thy part of the bargain and we must do ours. Men shall never say that we took away an honest man's work without making reparation for it, and here is what will keep thee in comfort to thy life's end." Then he vanished, and when the astonished seal catcher carried the bag into his cottage, and when he opened the bag it was full of gold! What the stranger had said was true, and that he would be a rich man for the remainder of his days.[9]

418 The idea that certain animals have spirit rulers is, in the imagination of native peoples, identical to the concept of species.[10] That is, they are identical to the archetype of the individual animals. Many native peoples call these animal spirit ancestors simply "eldest brother." The French Missionary Le Jeune reports from his encounters in 1634 with the Montagnais [Innu] tribe (Quebec and Labrador): "They say that all animals, of every species, have an elder brother, who is, as it were, the source and origin of all individuals, and this elder brother is wonderfully great and powerful."[11] Levy-Bruhl points out that all this indicates that these elders embody the life principle and origin of all individuals. The oldest brothers of all animal species are simultaneously the younger brothers of the supreme deity. "This principle, this 'elder brother', then, is a kind of personified genius of the species, in whom individuals of the species, the younger brothers, participate, and which makes them what they are."[12] If someone sees in a dream the oldest brother or the life principle of a species of animal, he will have success in hunting the younger brothers [i.e.,

---

[9] Grierson, pp. 57–65.

[10] According to Lévy-Bruhl, it denotes a kind of essence or type, too general to be an image, and too emotional to be a concept. . . the primitive's mind does not picture either the individual or the species exactly, but both at the same time, one within the other"; see *The "Soul" of the Primitive*, New York, 1928 pp. 59–60.

[11] P. Le Jeune, *Relation*, Cleveland, 1634, p. 157.

[12] Lévy-Bruhl, *The "Soul" of the Primitive*, p. 64. [Von Franz and von Beit might also be leaning on the meaning of *genius* in the sense of a guardian spirit in Roman mythology, the individual instance of a general divine nature that is present in every individual person, place, or thing.]

the real animal] of that species. The totem-ancestor is not simply that animal or that plant, rather the mystical, whole nature of the shared life-stuff together. At the same time it is a being of human nature.[13] "As far as the individual is concerned, he undergoes all possible catastrophes, and even death, but in so far as he is the type, he is imperishable, indestructible; comprising in himself the infinite multiplicity of the individuals of his species. . . To use the terms of Plato, the Baila represent to themselves the 'idea' of him"[14] (the unity in the multiplicity). That the ancestor of a genus is also represented as their chief, lord, or king, leads Lévy-Bruhl to call this a symbol.[15]

419 Sometimes, such a totem spirit in tales of primitive cultures amplifies into a powerful and dangerous deity as, for instance, in the Arawak tale, "Makonaura and Anuanaitu":

420 "In ancient times, when the grandmothers of our grandmothers were not yet born, the world was very different than today. The trees bore fruit continuously throughout the year. The animals lived in perfect harmony, and the little agouti played with the beards of the jaguars without fear. The snakes were not poisonous." There were no people yet and Adaheli, whom we now call our God but called himself the sun came down from the heavens, and human beings were born from the caiman (alligator). There were two sexes. The women were all of a fascinating beauty, but among the men there were a number of heinous and repulsive features. At that time among the group of beautiful people there lived a young man named Makonaura, and his very elderly mother. One day when Makonaura went to inspect his fish trap, he found to his surprise that it was broken open and all the fish in it were partly eaten. A woodpecker and then a Cassicus bird stood watch to warn him if the thief came again. One day the Cassicus bird woke him up and Makonaura saw a caiman near his trap. He quickly let an arrow fly and with a hiss it struck right between the two eyes of the animal and with a terrible "Glu-Glu" sound, it dove into the water and disappeared. Hardly had an hour passed, when suddenly he again heard the call of the Cassicus. Makonaura ran back fast. Panting, he arrived. But what a surprise! A young girl of dazzling beauty was there, all in tears. Moved by her tears, he asked her the cause of her grief, but she refused to tell the reason for her grief, nor did she want to accompany the young man home. Then he carried her to his mother. She said her name was Anuanaitu and she came "from

[13] Lévy-Bruhl, *The "Soul" of the Primitive*, pp. 59–67.

[14] Ibid., p. 60. [The Ba-ila are a tribe from northern Zimbabwe.]

[15] ". . . [T]he genius of the species is a more or less expressive and living symbol, according to the imaginations engaged by it"; see Ibid., p. 64.

far away." She refused to answer questions about her relatives. Makonaura and his mother did not push any further into her, and gradually she took part in her life.

421 Makonaura burned with love for her and, despite her secret, wanted to marry her. At first she refused, crying, but finally agreed. After they had lived happily for a while, she wanted to visit her mother to get her family's consent to her marriage. Although she was frightened at first that Makonaura insisted on accompanying her, they traveled together in a big canoe. When Anuanaitu arrives, she goes ahead to look for her mother, who, as the girl explains, will put Makonaura to a first test by offering him two calabashes to choose from, one full of blood and flesh, the other full of wine and bread. Makonaura chooses the latter and thereby wins the consent of the elderly woman to his marriage. It is more difficult to overcome the resistance of Anuanaitus' father Kaikutschi,[16] because he is relentless and wants to avenge the kidnapping of his daughter with blood. After three days he agrees to see Makonaura. He gives him the test task to make a stool in one night, one side of which has to carry a jaguar's head, the other Kaikutschi's features. Around midnight the stool is finished except for Kaikuchi's head. Since he usually carries a calabash in front of his face, Makonaura has not yet seen his face. He crept into Kaikutschi's hut to try to see what his face looked like, but Kaikutschi lay in his hammock "rolled up in a ball". With the help of an army of ants that stabs him, Makonaura succeeded in seeing the "terrible face." But that was not enough, he was given a second task, to "build a hut whose entire roof is made from the finest feathers, in one night." This time the young man thought he was really lost. But then suddenly, thousands upon thousands of hummingbirds and other birds flew to him, all with wonderful plumage. The cabin was finished before sunrise. That was the end of the difficult tests and Kaikutschi made Makonaura a member of the family and the honorable husband of Anuanaitu.

422 Several months passed and then Makonaura yearned to see his mother again. He had to return home without Anuanaitu. When he traveled a second time to the Anuanaitus clan, he was warned not to visit Kaikutschi. Makonaura did not heed them. Kaikutschi awaited him on the threshold of his hut and with a stroke of his club, he laid down at his feet and shot him with an arrow in the forehead between his two eyes. An owl reports Makanauro's death to his mother, who takes her son's body home in her boat. At the funeral ceremony two men vow

[16] Kaikutschi = caiman, alligator in the Arawak language. Note by Koch-Grünberg.

to avenge Makonaura. One is the soul of a giant snake, the other the soul of a jaguar. They go and kill Kaikutschi and his relatives at a drinking festival. But Anuanaitu, who did not take part in the feast, finds her dead brother and "With a vibrant voice, she began to sing the terrible Kenaimu song. She also danced. The soul of a rattlesnake had taken possession of her!" She went to Makonaura's mother. There, in the hut so full of memories, "Anuanaitu felt a terrible battle rising up in her soul, a battle of love for what she called her duty. But when she heard the words, 'You are now happy, my son, for thou hath been avenged in the blood!' impressing in her ears, she could think no more! Furious, she threw herself on the old woman, grasped her tongue, pulled it out of her mouth and drove in the fangs of the rattlesnake."

423 Anuanaitu told the dying woman that the caiman that her son had killed at the fish trap was Anuanaitus' brother. She had forgiven Makonaura, but her father had avenged his son. The relatives of Makonaura had now slain her, Anuanaitu's father and all her relatives. She would also be able to forgive this if they had only spared her mother, "the most precious thing she had ever had." So she spoke, and with a terrible cry she fled into the forest. "With a frightful, awesome scream, nature experienced an unprecedented change. The winds responded with a howl that tore down trees and uprooted everything along the path that Anuanaitu took. Thick clouds hid the sun god's face and ominous lightning struck into the darkness accompanied by terrible peals of thunder. A deluge of rain mingled with the emergence of springs. The animals, who had until now been peaceful, began killing each other. The snake began to bite, the caiman clashed his terrible jaws, and the jaguar tore up and devoured the innocent agouti.

424 Anuanaitu continued her fearful run and with her passing tore up all wild guests of the forest. She came to the summit of a huge rock from which a waterfall tumbled down. There, on the edge of the abyss, she stretched out her arms, leaned over and sprang into the void. The water in the depths took her in and closed over her. At that place you can see now only a terrible abyss. Even today, should a stranger pass by a certain waterfall, the Arawaks will warn him not to speak its name. This would surely bring his death, for at the bottom of these waters, Makonaura and Anuanaitu dwell together in the wonderful palace of the goddess who is the soul and the spirit of the waters."[17]

---

[17] Koch-Grünberg, *Südamerika*, pp. 40–52. [Translated from the German. The original source is given as P. C. van Coll, *Contes et Legendes des Indiens de Surinam*; in: Anthropos, vols. 2 and 3, 1907 and 1908. A version of the English text is also included in Hartley Burr Alexander, "Latin-American Mythologies," in: Herbert Louis Gray (ed.), *Mythology of All Races*, vol. 2, Boston, 1920, pp. 262-268.]

425 The spirits of the underwater kingdom gain access through an encroachment on the hero, he gains a magical girl, but only after he unknowingly and unintentionally kills her daemonic alligator brother. He accepts only the beautiful appearance of the magical kingdom and does not accept its animal, instinctive dark side. He violates the spiritual power of his tribe in that he kills the totem animal from whom, as a caiman, his people emerged. The totem animal is for the primitive taboo, and the slaying of a representative of this genus, due to the deep identity of the members of the tribe[18] with the totem animal, as the murder of a tribal brother and of his own totem ancestor, even as the murder of the totem divinity itself. Primitive man sees in the totem animal, as stated above, an "older brother" or the "old grandfather." Each person is the reincarnation of an ancestor or the spiritual substance of an animal from the *Alcheringa* time.[19]

426 As a result of this debt, Makonaura and his wife must confront the mysterious god in the center of the magical world.[20] The most important test of the hero is to gaze at the "horrible face" and to map out his features, even though the god himself disguises his terrible side, and wants to remain anonymous. To see the lethal aspect of the unconscious is so frightening that only a few elected ones can bear the sight.[21] Kaikutschi's face is that of an alligator. The Maya of Yucatan imagine the crocodile to be a fish-like creature, from which the Earth was made.[22] The Egyptian crocodile god, Sobek, was a god of the Nile (which was believed to have come from his sweat) who was worshipped at the places where celebrations were performed at the initiation of the Nile flooding. He gave life to vegetation and fertility to the land. The "Lord of the Waters" was believed to have risen from the primeval waters of Nun to create the world. This worship was carried so far that Sobek was described as having a "beautiful face." Possibly, as Erman has written, nourishment of the Earth was the purpose of the prayers,[23] particularly as the

---

[18] Lévy-Bruhl called this mystical identity of the tribal members, both among themselves and with animals and objects, *participation mystique*. See his *How Natives Think*, New York, 1966, chap. 2; see also Bächtold-Stäubli under *Sympathie*.

[19] [The dream time of the Australian Aborigines.] See Lévy-Bruhl, *The "Soul" of the Primitive*, pp. 28, 49, 50, 186, and *How Natives Think*, pp. 90, 92.

[20] In a certain way, here is a hint of the primitive stage of the Oedipus problem. Like Oedipus, Makonaura unwittingly kills an ancestor (here the totem ancestor), and binds himself to the female relatives and brings a terrible fate upon himself. [Interestingly, H. B. Alexander, "Latin-American Mythologies," Boston, 1920, p. 268 makes a similar remark after retelling "Makonaura and Anuanaitu:" "Here we have an American *Job* or *Oedipus*, presenting, as *Job* presents, the problem of evil; and, like Greek tragedy, portraying the harsh conflict between inexorable justice of the law of retribution and the loves and mercies which combat it, in the savage heart perhaps not less than in the civilized."]

[21] On the fatal consequences of viewing the realm of the dead, see Lévy-Bruhl, *How Natives Think*, pp. 119–120.

[22] See "The Creation" (Aztec), collected in Krickeberg, *Azteken and Inka*, pp. 4–5; see also Ibid., "Deity and world view of the Maya of Yucatan," note 27, p. 373.

[23] Erman, *Religion der Ägypter*, pp. 44–45.

crocodile was the enemy of Horus (Re-Harakhty) and is called "Stinkface" in the *Book of Apophis*. Also the hell dog had a crocodile head.[24]

427 In the personage of Kaikutschi, the same threatening aspect of the unconscious appears to Makonaura as Kaikutschi's son did, only now more sinister and menacing, as always when a person tries to keep the unconscious at bay. It tends to take on various forms, and it should have been clear to Makonaura as a result of his view of the unity of the tribe, that the god of the depths had already approached him in the guise of his son.

428 The stool that Makonaura completed had on one side the features of a caiman, and on the other side of a jaguar. It can be presumed, therefore, that the god of the depths also occasionally takes on the latter form. He has two faces, therefore, which expressed the two aspects of his nature.[25] For the Aztecs, the jaguar is the demon of the darkness of the Earth, and therefore, the gods of darkness are depicted in the shape of jaguars. The jaguar eats the sun during solar eclipses.[26] When Makonaura succeeded in representing the two faces of the dark god on his stool, according to the native view, he captured and recorded those parts of the god's being that he tries so hard to conceal. Although Makonaura then had to come to some kind of agreement with Kaikutschi, he could, especially after he had returned to the profane world, not bear the nature of the dark god and succumbed to him, and was killed by Kaikutschi. This act of revenge now causes a whole series of terrible disasters, ending in a general destruction, which even included the whole of nature. Anuanaitu, in her awesome run, unleashed raging storms, thunder, darkness, and floods. The magical powers of nature, including the animals, now show their evil sides. But in the waters, that is, the unconscious, the lovers are finally united and continue to live eternally as water spirits.[27] They have now become *eidola* or *imagines*, who tarry under the waterfall. This is a return to the primordial ground. The murder of the animal ancestor indicates psychologically a detachment from this life source, a dissociation. Because it was done without awareness, it was followed by a destructive flooding of the unconscious, an outbreak and a whole chain of affects, in which all the contents that had previously emerged now sink back into the depths. The archetypal image of a reunited loving couple, which rests timelessly at the

[24] Roeder, *Urkunden*, pp. 112, 123, 281.

[25] In Egypt, the crocodile that attacks the body of Osiris has the name "two faces" [turning face]. See Roeder, *Urkunden*, p. 87.

[26] See Krickeberg, *Azteken and Inka*, pp. 6–7. See also the myth, "World Time Age," where Tezcatlipoca, the ancient sun god, transforms into a jaguar, which now carried off the new sun in a storm; see Krickeberg, *Azteken and Inka*, p. 5 [Tezcatlipoca's nagual, his animal counterpart, was the jaguar and his jaguar aspect was the deity Tepeyollotl ("Mountainheart").] For a description of the Egyptian underworld sun (god of death) as "the lord of the two faces," see Roeder, *Urkunden*, p. 259.

[27] In folk belief, emotional outbursts are in close relationship with the spirits. On the personification of emotions as demons see C.G. Jung, "Spirit and Life," in: Sir Herbert Read et al. (eds.), *The Structure and Dynamics of the Psyche*, 2nd ed.; see also CW 8, ¶627 f.

bottom of the waters, i.e., the unconscious, and is dangerous for passers-by, is a symbol of the eternal continuation of an indestructible spirit hidden in the waters. This latter continues to threaten the world of human consciousness.[28]

429 Just as in this story the totem ancestors appear to have been raised to individual divine forms of general significance, tales from other native cultures indicate that the genius of animals and plants have coalesced into a kind of guardian spirit of nature. For instance, in another Siberian tale, "A Lamut Man Turned Into Stone," a cruel Lamut (a neighboring tribe to the Yukaghir of Siberia) had a vision. "High on the rock there stood an old man, large and white, as high as the sky." This great guardian spirit had come to punish him for his cruelty and disregard for his fellow men.[29] Elsewhere, the great guardian spirit can take the form of "the Lord of the Forests." As far as the forest represents the unconscious, this guardian spirit can be regarded as a personification of the whole magical realm.[30] He is described vividly in the fairytale, "A Tale About the Wood-Master," from the Yukaghir people of the Siberian tundra:

430 A poor Lamut hunter once desired to see the Wood-Master [i.e., lord of the forest animals] for himself. The next morning he set off to examine his deadfalls and all at once he became caught in a heavy snowstorm. He lost his way and struggled on not knowing where he was going. All at once, not far off, he saw a huge iron sledge. An iron reindeer-buck just as big was attached to the sledge, and a black-faced man as tall as a larch tree was walking along with enormous strides. He asked himself, "What are these? I wanted to see the Wood-Master. Goodness! Is this not the Wood-Master himself, with his appurtenances?" He was so frightened that he cried aloud, "God help me!" In a moment the iron sledge broke into a number of small pieces, and the iron buck was shattered to ashes. The tall man, however, did not fall at all. He looked at the man, and called angrily, "You, man! Come over here!" So the man went to the Wood-Master and awaited his words. "What have you done to my property?" cried the Wood-Master. "You have broken my sledge, you have destroyed my driving-reindeer, and you have even frightened me. I was frightened no less than you. And now you want me to walk on foot! I will not. You must

---

[28] The water spirit can also be positive; see the Native American myth, "The Traveler," Radin pp. 182–186, of a young man who is about to undertake an underworld journey to the water spirits. Before he sets out, he seeks the blessings of his ancestors who respond to him as their "grandchild." On the ancestral cult among the Greeks, see Rohde, *Psyche*, vol. I, pp. 167–168, 170–171.

[29] For the complete fairytale, see Bogoras, *Tales of the Yukaghir*, 1918, pp. 34–35.

[30] The Japanese know of the forest spirit Amanoyaku who eats children who have stayed at home alone and carelessly open up the door to strangers. See Rumpf (ed.), *Japanische Volksmärchen*, (*MdW*), ed. Fr. v. d. Leyen, 1938, p. 11.

> repair my sledge, and restore to life my driving reindeer- buck. This is the task that you must perform."

> 431 Then the black giant set off. The Lamut walked around some small bushes, saying "Sledge, O sledge! Be whole again! Buck, O buck! Be whole again!" And, indeed, the sledge and the buck were whole, as before. Then he touched the reindeer-buck with his right hand. "Buck, O buck! Come to life!" But the buck remained without life and motion. He touched the buck with his left hand, and said likewise, "Buck, O buck, come to life again!" And, indeed, the reindeer-buck gave a start and came to life. "Ah, ah!" said the Lamut, "where are you, black giant, Forest-Owner?" At once the black giant appeared. "Oh, it is all right! What do you want me to pay you for this? I can give you immense wealth." – "I do not wish any wealth at all. I want plenty of food for all of my life." – "All right, go home! You shall have as much food as you want. Have no care. Go home and sleep! Tomorrow morning go into the forest, and set there five large self-acting bows. They shall give you ample food." The Lamut went home. His wife said to him, "O husband! I thought you would never come back home. It is several days since I last saw you!" – "I was caught in a heavy snowstorm, so I sat crouching under the steep bank, before a small fire." – "What snowstorm?" asked the old woman in great wonder. "We have not had the slightest trace of any storm." The next morning the Lamut went into the woods and set five self-acting bows; and that very night five big elks were killed. He took them home. After that, he would catch five elks every time. He collected a great mass of meat and a number of skins, and so became very rich. He lived in plenty until his death.[31]

432 The black giant embodies the living spirit of the forest and, therefore, he can drive the animals, the life sustenance of the people of the tundra, to the devoted and correct Lamut and Yukaghir. In this, he recalls the spirit of the moon in "Flight to the Moon." The fact that a call of the hunter destroys his equipment, recalls how in "Blue-Jay Visits his Sister Io'i in the Land of the Dead," the call of Blue-Jay causes all items in the land of spirits suddenly to disintegrate and appear worthless. As stated above, the motif can be explained by the fact that the sound of his own voice shocks the man into conscious awareness of his own confusion, and releases him from being trapped in his unconscious state. Comparison with parallel motifs indicates that the Lamut in the above tale had slipped into dreamland.

[31] Slightly shortened from W. Bogoras, *Tales of the Yukaghir*, pp. 10 –12: "told by John Korkin, a Tundra Yukaghir, on the western tundra of the Kolyma country, spring of 1895."

433 In some regions of Europe, the figure of a "Lord of the Forest" also lives on. In the Celtic legend, "Owein, or the Countess of the Fountain," from *The Mabinogion*, Kynon reports on his adventures to Owein in the chambers of King Arthur. At the outset, Kynon was advised by an unknown man about where he should travel:

> 434 "Since you wish me to tell you of evil rather than good, I will do so. Spend the night here, and tomorrow rise and take the road that brought you to this valley until you reach the wood, which you passed through, and a short distance into that wood you will find a fork: take the right hand path and continue until your come to a great cleared field with a mound at the center, and on that mound in the centre you will see a great black man, no smaller than two men of this world. He has one foot, and one eye in the middle of his forehead and he carries an iron spear that you can be certain would be a burden for any two men. Though ugly, he is not an unpleasant man. He is keeper of the forest, and you will see a thousand wild animals grazing about him. Ask him where to go from the clearing; he will be cross with you, but nevertheless he will show you how to find what you seek."
>
> 435 That night seemed endless. In the morning I rose and dressed and mounted my horse and set out for the valley and the forest, and I found the fork in the road and the clearing that the man had described. When I arrived, the wild animals I saw were three times as pleasing as the man had said. The black man was sitting on the mound; my host had told me he would be big, but he was far bigger than I expected, and as for the iron spear, which was to be a burden for two men, Kei! I am certain it would be a burden for four warriors and yet this black man held it in his hand. I greeted him but he replied uncivilly, so I asked him what power he held over the animals. "Little man, I will show you," he said, and he took a cudgel and struck a stag a great blow so that it roared; with that wild animals gathered to him like stars gather in the sky on a clear night. There was scarcely room for me to stand among the serpents and vipers and lions and animals of all sorts. The black man looked at them and ordered them to graze, and they bowed their heads and worshipped him as obedient men worship their lord.[32]

436 The great Celtic-Britannic magician Merlin, the "face and voice of the forest," as Zimmer calls him, is also such a figure. He lives in the enchanted forest in

[32] Gautz, *Mabinogion*, pp. 196–197.

the valley of no return, is a soul guide, and a master of initiations.[33] In volume II of the present work, we will discuss the Russian fairytale, "Och," about a farmer in the forest who once sat down on a charred tree stump and groaned, "Och!" Then a small old man with wrinkles and a green beard down to his knees appears and reveals himself as the forest king Och. He later proves to be a powerful, part helpful, part evil wizard. The Indians of South America know of a strange forest spirit they call *Curupira*. He is the guardian spirit of the woods and master of the wild animals. He can do good and evil, he eats people, and also gives the hunters lucky snake arrows. The tribesmen call him "Grandfather." He often appears angry, rude, brash, and again good-natured, weak, stupid, or compassionate. To him are attributed the crashing of trees and the knocking of woodpeckers. He shows people medicinal plants. In the Amazon, he appears as a small man, not three feet in height, bald, but the rest of his body covered with long hair. He has only one eye, features blue or green teeth, his feet are always bent backward and he has exceptional physical strength. He lives in hollow trees and imitates all animals. Those who get lost in the forest have been enchanted by Curupira. Sometimes Curupira lets himself be killed then he comes back to life.[34] The Ainu have a similar figure, as described in the tale, "A Hobgoblin Originates Flies":

437 > "Once upon a time," they say, "many years ago, there was a great demon, who had his home far away in the midst of the mountains of Ainu-land..." In bodily shape he was like a man. He was exceedingly large, and was closely covered with hair; in fact, his skin was like that of a bear, so hairy was he. He had but one eye, however, and that was situated in the middle of his forehead, and it was as large as a common pot lid. This creature was a very great nuisance to the Ainu, for he had such a tremendous appetite that he was actually in the habit of catching, killing, and eating everything and everybody coming in his way. For this reason the people were afraid to go far into the mountains to hunt, for, though the one-eyed monster had been shot at many times, no arrow had yet made any effect upon him. Now it happened one day that a brave hunter, who was an expert with the bow, unknowingly went near the haunt of the cannibal. While he was in the midst of his pursuit of game he was astonished to see something brightly glaring at him through the undergrowth of the forest. Upon drawing near to see what it was he discovered it to be the big-bodied, hairy, fierce-looking demon.

---

[33] Zimmer, "Merlin," p. 265.

[34] See "The Snake Arrow," a tale from Rio Branca Tupi (NW Brazil), including the notes by Koch-Grünberg, *Südamerika*, pp. 323–324.

438 When he saw what it was, the hunter became so frightened that he knew not what to do. As soon as he mustered sufficient courage, however, he drew an arrow from his quiver, and, fitting it to his bow, stood on the defensive. As the creature drew nigh the Ainu took a steady and deadly aim at his solitary eye, and, being a good shot, hit it fair in the centre. The demon immediately fell down dead, for the eye was the vital– the only vital – part of his body. To make sure that so foul a creature and so deadly an enemy was quite killed, and would not come to life again to trouble the people, the brave hunter made a great bonfire over his body, and burnt it quite up, bones and all. When this was done he took the ashes in his hands and scattered them in the air, so as to make doubly sure that the monster was thoroughly destroyed. But lo, the ashes became gnats, mosquitoes, and gadflies as they were tossed up-ward. However, we must not grumble at these things, for the lesser evil of flies is not so bad as the greater evil of having the one-eyed man-eating monster amongst us.[35]

439 Another tale from a Samoyed-speaking people in Siberia, "The One-Sided Old Man," depicts an eerie, ghostly vision of the image of the father or the old man in the soul:

440 Once upon a time stood seven hundred tents and there lived seven hundred people. Seven lords ruled them. These seven would go around as guests to their people but themselves never did anything. The seven were brothers and had seven women, but no children. Only the oldest had one son, who was small. The boy did not go around, but slept day and night. One day he woke up and saw that the whole tribe had been destroyed in one night.[36] He then embarked on a long hike to other people. He found a woman there, but she was hostile to him and attacked him again and again. He was then killed by one of the enemies. Soon after came a one-legged, one-handed, and one-eyed old graybeard. In his hand he carried an iron rod. He hit the dead with his rod and said, 'Why are you lying there? It's time to get up! Get up and go back, your father lives, and all your brothers are alive again.' The dead man woke up and began talking to himself, 'I must have

[35] J. Batchelor, *Ainu Folklore*, London, 1891, pp. 73–74. For the Thonga tribe (Africa), ". . . the dead do show themselves in human shape in the sacred forest, but very rarely. Far more frequently they appear in animal disguise, as the praying mantis, for instance, or the small blue grey snakes..." A member of the tribe relates that "I went to the [sacred] wood, too, and then it came out. It was a snake, the father of Makoundjou, the master of the forest, Elephant-Face"; see H. A. Junod, *Ba-Ronga*, Neuchatel, 1898, pp. 392–93, cited in Lévy-Bruhl, *The "Soul" of the Primitive*, p. 296.

[36] [The rest of this tale has been shortened and summarized by von Beit and von Franz. The original tale is told in the present tense. We have translated their summary, using the past tense to conform with the other tales in this volume.]

slept for a long time. But what kind of a man was that who told me that my father lives and I should go home?' When he looked around, he saw no one, that is why he thought he must have been dreaming. Despite what the old man said, he did not return to his home and again was beaten and killed. This happened repeatedly until he beat his opponents so hard that they died. Then the old man reappeared and carried the bones of the hero into a cave.

441 He found himself in a dark place where he heard screams, whistling, and singing. People tried to snatch away the sack that the old man was carrying. Straight in front of him he saw something bright, like a window. By this light he saw that the people were naked, without skin, without coverings, and just bare bones. Their teeth grinned in their mouths. The old man walked up to the light, he saw a tent and entered it. Inside was no one but a woman who sat on the hearth. On the other side were two monsters who neither moved nor spoke. Their eyes were very large and lay on the top of their heads facing upwards. The old man threw the bag on the floor and said to the woman, 'Here you have firewood, throw it into the fire.' 'That is good, what you brought,' said the woman, 'I was already completely without wood.' The old woman lit a fire and threw in the bones from the sack, and they all burned to ashes. She took the ashes out, scattered them over the bed and then lay down to sleep on the ashes. After three days a man was born from the ashes.

442 This man had a terrible fear of the guardian animals[37] of the cave but finally found a way out. He had to marry the old woman at the hearth, however, as his second wife. He took her to his first home, and asked his first wife and her parents to join him. They did this and as they all approached his home, he saw all the seven hundred tents, many people, and many reindeer. All were alive again. A short ways away on the road, he saw the one-legged, one-handed, and one-eyed old man. The old one ran up to him, along with a different person, the one who had killed him three times. He began to beat his murderer, and knocked him down. Here he lost all his senses and in his frenzy killed the old one-eyed, one-handed man. Then he went back to the tents, but now all the people and reindeer lay dead. And the two women also died. So they all died, and he was alone again, after he had killed the one-legged, one-handed, and one-eyed old man.[38]

---

[37] [The woman calls them her "parents".]

[38] Kunike, *Sibirien*, Jena, 1940, pp. 13–22. For the original (German) version, see Castren, *Ethnologische*, St. Petersburg, 1857, pp. 157ff.

443 One can see clearly from this story that the daemonic old man guides the lives of all individuals and an entire tribe into the realm of the invisible. The cave where he lives seems to be some sort of kingdom of the dead with clear motifs of the afterlife. The enemy of the hero is another aspect of this one-sided old one. Together they build a unity, which is shown at the end where the hero kills both together. So this mysterious old man is at the same time a threatening and a helpful figure, and, considered together with the murderer, both a life-giver and a death-bringer. His one-sidedness indicates an impairment that also affects other similar mythological figures. As Jung points out, "The old man has therefore lost part of his eyesight – that is, his insight and enlightenment – to the daemonic world of darkness; this handicap is reminiscent of the fate of Osiris, who lost an eye at the sight of a black pig (his wicked brother Set), or again, Wotan, who sacrificed his eye at the spring of Mimir."[39] The good, useful side of the old man finds its dark complement to his wholeness in the murderer. Psychogically, such a manifestation usually indicates that the human being must liberate the spirit, adhering as it does to matter and darkness.

444 The transparent figures gain life through the old glass windows since the light penetrates them; their colors testifying to the nature of that light. Similarly, the psychic images reveal the nature of the archetype that becomes visible through their various manifestations. It is the archetype of the spirit reflected in the soul,[40] therein irradiating and mixing with the human, that produces the wide variety of images of the daemonic old man, which set humans in reverent fear. So far we have met with the overpowering father figure as a giving or killing ancestor, the daemonic father of the magical bride in the depths of the waters, or as the old one who suffers through being stuck in matter.

445 This archetypal figure of a revered father deity that is still in its full double aspect is particularly prevalent in fairytales of primitive peoples. In European tales, such images also play a role in as much as their motifs come largely from a pre-Christian epoch. However, the Christian cultural overlay masks the original image, which is often difficult to discern. One example occurs in the Grimm's fairytale, "Ferdinand the Faithful and Ferdinand the Unfaithful,"[41] where an unknown beggar appears as godfather of the hero. The beggar gives the hero a key to a magic castle where he later finds his magical horse. In French and Hanoverian versions of this tale, the unknown beggar is none

---

[39] C.G. Jung, "Archetypes of the Collective Unconscious," CW 9i, ¶413.

[40] On the idea of reflection in the soul, see Meister Eckhart, Sermon 27 (Matthew 10:28): "The reflection in the mirror lying in the sun is the sun but it is also what it is in itself. It is the same with God. God is in the soul with his essence, his being and his divinity, and yet he is not in the soul. The reflection of the soul is God in God, and yet she, the soul, is what she is in herself"; see Meister Eckhart, *Selected Writings*, trans. Oliver Davies, London, 1994, p. 232.

[41] [Retold and discussed below; see p. 408.]

other than the Lord God himself. According to a Dutch version, he is the devil. In yet other versions, this godfather proves to be identical with the beautiful mount of the hero that appears later in the tale.[42] The designation, "God" or "Devil," is thus a later name for a figure that in its original unitary form contained both sides of the deity and probably corresponded to an ancient Indo-European pagan god. The unknown beggar most likely points to Odin/Woden. Güntert describes this primordial god as follows:

446 It is usual . . . to view Odin/Woden above all as a god of death, the Lord of Wild Hunt, the *Seelenscharen* [host of wild souls] who the roar of the storm, as in the wild huntsmen or the Black Riders of folk legend . . . so much appears . . . sure that Odin/Woden in the north inherited traits that are familiar to the ancient "World Lords" and "World Wizards," traits that he has in common with the Vedic Varuna, who had close ties. . . with Yama, the god of death. Woden is the master of the world and king of the gods, and like Varuna, he looks from the highest heaven down to the earth in the morning, the sun is his eye. . . The blue cloak is a widely used symbol of power like scepter and crown, it is the divine, star-embroidered heavenly cloak. It is known indeed from a later period from the epithet *Hakelberend*, "coat-bearers," like Faust's magic cloak, that empowered Odin to be carried through the air (Saxo I, 40). This cloak is called sometimes dark, sometimes blue, as is said of Varuna. Odin was always "changing the light and dark garments."[43] But above all, Odin is the lord and master of magic, he is the magician and rune master par excellence, and all that was imaginable in spirituality and world wisdom that the ancient German could imagine: his many names, his ability to transform himself, his knowledge of runes, everything is based on this. Even his name suggests the basic nature of this god as a magician. [44]

447 Closely related to the views of natural cultures are the mythical ideas about the "father" in more civilized cultures in which the people still believe in a

[42] See Bolte and Polívka, *Anmerkungen*, vol. 3, pp. 18ff.

[43] See the blue coat of the old man in the "The Isle of Utrost."

[44] Güntert, *Weltkönig*, pp. 152–153. The Indian god Shiva is closely related to this archetypal figure. According to Heinrich Zimmer, he is the lord of animals, master of all the horrors, ghosts, and demons; the wandering stranger. He is the daemonic ruler of the wilderness, he who sends the fever arrows, and so strange that one only dared to perform sacrifices to him outside the town walls on the march; see his *Maya*, pp. 417, 473–475. [The *Bhagavata Purana*, 3.14.23–24, mentions a connection to the wild huntsman and flock of souls, "This particular time is most inauspicious because at this time the horrible-looking ghosts and constant companions of the lord of the ghosts are visible. Lord Shiva, the king of the ghosts, sitting on the back of his bull carrier, travels at this time, accompanied by ghosts who follow him for their welfare."]

pagan pantheon. Some stories therefore integrate well-known mythological figures or take place in their temples. These stories depict how ritually revered gods are experienced anew in the unconscious or help to mediate unconscious experience. This is the case in the Chinese fairytale, "The Dangerous Reward":

> 448 Once upon a time a man named Hu-Wu-Bau, who lived nearby, went walking on the Great Mountain. Under a tree, he met a messenger in a red robe who called out to him, "The Lord of the Great Mountain would like to see you!" The man was much frightened, but dared offer no objection. The messenger bade him shut his eyes, and when he was allowed to open them again after a short time, he found himself standing before a lofty palace. He entered it to see the divine one. The latter had a meal prepared for him and said, "I sent for you today because I had heard you intended to travel to the West. And in that case I should like to give you a letter to take to my daughter. She is married to the river-god. All you need to do is to take along the letter lying there. When you reach the middle of the Yellow River, beat against the side of the ship and call out: 'Greencoat!' Then someone will appear and take the letter from you." And with these words he handed Hu-Wu-Bau the letter, and he was taken back to the upper World.
>
> 449 Once on his journey to the West, when he came to the Yellow River he did what the Lord of the Great Mountain had told him, and cried, "Greencoat!" And sure enough, a girl in green garments rose from the water, took him by the hand and told him to close his eyes. Then she led him into the palace of the river-god and Hu-Wu-Bau delivered the letter. The river-god entertained him splendidly, and thanked him as best he knew how. At parting he said, "I am grateful that you have made this long journey to see me. I have nothing to give you, however, save this pair of green silk shoes. While you are wearing them you can keep on walking as long as you like and never grow weary. And they will give you second sight, so that you will be able to see the spirits and gods." The man thanked him for the gift and returned.
>
> 450 One year later back home, the man visits the Lord of the Great Mountain to report what had transpired. The Lord greets him, invites him to his court and thanks him generously. Walking around the courtyard, the man suddenly sees his deceased father in chains, who has to do unworthy service together as punishment for stepping on some bread. The father asks the son to put in a good word for him, so that he can become a field god in his native village. The mountain god shows himself inclined to the requests of Hu-Wu-Bau, but he warns:

> "The quick and the dead tread different paths. It is not well for the dead and the living to abide near one another permanently." After Hu-Wu-Bau return home, all his children soon died one after the other. In fear the man returns to the mountain god who reminds him of his warning, but then calls the father. "I forgave you your offense and sent you back to your home as a field-god. It was your duty to bring happiness to your family. Instead, nearly all of your grandchildren have died off. Why is this?" The father said: "I had been away from home so long that I was overjoyed to return. Besides I had meat and drink in overflowing measure. So I thought of my little grandchildren and called them to me.' Then the Lord of the Great Mountain appointed another field-god for that village, and also gave the father another place. And from that time no further misfortune happened to the family of Hu-Wu-Bau.[45]

451 Wilhelm, who recounts this tale, adds in a note that the Lord of the Great Mountain was originally Huang Fe-Hu, a faithful servant of the tyrant Dschou-Sin. Because of an insult against him, he joined King Wu. When the latter overcame the tyrant, Huang Fe-Hu was made Lord of the Mountain and overlord of the ten princes of the nether world.[46] He stands above the god of death; his temple, which is located in every county town, plays an important role in preparing the dead for burial. He presides over "good and evil, reward and punishment, life and death of the people," and rules "over the ten Princes of Hell."[47]

452 Hu-Wu-Bau's experience of the unconscious is projected onto this well known divine figure. Or one could also say that the father archetype appears to Hu-Wu-Bau in the form of the Lord of the Great Mountain. Hu-Wu-Bau lives near the mountains, that is, the magical region. Psychologically, this means that he is inclined to give free reign to his inner visions, and therefore can see the red-dressed messenger of the magical world. The color red often characterizes demons, ghosts, and spirits.[48] The closing of the eyes indicates

---

[45] Wilhelm, *The Chinese Fairy Book*, New York, 1921, pp. 174–177, shortened.

[46] Wilhelm, *The Chinese Fairy Book*, p. 177.

[47] See "Nü Wa," in: Wilhelm, ibid., pp. 51–55 and footnote to "The Constable," p. 177. See also Odin/Woden as "Ancient from the Mountains," i.e., as a god of death. See Mogk, *Germanische*, p. 72; on the deified Grecian heroes now living in enraptured retreat in caves or mountains, see also Rohde, *Psyche*, vol. I, pp. 89f. and 92f.

[48] SSee Bächtold-Stäubli under *rot* [red]. Those authors delve into wider meaning of the term red in the folk views. Sometimes, red stands close to brown, such as in "red" cow and has the general meaning of "beautiful." The color red in popular tradition can often be traced back to magic, as exciting and warming psychological effect, red occupies the most active end of the scale. Due to its luminosity, something red generally acquires the attribute of seriousness and royal power and use in a cult implies an appropriate magnificence of the deity. "In this way, the concept of the Holy Divine attaches itself to the color purple."

sinking or diving inside, as stated in the first chapter of this book [see page 17].

453 At first, Hu-Wu-Bau experiences only the lighter side of the magical kingdom, where he is well received. In this respect, the Lord of the Underworld is a God-image and as such part of the hero's soul. It originated there and is intricately interwoven with his soul. He[49] knows the hero's conscious plans, namely, in this case, to embark on a trip to the West. In the guise of the river god, the magical kingdom shows its benevolent side. The shoes that Hu-Wu-Bau receives as a gift confer a special power, they carry the color of nature and water, the magical world and make their wearer clairvoyant. As a result, he suddenly can see the "other," dark side of the mountain god in that he now recognizes his tormented father. But then it turns out that the degrading services required by the mountain god are a result of a crime against nature since bread, upon which the father had evidently trodden, is a vital substance and, therefore, must be treated as holy.[50] The father would be happy to be rehabilitated as a field god. Since Hu-Wu-Bau meets his father while walking in his own interior, the father must then be regarded as a part of his own being. Hu-Wu-Bau's petition for his father shows that he believes that atonement for the offense can be easily acquired. But he thereby misses the warning of the mountain god and the situation becomes dangerous for the living. The ghostly father magnetically attracts his grandchildren into the realm of the dead. With demonic, irresistible force the dead destroy the living, when the separation of the two kingdoms is not absolutely upheld. Since Hu-Wu-Bau would like to have his inner transgression forgiven without a propitiating sacrifice, he must endure punishment and involuntarily lose his children. He tried to usher the dark culpable part of his soul into his daily life without expiation in his daytime world. He must experience that the deeper will of his soul is stronger and threatens the conscious attitude. The message, "I am stronger than you," from the unconscious part of his being is expressed in the fact that it has become a nature god. A renewed and more humble devotion to the demands of this magic realm would arrest the destructive fate; but this still does not remove the polarity between the two worlds.

454 The righteous goodness of the Lord of the Great Mountain reveals yet another positive aspect of the father archetype, which goes beyond the giving of goods: that of wisdom. Human beings of all epochs have needed an inner guide to help them master the trials of life. This necessity has prompted humans to see in particular individuals, gods, or deified inspired personalities, the epitome of all abilities that they are seeking. When one is confronted by this drive, the archetype of the father often appears, carrying the image of the

---

49 [i.e. the godhead, Self, Lord of the Underworld.]

50 [The authors here suggest that any transgression, even if unconscious – or perhaps exactly because it is unconscious – should be taken seriously and correctly atoned for.]

god-like or deified advisor.[51] Not only the Chinese god, Lord of the Great Mountain, was once a man who had distinguished himself by wisdom. Also Byamee in the tale, "A Legend of Flowers," now guardian of the flowers and master of the magic arts, was once a medicine man and magician who was enraptured and taken up into the sphere of the gods. He has lived ever since on a mountain in heaven and sits on a throne of crystal clear water bordered on both sides by high crystal pillars. His son guides the souls of people to Byamee after they die. His son also created the first man who once visited Byamee by climbing up a spiral staircase and then further a ladder to heaven to receive the laws from him. Byamee was a healer and later venerated as the all-father, the creator and also the god of death. "But no man must look upon his face, lest surely he shall die."[52]

455 Insofar as this figure is equipped with all the mysterious attributes of the father god of the magical kingdom and also was once a great medicine man and mortal,[53] it corresponds to the "archetype of the mighty man in the form of the hero, chief, magician, medicine-man, saint, ruler of men and spirits, the friend of God."[54] The figure of the wise old man is in possession of secret names or esoteric knowledge;[55] "he is the superior master and teacher . . . a sage of the ways, of the pre-existent, of the meaning hidden in the chaos of life."[56] In Indian philosophy, he is called:

456 The wise who, by means of meditation on his Self,
recognizes the Ancient, who is difficult to be seen,
who has entered into the dark,
who is hidden in the cave,
who dwells in the abyss,
as God, he indeed leaves joy and sorrow far behind.[57]

---

[51] On the concept of the "numinous old one," see Bächtold-Stäubli under *Alte Mann* [old man].

[52] [Yahweh said exactly the same to Moses.] See the tale from the Noongahbourrah tribe: "The Borah of Byamee," collected in Parker, *More Australian*, London, 1898, pp. 94–105; see also the notes in Hambruch, *Südsee*, p. 342; see further G. v. d. Leeuw, *Religion in Essence*, vol. 1, p. 162f.

[53] See "A Shawnee Legend," in which a pious and affectionate brother so grieved the loss of his beloved sister that he resolved to follow her. Traveling a long way, past where the sky and earth meet, he came to the abode of his grandfather. This wise medicine man transformed him into spirit so that he could pass into the celestial realm and gave him instructions on how to find and bring back his sister. After performing the deeds as advised, the brother returned to the earth with his sister, bringing sacred dances and other religious ceremonies for the tribe with them. Told in Gregg, *Commerce*, Philadelphia, 1855, pp. 239–240.

[54] C.G. Jung, "Relation between the ego and the unconscious," CW 7, ¶377. Natural peoples often look upon their elder men as guardians of the sacred tribal secrets; see Lévy-Bruhl, *The "Soul" of the Primitive*, pp. 215ff.

[55] See C.G. Jung, "Relation between the ego and the unconscious," CW 7, ¶393.

[56] C.G. Jung, "Archetypes of the Collective Unconscious," CW 9i, ¶74.

[57] *Katha-Upanishad* [First Adhyaya, First Valli, Verse 12; see Mueller, *Upanishads*, p. 10.]

457 In fairytales and folktales, the importance of this figure is usually hinted at with a few terse but vivid strokes. Some stories emphasize the more mysterious, daemonic traits of this character, others more the goodness and wisdom in the form of benevolence or guidance. Still others describe particularly the ruler of the dead, while a number of stories reveal the same powerful archetype in the form of a terrifying nature spirit. To these latter tales belongs "The Mountain Elf." The collector notes that "Mountain Elves are mountain spirits, they live in trees and rocks and love to scare people."

> 458 There once was a scholar who had retired to a mountain temple, to study. One summer evening he sat in the courtyard, enjoying the cool air. Suddenly he heard a blast, and the gate of the temple broke wide open. Out came a monster that looked like an ogre. It was ten feet tall and sat down on the roof. His legs were spread as thick as tree trunks, his hair was like an expanse of grassy undergrowth. The scholar hid in his room, shut the door tight, and crawled onto his bed. Crash! The door opened and the monster came straight into the room lit by the lantern. His face was several feet long and black as smoke and coal. He groped his way toward the bed. In his death agony the man, who did not know what else to do, grasped his sword and tried to pierce the ogre in the stomach, but the sword bounced off as a pebble from hard stone. The spirit became angry, yanked the sword from the scholar's hand and broke it in two like a dry twig. The man wrapped himself in his blankets, and the spirit seized him with his enormous fist, just as one reaches for a mosquito or a flea. But because his fingers were too clumsy, the scholar managed to escape and hid under the bed again. So the ogre was left holding only the blanket in his hand. And he went away.
>
> 459 When morning broke, the scholar returned home as fast as he could and never dared to go back to the mountain temple again.[58]

460 The appearance of this mountain demon is preceded by a gust of wind. A cool breeze is often a harbinger of ghosts. The wind (Greek: *α΄νεμος anemos* or *pneuma*) is a symbol of the spirit, of the spiritual principle in general.[59] The scholar, who is struggling in solitude to understand things mentally [i.e. by means of the spirit] experiences the negative aspect of the spirit, which

---

[58] [Translated from Wilhelm, *Chinesische Märchen*, 1958, pp. 132–133.]

[59] See Bernhard Schweitzer, *Herakles: Aufsätze zur griechischen Religions- und Sagengeschichte*, 1922, p. 75f., who reports that Greek *Tritopatores* (see p. 79) are simultaneously deceased fathers and wind demons.

prompts him not to go back so carelessly into spheres where he will be exposed to attacks of the spirit.

461 The god of death and the underworld appears not as a nature demon, but as lord of the dead in "How a Scholar Chastised the Princes of Hell." Once a drunken scholar insulted a God-image in the temple of the Lord of the Netherworlds. Suddenly a red devil stood with a tablet and called out in a harsh tone: King Yän summons you! The red devil dragged him through five chambers and then to the Mountain of Death. There, he beheld the ruler Yän Lo (Yama), "In the hall sat a king with a fringed hat, a scepter in his hand, wearing dark clothing and red, square shoes. His face was violet-black and shiny. His hair and eyebrows were red, and his mustache hung down like two long tassels. He leaned on his table and sat upright. To his right stood the head of an ox and to his right the face of a horse, both leaning on their spears." According to Richard Wilhelm, the translator, this description corresponds to popular conceptions of this figure.[60] The clothing of the highest of the gods of the dead (Yama) is that of a ruler, his fringe hat indicates his special crown. Yama is the one who imposed the punishments of hell according to the level of sins committed. He rules over the book of life in which is noted the year of death of every human being.[61]

462 In European fairytales, this figure of a secular ruler over life and death is personified as "Death," as in the Grimm's "Godfather Death":

> 463 Once upon a time there was an old man who already had twelve children, and when the thirteenth was born he did not know where to turn for help. In desperation he went into the woods. There the good Lord happened upon him and said to him, "I feel sorry for you, poor man. I will lift your child from his baptism and take care of him. He will be happy on earth." The man answered, "I do not want you as a godfather. You give to the rich and let the poor starve." With that he left him standing there and continued on his way. Soon thereafter Death happened upon him and also said to him, "I will be godfather for you and pick up your child. And if he has me as a friend, he will lack nothing. I will make a doctor of him." The man accepted the deal.
>
> 464 The next day, Death arrived and held the child for his baptism. After he had grown up, Death came again and took his godchild into the woods, and said to him, "Now you are to become a doctor. When you are called to attend to a sick person you must only pay attention to

[60] Wilhelm took this long narrative from a popular play [in the early 1900s]; see his *Chinesische Märchen*, pp. 383–384.

[61] See also A. Dieterich, *Nekyia*, Leipzig, 1893, pp. 47–48 on the idea of the Lord of the Underworld among the Greeks, who is dark blue or black in color and feasts on human flesh.

where I am standing. If I am standing at his head, without further ado let him smell from this flask, then anoint his feet with its contents, and he soon will regain his health. But if I am standing at his feet, then he is finished, for I will soon take him. Do not attempt even to begin a cure." Soon the young man became a famous and rich doctor, he only needed to see a patient, and he could immediately predict whether he would regain his health or die.

465 Once he was summoned to the king, who was suffering from a serious illness. When the doctor approached him, he saw Death standing at the king's feet, and knew that his flask would be of no use. But it occurred to him that he might deceive Death. Thus he took hold of the king and turned him around, so that Death was now standing at his head. This trick succeeded, and the king regained his health. After the doctor returned home, Death came to him, angry and grim-faced, but forgave him only because he is his godfather. Soon afterward the king's beautiful daughter took ill. The doctor came and saw Death standing at her feet. Astonished at her beauty, he forgot the warning, turned her around, let her smell from the healing flask, and anointed the soles of her feet with its contents. Instantly her cheeks flushed and life stirred afresh in her. On his way home, death grabs the doctor "with his ice-cold hand" and leads him into an underground cave.[62] There the physician saw how thousands and thousands of candles were burning in endless rows, some large, others medium-sized, others small. Every instant some died out, and others were relit, so that the little flames seemed to leap hither and thither in perpetual change. "Look!" said Death. "These are all the living. And here is a light that will burn only a little longer, and then go out. This is your life! Take heed!" When the doctor sees his own very small light, he is frightened and begs for a new light. Death pretended that he was going to fulfill this wish and took hold of a large new candle, but, desiring revenge, he purposely made a mistake in relighting it, and the little piece fell down and went out. The physician immediately fell to the ground, and now he himself was in the hands of Death.[63]

---

[62] In other versions, the doctor is led to the forest or to a castle; see Bolte and Mackensen, *Handwörterbuch*, under "Gevatter Tod" (The Godfather's Death).

[63] J. and T. Grimm, *Complete Grimm's*, London, 1975, pp. 209–212 [and Ashliman, *Grimms*, (1998-2009)]. For a friendlier but weaker variant, "The Poor Weaver who Sought a Godfather," see Zaunert, *Deutsche Märchen aus dem Donaulande*, p. 194. For a general account of the different versions by the Grimm Brothers, see Hermann Hamann, "Die literarischen Vorlagen der Kinder- und Hausmärchen und ihre Bearbeitung durch die Brüder Grimm," in: *Palaestra XLVII, Untersuchungen und Texte aus der deutschen und englischen Philologie*, vol. 47, eds. Alois Brandl, Gustav Roethe and Erich Schmidt, 1906, p. 69ff. On the use of this motif in folk poetry, see Johannes Bolte, "Das Märchen vom Gevatter Tod," in: *Zeitschrift des Vereins für Volkskunde*, ed. Karl Weinhold, vol. 4, 1894, no. 4, p. 34.

466 The Godfather is to be understood essentially as the "spiritual father."[64] Fairytales generally reflect emerging natural images from the unconscious. We witness in this tale a representation that latently exposes the lord of fate and a ruler of this world in a form containing and unifying both light and dark. Thus, the adopted child is neither a child of God nor a child of the devil, but rather from the beginning a "child of death" from which it receives his magical abilities.[65] Death is portrayed as that mysterious deity in its double aspect, a depiction aptly suited to the whole magic kingdom: he bestows the herb of life and guards the life-lights in the dark cave, which evidently he commands as he wishes.[66] The connection between death and life in one and the same figure was widespread before Christianity and represented as such in the Greek mysteries. We see that the figure of death was the carrier of the symbol for the deity of the magic kingdom, begging for reverence, albeit with contradictory attributes. The doctor has been given insight into the double-natured essence of this spirit, to whom he must relinquish his powers over the fate of the patient. Death indicates the connection to the areas of chthonic powers: when he stands at the head, where consciousness prevails, then the doctor can use his knowledge to heal. If Death stands at the feet, the connection to the earth, then the doctor has no power to heal.[67] It seems that the spirit is subject to this rule. If the human, however, misuses this linking of the spirit, that is, his insight into the nature of the unconscious, for instance, in an arrogant way for selfish purposes, it turns out that this god of death presides over the laws of life and knows no mercy, he extinguishes the light.

467 The cave full of bright lights (the candles of life) is reminiscent of a related idea in a Nordic fairy tale, "The Lord of the Hill and John Blessom":

> 468 One Christmas Eve, John Blessom had finished some business in the city and was homesick. As he went along, a large, heavily built man passed him by in a hurry. John asked him where he was going. "I have

[64] See A. Dieterich, *Eine Mithrasliturgie*, Leipzig and Berlin, 1923, pp. 153–154. An Icelandic version portrays death as teacher of the hero; see Bolte and Polívka, *Anmerkungen*, vol. 1, Leipzig, 1913, p. 378.

[65] According to Bolte and Polívka, in some parallels the father became a doctor instead of the baptized child. Since the son is a piece of the father, and in those parallels plays only the role of getting his father to meet death and is not further intrinsic to the story, the two figures can stand for each other; see *Anmerkungen*, vol. 1, pp. 377ff.

[66] For an example of this double aspect of the figure of the old man, see "The Unsatisfied Son" (*Vom unzufriedenen Sohn*, M. Boehm and F. Specht, *Lettisch-litauische*, Jena, 1924, no. 47), in which the hero is first made all-seeing and then blinded by the magic potion.

[67] In a number of parallels (cf. Bolte and Polívka, *Anmerkungen*, vol. 1, pp. 377ff), death is powerless when standing at the feet and dangerous when at the head. This seems less logical, but could be explained thusly: the demon is fatal when he goes beyond his depth range and has taken control of consciousness. See, however, that Laistner mentions tales in which the demons approach the sleeper from the foot of the bed; *Das Rätsel*, vol. 1 p. 54 and vol. 2, p. 20. In *Psyche*, Rohde discusses the custom of carrying the dead feet first out of the house (vol. 1, p. 23, fn. 2). Under *Fuss* [foot], Bächtold-Stäubli reports that in some places the baby must be carried into the room feet first, otherwise it will die: "One may not stand at the feet of the dying, for this will impede the passing over."

to get back to Vaage this very evening." "I only wish that I could get there too!" sighed John. "You can stand on the runner of my sledge," said the man, "for I have a horse that covers a mile in twelve steps. So they set out, and Blessom had all that he could do to hold fast to the runner of the sledge; for they went through weather and wind, and he could see neither heaven nor earth. Once they stopped and rested. He could not tell exactly where they were, but when they began to hurry on again, he thought that he spied a skull on a pole. John began to freeze.

469 At a bridge near Vaage the stranger stopped and let John step off. "Now you are not far from home," said the stranger, "but you must promise me that you will not look around, when you hear a roaring and see a flare of light." As John went along he heard a roaring in the Jutulsberg, and the path before him suddenly grew so bright that one could have picked a needle from the ground. And he forgot what he had promised, and turned his head to see what was happening. There stood the giant gate of the Jutulsberg wide open, and out of it streamed a light and radiance as of thousands of candles. In the midst of it all stood the giant, and he was the man with whom he had driven. But from that time forward John's head was twisted, and so it remained as long as he lived.[68]

470 Here, the chthonic power is a giant in the mountain like the demon in "The Mountain Elf," his relationship to death is hinted at in the vision of a skull on a pole and the cold felt by the passenger. Forbidden is the glimpse "back" into the magic kingdom with its mysteriously concealed ruler. John Blessom transgresses the prohibition, and for this his head is forever "turned." Whoever sees the demon becomes crazy in the head.

471 Another tale from the Grimm Brothers, "The Godfather," begins in a very similar manner to "Godfather Death," but then clearly emphasizes the threatening, evil, or "devilish" aspect of the mysterious ruler of the underground kingdom, the unconscious. As one knows from studying the history of religions, when in one area a new religion claims victory over an older religion, then the older gods are demonized, as the process is called. That is, their friendly aspects are transformed into dark and evil characteristics. In Christianity, as the victorious religion, the older gods with their chthonic and destructive forces easily fit into the Christian image of the arch-demon and

[68] [The original fairytale is in Norwegian; see Asbjornsen, *Huldreeventyr*, vol. I, p. 189.) For a version in English, see Stroebe, *Norwegian Fairy Book*, pp. 263–266.]

adversary, popularly known as the "devil."[69] In "The Godfather," death and the devil coalesce into one figure:[70]

472 A poor man had so many children that he had already asked everyone in the world to be godfather, and when still another child was born, no one else was left whom he could ask. Following a dream, he went outside the gate and asked the first person who came his way to be godfather. The stranger gave him a little bottle of water, and said, "This is miraculous water. You can heal the sick with it. But you must see where Death is standing. If he is standing by the patient's head, give the patient some of the water and he will be healed, but if Death is standing by his feet all efforts will be in vain, for then the sick man must die."

473 From this time forth, the man could always say whether a patient could be saved or not. He became famous for his skill, and earned a great deal of money. The man went to visit his godfather and tell him what had happened with the water. He entered his godfather's house, but the strangest things were going on there. On the first flight of stairs, the dustpan and the broom were fighting, and violently hitting one another. He asked them, "Where does the godfather live?"

474 The broom answered, "Up one more flight of stairs." When he came to the second flight, he saw a heap of dead fingers lying there. He asked, "Where does the godfather live?" One of the fingers answered, "Up one more flight of stairs." On the third flight lay a heap of dead men's heads, and they directed him to still another flight higher. On the fourth flight, he saw fish on the fire, sizzling in a pan and baking themselves. They too said, "Up one more flight of stairs." And when he had climbed the fifth flight, he came to the closed door of a room. He peeped through the keyhole. There he saw the godfather who had a pair of long horns. When he opened the door and went in, the godfather quickly got into bed and covered himself up. In response to the man's curious questions about what he saw, the godfather explains that the broom and shovel were the servant and maid, the fingers were roots of a vegetable, the skulls as heads of cabbage, and

---

[69] See, for example, the name of the devil as "lord of the forest" in Hertz, *Werwolf*, 1862, pp. 103–104. See further Reitzenstein, *Hellenistic Mystery-Religions*, pp. 342–343, and *Iranische*, p. 137f.

[70] As a consequence, it is understandable that, for instance, in a Ukrainian version of "Godfather Death" [cited in Bolte and Polívka, *Anmerkungen*, vol. 1, p. 387] a cross, a saint, or holy water are placed at the bedside to prevent death standing at the feet. When Christian figures, such as Archangel Michael in a Bulgarian version, take over the role of death, this points to a christianization of a much older motif. Similarly, it may be a late overlay when told that death comes to get the man for neglecting the commandment to love thy neighbor. On the connections between concepts of the devil and the angel of death in the *Talmud*, see also Wünsche, *Vom geprellten Teufel*, Leipzig, 1905, pp. 16ff.

the fish were cooking themselves. About the long horns, the godfather just says that was not true. The man became frightened and ran out. If he had not done so, who knows what the godfather would have done to him?[71]

475 The unity of death and the devil is expressed by the skulls and skeleton fingers that the man meets and in his finally recognizing the horns of the devil. There is a French variant of "Godfather Death," called "The Doctor of Fougeray," in which the devil himself lets the doctor know when his patients will die by seeing the lights of life.[72] When the doctor, in return, fails to note the mistakes of the people, he will disappear from this world. "When it thawed out, the body of the shepherd was found on a broom (genus *Genista*) bush. The unfortunate doctor was holding a lamp of a very odd-shape made of unknown metal." Apparently, the doctor had found his own life lamp/light; he had so deeply penetrated into the secrets of the underworld that he himself perished. Even in "The Godfather," the curiosity of the visitor almost cost him his life.

476 The statements by the devil on the oddities of his house are euphemistic and at the same time disclose the "inverted world" of the unconscious. Even at the lowest level, the animated objects astonish the visitor to the magical realm. Apparently, the devil, as the tunghâk (see page 135) in the Inuit fairytale, "The Fire-Ball," can animate dead objects, indicating his life-giving side next to his death-bringing aspect. This was also shown when the godfather gave a bottle with life-healing water to the doctor at the beginning of the tale. Similarly, in a Finnish fairy tale, "The Devil's Castle," the devil has in addition to killing swords and guns, a healing ointment that can make one whole and a flute at whose sound doors open. In our tale, the devil is nourished by fish, which prepare themselves as food. Since fish live in the water, we can initially regard them as being contents of the unconscious. So here, the devil is also the lord of the water as the unconscious. He lives on the fifth floor, which is not without significance, because five is the number of materiality.[73]

477 Whilst in the last tale the devil, who traditionally in regard to some of his traits has an affinity to pre-Christian and pagan conceptions of the deity, has lost some of his demonic character through humorous traits, a central hidden deity (as the power of the unconscious) of undiminished size appears in the

---

[71] [Originally told to the Grimm Brothers by twelve-year-old Amalie Hassenpflug (without the last sentence). This is shortened from Margaret Hunt's (1884) translation, revised and corrected by D.L. Ashliman, For a nearly identical translation, see *Complete Grimm's*, pp. 206–208.]

[72] Tegethoff, *Französische Volksmärchen*, vol. 2, pp. 111–115.

[73] See Bachofen, *Mutterrecht*, pp. 58ff, esp. p. 60; see also C.G. Jung, *Mass*, CW 11, ¶89, on the ancient conception of the five as the number of natural (hylic) people, who make a pentagram with their outstretched arms and legs.

following powerful mythical narrative of Ireland, "Balor and the Birth of Lugh":

478 In ancient days, which sank in the long night of time, lived three brothers of the Tuatha de Danaan. The oldest had a forge in Druim na teine.[74] The youngest brother, Cian was lord of the land and had a wonder cow, Glas Gaibhnenn (*green cow*), which gave such enormous amounts of milk that it aroused the envy of the neighbors. Across from Druim na teine on the isle Tory[75] lived a famous warrior named Balor. He had only one eye in the middle of the forehead and also one in the back of his head. This eye on the back of the head could shine like a basilisk and kill people with its evil, squinting gaze and poisonous colors, but Balor kept it closed unless he wanted to petrify his enemies with a glance. It was prophesied by a druid that Balor would be killed by his own grandson despite his mighty power. As he had only one daughter, Ethlinn, Balor locked her in an impregnable tower on a rock that rose steeply from the sea into the clouds. There, he had Ethlinn guarded by twelve old women, whom were ordered to hide from her the existence of the male sex. Meanwhile, Balor decided to rob that wonder cow from Cian. He put on the appearance of a little boy with red hair and used a ruse to kidnap the cow. He changed back into his Balor form and dragged the cow back to his island.

479 Cian went then to a woman-Druid, Birog of the Mountain, for her help. She dressed him in woman's clothes, and brought him across the sea in a blast of wind, to the tower where Ethlinn was. Then she called to the women in the tower, and asked them for shelter for a high queen that was having hardship. The women in the tower did not like to refuse a woman of the Tuatha de Danaan, and they let her and her comrade in. Then Birog by her enchantments put them all into a deep sleep, and Cian went to speak with Ethlinn. And when she saw him she said that was the face she had seen in her dreams. So she gave him her love. After a while he was brought away again on a blast of wind.

480 When her time came, Ethlinn gave birth to a son. Balor learned of the news and bade his people put the child in a cloth and fasten it with a pin, and throw him into a current of the sea. As they were carrying the child across an arm of the sea, the pin dropped out, and the child slipped from the cloth into the water, and they thought he was

[74] Müller-Lisoswski translates this as "firewoman," or literally "ridge of fire"; see *Irische Volksmärchen*, p. 19.

[75] Tory means "sky-aspiring rock."

> drowned. But he was brought away by Birog of the Mountain, and she took him to his father Cian and he gave him to be fostered by Taillte, daughter of the King of the Great Plain. It is thus that Lugh was born and reared. In time he was given to his uncle, the blacksmith Goibniu, to learn a trade. Goibnu took Lugh to heart and taught him well. Then Balor killed Cian, Lugh's father and set out to destroy Lugh and Ireland with him. During a fierce and bloody battle, Lugh and Balor met. Lugh called out reproaches to Balor; and Balor become even more furious. He said to the men that were with him, "Lift up my eyelid till I see this chatterer who dares to talk like this to me." Then they raised Balor's eyelid, but Lugh threw his red spear at Balor, and it hit his eye with such force that it thrust the eye out through the back of Balor's head. The eye burst out towards Balor's own army, and three times nine of the Fomor died when they looked at it. "And if Lugh had not put out that eye when he did, the whole of Ireland would have been burned in one flash. And after this, Lugh struck off Balor's head. To avenge his father's death, the grandson killed his grandfather."[76]

481 The one-eyed Balor, who resides far from the human world and is surrounded on all sides by the sea, has a parallel in Polyphemus, the son of the sea and earth god Poseidon. Polyphemus is also a figure of the magical world who lost one eye when somebody whom he wronged thrust a glowing rod into it. In contrast to Polyphemus, however, Balor had another eye at the back of his head, which allowed him to see not only to the front into the secular world but also to the rear into the magical realm. A glimpse from this invisible, destructive eye can petrify his enemies. Here, the dual nature of the magic figure is perfectly illustrated; one of Balor's eyes is turned toward death and the night side of the world, and with his other single eye he can look into conscious human reality. In this he is like the "blind guest," Odin/Woden, with his dark hat and cloak. Odin/Woden is the old Norse/Germanic god of all that is magical including the dark wisdom of nature, who sacrificed one of his eyes to the giant Mimir to gain the power of prophesy. Also the Egyptian Horus is one-eyed. He lost his one eye to Seth, and when he regained it, he sacrificed it to revive his father.[77] In the collection of Welsh bard songs, *The Mabino-*

[76] The Balor-Lugh legend is mentioned already in the 8th and 9th centuries. In one version, Lugh burns "the nine-times veiled eye of Balor with an iron rod, after which seven sheaths fall." Cf. Georges Dottin, *Manuel pour servir à l'Etude de l'Antiquité Celtique*, 2nd ed. Librairie ancienne Honoré Champion, Édouard Champion, Paris, 1915, pp. 281–282, "A la bataille Moytura, Lug, le héro aux mille métiers, d'un coup de fronde, crève à Balor son mauvais œil qui ne s'ouvrait que sur un champ de bataille et dont la paupière ne se soulevait que sous les efforts de quatre hommes." According to James Hastings, *Encyclopaedia of Religion and Ethics* (1910) under "Celts," Balor apparently belonged to a group of the primordial gods of Ireland, from which the Irish trace their mythic descent. After the arrival of the Celts, these older gods became demonic and evil. Balor became the personification of the evil eye.

[77] See Erman, *Religion der Ägypter*, p. 71.

gion,[78] the hero, Peredur, fights a huge, black, one-eyed man, who had lost one of his eyes in battle with the "Black Snake" on the "Hill of Grief." This giant is called the "Black Oppressor." Such an eye, sacrificed to a daemon of the underworld, corresponds to Balor's death eye in that it combines both aspects of the daemonic.[79] The eye that looks to the back symbolizes "unlocking of the inner meaning."[80] The basilisk gaze of the lord of the small island, whose power transcends time and space far beyond the visible world, suggests an affinity to the dragon of the chthonic spheres and to its emergence from the muddy depths. This daemon is thus the lord of the depths, the typical image of a hidden dark god as the embodiment of the unconscious, the magical kingdom, in its destructive aspect. Living on an island marks him as a god of death, for according to the Norse/Germanic view[81] the realm of the dead is often taken to be in a remote sea island and, therefore, the burial service was often in a boat.[82]

482 Balor also has the ability of the Greek sea god Proteus to transform himself, and he appears in the form of a red-haired boy as a robber. We have already indicated that red is the color of the magical world. It is also the color of fire and, therefore, associated with the Norse and Germanic gods Loki, the fire god, and Thor, the red-haired and red-bearded god of thunder and storms. Red is also an attribute of Odin/Woden as the wild hunter. With the introduction of Christianity, the devil took on more and more aspects of Odin/Woden/Thor, inheriting his red beard, cap, and gown. According to folklore, red-haired people are, therefore, not to be trusted. Even death has a red hat, as do dwarves and spooks. Red is the color of blood, passion, and life and, therefore, of the utmost importance in the magic that has as its goal to influence the will of the gods, demons, or people in order to harm or bring personal gain.[83] The Egyptians, who hated the color red, transferred their emotion to the god Seth, whom they feared more than loved. He was red in color, had red eyes, and his evil deeds were "red things."[84]

483 Balor's opponent was, besides his own brother, Gloibniu, the blacksmith of the Tuatha De Danaan, who teaches Lugh, the boy hero. His forge is called the "fire demoness." The ancient image of the blacksmith is the lame Hephaestus, the god of volcanic fire, a dark deity, creating in the earth. Another name for the site of Goibniu's forge is Druim Na Teine, the Ridge of Fire. The blacksmith is creative because of his art and is master of fire, and the

---

78 Guest, *Mabinogion*, pp. 200ff.

79 [i.e., looking towards night and death – the unconscious, and the ability to see forward into conscious, human reality.]

80 See Ninck, *Wodan*, p. 133. For a detailed interpretation of the one-eyed god of the underworld, see Volume 2 of this work.

81 [And also many native American tribes of western North America such as the Hopi.]

82 See Mogk, *Germanische*, p. 60.

83 See Bächtold-Stäubli under *Rot* [red] or *Haar* [hair].

84 See Erman, *Religion der Ägypter*, pp. 37 and 39.

embers hidden in matter. The flames lick golden or red. In folklore, the descriptions of red and gold are interchangeable.[85] Fire is a symbol of the spirit and, here in the possession of the blacksmith, in the conceptual world of the primitive, the medicine man. Fanning the flames is a symbol of cunning, a well-known attribute of Loki. When Balor turns himself into a red-haired, little boy, he symbolizes aligning himself with a demonic ruse, which is not possible to resist, even less as he incorporated the fire aspect of his opponent. In that he shows related traits, he beats his opponents at their own game. The variety of enemies is only hinted at in the characterization of their empire: the sea and fire. It is as though various aspects of a magical being fight one another, or, formulated more psychologically, different tendencies in the unconscious, comparable to two different instinctual drives in the same human being, one a destructive and the other a creative.

484 Balor steals the nourishing, wonderful cow, Glas Gaibhnenn (*green cow*), from the three brothers. This cow symbolizes first and foremost a living power, life-nourishing, and for the primitive stage of civilization, the highest value: a symbol of fertility, the maternal and giving nature and, therefore, an Earth and mother goddess. This indispensable life force comes by way of a deceitful ploy under the power of a great underworld demon, but this incident engendered the incentive to destroy Balor and help the good to victory.[86] Balor's daughter is Ethlinn.[87] In the darkness of the unconscious, bound and guarded by the will of the demonic father, lives[88] a spiritual power, which takes up the connection to the living, opposite to the Balor principle, and will give birth to a child who destroys him. Help must arise out of the magical itself, the soul hidden in the dark depths of creation must intervene in the process by participating and connecting with the light side, to bear forth the one who unites the two worlds and can overcome the evil demon. From dreams, the young virgin already has a premonition that there are beings who can redeem and complete her that are of a different nature than herself and her environment. The wings of the wind carry the youngest brother Cian [= Mac Kineely], who has been robbed of his cow, into the closed magical center, thereby confirming the forebodings of her dreams. In lush fertility, Ethlinn gives birth to three children, but her father aspires to live and, like the dark gods Uranus and after him again Chronos, he must destroy his male offspring. But like them, one son escapes and overcomes him. Lugh is the young culture hero who ends the persecution of his grandfather Balor. Just when the darkness seems to have completely conquered the light, having destroyed the

---

[85] See Bächtold-Stäubli under *Rot*.

[86] ["Execute the will of the fates." For the earliest written account, see O'Donovan, *Annals of the Kingdom of Ireland*, 1856).]

[87] [This transliteration follows that of Lady Gregory (1904); other spellings are possible, such as *Ethnea*; see Rhys, *Hibbert Lectures*, p. 56.]

[88] [The present tense is used throughout in the original.]

father of the boy and the owner of the cow and even subjugated the blacksmith, the creative forces survive and grow. Lugh knows "the secret of his birth and Balor's attack on him and his brothers and also of the killing of his father." Balor unwittingly takes the young blacksmith to heart, as if he had a secret longing for the world of his opponent.[89] It is the longing for light and a sense that the fair grandson is somehow related to him, and that the darkness cannot do without the light. It is written in the Chinese oracle and wisdom book *I Ching*, therefore, that the power of darkness destroys itself when it has completely consumed the light, to which it owes its existence.[90] The young hero destroys Balor's eye, however, and thus Balor himself, thereby avenging the death of his father. This killing of Balor is reminiscent of the blinding of Polyphemus. It is a lifting of the destructive spirit in the unconscious. Thus the hero wins back the cow; this means that he brings again the life force out of the depths of the unconscious. Just how much this narrative makes use of archetypal material, is evident from the fact that one meets it again in a completely different culture in a similar way. Laistner mentions a Finnish story in which the daughter of a king sits "a hundred fathoms deep under the ground in an iron room imprisoned by a one-eyed, almost blind rock spirit."[91] The hero, whom the demon smells but cannot see, succeeds in poking out his eye with a glowing rod.

485 A gripping story whose main characters are as powerful as those in the story of Balor, is an old tale, "Golden Feet," collected in the late 1800s in the area of Lectoure, a small town near Gascogne in southern France.

> 486 There was once at Pont-de-Pîle a blacksmith who was just over a fathom in height, and as strong as a yoke of oxen. He was blacker than the chimney, with a long beard, bristly hair, and eyes as red as coals. He never set foot inside a church, and he ate meat at all seasons, even on Good Friday. Men said that the smith of Pont-de-Pîle was not of the race of Christians. The smith had not his like for working in iron as well as in gold or silver. Work showered down on him like hail. He saw to everything with no helper but a black wolf as big as a horse. Seven young men had come to the master to learn the trade. But the tests were so hard, that they had died of them within three days.
>
> 487 At that time there lived at the hamlet of La Côte. a poor widow who dwelt alone in her cottage with her son. When the lad had reached the age of fourteen, he said to his mother one evening: "Mother, we

[89] [That Balor shows a liking for the young blacksmith (Lugh), follows the text of O'Donovan (1856); this is the source for von Franz and von Beit. Later translations state that it is Lugh's uncle Goibniu, who, as in the version used above, takes a liking to Lugh.]

[90] Hexagram 36, "Darkening of the Light," Wilhelm/Baynes, *I Ching*, p. 142f.

[91] Laistner, *Psyche*, vol. II, p. 113.

are both killing ourselves with drudgery, without even making a livelihood. Tomorrow I shall go and see the Smith of Pont-de-Pîle, and become his apprentice." His mother warned him of the terrible blacksmith, but the boy paid no heed. Next day at dawn the lad was in front of the shop of the Smith of Pont-de-Pîle. "Ho, Smith of Pont-de-Pile. Ho, Ho. Ho. I want to be your apprentice." "Come in here, boy." The boy went into the shop without fear or flinching. "Boy, show me that you are strong." The boy took up an anvil of seven quintals. "Boy, show me that you are skillful." The boy went to a spider's web and disentangled it and wound it up from one end to the other without ever breaking the thread. "Boy, show me that you are brave." The boy opened the door of the wheel where lived day and night the black wolf as big as a horse that worked the bellows of the forge. At once the wolf leapt out. But the boy seized him in mid air by the neck, cut off his tail and his four paws on an anvil and burnt him alive in the fire of the forge. "Boy, your tests are over. You are strong, skillful, and brave. In three days you shall be in my employ. I will pay you well. But I do not mean you to live or to eat with me." "Master, you shall be obeyed."

488 The new apprentice bowed to the Smith of Pont-de-Pile and went out. Once outside, he thought: "My mother is right. My master is not a man like other men. For three days and three nights I will hide myself and watch him without his seeing me. Then I shall know whom I have to do with."

489 The apprentice took leave of his mother, and made as if to set off. But he went to hide himself, in secret, quite near the house of the Smith of Pont-de-Pile, in a rick of straw, whence he could see and hear everything without being seen or heard himself. He discovered that the blacksmith called his daughter, the queen of snakes, to him at night. The Queen of the Vipers was long and as thick as a sack of com, with a black fleur-de-lis on her head. The father and daughter fondled each other and devoured each other with kisses. He promised her the apprentice as her husband. The Queen of the Vipers went away. Immediately, the Smith of Pont-de-Pîle went down to the edge of the river Gers, in a meadow bordered with ash trees, poplars, and willows. The Apprentice came out of the rick of straw and followed his master quietly, very quietly, hiding himself behind the trees. The Smith of Pont-de-Pîle stripped himself as naked as a worm, and hid his clothes in a hollow willow-trunk. Then he pulled off his skin from his head to his feet and appeared in the form of a great otter. "Let us hide my man's skin," said he. "If I did not find it again, and put it on before the

sun rose, I should be an otter for evermore." He hid his man's skin in the hollow willow and leapt into the Gers, just at the moment when the stars were marking midnight. The Apprentice saw him swim, and dive to the bottom of the river, and come up with a carp or an eel which he ate by the light of the moon. This went on till the dawn. Then the Smith of Pont-de-Pile came out of the water, put on his man's skin and his clothes again, and went back home, not thinking that he had been watched.

490 The apprentice began his apprenticeship without ever betraying what he had witnessed. He became an even better goldsmith than his master. One time, he received the order to forge the wedding jewelry for a marquis's older daughter. Upon delivering his jewelry, he became entranced with the marquis's youngest daughter and soon they were engaged. He made her a golden necklace, which he had hardened with his own blood, and which attached itself so firmly to the wearer that neither God nor the devil could tear it off. The necklace was also endowed with the power to indicate when one of the beloved was in a bad way.

491 When the apprentice returned home, the blacksmith beat him severely out of jealousy for his skills and demanded that he marry his snake daughter. But when the apprentice refused, the blacksmith cut off his feet and threw him into a roofless tower a hundred fathoms high on the seashore in the land of snakes where he had to do goldsmith's work. For seven years the Apprentice lived and worked there. His bed was the ground and his roof the sky. When he was thirsty he drank the water of the well. He wanted not for iron, silver or gold, nor yet for diamonds and precious stones. All that he made, the great eagles of the Mountain took to the Smith of Pont-de-Pîle. When the apprentice had earned it a hundred times over, they would throw him a loaf of bread, black as the chimney, and bitter, bitter as gall. But during the seven years, he did not only make the finest jewelry but also secretly forged treasures for himself: a fine steel axe, an iron belt with three hooks, and well-fitting feet of gold. Finally, he made himself large feather-light wings. When after seven years the snake queen, who visited him every day in a seductive fashion, appeared, he severed her head with his axe and hung it on his belt. With his feather-light wings he flew home to the Gers River at night.

492 He looked down towards Pont-de-Pîle and saw by the light of the moon the Smith coming out of his house to change himself into an otter and swim in the Gers till the break of day. He waited till the last stroke of midnight. Then the Apprentice swooped down, a hundred

> times swifter than a swallow, upon the hollow willow where the Smith of Pont-de-Pîle hid his man's skin every night. In an instant, the man's skin was hanging on one of the hooks of his belt of iron, and he was hovering a hundred fathoms above the river Gers. "Ho, Smith of Pont-de-Pîle! Ho, Ho, Ho." "What do you want of me, big bird?" "Smith of Pont-de-Pîle, I bring you news of your daughter, news of the Queen of the Vipers." "Speak, big bird." "Big bird am I none. I am your Apprentice. For seven years past I have suffered death and torment on the shore of the great sea. Your daughter is in two pieces, head and body, hooked to my belt of iron. Pick them up in the Gers and try to sew them together." The Smith of Pont-de-Pîle was screaming like an eagle, in the river. "Smith of Pont-de-Pîle, you have not done with suffering. Look for your man's skin in the hollow willow. Look, friend. Look well. I have it, hooked to my belt of iron. And now you are an otter for evermore." The Smith of Pont-de-Pîle dove into the Gers. Never, never again has he been seen.

> 493 Then the hero visited his mother, told her of his times, roasted the skin of the blacksmith, and ate it. Then he went to his beloved, who knew of his distress through the necklace and, as they had agreed to do in this case, had herself buried in a seemingly dead state in bridal attire. He woke her up, asked her parents for her hand and they were married that morning. They lived long and happily, and they had twelve sons. The eldest was the strongest and handsomest of them all. But his stomach was covered with a fine soft yellow fur, like that of an otter. This was because (on the first day of the wedding) his father had eaten, fried on the gridiron, the skin of the Smith of Pont de-Pîle.[92]

494 As with the story of "Balor and the Birth of Lugh," so "Golden Feet" shares essential features with the legend of Wayland the Smith.[93] The otter form of the evil blacksmith could be related to the Norse legend in which Loki killed King Hreidmar's son Ótr in the shape of an otter and let his fur skin be coated with gold by the gods.[94]

---

[92] Shortened from Montagne Rhodes James, *Tales from Lectoure*, 2006, pp. 11–19. "Pieds-d'Or" was told to Jean-Francois Bladé (1827-1900), the collector, by three people: the old man Cazaux; Bladé's servant, Cadette Saint-Avit of Castera-Lectourois; and Pierre Laterrade of Saint-Martin-de-Goeyne (six miles northwest of Lectoure). Each placed the action in the area of their birth. Others in Lectoure knew the story, but their versions were less full and detailed than Cazaux's, which Bladé followed here.

[93] [In his introduction, the translator, M. R. James, notes that "Golden Feet" is essentially the same tale as "Waylend the Smith," the Völunder of the elder *Edda*, which is told in one of the oldest layers of that work, and of which our first record is a carving on the ivory casket in the British Museum called Franks Casket, and was made in Northern England in the eighth century.]

[94] [In Norse mythology, Ótr (alternately: Ott, Oter, Otr, Otter) is a dwarf. He is the son of the king Hreidmar and the brother of Fafnir and Regin.]

495 The dark, powerful, daemonic figure of the blacksmith of the Pont de Pîle points mainly to his evil destructive nature. The productive and positive side of his craft is significant, however, even when the dark aspect is highlighted as in "Balor and the Birth of Lugh." As a result of his mastery over the mysterious art of metalworking and the manufacture of high-quality equipment, in particular weapons, the smith has always had in popular belief the reputation of magical relationships and skills (even in regard to medical folk knowledge).[95] Various legends celebrate the blacksmith's art, for instance, those telling of the skills of Haephaestus, Wayland, and Mimir.[96] Traces of his godlike nature still appear in the earthly smith who is connected with otherworldly beings such as the metal and blacksmith crafts of dwarfs or the relation between the farrier (wrought iron, horseshoe blacksmith) with the wild hunt. The blacksmith on earth can fetter Lucifer, he can even banish, outwit, or be in league with the devil. The devil himself appears as a blacksmith.[97] Thus, in this fairytale the opponent of the hero is characterized as a smith who wreaks terror and expresses his underlying nature as a dark god. Another trait further emphasizes this aspect: the blacksmith reveals himself in his otter form as a water demon, as an element of the unconscious. At the end of the tale the otter disappears into that sphere, while the primal creative force, as that unfolds in the art of the blacksmith, passes on to the boy hero. (The hero takes on a little of the essence of the otters, however, by "incorporating" the skin of the blacksmith. He at first burnt the skin, that is, he purified it by fire.) Through the confrontation with the demon, man gains creative energy from the unconscious, much like the hero in "Balor and the Birth of Lugh" wins back the fertile cow. Significantly, it is said of the smith of Pont de Pîle that he was not of the tribe of Christians, because an old pagan primeval god lives on in him, and his human appearance deceives, he is more than a man because he also becomes an animal.

496 The smith does not always appear as an outwardly violent demon, on the contrary, dwarves are equally vaunted masters of the forge. Mimir is a well-known dwarf smith.[98] Laistner[99] reports a Swedish story in which a hunter met

---

[95] In a magic spell from Merseburg [Germany], Odin appears as a horseshoer.

[96] [Norse god of the forge.]

[97] See Bächtold-Stäubli under *Schmied* [Blacksmith]. In *Weltkönig* (1923, p. 111), Güntert mentions the distrust that the masses show when confronted with arts they do not understand. In primitive minds artists become magicians. This trait appears in legends, like that of Daedalus and Wayland, and even today [i.e., 1920s.]. The German language retains phrases such as *schemer*, related to *Schmied*, "to *hammer* something home" or "forge a lie." See Wünsche, *Vom geprellten Teufel*, pp. 11, 88ff., 96–98, on the relationship of Donar's form to that of the devil. Wünsch refers to legends in which the smith outwits the devil or trounces death as the devil. He relates a tale at the end of which the smith, since he finds no admittance to heaven or hell, becomes the blacksmith for the Emperor Barbarossa in Kyffhäuser (see *Vom geprellten Teufel*, pp. 91–92). Barbarossa, who was transported (*entrückte*) to the place known as Kyffhäuser, should be regarded as an underworld deity.

[98] [In the *Poetic Edda*, Mimir is a man who has been beheaded and lies beneath the World Tree Yggdrasil and from whose head Odin/Woden receives wisdom.]

[99] See Laistner, *Das Rätsel*, vol. 2, pp. 65–71.

"a sleeping mountain smith on the Oernekulla and seized him with power. The mountain smith cries and promises to forge everything asked for, one should only place iron and steel on the mountain cliff. Nevertheless, the hunter refuses to release the dwarf. Then speaks the dwarf: 'If I had my fog hat, you should not carry me away, but if you do not let me free, so you will pay with the demise of your house.' Three days the mountain dwarf sat imprisoned, then he suddenly disappeared, but his prophecy was fulfilled." In the Upper Palatinate, one knows the Earth-Smith (*Erdschmied*). Although in the Swedish legend the hunter met a mountain smith, the prisoner, a single representative of the dwarves, can still be considered part of an underground aspect of God, in which the multitude of dwarves are condensed in a single form. And in fact - characteristic of the double aspect of the magic kingdom - smallness is a major manifestation of that God[100] where, of course, his power, which still manifests itself, in turn emphasizes the oppositions prevailing in that world.[101]

497 In a fairytale from the Fiji Islands, "The Story of Longa-Poa," we meet another very small man who can work wonders:

> 498 There was once, so our fathers said, a chief in Tonga whose name was Longa-poa, a chief great and mighty, strong of arm, bold of heart, wise in council, and mighty in war. But, great and mighty as he was, there was nevertheless one before whom he trembled and quaked, and that was Fekai, the "Ferocious One," his own wife, the daughter of the king, a woman tall of stature and loud of tongue, whose soul was altogether evil. But she was the daughter of a "Sacred King," and he could not lift his hand against her, for she was nearer to the gods than he.

> 499 Once after again being fiercely criticized by Fekai, Longa-poa decided to leave the island and seek peace from Fekai in other lands. He embarked on a war-and-ravage tour with his faithful warriors. On one of their exploits they managed to kill a whale. In his *hubris* Longa-poa claimed this made him and his men into gods. But once more when at sea he met up with Fekai in her boat on the warpath against him. In his attempt to escape her wrath, he sailed right into a whirlpool where all his men died. Fekai, her boat, and her crew followed them into the whirlpool and also perished. Longa-poa alone escaped to an island and fell down exhausted at the foot of a palm tree and slept. In the night, he heard a shrill voice from the darkness above him calling, "Longa-poa! Longa-poa!" "Who calls me?" he cried, and sprung to his feet in great fear. But still the voice continued its call, "Longa-poa! Longa-poa!" Who is it that speaks to me?" he asked. He

[100] See the previously mentioned forest sprites Och and Kurupira.
[101] [I.e., the realm of the unconscious.]

> went around the palm-tree where he had been lying and saw a strange thing between him and the star-lit sky. On the very end of a long palm-leaf, which would not have supported the weight of a rat without bending, sat a little old man, who bobbed up and down as the leaf swayed and tossed in the night wind. Small he was, no taller than the length of an arm from hand to elbow; but his head was big, and so were his eyes, which glared through the darkness, glowing like firebrands. Longa-poa could see the face of the little old man because of the brightness that shone from his eyes; and his heart died within him, for he knew that it was a god who had spoken to him.

500 The little old man mocked the now deflated chief, challenging him to save himself since he was a god, no? He made fun of Longa-Poa until the poor fellow became quite humble. Then, while the little man continued to bob on the end of the palm leaf, he ordered Longo-Poa to prepare a fire and cook food. Magically the pit was filled with delicious food, of which the little man ate ten times as much as the big and starving Longa-Poa. Then the little man sent Longa-Poa back home on a magic bird. After further adventures, Longa-poa was made Tui, or Master, of Tonga and all the people honored him. A good king was Longa-poa, for he learned many things from what had befallen him during his travels; so that he became kinder of heart, and more humble of soul, than he was when Fekai threw the tuft of hair in his face, and drove him away with her stick.[102]

501 At the moment of the hero's greatest need, a strange deity appears on the scene. Its appearance is paradoxical: it is so small and lightweight that it teeters on the tip of a palm leaf. His head and eyes are bigger, however, than those of a full-grown man; his appetite, too! The little man expresses cruel mockery and infinite goodness in rapid succession, he combines demonic features and humorous, eerie laughter, derision and graciousness; he punishes, educates, and rewards. The large head is reminiscent of figures that consist only of a head, such as the rolling skull. When he squats on the palm frond he appears like a forest spirit. The little old man lives like Balor ("Balor and the Birth of Lugh") on a desert island in the sea and dominates all the processes of nature. He is like Balor, an image of the hidden but active spirit of nature in the depths of creation.

502 In this Fiji fairytale, the spirit, as far as it can be visually imagined, is admirably represented.[103] It is at the same time something so small that,

[102] Shortened from Fison, *Tales from Old Fiji*, 1904, pp. 65–85. Told to Fison by Chief Taliai Tupou from Naiau, Fiji.

[103] See J. Hoffmeister, *Wörterbuch der philosopischen Begriffe*, Leipzig, 1944, under *Geist* ("spirit"). The word "spirit" in Old High German is *gaist*, and *geist* in Middle High German. Etymologically, it is related to Norse *geysa*, "wild outbreak" or "to flow out." The same root occurs in English "geyser." In the course of its development, *Geist* acquired the meaning of air, breeze, and especially breath, as the vehicle of life, the life-preserving principle.

compared to the size and manifest reality of gross material one does not notice it at all, but the development of the eye as the organ of the faculty of perception is immense. Although physically as small as the pupil, the eye can "see" and thus encompass the whole universe. As "spirit," it towers above all things since it has an overview of the physical, concrete world. Also its ability to take in food is of course enormous; the spirit can actually take in, break down, utilize, metabolize, and digest everything material. It is ageless old, and yet is a part of the nature of the spirit. We refer here to an ancient Indian parallel, a pictorial description of the nature of the spiritual being, the *purusha* of the *Kathaka Upanishad.*[104] See also in the *Śvetāśvatara Upanishad,*[105] where the "first-begotten red wise seer" refers to "the golden (therefore red) embryo." Also the "ageless old one," or the "wise master of the universe."[106] He is also called the flaming arch-fire blazing through the world and also means the inexhaustible, through which food is produced fresh again and again.[107]

503 The "smallness" of the divine being is sometimes expressed in fairytales in the form of a dwarf and sometimes as the child, as when Balor (in "Balor and the Birth of Lugh") steals the cow by taking the shape of a *boy*. The boy, a figure of the divine child as a counter aspect to the old wise one and other aspects of the pagan nature god, the daemon of the unconscious, and as the epitome of the magic kingdom and its values, appears in fairytales of all cultures and times. At this point, it is not yet possible to identify all forms and relationships of this powerful central figure, for instance, the motifs of the old, sick, or blind king, or his other animal aspects. Now that the broad features of this archetype have been outlined, these other aspects will be discussed in the course of further treatment below. First, however, we will next review the archetypal aspects of the Great Mother as depicted in fairytales.

---

[104] In Hinduism, *purusha* (Sanskrit *purusa*, "man, cosmic man,") is the "self" which pervades the universe. See the *Kathaka Upanishad*, Fourth Vallī, 12:

As high as an inch (thumb) in size,
the Purusa dwells here in the body,
the lord of the past and future,
One, who knows him, does not feel alarmed at anything anymore.

(Deussen, *Sixty Upanishads*, p. 292.) Or in the *Śvetāśvatara Upanishad*, Third Adhyāya, 13, where it is written:

The Purusa, inch-high, as the inner soul,
is always to be found in the hearts of created beings;
Only he who is prepared by the heart, mind, and spirit, –
They who know him, thus, become immortal.

(Deussen, *Sixty Upanishads*, p. 313.)

[105] Fifth Adhyāya, 2 and footnote 2 (Deussen, *Sixty Upanishads*, p. 319).

[106] Deussen, *Sixty Upanishads*, p. 319, *Śvetāśvatara Upanishad*, Third Adhyāya, 21, [describing Brahman], Deussen, *Sixty Upanishads*, p. 314.

The Purusa, who is all this,
Who is the enlivener of the world,
The wise lord of all, who,
Omniforam, resides in the waters.

(*Mahā Upanishad*, Deussen, *Sixty Upanishads*, pp. 800–801).

[107] *Brhadāranyaka Upaninad*, Fifth Brāhmanam, 2 (Deussen, *Sixty Upanishads*, p. 418f).

Chapter 17
The Great Mother

504 In the fairytale, "Flight to the Moon," we already met the wife of the man in the moon whose empty back represented the other, dark, frightening side of her generously giving husband. Also in the tale, "Makonaura and Anuanaitu," the rulers of the magical kingdom were thought of as a couple,[1] but the male counterpart took a leading role in the plots of these tales. In a number of narratives, a female main character appears however, who dominates the magical realm.[2] For example, the primal mother with giant breasts in "Ngeraod's Bundle;" or the Aztec earth goddess, Tlatleotl, and ancestress of the tribe, Caotlicue, in "How Motecuzhoma Sought the Seven Caves;" or in Europe where in some variants of "Godfather Death," death appears in female form.[3]

505 While in these stories the female deity and her divine partner together symbolize the double aspect of the magical realm – or sometimes she alone embodies the partly giving, partly demanding power, a number of fairytales tell of the purely evil and malevolent nature of this figure as that of a witch. For instance, in the traditions of the Skidi-Pawnee (North America), the Spider-Woman spins webs in the center of the earth. In one tale it is said of her that she was one of those great red spiders, a tarantula, the daughter of Sun and Moon. Here is the fairytale, "Death of the Spider Woman":

506 There were many villages in a country where the people enjoyed many buffalo and plenty of corn; but there lived also the Spider-Woman[4] to the northeast of the villages. If a hunter got near to this Spider-

[1] See Bachofen, *Gräbersymbolik*, 1859, pp. 324–325; see also his *Mutterrecht*, 1861, p. 22, on the androgynous nature of the moon. See also the god/goddess pairs who govern the realm of the dead (e.g., the Greek Pluto and Persephone, or Mictlantecuhtli and his wife Mictecacihuatl who rule the Aztec land of the dead, Mictlan; on the latter, see Graulich, *Myths of Ancient Mexico*, p. 251).

[2] On this archetype, see the material collected in Leeuw, *Religion in Essence*, vol. 1, pp. 73ff.

[3] Cf. "Death as Godparents" and "The Soldier and his Knapsack"; see also Bolte and Polívka, *Anmerkungen*, vol. 1, p. 383f. There is a French version in which the husband gives this female figure of death preference over the Virgin Mary as the godmother of his child.

[4] [The collector of this tale, George Dorsey, notes that "There was not only one, but many Spider-Women. Contrary to that of the Witch-Women, their influence was uniformly good, inasmuch as they helped people, giving them seeds, the lariat rope, and teaching them to climb mountains and trees, etc. It was believed that they inhabited the sides of the mountains, where they stayed with their legs far apart, and were the source of springs which furnished sweet water"; see Dorsey, *Skidi Pawnee*, p. 335.]

Woman's place, she would feed him and put poison in the food she gave so that the hunter would die. She would then cut his head off, place it in her lodge, take the body and cut it up, or sometimes throw it into the creek which was near her, so that the animals in the stream ate up the body. She seemed to have had power from some mysterious animal in the earth.

507 Tirawa[5] looked down upon these people, and took pity on them. He commanded the Sun and Moon to send their two boys to the village, saying that he wanted them to help the people by destroying this Spider-Woman; evidently some mysterious animal had taken the old woman to their home and had taught her their mysteries. Tirawa had given seeds to this Spider-Woman to plant and reap, and when she had many seeds she was to have divided them among the people. Instead of doing this, she put the seeds in sacks, dug holes in the ground, and put them in the holes. She did not give a kernel to anybody, but kept all for herself.

508 When the sons grew up to be men, they started for the northern country, slinging special quivers over their shoulders. The old woman knew that they were coming so she sent her snakes to meet them. When the young men saw the snakes they were scared, in the center was a huge rattlesnake, which seemed to be the leader of all the other snakes. The oldest of the two boys took his bow and arrows and shot at this snake and killed it. After the snakes saw that the chief was killed, they all ran to their holes and disappeared. [This continued with mountain lions and bears...] Then the old witch-woman knew with whom she was dealing. She said; "They must be wonderful boys!" The boys went on, and they came to a thickly timbered country; they went through the forests, down the hills into a valley. There was the old woman standing outside, welcoming them. [She greeted them kindly and had a special meal prepared, but this was with poisoned human brains. The hero boys ate the food and the witch-woman happily gloated over how she would take their heads off and make nice corn sacks. But they excused themselves from her tent, went out to the woods, swallowed an emetic mixture, and vomited up the food.] They went back into the lodge, and the old woman was surprised. Said she: "These must be wonderful boys." Then she did the same with pumpkins, and again the boys went out and vomited up the poisoned food. When they came back, they told the old woman that they thought they had made their visit long enough, and they thought they

[5] [The Skidi-Pawnee supreme creator god.]

> would go home. She said: "No, no, my grandsons, stay with me; I shall give you plenty to eat and a good place to sleep; stay with me! Tomorrow we shall have the Skull bundle ceremony and dance." She now went out and prepared a place east of the lodge near a steep bank. She thought they would get dizzy and fall over this steep bank and be killed. She began to sing and evoked a raging dark snowstorm and icy frost. But the youths turned into snowbirds and danced with their faces turned to the north. They conjured up their sun father, who shone ever more glowingly down on the spider woman and sent down a cloud of locusts. The locusts seized the spider woman and carried her up to the moon. And that is the old woman that you see upon the full moon, dragging her dress at the bottom of her feet. The boys then went up to the old woman's lodge and freed her daughters. These girls were good, they had not known the doings of the old woman. Each picked up all the seeds they could, went to the different camps, to the four villages, and gave the seeds to their people. So they were married into the four tribes, so that each band of the Pawnee had seeds.[6]

509 This Spider Woman comes from the moon and is a mythical figure who is sometimes favorably disposed and helpful to humans, but just as often acts as a dangerous witch. For the Hopi, she existed before the creation and took part in it by creating the quarrelsome people.[7]

510 The animal form of the spider characterizes an evil mother, because the spider is a treacherous predator and a manifestation of blood-sucking night spirits. The spider is also the image of a witch soul that drives a woman to be a witch, and often appears as a witch's animal that brings ruin. For example, in the folklore of the Wends,[8] vampires take the shape of giant spiders. According to Japanese folk belief huge spider demons live in burrows, and in Wallonia,[9] a grandmother in the shape of a spider kills her grandchildren.[10]

511 Since spiders weave webs, they are also associated with the activities of spinning and weaving. Due to the connections that our well-ordered systems of thought make, sewing is associated with the concomitant hazards and can carry a tone of danger. Out of jealousy Athena, mistress of the art of weaving, transformed the ambitious weaver Arachne into a spider (Greek: *arachne*). Spinning or weaving is associated with the great mother goddesses. Thus the

---

[6] [Considerably shortened: "Told by Fox, usually known as John Box, one of the prominent members of the Skidi band"; see Dorsey, *Skidi Pawnee*, pp. 39–44.

[7] See Krickeberg, *Nordamerika*, p. 386; Ibid., p. 370, notes to "Giviok (Kiviok)"; see also the Hopi "Origin Myth"; see further Ibid., pp. 408-409, and "The Navajo Origin Legend," p. 412. On the spider as creator, particularly among the Spanish, see also A. v. Deursen, *Der Heilbringer*, pp. 137ff.

[8] [Germanic people of Slavic origin, including Poles, Czechs, Slovaks, Lusatian Sorbs, and the historical Polabians.]

[9] [The Walloon Region, commonly called Wallonia, is one of the three federal Regions of Belgium.]

[10] See Bächtold-Stäubli under *Spinne* [spider].

Greek Fates and the Germanic Norns, who can be seen together as a mother goddess, "spin" fate.[11]

512 In some regions, spinning is associated with fantasizing. For instance, a new Greek fairytale, "The Beardless One," begins with the verse:

513 Red thread tied,
winding around the spindle.
Give her the gentle push that she spins
So that the fairytale goes on by itself,

514 And the sweet evening passes pleasantly away.[12] The uniform activity of the hands in spinning and the monotonous hum of the wheel seem to invite the smooth drift into dreamland. Spinning, therefore, was probably a symbol that appeared frequently at the entrance to the magical kingdom.[13]

515 In the Grimm's fairytale, "Mother Holle," the girl is pulled straight from the spindle into the well and the kingdom of Mother Holle, who is a form of the Germanic original mother named Frigg. She was the protectress of spinning, just like almost all great natural mothers, such as Penelope (also originally an underworld goddess), Proserpina, and Aphrodite, the Ilithyian goddess of birth. Bachofen explains their meaning thus: "In the image of the spinning and weaving is the activity of the forming, shaping force of nature represented. The work of the great material primeval mothers is compared to the artful weaving and knitting, which provides the raw materials of division, symmetrical form and shape and refinement."[14]

516 Already the ancients spoke of the "web" and fabric of nature. In this respect, the spider is a symbol of the great weaver, who produces an extensive web of its own. Because the nature of a spider's web is to catch animals and their captivity in the network inevitably leads to their demise, the spider and her web became associated with the goddess of fate Ananke (= the force[15] of fate), often represented with skirt and spindle. Psychologically, this may mean that a person becomes caught in the chaotic mesh of their instincts. This is shown in the mythical image as a human transformed into an animal. There are many variations of such transformations in myths. The Babylonian Ishtar turned all her lovers (except Tammuz) into animals, the Greek demon Circe transformed her enemies, or those who offended her, into pigs and other

[11] See the Grimm's fairytale, "The Three Spinners," where the three Norns are shown in a popular view.

[12] Translated from Kretschmer, *Neugriechische*, 1917. For an English version, see Ruth Manning-Sanders, *Damian and the Dragon: Modern Greek Folk-Tales*, Oxford, 1965.

[13] Just how strongly the image of the cocoon and the spider hang primordially together with the Great Mother is shown by the following: in Malekula participants in the initiation rites wear garments made of spider webs, which symbolize being ritually reunited with the mother; see Layard, "The Making of Man in Malekula," pp. 259–60, plate 6 and table 3 of figure 1 therein.

[14] Bachofen, *Gräbersymbolik*, pp. 308, 309-310, 310ff.

[15] [Literally "compulsion."]

animals through the use of magical potions. Mother Holle also turns people into animals. The mountain giantess in the fairytale, "Trunt, Trunt, and the Trolls in the Mountains," "animalizes"[16] those who fall into her power. Due to its dangerous fascination for humans, the image of the spinning primal mother has been distorted into a witch. Thus, according to one variant, Mother Holle is "a mermaid with horrible hair, which had certainly not been combed for a year,"[17] and thus formed a "fabric." Sleeping Beauty ("Sleeping Beauty (Little Briar Rose)") pricks her finger on the spindle of an old mother (the wicked fairy) and sinks into a one hundred year slumber. In the Russian fairytale, "The Virgin Tsar," the great witch Baba Yaga enters on her revolving house standing on a green meadow and held high up in the air on three "spindle feet" in the form of chicken legs. She stokes her fire with her nose, herds geese, and combs silk strands.

517 The unpredictability that the mother archetype expresses in the form of a spider characterizes this image in other manifestations. In "The Story of Haburi," for instance, the mother is at first helpful, but essentially devouring and dangerous in her love:

> 518 Long ago, there were two sisters minding themselves; they had no man to look after them. One day they cut down an *ite* tree (genus *Mauritia*), from which they commenced to manufacture flour. It was now late, so they left their work and went home. Next morning when they went back, the starch was lying there already prepared, and they were much puzzled to know how this came to be so. Next day, the same thing happened – all the *ite* starch was found ready; and this happened again, and often. So one night they watched, and about the middle of the night they saw one of the leaves of the neighboring manicole palm tree bend gradually over and over until it touched the cut which they had made in the trunk of the *ite* palm lying beneath. As soon as the leaf actually touched, both sisters rushed up and caught hold of it, begging it earnestly to turn into a man. It refused at first, but as they begged so earnestly it did so. His name was Mayara-kóto. The big [elder] sister was now happy and by-and-by she had a beautiful baby boy, called Haburi.
>
> 519 [The palm father was eaten by a jaguar. The jaguar took the shape of the eaten husband and went back to the women. After some time they became suspicious and fled with the child.] While going along, they heard Wau-uta singing. Wau-uta was a woman in those days, indeed

[16] [Literal translation of *vertieren*, to brutalize.]

[17] See Bolte and Polívka, *Anmerkungen*, vol. 1, pp. 209, 216–217. See also the fairytale, "The Man Who was Changed into a Wolf," where a farmer is turned into a wolf by the belt of an unknown old woman. See also "The Devil's Deception and God's Power," where a figure similar to Circe appears.

she was a piai woman, and she was just then singing with her *shai-shak* [rattle]. The two women went on and on, quickly too, for they knew that once they arrived at Wau-uta's place they would be safe.

520 [Wau-uta hid the women because they brought the boy with them. She killed the persecuting jaguar by tricking him with a door covered with thorns.]

521 Then Wau-uta made the child grow all at once into a youth, and gave him the *harri-harri* to blow and the arrows to shoot. As the mother and aunt returned from the fields where they worked during the day, they heard the music playing and said to themselves, "There was no man or boy there when we left the house; who can it be? It must be a man playing." And though ashamed they went in and saw the youth blowing the harri-harri. As soon as they had taken the quakes [baskets] from off their backs and placed them on the ground, they asked after Haburi, but Wau-uta said that as soon as they had left for the field, the child had run after them, and she had thought it was still with them. Of course all this was a lie. Old Wau-uta was desirous of making Haburi grow quickly, with the intention of making him ultimately her lover. She still further deceived the two sisters by pretending to assist in the search which was then undertaken in the surrounding bush, but she took good care to get back to her house first, and told Haburi to say that she, Wau-uta, was his mother, and gave him full directions as to how he must treat her.

522 Haburi was a splendid shot – no bird could escape his arrow – and Wau-uta directed him to give to her all the big birds that he killed, and to his mother and aunt all the little ones, which he had to pollute first by fouling them. The object of this was to make the two sisters so vexed and angry that they would leave the place: but this they would not do; they continued searching the neighborhood for their little child. This sort of thing went on for many days, big birds and dirtied little birds being presented by Haburi to Wau-uta and the two women, respectively. Haburi, however, did one day miss a bird for the first time, his arrow sticking into a branch overhanging a creek where his uncles, the water-dogs [i.e., otters], used to come and feed. It was a nice cleared space, and here Haburi eased himself, covering the dung with leaves. He next climbed the tree to dislodge the arrow, but just then the water-dogs arrived, and, scenting the air, exclaimed, "What smell is this? That worthless nephew of ours, Haburi, must be somewhere about." So they looked around, and down, and up, and finally discovering him on the tree branch, ordered him to come down. They then sat him on a bench, and told him he was leading a

> bad life, that the old woman was not his mother, but that the two younger ones were his mother and aunt, respectively. They furthermore impressed upon him that it was very wicked of him to divide the birds so unfairly, and that in future he must do exactly the opposite, giving his real mother, the bigger of the two sisters, the larger birds. They told him also to let his real mother know that the way he had hitherto treated her was due entirely to ignorance on his part, and that he was sorry. [From then on, Haburi distributed the birds fairly, which angered Wau-uta sorely. Haburi and the two women decided to leave and Haburi made a boat out of beeswax. But then a black duck stole it. Haburi then made new boats in different shapes from different materials, but all of these were also stolen away. Then he made a boat out of the wood of the Samauma tree. Haburi's boat became so big overnight that it could hold the three people and some food. He secretly slipped away from his field work, but the parrot betrayed him to Wau-uta. The three set off in the Samauma boat but the parrot clung tightly to the side even when everyone hit her on her claws with oars. Haburi climbed ashore again and ordered Wau-uta to sip the honey of a bee's nest in the hollow of a tree. She crawled in, and Haburi closed the opening. "There she can still be found today as the Wau Uta frog, which lives only in hollow trees."[18]

523 Wa-uta is a witch-magician who at the end of the tale is transformed into a frog. In another Warrau tale, "Black-Tiger, Wau-uta, and the Broken Arrow," she is a magical advisor to the hero. The transformation of the mother figure into a swamp animal that constitutes the swamp as a part that stands for the whole is a significant image.[19] Marshes are habitats often overgrown with a rich and diverse life. According to the ancient Egyptian view, all life arose from the hot mud of the Nile. Some Gnostics called the primeval chaos out of which the world was created, a bottomless mud or an "aqueous spasm."[20] Mother deities are often presented in conjunction with the swamp, for instance, the Egyptian Helen, who lives on an Island of mud, or the Great Mother Isis, to whom the frogs sing their hymns of the Lycian lake bottom.[21]

524 Like the swamp, the frog and the toad are symbols of the fertility of nature, and sometimes a picture of the Great Mother. For example, in "Sleeping

---

[18] "The tree-frog above referred to is probably the *Icono(bo)-aru*, or rain-frog, the name given to the old woman in the Carib version of the story. The croaking of this creature *Hyla venulosa* is a sure sign of rain." Note by the collector, W. E. Roth, *Inquiry into Animism*, 1915, pp. 122–125.

[19] As Wodan rules over the rest of the dead, so does the mother goddess Frigg rule over those sunk in the swamp; see Mogk, *Germanische*, p. 112.

[20] Leisegang, *Die Gnosis*, p. 149. [This could be from "On the Origin of the World"; see Robinson, p. 162f.] See also Bachofen, *Gräbersymbolik*, p. 324. For Thales, water is the primary matter of the world.

[21] See Bachofen, *Gräbersymbolik*, p. 332f.

Beauty (Little Briar Rose)" a frog comes to the queen in her bath and promises her that she will have a child. In the fairytale, "The Story of Haburi," Wau-uta appears as a protective Mother Goddess and saves the sisters and their child from the tiger, who represents the evil dark father (he takes the place of the father whom he has eaten). But Wau-uta proves to be selfish, her love is greedy, she wants the boy to stay with her forever, without having to develop further. Likewise, the swamp is not only germinating life, but also "stagnation" (Latin *stagnum* = standing water). With this inhibiting love the negative aspect of this figure comes to the fore and she becomes a "devouring" mother for the son. This situation is described very clearly. Wau-uta makes Haburi into her son-lover. This is an archetypal motif, the mother goddesses of the Near East were accompanied by a young hero, as a son-lover. Thus Ishtar had her Tammuz, Cybele had her Attis, etc. When the sorceress Wau-uta makes the boy Haburi grow up so fast, it means psychologically that the connection with the unconscious and the wisdom resting in it matures the human being and furthers an increase of creative power. But if the increase in strength is not truly worked for, and is (only) a gift from the magical, then it (the magical, the unconscious) will take back its voluntary gifts. Wau-uta demands, therefore, most of the hunting spoils and Haburi becomes her working slave.

525 The legend, "The Origin of the Echo," from the Ute tribe of the North American prairie, describes the same problem most impressively:

526 I'-o-wi (the turtle dove) was gathering seeds in the valley, and her little babe slept. Wearied with carrying it on her back, she laid it under the ti-ho-pi (sage bush) in care of the boy's sister, O-ho-tcu (the summer yellow bird). Engaged in her labors, the mother wandered a distance away, when a tso-a-vwits (a witch) came and asked the little girl, "Is that your brother?" O-ho-tcu answered, "This is my sister," for she had heard that witches preferred to steal boys, and did not care for girls. Then the tso-a-vwits was angry and chided her, saying that it was very naughty for girls to lie; and she put on a strange and horrid appearance, so that O-ho-tcu was stupefied with fright; then the tso-a-vwits ran away with the boy, carrying him to her home on a distant mountain. Then she laid him down on the ground, and, taking hold of his right foot, stretched the baby's leg until it was as long as that of a man, and she did the same to the other leg; then his body was elongated; she stretched his arms, and, behold, the baby was as large as a man. And the tso-a-vwits married him and had a husband, which she had long desired; but, though he had the body of a man, he had the heart of a babe, and knew no better than to marry a witch. [Chief among I'-o-wi's friends was her brother, Kwi'-na (the eagle), who traveled far and wide over all the land. One day he heard a strange

noise, and coming near he saw the tso-a-vwits and her husband, but he did not know that this large man was indeed the little boy who had been stolen. When he found out, he stole the child back and saved him. Out of fear of Kwi'-na, the witch crawled into the stomach of her grandfather, the rattlesnake.] Then the grandfather tried to throw her up, but could not, and became sick nigh unto death. At last, in his terrible retchings, he crawled out of his own skin, and left the tso-a-vwits in it, and she, imprisoned there, rolled about and hid in the rocks. When Kwi'-na came near he shouted, "Where are you, old tso-a-vwits? Where are you, old tso-a-vwits?" She repeated his words in mockery. Ever since that day witches have lived in snake skins, and hide among the rocks, and take great delight in repeating the words of passers-by."[22]

527 If the contact with the unconscious spiritual sphere can make people mature– in the negative sense also precocious – it can also bestow eternal youth. The beloved of the Great Mother are, therefore, eternally youthful heroes. The permanent intimate union with the creative source – seen from the inside – always gives fresh life. At the same time in this situation – seen from the outside – against the background of the primordial Great Mother, everyone appears young.

528 In "The Story of Haburi," however, the negative effect of the binding to the primal mother is emphasized, because the development of the stage of childlike awareness is the task of indigenous peoples. Haburi receives precocity and adulthood, but only in the service of Wau-uta. He is in the clutches of the Great Mother and must be kept in her house with the thorn-cloaked door (like Sleeping Beauty = Little Briar Rose beneath the hedge of thorns). But through the otters, representing his animal instincts, he is warned and decides to flee.

529 But he is hindered by a black duck that steals the boat, his means of escaping from the magic kingdom. It is, of course, Wau-uta herself who appears in this form, since the duck is a typical image of the Mother Goddess. The black color of the duck points to her dark aspect. Often in fairytales a duck steals the sought-after treasure.[23] Wau-uta, in her duck form, takes control of the boat, so that Haburi remains bound to her, the devouring primal ground of the unconscious. Only perseverance and continually trying again and again creates a new boat that resists her magic.

530 Haburi takes the wood of a certain tree, which is helpful, and at the same time he lures Wau-uta into a hollow tree, and locks her up. He thus finds

---

[22] Powell, *Mythology*, 1881 pp. 45–47.

[23] See Bächtold-Stäubli under *Ente* [duck] for her witchcraft; see also Bolte and Mackensen, *Handwörterbuch*, under *Ente*. The duck, along with the goose, flocks to the witch and is eaten in the land of the dead. It is also a soul-bird.

protection in trees, which also, as a boat, bear him across the waters and which entrap the angry witch-mother. Thus cure is obtained by applying "like cures like" since the tree is also a symbol of the maternal world principle. Moreover, Haburi was generated from a palm tree. Among primitive peoples, there is a widespread belief that ancestral souls from a tree such as Ratappa (= child seeds) can enter a woman and make her pregnant.[24] In such cases, the tree is androgynous, and both sexes can give birth, male, as for instance, Haburi's palm father,[25] and female, as the tree mother who shelters the dead.[26] In most cases, the tree plays a purely maternal role, as is apparent from the popular belief according to which small children are brought down by "children's trees" (*Kinderbäume*).[27] The Herero people of Namibia trace their origins back to a very old tree from which they emerged.[28] According to the Aztecs,[29] there is in the hereafter a "nursemaid tree" in the so-called Xochitlapan ["garden-land"], or Chichihuacuauhco ["Place of the Nursemaid Tree"], at whose foot lie "unsullied" children (i.e., the "precious stones") who have died. When they open their mouths, a nourishing liquid drips from the tree. In the Persian (Iranian) myth there is the white Haoma, a celestial tree that grows in the lake Ourukasha, which confers eternal life, gives children to women, and horses to men.[30] The Norns, the Germanic goddesses of fate, live in the roots at the base of the World Ash, where they not only cut the thread of destiny, but also donate wealth as matrons.[31] According to Plutarch, the dead Osiris is washed up on a beach in Byblos and there enveloped by an erica (tamarisk) bush that becomes a tree so beautiful that the king of Byblos has it made into columns for his palace.[32] The Great Mother was often represented as a tree, from which her son-lover emerged. The evergreen pine tree and the almond tree were sacred to Attis, out of which he came and into which he was transformed.[33]

---

[24] See Thurnwald, "Primitive Initiationsriten," 1940, p. 347–348.

[25] On the light tree, see also A. Dieterich, *Abraxas*, Leipzig, 1891, pp. 98ff., and W. Mannhardt, *Wald- und Feldkulte*, vol. 1, Berlin, 1875, vol. 1, pp. 242ff.

[26] The tree as forefather of the human race, therefore, was often considered a double tree, *Ask* and *Embla*, ash and elm, as the original Germans, from which the gods created humans. Cf. M. Führer, *Nordgermanische*, München, 1938, pp. 43–44. On the bisexual nature of the tree, see also C.G. Jung, *Symbols of Transformation*, CW 5, ¶324ff., ¶659.

[27] See O. Rank, *Myth of the Birth*, Baltimore, 2004 p. 98; see further H. Silberer, *Problems of Mysticism*, New York, 1917, p. 64. See also, "Aspenclog," where the hero is the son of an aspen. In "Fundevogel" [Bird-foundling], the hero is found by a forest ranger high up in a tree, where it has been abducted by a bird of prey. He is later pursued by a wicked mother figure. On the personification of the tree and its intimate relationship to human life, see Mannhardt, *Wald und Feldkulte*, vol. I, and vol. II, ch. 1, section I.

[28] See Lang, *Myth*, London, 1887, vol. 1, p. 176.

[29] See Krickeberg, *Azteken and Inka*, p. 30, and Graulich, *Myths of Ancient Mexico*, p. 249.

[30] See C.G. Jung, *Symbols of Transformation*, CW 5, ¶367, fn 77 and and under *Baum* [tree]. See also Leeuw, *Religion in Essence*, vol. 1, pp. 55–58.

[31] See Ninck, *Wodan*, pp. 207–208. On the *Vardträd* as a protecting, nourishing tree, see *ibid.*, p. 216.

[32] Even columns have a maternal meaning. Cf. Erman, *Religion der Ägypter*, pp. 83ff. See also the connection between the tree and the primal in "Ngeraod's Bundle," where the hero while walking to his mother must pass through an opening and closing tree.

[33] See Reitzenstein, *Hellenistic Mystery-Religions*, pp. 176–177; see also Cumont, *The Oriental Religions*

In the German fairytale, "The Old Woman in the Woods," the prince who saved the poor girl had previously been transformed into a tree by an old woman. Given its maternal meaning, the tree can also be a symbol of the original homeland. In the view of the Aztecs the country of origin, the lost paradise, is a broken yucca tree, Tamoanchan, the home of all foods.[34] The Gnostic Simon Magus claimed that all flesh and all sensible things would be nourished by a big tree, which was identical to the visible and invisible celestial fire, the raw material of the world.[35] Thus, the tree symbolizes also the spiritual basis of the world. The same idea is already found in the *Brihadaranyaka-Upanishad*, where it is stated: "If it (the spirit) now falls asleep, he takes this all-containing World-Wood (mâtrâm matter), cuts itself down, and rebuilds itself by virtue of its own glory, according to its own light. . . "[36] According to a text from the Pyramids, a tall sycamore stands in the eastern heavens upon which as the tree of life the gods sit and they and the blessed ones are nourished from its fruits.[37]

531 Since the tree symbolizes not only the maternal in general, but also the basic structure of the spirit, it also confers secret wisdom. In addition to the Tree of Life, there is a Tree of Knowledge in paradise.[38] To acquire wisdom, Odin hung nine days on the World Ash Yggdrasil, which symbolizes a rebirth from the mother.[39] (The tree as an evil mother already appeared in "Hitchinna," which is the cause of suffering, when the man was dismembered on the spruce. There also occurred the destruction of a man whom the mother

---

in Roman Paganism, pp. 44–45. In ancient Rome, the corpse in the mourning procession was decorated as a pine tree as a symbol of the dead Attis; see Cumont, p. 52.

[34] Cf. Krickeberg, *Azteken and Inka*, p. 342, esp. the footnote about "Quetzalcoatl's fall and the Demise of Tollan"; see also and footnote on p. 358 about "The Creation of the World." [In English, this is mentioned by Graulich, *Myths of Ancient Mexico*, p. 195.]

[35] See Leisegang, *Die Gnosis*, p. 68, See a modern English translation by Price of *The Great Declaration* attributed to Simon Magus:

> And this is what is meant by "The flaming sword that turned this way and that to guard the path to the Tree of Life." This because the blood turns this way into semen and that way into milk, and like the tree, this power becomes both mother and father, father of all who are born and mother of those who are nourished. It stands in need of nothing, self-sufficient. And the Tree of Life, guarded by the whirling, fiery sword, is the seventh power which proceeds from itself, containing all and yet latent in the six powers. (Price 2006).]

See also Mead, *Fragments*, pp. 171–172, and Guest, *Mabinogion*, p. 203. In the *Mabinogion*, Peredur comes to a tree, of which one half is in flames and the other half in living green foliage.

[36] See Deussen, *Sixty Upanishads*, p. 467. For an English translation, see Max Müller, *Upanishads: Sacred Books of the East*: "And when he falls asleep, then after having taken away with him the material from the whole world, destroying and building it up again, he sleeps (dreams) by his own light. In that state the person is self-illuminated" (p. 164); see also Deussen, *Sixty Upanishads*, vol. 1, p. 203 (*Chandogy-Upanishad*: Eighth Chap. Twelfth Part); see further Deussen, *Sixty Upanishads*, vol. 1, pp. 305ff. (*Śvetāśvatara-Upanishad*) [possibly Sixth Adhyaya].

[37] See Erman, *Religion der Ägypter*, p. 215.

[38] See the prophetic and speaking trees in fairytales in Bolte and Mackensen, *Handwörterbuch*, under *Baum* (tree). The Buddha was enlightened under the tree. On the symbolism of the tree, see C.G. Jung, *Tree*, CW 13, ¶304–482.

[39] See Ninck, *Wodan*, p. 180; C.G. Jung, *Symbols of Transformation*, CW 5, ¶672 fn. 79, ¶494; Wünsche, *Die Sagen vom Lebensbaum und Lebenswasser. Altorientalische Mythen*, pp. 13–14.

principle had turned demonic. According to the principle that "like cures like," the coyote outwits and kills him by assuming the form of an old woman.)

532 The tree is a symbol of the maternal, matter, the basic substance of the world, therefore, of unconscious growth and spiritual development both as a life-giving and as a deadly principle. So when Haburi traps the frog mother in the hollow tree, this is a form of burial, the destruction of the evil mother principle in itself and also its transformation into the tree symbol, rendering it positive and life-enhancing.

533 The tree figures clearly both as an evil and as a good mother in "The Fig Tree," a fairytale from the Awaiama tribe of Melanesia:

534 Once upon a time a woman gave birth to a child, and soon afterwards her husband went to the islands fishing for turtle and dugong; he intended to smoke their flesh where he killed them but expected to come back next moon. Now the old woman, his mother, had powers of sorcery, and she said to her daughter-in-law, "There are ripe figs on a fig tree not far away, climb up and get them.[40] The young woman was still weak and did not want to go; but the old woman urged her until she consented and climbed the tree. When she had got to the fork of the tree, the hag began to weave her spell. At this the fork of the fig tree (which was covered with a sticky substance) held the young mother so tightly that she could not struggle free. Then the old woman climbed up and cut off one of her daughter-in-law's hands. She climbed down and took the hand to her house and left it there while she went to get vegetable food to eat with it. [Nevertheless, the young mother gave her milk to the infant. After four days the mother died and the older children fled with food, biting insects, and snakes to a little tree, which bent down on call to them and sprung back up, so that they could reach a high palm tree.]

535 By and by the old hag came back but could not find the children. "Little ones, little ones, where are you?" she called aloud; and mumbled to herself, "I'm afraid I've lost my little meats, perhaps they know about their mother." Just then the children heard her and said, "Oh grandmother, we are here, up in this palm tree." "All of you?" "Yes, all of us." "This is lucky," she said to herself, "I was afraid my little meat provisions had run away from me." [When she tried to climb up the palm tree, the insects attacked her. This repeats several times and the children are thus spared.] Now it happened that their father dreamt of the children and changed his plans, and taking his nets and spears

[40] [Note by Seligman et al., *The Melanesians of British New Guinea*, Cambridge 1910: "The tree referred to bears a fruit of a rich red color when ripe."]

> and fish came back to his home. Now when he got to the woman's house there was no one there. "Ah!" said he, "where are the little ones and their mother?" As he went down the river to bathe he was startled by a coconut falling quite close to him; looking up he saw his children. "How did you get up there? Where is your mother?" said he. "Our grandmother killed her," said the eldest-born, "and we fled here to avoid being killed." Then calling to the gomida tree to let them down they descended to the ground and greeted their father. He went to his house and began sharpening his long cutting tool and he ground and ground it until it was very sharp.

536 When his mother climbed up the house ladder groaning in pain her son killed her, took all his things, and burnt the two houses and went down to the beach and got on board his canoe with all his belongings and his three children, to cross over to the islands. Now there was a strong current and the canoe made no headway, so the man threw out his youngest born to lighten the canoe. But by-and-by the waves grew higher and higher and the man threw his second born overboard, and he and his eldest son bailed hard to keep their canoe afloat. And when night came on the canoe filled and as they were in the open sea, they soon drowned.[41]

537 The grandmother ties the young mother to the tree that later serves the purposes of the evil old one. Stuck on the tree, the mother is cut up and eaten by the witch. Her loving, caring, and maternal behavior (she suckles her children to the end) is slowly overgrown (as in a disease) by the destructive power of the death mother. The dismemberment of a human in a tree is reminiscent of that recounted in "Hitchinna." It is the disintegration in death. The cannibal witch looks like a duplicate of the tree and embodies the reason that the maternal tree exposes its negative side. Grandmother, of course, means "great mother," that is, the archetypal Great Mother,[42] who begins to destroy the human soul of the hunter's family until the end when a "flood" reaches the father himself.[43] This grim figure contrasts with the touching and friendly image of the palm-mother, who helps the children and grants them

[41] Shortened from Seligman et al., *The Melanesians of British New Guinea*, pp. 404–408.

[42] See C.G. Jung, "Mother Archetype," CW 9i, ¶188: "As the mother of the mother, she [the grandmother] is greater than the latter. She is in truth the 'grand' or 'Great Mother.' Not infrequently she assumes the attributes of wisdom as well as those of the witch." In the genesis legend of the Menomini tribe ("Genesis"), the earth (Nokomis) is the grandmother of the trickster-hero-culture bringer Manabusch (Nanabozho). In the Ojibwe language, nookomis means "my grandmother" (see *The Ojibwe People's Dictionary*).

[43] The evil grandmother occurs in a similar form in "The Jaguar Who Ate Her Grandchildren." There, the mother is the good and the grandmother the evil animal. ["In masculine psychology, the evil stepmother is a symbol of the unconscious in a destructive role"; see M.-L. v. Franz, *Interpretation of Fairytales*, New York, 1970, pp. VII–6.]

protection. In this case, otherwise dreaded biting animals, insects, and snakes work their service. They all join forces against the destructive grandmother. But the overcoming of her magic is only temporarily successful. The man is devoured with his children, whom he sacrifices. The unconscious in its negative manifestations remains victorious. Once again, the sea means "the devouring mother" in a changed form. A Nordic fairytale, "Storm Magic," uses the same image when it describes how witches, who appear as ravens on the ship of the husband, stir up a storm to kill him.

538 In the three stories just mentioned, the Great Mother in various forms has banned children into her realm to take advantage of them. Haburi (in "The Story of Haburi") is her lover and must give her the bulk of his catch, and the tso-a-vwits, the old witch in "The Origin of the Echo," dominates her child-like lover who worships her with her mind. In "The Fig Tree," the old mother devours the young mother – and here the "imprisonment" by the magical-maternal (or in psychological terms, being bound to the unconscious) is particularly vividly illustrated – after preventing her with words from freeing herself from the sticky goo of the tree. The grandchildren succeed, initially, until with their father they fall victim to the Great Mother.

539 The European fairytale also knows the theme of a confrontation with this primal image (archetype) and describes it – with a positive outcome – in "Hansel and Gretel," the well-known Grimm's fairytale:

> 540 Hard by a great forest dwelt a poor woodcutter with his wife and his two children. The boy was called Hansel and the girl Gretel. He had little to bite and to break, and once when great scarcity fell on the land, he could no longer procure daily bread. Now when he thought over this by night in his bed, and tossed about in his anxiety, he groaned and said to his wife, "What is to become of us? How are we to feed our poor children, when we no longer have anything even for ourselves?" "I'll tell you what, husband," answered the woman, "Early tomorrow morning we will take the children out into the forest to where it is the thickest, there we will light a fire for them, and give each of them one piece of bread more, and then we will go to our work and leave them alone. They will not find the way home again, and we shall be rid of them."
>
> 541 The children, who could not sleep because they were hungry, heard what the stepmother said, and with the help of small white pebbles that Hansel took along, they found their way back home the next night. They were received angrily by the mother, while the father rejoiced at their return. Not long after, the process repeated itself. This time the children tried to save themselves with the help of scattered breadcrumbs, but these were picked up by birds, so that they got lost.

On the third day they saw a snow-white bird sitting on a branch and followed it until they reached a little house made of bread, cake, and sweets. There they were welcomed by a very, very old woman. But the next morning the old witch (for the old woman ate lost children) locked Hansel in a small stable and Gretel had to cook food to fatten up her brother. Every morning Hansel had to put his finger through the barred door so that the witch could feel if he had become fat enough to eat. But he stuck out a small bone, and this fooled the old woman since her eyes were so bad. She was surprised that he was not getting fat. She was just waiting to slaughter Hansel and cook him up. Her hunger grew and she could not wait any more for Hansel to get fat so she ordered Gretel to crawl into the oven to check the heat. Of course, she wanted to shove Gretel in and cook her up. But Gretel saw what she had in her mind, and said, "I do not know how I am to do it; how do you get in?" "Silly goose," said the old woman, "The door is big enough; just look, I can get in myself!" and she crept up and thrust her head into the oven. Then Gretel gave her a push that drove her far into it, and shut the iron door, and fastened the bolt. Oh! then she began to howl quite horribly, but Gretel ran away, and the godless witch was miserably burnt to death.

542 They collected some precious stones and pears and set off through the forest. A duck helped them get over a river and they found their way back home "and threw themselves into their father's arms. The man had not known one happy hour since he had left the children in the forest; the woman, however, was dead. Gretel emptied her pinafore until pearls and precious stones ran about the room, and Hansel threw one handful after another out of his pocket to add to them. Then all anxiety was at an end, and they lived together in perfect happiness. My tale is done, there runs a mouse, whosoever catches it, may make himself a big fur cap out of it."[44]

543 The negative power of the mother appears clearly here in two figures simultaneously: as the demonic-primitive witch and as the wicked stepmother [in the original version, the biological mother]. That the mother also died after the destruction of the witch proves the secret identity of the two women.

544 While the (step)mother is characterized by callous hardness and she provides nothing to eat, the witch, on the contrary, is at first giving and hospitable.[45] Providing food and nourishment is, as we will show, the

[44] Summarized from Grimm, pp. 52–58.

[45] In a Portuguese version, she is one-eyed like Balor (in "Balor and the Birth of Lugh"). See also Bolte and Polívka, *Anmerkungen*, vol. 1, p. 117.

prerogative of the great mother goddess. In the realm of Mother Holle (in "Mother Holle") is an oven (often a symbol of the womb), full of baked bread, an apple tree full of ripe apples, and in her house "every day there was boiled and fried food." The cake house in "Hansel and Gretel" is, however, not a case of kind donation from the Great Mother, but a trick of the witch to attract the children and to eat them. This negative side reveals itself to those who lose themselves in such a deception, that is, in wishful fantasies of childhood, and so they tarry into the danger of being "eaten" by the unconscious.

545 Considered psychologically, this positive creative imagination stands against a sterile hardness embodied by the stepmother, who represents the same process seen from the other side: they are both an enslavement to the archetype of the Great Mother, whereby the human believes he or she can escape the hard reality of the world through unconscious fantasies.[46]

546 This problem is very nicely illuminated in a Spanish fairytale, "The Story of the Old Witch." There, an old witch from the "Witch's Mountain," who has a head of iron, puts all the people who look up at her in a bag in which they perish. This symbolizes losing one's self in the unconscious by a dreamy, childlike gazing into the air. A hero defeats the witch by restraining himself from looking up at her and forcing her to look down at him, whereby with her heavy iron head crashes, "very deep into the earth, so that only one leg stuck out." The determination of the conscious human being forces the unconscious negative soul images down to the ground of reality, thereby eliminating their dangerous nature.

547 In the fairytale, "Hansel and Gretel," one cannot consider the evil stepmother generally as only a negative aspect of the Great Mother, she is also a part of the anima, the soul of the father, as a wrong or evil spirit that takes possession of him, drowning out his original being with her evil whisperings. According to the beliefs of primitive peoples, a "foreign" soul can take possession of a man as if it owned him and set him in an inappropriate state not in accord with his natural intentions. He feels himself "bewitched" or "enchanted."[47] Under this misguided influence, the father drives his two children, who symbolize his future, his becoming, into the clutches of the witch. That is, the mother-image as a negative force within him gains more and more the upper hand.

548 A bird leads the children to the witch. The bird is a symbol of intuitive ideas, flights of fancy, and this streaming out into the air invites the deadly power of the unconscious to come forward. Overcoming the evil mother-

[46] See the connection between the images of the cake house and the cold in Volume II under the discussion of the Chuckchee fairytale, "The Children Carried Away By the Giant." In that tale, a giant steals a boy and a girl and takes them to the center of the *sea* where a dark, cold, empty cake house stands. Seagulls carry them back to their father.

[47] See Lévy-Bruhl, *How Natives Think*, New York, 1966, p. 232.

power takes place in one's self, because the oven in which she burns is (as we have already said) a maternal symbol.[48] In the center of the unconscious a reversal takes place, in which the negative aspect is destroyed itself and turns positive. Then it reveals itself in the form of the treasures that Hansel and Gretel take home. That the stepmother dies at the same time is based on an old Germanic idea, also found elsewhere, that when a witch spirit is destroyed – in whatever form she may take – the human shape that the witch has embodied is also affected.[49] The state of being "bewitched" ends with one stroke, and the unconscious life-enhancing effects can work anew. The children are carried back over the unfordable waters by a white duck (!). Again, this represents a completely symmetrical reversal of the initially luring behavior of the white bird.[50] This tale portrays the transformation of the mother-imago that in itself is intuitively comprehended but which runs completely in the unconscious as an inner process. This transformation is performed by the fire in the oven. The hidden inner fire, a symbol of passion, is in the magic realm a common attribute not only of the father god but also, in the magical realm, of the mother deity, who as Mother Earth carries a fire hidden in her depths. This one's inner fire, the maternal substance and the unconscious spiritual force, is purified and transformed by it. The transformation of the "Mother," of "matter," by self-destruction is one of the basic motifs of all fairytales which primarily depict images and functions of the mother archetype.

549 A pure fight – in this case of a grown man – with the destructive maternal force is described in "Giviok (Kiviok)," an Inuit fairytale:

> 550 Kiviok, it is told, lost his wife, and in despair was about to leave his child and the place where she was buried. He only waited till the boy had gone to sleep, and then he let himself down from the ledge to the floor; but when the child began crying, he again lay down beside him. Once he was all ready, stooping down to get out of the entrance, but went back unable to leave his son. One day the little boy entered the room in a highly agitated state, saying, "My mother is walking outside with a stranger." Kiviok answered, "Thy mother is not here; she is lying under the big stones yonder." But the little boy persisted, saying, "Look for thyself, then," and when Kiviok did look out of the window, he saw his wife in the arms of another man. At this he got into a great rage, went out, killed them, and threw their bodies on top of each other

48 See Bächtold-Stäubli under *Ofen* (oven) and *Backofen* [backing oven].

49 See Mogk, *Germanische*, pp. 50–51.

50 On the duck as a soul bird, see Bolte and Mackensen, *Handwörterbuch* (1930) under *Ente* (duck); see also Ninck, *Wodan*, p. 227, on the Valkyries in duck form.

into a stone grave. Father and son now went to rest, but when the boy slept, the father carried out his intention of taking flight.

551 Kiviok fled in his kayak across the wild sea, barely escaping a whirlpool and sea lice that devoured his kayak paddle. Finally he fell into a patch of seaweed that was matted to such an extent that he could lie down in it and he slept. When he awoke, he laboriously pushed his kayak onwards with his hands, then rowed up to two icebergs, between which there was a narrow passage that alternately opened and shut. He just managed to pass through but the tip of the stern of his kayak got crushed. He reached land and shelter and hid. A woman living nearby noticed Kiviok and invited him to enter her abode. On entering, he saw a hideous old hag lying beneath a coverlet, who ordered her daughter to go and fetch some berries. She returned with a great quantity of them, profusely mixed with fat. Kiviok, while he was eating them, remarked, "They are really delicious," and Usorsak (this was the name of the old hag) rejoined, "No wonder; the fat is of quite a young fellow." Kiviok responded, "Fie! Anything of that kind I cannot eat," and stooping down, he noticed many human heads all in a row beneath the ledge. When the hag uncovered herself a little, and turned her back towards him, he saw something glittering close behind her. When they were all ready to go to rest, Kiviok said, "I shall just go outside for an instant." Accordingly he went out and soon found a flat stone to cover his breast with. Upon re-entering the hut, he lay down on the ledge beneath the window. No sooner did he seem to be sleeping, then he heard the daughter saying, "Now he is sound asleep," and instantly the old hag came jumping down from her place on the main ledge. But she noticed that he was feigning not to be quite asleep and she cautiously returned. When he again had become quiet, and lying on his back, exposing his breast, the daughter again said, "He surely sleeps now," and again the mother let herself down, even quicker than the first time. Jumping up where he was lying, she sat down with all her weight upon his chest, crying out, "Oh dear!" but then she instantly tumbled down. "What a pity!" cried the daughter, "Usorsak has broken her tail! She provided so nicely for all of us." (Meaning that she had been killing men with the help of her tail.) Kiviok now got up from his couch, let fall the stone, and escaped through the door, the daughter shouting after him, "Thou rascal! Wouldn't I like to have had a taste of thy fine cheeks!" But he was already in his kayak, where he nearly capsized in his hurry. Rising again, he broke out, "Shouldn't I like to harpoon her!" and so saying, he killed her on the spot.

552 He continued on his journey and landed at another place and again a woman appeared, who invited him into her hut. Mother and daughter complained that they had no one to bring in their catch. Kiviok offered to help and told of his experiences. The women thanked him for killing the old witch, for she had killed all the men in their village. They explained that when he helped to bring in the catch, he must pay attention to the sea roaring, "When the high tide sets in, thou must be back on shore." As soon as he heard the sea roar, the great waves came rolling over him, so that he narrowly escaped up the beach. The harpooned fish, on account of their full bladders, kept floating on the surface, but were driven across to the opposite shore. Kiviok fetched them back in his kayak, however, for which the women were very thankful. He remained with them for some time.

553 After a while, the memory of his son haunted him, and he said to himself, "My poor little son! What a pitiful thing it was to hear him cry when I went away! Someday I must go and see him." So he left that place and travelled on and on. He encountered again all the dangers he had met with on his departure from home, but once more happily got past them. At last he reached the opposite country, and he heard people singing. He followed the song, and fell in with a great many boats tugging a whale along, on which stood a vigorous man. He did not recognize him, but this was his son, and he had been catching whales. The father left him as a weeping child and now beheld him as a great hunter, standing proud on a whale's back.[51]

554 A variation of the legend, "Kiviung," shows the image of the mother in other facets:

555 An old woman lived with her grandson in a small hut. As she had no husband and no son to take care of her and the boy, they were very poor, the boy's clothing being made of skins of birds, which they caught in snares. When the boy would come out of the hut and join his playfellows, the men would laugh at him and tear his outer garments. Only one man, whose name was Kiviung, was kind to the young boy: but could not protect him from the others. Often the lad came to his grandmother crying and weeping, and she always consoled him and each time made him a new garment. She entreated the men to stop teasing the boy and tearing his clothing, but they would not listen to her prayer. At last she got angry and swore she

[51] Rink, *Eskimo*, pp. 157–161: "This tale is chiefly taken from a single manuscript, but nevertheless it is well known all over Greenland. Some slight traces will be found in it of the Indian *Hiawatha* tale."

would take revenge upon his abuser, and she could easily do so, as she was a great angakoq. She commanded her grandson to step into a puddle, which was on the floor of the hut, telling him what would happen and how he should behave. As soon as he stood in the water, the earth opened and he sank out of sight, but the next moment he rose near the beach as a yearling seal with a beautiful skin and swam about lustily.

556 The seal lured the men far away from the coast out into the sea. Then a great storm arose and all the men drowned as a result of a storm, the seal returned home and transformed back into the boy. Of the men, only Kiviung, who was also a great angakoq and had never abused the boy, escaped the wind and waves. Being now alone, Kiviung set out to sea. After several days of paddling in the wild sea, he saw a coast with a stone house in which he entered and in which he was warmly welcomed by an old woman named Arnaitiang. At her request, he hung his stockings on a frame to dry. Later, when he reached out for them, the drying frame rose out of reach. When he asked Arnaitiang for help she answered, "Take them yourself, there they are, there they are," and went out again. Actually she was a very bad woman and wanted to eat Kiviung.

557 Seeing through the evil machinations of the old hag, he conjured up his tornaq, a huge polar bear that immediately rose from the depth under the floor of the house. When Arnaitiang heard the bear's loud roar, she offered Kiviung his stockings and boots. But Kiviung would not stay any longer with this horrid witch and did not even dare to put on his boots, but took them from Arnaitiang and rushed out of the door. He had barely escaped when it clapped violently together and just caught the tail of his jacket, which was torn off. He hastened to his kayak without once stopping to look behind and paddled away.

558 He had only gone a short distance before Arnaitiang, who had recovered from her fear, came out swinging her glittering woman's knife and threatening to kill him. He was nearly frightened to death and almost upset his kayak. However, he managed to balance it again and cried in answer, lifting his spear: "I shall kill you with my spear." When Arnaitiang heard these words, she fell down terror stricken and broke her knife. Kiviung then observed that it was made of a thin slab of fresh water ice.

559 He traveled on for many days and nights, following the shore. At last he came to a hut, and again a lamp was burning inside. There he found a woman who lived all alone with her daughter. Her son-in-law was a log of driftwood, which had four boughs. Every day about the time of

low water they carried it to the beach and when the tide came in it swam away. When night came again it returned with eight large seals, two being fastened to every bough. Thus the log provided its wife, her mother, and Kiviung with an abundance of food. One day, however, after they had launched it as they always had done, it left and never returned. After a short interval Kiviung married the young widow. Now he went sailing every day himself and was very successful. Soon the old mother became jealous of her daughter, for the new husband of the latter was a splendid hunter and she wished to marry him herself. One day when he was away hunting, she murdered her daughter, and in order to deceive Kiviung, she removed her daughter's skin and crept into it, thus changing her shape into that of the young woman. When Kiviung returned, she went to meet him, as it had been her daughter's custom, but when Kiviung saw the bones of his wife he at once became aware of the cruel deed and of the deception and fled.

560 Kiviung traveled on for many days and nights, always following the shore. At last he again came to a hut where a lamp was burning. As his clothing was wet and he was hungry, he landed and went up to the house. Before entering the hut it occurred to him that it would be best to find out first who was inside. He climbed up to the window and looked through the peephole. On the bed he saw an old woman whose name was Aissivang (spider). When she saw the dark figure before the window she believed it was a cloud passing the sun, and as the light was insufficient to enable her to go on with her work she got angry. With her knife she cut away her eyebrows, ate them, and did not mind dripping blood, but sewed on. When Kiviung saw this he thought she must be a very bad woman and turned away.[52] Still he traveled on days and nights. At last he came to a land that seemed familiar to him and he soon recognized his own country. He was very glad when he saw some boats coming to meet him. They had been on a whaling expedition and were towing a great carcass to the village. In the bow of one of the boats stood a stout young man who had killed the whale. He was Kiviung's son, whom he had left a small boy and who was now grown up and had become a great hunter. His wife had taken a new husband, but now she returned to Kiviung.[53]

561 Through the death of his wife, the danger arises for Kiviok that he too could be pulled into death, and the magic kingdom soon approaches him in various destructive forms. All unconscious phenomena are present here; the mother

[52] Krickeberg, *Nordamerika*, pp. 370–371, notes that in other versions Kiviung cuts off her head.
[53] Some parts summarized, based on Boas, "The Central Eskimo," 1888, pp. 621–624.

symbols that fill the psychic void left by the loss of the spouse. The image of the mother clearly represents the realm of the dead, the unconscious in its negative aspect. It appears as whirlpools, as hungry hordes of sea lice, as matted seaweed, as crashing rocks, and is finally personified as a man-eating witch. The sea lice symbolize the imminent danger of dissolution of the smallest units (psychologically, mental illness), to lose oneself as a particle in nature. The matted seaweed reminds us of spider's nets and weaving, especially in relation to untangling the knotted hair of Frau Holle.[54] The witch is accompanied by her daughter, a younger figure who seems to be just as bad.[55] The hero recognizes the risk, hardens and protects himself with the stone on his chest and causes the witch to perish at the hands of her own wickedness.[56] Thus, the purely negative aspect of the mother-imago is removed, but the hero experiences a repetition of the pair in which the mother aspect is admittedly not so evil but the danger of over-sleeping and of being flooded (!) still threatens as a sinking into the unconscious. After he escaped that final danger, his future appears rosy – symbolically embodied by his son who has grown up to be a great hunter. The variant tale also shows a series of evil mother images that speak for themselves. While Kiviok, according to primitive peoples, at best only escapes the imago of the devouring mother, other tales describe in detail the difficulties and the problems of a deep *auseinandersetzung* with the Great Mother. One example is the Irish fairytale, "The Knight With the Sinister Laugh":

562 And so it happened that a man and a woman had just married. Soon after their marriage, the man died and the woman was left alone. Nine months after the wedding – not one day more and not one day less – she gave birth to a boy child. Because she was so lonely, she loved him above everything; she would not have given him away for a mountain of gold. She suckled her boy, Cathal, as a baby at her breast for twenty-one years. She did not even allow him to cross the threshold of their house and nearly worked herself to death for him.

---

[54] See the important Inuit theme of the shaman's task to untangle Sedna's hair to obtain and preserve the nourishment of sea animals; see also page 239. On the crashing cliffs being caught by the mother, see C.G. Jung, *Symbols of Transformation*, CW 5, ¶367 fn. 72. See further the opening and closing tree at the entrance to the land of the Mother Goddess in "Ngeraod's Bundle."

[55] In her original form, this figure is often the same as the evil mother. See, for example, the terrible Gorgon as the companion and original form of Athena; on the identity of mother and daughter, see also Ninck, *Wodan*, p. 179.

[56] See the destruction of the witch in "Hansel and Gretel." See also the outwitting of the witch in the Japanese fairytale, "Ox-Cart Puller and Mountain Witch," collected in Rumpf, Japanische Volksmärchen, Jena, 1938, p. 179f. There, the driver of an ox hides from the witch Yamauba, first on a tree, then in the reeds, and finally in a boat. Eventually, he reaches the witch's hut and scalds her to death with hot water.

563 When the widow came into "the childish age" (i.e., senility), the son decided to care for her. He jumped out of bed, stretched, and was so tall his head stuck out of the house's rafters. The mother thought he was naughty and was leaving his "basket." But he let her sew together the necessary clothing from her bed linen, dressed, and hurried as fast as he could until he reached a castle. The laborers on the square before the castle fled from this tall skinny guy. He managed to hire himself out by showing his enormous powers and helped to build the palace. He sent all the money he earned back to his mother. One day, the king promised that whoever could get a huge snake in the forest to enter into service for the building, could then marry his golden-cheeked daughter, Leámuinn. Anyone who failed in this endeavor, however, would perish. Despite the warnings of his mother, the hero gave notice that he wanted to take on the task. He had been nursed for so long that he felt like he had the strength of a hundred men. He promptly overpowered the serpent by the forest lake. Although he earned his prize, the princess demanded that before she would marry him, he must first take the snake back to the forest and kill it, and then travel to the East and within one year's time find out why the "knight with the gloomy laugh" had not laughed for seven years. He must also return back with evidence of the death of the "terrible old woman with the cold cruel tooth." If he failed in this endeavor he would be punished with death. Cathal immediately took on the task, drove the snake back into the woods, slugged it dead and cut off her[57] tongue, lest anyone else should boast of his deed. Then he sailed to the East Indies in a miraculous boat that steered itself.

564 Forthwith, Cathal invaded the land and made his way to a homestead. To enter, he had to get down on hands and knees to crawl through a low door. Once inside, he found a slim, tall man lying stretched out motionless on his back in a bed. As soon as Cathal saluted him, the man jumped up and grabbed Cathal by the throat. A great struggle ensued. "The two huge men fought a fight that the world had never seen before or since." Finally Cathal thought of his mother and with the utmost effort pushed his opponent into the fire. The stranger begged for mercy and when Cathal asked him to identify the "knight with the gloomy laugh" who had not laughed for seven years, the man admitted it was indeed he himself. Cathal healed his wounds with his saliva. Then they observed each other warily. Suddenly they heard a woman's shriek that shattered the walls, and the knight's face distorted in pain.

---

[57] [In German, the snake is female.]

565 The next morning, Cathal wandered through the area, searching for the cause of the screaming. Two mouse-colored horses lured him into a round place in the forest. At the neighing of the animals, a terrible, huge old woman appeared, foaming at the mouth. She offered Cathal a deal: either he fought with her on "the blood-soaked stone" or he should allow her to cut "three times with a sharpened knife all his ribs into pieces." The son of the widow chose to fight on the blood-soaked stone, and returned the threat to his female opponent. Then ensued a battle of such terrible fierceness, unknown from one end of the world to the other. Towards evening, Cathal became exhausted. The old witch noticed his weakening and began to rejoice. A wren landed on the witch's nose, however, and jabbed its beak into her eyes. and immediately she became weak as a goose. Cathal finished her off with a blow to her neck at the artery and cut off her tongue.

566 Then he went to her palace and rummaged through all the rooms. He found no people, but gold and silver that filled every room. He harnessed up the horses and hastened to the knight without betraying what had happened. When the knight with the gloomy laugh heard no shrieks that evening, he was surprised. He told Cathal that the witch had lived there ever since time immemorial. Every night she ravaged, scorched, and burnt the island and everything and everybody that was on it. Only he and his caretaker lived there, nothing and nobody else. All his fights were in vain, and every night "in the dead hour" the agonizing scream came again. When Cathal asked the knight about the cause of his gloomy laugh, he related that he had once possessed a great empire. Seven years earlier, he had prepared a great feast and just when he had been about to cut the meat, he glanced at the window and saw the "rabbit with foul breath." This huge hare rolled around in the pool, then soiled the linen that was nicely spread out, and finally stuck his head through the window so that his breath ruined all the food. The outraged knight immediately called his men and dogs, mounted their horses and, went out on the hunt. But the rabbit tricked the hunters and lured them into a valley between two hills, which suddenly closed behind them and swallowed them all up.

567 The knight and his men found themselves confronted by twenty-four robbers who mocked their prisoners. The leader jeered even more when, having offered to feed them all, the knight could not even lift the boar onto the spit. He did not even have the strength to turn the spit! Then the leader of the robber band threw a big block of iron into the fire. Perpendicular to the block was a chain. When the block was

glowing hot, the chief and his band took it out of the fire. The knight continued his sad story: "Then the chief put his men on one side and my men on the other. Each side grabbed the chain and began to tug; each team tried to draw the red hot block towards the other. The robber band succeeded in dragging the iron block so that it came up to my men. It scorched and sizzled them until there was not an inch of their bodies left that was not melted together. Then the robber chief transformed my horses and dogs into stone by means of a magic wand. His men wanted to do the same with me, but the chief let me go free. It took a year before I could reach my home from whence I had set out to chase the rabbit. Since then, I have lain in my bed and laugh no more. The robbers enchanted the whole palace and my property with the exception of me and my old caretaker. For seven years the witch has prevailed with her burnings and screechings."

568 Cathal thanked him for revealing the reason he could not longer laugh. He said that the knight had good reason to have lost his laughter, but now he must no longer fear the old hag, since he, Cathal, had killed her. Then said the knight to Cathal: "I had even secretly planned to fight you, but now that you have killed the witch, the destroyer of this land, I have nothing against you." The next day at noon, the "rabbit with the foul breath" appeared again. With Cathal's help, they mounted the horses of the witch, and everything happened again just as it had seven years earlier. They were again received by robbers with mocking laughter, but now Cathal asked, "What is so funny?" He swept up all the dust and dirt that had collected on the land over the last seven years and heaved it into the mouths of the robbers. He then took the boar like it was a bundle of straw and roasted it on the fire in two minutes. Having shared the well-cooked meat with the knight, Cathal set the iron block in the fire. As soon as it was glowing red, he hauled it out of the fire and challenged the twenty-four robbers to a tug-of-war. This time Cathal pulled the block to the robbers, even if they pulled as hard as they could they lost their breath. In the end they were squeezed and cooked so that there was only a lump of fat left. At the request of the knight, the captain was spared and given the chance to return all the men, horses, and dogs that he had taken seven years earlier. The robber chief feared for his life and brought everything he had once stolen from the knight back to life. Cathal and the knight returned home and found the castle and farm blooming like it once had.

569 Cathal then returned to King Leámuinn and found that the king was just about to marry his daughter to another man. This man claimed

> that he had gone to the East Indies after Cathal and had brought back the head of the old witch and also that of the dead snake. He also reported that Cathal had been killed. Now everyone saw that Cathal was still alive but although he had brought back the tongue of the snake, he had not brought back the head of the witch. All had believed that Cathal had become lost between the millstone and the dough (i.e., he was completely ground to death). Cathal told them that he had cut out the tongue of the serpent and if they wanted to see who was telling "the true brew," then they should look inside the head. The king looked into the head and saw that it was indeed missing the tongue. Upon this, he recognized the true hero, embraced Cathal and took him into his heart and granted him the hand of his daughter. After their wedding, Cathal and his wife moved to the witch's palace, whose treasures belonged to their children and grandchildren.[58]

570 The tale includes several confrontations with the mother-imago, almost as if the unconscious wanted it to be imprinted with other images. Cathal's mother embodies the positive side of the mother image. She cherishes and nourishes the hero especially long until he suddenly enters secular life. Since the mother is widowed, she devotes herself entirely to her son and, as often happens in real life, makes him dependent, in a so-called maternal bond.[59] Through this, the forces of the unconscious are especially close; like Parsifal the man is gifted with creativity and marked to be a hero. But precisely this bond threatens the hero as a destructive mother-imago. The separation from the world of the mythical, with its even more powerful surrounding, controlling images, is a painful yet necessary act. Like the innocent fool who always listens to his mother, the separation happens only gradually; the tale consistently identifies Cathal as the "son of the widow," emphasizing that the fact of the mother-problem is ever-present. After he spends the first twenty-one years of his life in the house of his mother and never crosses the threshold, there comes the moment in which the positive image of the mother decreases in importance. The mother's becoming childlike (as the fairytale puts it) reflects that the world of unconscious fantasy life appears gradually infantile to the hero so that he now turns away from it and faces the real world.

571 The portrayal in a legend from a tribe on the lower Fraser River clearly equates tarrying with the mother with being unconscious:

---

[58] Slightly shortened and translated from Müller-Lisowski, *Irische Volksmärchen*, pp. 265–282. [This tale is related almost in full because no English translation exists.]

[59] On the natural "longing for the mother," the "looking back to the source from which one once arose," see C.G. Jung, "Relation between the ego and the unconscious," CW 7, ¶260. See also the hero as an "oven stool" in the Russian fairytales "Story of Ingnerssuit" and "The Virgin Tsar."

> 572 Ialepkelem, the ancestor of the Lekämel, lived *with his mother*. At that time the people had no fire and lived *as in a dream*. When the sun saw this, he felt sorry for them, and descended from heaven in the form of a man. The sun gave fire to Ialepkelem. He awoke from his dream life to real life. The sun taught him and his people all the arts. Later Qäls came along the way and fought with Ialepkelem. They stood facing each other, trying to transform each other. Ialepkelem took some white wood, spread the ashes on himself, and boasted of his power and wisdom through the help of the sun. He sprung high in the air. Qäls cried out: "Fare well in the water in the future!" and transformed him into a sturgeon.[60]

573 In the Irish tale, Cathal rushes out, ridiculously dressed, into the secular world to prove himself. He plans to care for the mother and send her money, which hints that his life force streams back to her, and that he is still connected to her as by an umbilical cord. This relationship hinders any new development (such as entering into a marriage), however, and so bonds him to the mother. This tie, initially the source of power, is now negative. Thus the hero is given the task to overcome and control this connection.

574 The big snake in the forest lake is a mother image, the personification of the unconscious in its negative aspect. The snake signifies the animal life force and symbolizes the dark instinct, which has for humans a double aspect: on the one hand, promoting, on the other inhibitory.[61] In the former case, the snake signifies life-saving wisdom. From this layer of the soul, which is directly connected with nature, often stems mantic wisdom, inspiration, and the gift

---

[60] F. Boas, *Indianische*, Berlin, 1895, p. 25.

[61] On the comprehensive symbol of the snake, on the one hand as a positive force and as a good principle in India, see Zimmer, *Maya*, pp. 44, 52, 105, 111 (as a cosmic principle); on Gnostic ideas, see Leisegang, *Die Gnosis*, pp. 111f, 113, 141, 147f, 150, 180; on the snake as a world- creating original being, as moisture, as the ring-shaped world-encircling ocean, as a symbol of the cycle of becoming, as its own tail eater, as a symbol of the redeemer, as a winged creature, and as the depth of the godhead, see Leisegang, *Ibid.*, pp. 214–215, 222–223, 232; see also Mead, *Fragments*, pp. 194–197, 214–215. On the other hand, the snake can be a negative force and a principle of evil: for instance, in Egypt. See Roeder, *Urkunden*, pp. 138ff (Isis kneaded a snake from her saliva, which then killed Re with its bite); see further *Ibid.*, pp. 154–155 (the name of the snake was "Earthson" and it destroys its enemies with its acid breath); Erman, *Religion der Ägypter*, p. 233 (Re is the night sun as a snake); Leisegang, *Die Gnosis*, pp. 179, 216–217; Mead, *Fragments*, p. 503 (the Gnostics called it *draco caelestis*, the dragon of the outer darkness, and it symbolized the spheres of Saturn); C.G. Jung, *Symbols of Transformation*, CW 5, ¶681, fn. 87, as in the Norse Midgard (Middle-earth), which is surrounded by an impassable world of water. This ocean is inhabited by the great sea serpent Jörmungandr (Miõgarõsormr), who is so huge that he encircles the world entirely, grasping his own tail. The concept is similar to that of the Uroboros. In Germanic belief, this snake is identical with the Flood. It is interesting that in the *Edda* (vol. I, p. 111, verse 30), the mother, Atli, in the shape of a snake, fatally bites King Gunnar:

> Crawling the evil mother of the King came;
> murder should she!
> In Gunnar's heart she dug her way in;
> I could not save the king's life.

of prophecy.[62] Therefore, the snake is the animal that advised the first parents in Paradise to eat of the Tree of Knowledge. The hero who overcomes this evil, must therefore, usually have snake wisdom, a snake soul that helps him.[63] In the second case, this unconscious instinctual psyche gives power to the hero's actions, and at the same time is the element that causes him to withdraw and paralyzes his capacity for acting. It is a symbol of the heavy female earth principle, the archetype of inhibition and passivity. Overcoming the serpent or the dragon, therefore, stands at the beginning of the hero's career in many fairytales. A Roma [Gypsy] tale, "The Evil Mother," tells of how the mother of a hero lets herself be imprisoned in a barrel with a dragon demon that her son had vanquished. Following the suggestions of the demon's whisperings, she tries to destroy her own son and eventually succeeds in dismembering him. It is the "retrospective longing" that makes a man into a child again. If the fight with the dragon initiates the career of the hero, then this represents the separation of the hero from the paralyzing and laming mother. Not only the personal mother is meant here, but the maternal source of the unconscious in general. In this sense, the snake symbolizes the maternal primal unity, the paradisiacal original homeland, and also death.[64]

575 Overcoming unconscious, nature-like eternal bonds, and stepping out of the "immortality" of creation, gives one the sense of one's own individual existence, but it also brings with it the awareness of one's own mortality. Since humans experience their reality as independent beings only after separation from the "mother" – a kind of psychological cutting of the umbilical cord – so it seems that mortality is connected to the relationship with her, as if death were latent in the Great Mother and is received from her hand. In this respect, the snake becomes a typical symbol of the fear of death. The snake has this double aspect: on the one hand, it is a knowledge-conferring being, bestowing the hero with wisdom and power and, on the other hand, a poisoning, strangling enemy. As a symbol, the snake thus indicates that deeper, unconscious, inherited instinctual reactions evidently have this double aspect. It depends primarily on the person's insight whether they serve good or evil.

576 In the fairytale about Cathal, the mother warns her son before the fight with the snake and wants to prevent him from his hero's work. This reveals the negative side of her all too great love. Cathal, unaware of the plot in the background, thanks her for her gifts, but does not let himself be led astray. He overcomes the dragon-like monster in a fierce struggle, makes this demonic

[62] See Leisegang, *Die Gnosis*, p. 111. In legends and fairytales, consuming a dragon heart therefore conveys secret knowledge.
[63] On the identity of man and snake, see Zimmer, "Indische Mythen," Einsiedeln, 1934, pp. 115–116. Krishna as the demon slayer embodies a part of the world snake.
[64] See C.G. Jung, *Symbols of Transformation*, CW 5, ¶351, 455ff., 540f., 577f.

power of the unconscious, the world of animal instincts, subservient and directs them, now tamed, to serve in the profane world.

577 But the hero still cannot find his place in life, which is embodied in the king's beautiful daughter. He has yet to break through to the more distant layers of the unconscious, to a final confrontation with the roots of the mother-imago in its negative form. The task that the princess places on him is dressed in a question on the fate of the knight with the gloomy laugh. This can be interpreted as the inner reflection of Cathal, his darker brother. It is part of Cathal's inner personality, which has fallen under the spell of the evil mother-imago. While Cathal, on the one hand, apparently receives enormous powers, on the other hand in his unconscious, he is condemned to bleak despair. Cathal encounters the knight by crawling on all fours through a low door, he must be able to shrink modestly and even adjust to his animal instincts to get to this other side of himself. But the knight greets the son of the widow not only with suspicion, but even hostility, and it comes to a fight between the "two big guys." This is because Cathal and the knight, that is, the one under the sway of the overly good mother and the other under the sway of the witch, cannot reach an agreement at first. Cathal cannot accept this aspect of his inner destiny. Remembering his benevolent mother and aware of his own primal force, he finally manages to push the enemy into the purifying fire. Thus Cathal opens the way to his redemption. The knight now reveals himself as the one Cathal was looking for, the one on whom it all depends. After a violent struggle with himself, Cathal now recognized with whom he was fighting.

578 The old woman screeches and threatens both heroes. Cathal is lured by two mouse-gray horses into her sanctuary. Horses are mother symbols. An illustration of this is found in the Balkan fairytale, "The Witch Who was Vanquished with Horseshoes," where every night a female master blacksmith enchanted one of her fellow smiths into a horse so that she could ride to the witch's party. Another blacksmith outwits her by transforming her into a horse and putting horseshoes on her. After she reverts back into her human form, her passion for witchcraft was forever lost.The fight with the horrible woman on the round place in the forest in the Irish tale is much worse than it was with the snake. The old woman has a "cold cruel tooth." Here, the tooth is perhaps a phallic symbol, and this attribute would have the same meaning as the big thumb of the Fates (the Parcae, the three Roman personifications of destiny: Nona, Decima, and Morta) and the large nose of the Russian witch Baba-Yaga.[65] But when Cathal's need is greatest, the wren appears as a magical helper. A bird means (as in "Hansel and Gretel") something spiritual, an idea, an inspiration, a helpful idea, which despite its apparent irrelevance (small

[65] See the fairytale, "The Visit to the Manabozho."

size of the bird), saves the hero. Through his honest effort in the fight against the power of the unconscious he obtains help from the unconscious, through creative intuition. This confers on the hero the capacity to recognize the nature of the negative mother-imago, and so identify its weak point whereby her threatening aspect suddenly loses all its power. The "son of the widow" can now put an end to the witch demon in exactly the same way as he killed the snake. Through her death, he gains a big increase in strength, symbolically in the form of immense riches. From the story the knight tells him, the hero learns that the witch has lived there since "time immemorial," that is, she is older than the human race, and has always had power over humans. "In the dead hour of night," that is, when waking consciousness is shut off and the magical is most potent, she was able to torment people exactly when her "screeching" stood in maximal sharp contrast to the stillness of the hour.

579 The knight once lived happily on the island until a harbinger of the witch, the rabbit with the foul breath, pollutes his kingdom and lures him into the power of the robbers. The valley which opens between the mountains like a vagina is "the womb of Mother Earth." In Germanic superstition, the rabbit is unlucky if you meet him first thing in the morning. Rabbit meat is an aphrodisiac.[66] It is an attribute of Diana, the primordial mother of all witches, as well as of Venus and Bacchus. "Bunny women" was a term for witches in Germanic countries. As an animal of witches, rabbits could generate fog and wind.[67] Psychologically, the rabbit in this appearance is an aspect of instinctual nature, in the extruded state, a "fogging," a confusing and misleading of consciousness with his bad breath, creating a state of psychic-mental corruption.

580 The "rabbit with the foul breath" is the emissary of the robber chief, who had lured the knight into the darkness. This initial turbidity of inner life led to even more dangerous inner demons: to greed, thievery, and enmity with people. These are the invisible forces that had been engendered in Cathal through the maternal bonds in the background of his manifested superhuman strength and also a part of himself that had been condemned to a bleak melancholy. They cause even a partial inner fossilization (symbolized by his horsemen and servants). The whole gang of robbers, with their leader, embodies the negative side of the dark companion of the Great Mother, the hidden male nature demon.

581 In that Cathal now learns the fate of the knight and redeems him in the fight against the Great Mother, he (Cathal) – psychologically speaking – becomes fully aware of the negative side of his own attachment to his mother

---

[66] [Possibly in connection with the popular notion of the fertility of rabbits; see also the link between eggs and the Easter bunny.]

[67] See Bächtold-Stäubli under *Hase* [hare] and Mogk, *Germanische*, 1927, p. 48.

and frees himself from its pernicious, inimical effects, so that he restores the kingdom to bloom.

582 A fairytale that describes, albeit in simpler images, the extraction of vital energy from the maternal realm is illustrated in the following summary of "Strong Hans":

583 A farm woman suckled her boy-child for fourteen years. He became so strong that he could tear up oak trees and he carried a heavy iron rod weighing fifteen "ship-pounds"[68] around as a weapon. One day he went out into the world. On his way, he resolved a dispute between two ants and a worm, two snakes bickering about a bone, two wolves fighting over an old horse, and two bears quarreling over a beehive, thus gaining the gratitude of these animals. When he goes to sleep on an earth mound, a large woman appears and says, "Hansy, my little son, if I wanted to, I could make you a head shorter, but I prefer that it remains standing." And the woman lies down not far away from him. Soon after, he stands up and says, "If I wanted to, I could now make *you* a head shorter, but I want that it stays standing on the shoulders. I'm leaving!" He comes to an old hut in which a little old mother greets him with the words: "Hansy, my son, you came here?" Hans hires himself out to this second mother for three days to guard three white mares against one of the colts. Every day, after the old woman brings him his midday meal out to the pasture, he fell asleep. When he awoke, the mares had disappeared. The first and the second time his grateful animals join together to bring the mares back, first out of the forest and then out from the earth. The third time only the winged snakes succeed in bringing the mare down from the clouds. The witch is disappointed because she liked to kill delinquent shepherds. Two of the foals of the mares are white, the third is black and has a spot on the forehead, and each one has an apple, his heart, in his mouth.

584 The old woman takes the apples from the two, cuts them in half and sets the halves together in the mouth of the black mare in the mouth, whose apple is still whole. Then the witch crumples the black colt to make it limp, and hides it. Despite this trick Hans, who has observed how the black colt became flaccid, chooses it. When he saddles and bridles it up, it becomes a great horse, which he mounts and rides on to his further exploits.[69] Later, the heroic colt becomes the man's human servant.[70]

---

68 [Schiffspfund : a weight measure for freight (about 400 pounds) used in northern Europe.]

69 The continuation of the story is identical with the tale, "Ferdinand the Faithful and Ferdinand the Unfaithful," which will be discussed below.

70 Translated from the authors' summary of Boehm and Specht, *Lettisch-litauische*, 1924, pp. 74–82.

585 The hero of this tale has also remained long with the mother,[71] which points both to his vocation and to the danger of being exposed to the Great Mother. The point is to wrest the creative force in the form of the horse and the magical powers of the servant from the sorcery of the magical and motherly. This succeeds because the hero sees through the unconscious opposing and warring impulses (he settles the animals' dispute) and keeps his quiet self-assurance at the first encounter with the mother-imago, the young woman who lies down next to him. As a result, he has gained an instinctive certainty for the subsequent *auseinandersetzung*, which he can even depend on while sleeping. All animals, even the miraculous animals, assist him. That is, the forces of the unconscious stream towards him and give him the supernatural skill necessary to gain control over the forces (the mothers' mares) and to bring them back out from the forest, earth, and clouds, which, as we have seen, are symbolic spheres of the unconscious.

586 As the tales of Cathal and "Strong Hans" show, "the mother" is something other than the actual mother; for the man she is the unconscious in general, out of which his fate unfolds. The African fairytale, "The Adventures of Mrile," melancholically describes the tragic ending of a young man who had tried to shape and determine his own life:

> 587 In the course of time, a man had three sons. One day, the oldest one, Mrile, went with his mother to dig up eddo tubers. As they were thus occupied, he saw a seed-bulb. And he said, "Why, there is a seed-bulb as handsome as my little brother." But his mother said to him, "How can a seed-bulb be as handsome as a human child?" He hid the seed-bulb, however, and the mother tied up the eddoes to carry them home. The boy hid the seed-bulb in the hollow of a tree and, using a magic formula, said, "*Msura Kwivire-vire tsa kawhingu na kasanga.*"
>
> 588 The following day he went there again. The seedling had now become a child. Whenever his mother cooked food, Mrile carried some of it to the seed-child, but he himself grew leaner and leaner. His fatherand mother noticed how lean he had grown and asked him, "Son, what is it that makes you so lean? Where is the food going that we always cook for you? Your younger brothers have not become so lean!" Then his younger brothers watched what Mrile did and reported back home, "We saw how our brother put the food there into the hollow of a tree

[71] See also "The Tale of the Devil" and "Strong Hans" (Grimm Brothers). There, the hero not only remains with his mother for a long time, but is imprisoned with her in a den of thieves. This is a doubling of the mother motif since the cave is symbol of the mother, inasmuch as the image reminds one of the womb. Accordingly, many ancient Greek heroes were transported, enraptured (*entrückt*), to caves (cf. Rohde, *Psyche*, 1925, vol 1, p. 91). [The translator of *Psyche*, W. B. Hillis, renders *entrückt* as "translated out of this life," which is a good alternative.]

and brought it to a child living there." The mother went to see for herself and killed the seed-child. Now when Mrile carried food to the tree he found the slain seed-child. Thereupon he went home and wept copiously and the tears could not be stopped. His parents advised him, "Take your father's chair along with you and go into the courtyard and sit down!" He took the chair, sat down on it in the courtyard, yet the tears continued. Then Mrile said, "Chair, raise yourself up high like my father's rope whereby he suspends the honey barrel in the virgin forest and in the steppe." About this time his younger brothers entered the courtyard. They saw how he was traveling upward toward the sky. They informed their mother, who did not believe them until she went herself. She called out to him, but Mrile did not let himself be softened by her requests nor by those from the rest of his family. He disappeared from their sight. After a while, Mrile encountered wood-gatherers. He greeted them, "Wood-gatherers, good day! Please show me the way to Moon-King." But they answered him, "Gather some wood, then we will direct you there." So he cut some firewood for them. Then they told him, "Just go straight ahead, and you will encounter some grass-cutters!" So he went on and soon encountered some grass-cutters, then tillers, herdsmen, bean-harvesters, millet-reapers, banana stalk seekers, water-carriers. Each time he helped then and they directed him to the next people.

589 After a while he encountered people who ate raw food. They were the people of the Moon-King. And he said to them, "Why do you not cook with fire?" But they answered him thus, "What is that, fire?" He said to them, "One cooks food with it until it is done." Then they said to him, "We know nothing about fire!" And he said to them, "If I prepare you some tasty food by means of fire, what will you give me?" The Moon-King said, "We shall send you large cattle and some small stock." Mrile taught the people and the Moon-King how to cook food and he received a cow, a goat, and things from the granary.

590 Mrile decided to go home, but wanted to send a message of his coming first. He asked different birds but decided on the mockingbird who offered to sing, "Mrile will come the day after tomorrow, save some fat for him in the spoon!"

591 After the mockingbird returned with proof that he had delivered his message, Mrile set out with his cattle. On the way he grew tired. Now he had a bull with him, and the bull spoke to him and said, "Since you are so tired out, if I take you upon my back, what will you do? If I take you upon my back, will you eat me when they slaughter me?" And Mrile answered him, "No, I will not eat you." So he climbed on

> the bull's back, and the bull supported him. And so Mrile came home singing proudly of his gifts. When he arrived at home, his father and mother smeared him with fat. Then he spoke to them thus: "This bull you shall feed until he grows old. Even when he grows old, I shall not eat his meat." But when the bull grew old, the father slaughtered him; thereupon the mother said, "Should this bull, that my son has taken so great trouble with, be devoured without his eating therefrom?" And she hid the fat, she hid it in the honey pot. When she knew that the meat had been used up, she ground flour, took the fat and added it thereto. So she brought it to her son, and Mrile tasted it. When he had tasted it with his mouth, the meat spoke to him: "Do you dare to consume me, me who have taken you on my back?" And it said to him, "Therefore be consumed, as you consume me!" Then Mrile sang: "My mother, I told you serve me not the meat of the bull!" But when he tasted it for a second time, his foot sank into the ground. And he sang: "My mother, I told you, serve me not the meat of the bull! " After continuing to consume the meal to completion, he was swallowed up. And this is the end of the story.[72]

592 In this fairytale, the final catastrophe is brought about by the incident told at the outset in which the mother kills the child of the eddo seed-bulb that belonged to the hero. A *participation mystique* joins Mrile with the seed-bulb of the tubers, which he holds to be his little brother. This is demonstrated by making a fetish endowed with magical power,[73] which represents the boy's alter ego and, as his child, also expresses his future personality. In another African tale, "The Tale of Chuveane," a boy creates a magical child by forming a figure out of clay and blowing his breath into it.[74] He takes care of this clay-child like a mother. The parents hide it away from him, but as they realize his desperation, they give it back. Later, he became famous through his heroic deeds and is even equated with a primordial god. Similar to Mrile's and Chuveane's bringing a root and a clay figure to life, Krishna and, in apocryphal gospels, Jesus enliven animal figures as a sign of their divine creative power. From this, one can assume this is a typical motif of fairytales and legends.[75] The doll in "The Adventures of Mrile" is a magical image of the hero and can be described, therefore, as the core of his personality. When this core is destroyed by his mother, the hero himself is struck in his life center. Everything that happens subsequently no longer results from his actions or

---

[72] TENT (retrieved June 2011).

[73] On the primitive belief that certain roots have magical power, see Lang, *Custom and Myth*, London, 1885, pp. 148ff. In Africa, this power is mainly apotropaic (i.e., designed to avert evil).

[74] [See also the story of the Golem.]

[75] See E. Abegg, "Krishnas Geburt," Zürich, 1937/1938, p. 54.

his own will; instead, he succumbs, passively, to all the consequences of his tragic fate. When he sits on his father's chair – this is a wish of the family and normally would console Mrile – it means an identification with the father, his mother's husband, and in fantasy an inner union with the parents as the essence of nurturing. He thus becomes bound to the maternal prenatal world.

593 If Mrile achieves great feats in the kingdom of heaven, to which he was transported by expressing a wish, that is, by his imagination alone, and to whose inhabitants he brings fire, then we should remember that all this happens in the hereafter. By identifying with his father, the youth imagines great deeds, which, however, do not take place in reality. Luminous fire is indeed a symbol of consciousness: Prometheus brought fire from the other world to the people of this world. The figures of the magical actually enter into a living fruitful relationship with Mrile as a result of the gift, because he turns his attention and spiritual energy to them. This turn to the unconscious that Mrile should avoid as a primitive man is, however, the fatal consequence of the destruction of that seed germ that is just developing, which symbolizes the tender inner being of his soul. Even in spite of this annihilation, there would still be hope if the hero would succeed in realizing something of what was planned and seen in the beyond. He could, for example, have become a shaman and brought his discoveries in the realm of the soul back across for the good of his fellow people. This possibility is indicated by the fact that Mrile receives herds and riches from the Moon King in gratitude for the gift of fire. Even if Mrile's journey to the otherworld should be evaluated negatively, as evading life in this world, as returning, inappropriately, to the realm of the dead and the ancestors of the moon, such a spiritual regression has a positive side: it brings about an unusual illumination and enlivening of the unconscious, symbolized here in the bringing of fire. Psychologically, the motif of teaching people in the hereafter signifies the transfer of consciousness into the unconscious. This motif is unusual, but is also found in a Balkan fairytale, "The Nightingale Gisar." There the hero shows a tigress how to shove bread into the oven without getting hurt. In return he receives her help. In a similar manner, he acquires the friendship of a lioness and an eagle woman. He teaches human arts to the animals. This clearly demonstrates a domesticating and conscious enlightening of a hitherto purely animal unconsciousness. The psychological conclusion is that the unconscious loses its threatening aspect and becomes life-promoting when consciousness turns a befriending face to it.[76] Thus, Mrile is also rewarded for his gift of fire. The cattle that he receives symbolize the increase in psychic energy that resulted from the attention he gave to the unconscious. But as soon as the hero makes his way home, he becomes tired and is unable to muster the strength to bring

[76] [see B. Hannah's notion of the "active imagination" for a similar formulation.]

the elements that he gained in the sphere of the unconscious back into consciousness. So Mrile must let himself be borne by the bull. In a certain sense, the bull must subordinate himself to his unconscious instinctual forces.[77] In a certain sense, the bull replaces the killing of the seed-bulb child. It also symbolizes Mrile's essence; not like a child in human form, but as non-human nature and instinctual driving force. As such, the bull embodies specifically the male generative and creative power that Mrile recovered by travelling to the beyond as a substitute for his lost child. Not only is the hero so tired that he must let himself be carried by the bull. He is also too weak and indifferent to protect this symbol of his very own personality, which he has gained a second time, against his mother's treacherous attacks.[78]

594 The imposed taboo, that Mrile may not eat his own bull, bestows a divine-magical and inviolable quality on the animal. In old Germanic cultures, it was forbidden to eat the meat of revered divine horses, while in modern India it is not allowed to partake of cows as food. The bull is Mrile's divine escort and also a primitive father image.

595 Mrile placed too much confidence in the profane world and so betrays his divine helper. His mother tries to nourish the boy hero in wrong and deadly ways, as is so often the case as here out of apparent love. She says: "Should this bull, with which my son had such trouble, be completely eaten without him eating any of it?" Being unconscious, Mrile lets himself be convinced to accept this love and then comes the revenge of the magical: the bull pulls him down into the earth, i.e., into the underworld, the beyond, where he came from. The Earth is an image of the mother in the broadest sense, and Mrile's sinking is equivalent to being engulfed by the Great Mother. Strangely, Mrile continues to eat the meat of the bull knowing whom he is consuming. He thus seems to succumb to an attraction that extends beyond his willpower.

596 In this fairytale, we find all levels of the mother imago. The *auseinandersetzung* begins with the personal mother, behind whom are revealed all the other deeper-reaching symbols of the Great Mother. Whereas Cathal in "The Knight With the Sinister Laugh" tries to defy her with his struggle with the Great Mother and develops into a hero, the sad and passive Mrile lets everything happen by itself and thus from the beginning is doomed to destruction. The land beyond, the unconscious, with all its alluring and threatening aspects, swallows him up.

597 The same process, the destruction of the vital driving force of mankind by the maternal bond, is also described briefly in the short fairytale, "The Otherworld":

---

[77] The fact that the bull is a part of himself is, for natural peoples, a self-evident notion since the owner lives in *participation mystique* with his animals and takes them to the grave; see Lévy-Bruhl, *The "Soul" of the Primitive*, pp. 120, 146, 192.

[78] See, among others, "An Elfin Combs the Woman's Hair," where the evil stepmother wishes to kill the magical oxen of the hero; collected in Leskien, *Balkanmärchen*, pp. 197–199.

598 There was once a little child whose mother gave her every afternoon a small bowl of milk and bread, and the child seated herself in the yard with it. But when she began to eat, a toad[79] came creeping out of a crevice in the wall, dipped its little head in the dish, and ate with her. The child took pleasure in this, and when she was sitting there with her little dish and the paddock did not come at once, she cried:

599 "Toady, toady, come swiftly
Hither come, thou tiny thing,
Thou shalt have thy crumbs of bread,
Thou shalt refresh thyself with milk."

600 Then the toad came in haste, and enjoyed its food. It even showed gratitude, for it brought the child all kinds of pretty things from its hidden treasures, bright stones, pearls, and golden playthings. The toad drank only the milk, however, and left the bread-crumbs alone. Then one day the child took its little spoon and struck the toad gently on its head, and said: "Eat the bread-crumbs as well, little thing." The mother, who was standing in the kitchen, heard the child talking to someone, and when she saw that she was striking a toad with her spoon, ran out with a log of wood, and killed the good creature.

601 From that time forth, a change came over the child. As long as the toad had eaten with her, she had grown tall and strong, but now she lost her pretty rosy cheeks and wasted away. It was not long before the funeral bird began to cry in the night and the redbreast to collect little branches and leaves for a funeral wreath, and soon afterwards the child lay on her bier.[80]

602 This story conveys a part of the primitive mentality, because the toad represents through *participation mystique* the vital center of the little girl herself. The toad gives her golden toys showing that it represents the richness of the child's fantasy life. It symbolizes a part of her unconscious soul, and when her mother kills it, she murders the child's soul, similar to Mrile killing his imagined child, his fantasy life. Significantly, *Unke* as frog or toad is a known mother symbol. The toad often symbolizes the uterus.[81] The Chinese see it in connection with the moon, in which sits a three-legged rain toad

---

[79] [German *Unke* is traditionally translated into English as "paddock" (archaic English for frog or toad) as in *Complete Grimm's*, London, 1975. However, literary research by Sonja Loidl, *Das Märchen von der Unkel (KHM 105) unter spezieller Berücksichtigung des Seelentier-Motiv* (2006) shows that in those parts of Germany where this tale was collected (it was told to the Grimm Brothers by Dortchen and Lisette Wild from Kassel in Hessen) *Unke* meant a ring or grass snake.]
[80] *Complete Grimm's*, pp. 480-481.
[81] See Silberer, *Problems of Mysticism*, p. 225.

named "Tschan" (a parallel figure to the rabbit in the moon that brews the elixir of life).[82] The maternal significance of the toad is of course not limited only to its positive aspect, the toad is also the animal of the witch.[83] Through her uncomprehending behavior, the real mother in "The Otherworld" kills the life-giving archetype of the mother in the child. The intimate, necessary, and natural connection between real mother and child, which is based on the chthonic archetype of the mother, is severed, and thereby also the child's capacity to live.

603 While in some of the previously discussed tales, the mother-imago was overcome, either by magic, by trickery, open combat, or by the hero successfully fleeing from it (the mother-imago), in other tales it overpowers him. In contrast, the Irish fairytale "Fionn MacCumhaill and his Mother," succinctly tells how the legendary hero Fionn gradually separates himself from his mother and gains his independence. Although Fionn shakes off the bond, the mother figure remains as the source of his wisdom, without which he could not have become a great hero:

> 604 Fionn MacCumhaill and his mother once went out. She carried him on her back. [They passed a group of men playing a betting game. The boy, Fionn,] watched how the men threw the "Anger Ball."
> "Let me down, Mother," he said, "so I can see the betting game."
> "Dearest," she said, "the big men will kill you."
> "Nonetheless, Mother, I want to go to them."
>
> 605 She let Fionn climb down off her back and he stood among the group of men. [He played the game too.] There was no one that exceeded him. After the game Fionn returned to his mother. She took him again up on her back. Then they continued on their way without interruption, until they reached Mota Dealgál or Dún-Dealgáin. Here, she lost her breastpin and left a marker at the place so that she would be able to find it again. They then came to an embankment. This is now called today "Wall of the breastpin." Now Fionn took his mother on his back, and they went on without pause until they came to the crest of the mountain Cuileann.
>
> 606 Fionn had only the two feet of his mother (everything else he had lost on the way). He threw these feet in the "Lake of the Old People of Béara." Then he entered a house nearby and asked for shelter. The

[82] See Wilhelm, *The Chinese Fairy Book*, p. 390, note to "The Lady of the Moon"; see also Róheim, *Spiegelzauber*, pp. 242–243. In China, the tortoise is the maternal primordial womb and the bearer of the world, and thus a sign of luck. See also Zimmer, *Maya*, pp. 8ff.; see further C.G. Jung and C. Kerényi, *Essays on a Science of Mythology: The Myth of the Divine Child and the Mysteries of Eleusis*, Princeton University Press, Princeton NJ, 1969, p. 57f.

[83] See Róheim, *Spiegelzauber*, p. 220, under *Frosch* [frog] and *Kröte* [toad].

> hostess (it was the old witch of Béara) said she would offer him lodging only if he caught two trout. He went and caught two trout in the "Lake of the Old People of Béara." (The trout were the feet of his mother.)
>
> 607 "Well," said the woman of the house as she set the trout on the fire, "now pay attention that no dark, black, or burn spots appear." Bubbles formed on one of the trout. Fionn put his thumb on it and got burned. Then he quickly slipped his thumb into his mouth. From that day until his death he fetched his wisdom from his thumb when he stuck it into his mouth and chewed from the tendons to the bone marrow.[84]

608 The motif of mutual carrying is significant: first the mother carries the son, and then the son carries the mother. The former applies to the personal context and also the meaning that the individual is carried into his or her life and fate by the forces of the unconscious. Later it is the opposite, however, it is the individual who bears, or has to endure, all the traditions and the unconscious past, as a spiritual power. To be borne by the mother means to be carried by the unconscious; to bear the mother would, therefore, mean carrying the unconscious, that is, the fate taken over from the ancestors of completing the fate that is bequeathed by the past. Losing one part of the mother after another, which begins with the fact that the mother drops her breast-pin, is a motif indicating a coming development: the hero gradually grows out of the "arrested" state driven by problems of life belonging to the personal mother. In that Fionn loses the concrete mother, he comes to the witch of Béara, an image of the Great Mother. One could say: in the measure that he loses his mother in her personal aspect, the archetype of the mother increases in importance for him. What remains for him, namely, what he pulls up out of the water (the unconscious) in the form of the trout as living values, are the feet of the mother. This refers to the base upon which she stood, the foundation of the concrete mother image. He must fry the rest of the mother, that is, he must submit it to a process of development. Through the fire, this part of the mother is made edible, which symbolizes that he can ingest her essence, in this case its transformed state as wisdom. The witch, of course, would like this wisdom for herself and tries to hinder Fionn from gaining access to it. The unconscious always tries to get its gifts back. Fionn obtains his wisdom only by the fact that, through self-inflicted wounding, he takes suffering upon himself.

609 Thumb sucking is a gesture of self-sufficiency in which the child becomes independent from the environment. In German, this image is used to describe independent creation as "sucking something out of the fingers." The thumb is

---

[84] Müller-Lisowski, *Irische Volksmärchen*, pp. 42–43. [One modern instance is Michael Towner's novel, "The Ogre" (*Le roi des Autres*, 1972), which concerns precisely this symbol of bearing or carrying.]

a phallic symbol and, therefore, secret power is attributed to it. As "Tom Thumb" it is even considered as a separate being. In the fairytale, "Fionn and Lorcán," Lorcán, a friend of Fionn's, has a thumb with which he can heal wounds. Siegfried is also able to understand the language of birds when he dips his fingers into the hot dragon's blood and then brings them to his lips (the devouring dragon is also a mother symbol). And the Welsh *Mabinigion* legend of the origin of Taliesin tells how the boy, Gwion Bach, is employed by a mother-witch, Caridwen, to see that a cooking vessel does not boil over. After almost a year of watching the cauldron, three drops fly out and scald his thumb. When he licks it, he acquires the wisdom and knowledge of the future. He sees that his future is endangered by Caridwen and flees. The woman follows him, and she turns into a hare and a series of other hunting animals to chase him as he changes form again and again. In the end, he transforms himself into a grain of wheat and the old witch into a hen who finds and swallows the grain. She then gives birth to Gwion as Taliesin, the poet-seer, whose name means "radiant brow."[85]

610 Thus the tale of Fionn shows remarkably clearly how the image of the actual mother gradually changes in the soul of man and comprises a greater element, that is, a source of superior knowledge.

611 The fairytale previously discussed in this chapter, "The Knight With the Sinister Laugh," only faintly alludes to an important characteristic of the Great Mother, namely, its connection with the male deity of the magical kingdom. In "The Lady of the Moon," the emperor saw next to the Lady of the Moon a quiet gardener, who cut the cassia tree, but he did not take part in the events of the fairytale. Working with the same intent as the Great Mother, only the chief of the robber gang actually acts in the fairytale and was also destroyed about the same time as the witch. One can interpret this figure, therefore, as the male component of the original mother, as her personalized spiritual energy, her demonic will (similar to the relationship between the devil and his grandmother, the image arises from the same archetypal idea).

612 In the following fairytale, "The Wolf with the Iron Head," the male figure appears as a wolf in conjunction with the Great Mother and is destroyed by her. The mother figure even appears in a double aspect, in which the shape of a kind mother is opposed to that of the devouring mother, because in the end that which is spoiled by the mother can only be made good again by the mother:

---

[85] See Guest, *Mabinogion*, pp. 263ff. On the mother image as an inspirational force, see "The Adventures of Matandua, the One-Eyed," a fairytale that tells how a hero protects the spirit of his drowned mother from many dangers and is driven to great feats while at the same time he is guided through them. The dead mother speaks to him in his sleep and flies before him as a guiding bird. In a Roma (Gypsy) fairytale, "The Flower of Happiness," a blue flower that grew on the grave of the mother and calls itself the soul of the mother, leads the hero through various adventures to great happiness. It floats, invisible to others, in front of him and shares her wise counsel.

613 The wolf with the iron head once wanted to eat the shepherd Peter. The shepherd pleaded for his life, however, and the wolf agreed to wait until Peter's wedding. Peter soon forgot all about the wolf, but as the wedding wagon passed through the forest, the wolf called out for him. Peter fled, the wolf pursued. Towards evening, he took refuge in a house where he saw a woman stoking the fire with her bare hands. She was the mother of the sun. Peter ripped off a piece of his shirt and wrapped her hands in it. She fed him and in the morning gave him a red cloth that when swung once, could divide a body of water or a forest. When swung two times, the waters or forest would close up again. Peter got a head start on the wolf with the iron head but it chased Peter across a stretch of a water. Peter swung his red cloth two times and the waters engulfed the wolf. Peter arrived in the evening at the house of the moon mother, whom he kissed on her hands. In the morning she gave him a loaf of bread, which would show him what was going to happen when used as a pillow. With the help of the red cloth he came to a wood, and after sleeping on the bread loaf, in the morning he saw a lion, a bear, and a lynx circling around him in a friendly way. He fed his loaf of bread to the animals. When the wolf with the iron head gnawed his way into this forest, Peter's red cloth made a way for him and his animals to reach the outside and imprisoned the wolf behind them. Peter then arrived at a hut and told the old lady there his story of being chased by the wolf and meeting the mother of the sun and the mother of the moon. Unbeknownst to him, the old woman was the mother of the wolf. He let himself be persuaded to watch over herds and gave her his red cloth for safe-keeping. With this, she freed her son the wolf from the woods. The wolf was afraid of Peter's animals and tried to spring on Peter out of a ditch but the animals laid down over the pit and defeated his plan. Now, the wolf induced his mother to persuade Peter to let his animals stay with her when he went out herding. This time when the wolf lunged at him, Peter managed to escape up a tree, but then the wolf set to gnawing the tree down. In the meantime, the animals who had been locked up by the old woman heard the calls of their master and dug their way under the wall and reached him just as the tree was about to fall. They ripped the wolf to pieces and then went after the old woman whom they also destroyed. Peter found countless amounts of money in her hut, returned home with his animals, and lived with his young wife happy and contented forever after.[86]

[86] Summarized from Leskien (ed.), *Balkanmärchen aus Albanien / Bulgarien, Serbien und Kroatien*, (*MdW*), 1919, pp. 291–296.

614 Here the wolf signifies dark greed, "wolfing down," the devouring impulsiveness of the unconscious. The iron head points to the relentless harshness and cruelty of this greed. In German folklore, witches ride wolves,[87] and sometimes a gray wolf escorts the Russian witch Baba-Yaga.[88] In some religions, the wolf is considered the principle of evil, as Fenris, the wolf in Germanic mythology. Peter, the hero of the Balkan fairytale, flees from the demon who pursues him out of the dark area of his soul and arrives at a maternal goddess, who helpfully stands by him. The magic cloth that she gives him and with which he can open or close rivers and forests signifies a magical force through which the individual with the gift of consciousness gains safety from raw nature. In this sense, magic is in general the precursor of the scientific overcoming and mastery over nature, and therefore represents a first step towards the autonomy of human consciousness over the inner and outer devouring power of the unconscious. From the moon mother, the hero receives a loaf of bread, which attracts the three helping animals: lion, bear, and lynx. Bread nourishes and sustains the body; a loaf of bread can be seen, therefore, as a symbol of the human body and body consciousness. The latter contributes significantly to the feeling of being alive and conscious of the personality. In this sense, the gift from the moon-nature can be seen as a protection against the devouring aspect of the magical world. The bread also attracts helping animals, therefore, because they embody the drives, the instincts, which are integral to body-consciousness and even comprise its constituents.

615 But now follows a new danger: the harboring mother figure, which has so far been helpful, transforms into the pursuer (the mother of the wolf who tries to destroy Peter). She steals the saving magic cloth and imprisons his helpful animals. The scene in which Peter experiences sitting on the tree is signally oppressive, the wolf is gnawing at the tree and its collapse draws closer. This recalls a typical situation of nightmares. Once more, the tree symbolizes the helpful mother. Peter, however, needs not only the plant kingdom to support him, but also, in accordance with the animal nature of the wolf, even the power of the animals, because human beings must garner their life forces to defend themselves against the threat of the unconscious. And thus, the wolf and his mother are finally torn apart by the animals. This means that the healthy instincts have differentiated the demonic phenomena that emerged from the soul into lifeless parts. Through overcoming the Great Mother, the hero attains, as often reported, an increase of spiritual values, represented in the form of money, which he finds in the house of the old one, the heavenly mother. So, this fairytale describes in unusually gruesome and dramatic

[87] See Peuckert, *Volksglaube*, 1942, p. 15, fig.1.

[88] See the fairytale, "The Miracle Sleigh"; in German, see Loepfe, *Russische Märchen*, pp. 130ff.

pictures, the opposing natures of the unconscious, which are symbolized, on the one hand, by the pursuing wolf and his mother, and on the other hand, by the helping "star mothers" (*Gestirnsmüttern*) and animals. Furthermore, it describes how, with the correct behavior, the individual can emerge and benefit from the coincidence of these inner polarities.

616 In some fairytales, the masculine figure that accompanies the evil mother can appear not only as an individual daemon or as a group (such as the robber gang in "The Knight With the Sinister Laugh"), but also as a duality, trinity, or even quaternity. In the following fairytale, "The Great Fool from Cuasan," two giants have to be overcome before the witch can be defeated. The main theme of freeing the hero from the mother is represented in a variety of forms.

> 617 A long time ago there lived a poor widow, who had only one son. He was called Séaghan. He was such a simpleton, so terribly foolish, that when he received decent vestments, he still put on the shabbiest clothes he had. His mother owned in the whole world nothing more than two goats and, in the depths of winter, a billy goat. Séagan lived with his mother like such people live: one day they have something to eat, the next day they starve. Still, through good times or bad times, Séaghan's duty was to herd the goats. In the morning he took them out, during the day he watched over them, and in the evening, he brought them home to milk. One winter day, his mother sent him in his oversized coat out again to fetch the goats. At the end of the fields, he came to a big post. The snowdrifts had covered it over and Séaghan thought the post was a man. He asked it why he stood out there in such weather. The post remained silent and the boy in sympathy threw his cloak over the post and ran freezing home without the goats. After he explained to his mother where his coat was, she demanded that he retrieve the coat and goats. But he refused to rob the post, and she hit him on the legs with tongs from their fireplace. He had no leggings or socks on, so this hurt really badly and he ran out of the hut screaming. In the meantime, the wind had blown the coat off the pole into the snow. Séaghan raced around the post, indignant because of its bad treatment of his coat. He reprimanded the post and shook it until it fell over. On the spot where the post had stood, Séaghan found "only beautiful stones." He collected all that he could, filling his coat, which he heaved on his shoulder and thus returned to his mother.
>
> 618 The mother recognized that the stones were gold and they went out to where the post had stood, collected the rest of the gold, and lugged it back to their hut. They poured everything into an old chest, the only piece of furniture they possessed. Her mother made her son promise not to talk about their findings under threat of using the fire tongs

again. Séaghan promised. His mother demanded he bring in the goats before he went to sleep. Despite the freezing cold, he went out and found the goats and herded them home. The next morning fresh snow lay on the ground. His mother told him to take the goats out again. Séaghan went out but froze in the cold and returned quickly to the hut. With the help of the fire tongs, his mother sent him out again. She was worried that the goats would damage the neighbor's property. Weeping, Séaghan went out again. He again went to where the post stood to see if the man was dead or alive. There stood a distinguished gentleman with a hunting flint, who was curiously investigating the overturned post. The gentleman was about to go on his way when the boy asked him if the man (the post) was still alive. The hunter did not understand and Séaghan told him the whole story, mentioning the stones in the trunk, but not calling them gold. The gentleman asked to meet his mother and Séaghan was happy to find an excuse to get out of the snow. They came to the hut of the mother and the man introduced himself politely and asked about the "pebbles." The mother said she could not show them to him, and he answered back that he was the owner of the land, and therefore owner of everything that was found on it. He threatened to shoot her with his flint. The widow led him to the trunk and opened it. As the gentleman bent over the chest to look inside, she struck him a blow on the back of his head, so hard that he fell in the chest, dead, and she closed it over him. At nightfall, the mother told Séaghan to fasten the corpse on his back and tow it northwards to Portach an Caoil [Bog Waters]. There they found a bog in some woods and laid the corpse in the water and made their way home. The mother again threatened to "drive his soul out of his body" if Séaghan told anybody about what they did. That night, when the boy slept, the mother became afraid that he would again tell somebody the story. She went out and killed the billy goat, took it by the horns and lugged it to the moor where the body of the landowner lay. She pulled the corpse out and put the goat in its place. The gentleman's body she pulled to another bog and buried it there. The next day Séaghan met a lot of men who were looking for their master. He told them that it was perhaps the one his mother had murdered. For three pennies he showed them the moor hole and for another three he tried to lift the body. Then he recognized his little buck with tears, and while the men walked away angrily, he carried it sadly to his mother and said that the nobleman had slain the little buck and thrown it into the hole in his place. The mother gave him three pennies and chased him out with the fire tongs with the order never to come under her eyes again.

619 Poor Séaghan found employment with a farmer to herd twelve cows and a lamb in return for two meals of dry oats a day. The wife of the farmer despised the new shepherd who defended himself against her attempts to exploit him. When the farmer gave him sticks for herding, they broke under his hand and he demanded a rod six feet long weighing fourteen pounds and made of iron. The farmer wanted Séaghan to carry peat but the boy said he took service only to herd the cows and the lamb. They went out into the pasture together, Séaghan with his iron rod. The farmer told him: "There was one thing I forgot to tell you, you are not to let even one cow go into the woods. Because if you do, you'll never see it again and I no more than you. There are three giants in the woods and they will keep each cow that wanders in there. They have already stolen twenty cows from me this year." That day, Séaghan watched all cows very closely and returned to the house of the farmer with all twelve cows. The farmer was happy and gave him his evening meal. The next day, the farmer informed Séaghan that he had been summoned to the nearby palace of the king and that Séaghan dare not lose a cow. Séaghan said to him he should not worry, he would bring all the cows home that night.

620 But that day, knowing that the farmer was not around, Séaghan went into the forest with all the cows. Soon he heard a crashing, a din, a clanging, and a rumbling. The dried wood on the ground snapped and cracked and a giant appeared. He had three horns on three heads on three long thick necks. The giant cursed Séaghan for entering "his orchard" and then demanded that Séaghan pay him back for trespassing. Séaghan answered cheekily: "The way you pay me back is the same as the way I pay you back." The giant went after the impertinent boy with his sword, but Séaghan jumped aside and landed the giant a terrible blow with his iron rod. On the ground, the giant pleaded not to rob him of his head and life force and promised his "sleek brown horse and storehouse of weapons and equipment with dress and magic wand that lie here in the hole of my ear." The magic wand could bring back lost weapons and armor as soon as the owner touched it. Séaghan demanded the magical equipment. As soon as he got them, he said: "Not only those things, but your heads are also mine!" and with his iron rod, severed the heads from the body of the giant. He drew a slender but strong hawthorn rod through the cheeks of the heads and hung them on a tree branch. Then he went back to the farmer with his cows that were about to burst from the whole day pasturing on the giant's rich grass, but told his boss nothing of his adventure.

621 The next day Séaghan encountered a giant with five horns on five heads in the forest. Séaghan at first fled when the giant hit his legs, remembering his mother and the tongs of fire. But finally he defeated the giant, who offered him for his life his red-eared brown horse, which would carry the rider safely from every fight, as well as armor and robes. Séaghan found out where the horse and armor and robes were hid, then he cut off the giants' heads and hung them on a tree. The following day he heard a roar and a crashing twice as loud as two days before. He saw an old hag coming at him; she had a furious gaze and flaming red eyes. Her hair stood straight out from her head like swords. She cursed him because he had killed her sons, and ran wildly at him with her six foot long fingernails, each weighing seven pounds. She tried to grab him between her claws and had she caught him, she would have bored right through him from side to side with her nails. He swung and swung his rod, and managed to jump aside from her attacks. Two hours long they fought. Séaghan tired, her fingernails were longer than his iron rod, he was so exhausted he could hardly lift it anymore. Finally, he jumped behind an old oak. "You nasty old hag, you; try to get me now!" he enticed her. The witch went after Séaghan behind the tree, drilling all her nails right through the tree. But Séaghan had stepped aside and when all her nails were all the way through and stuck out the other side of the tree, he heaved his iron rod and smashed all the ends of the nails right off.

622 "Now you old maid, what are you going to do now!"

623 And what did she do? She ripped up the whole tree! But the tree fell to the ground with the witch stuck in the trunk. "Now I will take my time and cut your head off," says Séaghan.

624 "Please don't do that! I will give you my white slender horse, so white as snow and my armor and clothing which have never failed in battle. Half of my kingdom I will give you now and the other half after I die." "Those all I will thankfully take - and your head also, you old crone," and with a great heave of his rod, severed her head from her body. He took another stalk of hawthorn bush and strung her head up on a tree. Then he drove the cows home. On the way back, the lamb was so fat and haughty that it blocked up the gate to the cows coming behind. Séaghan chased it away. But when the shepherd came along with the cows, the little sheep stood there again at the gate. This time Séaghan hit him with his rod and killed him on the spot. He brought the cows in, carrying the lamb whom he took to the mistress of the house. He knew that this was her favorite lamb. The woman and

Séaghan never got on well together, and now their friendship was hardly strengthened!

625 As usual the wife acted as if she did not see him and gave him nothing to eat. Only the farmer, once again gave him supper. The farmer told Séaghan that the next day the king's daughter would be sacrificed to a sea snake that threatened the people. "Every seven years a great water snake rises up from the sea and will eat all the people unless a maiden be given. This year the lot fell on the princess. Only if a hero comes and fights three days with the worm will she be saved." The farmer said that Séaghan should come with him, surely the boy had never seen such a creature in all his life. Séaghan responded that it didn't interest him. If harm should come to the cows, then he would be to blame, and anyway, who wanted to see a snake eat a girl? The farmer went to the town and Séaghan took the cows to the forest again. There he sought out the barn of the first giant. He put on the armor and picked up the weapons of the first giant, but remembered to take his iron staff: in that he had the most trust! On the brown horse, he rode to the town and made his way through the crowd at the harbor. People jumped aside at the sight of this armored young man swaggering through. Séaghan did not stop until he had reached the maiden bound to a tree at the water's edge. He asked her what she was doing there. She explained her story and told him that if a valiant knight saved her, then she would marry him and he would receive half of her father's kingdom. "But you look tired; there is three-quarters of an hour before the monster comes. Come lay your head on my lap!" Séaghan lay his head in her lap and acted as if he had fallen asleep. She cut a lock of hair from his crown and hid it in her bodice. Soon she heard the crowd getting restless and realized the snake was approaching. The princess woke him up and said now it was time, the sea monster had arrived. The valiant warrior sprang up, grabbed his armor, and strode off to meet the monster. The seas parted, like mountains being pushed aside, the snake came with such might! All the people jumped back in terror, but Séaghan went to meet the snake. He struck it with his rod and bashed the monster so hard, it sank back into the sea. Nobody knew if the monster was really dead, just that the sea was red with blood. Séaghan stood and watched that the snake did not reappear that day. Seeing that the snake was not coming, he cut the maiden free of her bonds and told her to go home as the snake would not come, today she did not need to fear the snake. He went to his steed, but before he could ride away, she asked him to come with her to the king's palace. Séaghan turned down the invitation saying he had to return to his work, he had a job to do. She

pleaded that he come again the second day. "Let's hope for a good day tomorrow," called out Séaghan and rode away. Once back at the forest, he put his armor down and changed back into his old rags, rubbed and washed down his horse, and drove the fat cows back to the farmer's house. Again, the farmer returned only much later, excited to tell Séaghan all the news of the day. But the boy reported he was not interested in news, but only in his dinner.

626 On the second day he defeated the snake in the armor of the second giant. On the third day, the farmer's efforts to persuade Séaghan to watch the battle were once again in vain. Séaghan drove the cows out, put on the armour and clothes of the dead witch, and mounted the white horse. The steed was so agile that it caught up with the wind ahead, and the wind behind could not catch up with it. When he came flying up over the hill to the harbour, the assembled crowd thought he had come from the other world. The maiden noticed immediately that he was the same knight as before, but did not divulge her knowledge. Again he asked what she was doing there, and she answered as before. He lay his head on her lap to rest before the battle. The virgin noticed the place where the locks were missing and cut another with her little scissors. When the time came for the great worm to emerge, she woke him up. This time Séaghan had to wait a half-hour for the snake to appear. He let the snake advance with jaws open wide, this time even farther up the beach to where the princess stood bound to the tree. But before the monster could take her in its jaws, Séaghan struck it with all his might and this time until the snake really died. He cut off the head and proceeded to split the carcass from head to tail, slicing the great filets from the middle into five pieces. After he cut the princess free, and before she had time to invite him to the castle again, he was on his steed and away. In the forest again, he washed down the white horse, changed back into his shabby clothes, and drove the cows home. The mistress of the house offered him nothing to eat and he had to wait again until the farmer returned. Excitedly he told Séaghan of the saving of the princess and the whole town from the sea monster.

627 The next day, the farmer had taken the cows out himself before Séaghan awoke. "And where are they?" asked Séaghan.

628 "In the field with the two gates," answered the farmer. "And why did you do that?"

629 "Because today there will be the wedding and you must come to the great feast, whether you like it or not."

630 "I have no shoes, people will step on my feet."

631 "It does not matter what you have on your feet! There will be food for everyone and I want you to come and get your part of the meal!" said the farmer forcefully.

632 "Well, in that case, I guess I will come. Maybe I will get something good to eat."

633 They traveled together. At the great hall, Séaghan went to eat with the poor people. But the poor fought amongst themselves for the food so fiercely that Séaghan got nothing to eat. And the drinks all spilled when the people greedily grabbed at whatever was offered. Séaghan got so angry that he pulled out his iron bludgeon and went after them with a roar. At this moment, the princess looked through a window and recognized the iron rod. She ran to her father, the king, and asked him to request the presence of that man, for he might be the one who saved her.

634 "Hold her here!" ordered the king to his ministers, "She has lost her mind!"

635 The princess claimed she had proof and one of the king's ministers asked what kind of proof. But the princess retorted that she would show no man or woman before she had seen the one in the crowd. They brought Séaghan to her. When he entered the chambers, the princess drew out her three locks of hair and called to her father. She took off his old cap and there were the three missing locks of hair. She took those of hers and placed them in the correct spots. "This is the man who saved me! And there is no prince or knight in the whole land that I will marry but him." She turned to the false knight and told him that he was far from her the whole time, and should quit her presence. After he left, she said to Séaghan that she wanted to marry him – if he wanted her. "Not until I have the proper clothing," he answered.

636 "You can put them on when we are married," she answered. But the king spoke out and said that he would give the young man a proper suit.

637 Séaghan said he must put on his own clothing and despite protests from the princess, who did not want him to go, he left. In exactly one hour a wild, daring knight approached upon a white horse that glistened white as a swan. The ground shook as he neared. Séaghan did not follow a path but jumped over all hurdles. He even did not wait until the gates of the castle were opened, but sprang over the wall and the whole palace shook when he landed. Now the pride and joy

of the king was unsurpassed. Everyone recognized this horseman as the knight who saved them and the princess from the sea snake. Séaghan dismounted and went to the king's daughter. "How do you like me now?" He asked. "I like you as much as I did when I recognized you among the poor people with your iron rod. I knew the hero was in you."

638 The wedding took place on the spot. Séaghan inherited half the kingdom and the king granted the farmer, Séaghan's former master, the land and goods without taxes for the rest of his life. But he had to promise not to give his wife a single bit of food, because she had treated their servant so unkindly. Séaghan moved with his new wife to the palace of the giants in the woods and there they lived happily many years. One day, Séaghan remembered his mother who had gone after him with the fire tongs and rode on his gleaming white horses to his home. The cabin was still standing, but his mother and the goats were no longer there. He went to the neighbors who did not recognize him in his grandeur. They told him that the woman who lived there had died a long time ago and had left behind a lot of money that she had hidden somewhere. "It does not matter to me where she hid her money, if only she were still alive," spoke Séaghan. Therewith he turned his steed and rode off. The neighbors did not know who he was, but had seen the tears in his eyes. Séaghan and his wife lived happily to the end of their lives. And their children's children still live in the castle of the giants in the woods.[89]

639 This well-constructed and artistic fairytale works through its intriguing mix of lively fantasy in the style of a typical heroic tale and with extraordinarily vivid, dramatic, and carnival scenes. Unfortunately, the shortened version above does poor justice to the Irish original. The characters are very lively and consistently depicted. Once one begins to get to the bottom of the many impressions and to dissect the rich content, one discovers a tremendous rhythm and pace and how, in back-and-forth movements, the "great fool" gradually develops into a brilliant hero.

640 Like Cathal (in "The Knight With the Sinister Laugh"), Séaghan is the son of a widow, conditioned and enthralled in a particular degree by the mother-imago, and to this extent his adaptation to the world is disturbed and his relation to male energy remains undeveloped. He is completely caught up in the unconscious, and thus trapped in an infantile state. But at the same time he also is closer than ordinary individuals to the creative source of life. As a

[89] [Since no English translation of the original Irish appears to exist, we have used the 34-page German translation in Müller-Lisowski's *Irische Volksmärchen*, pp. 167–200, as the basis for this summary.]

result, he is one who is both called and threatened. Séaghan grows out of this situation in the course of the narrative, whereby the different rooms in the story (his mother's house near the bog, the farmer's house near the forest, the battle arena on the seafront, the royal court at the king's castle, the redeemed giant's castle in the forest) represent various stages of inner development. The voluntary choice to wear shabby clothes is a motif that is repeated when the hero, after his great deeds, deliberately returns to being a shepherd. This is a refusal to adapt to the world, at the same time a sign of strong character that rejects adapting to outer appearances and their dazzling brilliance. Under the guise of the poor fool, the hero maintains his inner independence, which was already revealed in the naive discovery of the murder committed by his mother.

641 His first encounter with the boundary post, which he considers to be a man and under which he later finds the gold, is symbolically important. Boundary stones and landmarks have phallic significance almost everywhere; ancient boundary markers were either a Priapos[90] or a Hermes Ithyphallikos[91] or simply a phallus, to which animals and fruits were offered. He guaranteed not only the integrity but also the fertility of the fields. As amplified by Bächtold-Stäubli under *Pfahl* [post, stake]:

> 642 "As a stake or post, rod, or stick hewn from parts of a tree, these markers naturally played a large role in daily life and in the mythological ideas of the earlier peoples. Among the Indo-European peoples, such posts also served as arable woods, to prepare fires, as border stakes, and other important and sacred tools. In addition, forms of these rods revered as divine have served as starting points for the development of the god images. . . Idols in the form of posts or stakes are still in use even up to modern times. . . Such posts appear not only as representatives of a specific deity, but also, like the tree of life, can represent a whole culture. A poacher once turned into a post. Therefore, many primitive peoples erected a post instead of a grave tree pile not as a monument, but as a surrogate for the seat of the soul."[92]

643 In one moment, after his mother had treated him in an especially hostile and harsh manner, Séaghan discovered his own creative future as a man. When he spoke to the post thinking it was a living man and gave him his coat, he

[90] [In Greek mythology, Priapus or Priapos was a minor rustic fertility god, protector of livestock, fruit plants, gardens, and male genitalia. Priapus was best noted for his large, permanent erection, which gave rise to the medical term priapism.]

[91] [Hermai were boundary or milestones, carved with the head and phallus of Hermes. They were rural markers which were also supposed to ensure the fertility of the herds and flocks and bring luck.]

[92] Bächtold-Stäubli under *Pfahl*.

demonstrated his devotion as if it were a fetish. Precisely because he evidenced such a positive attitude of reverence to this symbol, he later found the treasure of golden pebbles under the overturned stake. When the mother took the gold for herself, he relinquished to her the new opportunity and creative life value. Her ban on speaking about what happened isolated Séaghan even more from the environment and he remained completely engulfed by the mother. The gentleman who then appeared as the owner of the treasure (life resources) was an image of Séaghan's potential future. Accordingly, the mother "murdered" this source of masculine developmental power and even threw it into a trunk.[93] Since the box is also a mother symbol, this removal of the corpse again epitomized engulfment by the mother. She even killed her son's beloved billy goat and buried it in place of the gentleman in the bog. This fact corresponds to the tragic killing of Mrile's tuber seed child in "The Adventures of Mrile." The billy goat, like the ram, the animal of Pan, is a phallic symbol and as such a living equivalent to the post.[94] By killing the animal power of the hero, he was pushed down into the unconscious, but both his resistance to letting his soul be bent[95] and his sincerity prevented his destruction. He revealed the murder that his mother committed and thus brought down her wrath leading to her chasing him out of the house in a fit of rage. He avoided succumbing to the mother because inwardly he took no part in her malice and greed. As a symbol, he is[96] like an unassimilable spark of light that is spewn out by the darkness.[97]

---

[93] [In Swiss German, *Kiste* (box, trunk) is a common metaphor for "coffin."]

[94] On the role of the billy goat in pagan cults and superstitions, see Bächtold-Stäubli under *Ziegenbock* [billy goat].

[95] [*seelisch Unverbogenheit.*]

[96] [We use the present tense here because the authors are speaking of a symbol that is alive *now*.]

[97] Cf. also "Der ehrliche Vierschilling" [The honest four shillings]. "Once upon a time there was a poor woman, who lived in a wretched hut far away from the village. She had but little to bite and less to burn, so she sent her little boy to the forest to gather wood. . . When he had filled his barrow, and was wandering homeward, he crossed a field of stubble. There he saw lying a jagged white stone. "Oh, you poor old stone, how white and pale you are! You must be freezing terribly!" said the boy; took off his jacket, and laid it over the stone. And when he came back home with his wood, his mother asked him how it was that he was going around in the autumn cold in his shirt-sleeves. He told her that he had seen a jagged old stone, quite white and pale with the frost, and that he had given it his jacket. "You fool" said the woman, "do you think a stone can freeze? And with that she drove the boy out again to fetch his jacket." He went and found a box of silver coins under the stone. He decided that this must be stolen money and threw it into a pond. A four shilling piece remained floating on the water and, considering this to be honest, kept it. Back home he told his mother who admonished him, "You are a fool! If nothing were honest save what floats on the water, there would be but little honesty left in the world!" She then chased him out into the world to earn his own living. After many rejections he took up service as a kitchen boy with a merchant. One day before the merchant left on a journey, the boy gave him his four shilling piece to buy whatever "it will bring." At the last minute of his purchasing tour, the businessman bought a cat from a poor woman with the four shilling piece. On the ship traveling home, a storm carried him to a country in which mice were a plague and cats were unknown. The merchant sold the cat for a hundred shillings. Hardly at sea again, when the merchant saw the cat sitting on the highest mast of his ship. Again a storm arose and the merchant was driven to a new foreign land where there are even bigger mice. He sold the cat for two hundred shillings and later the cat was again on the mast. An even bigger storm came and he was driven to a country full of rats. Again he sold the cat, this time for three hundred shillings and upon sailing there she was, sitting on the mast.

644 Séaghan then came to the farmer and his wife, who function as a kind of parent-imagos in the place of his mother. Still, the mother image remains purely negative as the farmer's wife tries to starve the hero to death. Her wickedness is compensated by the farmer, however, who is not only the real master, but also represents, symbolically a male role model, a father figure for the hero. For the first time, Séaghan found an activity in which he could perform useful work (although the farmer's wife like his mother tried to thwart this). When the farmer asked for his name, he replied: "My mother called me Séaghan." Like Perceval, his whole world view and his idea of the self are initially entirely determined by the mother.[98]

645 By the time Séaghan's contracted work for the friendly farmer came to an end, it is clear that his self-esteem and strength had drastically increased from the time he began the job. We see this in his increasingly energetic demands for his meals and his use of the shepherd's stick; also in his attitude to the farmer's wife. And suddenly this fool, who used to be intimidated by the fire tongs of his mother, can swing a fourteen-pound club. Like the post, this iron cudgel is a phallic symbol. Through the separation from the mother, the hero gains possession of his masculine energy and now steps up against the domineering male part of the mother's nature.

646 With his bludgeon, he successively defeats the two forest giants; these many headed demons represent untamed, chaotic natural forces in his unconscious that threaten to overwhelm Séaghan. Similarly, the chaos of unconscious passion has endangered a piece of female maternal nature, which he has obtained in the form of cows. He subordinated them and they are well-disposed towards him and he is entrusted with their health and well-being. In an Iranian tale, "Little Fatima with the Moon Forehead," (told in full in Vol. 1, Book 2, "Quest of the Maiden") a daughter murdered her mother as a favor for her teacher, who was jealous and wanted to marry her father, which she soon did. But she then mistreated her stepdaughter and gave her the task of spinning a bale of wool into a ball of thread in one day. The girl, repenting her evil deeds, went out to the fields to tend the cows and spin the wool. Her dead mother had become a cow and licked the tears of her daughter, ingested the

---

This time such a dangerous storm arose that the merchant realized he must promise the boy the money earned from the cat. No sooner did he promise than the storm abated. Landing back home, "he gave the youth the six hundred shillings and his daughter to boot. For now the scullion was richer than the merchant himself, and thereafter he lived in splendor and happiness. He even took in his mother and treated her kindly. 'For I do not believe that charity begins at home,' said the youth." [English translation in C. Stroebe, *Norwegian Fairy Book*, New York, 1922, pp. 69–75. The original Norwegian is in Asbjornsen and Moe, N.F.E., p. 306, No. 59).] In this Norwegian version, the cat is a mother symbol. Here the image of the mother turns from her dark to her light aspect due to her honest conduct towards her son.

[98] This reminds us of Gornemant, who says to Perceval:

> "Must you always refer to mother,
> As if you did not want to know anything else?"

(translated from Wolfram von Eschenbach, *Parzival*, ed. Wilhelm Hertz, 1923, p. 78.)

wool, and later spat out a fully spun ball of thread (!). One senses here clearly the importance of the mother cow. In China, the female receptive principle (Yin), is represented by the image of the cow, a symbol of extreme docility and gentleness.[99] Here, Séaghan demonstrates that he can protect the gentle maternal nature in its animal appearance from the attacks of deadly unconscious powers. And later he proves to be ready to save and possess the same female principle on a higher level in the figure of the princess.

647 The battles with the giants intensify, reflecting the hero's inner development. The age and power of the enemies increase over time, as do the number of their heads and their ferocity. The second giant threatens to come at the legs of the hero, reminding him of the fire tongs of his mother so that he falls weak and flees. (Is this a threat to his "position" and the "progress" that he has made?) What this incident tells us is that the giants represent powers that were hidden behind the image of the mother,[100] and with the appearance of the old hag it is finally revealed that the struggle is ultimately to defeat the archetype of the terrible mother as the destructive power of the unconscious. By winning these battles, Séaghan acquires three horses: one earth-colored, one with red ears, and finally, the white horse of the witch-mother. The horse is, on the one hand – as we stated above – a mother symbol; on the other hand, it is generally the animal, instinctive side of the unconscious, the psychic power that supports the life force of the body. In a certain sense, winning the horses compensates for the killing of the billy goat. The hero has at his free disposal the post now in the form of his iron club as well as in the form of the newly acquired weapons of the giants and also the billy goat in the form of the horses. For the time being, he attends to the feminine in the form of several cows, which obey and nourish him. Thus the negative demonic aspect of the unconscious gradually transforms into a positive life-enhancing power.

648 The mother of the giants is defeated by the hero when she drills her claws as long fingernails into the tree he was hiding behind and there she is helplessly caught, an easy target. The hero overcomes her, as is the case in many fairy tales we have previously mentioned, through the law of "like conquers like" because the tree is a symbol of the Great Mother. Many female goddesses were worshiped under the image of wood or tree. In the Middle Ages trees were addressed poetically as women.[101] The sky goddess Hathor, the cow, who was revered in Egypt as a cow-mother goddess, was called "The

---

99 See Wilhelm and Baynes, *I Ching*, p. 273. [The translators of the *I Ching* note on page 273 that the receptive is also represented by the mare, as in *The Commentaries* on "The Receptive," pp. 386ff.]

100 For a parallel narrative, see "Mother Holle," where the dragons are the four sons of the old witch-demon.

101 See Mannhardt, *Wald- und Feldkulte*, vol. 1, *passim*. Like watercourses, trees are the home of mainly female spirits: hamadryads, tree nymphs, etc. Cf. Przyluski, "Ursprünge,"pp. 15ff.

Mistress of the Sycamore,"[102] and similar to the wishing cow Indra in Indian mythology, which arose out of what is desired, there was also a wishing tree that could make all fantasies become reality.[103] In fairytales, the tree is also a miracle shrine.[104] Since the tree as the world-tree means primordial world-matter (Greek: *hyle* = forest, wood, matter), so with the demon-witch nailed to the tree, Séaghan forces her to accept the immobility of matter. Insofar as the tree also embodies spiritual growth and inner development, overcoming the mother image actually symbolizes the transformation of the tree image into one of inner becoming and gradual individuation (i.e., self-realization).

649 On the way home, Séaghan kills the lamb, which, having become arrogant, blocked the path for the cows. And since it had been the favorite animal of the farmer woman, this act augments her hostility. The lamb here represents a piece of childish innocence, a naive "inability to find one's place in life," whereby Séaghan is at the mercy of the mother imago. By eliminating this trait in himself, he frees himself even more from the maternal bond. Killing the lamb also compensates for killing his beloved billy goat. In principle, while this behavior is brutal and vicious, it demonstrates that Séaghan had now overcome his own childlike innocence, which was also a helpless stubbornness.

650 From the moment Séaghan dons the armor of the giants and controls the magic realm begins the second phase of his heroic career: his transformation into a chivalrous liberator of the king's daughter. His appearance as a cowherd is now only maintained as a deliberate mask behind which he hides his nature, to give from time to time, a glance at the luster of his mysterious lordship. With iron determination he plays his game of hide-and-seek, with the surety of a mature knight who owns the treasures of the magical center. The approach of the hero-knight is told with an artistic power of perception: how he springs down over the bordering hills and walks through the middle of the crowd with the quality of a miracle-bringer, to bring his horse to a halt in front of the virgin who is tied to a tree. The virgin means the unconscious feminine principle in the hero in its worthy living aspect as the precious treasure to be won. This is still closely tied to the tree as the image of matter (the mother) and threatened by a sea monster, the snake. As in "The Knight With the Sinister Laugh," overcoming the dragon is a prerequisite for acquiring the princess, symbol of new fruitful life. Each day of battle brings, as earlier in the forest of the giants, a clear crescendo in comparison to the previous day. This we see both in the appearance and increasing speed of the knight, as well as in the force of his strokes and their impact on the more and more exhausted

[102] See Erman, *Religion der Ägypter*, p. 31.
[103] See Zimmer, *Maya*, pp. 128, 220-24, 388-91.
[104] See Bolte andMackensen, *Handwörterbuch*, under *Baum als Wunderschrank* [tree as a miracle cabinet].

approaching monster. With his most important weapon, the iron club, which also serves as his trademark sign at the end, Séaghan defeats the snake. Then he filets the monster with his sword, by which deliberate and conscious action he frees the spiritual power that will bring him new life, from its paralyzing attachment to the barren superiority of the past, which long held him dependent.

651 But then the hero vanishes over the horizon on the hill and maintains the secret of his superiority over the powers of the magic kingdom. On the fifth day the farmer irrevocably insists that the cowherd accompany him to the palace since the king has set his will on finding the mysterious liberator. The moment in which a false bridegroom appears, the hour of the hero has tolled. He rejects the clothes offered by the king, and appears in the armor he had acquired from the mother of the giants in the forest, cloaked in the splendor of the magical world. The power of the mother archetype, which had alienated him from life and had humiliated him, has been transformed by his manly effort into something extraordinary that will carry him into a towering personality. This time he approaches, in contrast to the struggle with the sea serpent, not "from above" like a celestial phenomenon, but "from below," from the valley's edge. It is as if the Earth opens to bring forth the hero of light. So he wins the princess and becomes heir of the empire.

652 Now follows a strange and enlightening sequel. In the armor of the giantess, as a sign that he has overcome the threat of the demonic female, he goes to find his mother. His previous dependence has been transformed into an understandable human attachment. But he does not find the mother, she has died. Just like in "Hansel and Gretel" the witch in the magical kingdom and the evil mother in the profane world perish at the same time. Since the mother, as an individual person, completely took on the archetype of the evil mother, she must die in the moment when she loses her effectiveness. Probably there was not enough "human" in her, through which she could transform and participate in the life of her son in the "disenchanted" castle. The castle is demystified because the unconscious changed. "Transform yourself and you wil enter a transformed world. . ."[105]

653 Between the hero and the farmer's evil wife, on the other hand, there is no human relationship, and therefore he insists on a penalty corresponding to her debt to him.

654 Returning to the mother not only marks an effective conclusion, in which the circle closes, but it also makes sense. The whole story circles in gradually increasing spirals revolving around the issue of the mother image in the life of the man. The mother appears as the natural mother, as the evil concrete power (the farmer's wife), as the animal archetype (the snake) and - trans-

[105] Zimmer, *Weisheit Indiens*, Darmstadt, 1938, p. 98.

formed – as the herd of cows, as a beautiful princess, and as a castle, which in its harboring grasp has a maternal significance. Once more, all these images are compared, most impressively, with the initial situation of the hero's youth. It is as if he sadly returns to the point from whence his sorrowful fate had begun, and out of which his meaningful fate later evolved in ever expanding spirals. Ultimately, the image of the mother is the cord, "the real bond through which we are connected with our origins."[106]

655 The stories we have examined here present us with the image of the Great Mother as she appears mirrored in the male soul. In many fairytales from all over the world the Great Mother appears as a major figure in relation to developing girls.[107] Here the mother-imago is a positive role model embodying the maternal. Here too she occasionally shows her negative side, however, and then transmits particularly gruesome features. The German fairytale, "Frau Trude," where, like in "The Great Fool from Cuasan," the mother figure appears with male companions, shows impressively the dual nature of this archetype:[108]

> 656 Once upon a time there was a small girl who was strong willed and forward, and whenever her parents said anything to her, she disobeyed them. How could anything go well with her? One day she said to her parents: "I have heard so much about Frau Trude. Someday I want to go to her place. People say such amazing things are seen there, and such strange things happen there, that I have become very curious." Her parents strictly forbade her, saying: "Frau Trude is a wicked woman who commits godless acts. If you go there, you will no longer be our child."
>
> 657 But the girl paid no attention to her parents and went to Frau Trude's place anyway.
>
> 658 When she arrived there, Frau Trude asked: "Why are you so pale?"
>
> 659 "Oh," she answered, trembling all over, "I saw something that frightened me."
>
> 660 "What did you see?"
>
> 661 "I saw a black man on your steps."
>
> 662 "That was a charcoal burner."
>
> 663 "Then I saw a green man."
>
> 664 "That was a huntsman."

[106] Cf. C.G. Jung, *Symbols of Transformation*, CW 5, ¶669.
[107] We will explore this theme in a later volume.
[108] See also the witch with the cold cruel tooth in "The Knight With the Sinister Laugh," p. 262.

665 "Then I saw a blood-red man."

666 "That was a butcher."

667 "Oh, Frau Trude, it frightened me when I looked through your window and could not see you, but instead saw the devil with a head of fire."

668 "Aha" she said. "So you saw the witch properly outfitted. I have been waiting for you and wanting you for a long time. Light the way for me now."

669 With that she turned the girl into a block of wood and threw it into the fire. When it was thoroughly aglow she sat down next to it, and warmed herself by it, saying: "It gives such a bright light."[109]

670 Frau Trude's gruesome features are drawn in lapidary lines, her answers are so matter-of-fact that the girl succumbs without resistance to the devilish fire, an image of the red coals in her soul. Frau Trude is particularly incensed that the cheeky girl has seen her witch aspect. She reacts in a peeved and angry way, just like the devil in "The Godfather." This is similar to Kaikutschi's reaction to exposing his hidden faces in "Makonaura and Anuanaitu."

671 In "The Witchdoctor Makanaholo," the Arawak of South America depicted the Great Mother as the Death Mother:

672 None was so far advanced in the art of sorcery than the witchdoctor Makanaholo. He could rise from the earth, jump over the trees; yes, he could even grow wings if he needed them. But the most wonderful of all his arts was the power to change his appearance and shape into any animal that he liked. And always the stag played a leading role. One fine day, Makanaholo was lonely and decided to find a companion. He turned himself into a dead stag and let his flesh begin to rot, which attracted vultures. He waited until the most beautiful of vultures, the queen vulture, settled close to him. Then Makanaholo had her, and she became his wife. After a time of happy marriage during which Makanaholo cured her of lice, she wanted to visit her mother. Makanaholo accompanied her up to the skies.

673 Akathu, the mother of the king [sic] of vultures, always remained in her hammock so that no one could see her face. To test the art of her son-in-law, she ordered him to make a sitting stool in the shape of her head. Makanaholo, thanks to his power over the animals, called up the red ants who bit Akathu so hard that she jumped out of the

[109] *Complete Grimm's*, London, 1975, pp. 208–209. The version reproduced here is a more modern translation by D. L. Ashliman (Princeton, 1998–2009).

> hammock. The sorcerer, who secretly lurked nearby saw "that she not only had a head, but no less than a dozen!" He made the stool which faithfully reproduced Akathu's features. She was so happy that she cried aloud: "Yes, yes, you are a very clever man!"

> 674 With the help of his powers of sorcery, Makanajolo passed further tests, whereupon Akathu called all her children to her and said, "Well, we want to make a beautiful garden for him, because we want such a clever man to remain with us forever." In her heart Akathu was full of fear and apprehension about the arts of the doctor of magic. She was afraid both for herself and for her daughter and her other children. She told them, "As soon as he falls asleep in his beautiful garden, we must kill him."

> 675 One of Akathu's children warned Makanaholo of the evil plan to kill him, but the sorcerer did not flee, he wanted to test his powers. The garden was prepared and sealed on all sides. The killers were quite sure that Makanaholo could not escape, and yet when they went after him, he was no longer in the garden! Makanaholo liked to play his flute and in one of the garden walls there was a small opening through which he guided his flute. When three flute holes were outside of the garden he turned himself into a fly, flew into a flute hole that was open inside the garden, and slipped through the flute and flew out through one of the holes that was outside. The would-be murderers heard Makanaholo playing his flute in complete freedom. After this feat, he returned to earth.[110]

676 The magical invisibility of Akathu is expressed through her permanent residence in the hammock (a woven fabric!). But when the ants force her to leave, it turns out that she has "no less than a dozen" heads. The queen of the vultures is very much a mother of death. Vultures eat corpses and thereby draw creatures back into themselves, which corresponds to a re-entry into the mother. Even the Indian Great Mother Kali is a devourer of all life and a bloody goddess. She drinks from the skulls of her victims on the night of their death and at their grave.[111] In the Orient, where the dead are left to be eaten by scavenging birds, vultures correspond to the sheltering grave.

677 Particularly in Egypt, the vulture plays a role as a mother symbol. The deceased come to the "two mothers, the vultures with the long hair and swelling breasts, sitting on the mountain Sehseh. . . " who offer their breasts to the dead one.[112] The connection of the concepts of death and matter =

---

[110] Summarized from Koch-Grünberg, *Südamerika*, pp. 52–54.

[111] Cf. Zimmer, *Maya*, p. 489.

[112] Cf. Erman, *Religion der Ägypter*, pp. 22, 215.

materia, can be considered as reflecting that death destroys life as a form of being and the parts of matter tied up with it in the primal matter. The material is what is mortal in the individual.[113] Vultures also take the dead to heaven, so they carry the image of the ascending soul as well.[114] Vultures can also occur as male demons. Along with the mother of the king/queen vulture, the father of the king/queen vulture appears in other South American fairytales[115] as a master of the demon empire who imposes impossible tasks upon the hero. Often he has two heads, is a man-eater, and he feeds on decaying animals.[116]

678 After Makanaholo escapes her attacks several times, the mother of death decides, as a last resort, to lock him in a garden and kill him. The garden itself is, however, a symbol of the nourishing but enclosing womb. Thus the Garden of Eden in which man was formed was already interpreted by some Gnostics as the uterus.[117] (Even groves have a similar meaning.) In some Christian concepts, the garden is a symbol of the Mother of God. As a symbol of the maternal primary ground of the human soul, the garden is the blessed land of origin and the human soul and the final destination of the journey at the same time.[118] The connection between the mother deity and the garden is impressively shown in a Russian fairytale ("Ivan, the Cow's Son") that we will discuss in the second volume. There the great witch Baba-Yaga decided to transform her second daughter-in-law into a beautiful garden with heavily laden fruit trees. If the hero should pick one of the fruits, "she will tear the fruit into pieces the size of poppy seeds." This fragmentation means the complete disintegration in the unconscious, the mental and physical destruction of personality. In the Uzbek fairytale, "The Beautiful Dunye," a witch appears who poisons all the people who come to her, all the birds that fly over her garden burn their feathers, and all people and animals who walk therein, burn their legs. The garden here signifies the realm of destructive passions of the unconscious, which make movement impossible for all beings. The kingdom of Frau Holle is called in a variant from Franconia, "the garden in the fountain."[119]

679 So if the evil death mother, the vulture queen, wants to lock up the hero in a garden, this means she wants to corrupt him, to swallow him. But Makanaholo escapes in a peculiar way as a fly, crawling through the finger holes of his flute. Figuratively, this escape resembles a rebirth: in an

[113] On the connection between death and impermanence with the material [as preached by the Apostle Paul], see Reitzenstein, *Hellenistic Mystery-Religions*, p. 447.
[114] See Dieterich, *Eine Mithrasliturgie*, pp. 204–205.
[115] [For instance in "The Visit to Heaven," retold here on page 398.]
[116] See notes to this tale in Koch-Grünberg, *Südamerika*, pp. 247ff.
[117] Cf. Leisegang, *Die Gnosis*, pp. 75ff. On the garden as a symbol of the female body, see also Silberer, *Problems of Mysticism*, p. 88.
[118] Silberer, pp. 187–188.
[119] Cf. Bolte and Polívka, *Anmerkungen*, vol. 1, p. 211.

unassuming guise, he traverses the devouring unconscious and returns to the world of consciousness.

680 It seems that knowledge about the secret of magical powers leads people to destruction, even when it was a task to gain this insight (as in the case of Makanaholo) or when insight is gained by curiosity (as in "Frau Trude"). Only through the further conduct of the person, and through the consequences he or she draws from what they have seen, can they assure a real gain. Further discussion of this important theme awaits a later chapter. Inspection of "Frau Trude" seems to indicate that the meddlesome girl who is in no way mature enough for such a show of magic, was not destined for this kind of submersion in the unconscious, because the primordial figure of death had not approached her, as in the case of Makanaholo in the shape of his wife. The impertinent girl lacks the inner attitude, which could support a meaningful turn to the magical. The overly cheeky visit to the witch and her transformation into a glowing ember means, therefore, that the girl hopelessly and inevitably succumbs to her own inner abyss; she is compulsively addicted to her destructive passions. All the more so as she previously sees the three male devil figures, which embody the demonic spiritual energy of the mother image.[120] Seeing these figures means becoming aware of the terrible mother's demonic energy in the heroine's own psychic realm. She is frightened to death and crumbles defenselessly against the witch. (In a Czech version[121] the child is killed with a hoe, its spiritual personality is literally "hacked to pieces" by the vision.) This enslavement to the unconscious acts like a triumph of the evil mother, that wild nature, which – without inhibition – seems to know the human being only as means to her ends. The onlooker's fascination leads, as it were, to the cheeky girl aligning herself with the powers of hell and becoming a glowing block of charcoal. This image of a piece of matter that is consumed by fire, symbolizes the girl's core of being that is no longer human-alive, but is sunk into petrification and destroyed in the flames of her unconscious visions. In a frightening irony, Frau Trude says to the girl, "She ought to shine for me!" since the poor child, unlike "The Adventures of Mrile," does not bring fire as an illuminating force in the magical world, but she becomes victim of unimaginable embers.[122] The dual nature of Frau Trude and

[120] See also an episode in "Vasilisa the Beautiful:" a girl is ordered by the evil stepmother to go into the forest in which the arch-witch, the Baba Yaga, lives. The girl manages to stay clear of the witch, but then her two stepsisters force her to go directly to the Baba Yaga to fetch light. On her way to the witch's hut on chicken legs in the dark woods, the heroine sees first a white knight riding a white horse, then a red rider passes her on a red horse, and finally a black horseman gallops by on a black horse. Later she learns from the witch that these horsemen are the bright day, the red sun, and the dark night.

[121] Cf. Bolte and Polívka, *Anmerkungen,* vol. 1, p. 377.

[122] On the figure of the Great Mother and her relationship to fire, Emma Jung writes: "This mother figure represents, in contrast to a heavenly light mother, the primordial woman as a heavy, dark, earth-bound, versed in magic, sometimes helpful, sometimes sinister, witch-like and often destructive power. Her son would be a chthonic fire spirit, reminiscent of the Logi and Loki of Norse mythology, which (after the Grimm Brothers) is conceived of as a creativity gifted giant and at the same time as a shrewd,

her three companions, which represents the undifferentiated male-female primordial psychic ground, will vary in other versions. Thus in a parallel her husband was a cane in the corner of the living room.[123] This represents the male aspect of the First Mother, pictured as a phallic symbol, like a pronounced tooth or large nose, or manifesting in the form of dark demons. The wooden block into which the girl is transformed [and burned], is reminiscent of the same symbol. It means an aggressive psychic condition of the primal female being, which can act both creatively and destructively. To the extent – psychologically speaking – that the visions of the events arise from the impertinent girl's own soul, this trait of the Great Mother corresponds to the child's obstinacy and impertinence, which were the cause of the girl's tragic end.

681 Mythologically, the figure of Frau Trude belongs to the great divine mother figures in the Germanic tradition such as Frau Perhta, Frau Rose, Frau Hulda, and Frau Gothel.[124] According to Bächtold-Stäubli under "Perhta," this figure is:

682 A mythical creature whose shape, worship, rich in suggestive appearances and interpretations, has always been a particularly living part of German folk belief. We find a whole series of mythical female beings having the same or similar nature. . . Most similar to Pertha is Frau (Mother) Holle (also Hulda or Holds), whose form is just as rich and variable. In both figures – Perhta and Holle – we see personifications of the same basic demonic nature: both were originally members of a whole horde of demons, both were accounted as ghosts, but gradually emerged as individual demons. . . They lead a whole host of companion demonic beings. . . Both Perhta and Frau Holle punish severely all the delinquent, lazy, careless, or overly inquisitive. Then they act like ghosts and dream figures. . ."[125]

---

seductive villain, who later became the Christian devil. In Greek mythology, he corresponds to Hephaestus, the god of earthly fire, but his work as a blacksmith points to a tamed fire, while as the Nordic Logi he is more the directionless elemental force of nature. This earth fire spirit is as a son of the lower mother of woman close and well-known. He manifests positively in practical work, especially in the handling of matter, also in the artful reworking; negatively in states of stress or emotional explosions and often in dubious and fatal ways as an ally of the primordial Maternal, as instigator or assistant in what is commonly known under the term 'female devilishness and witchcraft.'" Translated from Emma Jung, "Beitrag zum Problem des Animus," Zürich, 1934, pp. 339–340. By comparison, see "The Drummer," where the king's daughter does not succumb to the flames, whereas the witch burns. Although these two figures stand in a different relation than the situation of the girl in "Frau Trude," we would still like to note the essential difference.

[123] Cf. Bolte and Polívka, *Anmerkungen*, vol. 1, p. 377.

[124] [German "*Frau*" = English "Mrs."]

[125] Cf. Bächtold-Stäubli *Frau Rose*; see further Will-Erich Peuckert, *Deutscher Volksglaube des Spätmittelalters*, 1942, pp. 97ff.

683 But Perhta can also be helpful and rewards industriousness. Such demonic mother figures are familiar from folklore and fairytales from all lands. In Japan, the primeval witch is named "Yamauba," a "wild woman" or "forest woman." She has long body hair, a red naked body, covered with her thick black hair, and the eyes of her ugly old face are green. In Western Japan, she is a beautiful woman who has a second mouth at the crown of her head hidden by hair. She eats only when she cannot be overheard, but then gobbles huge amounts of rice with her second mouth. Her hair becomes snakes, which bring the food to her second mouth. Her feces change into silk and brocade fabrics. From drivers of pack animals she steals and devours their loads of fish, then the beast of burden, and even the driver himself. She carries men around in a basket on her head through the forest to her family as meat for a festive meal.[126]

684 Compare this figure to the Russian arch witch and archaic forest mother, "Baba Yaga, with her wooden legs, her head like a club face to the floor, her feet to the ceiling." She lives in a hut spinning on three chicken or spindle legs, "flies about in an iron mortar shell, which she steers and paddles along with her club or crutch, and covers her tracks with a broom." She feeds on human flesh and, therefore, steals children. Death, who often travels with her, hands over the dead, and she nourishes herself with their souls.[127] In "Vasilisa the Beautiful," her house is built of skeletons and is surrounded with skulls having glowing eyes. (Baba Yaga is sometimes helpful but, as Yamauba also occasionally does, mostly gives gifts to the lost.) The figure of the first mother appears even stranger in a Czech variant to "Frau Trude," in which the girl finds a fence with human heads, a finger as a doorpost, twelve heads as guard dogs, six barrels of blood as wine, in the hallway corpses as ducks, and on the hearth a child as roasted duck. "Spying through a keyhole she sees that the old witch has two heads, one of which delouses the other. . . "[128]

685 Noteworthy is the image of the two heads of the witch that delouse each other. She represents in the broadest sense the tension of opposites in the unconscious, which is a continual process, and which without the intervention of consciousness would aimlessly go back and forth forever. The mutual grooming of lice indicates a general exchange process. Mother Holle (in "Mother Holle") has indeed an aspect of witchcraft, a death-bringing side, which she invokes as she pours pitch onto the lazy girl (Pitch-Marie). In another version Pitch-Marie is taken to a neighboring hut full of snakes and toads, or she is made to fall into a swamp. Here again the archetype of the Great Mother appears clearly as Mother Death, a gigantic black-white woman

---

[126] See the Introduction in Rumpf, *Japanische Volksmärchen*, Jena 1938, pp. 10–11.

[127] See "Baba Yaga" in A. N. Afanaßjew, *Russische*, Vienna, 1906, vol. 1, no. 18; see especially the epilogue (pp. 67–68) and the fairytale, "The Maiden as Soldier."

[128] Bolte and Polívka, *Anmerkungen*, vol. 1, p. 377.

with the characteristic double aspect of this psychic phenomenon. In other variants, Mother Holle is a "little red mother" (see the red color of the Yamauba) or a troll-woman, or as "Mrs. Skullhead," or she has the head of a mare with which one must dance. She melts into axle grease, or becomes a wolf or snow demon whose head decomposes into gold and silver, or even becomes herself a head of iron. In still other versions an old man stands in her place, a hairy monster or man-eating ogre couple. She gives the girl either a glowing head, which burns her enemies or disintegrates into ducats, or she appears with three golden heads, or she gives the girl a green chest full of clothes, a magic wand, or silver and gold.[129] The Great Mother is even generally the guardian of treasures and of gold, and their hidden begetter. In an Icelandic fairytale, "The Hole of the Giantess," a man goes down through a hole into the Earth. There he meets a blind, ancient woman giant who mills gold. In China, the Mother Goddess appears as the "Queen Mother from Kulun Mountain," or as the "mother of metals," or "Queen Mother of the West." She leads the round dance of the fairies and presides over change and growth.[130]

686 The Great Mother who, on the one hand, is connected with dangerous powers, is, on the other hand, a helper and giver, as described by an indigenous tribe from British Guiana, "Makunaima and Pia." In this tale, a woman pregnant with twin boys[131] gets lost and is found by the queen of the rain frogs, the mother of the tiger who takes pity on her and protects her. When the tiger returns it kills the woman, but the twins are saved. Later they slay the frog mother and the tiger. Still later, they go on a journey to a very old woman who is actually a frog. They spy on her in secret and discover that the old one has a white spot on her shoulders. When she scratches the spot, out pours cassava flour. The tiger and his rain frog mother remind us of the devil and his grandmother (see the Grimm's tale, "The Devil and his Grandmother"). The female figure often assumes a benevolent role in helping and saving the hero from the devil.[132] In a Maori tale, "The Legend of Tawhaki," this figure is even the hero's mother, who had been forced to serve the demonic world. Like every archetypal image, the first mother is immortal and, when destroyed, reappears – as in the previously discussed story – again in a similar form and function.

---

[129] For all these variants, see *Ibid.*, pp. 207ff.

[130] Wilhelm, *The Chinese Fairy Book*, 1921, esp. the first section of "The Lady of the Moon" and also "How the Five Ancients Became Men."

[131] [Makunaima and Pia are twin heroes for several Amazonian-Caribbean tribes. "Makunaima or Makonaima, the alleged God or Supreme Being of the Akawai, the Maker of Heaven and Earth of the Makusi, was one of the twin children of the Sun. . . He and his brother Pia may be regarded as both Akawai and Makusi heroes. The name itself, Makunaima, signifies 'one that works in the dark'; the Being working in opposition to him, according to Makusi beliefs, is Epel"; see Roth, Inquiry into Animism, 1915, p. 130. Roth's remarks also refer to "The Sun, the Frog, and the Firesticks," a Warau tale cited below.]

[132] Cf. "The Devil with the Three Golden Hairs" and "The Werewolf."

The female frog symbolizes matter and the fertile swamp, and contrasts vividly with the destructive ferocity of the male tiger. Especially strange is the fertility shown with the image of the frog mother scratching herself, which releases cassava flour out of her body from which she bakes cakes. Her skin is like a plowed field and she herself the nurturing Mother Earth. According to a widespread popular belief in Germanic Europe, a mysterious old woman is sitting in a wheat field, called the "Corn Mother," "Harvest Mother," "Great Mother," or "Old Baba." The last sheaf of rye to be harvested is called "Grandmother" and the last ear of corn "cow."[133]

687 In general, the great mother goddess is in many places the originator of food.[134] The Inuit describe her in the tale, "Sedna's World." Summarizing one variant, Rink describes Sedna and the angakoq's journey to her thus:

> 688 In the depths of the ocean there lives a woman called *Arnarquagssaq* (= old woman in general). She sits in her dwelling in front of a lamp, beneath which is placed a vessel receiving the oil [from seal or whale blubber] that keeps flowing down from the lamp. From this vessel, or from the dark interior of her house, she sends out all the animals that serve as food [for humans on Earth]. In certain cases she withholds the supply, thus causing want and famine. Her retaining them was ascribed to a kind of filthy and noxious parasites (*agdlerutit*), which also signifies abortions or dead-born children), which had fastened themselves around her head; and then it was the task of the *angakok* to deliver her from these, and to induce her to again send out the animals for the benefit of man. In going to her he first had to pass the *arsissut*, and then to cross an abyss, in which, according to the earliest authors, a wheel was constantly turning round[135] as slippery as ice; and then having safely got past a boiling kettle with seals in it, he arrived at the house, in front of which a watch was kept by terrible animals, sometimes described as seals, sometimes as dogs; and lastly within the house-passage itself he had to cross an abyss by means of a bridge as narrow as a knife's edge.[136]

689 In another version,[137] this goddess of the sea is described as being one-eyed like Balor (see, "Balor and the Birth of Lugh"). The food-giving vessels of the

[133] See the "Corn Mother" in Frazer, *The Golden Bough*, New York, 1922 pp. 399ff.

[134] On the nurturing function of the first mother, see C.G. Jung, *Symbols of Transformation*, CW 5, ¶519f; see also *ibid* ¶530, fn. 73, which mentions that the sun-woman of the Nama People (South Africa) is made of bacon-fat.

[135] Cf. the milling Great Mother in "The Hole of the Giantess."

[136] Rink, *Eskimo*, p. 40.

[137] [This tale and other related Sedna myths are discussed in detail in Book 2 of this work in the section on the animus and the heroine's quest.]

mother goddess are also found in the Grimm's fairytale, "Sweet Porridge," where an old woman in the forest gives a magic pot to a pious girl in need. When the girl says, "Cook, pot, cook," it would cook good, sweet porridge. When the girl said, "Stop, little pot," it would cease to cook. All went well until one day when the girl was away and the mother got so hungry, she asked the pot to cook. However she had forgotten the words to make it stop. The pot cooked and cooked and buried the whole town and would probably have buried the whole Earth had not the girl come home and said the right words. The nourishing donation is here obviously bound up with the figure of the Great Mother.[138] In a parallel fairytale to "Makunaima and Pia" from the indigenous people of the Orinoco Delta (Venezuela), "The Sun, the Frog, and the Firesticks," there is a mother demon, a "very old, very big [i.e. fat] woman," who was a frog. One of the hero twins changed himself into a lizard and observed how she cooked. She had poisonous lice and could vomit out fire, and when she scratched her neck, something like balata milk (Mimusops balata) came out from which she prepared starch. She is, therefore, graphically associated with the cow and has – as Mother Earth – a secret fire, that is, hidden spiritual power and passion.

690 A charming pre-Grimm German fairytale, which was first written down around 1557 by Martin Montanus, is called "The Little Earth Cow":[139]

691 A widower remarried and his second wife hated Margaretlein, the younger of her two stepdaughters. She conspired with Margaretlein's older sister, Annelein, to get rid of Margaretlein. They decided one day to take the younger girl into the forest and abandon her there. Margaretlein overheard the conversation and told her old godmother of her worries. Her godmother advised her to sprinkle the way there with sawdust. Following these instructions, Margaretlein found her way back home. The next time she overheard the conniving of her sister and stepmother, her godmother advised her to sprinkle the way with chaff. Thus Margaretlein again traced her way back home. The third time the godmother advised her to sow hemp seed along the

[138] In the Aztec world creation myth, Quetzalcoatl and Texcatlipoca bring the goddess Tlalteotl "whose joints were full of eyes and mouths which she bit like a wild beast" down from the sky and put her in the waters. The two gods transformed themselves into snakes and tear Tlalteotl apart. "From the half towards the shoulders they formed the earth, and they took the other half to the sky." This irritated "the gods," and so to atone, Quetzalcoatl and Texcatlipoca created everything that humans need from Tlalteotl's body; her hair became trees, flowers, herbs; her skin became the short grasses and small flowers, from her countless eyes came wells, fountains and caves. "And at times this goddess wept at night, wanting to devour human hearts, and would not hush until they were given to her. Nor did she want to produce fruits unless she was sprinkled with human blood." See Graulich, *Myths of Ancient Mexico*, p. 50; the quotations are from Graulich's translation of Anonymous (1888–92).

[139] See Wesselski, *Deutsche Märchen*, pp. 32ff., and Ninck, "Älteste Märchen," pp. 153ff. On May 19, 1776, Goethe wrote as follows to Charlotte von Stein: "For the first time I have slept in the garden, and now I am forever a little earth-cow." [Wesselski notes that the source for this quote is unknown.]

path. But this time birds pecked all the hemp seed up, and the child got lost deep in the woods. She nearly gave up all hope, but then she decided to climb a tree to see if she could see some city, village, or house where she might go. Otherwise she would surely come to a sad end as food for the wild beasts. And, indeed, she spied a little column of smoke. She quickly descended and walked in the direction of the smoke. Soon she came upon "a little house, in which only one little earth-cow dwelt." The girl knocked and asked to be let in. . . [The] earth-cow answered, "Very well, all you need to do is to milk me in the morning, and again in the evening. . . But remember to be careful not to tell anyone about me! Even if your own sister should come to the door, do not let her in and betray my presence here. If you do, I shall lose my life." From the milk Margartlein nourished herself, and the earth cow gave her good clothes of velvet and silk. Then the earth cow went out "to her pasture."

692 After a year had passed, Annelein regretted her evil deed and went to look for her younger sister in the woods. She too lost her way and discovered, from the same tree as her sister did, the house of the earth cow. Margaretlein remained long steadfast, but then finally after many futile excuses, told her sister about the earth-cow. Annelein found her way back home and told her stepmother all about what she had seen and heard. The stepmother decided to go and bring the girl home with the earth-cow, which then she planned to slaughter and eat. Meanwhile in the forest, the earth-cow returned home in the evening. She already knew all that had happened and told the girl that the stepmother and her older sister were going to come and take them both back to their house. There Margaretlein would remain but the earth cow would be slaughtered. Margaretlein was inconsolable, and cried as if she would die. The earth-cow advised her to ask the butcher of the coolness of the earth for a tail, a horn, and a hoof, then to put the tail in the earth, the horn on it, and the hoof on it. On the third day a tree would grow up that summer and winter would bear the most beautiful apples, which no one but Margaretlein would be able to break off, and "through the same tree you will become a great woman." One day a great lord rode past the tree with his son who was sick with fever and chills. When the boy saw the beautiful apples, he asked to be given one to eat, they would surely make him healthy again. His father called for some of the apples, and promised to give large sums of money for them. Neither the older daughter nor the stepmother were able to take any of the apples, since when they tried to grab them, the tree pulled up its branches even higher. The great lord watched all of this in wonderment. When Margaretlein came, the

> tree lowered its branches and the apples let themselves be plucked. The lord thought that Margaretlein must be a saintly woman and asked for her presence. Margaretlein told him the whole story of her sister and stepmother, being lost in the forest, and the earth cow. The wealthy gentleman asked her if she would like to come with him and his son. Margartlein was very pleased, dug up the tree, and with her father and the tree, climbed into the gentleman's carriage. They were all warmly welcomed and rode away, leaving the mother and sister behind.[140]

693 In this tale, the archetype of the mother appears in multiple forms that mirror her varied aspects: the stepmother is purely evil against the girl and despises all creatures and magical powers in a profane manner. The godmother gives ambiguous advice: due to her counsel the girl twice returns safely to the profane world, but not a third time. Her advice can hardly be rated "good" or "bad," because although according to common sense it would be desirable to return from the dark forest, it seems that the internal development of the girl requires a deeper immersion in the magic kingdom; a longer sojourn at a safe distance from the evil stepmother and in the animal warmth of motherhood and nature-like earth cow. This is especially so since the human form of the positive mother image, the natural mother of the girl, is "dead." This is to say that her relationship to the world – expressed in the form of her family members – is poor, because the relationship with the mother shapes the nature of the child's relationship with the world. The godmother's first piece of advice concerns the secular mind, while her final counsel plays her godchild right into the magical realm. In this tale, the mother appears twice as a tree; a brief appearance as natural intuition pointing the way from the dark woods to the friendly house of the earth cow, from a total lostness and failure of rational orientation to a sense of security in the undreamt of and unconscious depths of the soul. The second time, the tree appears as a symbol of the mother at a much higher level as the bearer of wonderful, healing fruit.

694 Between the two trees lies the appearance of the original mother as the earth cow. According to Bächtold-Stäubli under *Kuh* [cow], the cow is "the most commonly comprehensible image of fertility and as such is the deity that people worshipped from the earliest times. For the ancient Egyptians, the cow is sacred to Hathor and Isis, who are often represented as a woman with bull horns, like the Greek Io. The chariot of Nerthus[141] is pulled by female cows."[142] Not only is the cow a symbol of the mother but also of a cosmic power. In the

---

[140] Summarized from Wesselski, *Deutsche Märchen*, pp. 36–45.

[141] [The pagan Germanic Mother Earth goddess.]

[142] See A. R. Birley's translation of Tacitus' *Germania*, esp. chapter 40. Cf. Bächtold-Stäubli for more on ghostly or witch-like cows.

view of the ancient Norse, the world arose from the fragmentation of the giant primordial cow, Audhumla, or the giant Ymir.[143] Egyptian mythology knows – as we mentioned earlier – that the celestial cow Hathor, who wears the solar disk between her female cow horns, emerged from the primeval chaos and is also called Neith, the mother, who "gave birth to the sun, she bore first, before he was born."[144] In India the cow is the most important and sacred of all animals, and some people believe themselves to be reincarnated from a cow. An ancient Indian rebirth ritual involved pulling the initiate through a golden statue of a woman or a cow.[145] The *Brahmana* mention Shabali, a wish-fulfilling cow: "So milk us. Juice and strength, a stream of wealth, Shabali, you are the most powerful among all creatures."[146] In Sanskrit, earth and cow have the same name![147] Indra, the prosperity-bestowing god, has a "wish-granting cow," just as the holy Vasischtha owns a "miracle-cow"; as a nurturing mother, this cow is a kind of magic (or wishing) table, but also gives jewelry and clothes. She also symbolizes the power of the Maya, who could conjure up wish images and phantasmagoria. Likewise, the Holy Jamadagni milked palaces, pleasure-gardens, and an entourage of blessed ones from his miracle cow.[148]

695 The symbol of the cow has the same meaning in fairytales. In "Balor and the Birth of Lugh," the green cow's color clearly points to nature and fertility and thus reveals itself to be an aspect of Mother Earth. In an Icelandic fairytale, "Bukolla, the Cow," the cow Bukolla disappears, the only commodity of an old couple. They send their only son, whom they do not like very much, out to find her. He must free Bukolla from two evil troll women who had stolen the cow (negative aspect of the mother!). He is assisted in a magical way by Bukolla so that they arrive safely home with her. The South Slavic fairytale, "The Shepherd Hero and the Little Spotted Cow," is summarized here:

> 696 Once upon a time a farmer refuses to give his shepherd enough to eat. A little spotted cow lets the boy twist his right horn and therein the shepherd finds cloth, which when spreads out, sets itself with victuals. When the employer wants to kill the spotted cow, it escapes into the night with the shepherd and says, "Sit on me, I will carry you, because I see better than you." Together they overcome a dragon and live together for many years on a lonely mountain top. The spotted cow keeps the shepherd with her until he is so strong he can uproot a tree with a jerk. Before he leaves, the cow lets him take from the left horn a handkerchief of which he gives him half. Whenever one sees that

143 Cf. Silberer, *Problems of Mysticism*, p. 71; see also Bousset, *Hauptprobleme der Gnosis*, p. 211, note 1.
144 Cf. Roeder, *Urkunden*, p. 146, xxi; Erman, *Religion der Ägypter*, p. 33.
145 Cf. Dieterich, *Eine Mithrasliturgie*, p. 136.
146 Cf. Güntert, *Weltkönig*, p. 368, and the additional material collected there.
147 Cf. Abegg, "Krishnas Geburt," p. 34, fn. 20.
148 Cf. Zimmer, *Maya*, pp. 220ff. and 391.

> the handkerchief shows blood he or she will know that the other has died. The shepherd finds three brothers[149] and they enter together into many fights. They triumph again and again until one time the shepherd forgets to say before a fight, "Stand by me, my spotted cow!" He and his brothers are defeated and killed. The spotted cow sees its handkerchief is bloodied, goes to find the "Shepherd Hero," and revives him and his "brothers." Because the little cow knows that his "'brothers' are planning an evil deed," it leaves the shepherd to die alone. The hero shepherd finds and buries the spotted cow. After the "brothers" force him into another fight through deception, he finally kills them, marries a Divdaughter[150] and becomes emperor.[151]

697 Here the cow is the wise, caring, selfless mother, waiting until the hero gains a solid, stable personality, which no longer relies on maternal guidance, nor on the forces of his elected brothers.[152] After the marriage, the maternal principle passes over to of the wife. From variations to "Mother Holle," we see how closely related the idea of the cow is to that of the Great Mother. In one parallel tale, the girl arrives at a "Moo-Calf," which bows at her command, or she must milk a (in one version a red) cow.[153]

698 In "The Little Earth Cow," this motherly creature, who lives alone and mysteriously moves and works deep in the magic realm, is initially a victim of the profane world. In "Makonaura and Anuanaitu" and in "The Witchdoctor Makanaholo," the inner power of the psyche was based on being hidden. Only in absolute secrecy from the profane world does the innermost depth of the psyche reveal its fascinating and exhilarating power. The earth cow becomes a victim of the girl's weakness towards the profane, but without becoming angry. This happens because in the end the experience of the unconscious is only productive for life if it is incorporated into consciousness. The inclination of the girl to the profane world, along with her stepmother, causes evil, but thereby nevertheless create the good. This is because the earth cow, which symbolizes matter and the animal-maternal instincts, becomes a

---

149 [*Wahlbrüder*; literally "brothers of choice."]

150 German: *Divtochter*, alternative translation: young female div. Divs are powerful malignant spirits of ancient Iranian (Zoroastrian) and Armenian tradition. The *daevas* were "gods that are were rejected" as being divinities that promote chaos and disorder. In later tradition and folklore, divs are personifications of every imaginable evil. They frequent in caves and forests, look like men and women and shape-shift into cyclopean wild animals with as many as seven heads.]

151 Friedrich Salomon Krauss, *Darstellungen aus dem Gebiete der nichtchristlichen Religionsgeschichte*, vol. 2: *Volksglaube und religiöser Brauch der Südslaven*, 1890, p. 346, no. 139 [original title: *Held Hirte und das scheckige Kühlein*].

152 On the three brothers as functions of the psyche, see below, "The Hero's Journey."

153 Cf. Bolte and Polívka, *Anmerkungen*, vol. 1, pp. 207ff. The color red points to the magical realm. See Mannhardt, *Wald- und Feldkulte*, vol. 1, pp. 125–26, who reports a legend in which a little girl in a beech-tree forest meets a big woman with a black hood and long fingers who grows larger and larger and pursues the fleeing child. The girl falls over and remains lying until the woman is transformed at sunset into a black cow. For three years the child goes about with a deranged mind.

fruit-bearing tree, the symbol of all inner and outer growth. Without losing contact with Mother Earth (burying the tail, horn, and hoof), a tree grows from these roots, whose crown at all times bears beautiful fruit. These lure the liberators who help free the girl from the world of the evil mother. It is significant that the girl takes the tree along with her, a symbol of the good mother. She even brings along her father, otherwise almost missing in the story. Thus accompanied, so-to-speak, by both parents, she goes off – we assume – to her wedding.[154]

699 This theme is also recorded in "One-Eye, Two-Eyes, and Three-Eyes":

> There was once a woman who had three daughters, the eldest of whom was called One-eye, because she had only one eye in the middle of her forehead, and the second, Two-eyes, because she had two eyes like other folks, and the youngest, Three-eyes, because she had three eyes; and her third eye was also in the center of her forehead. However, as Two-eyes saw just as other human beings did, her sisters and her mother could not endure her. They said to her, "Thou, with thy two eyes, art no better than the common people; thou dost not belong to us!" They pushed her about, and threw old clothes to her, and gave her nothing to eat. It came to pass that Two-eyes had to go out into the fields and tend the goat, but she was still quite hungry, because her sisters had given her so little to eat. So she sat down on a ridge and began to weep, and so bitterly that two streams ran down from her eyes. And once when she looked up in her grief, a woman was standing beside her, who said, "Why art thou weeping, little Two-eyes?" Two-eyes answered, "Have I not reason to weep, when I have two eyes like other people, and my sisters and mother hate me for it, and push me from one corner to another, throw old clothes at me, and give me nothing to eat but the scraps they leave? Today they have given me so little that I am still quite hungry." Then the wise woman said, "Wipe away thy tears, Two-eyes, and I will tell thee something to stop thee ever suffering from hunger again; just say to thy goat, 'Bleat, my little goat, bleat, cover the table with something to eat,' and then a clean well-spread little table will stand before thee, with the most delicious food upon it of which thou mayest eat as much as thou art inclined for, and when thou hast had enough, and hast no more need of the little table, just say, 'Bleat, bleat, my little goat, I pray, and take the table quite away' and then it will vanish again from thy sight." Hereupon the wise woman departed.

[154] Cf. "The Adventures of Mrile." There, the young man went against the prohibitions of the bull, so that the slaughter ended tragically. For more on the theme of separating from the mother through marriage, see the section below, *The Maiden's Quest*.

700 Two-eyes immediately tried out what she had been told and it came to pass exactly as the woman had said. The table appeared, Two-eyes said a short prayer and helped herself to the delicious food. When she was finished she bade the table disappear. In the evening Two-eyes went home with her goat and did not touch the food her sisters had prepared for her. She left the few bits of bread also untouched on the next day. After this happened for several days in a row, her sisters became suspicious. They decided that One-eye should go out to pasture the goat with Two-eyes. Two-eyes lulled One-eye to sleep with a song. She called her magic table and ate while One-eye slept. Afterwards, she sent the table away and woke up One-eye, admonishing her for sleeping while the goat could have run away. The next day their mother sent out Three-eyes to report on her sisters' doings. This time, however, Two-eyes mistakenly sang that two-eyes should sleep. So one eye in the forehead remained open. Three-eyes closed this eye, but only in cunning; she observed all that happened, and upon return told their mother. Outraged that Two-eyes did not share her food with them, the mother slaughtered the goat. Now the wise woman had foretold that this would happen and had told Two-eyes to ask for the goat's entrails and to bury them in front of the house door. Two-eyes did as the wise woman in the woods had counseled her. The next morning there stood a magnificent tree with leaves of silver and fruit of gold. The mother desired the fruit, but neither she nor the other sisters could reach the fruit as the branches moved away from their outreaching arms.

701 So they lived, the two sisters and the mother in envy of Two-eyes. One day a young knight rode by and stopped at the magnificent tree. Three-eyes and One-eye hid their sister under an empty barrel with a few golden apples that she had just plucked. The knight asked to whom the tree belonged, to which the two sisters promptly responded, "To us!" The handsome knight asked for a bough of the tree. But the sisters could not reach a branch. The knight thought this to be strange. The sisters admitted they had another sister, but that she was not allowed to show herself, for she had only two eyes like common people. The knight, however, desired to see her, and cried, "Two-eyes, come forth." Out rolled two golden apples from the barrel. The knight again called for Two-eyes who then crawled out, cut down a branch, and gave it to him. The knight took her to his castle and married her. The next morning the tree stood before their chamber. Two-eyes lived a long time in happiness. One day, two poor women came to her in the castle, and begged for alms. She looked at their faces, and recognized her sisters, One-eye and Three-eyes, who had fallen into

> such poverty that they had to wander about and beg their bread from door to door. Two-eyes, welcomed them in, however, was kind to them, and took care of them, so that they both with all their hearts repented the evil that they had done to their sister in their youth.[155]

702 Here, the cow is replaced by the goat, and the evil mother is again embodied in the shape of the barrel, since a vessel is also a symbol of the mother. In "The Little Earth Cow," the good mother first appears as a wise woman and plays the role of the godmother and the tree that shows the way. We have already mentioned the goat as a mother symbol in our discussion of "The Isle of Utrøst." In that tale, she accompanies a little old man dressed in blue, probably a remnant of the goat Heidrun of the Germanic legend. This goat grazes on the tree Laeradr and gives her milk to the residents of Valhalla.[156] The silver leaves and golden apples on the tree are the only indication that the Earth Mother carries metal and fire in her. A tale from Melanesia, "How Fire Came," tells of an old woman who cooks with fire that she brings out "from between her legs." A young boy stole a brand from the cooking fire and accidentally set a pandanus palm in flames. A snake lived in this pandanus and its tail caught fire and burned like a torch. The old woman caused rain to fall in great torrents so that the fire was put out, but the snake stayed in his hole in the pandanus tree and his tail continued to glow. The boys went out looking for remnants of the fire and noticed the glow in the pandanus tree, pulled the snake out, and used its tail to set fire to a pile of wood. Villagers came and took pieces of that fire home. This is how people obtained fire.[157] In the aforementioned Warau tale, "The Sun, the Frog, and the Firesticks," the hero twins decide to burn the old frog mother:

703

> Clearing a large field, they left in its very center a fine tree, to which they tied her; then, surrounding her on all sides with stacks of timber, the boys set them on fire. As the old woman gradually was consumed, the fire which used to be within her passed into the surrounding fagots. These fagots happened to be hima-heru wood, and whenever we rub together two sticks of this same timber we can get fire.[158]

---

[155] Cf. the Russian variant "Burenushka, the Little Red Cow"; for a general account of cows that help stepchildren, see "Little Fatima with the Moon Forehead."

[156] Cf. Mogk, *Germanische*, p. 70. [Laeradr/Lerad is a tree in Norse mythology, often identified with Yggdrasil. It stands at the top of Valhalla. Two animals, the goat Heidrún and the hart Eikthyrnir, graze its foliage. The *Poetic Edda* has, "The she-goat, she who is called Heidrún, stands up in Valhalla and bites the needles from the limb of that tree which is very famous, and is called Léradr; and from her udders mead runs so copiously, that she fills a tun every day."]

[157] Seligman et al., *The Melanesians of British New Guinea*, pp. 379–380.

[158] Roth, *Inquiry into Animism*, p. 133.

704 Strictly speaking, the old woman does not die, but lives on as firewood, inasmuch as wood is a symbol of matter, which contains the secret fire. The youths' deed makes fire serve the human being. The devouring aspect of the spiritual passion contained in the unconscious is overcome and can be used to bring culture.

705 In mythology, ideas about who originally owned fire are sometimes confounded. It is not always clear whether this treasure, this symbol of human passion, originates in the primordial mother or father. One personification of earthly fire, for example, is the Germanic (Norse) god Loki. His mother is Laufey, "full of leaves," possibly associated with lightning hitting the leaves or needles of a tree to give rise to fire, and his daughter is Hel, goddess of the dead. He also appears as a cunning witch-like woman, or he sits as a giantess in a mountain cave,[159] or as a maiden he milks cows in the underground.[160] Carus in a sentence from *Psyche* offers us a possible clue as to why it is possible not only to see the god of the chthonic realm as Lord of Fire, as a symbol of spiritual passion, but also to honor the great mother as his guardian. He calls the unconscious, "the nourishing, originally conditioning principle. . . from which emanates all spiritual warmth of the life of the soul."[161] Sometimes the mother-imago appears next to the blacksmith, for instance, in ancient Eastern cosmologies as the mother of the smith,[162] and in North American myths as grandmother of the great healers who usually brought fire to the people. She lives with him in eternity, "because. . . matter does not exist without spirit, the mind cannot exist or function without matter. . ."[163]

706 The archetypes of spirit and matter, personified by the father and mother as the original parents, are reflected in all the myths of mankind. We have amplified them here as images of nature spirits that appear as wild men and wild women in legends[164] or in Gnostic visions.[165] Sometimes only one figure appears, but then it is bisexual like the hermaphroditic Cybele or the Roman Fortuna Barbata,[166] because the archetype of the Spirit, the Father, is needed to complete the foundations of the life of the soul, the Great Mother. The original parents appear, as mirrored in the magic kingdom as represented in fairytales, therefore, either separated or connected as a pair. Thereby the mother archetype (like the father archetype) makes use of various symbols

---

159 Cf. "The Hole of the Giantess," where the giantess grinds gold, the color of fire.
160 See Mogk, *Germanische*, pp. 76–77.
161 Carus, *Psyche*, p. 235.
162 Cf. V. C. C. Collum, "Schöpferische Mutter-Göttin," Zürich, 1939, p. 229.
163 Goethe, *Erläuterung zum Aufsatz "Die Natur"* [Notes on the Essay "Nature"].
164 Mannhardt, *Wald- und Feldkulte*, vol. 1, pp. 117ff. and *passim*.
165 Cf. Bousset, *Hauptprobleme der Gnosis* (1907), *passim*.
166 Cf. Przyluski, "Ursprünge," pp. 27–28. [Fortuna Barbata, that is, "Bearded" Fortuna, was the goddess to whom boys offered the first cuttings of their new beards as they became men. She represents a deity who watches over and blesses the transition from childhood to adulthood.]

and appears in positive and negative form not only as mother, grandmother, nurse, godmother, ancestress, demoness, and goddess, but also in the broader sense as, for example, city, forest, sky, sea, water, underworld, garden, rock cliff, cave, tree, well, all vessels, oven, flower, female animal, dragon, grave, and death. The Great Mother can be frightful, dark, and destructive, as well as good, cherishing, supporting, giving, and warm; a wise woman – the guardian of all things past, and knowing about the future.

Chapter 18

The Image of the Daemonic Son [the shadow]

707 The fairytales discussed above show that while the hero does not always reach the rulers of the magical kingdom, he meets other magical beings along the way, or they mediate the initial encounter with the central power of the unconscious sphere. They approach the hero as emanations of the inner power of the magical kingdom, sometimes as theriomorphic, other times anthropomorphic, or even as daemonic figures, more-or-less at the periphery of the psychic realm. The encounter and relationship with these characters are portrayed in all fairytales as momentous for the fate of the individual human being, especially if they appear concentrated in the figure of the son of the magical deities. The way in which the fairytale hero confronts him decides the fate of both, as shown in, among other tales, "Makonaura and Anuanaitu." And even if the tormented knight was not described specifically as the son of the demoness in "The Knight With the Sinister Laugh," the *auseinandersetzung* and agreement with him were preconditions for overcoming the old witch. The latter fairytale clearly establishes how strongly the fate of the magical son affects people. By sharing a common destiny, he resembles a brother or doppelgänger and, because he[1] belongs to the immaterial world of dreams, also the shadow.[2]

708 The shadow is, in the conception of many peoples, the alter ego or the real soul of a person.[3] Rohde describes the Homeric view, which is similar to that of indigenous peoples:

---

1 [We have chosen to follow the original German, which refers to this figure as "he." The shadow is, of course, an inner image, a psychological figure independent of gender.]

2 On the dead soul as shadow and reflection among the Greeks, see Rohde, *Psyche*, pp. 3ff,.

3 Cf. Lévy-Bruhl, *The "Soul" of the Primitive*, pp. 130, 134ff.; Róheim, *Spiegelzauber*, pp. 220ff. See also the comprehensive material in Bächtold-Stäubli under *Schatten* [shadow], where it is reported that in popular belief the shadow was considered to belong to its carrier and has the same power, however, the shadows suffers the opposite way to what the carrier experiences. The shadow is also conceived of as the life principle, the soul. "Ethnology shows with numerous examples from old languages how popular usage connects 'shadow' with 'soul.'" See the same reference for more about the autonomy of the shadow and the shadow as a walled-in shadow as a building sacrifice and the "spirit that follows one" as a doubling of the "natural" shadow.

709 Human beings exist twice over: once as an outward and visible shape, and again as an invisible "image," which only gains its freedom in death. This and nothing else, is the Psyche [sic] . . . It was not the phenomena of sensation, will, perception, or thought in waking and conscious man which led to this conclusion. It was the experience of an apparent double life in dreaming, in swoons, and ecstasy, that gave rise to the inference of a two-fold principle of life in man, and of the existence of an independent, separable "second ego" dwelling within the visible ego of daily life.[4]

710 In the psychology of C.G. Jung, this archetypal figure that emerges from the unconscious is referred to simply as the "shadow."[5] The shadow is of the same gender as the ego but of a different nature, like a dark mirror image that is not lit by the light of ego-consciousness. The shadow thus represents the unknown side of human nature, which is less developed than the conscious mental properties. As a mirror image, the "shadow" always stands on the "other side," opposite to the ego. It contains, therefore, all the equivalent values of the ego as an alter ego, like a dark brother who accompanies ego-consciousness everywhere and supplements it. The shadow behaves, therefore, in a complementary way to the conscious personality.[6]

711 As we will show below, the reactions of the "shadow" figures, as the phenomenon is defined by Jung, match the behavior described in fairytales in the figure of the daemonic son of the magical god and goddess couple as he appears in the role of a dark brother or antagonist to the hero. The figure of the shadow, whether in the form of animals, demons, or men, personifies the entire magical realm in concentrated form. Deeper investigation reveals its broader aspects. As seen from the fairytales so far discussed, the hero is not just defenseless and at the mercy of this demon, but there is a secret interaction with indistinct boundaries between him and the magical realm. As tempting as it would be to derive general rules for the relationship to the unconscious from fairytales. However, on closer examination, this task proves to be impossible. Even the apparent laws that seem absolutely true prove to

[4] Rohde, *Psyche*, pp. 6 –7. [Hillis' translation of 1925 has been altered to conform to the 1910 edition. It may be of interest to note that Rohde differentiates "psyche" and "spirit" in Homeric belief: the spirit is only active while the person is alive, whereas the psyche remains untouched by death (*ibid.*, p. 5).]

[5] See Wünsche, *Vom geprellten Teufel* (1905, p. 116), for a Spanish legend in which a certain count whose soul falls into the hands of the devil succeeds in getting the devil's own shadow, "the man behind," to take the place of his own. Thereafter the count has no shadow, however, even if he stands in the sun (i.e., he is incomplete). Cf. Chamisso's "Peter Schlemihl's wondersame Geschichte" [Peter Schlemihl's wonderful story].

[6] Perhaps this equalizing, balancing character of the shadow figure explains why in ancient times mythical peoples were often rumored to personify justice. See Dieterich, *Eine Mithrasliturgie*, pp. 35–36; see also Toni Wolff's summary of Jung's psychological concepts in "Einführung in die Grundlagen der komplexen Psychologie," in: *Die kulturelle Bedeutung der komplexen Psychologie. Festschrift zum 60. Geburtstag von C.G. Jung*, 1935, pp. 107ff.

be contradictory; they are all correct and incorrect at the same time. "Nothing is more contrary to the spirit of a fairytale," writes Novalis, "than a moral code or a law of relationships."[7] Often blind obedience is the correct behavior, absolute submission to the characters of the magic realm.[8] Sometimes a stout refusal to obey leads to the salutary detours and complications, which then lead the hero to experience the deeper layers of his soul and achieve more important aims.[9] But the unconscious always remains the stronger power; it is concerned with understanding its intentions and complementing them with consciousness. It is as if one were to recognize the wind as a given fact and step into a boat with the conscious intention to sail with the breeze. While there are no fixed, determinate laws, there are nevertheless something like hidden rules of conduct. The unconscious at first appears "as far as moral sense, aesthetic taste, and intellectual judgment go," as a completely neutral, natural entity[10] and requires great attention. Zimmer aptly describes the difficulties of working with the unconscious as follows:

712 ... we are met by one who is more powerful, more mysterious, and greater than ourselves. You can search for him, try to be friends with him by regarding him daily with reverence and your mindfulness in cultic rituals. It depends on the regularity of your contact, otherwise the power eludes us; it is diverse, dark and sinuous. It evades, teases, surprises, and plagues us with unwanted presence and absence, and declarations and threats. It fails to meet our needs, becomes alien to us, hostile and impish, it does not allow itself to be addressed or petitioned. Through daily and respectful contact . . . one can ensure its presence and sympathy.[11]

713 One of the guidelines for the correct attitude of people towards the unconscious lies in the knowledge about the fact that the unconscious is not only self-contradictory and bipolar, but, as already mentioned, that it also behaves complementary to consciousness,[12] which is depicted graphically in the motif of the "inverted world."[13] But this is only the case (and herein the rule is again relativized) when consciousness is one-sidedly oriented and is

[7] Novalis, *Fragmente*, Dresden, 1929, p. 670, no. 2068.
[8] See, for example "Godfather Death"; see also Bolte and Mackensen, *Handwörterbuch* (1930) under *Gehorsamsproben* ["obedience tests"].
[9] Cf. "The Golden Bird," in: *Complete Grimm's*, pp. 272–279.
[10] C.G. Jung, *Practical*, CW 16, ¶329.
[11] Zimmer, "Tantra-Yoga" (1934), p. 53. See also Zimmer, *Mother* (1968), p. 95: "Every being has a two-fold aspect, reveals a friendly and a menacing face. All gods have a charming and hideous form, according to how one approaches them."
[12] Cf. C.G. Jung, *Psychological Types*, CW 6, ¶839ff., 969; see also his *Dream Psychology*, CW 8, ¶477, 484.
[13] Such as occurs in "The Black-Brown Michel," in which two brothers, a holy hermit, and a robber, appear. In the end, the robber goes to Heaven and the holy hermit is damned. These two figures represent the two poles of one and the same personality.

blind to the conditions of the unconscious. For then, the internal polarities of the unconscious act as a sharp contrast between the conscious and the unconscious. If consciousness can encompass the primordial opposites within the soul, however, then this is also constellated within that sphere and initiates a process of transformation. Such a conversion from one pole of the unconscious into the other has appeared in some tales discussed already, such as when the hero forces the mother demon to self-destruction and transformation. In dealing with the forms of the magical kingdom, the rules for individual behavior that are generally to be observed but sometimes disobeyed, will become clear in the course of the following fairytale. In the opinion of all the magical arts, ghosts are also bound to rules.[14] As one example recall the fairytale, "Godfather Death," in which the position where death stood, whether it be at the head or feet of the patient, was the essential point. Or recall the magical food that banishes one to the land of the dead, but in other cases is a special source of power.

714 The psychological figure of the shadow, the son of the magical world and dark brother of the conscious human being, usually initially appears in an encounter with the dream world where the ego personality first experiences the conditions and the nature of the magical world.[15] Due to the importance of this figure, we will take a closer look as he appears in fairytales. A subtle yet slyly humorous depiction of the confrontation with the unconscious as a questionable opponent is the tale, "The Piper and the Púca":

715 In the old times, there was a man, the town fool, who lived in Dunmore, Galway County. Although he was very fond of music, he was unable to learn more than one tune and that was "The Black Rogue." One night the piper was coming home from a house where there had been a dance, and he was half drunk. When he came to a little bridge that was up by his mother's house, he squeezed his bagpipes on, and began playing "The Black Rogue." The Púca[16] came behind him, and flung him up on his own back. There were long horns on the Púca, and the piper took a good grip on them, and then he

[14] On the subject of laws in behaving towards demons, see "The Prior and his Servant," in: Jegerlehner, *Herdfeuer*, Bern, 1929, p. 182. Who calls them, must give them work to do, so they do not crush him. Those who know them read the book of magic backwards when the called should return to their custody.

[15] See also R. Meyer, *Weisheit Schweizer*, Schaffhausen, 1944, p. 83.

[16] The Púca or Pooka is an Irish leprechaun, with goat-legs and horns like Pan. In Shakespeare's "A Midsummer Night's Dream," this is Puck, the mischievous elf. [Cf. Brothers Grimm, *Irische Elfenmärchen*, Friedrich Fleischer, Leipzig, 1826, p. xvii; for an English translation, see Thomas Crofton Croker, *Fairy Legends and Traditions of the South of Ireland*, Part III, John Murray, London, 1828, p. 11, who notes: "... the Welsh word Gwyll, which signifies darkness, night, shade, mountain-spirit, fully corresponds with the Irish Phooka. It is the Alp of the Germans."]

shouted: "Destruction on you, you nasty beast, let me go home. I have a ten-penny piece in my pocket for my mother, and she wants snuff."

716 "Never mind your mother," said the Púca, "but keep your hold. If you fall, you will break your neck and your pipes." Then the Púca said to him, "Play up for me the "The Poor Old Woman" (*an t-seann-bhean bhocht*)."

717 "I don't know it," said the piper. "Never mind whether you do or you don't," said the Púca. "Just play, and I'll make you know it."

718 The piper put wind in his bag, and he played such music as made himself wonder.

719 "Upon my word, you're a fine music-master," says the piper then, "but tell me where you're for bringing me!"

720 "There's a great feast in the house of the Banshee, on the top of Croagh Patrick[17] tonight," says the Púca, "and I'm for bringing you there to play music, and, take my word, you'll get the price of your trouble." "By my word, you'll save me a journey, then," says the piper, "for Father William put a journey to Croagh Patrick on me, because I stole the white gander from him last Martinmas."

721 The Púca dragged him across hills and bogs and rough places, till they came to the top of Croagh Patrick. Then the Púca struck three blows with his foot, and a great door opened, and they passed in together, into a fine room.

722 The piper saw a golden table in the middle of the room, and hundreds of old women sitting round about it. One old woman rose up and said, "A hundred thousand welcomes to you, you Púca of November. Who is this you have brought with you?" "The best piper in Ireland," said the Púca.

723 One of the old women struck a blow on the ground, and a door opened in the side of the wall, and what should the piper see coming out but the white gander that the piper had stolen from Father William!

724 "By my conscience, then," says the piper, "myself and my mother ate every taste of that gander, only one wing, and I gave that to the Red Marie, and it was she who told the priest that I stole his gander."

725 The gander cleaned the table, and carried it away, and the Púca said, "Play up music for these ladies."

[17] [The Croagh Patrick (Irish: *Cruach Phádraig*), nicknamed the Reek, is a 764 meter tall mountain and an important site of pilgrimage in County Mayo, Republic of Ireland.]

726 The piper played up, and the old women began dancing, and they were dancing till they were tired. Then the Púca told them to pay the piper, and every old woman drew out a gold piece and gave it to him. "By the tooth of Patrick," said he, "I'm as rich as the son of a lord." "Come with me," says the Púca, "and I'll bring you home." They went out then, and just as he was going to ride on the Púca, the gander came up to him, and gave him a new set of pipes. The Púca was not long until he brought him to Dunmore, and he threw the piper off at the little bridge, and then he told him to go home, and said to him, "You have two things now that you never had before – intellect and music." The piper went home, and he knocked at his mother's door, saying, "Let me in, I'm as rich as a lord, and I'm the best piper in Ireland." "You're drunk," said his mother. "No, indeed not," said the piper, "I haven't drunk a drop."

727 The mother let him in, and he gave her the gold pieces and said, "Wait till you hear the music. I'll play now." He buckled on the pipes, but instead of music, there came a sound as if all the geese and ganders in Ireland were screeching together. He awakened the neighbors and they all mocked him until he put on the old pipes. Then he played melodious music for them; and after that he told them all that he had gone through that night.

728 The next morning, when his mother went to look at the gold pieces, there was nothing there but leaves. The piper went to the priest and told him his story, but the priest would not believe a word from him. Then he put the pipes on, and the screeching of the ganders and geese began. "Leave my sight, you thief," said the priest. But nothing would do the piper till he would put the old pipes on him to show the priest that his story was true.

729 He buckled on the old pipes and he played melodious music. From that day till the day of his death, there was never a piper in County Galway as good as he.[18]

730 The most striking thing about this tale, reminiscent of Shakespeare when he wove art and coarse humor together, is the life-like nature of the pagan past that bubbles up from the unconscious, overwhelming the Christian morals and installing its own as opposite.

731 The bagpiper is called the town fool, which testifies that he is open-minded towards the spirit-world. He also appears to be particularly dependent

[18] Douglas Hyde, translator from the Irish of the Leabhar Sgeulaigheachta; see sacred-texts.com (accessed 2011).

on his mother and lives for her. He is an artist, a man bound to the creative ground of his soul, a sage, and yet a "holy" fool. He lives for his music, emerges up out of the world of Eros, which expresses the feelings of inner mental processes. Music rises from a kind of intoxicated rapture (which is why the Emperor in "The Lady of the Moon" brings "songs" back from the realm of the moon fairy). It is the manifestation of the "enthusiasm of the heart" that resolves all tensions.[19] It transports[20] the audience into a world of feeling and for many cultures is associated with the cult of the mother goddess.[21] It is no coincidence that the piper still lives with his elderly mother and that his "underworld journey" leads him to the "mothers." Music serves the magical characters as bait for corruptible humans. Thus did the Sirens of ancient Greece lure sailors, and the piper in "The Pied Piper of Hamlin" entranced the children to follow him.[22] In that music is the purest expression of feeling, it serves to express the highest bliss and inner harmony. Also since music comes straight from the unconscious, the musician is very close to the dream world. Seen from the profane world, the musician is alien; this is probably why in the tale of the Irish piper music and foolishness were connected.

732 The initially "foolish" piper can play only one song, "The Black Rogue." The unconscious power, which he announces in his art, is his own dark side that he suspects but does not yet know and which he has so far only experienced as being the village scoundrel.[23] He proclaims his own nature in the song he sings, after all he had stolen a gander from the priest. His shadow, this "black rogue," Púca, is really the devil, but in his historical-original form is a pagan nature deity. He is identical to the Púca who later appears as a horned forest troll. Christianity seems, at least in this Irish fairytale, not to satisfy the deeper layers of soul; this impish devil pokes his head out of the pagan imagination, which remains alive in the unconscious. At the beginning, the picture of a dark demon so completely dominates the piper that his creative faculties are stunted and he can play only one song.

733 The piper then gets drunk on a Christian holiday, and steps down entirely into the pagan unconscious, the realm of his black villain.[24] While crossing a

---

[19] Cf. Wilhelm and Baynes, *I Ching*, p. 68, esp. the discussion of the hexagram *Enthusiasm*: "So, too, music has power to ease tension within the heart and to loosen the grip of obscure emotions. The enthusiasm of the heart expresses itself involuntarily in a burst of song, in dance, and rhythmic movement of the body."

[20] [German: *entrücken*.]

[21] See Collum, "Schöpferische Mutter-Göttin," pp. 231, 281, 285. It is thus significant that the hero of a fairytale often receives a magical musical instrument from a figure of the Great Mother's entourage such as in "The Flute, that Brought Everyone to Dance" and "The Fairy Harp" (in German, see Ehrentreich, *Englische Volksmärchen*, p. 174f).

[22] Cf. also the well-known tale "The Pied Piper."

[23] On the relationship between music and the devil, see "The Musician Who Got the Devil to Play at a Wedding." A devil passes his handkerchief over the hero's left eye, after which the hero can recognize devils wherever they cause harm. [In German, see Boehm and Specht, *Lettisch-litauische*, p. 170f.]

[24] See "How the Farmer Went to Hell," a tale about a drunken peasant who in his stupor falls into hell and tries to build a church there. [In German, see Boehm and Specht, *Lettisch-litauische*, p. 132f.]

bridge, his song finally attracts Púca who lifts the piper onto his back. A bridge connects two pieces of land that are separated by water. This refers to a psychic situation in which consciousness is interrupted and there is a gap in the continuity of the conscious world. Hence a spook can come up out from the unconscious. The bridge is also a "transition" to another region, and at this place lurk demons from the unconscious realm.[25] The piper had always lived with his mother, "by the bridge," i.e., in the psychic borderland between this world and the hereafter. This corresponds to his "foolish" essence. (Also Hu Wu-Bau, in "The Dangerous Reward," lived near the Great Mountain and saw the red-robed messenger of God.) In mythology, the bridge is a common image for a dangerous place of passage over water or a border river[26] and with the crossing often begins the entrance into the magical.[27] This is the moment in which humans let go of their own activity and give the psychic events and leadership over to the soul guides that arise from the other world. This is why the much celebrated and oft invoked black rascal jumps onto the piper. A piece of creative nature force waylays the piper and causes him to part from the real mother. The Púca says, "Oh! Don't worry about your mother!" This is because the solution to the fixation on the mother, which shuts one off from the outside world, is a precondition for any independent action.[28] At the same time, the Púca inspires him to a new song, "The Poor Old Woman." He forces him to confront the image of the mother and prepares him for a much more profound transition "to the mothers," to the source of all unconscious life itself. The

---

[25] Cf. "The Lady of the Moon," the bridge to the kingdom of the moon conjured up by the wizards. Also Bächtold-Stäubli under *Ort* [place] on superstitions about places of magical power.

[26] Cf. "Sedna's World, Version 4" (Krickeberg, *Nordamerika*, p. 9 [whose source is Rink, *Eskimo*, p. 40]. In the depths of the sea dwells a personification of the Great Mother [*arnarkuagsak*, "signifying old woman in general"]. On the way to this woman the Angakoq must traverse an abyss in which a wheel, slippery as ice, continuously rotates. Once he has overcome this, another obstacle stands in his way. If the guarding animals let him pass, he finds himself standing before another abyss over which he must cross "by means of a bridge as narrow as a knife's edge," (see page 266). According to "The Beyond," the Inca believed that the souls of their dead could reach the "the land of the silent" only if they had crossed a river, "over which a very thin bridge of hair hangs." Compare this with "How a Scholar Chastised the Princes of Hell," where we are told that "a rainbow bridge in golden sparkling radiance" spans the river of hell over which the good people can walk while the criminals have to wade through the water. In Zoroastrianism the Chinvat Bridge separates the world of the living from the world of the dead. All souls must cross the bridge upon death. The Chinvat Bridge's appearance, however, varies depending on the observer's asha, or righteousness (cf. Bousset, *Himmelsreise*, 1901, pp. 155ff). Sometimes even the demon lives in the river or chasm and tries to prevent the building of the bridge by which humans attempt to avoid his powers. One example is the Japanese fairytale, "The Bridge-Builder and the Demon," in which the demon who lived in a raging river first impeded the building of a bridge, but then a famous carpenter who overcame a series of arduous conditions arrived to help. He finally manages to get rid of the conditions whereupon the devil jumped back into the river's currents. For additional material on the relationship of the devil to building bridges, see Wünsche, *Vom geprellten Teufel*, pp. 31–37.

[27] Cf. with the exception of the river Styx, which borders both Hades and the realm of the dead, as mentioned by Reitzenstein, *Hellenistic Mystery-Religions*, p. 306: according to the Apocalypse of Baruch, the dead in hell wet their lips with living water, "that separates the world of the senses from the world of the supernatural." In India, the dead go to the ageless river, where they are received by the Apsarases, the [five hundred] women of heaven; see Zimmer, *Death and Rebirth*, p. 329.

[28] See C.G. Jung, *Symbols of Tr41ansformation*, CW 5, ¶329, and "Relation between the ego and the unconscious," CW 7, ¶314.

separation from the personal mother leads to the confrontation with the Great Mother, the recognition of that figure who was hidden behind the personal mother and who accounted for the larger-than life fascination with her.[29] The black rogue, whom the unsuspecting piper entertained with his song, was a piece of future creativity, an emissary of the mothers, the fairies in Patrick mountain, "Croagh, the Reek." By being "smitten" and "taken" in a trance, i.e., emotionally carried away, he reaches the fairies.[30]

734 The house of the fairies lies on the crest of a hill that was named after St. Patrick, the missionary who converted the Irish to Christianity. There is a certain humor in the fact that the demon helps the piper take a penitential pilgrimage to the priest for the theft of his gander, especially as it is indeed the black rogue [i.e., the Púca] in the soul of the piper, who actually stole the gander. That is of course precisely why he finds it again in the rogue's kingdom.

735 The goose originates in primordial matter and symbolizes earthly matter. One Greek myth portrays the primordial mother and revengeful goddess Nemesis as a goose. Since this animal is associated with the groundwater that fertilizes and moisturizes the soil and so creates mud and swamps, the goose can be viewed as a symbol of the primeval chaos.[31] This fits Bächtold-Stäubli's descriptions of *Gans* [goose] : witches haunt humans in the form of geese and the goose is a manifestation of Frau Holle.[32] Here in the Irish tale it is a gander, and in fact the devil can also appear as a goose.[33] The gander is closely related both to the "black rogue" and the "mothers," where the piper meets him again. First and foremost, however, the goose belongs to the priest, who is also connected to it by the black rogue. The gander is a male animal and in this respect can be likened to the male swan. Bachofen writes on "the female goose. . . that it corresponds to the male side of the swan."[34] And in an Egyptian creation myth, the goose emerges from an egg lying on the primeval slime, "and with her it was light, because she was the sun," the first light.[35] This luminous nature emphasizes the character of the goose as a symbol of the soul. This part of the soul, connected as it is to nature and magical powers, was stolen from the priest by the young piper and had sunk into the unconscious world of chthonic figures. Fairytales of many folk cultures reflect a psychological situation in which Christianity with its differentiated teaching was only partially

---

[29] The Púca corresponds to *Goethe's* Mephistopheles, who leads Faust to the mothers. There, too, the unconscious first approached Faust as a black poodle (a rogue), and from this encounter, the whole drama emerges.

[30] Cf. the role of the magician in "The Lady of the Moon," and in "King Mu of Dschou," who conjures the emperor, or King, into the afterlife. See also "The Spirit of the Wu-Lian Mountain," in which a monster grabs a scholar by the hair and carries him near a god.

[31] Cf. Bachofen, *Mutterrecht*, pp. 69–70.

[32] Cf. Laiblin, "Urbild," p. 107.

[33] Cf. Bolte and Mackensen, *Handwörterbuch*, under *Gans*.

[34] Cf. Bachofen, *Mutterrecht*, p. 70. See the same reference for aspects of the swan ranging from an earthly (telluric) to a heavenly light power.

[35] Cf. Erman, *Religion der Ägypter*, pp. 61–62.

understood and not yet really absorbed. Pagan concepts continued to fulfil the people's religious needs. These tales like to depict priests and their demands, therefore, in a dry, rational, and profane light; in stark and hostile contrast to the colorful and fantastic world of nature spirits who in this whole story stand on the side of the piper.[36] That the piper steals the gander from the priest means that the chthonic aspect in the eyes of the piper belongs more to him than to the minister (whereby the piper is inwardly "possessed" by the "black rogue"). The piper takes the blame on himself, therefore, and has to go over to St. Patrick's mound on St. Martin's Day. This is not without reason, because according to ancient custom, geese are slaughtered on St. Martin's Day. This is probably the remnant of earlier Odin/Woden rites, because in pagan times the goose was an animal sacrificed for Odin (Odin/Woden). In later times, geese joined the Valkyrie swans and St. Martin goose heaven (according to folk belief, a house in the back of Heaven). The goose stall is a continuation of the heavenly hall of Woden and Freyja.[37] Thus the gander builds the bridge between the pagan and Christian conceptual realms, as he belongs to a certain extent to both worlds. From the Christian point of view, the penitential pilgrimage on St. Martin's Day has the meaning of sacrificing the pagan aspect of the personality, but the pastor had apparently underestimated the significance that this chthonic essence of the personality held in the soul of the Irish piper. He did not comprehend this direct [symbolic] appropriation by the theft. But the unconscious breaks through in the elementary form of Púca, who prevents the sacrifice and leads the piper to the mothers, whose attribute is known to be the goose. Quite logically, there he also meets the gander again, in that deep spiritual center where the tension between his artistic nature and the laws of the secular world can be resolved. There is a "fine room" in the house of the Banshees in the midst of which stands a square or circular golden table. Around this golden table sit hundreds of old women. They form a circle around a golden center. On the magical significance of geometric figures, and in general, self-contained forms among primitive people Bächtold-Stäubli reports:

736 In its unity and enclosure lie the main characteristic and the major forces of the magic circle. The circumference indicates a separation

[36] In Irish tales, Christian religion is often depicted negatively; this also concerns Nordic peoples in particular, as Jung explains: "We must never forget our historical antecedents. Only a little more than a thousand years ago we stumbled out the crudest beginnings of polytheism into a highly developed Oriental religion, which lifted the imaginative minds of half-savages to a height that in no way corresponded to their spiritual development. In order to keep to this height in some fashion or other, it was inevitable that the instinctual sphere should be largely repressed. . . The repressed elements naturally did not develop, but went on vegetating in the unconscious, in their original barbarism. We would like to scale the heights of a philosophical religion, but in fact are incapable of doing it. To grow up to it is the most we can hope for"; see Jung, *Golden Flower*, CW 13, ¶70.

[37] Cf. Ninck, *Wodan*, pp. 139–140, fn. 1.

> of the interior of the circle of the area; a division of space into an "inside" and "outside," where the "inside" is the area enclosed by the circumference that forms its own power and sphere of action. . . Within the circle, one has power over everything inside. . . The magical power over the enclosed can also be used to exclude and ward off all that is alien and hostile; the circumference is the magic mark. . . Often this is symbolized by movement around the circle. . . An additional significant factor is the person or thing that performs the circular motion. Hereby the law applies that the effect of the magic circle stretches from the environment encircled as well as those who perform the circling, where a mutual exchange of roles without a change of meaning is typical. A special kind of circular movement is the circle dance, like the circumambulation that is a magical increase of circumventing. The apotropaic power of the circle not only excludes and fends off the evil which is outside, but by circling something one can invoke its cleansing cathartic power to remove evil that has already penetrated inside. . . In any case one can clearly observe in these traditions that often one cannot separate the apotropaic from the cathartic magical powers inherent in the circular form. . . In some cases, the circle prevents a particular action originating in the outer secular environment from taking place, in order to protect and consecrate the place of the deed . . . The circle is probably the most natural form for a meeting, the circular form also lent a secret power, creating a sacred protected area, a place of peace. . . Also the circle plays a role in many games and dances, which both often include remnants of cultic practices.[38]

737 In most cults where such notions of circularity play a role, they reflect a religious goal or an intrapsychic center, expressed in images, architecture, or descriptions.[39] In Eastern cultures, such representations of ritual circles are called "mandalas." The Sanskrit word mandala "means 'circle,' also 'magic circle.' Its symbolism includes – to mention only the most important forms – all concentrically arranged figures, round or square patterns with a center, and radial or spherical arrangements."[40] For Jung, there is no question that

738 > ...these Eastern symbols originated in dreams and visions, and were not invented by some Mahayana church father. On the contrary, they

---

[38] Bächtold-Stäubli under *Kreis* [circle].

[39] On India, see Zimmer, *Kunstform*, Berlin, 1926, esp. pp. 94ff.

[40] C.G. Jung, *Psychology and Alchemy*, CW 12, ¶46 fn. 1; see also ¶122ff. on the use of mandalas in Tantric yoga and in Tibetan Buddhism as an instrument of contemplation. See further C.G. Jung, *Golden Flower*, CW 13, ¶31ff., and *"Psychologie und Religion,"* CW 11, ¶109. Finally, see Wilhelm, *Secret of the Golden Flower* (pp. 30ff) on the "circulation of the light" aspired to in Eastern meditation.

> are among the oldest religious symbols of humanity... and may have even existed in paleolithic times... The mandalas used in ceremonies are of great significance because their centers usually contain one of the highest religious figures... It is not without importance for us to appreciate the high value set upon the mandalas, for it accords very well with the paramount significance of individual mandala symbols, which are characterized by the same qualities of a so-to-speak 'metaphysical' nature. Unless everything deceives us, they signify nothing less than a psychic center of the personality not to be identified with the ego."[41]

739 The mandala is not only a means of expression but produces an effect. It reacts to its maker. Or, as Jung adds:

740
> ... It has the obvious purpose of drawing a *suculus primogenius*, a magical furrow around the center, the temple or *temenos* [sacred precinct], of the innermost personality, in order to prevent "out-flowing" or to guard by apotropaic means against distracting influences from outside. Magical practices are nothing but projections of psychic events, which then exert a counter-influence on the psyche and put a kind of spell upon the personality. Through the ritual action, attention and interest are led back to the inner, sacred precinct, which is the source and goal of the psyche and contains the unity of life and consciousness. The unity once possessed has been lost, and must now be found again.[42]

741 The piper reaches the mandala center of his soul, and for the effect that the experience there has for him, it is important to keep in mind the above amplifications of the symbol of the circle and circular movement. The circle has a cleansing, cathartic effect and also represents a sacred precinct. It symbolizes the connection to life and consciousness. These symbolic meanings of the mandala are essential to the experience of the piper because he is possessed by the demon, arrested in his artistic ability, and also a thief.

742 The mandala at St. Patrick's Hill appears several times because in the room, which as a rectangular closed space is a mandala – and that is the most striking image – sit the old women in a circle around a table. Whether round or square, its shape is a mandala and it is placed at the center. This table is golden. Gold is a symbol of the highest value. Here it is the treasure that surrounds and cherishes the maternal psychic forces. As the mother

---

[41] Jung, *Psychology and Alchemy*, CW 12, ¶124–126.

[42] Cf. Jung, *Golden Flower*, CW 13, ¶36. See also J. Jacobi, *Die Psychologie von C.G. Jung*, pp. 151–152.

symbolizes the creative ground of the soul, the symbol of the most precious treasure is often presented as being initially hidden in her possession in the bosom of the earth. Even Frau Holle, the great mother, gives gold to her favorite people. According to an old folk song, she grinds fate at the mill every morning, "silver in the morning, the red *gold*."[43] In the aforementioned Icelandic fairytale, "The Hole of the Giantess," an exceedingly large old woman lives in a hole in the earth and grinds gold in a mill there.[44] In our present tale, hundreds of mother figures sit around the golden table. "Sitting together at one table means relationship, being connected, a 'putting together.' The round table indicates that the figures have been brought together for the purpose of wholeness."[45] It is as if a current circles the ring of the table around which sit the united daemonic mother figures. The scene of the mothers sitting around the golden table means for the piper, therefore, the experience of inner balance and enlivened harmony. Thanks to the Púca, he gains access to the secret center of his soul, his potential inner wholeness. The multitude of female nature demons that he finds there corresponds to the primitive mental level, from which the fairytale clearly arises, and for which the soul is not a unity, but consists of a plurality of ancestral souls. Even for the childlike mentality of the piper, therefore, the image of the primordial mother that stands behind his own personal mother is a multiplicity. (That the piper beholds "old" women points to the childishness of his conscious state, since for the child all adults seem old.) On the other hand, the roundness of the golden table suggests that this multiplicity is arranged around a psychic center.

743 After his passage into the earth, the Púca suddenly announces that the piper is "the best in Ireland." He actually can play not just one song, but can also strike up a dance. Since the unconscious behaves complementary to consciousness, the piper can do things in the dream world he could not perform in waking consciousness, but that he probably longed to do. But before that can take place the gander enters the scene. Initially, the stolen and devoured gander represents the piper's bad conscience. Indeed, he swears, "By my conscience!" Through this honest and impulsive confession, the atmosphere remains cheerful and light. It also shows how the unconscious touches and modifies, as it were, the morality of consciousness: the evil deed reveals itself as a source of spiritual enrichment and as the impetus for fertile inner experience. The astonished piper learns here that "livingness"[46] escapes destruction and lives on in the world of nature. In fact, because of that, every deed remains alive as a warning in one's own psychic sphere. In this respect, the effect of the journey to the nature spirits is similar to the penitential

[43] Cf. Laiblin, "Urbild," p. 104.
[44] H. and I. Naumann (trans.), *Isländische*, p. 297.
[45] C.G. Jung, *Psychology and Alchemy*, CW 12, ¶242, fn. 118.
[46] [*Lebendige*, i.e., the incorruptible essence of one's being, the self.]

pilgrimage imposed by the priest. In what sense it goes beyond that, is expressed in the wild dance of mothers. This dance to the piper's music is the intensification of that circle of current; it is the revival of hidden powers slumbering latent in his soul insofar as "mother" symbolizes the basic substance of what has become and what is becoming. This primordial matter begins whirling; the intervention of consciousness (the arrival of the piper) spurs the previously latent powers of the unconscious – inspired by feeling (the music) – into motion.[47] The soul becomes creative because the dance is both trance and unconsciousness, which are both able to change psychic disposition. In ancient Greece, ecstatic dances served healing purposes,[48] especially in the mysteries of the Great Mother. Dance also played a role with the chthonic gods of the dead. All the gods, river, and star beings danced at the "Source at the Place of the Beautiful Dancer" in honor of Demeter and her daughter Persephone.[49] The whirlwind in the piper's soul – the insight into the movement of natural forces, which correspond to a shift in himself – releases his creative powers.

744 Upon his dismissal, the piper receives money, and Púca attests that he now has even more: intellect and music. In the light of day, the pieces of gold turn out to be leaves, for that which has the highest value in the unconscious, is considered by consciousness, with its worldly aspirations, to be without value. It is an inner enrichment that does not count in the eyes of the world.[50] Here again, the value of gifts from the unconscious depends on the receiver's attitude. The real gain of the piper's journey to the depths is the acquisition of "intellect and music," that is, of insight into the inner workings of the realm of the soul and creative inspiration from the feeling function.[51] The piper was previously a fool, that is, he was fascinated by the unconscious, but without access to its gifts. Yet now, he has found his creative powers. From now on, he has two bagpipes: his old one, from which he is able to elicit unknown beautiful melodies; and a new one, which only produces the screeching sound of geese. This was handed to him by the strange and almost silent, but insistent, main supporting character, the gander who wanders through the scene like a ghost. This is but a small punishment for his theft. Beforehand,

---

[47] In India, the Goddess Maya is the world of the Dance of the Divine, in which she enjoys itself; see Zimmer, *Maya*, pp. 211ff.

[48] Cf. Rohde, *Psyche*, vol. 2, pp. 47ff.

[49] K. Kerényi, "Göttl. Mädchen," p. 75; see also pp. 51, 55ff, 65. [For an English version, see Kerényi, *Kore*, Princeton, 1969, pp. 113f., 135f.] See also Betty Kovács, "Journey of the Mothers," in: Leila Castle (ed.), *Earthwalking Sky Dancers: Women's Pilgrimages to Sacred Places* (1996); see further the dance of the spirits of the dead in the afterlife in "The Woman who Followed her Husband to Aguarerente" and "Blue-Jay Visits his Sister Io'i in the Land of the Dead." In "Death of the Spider Woman," the Spider-Woman tries to get the two heroes to dance to death.

[50] The medieval alchemists emphasized that their gold is not an *aurum vulgi* [vulgar gold] but was plain and unattractive. Cf. C.G. Jung, *Psychology and Alchemy*, CW 12, ¶99, 103.

[51] Cf. the English fairytale, "The Fairy Harp," in which out of gratitude an hospitable farmer receives a harp from the fairies that plays wonderful melodies and inspires people to dance.

the piper could only play the "black rogue," whereas now he occasionally pipes the "goose song" in the service of the magical world, which, besides the highest values, also comprises the mad and also the earthly. In a small part of his soul, the piper remains a fool. Since the vibrations of the soul now flow uninhibited through his art, which now displays the double aspect of the magical world and reflects, on the one hand, the valuable and, on the other hand, the ridiculous. The tale of the piper and Púca expresses in a very rare, realistic, and surprising dream-like way the confrontation with the unconscious. It shows how subtle and, to the ordinary mind, paradoxical, even strange, its moral views are: the hero's guilt leads him down to the creative source of life, the black villain in him reveals himself to be the spirit that separates him from the mother and develops his artistic skills. The unconscious contains not only a pagan naturalistic amorality, but also remembers ill-deeds and even highlights their traces; it ridicules worldly greed and sets a limit to the possible threat of hubris with the bagpipes that play the honkings of geese constantly to remind the piper of his guilt.

745 If one tries to deduce a law for proper conduct from this tale, it would most likely be that in all circumstances one can follow and trust one's own inner daemon, even if this experiment initially brings one into conflict with prevailing opinion. If one opposes his or her inner voice, one loses the support of the unconscious and is punished by misfortune. (Had the piper not let himself be guided by the Púca, he would have forever remained a poor incompetent fool.) If one lets oneself be guided by the unconscious, without losing his or her head or sense of humor, the journey into the depths rewards one with unexpected riches.

746 The most remarkable figure in this tale is the Púca, a half-animal, half divine elf who accosts the piper at the bridge and takes him into the world of magic. He becomes his soul guide in the underworld journey and is reminiscent of the *tunghâk*, who brought the young Inuit fisherman into contact with the unknown beautiful woman in the fairytale "The Fire-Ball" (see page 134). Similar to Púca and the *tornaq* is the guardian bear spirit, who kidnapped the shaman in "Flight to the Moon." This journey is a kind of berserker trip and it is also called, significantly, a possession by anger, a shape-changing frenzy, a condition that was sometimes explained by the ancient Germanic tribes as the donning of a magic shell, "hamr," and which is also called the shadow, or protective spirit. "It concerns," as Ninck writes, "the widespread concept of the image . . . shadow . . . or the figure of man, which, removable from the body, extends outwards in a dream or deep sleep."[52]

747 One revealing example of the nature of the shadow, and how it affects us, is "The Neighbor Underground":

---

[52] Ninck, *Wodan*, pp. 42–43.

748 Once upon a time there was a peasant who lived in Telemarken, and had a big farm; yet he had nothing but bad luck with his cattle, and at last lost his house and holding. He had scarcely anything left, and with the little he had, he bought a bit of land that lay off to one side, far away from the city, in the wildwood and the wilderness. One day, as he was passing through his farmyard, he met a man. "Good-day, neighbor!" said the man. "Good-day," said the peasant, "I thought I was all alone here. Are you a neighbor of mine?" "You can see my homestead over yonder," said the man. "It is not far from your own." And there lay a farm-holding such as he had never before seen, handsome and prosperous, and in fine condition. Then he knew very well that this must be one of the underground people; yet he had no fear, but invited his neighbor in to drink a glass with him, and the neighbor seemed to enjoy it. "Listen," said the neighbor, 'there is one thing you must do for me as a favor." "First let me know what it is," said the peasant. "You must shift your cow-stable, because it is in my way," was the answer he gave the peasant. "No, I'll not do that," said the peasant. "I put it up only this summer, and the winter is coming on. What am I to do with my cattle then?" "Well, do as you choose; but if you do not tear it down, you will live to regret it," said his neighbor. And with that he went on his way. The peasant was surprised at this, and did not know what to do. It seemed quite foolish to him to start in to tear down his stable when the long winter night was approaching, and besides, he could not count on help. One day as he was standing in his stable, he sank through the ground. Down below, in the place to which he had come, everything was unspeakably handsome. There was nothing which was not of gold or of silver. Then the man who had called himself his neighbor came along, and bade him sit down. After a time food was brought in on a silver platter, and mead in a silver jug, and the neighbor invited him to draw up to the table and eat. The peasant did not dare refuse, and sat down at the table; but just as he was about to dip his spoon into the dish, something fell down into his food from above, so that he lost his appetite. "Yes, yes," said the man, "now you can see why we don't like your stable. We can never eat in peace, for as soon as we sit down to a meal, dirt and straw fall down, and no matter how hungry we may be, we lose our appetites and cannot eat. But if you will do me the favor of setting up your stable elsewhere, you shall never go short of pasture nor good crops, no matter how old you may grow to be. But if you won't, you shall know naught but lean years all your life long." When the peasant heard that, he went right to work pulling down his stable, to put it up again in another place. Yet he could not have

> worked alone, for at night, when all slept, the building of the new stable went forward just as it did by day, and well he knew his neighbor was helping him. Nor did he regret it later, for he had enough of feed and corn, and his cattle waxed fat. Once there was a year of scarcity, and feed was so short that he was thinking of selling or slaughtering half his herd. But one morning, when the milkmaid went into the stable, the dog was gone, and with him all the cows and the calves. She began to cry and told the peasant. But he thought to himself, that it was probably his neighbor's doing, who had taken the cattle to pasture. And sure enough, so it was; for toward spring, when the woods grew green, he saw the dog come along, barking and leaping, by the edge of the forest, and after him followed all the cows and calves, and the whole herd was so fat it was a pleasure to look at it.[53]

749 Here the shadow is the "neighbor underground." He is portrayed as a threatening and yet gift-bestowing companion spirit. He lives under the barn, under the animals. He is an earth spirit from the wild forest who imperiously demands submission. But when he is graciously accommodated, he invisibly protects the farmer's animals, since the shadow is psychologically linked to the world of instinct, as illustrated by the presence of the farm animals in the tale.

750 In many accounts, he has less ghostly traits, however, and appears rather as a companion of inferior human quality. Not only in the sense of a lesser person, but rather as an individual in an earlier stage of development. Sometimes the shadow appears as the historically older person, or in animal-human form, often in the figure of an animal that embodies the world of natural impulses and instincts.[54] The shadow, an image of the incomplete and in some ways inferior part of the personality, is bound to the earth, to nature. For most people, contact with the shadow is the first encounter on their passage to the unconscious. Considering the shadow, Jung observes:

> 751 The meeting with oneself is, initially, the meeting with one's own shadow. The shadow is a tight passage, a narrow door, whose painful constriction no one is spared who goes down deep into the well. But one must learn to know oneself in order to know who one is. For what comes after the door is, surprisingly enough, a boundless expanse full of unprecedented uncertainty, with apparently no inside and no outside, no above, no below, no here and no there, no mine and no

---

[53] Stroebe, *Norwegian Fairy Book*, pp. 22–25.

[54] Cf. C.G. Jung, "Rebirth," CW 9i, ¶244; see also "Archetypes of the Collective Unconscious," CW 9i, ¶55.

> thine, no good and no bad. It is a world of water, where all life floats in suspension; where the realm of the sympathetic system, the soul of everything living begins; where I am indivisibly this and that; where I experience the other in myself and the other-than-myself experiences me."[55]

752 The shadow accompanies the soul since it can cross rivers and transform the waters. Zimmer retells a Hasidic story of a miracle-working rabbi:

753 The consciousness of His Holiness was plagued by the question, next to whom would he sit when the Lord at the end of time gathered his people together at his table. A voice called to him in a dream and gave him the name of a fellow believer that he did not know. The voice also mentioned the name of a place, a spot unbeknownst to him. The rabbi awoke from the dream quite contrite, as he saw himself to be in the crowd of the nameless and insignificant, and he was overcome by only one wish: to be able to see now the face of him whom he would sit next to in order to judge his righteousness before God. He wandered to that place and after a long search came upon a dilapidated house. It was at the time of the Sabbath meal, but the house was not cleaned nor prepared. Sighing, the rabbi was astonished that such an unsaintly fellow believer was his neighbor before God. Having waited a long time, late in the night a grimy man wandered in and invited the rabbi to join him. The rabbi shuddered in the face of such disregard for the Sabbath customs. Horrified by his alleged likeness, the rabbi tried to sleep wrapped in his cloak. The next day he made his way home, broken, carrying the verdict of God on his unworthiness. He came up to a river running high water, and he just barely succeeded to make it across a tottering bridge before the flood washed it away. He realized that he had forgotten his coat but now could not return to fetch it. Suddenly he saw from afar a man approaching him with great swinging strides, swiftly as an angel. He recognized him as his host carrying his forgotten coat. Whilst the rabbi beckoned to his comrade that it was impossible to cross over the surging river, the man had already thrown his own coat onto the waters and was crossing over as if on a light canoe over the gurgling waters. Arriving at the side of the rabbi, the man handed him his coat and disappeared.[56]

[55] C.G. Jung, "Archetypes of the Collective Unconscious," CW 9i, ¶45.
[56] Zimmer, *Weisheit Indiens*, pp. 46–48.

754 The shadow constitutes a bridge, therefore, to humankind per se. It guides human beings back to their natural roots, instinctual abilities, and connection with the earth. Alfred de Musset describes the experience as follows:

755 Partout où j'ai voulu dormir,
Partout où j'ai voulu mourir,
Partout où j'ai touché la terre,
Sur ma route est venu s'asseoir
Un malheureux vêtu de noir,
qui me ressemblait comme un frère."
(Wherever I wanted to sleep,
Wherever I wanted to die,
Whenever I touched the ground,
On my way came and sat
An unfortunate one dressed in black,
Who resembled me like a brother.)[57]

756 But the shadow can also appear as a ghostly spirit who misleads people into crooked ways. An impressive description of the first encounter with the shadow is contained in the Norwegian fairytale, "Per Gynt":

757 In the old days there lived in Kvam a marksman by the name of Per Gynt. He was continually in the mountains, where he shot bear and elk, for at that time there were more forests on the Fjall, and all sorts of beasts dwelt in them. Once, late autumn, when the cattle had long since been driven down from the mountain pastures, Per Gynt decided to go up on the Fjall again. With the exception of three dairymaids, all the herd-folk had already left the mountains. But when Per Gynt reached Hb'vringalm, where he intended to stay overnight in a herdsman's hut, it already was so dark that he could not see his hand before his eyes. Then the dogs began to bark so violently that he felt quite uneasy. And suddenly his foot struck something, and when he took hold of it, it was cold, and large and slippery. Since he felt certain he had not left the path, he could not imagine what it might be; but he sensed that all was not in order. "And who are you?" asked Per Gynt, for he noticed that it moved.

758 "Oh, I am the crooked one," was the answer. And now Per Gynt knew as much as he had before. So he went along its length, "for sooner or later I will come to the end of it," thought he. As he went along he

[57] From "La Nuit de Décembre," in: Alfred de Musset, *Poésies Nouvelles,* 1836–1852, Paris, 1883, p. 75; emphases added.

again struck against something, and when he felt it, it was again something cold and large and slippery.

759 "And who are you?" asked Per Gynt.

760 "I am the crooked one," was again the answer.

761 "Well, whether you be crooked or straight, you will have to let me pass," said Per Gynt; for he noticed that he was going around in a circle, and that the crooked one had coiled himself about the herdsman's cottage. At these words the crooked one moved a little to one side, so that Per Gynt could get into the cottage. When he entered he found it as dark inside as it was out; and he stumbled and felt his way along the walls; for he wanted to lay aside his firelock and his hunting bag. But while he was feeling his way about, he once more noticed something large, and cold and slippery.

762 "And who are you now?" cried Per Gynt.

763 "Oh, I am the big crooked one," was the answer. And no matter where he took hold or where he set his foot, he could feel the coils of the crooked one laid around him.

764 "This is a no good place to be in," thought Per Gynt, "for this crooked one is outside and inside; but I will soon put what is wrong to rights." He took his firelock, went out again, and felt his way along the crooked one until he came to his head.

765 "And who are you really and truly?" he asked.

766 "Oh, I am the big crooked one of Etnedal," said the monster troll. Then Per Gynt did not waste any time, but shot three bullets right through the middle of his head.

767 "Shoot again!" cried the crooked one. But Per Gynt knew better, for had he shot another time, the bullet would have rebounded and hit his own head.[58]

768 The last sentence points to a secret identity with the shadow. Simple and vivid is the presentation of the shadow in the well-known Grimm's tale, "Bearskin":

769 Once upon a time there was a young fellow who enlisted as a soldier, conducted himself bravely, and was always at the very front when it was raining bullets. As long as the war lasted all went well, but when peace was made he was dismissed, and the captain said he could go wherever he wanted to. The soldier had nothing left but his gun, so,

[58] Stroebe, *Norwegian Fairy Book*, pp. 1–8. [This is merely the beginning of the tale.]

putting it on his shoulder, he went forth into the world. He came to a large heath, on which nothing was to be seen but a circle of trees. Filled with sorrow, he sat down beneath them and thought about his fate. "I have no money," he thought, "and the only trade I have learned is that of making war, and now that they have made peace they can no longer use me, so I see that I shall starve."

770 Suddenly he heard a rustling sound, and when he looked around, a strange man was standing before him. He wore a green jacket and looked quite stately, but he had a hideous horse's foot.

771 "I know what you are in need of," said the man. "You shall have money and property, as much as you, with all your might, can squander away, but first I must know if you are fearless, so that I won't be giving away my money for nothing."

772 The soldier proves his courage by not being frightened by a bear suddenly approaching from behind, but by killing him. Then the devil makes the following condition of him: "For the next seven years you are neither to wash yourself, nor comb your beard and hair, nor cut your nails, nor say the Lord's prayer. I will give you a jacket and a cloak, which you must wear during this time. If you die during these seven years, you are mine. If you stay alive, you are free, and rich as well, for all the rest of your life." The soldier thought about his desperate situation, and having faced death so often before, he decided to risk it now as well, and he entered into the agreement. The soldier received the devil's green jacket and the bear's skin, saying, "This shall be your cloak, and your bed as well, for you are to sleep on it, and you are not allowed to lie in any other bed. Because of your clothing you shall be called Bearskin." With that the devil disappeared. The soldier put on the jacket, immediately reached into the pocket, and found a handful of money. Then he put on the bearskin and went forth into the world. He did whatever he pleased, refraining from nothing that did him good and his money harm.

773 During the first year his appearance was still acceptable, but during the second he looked like a monster. His hair covered nearly his entire face. His beard looked like a piece of coarse felt cloth. His fingers had claws, and his face was so covered with dirt that if someone had planted cress on it, it would have grown. Everyone who saw him ran away. However, because everywhere he went he gave money to the poor to pray that he might not die during the seven years, and because he paid well for everything, he always found shelter.

774 In the fourth year he met a poor man in great financial need in a hostel, whose debts he paid. In return, he promised him one of his three beautiful daughters. But the two older ones spurned him because of his deformity. But the youngest said, "dear father, this must be a good man who has helped you out of trouble, if you have promised him a bride for this, your word must be kept." Bearskin got engaged to her by giving her half of his broken ring and promising to return after three years time. In the meantime, she should pray for his life. The bride remained bravely faithful to him despite her sisters' mockeries. After seven years Bearskin met the devil again in the forest and gave him back his green jacket. Whether the devil wanted to or not, he had to fetch water and wash off Bearskin, comb his hair, and cut his nails. After this he looked like a brave soldier and was much better looking than he had ever been before. When the devil was safely gone Bearskin was quite lighthearted. He went to town, bought splendid clothes and went to his bride-to-be. The two older sisters wanted to marry the unknown man at any price, and went to put on their best dresses. But Bearskin revealed himself to the youngest sister through his half of the broken ring. In the meantime the two sisters came back in full dress. When they saw that the youngest sister had received the handsome man, and heard that he was Bearskin, they ran out filled with anger and rage. One of them drowned herself in the well. The other hanged herself on a tree. That evening, someone knocked at the door, and when the bridegroom opened it, it was the devil in his green jacket, who said, "You see, I now have two souls for the one of yours."[59]

775 Closely related is the tale, "The Devil's Sooty Brother":

A discharged soldier had nothing to live on, and did not know how to get on. So he went out into the forest and when he had walked for a short time, he met a little man who was, however, the Devil. The little man said to him, "What ails you? You seem so very sorrowful." Then the soldier said, "I am hungry, but have no money." The Devil said, "If you will hire yourself to me, and be my serving-man, you shall have enough for all your life. You shall serve me for seven years, and after that you shall again be free. But one thing I must tell you, and that is, you must not wash, comb, or trim yourself, or cut your hair or nails, or wipe the water from your eyes." The soldier said, "All right, if

[59] Partly summarized from *Complete Grimm's*, pp. 463–472. [See also D. L. Ashliman (ed.), *The Grimm Brothers' Children's and Household Tales (Grimm's Fairy Tales)*, Princeton University Press, Princeton NJ, 1998–2009.]

there is no help for it," and went off with the little man, who straightway led him down into hell.

776 He had to poke the fire under the kettles without looking inside and carry out the rubbish. The soldier nevertheless looked into the cauldrons. But because he saw his former superiors in it, he stirred up the fire even more. At the end of his seven years of service, the devil pardoned him for peeping into the kettles since he added wood to the fire, otherwise his "life would have been forfeited." The devil then dismissed the man, and said, "In order that you may receive the wages you have earned, go and fill your knapsack full of the sweepings, and take it home with you. You must also go unwashed and uncombed, with long hair on your head and beard, and with uncut nails and dim eyes, and when you are asked whence you come, you must say, 'From hell,' and when you are asked who you are, you are to say, 'The Devil's sooty brother, and my King as well.' " The ex-soldier held his peace, and did as the Devil bade him, but he was not at all satisfied with his wages.

777 Then as soon as he was up in the forest again, he took his knapsack from his back, to empty it, but on opening it, the sweepings had become pure gold. He went to a nearby town and stayed at an inn, not washing or combing himself, just as the devil had said. But the landlord had seen the knapsack with gold, and stole it. The next morning, when Hans the ex-soldier got up and wanted to pay the landlord and travel further, behold his knapsack was gone! But he soon composed himself and thought, "Thou hast been unfortunate from no fault of thine own," and straightway went back again to hell, complained of his misfortune to the old Devil, and begged for his help. The Devil said, "Seat yourself, I will wash, comb, and trim you, cut your hair and nails, and wash your eyes for you," and when he had done with him, he gave him the knapsack back again full of sweepings, and said, "Go and tell the landlord that he must return you your money, or else I will come and fetch him, and he shall poke the fire in your place." Hans went up and thus threatened the landlord, who returned the money, and more besides, begging him to keep it secret, and Hans was now a rich man. He set out on his way home to his father, bought himself a shabby smock-frock to wear, and strolled about making music, for he had learned to do that while he was with the Devil in hell. There was an old King in that country, however, before whom he had to play, and the King was so delighted with his playing, that he promised him his eldest daughter in marriage. But when she heard that she was to be married to a common fellow in a smock-frock, she

said, "Rather than do that, I would go into the deepest water." Then the King gave him the youngest, who was quite willing to do it to please her father, and thus the Devil's sooty brother got the King's daughter, and when the aged King died, the whole kingdom likewise.[60]

778 The hero's becoming dirty and animal-like are assimilations to the shadow.[61] This points to unlived instinctuality and wildness and also rebellion against all human adaptation.[62] First, there appears behind the soldier a bear that embodies his own animality. (In popular German belief the bear is both a manifestation of the soul and the devil!)[63] He dons the bear's skin, and thus partially transforms into a bear. The belief in the Nordic-Germanic berserkers lives on in this motif.

779 The Berserkers are men who have sudden fits of rage and then behave like wild animals. . . they become superhumanly strong and invulnerable. By calling them by their name the possession can be removed, the magical spell averted. The name "berserker" suggests not only bearskin instead of breastplate, but also has deeper meaning, as is apparent from the Saga of Hrolf Kraki (Scandinavia). During a great fight, involving all of King Hrolf 's men, the valiant warrior Bodvar Bjarki sits idle in the hall. Hrolf goes to battle but a big bear sloughs off all the slashing weapons and thrusting lances, smashes down men and horses and tears the people with claws and teeth. Hjalti, one of Hrolf 's best warriors and a friend of Bjarki, misses his comrades and hurries into the hall, where he finds Bjarki asleep and yells at him to wake up. Sighing, Bjarki arises, goes to the battlefield, and the bear disappears. So here the hero fights in the shape of a bear while his body remains asleep, in a trance. . . The berserkers are like vampires, people who turn into wolves and cause damage. Berserkers are originally men who go out as bears.[64]

---

[60] Partially summarized from *Complete Grimm's*, pp. 463–466. See also the parallel Lithuanian tale, "Von einem Mann, der dem Teufel drei Jahre diente" (The man who served the devil for three years).

[61] See, for example, "Trunt, Trunt, and the Trolls in the Mountains."

[62] On this meaning of the "wild man" in children's dreams, see C.G. Jung, *Children's Dreams, Notes from the Seminar Given in 1936–1940*, eds. Maria Meyer-Grass and Lorenz Jung, trans Ernst Falzeder and Tony Woolfson (Princeton: Princeton University Press, 2008), pp. 104ff.

[63] Cf. Bächtold-Stäubli under *Bär* [bear].

[64] Bolte and Mackensen, *Handwörterbuch*, under *Bärenhäuter* [Bearskinners]. On the werewolf, see Hertz, *Werwolf*, pp. 57–58, also Bächtold-Stäubli under *Bärenhäuter*. The latter authors mention the Bjarki Saga and particularly the fact that when Bjarki's alter ego stops fighting in bear form, and awakens as Bjarki, he can no longer match the power of the bear. See also Bächtold-Stäubli under *Bär* concerning the popular belief in various countries that the bear is a transformed person. [In this context, see also C.G. Jung, "Wotan," in: Sir Herbert Read et al. (eds.), *Civilization in Transition*, Princeton University Press, Princeton (CW 10, trans. by R. F. C. Hull), where he discusses the possible origin of Nazi fanaticism in the Berserkers.]

780 Ninck suggests that the notion of the word berserker in "Bearskin" is still alive. In the Grimm's version of this fairytale, the experience of the berserker is still reflected strongly and can be traced back to Woden (Odin).[65]

781 We recognize Odin in those evil ones with horses' feet and green skirts who go thundering over the heath and appear as soldiers in the ring of trees. Horses' feet and green skirts are characteristics of Odin/Woden. To go abroad and roam for seven years is a condition that the bearskinners enter into Odin's service. For this they received God's dress of rapture, the fur of the berserk, money, possessions, and wealth, such as those that Odin bestowed upon Starkad.[66] For seven years the bearskinner may not wash, comb, or cut his nails, just as was the custom among the berserker-like warriors of the Chatti[67]. . . A bride awaits his salvation and the fulfilment of his vow. She is granted to him in the inn and the shared ring holds them connected to each other: a motif that we will encounter over and over again in the sagas of rapture[68] from the followers of Odin/Woden.[69]

782 This connection to the pre-Christian background of the tale facilitates its psychological interpretation: the hero suffers a state of possession by his unconscious, which forces him into a negative role, alienated from human society. It is a typical effect of the shadow to induce an isolation from other people, and just in this fact lies something positive. Being alone is one of the preconditions of all psychic development.[70] As in "The Piper and the Púca," it is also shown here that the shadow in the individual human being has not only a personal side as the black villain, but that in the deeper sense it is a magical figure of divine power. It corresponds to a daemonic figure that bestows gifts and riches as rewards, but also imposes punishment. Thus, this dark figure is also a soul guide, who confers not only worldly adventure upon the hero, but also eventually leads him to his mistress, who, similarly to the shadow, symbolically embodies his own soul. There is a significant Russian

---

[65] The Grimm's version of "Bearskin" was strongly influenced by Hans Jakob Christoffel von Grimmelshausen's *Der erste Bärenhäuter* [The First Bearskinners] (1670), in which the bearskinners are linked to the figure of the devil and the soldiers of Odin/Woden.

[66] [A legendary hero in Norse mythology.]

[67] [The *Chatten* were an ancient Germanic tribe.]

[68] [German: *entrücken*.]

[69] Ninck, *Wodan*, p. 67.

[70] Cf. the practice by Hindu saints of never washing themselves. The Buddha admonished his monks to live an ascetic life (K. Neumann, *Reden Gotamo*, München, 1921, vol. 1, pp. 81ff.) [Here is a quote from the *Majjhima Nikaaya*: "Sariputta, I recall having lived a holy life possessing four factors. I have practiced asceticism – the extreme of asceticism; I have practiced coarseness – the extreme of coarseness; I have practiced scrupulousness – the extreme of scrupulousness; I have practiced seclusion – the extreme of seclusion."] See also the vow of a Nazirite offered to Jehovah of not cutting one's hair, Numbers 6:5.

parallel to "Bearskin," called "Nü Wa," in which at the end the devil, in order to clean the hero, chops him up into small pieces, cooks the pieces in a kettle, and afterwards puts them back together again. "Just as how they belonged: bone to bone, joint to joint, tendon to tendon, and then he sprayed the water of death and of life. And there stood the soldier as such a lad, so handsome that no fairytale can relate, no pen can describe."[71] This, as will be explained later, is a shamanistic initiation, a rebirth ritual. Thus when he appears in the role of the shadow, the devil proves to be a magical helper or soul-guiding daemon, who works for the inner rebirth of the individual.

783 It is also significant that the devil cannot possess the soldier who has a "pure heart," but indeed possesses the envious sisters of the bride.[72] He has there just a handle on the hero, where a piece of his personal "shadow," an inferiority complex, is present.[73] Thus, the shadow comprises to some extent a double condition: on the one hand, a personal inadequacy; and on the other, the unconscious as an untamed nature being. While the former necessarily requires to be overcome, the latter calls for a serious *auseinandersetzung* and a human effort, because in this part of the shadow the deeper roots of the personality lie hidden.[74]

784 The consequences of a rejection of the *auseinandersetzung* with the shadow and his world are shown in the Norwegian tale "The Secret Church":

> 785 Once the schoolmaster of *Etnedal* was staying in the mountains to fish. One Sunday morning, as he was lying there pleasantly reading a book, it seemed as though he could hear church bells; sometimes they sounded faintly, as though from a great distance; at other times the sound was clear, as though carried by the wind. He became curious, so he laid aside his book, stood up, and went out. The sun was shining, the weather was fine, and one group of churchgoers after another passed him in their best Sunday clothes, and then the priest came by, and he was so old and decrepit that his wife and daughter led him.

[71] August von Löwis of Menar (ed.), *Russische Volksmärchen,* (*MdW*), ed. Fr. v. d. Leyen and P. Zaunert, 1927, pp. 156–159 [in German].

[72] [The part about the sisters is a late addition by the Grimm brothers and only present in the last edition of their *KHM*. It is not recorded in their sources.]

[73] This is also the main theme of "The Three Apprentices."

[74] "What seems evil, or at least meaningless and valueless to contemporary experience and knowledge, might on a higher level of experience and knowledge, appear as the source of the best everything depending, naturally, on the use one makes of one's seven devils. To explain them as meaningless robs the personality of its proper shadow, and with this it loses its form. The living form needs deep shadow if it is to appear plastic. Without shadow it remains a two-dimensional phantom, a more or less well brought up child"; see C.G. Jung, "Relation between the ego and the unconscious," CW 7, ¶400. See also: ". . . for the inferior and even the worthless belongs to me as my shadow and gives me substance and mass. How can I be substantial without casting a shadow? I must have a dark side too if I am to be whole; and by becoming conscious of my shadow I remember once more that I am a human being like any other"; Jung, *Spiritual Problem*, CW 10, ¶134.

And when they came to the spot where the schoolmaster was standing, they stopped and invited him to come to church and hear mass. The schoolmaster thought for a moment; but since it occurred to him that it might be amusing to see how these people worshiped God, he said he would go along, if he did not thereby suffer harm. No, no harm should come to him, said they, but rather a blessing. In the church all went forward in a quiet and orderly manner, there were neither dogs nor crying children to disturb the service. The singing was good but he could not make any sense of the words. When the priest had been led to the pulpit he delivered what seemed to the listening schoolmaster a really fine and edifying sermon but one, it appeared to him, of quite a peculiar trend of thought, which he was not always able to follow. Nor did the "Our Father in heaven. . . " sound just right, and the "Deliver us from evil. . . " he did not hear at all. Nor was the name of Jesus uttered; and at the close no blessing was spoken.

786 After Mass he was invited to dinner with the priest's family, and thinking that the schoolmaster was such a strong and able man, the priest's daughter asked him if he wanted to become the successor of the old man. She insisted that he did not need to have special studies, he had more than was needed in their case. The schoolmaster said he needed a year to think it over. When he had said that he found himself standing by a pond in the wood, and could see neither church nor parsonage. So he thought the matter was at an end.

787 But a year later when he was working on a house on his school vacation, he saw the pastor's daughter coming straight toward him. She asked him if he had thought over the matter. "Yes," said he, "I have thought it over, but I cannot; since I cannot answer for it before God and my own conscience." That very moment the pastor's daughter from underground vanished; but immediately after he cut himself in the knee with the ax in such a wise that he remained a cripple for life.[75]

788 By rejecting the magical sphere and due to his apprehension concerning the task towards the natural forces, the schoolmaster crippled himself. He injured his leg, his connection to the earth. The world that approached him, however, threatened his conscious attitude and his whole secure grip on his life. It is certainly questionable whether it would have been proper unconditionally to prescribe himself to the spirits. But he would have done well to have asked the spirits why they now wanted just him, a living man and a Christian, to be their

[75] Shortened and edited from Stroebe, *Norwegian Fairy Book*, pp. 26–29.

pastor. Maybe they wanted to be redeemed by him? The schoolmaster denied them the effort, however, out of inner cowardice, and literally cut himself in the flesh.

789 In "The Neighbor Underground" and "The Secret Church," the figure from the other world has human features and traits. The "schoolmaster" confronted a "priest" and he was invited to be a priest in that other realm. In "The Neighbor Underground," the farmer met another "neighbor," that is, another farmer. Only in one case is the priest not a Christian, and in the other case, the neighbor is much more rich and powerful than any ordinary farmer. In the next fairytale, the Icelandic "Sigurd and the Ghost*," the hero and his magical counterpart are very similar but exhibit slight differences in their nature. This shows how the magical counterpart is a shadowy part of the human personality.

> 790 The son of a farmer, Sigurd, was a strange boy, a bit odd, and not very popular. One winter a strange man came to the farm, who was also called Sigurd. But he understood nothing, and could only play the harp. Between the two namesakes there grew a close friendship. When spring came to the farm, the stranger took to the road again. The farmer's son began to pine and grieve to such an extent, that he decided to set off in search of the other Sigurd. He traveled from farm to farm, church to church, town to town, everywhere asking the whereabouts of a man called Sigurd who played the harp. He finally came to the rectory of a parish, where he was told that a man named Sigurd had just died and would soon be entombed in the church. The farmer's son asked to be shown where he lay. He found the coffin and there he stayed up all night sitting beside the dead man. Suddenly he saw how Sigurd arose from the coffin and went out. The farmer's son remained sitting next to the coffin.
>
> 791 Now it so happened that the wife of the pastor had just given birth to a child. After a long time Sigurd returned and desired to get back into the coffin. The farmer's son prevented him, however, until he told him what he was about. The ghost replied that he was just gambling with his money and would like now to return to his coffin.
>
> 792 "Not until you tell me where the money is." said the farmer's son. "That you shall never know," replied the ghost.
>
> 793 "Then you will not get back into your coffin," countered the boy. " It is under a corner of the bath-house," said the ghost.
>
> 794 "And how much?" "A quarter of a ton."

795 "Did you do nothing else in the night?" This went back and forth until the ghost admitted that he killed the pastors' wife. "Tell me why or you shall never get back in your coffin," demanded the farmer's son. "I wanted her affection but she refused me," answered the ghost. "How did you kill her?" asked the boy Sigurd.

796 "I stroked all of her life into her little finger."

797 "Can one bring her back to life? asked the farmer's son.

798 " Yes, if one were to carefully loosen the fine thread that I tied around her finger so that not a drop of blood flows. Now I want to finally get back in my coffin!"

799 "Only after you promise never to come out again."

800 This the ghost promised, so Sigurd let him climb in and closed the lid.

801 When morning came all the people in the pastor's house were grieving terribly. The farmer's son asked what had happened and was told that the pastor's wife had died in the night. The boy begged to be able to see her and was led to where she lay. He untied the thread on her finger and carefully stroked the blood back into all parts of her body so that she returned to life. He then told the pastor all that he had experienced in the night and as proof, explained where to find the money. This the pastor did and was so struck by the boy that he took him into his service. It is said that the pastor made a good man out of Sigurd, who remained so his whole life. And that is the end of this story.[76]

802 Sigurd, the farmer's son, is "strange" due to his unadaptedness to normal life. It is as if his excessive introversion were blocking a connection to other people, so that this unrelatedness reflects an image of his incompleteness. In the dark season, a man appears in the courtyard who only understands how to play the harp. The winter season, in which nighttime prevails, and in which the farmer has not much to do and spends idle hours in the living room dreaming, is fertile ground for bringing to life the images of the inner world. Hence the widespread folk belief that demons roam about especially in the winter. That the farmer's son and the stranger have the same name clearly indicates the two belong together; they are symbols of two parts of one and the same person, two tendencies of one soul.[77] A singer or musician can help compensate for the down-to-earthness of the unpopular farmer's son; music brings the world of eros and of music-induced intoxication, the weightless

[76] Translated from H. and I. Naumann (trans.), *Isländische*, pp. 225–226.

[77] On the "namesake" among primitive peoples, as a protective spirit or a dead ancestor, see Lévy-Bruhl, *The "Soul" of the Primitive*, pp. 338f.

expression of feeling, to his particular stubbornness. This being from "the other side" rose up during the wintertime to Sigurd's outer personality from an inner part of his soul of which he was unconscious. Once the light of spring approaches, and mundane activity returns, the doppelgänger disappears; not only into the distance, but even to the grave! However, he draws his namesake after him. It turns out that "death" in the fairytale world means separation from the profane world and enrapture[78] into the realm of the soul. But Sigurd is full of life and brave enough to investigate the problem and to explore the nature of his mysterious brother. What he first discovers is unpleasant: his brother is a gambler and a vengeful murderer. Here apparently lies the root of Sigurd's so-called oddness. He entertains thoughts of revenge because of rejected love and is internally a gambler and a dreamer. The fact that he acquires this awareness about the "other Sigurd" creates the opportunity to atone for his unconscious misdeeds and even to emerge enriched and respected from this experience.[79] The last unbearable remnant of this shadow figure is, however, definitely split off by the hero (in the coffin). And yet, he is still there in the background – perhaps as a mystic deity – and could possibly still lead Sigurd to much deeper layers of the unconscious. Apparently, however, Sigurd is not called: no further task awaits him. The Inuit tale, "The Fire-Ball" (see page 134), hints at what task this might be. In that tale, the hero receives counsel from the *Tunghaq*, "Release him!" The fisherman was not in a position to follow the advice and disappeared from the secular world. Sigurd succeeds in carrying through a meaningful and fruitful confrontation (*ausp*) with the daemonic brother. We will return to the redemption of these figures in later chapters.

803 A similar double and mirror image presentation of the ego personality is depicted in a Chinese fairytale from modern times, "The Tale of the Devil:"

> 804 In a city in the neighborhood of Kaiutschou there once lived a constable by the name of Dung. One day when he returned from a hunt after thieves and the twilight had already begun to fall, he waded through the stream that flowed through the city. He sat down on the bank, lit a pipe, and took off his shoes. Suddenly he noticed a man in a red hat dressed as a constable crouching beside him. They chatted awhile together, and together waded through the stream. And gradually they began to confide in each other and the stranger said: "I will be quite frank with you. I am the head constable of the Nether

[78] [German: *entrücken*.]

[79] Zimmer discusses the same problem in *The King and the Corpse*, Princeton, 1972, pp. 202ff: a king must drag a corpse from the graveyard, who embodies all that has happened in the king's life and his accumulated unconscious debts. The corpse tortures the king with his stories, but ultimately rescues him and reveals himself as Shiva.

World, and am subject to the Lord of the Great Mountain. You yourself are a constable of reputation here in the upper world. And, because of my skill, I have standing in the world below. Since we are so well suited to each other, I should like to enter into a bond of brotherhood with you."

805 Dung agreed and invited his colleague to stay at his home, and entertained him with wine and food. But the other only talked and touched neither the goblet nor the chop-sticks. Dung was concerned that the food was not good enough, but his guest replied: "Oh no, I am already surfeited and satisfied! We spirits feed only on odors; in which respect we differ from men."

806 Dung helped him with a mission from the Lord of the Great Mountain. When they were finished, the demonic henchman said, "Now all is in order: I am off! In two years' time you will go to Yaianfu, the city near the Great Mountain, and there we will meet again." In fact, after two years' time Dung had to travel professionally to Yaianfu. To his surprise, the inn-keeper already knew of him and his impending arrival. Dung asked how this was possible and the lower case inn-keeper explained: "The constable of the temple of the Great Mountain appeared to me last night and said: 'To-morrow a man by the name of Dung who is a good friend of mine is coming from the Bay of Kaiutschou!' And then he described your appearance and your clothes to me exactly, and told me to make careful note of them, and when you came to treat you with the greatest consideration, and to take no pay from you, since he would repay me lavishly. So when I saw you coming everything was exactly as my dreams had foretold, and I knew you at once. I have already prepared a quiet room for you, and beg that you will condescend to make yourself at ease."

807 Joyfully Dung followed him, and the inn-keeper waited on him with the greatest consideration, and saw that he had plenty to eat and to drink. At midnight the spirit arrived. Without having opened the door, he stood by Dung's bedside, gave him his hand, and asked how things had gone with him since he had last seen him. Dung answered all his questions and thanked him into the bargain for appearing to the inn-keeper in a dream. In return, the Devil's constable explained what had happened and thanked Dung for his assistance. Then he added: "When you reach home you must take constant care of your health. Fate has allowed you seventy-eight years of mortal life. When your time is up I will come to fetch you myself. Then I will see that

> you obtain a place as constable in the Nether World, where we can always be together." Having said all this, he disappeared.[80]

808 Here a doppelgänger belonging to the realm of the shadow comes to meet a Chinese thug, a theme already known among primitive peoples. Levy-Bruhl writes on this concept among folk people:

809

> So far we have seen the shadow or the similitude considered as an "essential appurtenance" of the individual, necessary to his life, and compatible with the outer appurtenances which are elements, prolongations, "extensions" of the personality. I have also presented another aspect, one still more difficult to interpret, when it is a "double" or a "replica" of the individual."[81]

810 This "second ego" is known as a shadow, reflection, or likeness. It is not "like" the original and at the same time exists outside the personality. For the primitives, while both the shadow and the reflection are the person, they are not confused.[82] Still, it is not enough to say,

811

> . . . that the shadow or the likeness is a 'second self,' as if it really had an existence apart from that of the 'first self.' Rather, they are only another aspect of the same 'self.'. . . To the primitive mind the reproduction is one being, the original another; they are two beings and yet the same being. It is equally true that they are two and that they are one: two in one, one in two. The primitive sees nothing extraordinary in that, although we think differently."[83]

812 The "second ego" comes close to being the "soul" of the same person. An idea related to the "shadow" is the *Ka* of the Egyptians.[84] The reflection goes beyond the shadow in the sense that it more closely matches the ego personality. If one takes possession of a person's mirror image, then, according to superstition, one has power over their life and death. Likewise, one must die

---

[80] Shortened from Wilhelm, *The Chinese Fairy Book*, pp. 168–174. For interesting examples of doppelgängers in life and literature, see G. Jacob, "Märchen and Traum," in: *Beiträge zur Märchenforschung des Morgenlandes*, Hannover, 1923, pp. 64–68.

[81] Lévy-Bruhl, *The "Soul" of the Primitive*, p. 141; see also *ibid.*, pp. 135ff.

[82] See *ibid.*, pp. 144 and 155.

[83] *Ibid.*, pp. 155–56, and also pp. 291–292.

[84] Cf. Güntert, *Weltkönig*, pp. 350–351, who refers to the Medieval *Schattenbuße* [shadow repentance], a rule mentioned in the *Sachsenspiegel* [Mirror of Saxony], the most important law book and legal code of the German Middle Ages, that people who were not considered honorable were only allowed to take revenge on the shadow of the offender. In one Indian legend, a certain demoness has the habit of seizing the shadows of those who approach her and thus attracting her victims so she can devour them.

if one sees one's spiritual double,[85] "because the person has given up this close connection to the body, and this signifies earthly death."[86] Although the double can be dangerous, it is evident from superstitions and ancient religious thought about both the shadow and mirrors that people felt the fructifying effect of this form of the soul. According to the myth of Dionysus, Persephone looked at herself in the mirror before she gave birth to Zagreus, which Rank states is a mythologem about "procreation through the interaction of personality and doppelgänger."[87] The spiritually fertilizing power of the shadow figure finds tragic expression in those sagas in which a person loses their shadow, for instance, when selling it to the devil.[88] In "The Constable," the Chinese fairytale retold above, the positive aspect comes to the fore in the figure of the magical double. This is not surprising after the reverential reception by the Chinese henchmen. Also, the shadow figure functions quite like a mirror image. As in "The Piper and the Púca," this is seldom the rule, because the "alter ego," which is connected to the person through *participation mystique*, need not be a likeness: similarity is not a necessary condition. *Participation mystique* may exist in the same sense and function between completely different beings (natures). The "alter ego" can also be an animal, a conception that leads to the idea of the dual nature (human-animal) and the double life (as in the werewolf).[89] We see this also in the related Mesoamerican

---

[85] In the conclusion of "The Housewife in Husavik," the dying person sees her double (doppelgänger) as a sign of approaching death.

[86] Güntert, *Weltkönig*, pp. 351ff. and 356f: "One can also find expression of popular views on the reflection and shadow in language. For instance, Old High German *scūchar*, 'mirror,' literally means "shadow container." Old Icelandic *skuggsjá* 'mirror,' is actually the 'shadow-seer.' (Anglosaxon *scuwo*, Old High German *scuwa*, to Old Icelandic *skugge*, 'shadow,' from which the Finnish *kuva*, 'image' is borrowed. Ancient Germanic *knuu[u]a*). Also similar is Old Irish *scathán* [mirror] undeniably a derivative of *scáth* [shadow]." See also *ibid* p. 377f. and Bächtold-Stäubli under *Der Spiegel* [the mirror]: "the fact that all over the world at all times special forces attributed to mirrors can be ascribed to a few simple facts of experience. The mirror shows everything in reverse, which suggests to a naive observer that something is strange and provides fertile ground for a "numinous" situation. . . The observer sees in the mirror what is behind him, the mirror seems to see more than one can observe oneself. This thought spun out into ideas of viewing through things and prophesying the future with the help of a mirror. The mirror mainly shows the viewer his own image. . . the mirror image is equal to the image and the shadow as a piece of extended self. . . Thus what has been said about the mirror image goes for the shadow as the soul and the double. . . Like the image and the shadow, the mirror image of a person is an essential part of his personality. . . Just as the shadow, the mirror image becomes the double. What happens to it happens to the person himself." See also Rank, *The Double*, pp. 69ff., and "The Misunderstood Mirror Image," a humorous Japanese tale collected in Hammitzsch et al., *Japanische*, p. 228 [in German].

[87] See Rank, *The Double*, p. 67, retranslated. [This is a quote from J. Negelein, "Ein Beitrag zum indischen Seelenwanderungsglauben," in *Archiv für Religionswissenschaften*, 1901.] See also *ibid.*, p. 67: the "late-Greek idea of the creation of the material world has its archetype in Indic cosmology, which took the reflection of the primeval essence to be the foundation of the material world." See the entire work by Rank with its rich material from legend and literature.

[88] This "generative effect" [in the sense of creative, giving birth, fertilizing, conceiving] is understood completely materialistically when, as in Lenau's poetic cycle *Anna* (taken after a Swedish legend), a woman without any shadow cannot conceive children. See also Bächtold-Stäubli under *Schatten* [shadow].

[89] Cf. Levy-Bruhl: ". . . what interests the primitive most, or even exclusively, when he sees his own image (shadow, reflection, etc.) is not the more or less faithful reproduction of his features, it is the

concepts of the *nagual* and the *tonal*.[90] For this reason the dark figure appears frequently in fairytales as an animal.[91] Contrary to the hero's expectations, this figure is helpful; without the animal's aid, he never would have attained his goals. By means of this image, the fairytale clearly indicates symbolically that the animal – unlike what the human thinks – is not inferior, but, in some respects, essential. A familiar example that addresses this issue is the fairytale, "Puss in Boots,"

813 There was once a miller who, when he died, left no more of his estate to his three sons than his mill, his mule, and his cat. The eldest son got the mill, the second the mule, and the youngest nothing but the cat. The poor young fellow was quite comfortless at having received such a poor lot. "My brothers," said he, "may get their living handsomely enough by joining their stocks together; but for my part, when I have eaten up my cat, and made myself a muff from his skin, I must die of hunger." The Cat, who heard all this, but made out as if he had not, said to his new master with a grave and serious air: "Do not thus affiict yourself, my good master. You have nothing else to do but to give me a bag and get a pair of boots made for me that I may scamper through the dirt and brambles, and you shall see that you have not so bad a portion in me as you imagine."

814 . . . When the Cat had what he asked for he booted himself very gallantly, and putting his bag about his neck, he held the strings of it in his two forepaws and went into a warren where there were many rabbits. Soon a rash and foolish young rabbit jumped into his bag, and Monsieur Puss, immediately drawing close the strings, took his bag and killed the contents without pity. Proud of his prey, he went with it to the palace and asked to speak with His Majesty. "I have brought you, sir, a rabbit of the warren, which my noble lord the Marquis of Carabas" (for that was the title which Puss was pleased to give his master) "has commanded me to present to your majesty from him." "Tell thy master," said the king, "that I thank him and that he does me a great deal of pleasure."

---

consubstantiality he imagines and feels between it and himself. Now this participation can in essence be also imagined and felt between himself and a being whose outward appearance is different from his own. This being will none the less be his double, his 'second self, his replica, his echo,' . . . Hence between this replica and the individual, at the same time as a real identity, there is a mystical resemblance, which does not depend for its existence on a material similitude of form and share." See Lévy-Bruhl, *The "Soul" of the Primitive*, pp. 157, 158–174, and 195–196.

[90] [See Daniel G. Brinton, *Nagualism. A Study in Native American Folk-lore and History*, 1894, *passim*.]

[91] Concerning the animal as an epiphany of the soul in superstition, see Bächtold-Stäubli under *Tier* [animal] and *Tiergestalt* [animal shapes]. See further O. Tobler, *Epiphanie*, Kiel, 1911, *passim*, esp. pp. 72ff, where Tobler indicates that the image of man riding an animal represents a doubling of the concept of the soul, which supports the interpretation of the animal as a shadowy double.

815 The Cat continued for two or three months thus to carry his Majesty, from time to time, game of his master's taking. One day he learned that the king was going to take his daughter for a walk on the riverbank. The Cat arranged that the son of the miller should bathe in the river during this time. When his master was bathing, the cat screamed for help, "the Marquis is drowning, thieves have stolen his clothes!" At this noise the King put his head out of the coach window, and, finding it was the Cat who had so often brought him such good game, he commanded his guards to run immediately to the assistance of his Lordship the Marquis of Carabas and to fetch one of his best suits for him. The fine clothes he had been given set off his good mien extremely well (for he was well made and very handsome in his person). So it was that the King's daughter took a secret inclination to him, and the Marquis of Carabas had no sooner cast two or three respectful and somewhat tender glances but she fell in love with him to distraction.

816 One time the king asked the marquis to join him in his carriage. The Cat ran ahead and told the mowers of a meadow and the reapers of a cornfield that when the king passed by and asked whose meadows and cornfields these belong to, they should on their lives say, "the Marquis of Carabas!" They did this and the King was quite impressed at the vast estates of my Lord Marquis of Carabas. Meanwhile Monsieur Puss came at last to a stately castle, the master of which was an ogre, the richest ogre that ever had been known; for all the lands which the King had then gone over actually belonged to him. Now the Cat, who had taken care to inform himself who this ogre was and what he could do, asked to speak with him, saying he could not pass so near his castle without having the honor of paying his respects. The ogre received him as civilly as an ogre could do, and made him sit down. The Cat proceeded to trick the ogre into changing himself into a mouse. No sooner had Puss perceived that than he but fell upon the mouse and ate him up.

817 Meanwhile the King, who saw, as he passed, this fine castle of the ogre's, had a mind to go into it. Puss, who heard the noise of his Majesty's coach running over the drawbridge, ran out, and said to the King: "Your Majesty is welcome to this castle of my Lord Marquis of Carabas." "What! my Lord Marquis," cried the King, "and does this castle also belong to you? There can be nothing finer than this court and all the stately buildings which surround it; let us go into it, if you please." His Majesty was perfectly charmed with the good qualities of my Lord Marquis of Carabas, as was his daughter, who had fallen

> violently in love with him, and, seeing the vast estate he possessed, said to him, after having drunk five or six glasses: "It will be owing to yourself only, my Lord Marquis, if you are not my son-in-law." The Marquis, making several low bows, accepted the honor which his Majesty conferred upon him, and forthwith, that very same day, married the Princess. Puss became a great lord, and never ran after mice anymore but only for his diversion.[92]

818 In the German version,[93] which was only included in the first edition of *The Nursery and Household Tales of the Brothers Grimm*, the boy expresses a certain contempt when he hears the Cat's request for boots. The German version has the boy saying, "What? A decent pair of boots you want, just like other people?" But then he sacrifices the last of his money for the boots. The same version also emphasizes that Puss "goes on two legs just like a man," and "because he looks so strange," and goes about "like a man in boots," the people fear him. And yet he becomes the head minister of his lord.

819 As the Cat, the shadow shimmers between human and animal form and is otherwise not choosy in his means. Considering his "boots," however, Puss is firmly on the ground, symbolizing a healthy instinct and a street "savvy" or cunning. As Jung pointed out, with the animal symbol, "we are dealing with an undisciplined, undifferentiated, and not yet humanized part of the libido, which still possesses the compulsive character of an instinct, a part still untamed by domestication."[94] Further: ". . . the animal symbol points specifically to the extra-human, the transpersonal; for the contents of the collective unconscious are not only the residues of archaic, specifically human modes of functioning, but also the residues of functions from man's animal ancestry."[95]This meaning, as untamed, impulsive, and instinctually driven nature, and at the same time supra-personal character, explains Puss's apparently odd behavior in the fairytale. This particular character emphasizes the earthy side (boots) with supernatural power and a connection to fraud and deceit, all in the service of the miller's son. To the extent that the son

---

[92] By Charles Perrault [original in French. English version (here slightly edited) by Lang originally published in 1889, reproduced in 1965, Andrew Lang, The Blue Fairy Book, Dover, New York, 1965.] The parallels include "The Cat and the Fool" (A. v. Löwis of Menar, Russische Volksmärchen, p. 68f) and the Russian fairytale, "Bukhtan Bukhtanovich" (see also the Caucasian version, "Bukutschichan," in Dirr, Kaukasische Märchen, p. 65f). In these tales, the helpful animal is a fox, whose cunning, lying, and humor contrast with the hero's colorless character. For an interesting variation, see "Die Federkönig" ["The Feather King"], collected in Zaunert, Deutsche Märchen seit Grimm, pp. 186–190. In this German tale, published "after Grimm," the helpful animal is a wildcat that abducts, robs, and then raises a boy. The wildcat later helps him find a bride and palace. After the hero beheads the cat she becomes a beautiful woman whom the hero calls "mother" and who marries the old king. Here images of the Great Mother and the shadow are combined. Both are symbols of the magical world in general.

[93] Cf. Bolte and Polívka, *Anmerkungen*, vol. 1, pp 325ff.

[94] C.G. Jung, *The Unconscious*, CW 7, ¶133.

[95] Ibid., ¶159.

represents ego consciousness, this portrayal represents the ego as being fairly weak and colorless. This is complemented from his unconscious by a perky cat. The acquisition of the boots is a conscious turning to the chthonic realm. The gifts to the king are insufficient efforts as long as it is the shadow who procures and presents them. That is why the Cat forces the hero to bathe in the river: to be immersed in the magical element and thus to experience a complete self- emptying (nakedness). Now begins his ascent, and the animal in him gradually overcomes the evil forces (mowers, reapers, ogres) that had possessed all goods without letting them become part of the young man's potential abilities to use them in order to come into life, just as they had not been available to his late father. The shadow figure thus creates a psychologically safe situation in which he can take command of his inner realm and resources in harmony with the princess. Now Puss the Cat fades into the background or - as in the German version - takes second place.

820 Just as an animal brother, at first scorned by the hero, becomes the mediator for obtaining the highest values, and just as an animal that has a very low standing in the animal kingdom is the only being capable of achieving the values of the upper world, is beautifully illustrated in the Mbundu (Angola) tale, "The Son of Kimanaueze and the Daughter of the Sun and Moon":[96]

> 821 I often tell of na Kimanaueze,[97] who begat a male child. The child grew up; he came to the age of marrying. His father said: "Marry." He said: "I will not marry a woman of the earth." His father said: "Then where wilt thou marry?" He said: "It must be that I marry the daughter of Lord Sun and Lady Moon." The people said: "Who can go to heaven, where is the daughter of Lord Sun and Lady Moon?" He said: "I indeed, I want her; I cannot marry her here, on earth."
>
> 822 He wrote a letter of marriage; he gave it to Deer. Deer said: "I cannot go to heaven." He gave it again to Antelope. Antelope said: "I cannot go to heaven." He gave it to Hawk. Hawk said: "I cannot go to heaven." He gave it to Vulture. Vulture said: "I can only reach halfway; I cannot get all the way to heaven." The young man said: "How shall I do it? " He laid it aside in his box; he kept quiet.
>
> 823 The people at Lord Sun and Lady Moon's used to come to get water on earth. Frog came; he found the son of Kimanaueze, and said:

[96] [The original, semi-literal translation in English is given here in full with only minor editing since von Franz and von Beit state that much is lost in the German translation. While the original mixes past and present, we have used the past for the sake of consistency.]

[97] ["Na" is an epithet of a name denoting veneration.]

"Young master,[98] give me the letter, that I may go with it." He, the young master, said: "Begone; where people of life, who have wings, gave it up, dost thou say: 'I will go there?' How canst thou get there?" Frog said: "Young master, I am equal to it." The son of Kimanaueze gave him the letter, saying: "If thou canst not go there, and thou return with it, I will give thee a thrashing."

824 Frog started; he went to the well, where the people of Lord Sun and Lady Moon were wont to come to get water. He put in his mouth the letter; he went into the well; he kept quiet. After a while, the people of Lord Sun and Lady Moon came to get water. They put a jug into the well; Frog entered into the jug.

825 They got the water; they lifted the jug up. They didn't know that Frog had entered into the jug. They arrived in heaven; they set down the jugs in their place; they went hence. Frog got out of the jug. In that room where they kept the jugs of water, they also kept a table. Frog spat out the letter; he set it on the top of the table. He went; he hid in the corner of the room.

826 After a while the Lord Sun himself came into the room where the water was kept; he looked on the table; a letter was there. He took it, asked, saying: "Whence comes this letter?" They said: "Lord, we don't know." Lord Sun opened it; he read it. It said, "I, son of na Kimanaueze kia Tumb'a a Ndala, on earth, I want to marry with the daughter of Lord Sun and Lady Moon." Lord Sun thought, saying in his heart; "Na Kimanaueze lives on earth; I am a man that lives in heaven; he who came with the letter, who is he?" He put away the letter into the box; he kept quiet.

827 Lord Sun finished reading the letter. Frog got into the jug. After a while, the water was out of the jugs; the water-girls lifted the jugs; they went back down to earth. They arrived at the well; they put the jugs in the water. Frog got out; he went under water, he bid his time. The girls finished bailing out, they went.

828 Frog came out of the water; he went to his village; he kept quiet. Many days passed. The son of na Kimanaueze asked Frog: "O fellow, where didst thou go with the letter, and how?'" Frog said: "Master, the letter, I delivered it; they have not yet returned an answer." The son of na Kimanaueze said: "O man, thou toldest a lie; thou didst not go there." Frog said: "Master, that same place where I went, thou shalt see."

[98] [Chatelain: "Na velu is the title of the son of a soba, used in addressing him. Velu is the native pronunciation of the Portuguese 'velho' (old man); but this cannot be its meaning in the present. 'Lord old man,' would not be a flattering title for a young prince."]

829 They spent six days; the son of na Kimanaueze wrote again a letter to ask about the former letter, saying: "I wrote to you, you Lord Sun and Lady Moon. My letter went up; not at all did you return an answer, saying, 'we accept thee,' or 'we refuse thee,' " He finished writing it; he closed it. He called Frog; he gave it to him. Frog started; he arrived at the well. He took in his mouth the letter; got into the water; he squatted on the bottom of the well.

830 After a while and the girls, the watercarriers, came down; they arrived at the well. They put the jugs into the water; Frog got into a jug. They finished filling; they lifted the jug up. They went up by the cobweb that Spider had woven. They arrived in heaven; they entered the house. They set down their jugs; they went. Frog stepped out of the jug; he spat out the letter. He laid it on the table; he hid in the corner.

831 After a while, the Lord Sun passed through the room where the water was. He looked on the table; a letter was there. He uncovered it; he read it. The letter said: "I, son of na Kimanaueze kia Tumbá Ndala, I ask thee, Lord Sun, about my letter, that went before. Not at all didst thou return me an answer." Lord Sun said: "You, girls, who always go to fetch water, are you always carrying letters?" The girls said: "We, master, no." Lord Sun, doubt possessed him; he laid the letter into the box. He wrote to the son of na Kimanaueze, saying: "Thou, who art sending me letters about marrying my daughter, I agree; on condition that thou in person, the man, comest with thy first-present; that I too may know thee." He finished writing; he folded the letter. He laid it on the table; he went away. Frog came out of the corner; he took the letter. He put it in his mouth; he entered into the jug; he kept quiet.

832 Evening came, Frog said: "Now I will take the letter." He spat it out; he arrived at the house of the son of na Kimanaueze. He knocked at the door; the son of na Kimanaueze asked, saying: "Who?" Frog says: "I am Mainu the Frog." The son of na Kimanaueze got up from bed where he had been reclining and said, "Come in." Frog went in; he delivered the letter; he went out. The son of na Kimanaueze he uncovered it; he read it. What Lord Sun announced, it pleased him. He thought to himself, "Frog, why, it was his truth that he told me, saying, 'Thou shalt see where I went.'" He paused; he slept.

833 In the morning, he took forty macutas; and wrote a letter, saying: "You, Lord Sun and Lady Moon, the first-present is coming; I remain to seek for the wooing-present. You there, tell me the amount of the wooing-present." He finished the letter; called Mainu the Frog. He came; he gave him the letter and the forty macutas, saying: "Carry." The Frog started, he arrived at the well. He entered under the well; he

kept quiet. After a while, the girls came down; they put the jugs in the water; Frog entered into a jug. The girls finished filling; they took the jugs up. They went up by the cobweb; they arrived in the room of the water. They set down the jugs; they left.

834 Frog got out of the jug; he put down the letter on the table with the money.[99] He went; hid in the corner. After a while, the Lord Sun came into the room of the water; he found the letter on the table. He took it with the money; he read it. He told his wife the news that came from the son-in-law; his wife assented.

835 Lord Sun said: "Who is coming with these letters, I do not know him; his food, how shall it be cooked?" His wife said: "We will cook it anyhow, and put it on the table, where the letter usually lie." Lord Sun said: 'Very well." They killed a mother hen; they cooked it. Evening came; they cooked the mush. They set the eatables on the table; they shut the door. Frog came to the table; he ate the victuals. He went to the corner; he kept quiet.

836 Lord Sun wrote a letter, saying: "Thou, son-in-law of mine, the first-present, which thou hast sent me, I have received. For the amount of the wooing-present, thou shalt give me a sack of money." He finished the letter; he laid it on the table; he went. Frog came out of the corner; took the letter. He entered the jug; he slept.

837 Morning came, the girls took the jugs; they went down to the earth. They arrived at the well; they put the jugs into the water. Frog got out of the jug. The girls finished filling; they went up.

838 Frog went out from the water; he arrived in their village. He entered into his house; he waited. The sun was gone; evening had come; he said: "I will now bring the letter." He set off; he arrived at the house of the son of na Kimanaueze. He knocked at the door; the son of na Kimanaueze answered: "Who?" Frog said: "I am Mainu the Frog."

839 Said he: "Come in." Frog went in; he gave the letter; he went out. The son of na Kimanaueze uncovered the letter; he read it; then he set it aside.

840 He spent six days; he collected the sack of money. He called Frog; Frog came. The son of na Kimanaueze wrote a letter, saying; "You, my parents-in-law, the wooing-present comes here; soon I myself, I shall

---

[99] [Chatelain: "A saku is thirty 'milreis fortes' which is nearly thirty-three American dollars. In the present case, it looks as though the saku was paid in paper (in macutas), and not in copper [as was normal]; for a saku of copper is exactly one man's load, and for the water-girl not to notice such an addition to the weight of her jug would be a big 'poetical license.'"]

find a day to bring home my wife." The letter, he gave it to the Frog, with the money.

841 Frog started; he arrived at the well. He went in underwater; he hid. After a while, the water-carriers came down; they arrived at the well. They put the jugs into the water; Frog entered into a jug. They finished filling; they take up. They went up by way of the cobwebs of Spider; they arrived in heaven. They set down the jugs in the room of the water; they went out. Frog got out of the jug; he laid down the letter on the table with the money. He went into the corner; he hid. Lord Sun came into the house of the water; he found the letter and the money. He took them; he showed the money to his wife, Lady Moon. Lady Moon said: "Very well." They took a young hog; they killed it. They cooked the food; they set it down on table; they shut the door. Frog came to eat; he ate. He finished; entered into the jug and slept.

842 Morning came, the water-carriers took up the jugs; they went down to earth. They arrived at the well; they dipped their jugs into the water, Frog got out of the jug; he hid. They finished filling and went back to heaven. Frog went ashore; he arrived in their village. He entered his house; he kept quiet and slept.

843 Next morning, Frog went to the son of na Kimanaueze and said: "Young master, where I went, I gave them the wooing-present; they received it. They cooked me a young hog; I ate. Now, thou thyself shalt choose the day of going to bring her home." The son of na Kimanaueze said: "Very well." They lived on; ten days and two.

844 The son of na Kimanaueze said; "I need people to go to bring home the bride for me; I cannot find any. They say, "We cannot go to heaven." "Now, what shall I do, thou, Frog?" Frog said:

845 "My young master, be quiet; I am equal to it, to go and bring her home." The son of na Kimanaueze said: "Thou canst not. Thou couldst indeed carry the letters, but bring her home thou canst not." Frog said again: "Young master, be quiet; be not troubled for naught. I indeed am able to go and bring her home; do not despise me." The son of na Kimanaueze said: "Let me try thee." He took victuals; he gave them to Frog.

846 Frog started on his way; he arrived at the well. He climbed into the well; he hid. After a while, the water-carriers came down; they arrived at the well. They dipped in their jugs; Frog entered them. They filled them up; they went back to heaven. They arrived in the room of the water; they set down the jugs; they went. Frog got out of the jug; he hid in the corner. The sun set; in the evening of the night, Frog went

out of the room of the water; he went seeking the room where the daughter of Lord Sun slept, He found her asleep here. He took out one of her eyes; he took out again the other. He tied them up in a handkerchief; he came in the room of the water, in his corner. He hid; he slept.

847 In the morning, all the people got up. The daughter of Lord Sun could not get up. They asked her: "Dost thou not get up ?" She said: "My eyes are closed; I cannot see." Her father and mother said: "What may have caused this? Yesterday, she did not complain."

848 Lord Sun takes up two messengers, saying: "Go to Ngombo, to seek divination about my child, whose eyes are sick." They started out; they arrived at the Ngombo-man's. The Ngombo-man took out his [divining] bundle.[100] They do not let [the Ngombo-man] know the disease; they say only: "We have come to be divined." The Ngombo-man looked into the paraphernalia, says: "Disease has brought you; the one who is sick is a woman; the sickness that ails her, the eyes. You have come, being sent; you have not come of your own will. I have spoken." The divining people said: "Truth. Look now what caused the ailment." The Ngombo-man looked again; he said: "She, the woman who is sick, is not yet married; she is chosen only. Her master, who bespake her, he sent the spell,[101] saying, 'my wife, let her come; if she does not come, she shall die.' You, who came to divine, go, bring her to her husband, that she may escape. I have spoken." Those who sought the divination assented; they got up. They found Lord Sun; they reported to him the words of the Ngombo-man. Lord Sun said: "All right. Let us sleep; tomorrow they shall take her down to the earth."

849 Frog, in his corner, heard all that they had said. In the morning, Frog got into the jug; the water-carriers came; they took up the jugs. They descended to the earth; they arrived at the well. They put the jugs into the water; Frog came out of the jug. He hid under the well. The water-carriers went up.

850 Lord Sun told Spider, saying: "Weave a large cobweb, down to the earth; for today is the taking down of my daughter to the earth." Spider wove; finished. They passed time in waiting.

---

[100] [Chatelain: "Literally kila = a bundle. . . It consists of bones, claws, rags, hairs, etc., which the diviner shakes in his divining basket before throwing them on the ground. From the positions taken by the different objects, he reads, or divines, what the visitors want to know."]

[101] [Chatelain: "U-anga, with which compare ng-anga, wizard, signifies witchcraft, both criminal and non-criminal. Here, as the young man is simply supposed to have secured the aid of spirits in order to obtain his due, and not to destroy wantonly, or unjustly, his u-anga is not of the sort that would stamp him a muloji (wizard)."]

851 Frog got out of the well; he went to their village. He found the son of na Kimanaueze, and said: "O young master! Thy bride, today she comes." The son of na Kimanaueze said: "Begone, man, thou art a liar." Frog said: "Master, truth itself. I will bring her to thee in the evening of the night." They kept quiet.

852 Frog returned to the well; he got into the water; he was silent. The sun set; the daughter of Lord Sun, they brought her down to the earth. They left her at the well; they went up again.

853 Frog got out of the well; he spoke to the young woman, saying: "I myself am thy guide; let us go that I may bring thee to your master." Frog returned her eyes to her; they started. They entered the house of the son of na Kimanaueze. Frog said: "O young master! Thy bride is here." The son of na Kimanaueze said: "Welcome! Mainu the Frog." The son of na Kimanaueze married the daughter of Lord Sun and Lady Moon; they lived on. They all had given up hope of going to heaven; the only one who could do it was Mainu, the Frog.

854 I have told my little story. Finished.[102]

855 While the winged creatures, which represent spiritual beings, do not reach heaven, a cunning swamp animal manages to attain the lofty goals of his lord. Here the frog plays the typical role of a shadow figure, which becomes clear when one considers the encounter of the "young master" with him. The son of na Kimanaueze is suspicious and arrogant towards Mainu; he calls him a liar and only at the end says "Welcome, Mainu!" Besides the frog, the spider, who as already stated is a symbol of the Great Weaver and Mother Nature, produces with her thread the delicate connection between above and below, heaven and earth. The spider's web is as fine as a sunbeam. Nature uses such a delicate way to maintain the cycle between above and below and to connect the interdependent spheres. Only the frog, who peeks out from the depths, knows this mysterious way. The frog is the instinct that knows the hidden connections. While a hint of malicious-inferior properties appears in the eyes of the Sun's daughter being stolen, this act brings about the hero's longed-for connection with his beloved wife. Floating on the light fabric of the Great Mother, she comes from the source down to Earth, where the magic helper returns her sight and leads her to the groom.

856 The shadow does not always have such a nourishing side. There are tales of primitive peoples in which the shadow is portrayed as a hostile brother, who destroys all people's good work. In such a case, the story reflects the situation of the primitive for whom the conscious cultural life, the formative

[102] Told by Jeremía dia Sabatelu to Chatelain in 1890–91, Chatelain pp. 131–141.

action, is the developmental goal they are striving for. Certain forces in the unconscious, however, work to divert the efforts. The shadow, therefore, becomes the cause of fatal dangers. A simple example of this type is the series of tales from Melanesia [Gazelle Peninsula, East New Britain, Papua New Guinea], "Three Stories of the Brothers To Kabinana and To Karwuwu:"

1 The Fish

857 To Kabinana carved a tuna from wood and threw him into the sea. There he became alive. As thanks for this he then always drove sardines onto the beach so that To Kabinana could comfortably catch and carry them home. When his brother, To Karwuwu, saw the great multitude of fishes, he also wanted to have some and asked his brother: "Tell me, where is this fish? I would like to eat some." "All right, then make yourself a fish. Carve it the way I did, it must be a tuna."

858 To Karwuwu now made a fish. But he did not do what his brother said, he carved a shark. He threw his carved shark into the waters, the shark swam to the sardines, but it ate them all up and To Karwuwu got none to eat. Weeping, he went back to his brother and said, "I could not make a fish like you did. Mine just ate all the sardines." To Kabinana asked him: "What kind of fish did you make?"

859 "Well, I whittled myself a shark," said To Karwuwu. His brother answered, saying only, "You are a terrible fool, and our demise. Your fish will eat up all the others and do us no good." Since then the shark eats not only the other fish, but also attacks people.

2 Shedding Skin

860 One day To Karwuwu was roasting breadfruit. Then came To Kabinana who walked straight up to him and asked, "Are you cooking there?" "Yes." "Why do you do it secretly? So that mother does not know it? Bring her also half a breadfruit."

861 To Karwuwu went to the hut of his mother. She had shed her skin and had become a young maiden. On that account her son did not recognize her. He asked, "Where are you, my Mother?"

862 "I'm here." "No," he replied, "You're not my mother."

863 "You're wrong," she said, "I am she." "But you do not look like my mother!"

864 "But I am. I just shed and got a new skin." To Karwuwu wept bitterly because his mother had a different skin and he did not recognize her.

"I cannot bear you anymore," said her son, "I do not like how you look in your new skin. Tell me, where did you leave your old skin?" She replied: "I threw it into the water, it has surely washed away." To Karwuwu cried: "Oh, your new skin, I do not like it, I will seek out the old skin."

865 He got up, went and searched and searched until he finally found the skin hanging in a thicket. The waters had washed it there and left it hanging. He took the skin with him and returned to his mother. He pulled the old skin onto her. In the evening, his brother, To Kabinana, came home and asked To Karwuwu: "Why did you pull the old skin over our mother? She had stripped it off! You are really a big fool! Now our children must always die. And only snakes will shed their skin."

866 To Kabinana was very angry about what To Karwuwu said because it meant that people could no longer shed their skins, only snakes could. Annoyed, he stamped on the head of the snake until it became wide. "You have made it so we cannot molt!" he said to To Karwuwu. And thus it is that people do not molt, only snakes. Actually, we could do it originally, and then we would become young again.

The Breadfruit

867 One day, To Kabinana went out and caught six live snakes, which he tied together with string. Then he went into the forest, to a place where breadfruit trees were standing. But these belonged to the devils. He climbed up a tree and tried to bring down some of the fruit. The devils kept a watchful eye on their trees, however, and guarded them carefully so that nobody would steal the fruits. In spite of this, To Kabinana picked a breadfruit, pulled a snake out from his bundle and threw them both down so that they struck the ground with force. The devils heard the noise and thought it was someone picking their breadfruit. When they saw the snake, they went after it and forgot about the breadfruit.

868 To Kabinana picked another breadfruit and again threw it down with a snake. Again the devils went after the snake. This he continued to do until he had no more snakes and then he climbed down the tree. While the devils were hunting the snakes in the forest To Kabinana gathered up the breadfruit and went home to his brother. To Karwuwu asked him, "Brother, what kind of fruit do you have there?" "These are breadfruit." "Where can I get them?" "Down there."

869 To Karwuwu spoke, "Fine, I'll go get some myself, I'll climb up that tree." To Kabinana told him, "You will probably do something stupid again." Ha, ha! I will fetch some for you and me, just you wait and see!" "Well, go ahead! But you better catch some live snakes first!" said To Kabinana.

870 To Karwuwu went to the breadfruit trees. He struck the snakes dead and then climbed up the tree. He grabbed one of the breadfruits and threw it down at the same time with a dead snake. This time the devils did not chase the snake because it did not flee; the snake just lay on the forest floor because it was dead. The devils saw the breadfruit lying there and said: "Who is throwing down our breadfruit and trying to hoodwink us? We will flush you out!"

871 So the devils climbed up and seized To Karwuwu and beat him terribly. He yelled for help: "Oh! To Kabinana, my brother! Come, stand by me! Blow the conch shell and beat the drums!"

872 To Kabinana blew the conch shell and beat the drums and the devils fled. To Karwuwu was able to descend from the tree and went to his brother. To Kabinana asked, "What have you done with the breadfruit?" "I killed the snakes, and when I threw down a bread fruit and a snake, the devils did not chase it."

873 "Oh, the world has never seen such a fool as you! I told you exactly what to do, you need the snakes to be alive! What kind of devil would chase after a dead snake? Now all our children will be afraid of the devils, and they will pursue them. And because you threw a dead snake from the tree, all that falls from trees will fall to death."

874 And so it is, that which falls from a tree remains dead.[103]

875 Hambruch notes: "From other stories not given here it is clear that To Kabinana, the inventor and representative of all that is good, the wise one, is the bright moon. He is contrasted with To Karwuwu, the blunderer and fool, the ne'er do well and mischief-maker, as the dark moon. The contrasting natures of the phases of the moon are excellently represented in these two personalities. The aboriginals revere them both as their ancestors, exerting a decisive influence on all aspects of the lives of their descendants. From the beginning they stand as real people who confront, play with, and provoke the spirits."[104]

---

[103] Hambruch, *Südsee*, Jena, 1921, pp. 50–54 [original source: P. Jos. Meier, "Mythen und Erzählungen der Kustenbewohner der Gazelle-Halbinsel (Neu-Pomern)," in: *Anthropos, Internationale Sammlung Ethnologischer Monographien*, vol. 1, Münster i. .W. 1909, pp. 58–76].

[104] Hambruch, *Südsee*, pp. 342–43.

876 These two characters, tribal ancestors of all humans, represent two basic functions of all humankind: on the one hand, the creative, life- promoting, and constructive activity of conscious humans; and, on the other, they are oafish caricatures, who play irrationally and destructively with their methods.[105] While the playful blunderer is not necessarily damaging, he is when he becomes an uncontrolled companion to people and usurps the plans of consciousness.

877 In the second story, To Karwuwu evolves into a personal superhuman demon who brings death into the world. He almost changes into the chthonic dark father god.[106] (Recall how, in "Makonaura and Anuanaitu," Anuanaitu's slain crocodile brother shared a secret identity with his father, Kaikutschi.)

878 Although the shadow can, on the one hand, be a hostile enemy power opposed to consciousness, human behavior, on the other hand, requires a certain sensitivity. Consciousness may not aggressively oppose the shadow because it mediates the connection to the Earth and represents human instincts; it is after all, "the other one in me."[107] The recognition and acknowledgment of this fact could show people the correct way to deal with the shadow. Often, however, the path to this awareness first leads through human suffering, as, for example, in the "The Two Travelers":[108]

879 Hill and vale do not meet, but the children of men do, good and bad. In this way a shoemaker and a tailor once met on their travels. The tailor was a handsome little fellow who was always merry and full of

---

[105] For further tales that juxtapose these two figures, see "The Old Man Who Brought the Withered Trees Back to Bloom," in which a kind-hearted man gets a dog out of nowhere. The dog shows the old man where to dig for gold. An envious neighbor borrows the dog for himself, but finds only garbage and kills the dog. The kind-hearted old man buries the dog under a pine tree and waters it with his tears. The pine tree grows quickly, and the old man cuts it down. He grinds the wood of the tree in a handmill and out comes gold and silver with the sawdust. Again, the envious neighbor borrows the handmill but it produces just rubbish, so he burns it. The ashes bring withered trees to bloom, and the prince hears of this wonder. He invites the old man to come and revive some of his trees. The old man comes, the trees live again, and he is richly rewarded. When the envious one again attempts to save the royal's trees, ashes fly into the prince's eye and the envious man is beaten up. See also three other Japanese fairytales, "The Golden Rain," "Should We Keep It, Should We Drop It?," and "Raven Stories." Also the following variants of the mill motif. One Icelandic tale, "The Mill That Mills Everything," tells of the all-grinding mill that an envious man took over but could not bring to a standstill so that his ship sinks and the mill now grinds salt on the seabed. See also the Danish fairytale "The Mill On the Ocean Floor," and the German "Why Seawater Is Salty," and the Japanese tale with the same title, "Why Seawater Is Salty." See also Grimm's fairytale "Simeli Mountain."

[106] The Aztecs distinguished Quetzalcoatl, the good god and savior, from Tezcatlipoca, his adversary and a dark deity. Texzcatlipoco appears also in human form as a shadow and is regarded as the sender of dreams and fantasies; see Róheim, *Spiegelzauber*, pp. 235ff.

[107] On this problem, see C.G. Jung, *Psychologie und Religion*, CW 11, ¶133ff.

[108] This story seems to have been moralized by the Grimm Brothers; see Bächtold-Stäubli, who mentions several variants under the heading "two unequal brothers": for example, "Veritas and Falsitas," "The Wicked and the Righteous," and, "Fa-bene and Fa-male." See also Bolte and Polívka, *Anmerkungen*, vol. 2, pp. 468ff. See especially "The Rich and the Poor" (Spain), "The Three Ravens" (Ireland), "The Lie and the Truth" (Donau), and "What is Better: Truth or Lies?" (Finland). This theme is taken up in a later volume.

enjoyment. He saw the shoemaker coming towards him from the other side, and as he observed by his bag what kind of trade he plied, he sang a little mocking song to him:

880 Sew me the seam,
Draw me the thread,
Spread it over with pitch,
Knock the nail on the head.

881 The shoemaker, however, could not bear a joke; he pulled a face as if he had drunk vinegar, and made a gesture as if her were about to seize the tailor by the throat. But the little fellow began to laugh, reached him his bottle, and said: "No harm was meant, take a drink, swallow your anger down."[109] They traveled onwards together, and " always set one foot before the other like a weasel in the snow." As they wandered through a forest, the tailor, who had trusted God and only took bread for two days, became so thin and starved that he asked his companion, the shoemaker, for a bite from his bread. This the shoemaker gave, but in return poked out the tailor's right eye. When the next day the tailor again could no longer walk and asked for a second bite, the shoemaker again gave him a morsel of bread and struck out his right eye. He led the now blind tailor onwards but left him beneath the gallows at the entrance to the next town. Above where the blind tailor lay, hung two men on the gallows, a crow sitting on each head. One of the hanged men said to the other:[110] "Brother, are you awake?" "Yes, I am." "Do you know that the dew, which this night has fallen down over us from the gallows, gives eyesight to anyone who washes himself with it?" Hearing this, the tailor took out his pocket handkerchief, pressed it on the grass, and washed out the sockets of his eyes. Immediately new eyes filled them. With the sun the tailor arose and now could see again as well as before. He thanked God for his mercy and prayed for the poor sinners hanging there swinging in the wind, and made his way into the town.

882 Along the way he met a young colt whom he would have liked to ride, but it asked to be spared since it was too young to carry him. Maybe later when it was older, it said. The tailor agreed, but his hunger drove him to hunt the next edible thing that crossed his path. He came upon a stork, seized it, and wanted to roast it up on the spot. But the stork

[109] [From here, the German version is translated as paraphrased by von Franz and von Beit.] See the full-length English version in *Complete Grimm's*, pp. 486–496.
[110] [In some versions, it is the crows that speak; see discussion below.]

pleaded for its life, saying it was a sacred bird that brings mankind great profit. Again the tailor acquiesced, and set the stork free. With his hunger biting deeper, he came upon some young ducks, whose father spoke up to the tailor just before he was about to wring the young one's necks. The tailor again set them free and came upon a hive of wild bees. About to devour their honey, the queen bee threatened him with stings and offered their services at a later time. The starving tailor entered the city, found work, and soon became famous. At last the king appointed him as court-tailor.

883 Odd things happen in the world, so did they in those times. On the very same day that the tailor was appointed, his old companion became the king's shoemaker. When he caught sight of the tailor with two good eyes, he feared that his evil would be revenged. His conscience troubled him and set his mind to kill the poor chap. The shoemaker counseled the king that his new court-tailor had arrogantly boasted that he would get back the gold crown that had been lost in ancient times. Long desiring the ancient crown, the king ordered the tailor to bring back the crown or leave the town. Sadly, the tailor decided to leave town immediately since he knew the task set him was impossible to fulfil. In the forest, he sat by a pond and mourned the loss of the good job he had. Then he saw the now grown-up ducks whose lives he had spared. They came to him and asked why his head was hanging down so. He told the ducks his story. They listened and said "If that be all, we can help you. The crown fell into these waters, and lies below at the bottom of this pond!" In five minutes the ducks had together brought up the heavy crown. The tailor took it to the king who rewarded him richly. The shoemaker, now vilified, informed the king that the tailor had in secret boasted he could make a copy in wax of the whole palace "and everything that pertains to it, moving or immovable, within and without." Such a wonderful thing the king could not let pass and ordered the tailor to fulfil his boast or be imprisoned for the rest of his life.

884 Again the tailor left the town before being put in imprisonment deep underground. This time the bees found him and reported his plight to the queen bee. She organized her bees to make the wax palace and the next morning the bees brought it the tailor. He wrapped it carefully and took it to the king. Again the tailor was richly rewarded, this time with an admirable stone house. The shoemaker could not bear this success and went a third time to the king and whispered that the tailor, hearing that no water welled up in the courtyard, boasted that he could make a spring as high as a man on horseback and as clear as crystal.

This time the king ordered the tailor to fulfil his boast or lose his head. Again, the tailor left town before he lost his head. This time he met the horse, whose life he had saved as a young colt. The horse had already heard the news and told the tailor to climb on his back and hold on. They galloped into the town and raced three times around the palace. Suddenly, with a clap of thunder, the horse and rider fell down and on that spot a fountain shot up as high as a man on horseback and as pure as crystal. The king embraced the tailor in joy.

885 Luck did not, however, last long. It so happened that the king had daughters, one prettier than the next, but none had born a son. Again the shoemaker whispered to the king that the arrogant tailor had announced that he could cause a son to be brought forth. The king summoned the tailor and said he must cause a son to be born within nine days, if he succeeded he would get the eldest daughter in marriage. "The reward is great," thought the tailor, "but the cherries grow too high for me. If I climb for them, the bough will surely break beneath me and I shall fall." Tying up his bundle the tailor went out of the king's gates. There in a meadow he met the stork, pacing back and forth like a philosopher, pausing at each turn and standing first on one leg, and then the other. Hearing the tailor's tale, the stork said, "For a long time now I have carried the children in swaddling clothes into the town, so for once I can fetch a little prince out of the well. Go home and be easy. In nine days I will come." Sure enough, at the appointed time the stork flew to the window of the tailor with a bundle. He brought the bundle to the queen. The eldest princess got none of the colored sweetmeats at the festival but she received the merry tailor as a husband. The shoemaker had to make the wedding shoes for the tailor in which he danced at the wedding festival. His evil conniving was uncovered and he was ordered to leave town. He came to the gallows, and worn out with anger, lay down to sleep. The two crows flew down from the heads of the men who were hanging there and pecked out his eyes. In his madness he ran into the forest and he must have died there of hunger, for ever since no one either saw or heard of him.

886 This tale highlights the contrast between the two travelers. The shoemaker with his evil, dully materialistic, and earthbound ways personifies a typical shadow. He contrasts and complements the light, merry, cheerful but air bound, impractical side of the little tailor. While the latter lives life from the light-hearted side, the one "from the other side" joins him, the ill-tempered villain. In parallel versions,[111] this alter-ego character is called "the evil

[111] See Bolte and Polívka, *Anmerkungen*, vol. 2, p. 476.

brother." Soon after their initial meeting (probably closely related to the emergence of the shadow), the trail leads the two into a large forest. This tells us that the tailor's shadow entangles him in the depths of the unconscious. There it turns out that only the shadow has packed enough bread for the worst case and the merry tailor is now dependent on him for nourishment. Bread loaves symbolize the body itself, which belongs to the realm of the shadow. The tailor took this valuable possession of the shadow, that is, his bodily needs, too little into account. The shadow possesses the nourishing substance without which consciousness would starve.

887 The shoemaker sells the bread for the tailor's eyes and leads the blind man to the gallows. This "blinding" means that the material side of the tailor, personified here as his cobbler companion, suddenly "deludes"[112] the ego, the lighter side. That is, we might even say that the tailor, having overshadowed his real needs for material nourishment, succumbs to an unconscious overcompensation and falls into the illusion of material reality. As a result, he loses orientation, towards both his inner world (awareness of bodily needs) and his outer world (environmental realities). By leading the cobbler to the gallows, the shadow leads him into contact – at least in the auditory sense – with the criminals' sheer despair and to total spiritual darkness. The conflict with the shadow as the opponent has brought the ego to the brink of annihilation. Only then can a different inner voice, that of nature, be heard. In the moment of complete hopelessness and demolishment of human will, transformation occurs: the shadow appears in another form, here as the savior. The two corpses begin to speak and proclaim the healing message; according to some versions, even the whole future. In a parallel Irish version, "The Three Ravens," it is the crows that begin to speak, as in other parallel versions.[113] The dead sinners are practically identical with the crows (or ravens) perched on their heads. They are the dead within us, the side that has not yet come to life, and at the same time our dark bird of ill omen. In a tale from Rote Island (Indonesia), "The Story of the Blind King Who Lived in the Western Lands," the hero must first serve a dead man, symbolizing the shadow, before the latter gratefully helps him further.[114]

888 The crows sitting on the hanged men's heads are birds of ill omen, and hover, like the raven, over battlefields and gallows.[115] According to old Germanic folk belief, the crow is a very clever animal.[116] Mythologically, crows are in some places good, elsewhere evil spirits. They are sacred birds or even gods, as "Raven" in Siberian, Inuit, and many Native American tribes from

---

[112] [German *verblendet*, literally "blinded."]
[113] Cf. Bolte and Polívka, *Anmerkungen*, vol. 2, pp. 468ff.
[114] Hambruch, *Malaiische*, pp. 143–155.
[115] Cf. Ninck, *Wodan*, p. 99.
[116] See Bächtold-Stäubli under *Krähe* [crow].

the Pacific Northwest. In India, crows were assigned to the deities Kali and Yama, the gods of the dead, whereas in Estonia it was a bird of light. The Romans regarded crows as demonic beings and the Germanic Valkyries, which were originally considered birds that devoured corpses, wore crow shirts (vestments). Superstition had it that crows were companions of the devil and witches appeared in their form. In India, the crow was the shadow of the dead(!) and received food offerings. On the other hand, popular belief held that the crow knows the source of living water and is an oracular animal. The crow is the wife[117] of the raven; in general, crows and ravens were often confused.[118] The raven is the animal of the churchyard and High Court. It knows the mysterious forces of nature and can speak. If one overhears crows chattering on the gallows, one can learn many things. In antiquity, two ravens were the messengers of the sun god and also of Mithras; they were attendants of Helios and Apollo, who himself appeared as a raven. While the raven appears in the myths of many people sometimes as a light and sometimes as a dark demon, in Buddhism the benevolent demon of fate had a raven's head. In Norse/Germanic mythology, the raven is both the animal of the world of the dead and the god of death, of the hanged, sacrificed Odin/Woden,[119] and the birds of corpses and souls of evil. They were also the birds of the poet: Odin/Woden stole the mead of poets in the shape of a raven or eagle. In ancient Germanic belief the two ravens, Huginn and Muninn (thought and memory), are Odin's companions. They sit on Odin's shoulders and bring him news of the world. Odin is also called the "raven investigator," and the raven that he sends out is always a bearer of fate, a messenger of death or victory.[120] These black birds signify death, tragedy, or grief.[121] Significantly, the hero of a

---

[117] [Crow is a feminine noun in German.]

[118] Cf. Bächtold-Stäubli under *Raben* [raven].

[119] [Translators and literary historians are at odds whether Odin/Woden as "the hanged/hung one" meant that he was hanged by others or by himself.]

[120] Cf. Ninck, *Wodan*, pp. 7, 15, 91–99, 174–175; Mogk, *Germanische*, pp. 65 and 70.

[121] Cf. also Weicker, *Seelenvogel*, Leipzig, 1902, p. 27. For the raven as a symbol of desolation see the Inuit tale, "The One Who Finds Nothing." Here, a small, ugly-faced young man who could never find anything that he looked for would return empty handed from his exploits and sit desolate in his hut. "Whenever this man, 'One-who-finds-nothing,' went out with his sled for wood, he returned without anything. He could not even find water for himself and had to rely on others. One day he took his miserable bed and rolled it up with his poor tool bag, put the bundle on his back, and went out to the landward side of the village, beyond the houses, and sat down. Once seated, he took his bundle from his back and, opening it, untied his tool bag. This being done, he scattered the tools about him and threw away the bag. Then he spread down his bed and, sitting upon it, lay back, saying, 'Here will I die.' Two ravens came; one wanted to pick his eyes out, but the other said that the man was not dead, and flew away. The other decided to go for the eyes, but at the last second One-who-finds-nothing snatched the raven's knife away. Back sprang Raven, and the man sat up. 'Give me my knife,' said Raven. One-who-finds-nothing answered, saying, 'I have no knife, and this shall be my knife.' Raven replied, 'I will pay you for it with all kinds of game.' 'No,' said the man, 'I will not give it back. I always go out hunting and can get nothing.' 'Then,' said the Raven, 'if you wish to go back to the village you will not reach there when you try.' 'I have no knife,' replied the man. Raven coughed and fell down, saying, 'Thus will you do. Keep my knife, if you prize it,' said he, and flew away. The man sat up, still keeping the knife. Then he started to go back to the village. As he was going his throat contracted, his back bent over in front, and he rested his hands on his knees. Suddenly he became an old man. He could not walk. He

Spanish variant, "The Rich and the Poor," overhears devils conversing instead of crows. The crows that appear in the tale of the tailor and the shoemaker emphasize the hero's gloom and blindness, a prerequisite for the wise intuitions that later arise from the depths.[122]

889 The fact that *two* crows tell of the future and perch on *two* gallows below which the blinded tailor lies suggests a dissolution of the shadow into an internal opposition. The cobbler no longer stands opposite the tailor as a concentrated charge of hostile energy, but instead personifies a healing alongside a destructive force.

890 The two crows reveal that dew can heal the tailor's eyes. Dew appears here as a healing water. It is regarded as pure water from the heavenly hereafter and, therefore, contains divine spirit. In the Christian allegory, therefore, dew means the coming of the Holy Spirit or the Logos.[123] Thus the healing of the hero's blindness by the dew reflects a recovery of spiritual knowledge and a new vision of reality. In the Irish tale, "The Three Ravens," it is the herb of life instead of dew. In this tale, three boys go into a forest. Two of them blind the third one, who, overhearing a conversation between some ravens, learns that a curing herb grows at the place where his gouged out eyes are lying. If he picks this herb, he can cure the princess.[124] When he recovers his eyesight, he can see even better than before! Equipped with the herb, he cures the king's daughter and strikes open a spring for drinking water from a cliff near the city, which is dying of thirst. For these deeds, he receives the king's daughter as wife. The two villains, however, are then blinded by ravens. In still other parallels, the healing water comes from a burned toad and water.[125] Blinding through evil workings and healing by the water of life is a common fairy tale motif. In "Prince Hassan Pasha,"[126] for example, the hero is blinded by his brothers and, after forty days of prayer to Allah, he finds a healing spring and sees "God's light" again. In the Grimm's tale, "The King's Son, Who Feared Nothing," the hero is blinded by a giant, and with the help of a lion, discovers the healing waters of a river and regains his eyesight.[127]

---

lay on his face. He did not stir. He was dead." W. E. Nelson, *Eskimo - Bering Strait*, Washington, D.C., 1900, pp. 474–475.

[122] See Tiresias and Phineas, the ancient Greek seers, who were blinded, in some versions, for revealing too many of the god's secrets.

[123] On the widespread symbolism of the water of life, which to the minds of the medieval alchemists signified the eye water of the philosophers or as the *ros Gedeonis* (= dew of Gideon) see C.G. Jung, *Psychologie und Religion*, CW 11, ¶160–161, esp. fn. 69; see also his *Psychology and Alchemy* CW 12, ¶154ff, 336ff, 475ff. See also Reitzenstein, *Hellenistic Mystery-Religions*, pp. 306–307.

[124] Bolte and Polívka, *Anmerkungen*, vol. 2, pp. 470–471: "the blinded one learns by eavesdropping on the birds not only the secret of how to regain his eyesight, but also how he can cure the king's sick daughter and make a dried up well flow again."

[125] Ibid., vol. 2, p. 468.

[126] [Discussed in detail in von Franz's *Individuation in Fairy Tales*.]

[127] See also "The Blind Man Who Recovered His Sight," where the hero is blinded by his evil mother and healed by the excrement of wild geese. For more examples. see Bolte and Mackensen, *Handwörterbuch*, under *Blendung* [blinding] and *Blindheit* [blindness].

891 It appears that the tailor has learned something from his difficult experience because he spares the animals he meets, although this seems at first to be to his disadvantage. He now considers the demands of the instinctual world and thereby gains the help of the positive, natural side of his shadow. From now on, he is successful and even finds a position at the court of the king. But since he has returned to the world of consciousness, the evil cobbler, his unconscious rival, turns up again. The latter secretly spreads rumors of the tailor's supernatural skills, and causes him to be challenged with impossible tasks. The shadow poisons the tailor by secretly aspiring to particular heroism. But although he always works evil, he ultimately brings good since with the help of friendly animals, that is, on the basis of his acquired instinctual security and closeness to nature, the tailor manages to bring his actual superiority to light and to act as a savior.

892 This role of the shadow as a stimulus to developmental movement is clearly illustrated in a Koryak tale, "The Daughter of Floating-Island." There Eme'mqut, the hero, is constantly accompanied by a neighbor called "Envious-One" (!), who spoils every enterprise he undertakes. One day, Envious-One mockingly says that Eme'mqut could not win the "daughter of the floating island" to be his wife. Eme'mqut became fraught with anger and finally embarked on the great adventure, forcing Envious-One to come along. Together they win many beautiful women from the spirit-land and sea. Here it becomes clear that Envious-One, who is also a braggart (he boasts of being able to jump over reindeer, even though he obviously cannot), embodies the jealous and boastful side of the hero himself. This shadow is actually the one that coerces the ego to an *auseinandersetzung* with the unconscious. Precisely because of this prodding and badgering, he gains contact with his soul, which appears in the form of the woman as the highest value.

893 In the Grimm's fairytale, the tailor must rescue a crown from the bottom of a lake. This task is similar to that of the Koryak hero, Eme'mqut, since the crown that the ducks dredge up from the depths, that is, from the unconscious, also symbolizes the highest value, inner wholeness. Even the small castle, which the bees build for the tailor with their wax, is a geometrical structure that may be regarded as a mandala and, therefore, as a spiritual center. Another mandala is the magical circle that the young horse pulls into the yard. At its center, a crystal-clear light fountain gushes forth from behind a spherical piece of land.[128] If the crown signifies supreme value, the castle the pristine source of strength, and the flowing fountain vitality and eternal renewal, then finally the fourth arrives: the long-awaited grandson of the king, brought by

---

[128] In a variation on this tale (cf. Bolte and Polívka, *Anmerkungen*, vol. 2, p. 468), all the fountains of the city have dried up, "and no one knows that the big square stone in the center of the marketplace must be removed for underneath there swells the purest water."

the stork. In a South Slavic version,[129] a dove brings the child, possibly reflecting the original concept of the dove representing the Holy Spirit. When the tailor first meets the stork, it says about itself: "I am a sacred bird that does no one harm. . . " In the child, the highest spiritual value has finally arrived in human form, because it is a symbol of inner renewal and points to the future. The fourth stage brings the completion and the union of the tailor with the king's daughter. Once this is achieved, the evil aspect of the shadow disappears, overcome by the instinctual world represented as animals, the only counter-forces that can match him since they also belong to the realm of the unconscious. In engaging in the tasks, the hero does not participate actively in the *auseinandersetzung*, but stands above them, "free of contradictions," and lets the light and dark sides of the unconscious fight each other. A reversal takes place: the dark companion now proves to be the blinded[130] one; the animals have turned against him and he disappears into the forest, whence he came.

894 This naive fairytale proves to be a far-reaching psychic drama that culminates in the obtaining of the treasures. As noted, each of these treasures symbolizes the highest psychic value, which Jung calls, in psychological language, the Self.[131] He is referring here to a midpoint between consciousness and the unconscious. "This something is the desired 'mid-point' of the personality, that ineffable something betwixt the opposites, or else that which unites them, or the result of conflict, or the product of energetic tension. . ."[132] When an individual in the course of their psychic development has found the center of personality, they are balanced and at peace with themselves. Attaining this goal is so significant that it amounts to a transformation. Therefore, psychic effort focuses on this central place.[133] In Jung's concept, the Self is not only a psychic "place," but an archetype, a primordial image that is energetically charged and functions because it is supraordinate to and includes the conscious ego.[134] It determines the fate of individuals, always as an archetype, depending on the attitude of the ego, in a positive or negative sense.[135] The symbolic image of this archetype appears in dreams of

---

129 Cf. Bolte and Polívka, *Anmerkungen*, vol. 2, p. 471, fn. 1.

130 [In German, literally "deluded."]

131 Cf. C.G. Jung, "Relation between the ego and the unconscious," CW 7, ¶399, 404f.; "Rebirth," CW 9i, ¶247f.; *Mass*, CW 11, ¶396; *Psychologie und Religion*, CW 11, ¶140.

132 C.G. Jung, "Relation between the ego and the unconscious," CW 7, ¶382.

133 In "Relation between the ego and the unconscious," Jung writes that the Self is "a virtual center of . . . mysterious constitution" (CW 7, ¶398). In his *Commentary on 'The Golden Flower,'* the goal is to shift the centering in the ego to a new center taking into account demands of the conscious and the unconscious. This "hypothetical point" between conscious and unconscious might be called the self (CW 13, ¶67).

134 Cf. C.G. Jung, "Relation between the ego and the unconscious," CW 7, ¶274.

135 Cf. J. Jacobi, *Die Psychologie von C.G. Jung*, Zürich, 1939, p. 145: "The Self, however, is also a psychological category, as such, one can experience it. When we step out of psychological language, we can call it the 'central fire,' our individual share in God or the 'spark' to use Meister Eckhart's word."

individuals, in the myths and fairytales of many peoples, and in the reports of religious experiences. It is also expressed in visions, and – as far as it does not represent something living such as the "divine child" – occurs in the form of a mandala. The unity and regularity [i.e., conforming to laws] of the mandala symbolizes wholeness. "Most mandalas take the form of a cross, or wheel, and show a distinct tendency towards a quaternary structure. . ."[136]

895 In the tale of the two wanderers, it is the shadow figure that prompts the tailor to seek this psychic center, a symbol of his soul's inner fortitude. It turns out that the shoemaker's sinister plans help the tailor to mature and become a royal person.

896 The alter ego appears in fairytales also as a servant or ministering spirit of the hero, because of its affinity to the hero – both in terms of subordinate dependency and its commitment to engaging in helpful efforts. A fairytale that depicts the dangerous encounter with one's own demon and uniquely represents how this form achieves the goods that are available, and which beautifully illuminates the magical character of the servant, is "Lasse, My Servant":

> 897 Once upon a time there was a prince or a duke or whatever you choose to call him, but at any rate a tremendously noble highborn, who did not want to stay at home. And so he traveled about the world, and wherever he went he was well received. He hobnobbed with the very finest people for he had an unheard of amount of money. He at once found friends and acquaintances no matter where he went, for whoever has a full trough can always find pigs to thrust their snouts into it. But since he handled his money as he did, it grew less and less, and at last he was left high and dry, without a red cent. And there was an end to all his many friends; for they did just as the pigs do. When he had been well fleeced, they began to snivel and grunt, and soon scattered, each about his own business. And there he stood, after having been led about by the nose, abandoned by all. All had been glad to help him get rid of his money; but none were willing to help him regain it, so there was nothing left for him to do but to wander back home again like a journeyman apprentice, and beg his way as he went.
>
> 898 Late one evening he found himself in a big forest, without any idea as to where he might spend the night. And as he was looking around, his glance happened to fall on an old hut, peeping out from among the bushes. Of course an old hut was no lodging for such a fine gentleman; but when we cannot have what we want, we must take

[136] C.G. Jung, *Golden Flower*, CW 13, ¶31ff; see also Jacobi, *Die Psychologie von C.G. Jung*, p. 151.

what we can get, and since there was no help for it, he went into the hut. There was not even a cat there, not even a stool to sit on. But against one wall there was a great chest. What might there be in the chest? Suppose there were a few moldy crusts of bread in it? They would taste good to him, for he had not been given a single thing all day long, and he was so hungry that his innards stuck to his ribs. He opened the chest. But within the chest was another chest, and in that chest still another chest, and so it went, one always smaller than the other, until they were nothing but little boxes. And the more there were of them, the more trouble he took to open them; for whatever was hidden away so carefully must be something exceptionally beautiful, thought he.

899 At last he came to a tiny box, and in the tiny box was a slip of paper and that was all he had for his pains! At first he was much depressed.

900 But all at once, he saw that something was written on the piece of paper, and on closer examination he was even able to spell out the words, though they had a strange appearance. And he read: "Lasse, my servant!"[137]

901 No sooner had he spoken these words than something answered, close to his ear: "What does my master command?"

902 He looked around, but saw no one. That's strange, thought he, and once more read aloud: "Lasse, my servant!" And just as before came the answer: "What does my master command?"

903 [Being desperate for something to eat, he asked for some food. Immediately there appeared a richly laid table covered with all the good things to eat! With the help of his invisible servant, he is given a nice bed and the cottage is turned into a magnificent palace with servants. On the other side of the forest lay a king's palace. That king was astonished at the castle that had suddenly arisen on the other side of "his" forest. Enraged at this audacity, he sent out his soldiers to demolish it and hang the builder. The duke was again saved by his invisible servant who gave him twice as many soldiers as the king, so that the royal officers did not venture further. The duke entertained them and learned that the king had an incomparably beautiful daughter, who was so proud that she never even looked at a man. The duke asked the officers to carry his greetings to the king. In the evening he called, "Lasse, my servant" and told his unseen helper to carry the sleeping princess to him without awakening her. It did not

[137] The name "Lasse" is a common nickname for "Lars" in Swedish and "Lorenz" in German.

take long before she was lying on his bed, more beautiful than any woman he had ever seen. The duke commanded his servant to return her to her own castle, for he would pay a visit the next day and ask the king for her hand. Meanwhile the king became angry seeing that the castle still stood against him. His captain explained everything, which at first the king could not understand. Then the princess arrived and told her father the king that she had a strange and wonderful dream: she was in the new castle and met a beautiful and magnificent duke and now she wanted him for her husband. Even before the King had recovered from his surprise, the duke arrived with drums, trumpets, and glittering gold. The duke proclaimed his allegiance to the king and courted his daughter. The king dared not say no, but first wanted to see for himself the features of the other castle and the circumstances of the duke. Having confirmed the situation, he agreed. The wedding was lavishly celebrated and the couple left to live in the duke's castle.] After some time had passed, the duke one evening heard the words: "Is my master content now?" It was Lasse, though the duke could not see him.

904 "I am well content," answered the duke, "for you have brought me all that I have."

905 "But what did I get for it?" asked Lasse.

906 "Nothing," replied the duke, "but, heaven above, what was I to give you, who are not flesh and blood, and whom I cannot even see," said he. "Yet if there be anything I can do for you, why let me know what it is, and I will do it."

907 "I would very much like to have the little scrap of paper that you keep in the box," said Lasse.

908 "If that is all you want, and if such a trifle is of any service to you, your wish shall be granted, for I believe I know the words by heart now," said the duke. Lasse thanked him, and said that all the duke need do, would be to lay the paper on the chair beside his bed when he went to sleep, and that he would fetch it during the night.

909 This the duke did, and then he went to bed and fell asleep. But toward morning the duke woke up, freezing so that his teeth chattered, and when he had fully opened his eyes, he saw that he had been stripped of everything, and had scarcely a shirt to his name. And instead of lying in the handsome bed in the handsome bedroom in the magnificent castle, he lay on the big chest in the old hut. He at once called out: "Lasse, my servant!" But there was no answer. Then he cried again:

910 "Lasse, my servant!" Again there was no answer. So he called, out as loudly as he could: "Lasse, my servant!" But this third call was also in vain.

911 Now he began to realize what had happened, and that Lasse, when he obtained that scrap of paper, no longer had to serve him, and that Lasse had made this possible. But now things were as they were, and there stood the duke in the old hut, with scarcely a shirt to his name. The princess herself was not much better off, though she had kept her clothes; for they had been given her by her father, and Lasse had no power over them. Now the duke had to explain everything to the princess, and beg her to leave him, since it would be best if he tried to get along as well as he could himself, said he. But this the princess would not do. She had a better memory for what the pastor had said when he married them, she told him, and that she was never, never to leave him.

912 [When the king no longer saw the wondrous castle on the other side of the woods, he became worried and went to check for himself. Finding his weeping daughter, and his now wretched son, who could not bring himself to tell the king actually what had happened, he ordered the Duke to be hung. The princess spoke to the executioner and made a scheme so that the duke should be saved and she would flee with him.]

913 Now the duke was at the end of his rope, quite literally! Yet due to the special way the executioner had prepared the rope, he did not die, but dangled there. This gave him time enough to reflect about his mistake in not contenting himself with an inch instead of reaching out at once for an ell; that he had so foolishly given back the scrap of paper to Lasse annoyed him most of all. "If I only had it again, I would show everyone that adversity has made me wise," he thought to himself. But when the horse is stolen we close the stable door. And that is the way of the world. And then he dangled his legs, since for the time being there was nothing else for him to do.

914 It had been a long, hard day for him, and he was not sorry when he saw the sun sinking behind the forest. But just as the sun was setting he suddenly heard a most tremendous "Yo ho," and when he looked down there were seven carts of worn-out shoes coming along the road, and atop the last cart was a little old man in gray, with a nightcap on his head. He had the face of some horrible specter, and was not much better to look at in other respects. He drove straight up to the gallows, and stopped when he was directly beneath them, looked up at the duke and laughed, the horrible old creature!

915 "And is this the measure of your stupidity?" he said, "but then what is a fellow of your sort to do with his stupidity, if he does not put it to some use?" And then he laughed again. "Yes, there you hang, and here I am carting off all the shoes I wore out going about on your silly errands. I wonder, sometimes, whether you can actually read what is written on that scrap of paper, and whether you recognize it," said he, laughing again, indulging in all sorts of horseplay, and waving the scrap of paper under the duke's nose. But all who are hanging on the gallows are not dead, and this time Lasse was the greater fool of the two.

916 The duke snatched and tore the scrap of paper from his hand! "Lasse, my servant!"

917 "What does my master command?"

918 [The duke ordered Lasse to cut him down from the gallows, reinstate the castle and all as before, which of course Lasse performed. The next morning the king saw the castle again, but the gallows and even the son-in-law and daughter had disappeared. He had to sit down, take off his crown and scratch his head. So many strange things had recently happened! He went to the duke's castle and was greeted by his daughter and son-in-law. Totally astounded, the king asked for an explanation. The duke, totally self-assured, denied anything out of the ordinary and offered the possibility that the king had somehow temporarily lost his mind.]

919 "It must be as you say," the king told the duke, "and I believe that I have recovered my reason, and have found my eyes again. And it would have been a sin and shame had I had you hung," said he. Then he grew joyful and no one gave the matter further thought. But adversity teaches one to be wise, so people say, and the duke now began to attend to most things himself, and to see to it that Lasse did not have to wear out so many pairs of shoes. The king at once bestowed half the kingdom upon him, which gave him plenty to do, and people said that one would have to look far in order to find a better ruler.

920 Then Lasse came to the duke one day, and though he did not look much better than before, he was more civil and did not venture to grin and carry on. "You no longer need my help," said he, "for though formerly I used to wear out all my shoes, I now cannot even wear out a single pair, and I almost believe my legs are moss-grown. Will you not discharge me?"

921 The duke thought he could. "I have taken great pains to spare you, and I really believe that I can get along without you," he replied. "But the castle here and all the other things I could not well dispense with, since I never again could find an architect like yourself, and you may take for granted that I have no wish to ornament the gallows-tree a second time. I will not of my own free will, therefore, give you back the scrap of paper," said he.

922 "While it is in your possession I have nothing to fear," answered Lasse. "But should the paper fall into other hands, then I should have to begin to run and work all over again and that, just that, is what I would like to prevent. When a fellow has been working a thousand years, as I have, he is bound to grow weary at last."

923 So they came to the conclusion that the duke should put the scrap of paper in its little box and bury it seven ells underground, beneath a stone that had grown there and would remain there as well. Then they thanked each other for pleasant comradeship and separated. The duke did as he had agreed to do, and no one saw him hide the box. He lived happily with his princess, and was blessed with sons and daughters. When the king died, he inherited the whole kingdom and, as you may imagine, he was none the worse off thereby, and no doubt he is still living and ruling there, unless he has died.

924 As to the little box containing the scrap of paper, many are still digging and searching for it.[138]

925 The fateful encounter with the magical kingdom occurs here at the moment of a failure in the world. Through outer isolation, the ego hears inner voices. Significantly, in the Spanish tale "The Beauty of the World," the adventures of a young king also begin when he loses all his belongings to a bad courtier, who then abandons him on an island out a sea. Thus, the hero falls under the power of the shadow.

926 The duke in the Swedish fairytale also finds the dangerous and richly bestowing power of the unconscious in a scrap of paper within the smallest of four nested boxes. The box as something receptive, secure, a safe place, is a symbol of the womb,[139] and also, more generally, of the body.[140] It signifies the

---

[138] Stroebe, *The Swedish Fairy Book*, pp. 11–32.

[139] Cf. Bachofen, *Gräbersymbolik*, pp. 127–128; Silberer, *Problems of Mysticism*, p. 225; Rank, *Myth of the Birth*, pp. 55 and 83.

[140] Cf. Angelus [Johann Scheffier] Silesius, *The Cherubinic Wanderer*, Paulist Press, New Jersey, 1986, trans. Maria Shrady, p. 42 [slightly edited]: "Body, soul, and divinity:"

The soul is a crystal, the divinity is its radiance:
The body you inhabit hides both as in a shrine."
("Die Seel ist ein Kristall, die Gottheit ist ihr Schein:
Der Leib, in dem du lebst, ist ihrer beider Schrein.")

all-enveloping and dark body-soul.[141] In the Eleusian mysteries, the golden snake as the image of the secret divinity was carried around hidden in the sacred chest or ark.[142] In the Grimm's fairytale, "The Three Feathers," the Simpleton hero goes down some steps into the ground and comes upon a great fat toad who gives him a magic carpet und other wonder tools. [See future volume for complete tale.] In a Russian fairytale, "The Dead Maiden," a whole golden city is contained in a golden box.[143] In these examples, the chests, like Pandora's box, denote the unconscious. In the tale, "Lasse, My Servant", the duke must open three boxes until he comes to the fourth to find the paper with the magic words.

927 The psychological process thus concerns the duke, led by external need, who must dig deeper into his own soul and go through many layers until he reaches the living creative core in the unconscious. (The hut, which has the same shape as the box, is a mandala, a symbol of the psychic sphere.) The note that he finds gives him power over an invisible servant, who performs his every wish. It embodies the infinite possibilities of wishful thinking and the gift of letting the wealth and destiny-shaping possibilities of inner images become imaginatively "real" (effective). These possibilities are not directly accessible to the duke, but through a magic object, the piece of paper with the words "Lasse, my servant." The note and the words are an aid, a kind of key or formula to gain access to the unconscious.

928 The invisible servant turns out to be a small, gray old man with a stocking cap, who has a face "like a ghastly ghost." He is like the Púca (in "The Piper and the Púca"), a dark spirit whose sharp, pointed hat makes him look like a dwarf. Dwarves (like smiths) signify pictorial forces hidden in nature. Lasse also appears almost transpersonally like the chthonic deity itself. (See the figure in "The Story of Longa-Poa.") In the Spanish tale, "The Bear Hans," a small black man appears whom the hero must first fight, but then is overcome and fulfills all the hero's wishes. (The shadow is often presented in Spanish fairytales as a black man.) Although Lasse is initially submissive, acting like a true servant in procuring all the items that his master desires, he later reveals his entire dark aspect and brings the hero to the gallows, just as the shoemaker did to the tailor in "The Two Travelers." But Lasse also mediates the contact with the female, emotional side of the unconscious, which is represented by the king's daughter. Through her, the hero is even saved, because she bribes the executioner.

---

[141] German: *Körperseele.*

[142] Cf. A. Dieterich, *Eine Mithrasliturgie*, pp. 124ff.; Rank, *Myth of the Birth*, pp. 55, 76 –77. See also the Aztec "Chest of Hackmack" (housed at the Hamburg Museum for Folk Culture). This stone chest is "an image and symbol of the whole cosmos"; see Danzel, "The Psychology of Ancient Mexican Symbolism," p. 106. The Holy Ark of ancient Israel, a chest-shaped tabernacle, became a locus of religious energies.

[143] [See also "The Magic Box," in: *Russian Fairy Tales*, trans. N. Guterman, pp. 164–167.]

929 Since the duke brought the forces of the unconscious that had been under his spell by artificial means, he is not really lord over them. When the power slips away without his knowledge, the demon is freed and reveals his true nature, plunging the duke into an even more drastic situation than before. But then he realizes that he cannot illegitimately use the powers that lie in the unconscious for himself, but must acquire the treasures through conscious effort and performance and utilize them within certain human boundaries. As a result of this insight, the duke becomes so mature that he no longer needs an "art" or "method" of dealing with the demonic realm. The burying of the note very aptly expresses the attained goal, a person's meaningful relationship with their shadow and indeed with the unconscious. Each of them waives superiority over the other and thereby gains peace. The magical charm is humbly returned to nature, since the duke now knows the mystery of the unconscious in himself. The dark demon disappears, however, as the shoemaker did in "The Two Travelers," never to return to the magical realm.

930 A similar story is "The Imprisoned *Schratl* and Rich Julius,"[144]

931 The rich but lonely Mr. Julius set free a *schratl*[145] from a box in a wall. For this freedom the spirit fulfilled all his wishes. He made Mr. Julius a captain who sailed all the seas, but then he spoiled this happiness with a storm. Then the *schratl* made him a general, but did not allow him to kill anybody. Next, he made Mr. Julius into a Turkish Sultan, but Mr. Julius was shy of women and did not like the harem women and, as a hermit, he was grumpy. Then the *schratl* made him a gardener by secretly killing the real gardener and setting up Julius with his wife and children. Now Julius was happy. But this irked the *schratl*, because he could not suffer his Lord being happy, so he

[144] Cf. also the charming fairytale, "Go I Know Not Whither, Bring Back I Know Not What," in which an archer refrains from shooting a pigeon, who transforms into human form and becomes his wife. The king desires her and sends the archer off on an adventure. After many jobs and adventures in the end he must take on the task: "Go I know not whither, bring back I know not." While his wife remains loyal to him in the form of a dove, he wanders off until he meets her mother, a sorceress, with whose help he wins the servant-spirit, Shmat Razum. He lives in a cave where he serves two old men. On the return trip Shmat Razum gives him magical items, a castle and soldiers, so he defeats the king and with his wife receives the kingdom. Shmat Razum is no longer mentioned. Here the magical figure of the servant in the cave (!) is bound to the chthonic father deity (personified in the two old men in their double aspect). The hero asks Shmatz Razum to eat with him. Not in his thirty years of serve to the two old ones was Shmat Razum ever invited to sit with them at the table. By this invitation the archer rescues Shmat Razum and frees him from being bound to the realm of the unconscious. He disappears as soon as the hero is safe in his "kingdom." That the magical mother figure leads the hero to the cave indicates the link between the Great Mother and the shadow, both of which symbolize bestowing nature. See also the relationship between the Púca and the maternal fairies in "The Piper and the Púca." See also "The Blue Light." There, too, an evil witch first controlled the magical servant (a little old man), who served the hero whenever he lit his pipe with a blue light. At the end of the tale, the soldier becomes king and there is no further mention of the little servant.

[145] [A forest demon.]

> decided to destroy his good luck. One day he came to the gardener's wife disguised as an old man and told her that he was the *schratl*, a kind of demon, and the servant of her husband. He related the whole story of Mr. Julius and told her that he was not her rightful husband. She did not believe him even though he said he could prove it all and could show her before her eyes. He added that he could transform himself into anything she wanted. But she chased him away and told all to Julius. He then confessed everything and was very sad that his happiness and good fortune were over. But the woman was brave and said that it would turn out all right, but only if he were to marry her by a Christian pastor, which he did. The *schratl*, however, continued to molest her until she caught him up in her sewing box and cast it into the sea. From then on, the couple lived together in happiness.

932 The interpretation of this tale is clear from the preceding discussion. The tale succinctly depicts the double aspect of the shadow, as a magical helper and as a destroyer. It embodies the daemonic aspect of a person's unconscious, in which all the forces that can make someone a king or a murderer lie dormant. The *schratl* appears to be able to show its opposite [i.e., the ego, its vis-à-vis], the right attitude, which embraces wise self-restraint and the ability to differentiate between the ego and its daemons.

933 An important fairytale related to "The Two Travelers," but illustrating new aspects of the problem of the shadow, is "Ferdinand the Faithful and Ferdinand the Unfaithful." This tale clearly supports our interpretation that helpful animals portray positive aspects of the shadow:

> 934 Once upon a time there lived a man and his wife who so long as they were rich had no children, but when they became poor they had a little boy. They could find no godfather for him, however, so the man said he would just go to another place to see if he could get one there. As he went, a poor man met him, who asked him where he was going. He said he was going to see if he could get a godfather, that he was poor, so no one would stand as godfather for him. "Oh," said the poor man, "you are poor, and I am poor; I will be godfather for you, but I am so badly off I can give the child nothing. Go home and tell the nurse that she is to come to the church with the child." When they all got to the church together, the beggar was already there, and he gave the child the name of Ferdinand the Faithful.
>
> 935 [When he was going out of the church, the beggar gave a key to the nurse, and told her when she got home she was to give it to the father, who was to take care of it until the child was fourteen years old.] At the age of seven, the boy searched in vain for the lock, but at the age

of fourteen he saw it standing on the heath, unlocked it, and found a white horse, which he joyfully mounted and shouted to his father: "Now I have a white horse, and I will travel!" So he set out, and as he was on his way, he passed a (feather-)pen lying on the road. At first he thought he would pick it up, but then again he thought to himself, "Thou should'st leave it lying there; thou wilt easily find a (feather-) pen where thou art going, if thou hast need of one." As he began to ride away, a voice called after him, "Ferdinand the Faithful, take it with thee." He looked around, but saw no one (it was the horse who spoke), then he went back again and picked up the (feather-)pen. When he had ridden a little way farther, he passed by a lake, and a fish was lying on the bank, gasping and panting for breath, so he said, "Wait, my dear fish, I will help thee get into the water" and he took hold of it by the tail, and threw it into the lake. Then the fish put its head out of the water and said, "As thou hast helped me out of the mud I will give thee a flute; when thou art in any need, play on it, and then I will help thee, and if ever thou lettest anything fall in the water, just play and I will reach it out to thee." Then he rode away, and there came to him a man who asked him where he was going. "Oh, to the next place." Then he asked him what his name was? "Ferdinand the Faithful." "So! then we have got almost the same name, I am called Ferdinand the Unfaithful." And they both set out for the next inn.

936 Now it was unfortunate that Ferdinand the Unfaithful knew everything that the other had ever thought and everything he was about to do; he knew it by means of all kinds of wicked arts. There was in the inn an honest girl, however, who had a bright face and behaved very prettily. She fell in love with Ferdinand the Faithful because he was a handsome man, and she asked him whither he was going. "Oh, I am just traveling round about," said he. Then she said he ought to stay there, for the King of that country wanted an attendant or an outrider, and he ought to enter his service. He answered he could not very well go to any one like that and offer himself. Then said the maiden, "Oh, but I will soon do that for you." And so she went straight to the King, and told him that she knew of an excellent servant for him. He was well pleased with that, and had Ferdinand the Faithful brought to him, and wanted to make him his servant. He liked better to be an outrider, however, for where his horse was, there he also wanted to be, so the King made him an outrider. When Ferdinand the Unfaithful learnt that, he said to the girl, "What! Dost thou help him and not me?" "Oh," said the girl, "I will help thee too." She thought, "I must keep friends with that man, for he is not to

be trusted." She went to the King, and offered him as a servant, and the King was willing.

937 [The King was always lamented that he did not have his love with him. Ferdinand the Unfaithful suggested to the King that he give Ferdinand the Faithful the job to find the girl he loved. If he failed, the King should have his head struck off.] The King sent for Ferdinand the Faithful, and told him that there was, in this place or in that place, a girl he loved, and that he was to bring her to him, and if he did not do it he should die.

938 [Back in the stable with his little white horse Ferdinand the Faithful lamented his fate and called out for help. The little white horse told him not to worry, have the King give him a ship full of meat, and a ship full of bread, he would need this to pacify the giants and the huge birds on the island where the King's love, a princess, lay sleeping. Thus equipped, Ferdinand the Faithful went to the island and fed the giants and birds. Once they were satiated with the meat, Ferdinand got the giants to carry the princess in her bed to the King.] When she came to the King, she said she could not live, she must have her writings, they had been left in her castle. By the instigation of Ferdinand the Unfaithful, Ferdinand the Faithful was called, and the King told him he must fetch the writings from the castle, or he should die. Then he went once more into the stable, and bemoaned himself and said, "Oh, my dear little white horse, now I am to go away again, how am I to do it?" Then the little white horse said he was just to load the ships full again. So it happened again as it had happened before, and the giants and the birds were satisfied, and made gentle by the meat. When they came to the castle, the white horse told Ferdinand the Faithful that he must go in, and that on the table in the princess's bed-room lay the writings. And Ferdinand the Faithful went in, and fetched them. When they were on the lake, he let his feather-pen fall into the water; then said the white horse, "Now I cannot help thee at all." But he remembered his flute, and began to play on it, and the fish came with the feather-pen in its mouth, and gave it to him. So he took the writings to the castle, where the wedding was celebrated. The Queen did not love the King, however, because he had no nose; she would have much preferred to love Ferdinand the Faithful. Once when all the lords of the court were together, therefore, the Queen said she could do feats of magic, that she could cut off any one's head and put it on again, and that one of them ought just to try it. But none of them would be the first, so Ferdinand the Faithful, again at the instigation of Ferdinand the Unfaithful, undertook it and she hewed off his head,

and put it on again for him, and it healed together directly, so that it looked as if he had a red thread round his throat. Then the King said to her, "My child, and where hast thou learnt that?" "Yes," she said, "I understand the art; shall I just try it on thee also?" "Oh, yes," said he. She cut off his head, but did not put it on again, pretending that she could not get it right, it would not stay fixed. Then the King was buried and the Queen married Ferdinand the Faithful.

939 He always rode on his white horse, however, and once when he was seated on it, it told him that he was to go on to the heath that he knew, and gallop three times round it. And when he had done that, the white horse stood up on its hind legs, and was changed into a King's son.[146]

940 From the outset, Ferdinand the Faithful is surrounded by two shadowy companions. One is, of course, the evil Ferdinand the Unfaithful (who corresponds to the cobbler in "The Two Travelers"). His similar name indicates particularly well that he is a counter-image of the hero himself.[147] The second shadow figure is the helpful horse, which turns out to be a prince. According to a French version ("Thirty-From-Paris"), this figure is identical to the godfather who appeared at the beginning of the story, who is the Lord God himself.[148] The hero's vocation is already present in his parents' fate. Chosen to be a special child, he is born to them after their impoverishment in the world. It is a precondition for the appearance of the wonderful godfather. This person meets the father as a stranger, on the way to another village. From the beginning, one suspects he has mysterious and magical abilities, because everything unknown is easily enlivened by the unconscious, especially when one finds oneself in a predicament. The Godfather is, implicitly, the representative of the Father in Heaven (he is called the "godfather"!). In the French parallel, the beggar with the miraculous key is clearly a divine being. There is a custom of giving the baptized a "God-father" and a "God-mother," as Bächtold-Stäubli explains under *Gevatter, Pate* [godfather, patron]:

941 A form of artificial affinity that serves the purpose of fostering a greater security for the life of the individual and strengthened and sanctified by the cult of the individual. In ancient Germany, the practice was known in several forms, such as in the oath and kinship adoption, and with foster parents. . . (This artificial relationship is a

---

[146] Slightly edited from *Complete Grimm's*, pp. 566–571, based on the translation by Margaret Hunt (1884).

[147] Cf. also "The Snake Arrow."

[148] Cf. Bolte and Polívka, *Anmerkungen*, vol. 3, p. 22, who mention a similar version from the Lorraine. In a Swedish parallel, "Faithful and Unfaithful," a huldra, a seductive female forest creature, is a godmother who gives the hero his magical horse.

> breach of the narrow confines of the clan.) The church used the *patrini* and *matrinae*, the elder ones, those who stood surety of the newborn. . . as an effective power and guarantee for a means of education. The godfather (Old High German, *gevatero*) should be a spiritual co-father and relative (cf. French *compère, commère*) who can assist the sometimes unreliable parental educational authority. . . Despite the Church's participation in the godfather custom, this is carried today [i.e., early 1900s] by predominantly non-Christian concepts, especially as regards the number and choice of the patrons, the giving of names, the (sympathetic) relationship between godparent and child and the particular bestowal of gifts. . .[149] The intimate, spiritual kinship between the baptized and the godparents is amplified by many mysterious and sympathetic relationships in the superstitions of folk culture. Often the child is given the name of the godparents. . . and so "inherits" the spiritual and physical attributes of his godparents, which shows through in the temperament of the child. . . It is important, therefore, to ask the person to take the role of the godparent. . . Most notably, the development of the child is to a large extent dependent on the actions and omissions of the godparent at the baptism. . . The interconnected sympathetic relationships on the day of baptism are important for the child throughout his whole life, even until his death. The godfather carries a certain amount of blessing and even healing power. . . To be chosen as a godfather is an honor, but also a responsibility. . . The most visible expression of the intimate relationship between sponsor and child is found in the gifts, always gratefully received. . . Although the obligations to the godchild can be ended at the seventh year, in practice it usually extends to the confirmation or end of the obligatory school years; and sometimes even until the wedding day or for the lifetime. . . Of particular importance and superstitious preeminence is the sack[150] that the godparents give to the child at birth or at the baptism to be "put in the pillow". . . Inside is the all-important "godparent money," usually coins, often gold coins, meant to assure wealth for the godchild and ensure that the child does not appear empty-handed before God.[151]

942 It is obvious that behind these ideas lies the archetype of the father, the spiritual side behind the earthly father. Therefore, legends and fairytales always emphasize the relationship to the supernatural, a wonderful "spiritual kinship,"

---

[149] [The role of the godparents has a strong tradition in Switzerland and Germany that is still active today and can be very meaningful for the godchild.]

[150] [German: *Einbund, Eingebinde*].

[151] Bächtold-Stäubli under *Gevatter, Pate* [godfather, patron].

which guarantees the spiritual welfare of the child. The daemonic godfather in "Ferdinand the Faithful and Ferdinand the Unfaithful" appears as destitute because the inner treasure is usually invisible to the human eye.[152] A version of this tale from Hannover is called "The Lord God as Godfather." In contrast, in a version from Holstein, the hero is the godchild of the Devil and can lift a golden horseshoe with a feather.[153] The beggar-godfather is also a manifestation of the father archetype in its dual, sometimes light, sometimes dark aspect.[154] (Since he stands in secret identity with his horse as a shadow companion,[155] he could also be taken as an initial appearance, in two aspects – the horse and Ferdinand the Unfaithful – of the shadow. Later, these two aspects split apart.) As his only present, he gives the boy a key to an imaginary lock, which as yet does not exist.

943 The key as a tool to open locked up places and things is a symbol for the exploration of knowledge.[156] In the tales of otherworldly things this is, therefore, often in possession of a wise old man.[157] Thus, the daemonic beggar gives the boy a secret knowledge about things of magic, that is, his own spiritual kingdom.

944 The key first opens the doors of a castle on the heath. The heath, a lonely, sinister place, signifies the unconscious, like the forest or the desert. It is, therefore, the home of magical powers. The castle itself is a mandala[158] and as such, the center of the unconscious realm, which means the seat of the deity. This appears here as a white horse, which becomes the magic helper of the hero. In the French parallel, "Thirty-From-Paris," the mount transforms at the end into the Virgin Mary, who had been sent by the divine protector. From this emerges a kind of identity between the horse and the godfather, who gave the hero the gift of "opening up" the magical kingdom. The godfather thus shows him the path to himself.

---

[152] On the plainness and unsightliness of the *lapis philosophorum* in medieval alchemy, see C.G. Jung, *Psychology and Alchemy*, CW 12, ¶103.

[153] Bolte and Polívka, *Anmerkungen*, vol. 3, p. 19. See also the Roma fairytale, "Comerade," in which the Good Lord as a poor but magical journeyman joins a traveling gypsy. When the latter uses the journeyman's magic to make money fraudulently but does not share the proceeds, he flies off as a dove.

[154] Quite possibly, the original poor wanderer was a figure of Odin/Woden, whom the Christian storytellers renamed as the Devil to obscure his pagan character. When he did good things and showed his benedictory aspects, he was declared to be the Good Lord.

[155] Cf. "The Beautiful Hill," a Roma in which an old man on the street said to the hero: "Command me to transform myself into an old horse!" Hans did this and the horse said, "Climb on my back now, we will go on together." He climbed on and the old horse and Hans went on the road together.

[156] Cf. Silberer, *Problems of Mysticism*, p. 135, who mentions that Fludd, in his *Tractatus theologo-philosophicus de vita, morte et resurrectione*, wrote of a "true mystery" or "key of knowledge," which provides access to the paradise of joy; see also Ibid., p. 238. In *Die Gnosis* (1924, p. 386), Leisegang notes that in the *Pistis Sophia*, Jesus says that the Gnosis is the key to the mysteries of the kingdom of heaven. See also Carus, *Psyche* (1846): "The key to knowledge of the nature of conscious life of the soul lies in the region of the unconscious" (p. 1).

[157] See, for example, "The Story of Djihanshah," which is retold and discussed further below.

[158] Cf. C.G. Jung, *Golden Flower*, CW 13, ¶31, 32.

945 Taking the key, his godfather's gift, the hero mounts the white horse, full of confidence and courage, without knowing that the animal is a magic helper. "There is ample testimony from the Indo-European world that the horse is one of the initial manifestations of the deity. In the Germanic folk tradition, Odin/Woden is the human hypostasis of a former animal demon in equine form. This gives the basis for an explanation of many features with which the horse is associated in today's popular superstition."[159] Insofar as Odin/Woden is a god of death, lord and leader of the dead, the horse also becomes related to death. There is an "essential identity between the dead and the bringer of death, the god of death, and death itself."[160] Many concepts from ancient Greece are also found in the Germanic peoples of Northwestern Europe: death or the daemon of death is a horseman, and the horse is an "incarnation of the demonic, life-wresting powers."[161] In connection with "Ferdinand the Faithful and Ferdinand the Unfaithful," this relationship signifies in particular that the daemonic horse symbolizes a spiritual component. It is "prophetic": it possesses the power of intuition, of instinct, and has the capacity to understand beyond comprehension,[162] but thus also threatens people with extinction.[163]

946 Since it is emphatically a *white* horse, it should be noted that the "swan-like," "shining" horse has been especially esteemed by all peoples and in all times.[164] Both ancient Greek and pagan German customs recognize the white horse as a symbol of the Sun and as the horse of the sun god. Tacitus says that among the Germanic tribes, white horses were used in cult practices.

947 He also mentions that neighing had a prophetic significance, because white horses were regarded as the intimates and confidants of the gods. And also that the ghostly white horse "is a part of Odin/Woden's essence."[165] Thus Ferdinand's white horse symbolizes the fundamental energy that carries the hero to his tasks, and enables him to perform them.[166] It represents the

---

[159] See Bächtold-Stäubli under *Pferd*. In the same reference, see also the citation from the Norwegian *Song of Beiarblack*, a horse of "supernatural kind," which with the third jump reached the gates of heaven: "And when he came to heaven's gate, he had a sense, that he knew it already" [or "that he had been there before"; the original passage is written in rhymes]. There is thus an identity between Odin/Woden and Sleipnir, his eight-legged steed.

[160] See Bächtold-Stäubli under *Pferd*.

[161] See B. Schweitzer, *Herakles*, Tübingen, 1922, p. 77, where it is also mentioned that the dead can appear in the form of a horse and herds of horses belonging to the gods of the underworld are the dead themselves. See also Bächtold-Stäubli under *Pferd*.

[162] [German: *überverständlicher Fähigkeit*]

[163] See the interpretation in Rudolf Meyer, *Die Weisheit der Schweizer Märchen*, pp. 43–44, 81.

[164] See Bächtold-Stäubli under *Schimmel* [white horse]. Hence Sleipnir was white. Indian mythology knows the incarnation of the sun god Vishnu in the form of a white horse.

[165] See Bächtold-Stäubli under *Schimmel*.

[166] On the symbol of the white horse, see Erwin Rousselle, "Drache und Stute, Gestalten der mythischen Welt chinesischer Urzeit," in: *Eranos-Jahrbuch 1934: Ostwestliche Symbolik und Seelenführung*, ed. Olga Fröbe-Kapteyn, Rhein-Verlag, Zürich, 1935, p. 30, fn. 26; Rouseelle mentions the "Buddhistic white horse (one of the seven jewels of the Indian world ruler), which carries the wonder jewel," as well as "the white horse, which brought the sacred scriptures from India to China." See also Zimmer, *Maya*, pp. 128, 137–38.

bestowal of a high ideal, as manifest in the giving of the name, "Ferdinand the Faithful."

948 But the light challenges the darkness and calls the evil opponent to action. At first, the goal of the hero is completely undetermined. But when the girl in the tavern asks him whither he is going, he replies, "Oh, I am just traveling round about." He is evidently on an aimless walk in the magical realm. On the way he finds a pen (presumably a goose quill). He scorns it at first, but then the white horse advises him to pick it up. In most parallels,[167] as in the aforementioned French version, however, the animal helper warns the hero not to take the quill along, which will lead him into the fateful entanglement. Although the versions contradict each other in this respect, none of them is unlikely or psychologically wrong. The horse represents the hero's vitality and instincts. These are what, on the one hand, drive people to adventures and embroilments, while on the other hand, they are the sources of conservative fear of change and innovation. Actually, instinct leads the individual into temptation while warning them that the unconscious does not spare them from having to make ethical decisions.[168]

949 According to the Grimm's version, the horse clearly encourages the hero to pick up the quill. Although this seems at first glance to be unmotivated, there also appears to be a connection between this pen and the writings he is to fetch for the princess. The parallels support this assumption. Thus, according to a Danish version, an image of the princess whom he will later be seeking is pictured on the golden feathers that the hero picks up. Or the hero finds a golden quill pen and at the king's command he must find the bird to which it belonged. This bird then transforms into the virgin.[169] Gold always means the highest value and the feather quill is both a part of the whole bird and also the first hint of the nature and existence of the virgin.[170] Similarly, the fish episode is the first appearance of images that will be encountered in the future. Since fish live in water, they symbolize a content of the unconscious, which could be "caught." It is the task of mankind to bring these living beings into consciousness but first Ferdinand has other tasks to accomplish. Later he will be asked to put himself in the service of this major undertaking, but now he first must learn respect and sympathy. His dark brother, Ferdinand the Unfaithful, joins him, complementing his positive forces.

---

[167] See Bolte and Polívka, *Anmerkungen,* vol. 3, pp. 20, 22, 25. See also "The Beautiful Hill."

[168] See C.G. Jung, "The Development of the Personality," in: Herbert Read et al. (eds.), *The Development of the Personality* (1971): ". . . he who cannot lose his life; neither shall he save it. To develop the personality is a gamble, and the tragedy is that the daemon of the inner voice is at once our greatest danger and an indispensable help. It is tragic, but logical, for it is the nature of things to be so" (Jung, CW 17, ¶321).

[169] See Bolte and Polívka, *Anmerkungen,* vol. 3, p. 20; see further the Roma fairytale, "Threeson."

[170] On the importance of the virgin, the bird, and the feather as forms of the soul, see Tobler, *Epiphanie,* pp. 28ff, 51, 63ff. On the importance of the feather as a mediator of magical knowledge, see Lévy-Bruhl, *How Natives Think,* pp. 25, 84, 106–107.

950 They now come to an inn, that is, he becomes part of collective life. The "shadow" personifies the spiritual rootedness of humankind, which represents the connection to the undifferentiated nature of what is general, "normal," and "public" in all humans. It is here in the public room (bar) of the common man that the hero first meets a female figure who points the way further and higher up, to the King's court. She is a first manifestation of the virgin, which culminates in the recurring figure of the princess - an essential piece of fate that confronts him as a foreshadowing.

951 The evil intrigues of Ferdinand the Unfaithful begin at the court. He is the cajoler of the king and disappears from the scene – without any details of how exactly – when the king is assassinated. He is, thus, somewhat identical with the king, but at the same time, the evil brother and comrade of Ferdinand the Faithful. He possesses characteristics of Goethe's Mephistopheles: he has knowledge of the secret arts and appears to be telepathic; and he knows other people's intentions and thoughts. How closely related he is to the hero becomes clear from a comment by Bolte and Polívka: "In some versions this unfaithful companion forces the hero literally to 'change places with him'... A red knight, or an older brother of the hero appears as jealous counselors to the kings. . ."[171] Similarly, in a Swedish fairytale "Knos," the opponent of the hero, the so-called "Red Peter," acts as if he had committed all the hero's deeds and at the end is punished for that. Through the designation, "Red Knight" or "Red Peter," this figure takes on epithets of the Devil; the color red indicates a connection with affections, emotions, and fire. While passion in itself is not bad, it sometimes entangles one in dangerous situations, and overcoming it can be beneficial (as in "The Two Travelers"). It is dangerous because of the connections with the profane outer world, where power lies, here shown in the figure of the king. The hero does not separate himself from his horse, and this close connection points to the instinctual surety, that protects him against the temptations and encroachments of the secular world.

952 The king coerces Ferdinand the Faithful to go into the deepest regions of the magical kingdom, where the princess is sleeping in her bed in the castle (i.e., in a closed area and mandala). Apparently, she is in a kind of enchanted sleep, because she cannot be awakened and must be taken together with her bed. The king wants her for himself and tries to pull her into his profane sphere.[172] On the journey, only his natural instincts, symbolized by the mysterious voice of his magical horse, can advise him. From his steed, he learns that he can reach his goal only by appeasing the recalcitrant giants and birds by sacrifice and kindness. The giants are his inhibitions, which arise from the unconscious as his journey advances, while the birds pecking out the eyes

[171] Bolte and Polívka, *Anmerkungen*, vol. 3, p. 18, fn. 4.

[172] The same problem occurs in "The Young Hunter and the Beauty of the World."

symbolize evil blinding ideas and fantasies, which hinder insight. By confronting these threatening figures with his words and actions, Ferdinand the Faithful acknowledges them. Figuratively, he gives them bread and meat. Psychologically, this means that he grants them reality (by giving them food), and so they transform into forces that serve him.[173]

953 On his second trip, the hero must return with the writings of the princess. In some parallels, these rather remarkable "scriptures" (perhaps they are spellbooks, which she uses for her mental magic) are replaced by keys.[174] A Romanian version replaces them with the sword of God. Whatever the image, they all refer to spiritual items, a secret knowledge, which is in the possession of a beautiful virgin.

954 Despite all the tasks performed, the captured princess refuses to marry the king, because he has no nose. This sentence can almost be taken literally – he has no sense of smell.[175] In his profane way, he has no empathic understanding of the woman from the magical world, who fell in love with the one who managed to free her from her enchanted sleep.[176] She therefore starts to play mind games. She can – and this should also be taken literally – make men lose their heads, as she deprives them of reason and reflection. The head, as described, is a symbol of the self, which the virgin can deal with as she wishes: she eliminates the secular king and strangely enough, Ferdinand the Unfaithful disappears at the same time. This is not so surprising since his malice works only in conjunction with the king.

955 After the destructive part of the shadow has been eradicated, the helpful side, which until now had to appear in animal garb, can be seen in its real value; that is, it can be redeemed. The white horse advises the hero how to redeem him: by creating a mandala by riding a circle.[177] This cultic circumambulation shuts out all the tendencies invading from the outside, which debase the magical figure of the shadow. This creates a firm inner attitude, an inner center, which lies beyond all human opinions and judgments, and allows the shadow to become what it always was: a royal figure.[178] In the French parallel, "Thirty-From- Paris," at the end the horse changes into the Virgin Mary with

---

[173] In the French parallel, "Thirty-From-Paris," he must tame and subjugate four hungry lions, who symbolize wild instinctual drives.

[174] See Bolte and Polívka, *Anmerkungen*, vol. 3, pp. 21ff.

[175] [In Swiss-German, having "no nose" means having "no clue about what is going on."]

[176] For more on deliverance from the enchanted sleep, see the archetypal image of Brünhilde, who, when she could not marry the one who awoke her, wrought dreadful revenge.

[177] See Bächtold-Stäubli under *umkreisen* [circling] on the symbolic-magical power inherent in encircling. By circumambulating, "the one who is actively or passively encircling the godhead can bring it into a closer relationship, aiming at a "binding" to the divinity. See also Bächtold-Stäubli und *umreiten* [ride around], *Umzug, Umgang* [moving, procession], *Rund* [round], *Kreis* [circle]. On the psychological meaning of creating mandala figures, see the quote by Jung above on page 288.

[178] See Bächtold-Stäubli under *Pferd* [horse]. According to this reference, the prince, the king's son in the tale of the two Ferdinands, is a "helping god that emerges out of the skin of the horse. The fairytale preserves the double layers of the idea of the animal (in the form of the horse) and the human hypostasis of God."

the result that the figure of the horse merges into the main female protagonist of the tale, the princess in the golden castle. Insofar as the two figures are identical, they both transform into their shared archetypal background. The horse was originally an inhabitant of the castle at the beginning of the story, and so the center of this mandala, and was also in a secret manner identical to the daemonic godfather. It was, therefore, not only the shadow (in the sense of a dark daemon – it was, however, white!), rather it was also the higher personality of Ferdinand the Faithful, which compelled him to embark on the heroic journey.

956 In this fairytale, the shadow appears in many different forms: the evil counterpart in Ferdinand the Unfaithful; the driving impulses of the instincts; the higher personalities in the figure of the white horse; and the secular collective world as the king who conspires and thus blends with the personal opponent of the hero. The enchanted prince in animal guise proves to be a divine figure and escort on the way to the magical kingdom. He thus plays a role similar to the Púca in the Irish tale, "The Piper and the Púca," only here the demonic aspects are less dark and sinister, and the evil side appears autonomously as Ferdinand the Unfaithful. Behind the shadow stands the whole unconscious with all its images. Thus the fateful meeting with the shadow can signify the call to heroism. At the same time, these images bring all the destructive powers onto the scene.

957 One story that in a simple form illustrates the fact that the animal-shaped shadow figures represent the alter ego and an all-encompassing human essence that, if rejected, become demonic opponents, is "The Old Rooster":

> 958 There was once a castle, whose lord had an old rooster. Because this rooster was already quite old, the master of the castle did not want to feed him anymore and shooed him out. The old cock had to go around in the neighborhood begging in order to find his food. But as this did not bring enough to preserve his life, the poor rooster decided to return home. On the way he met a fox, who asked him: "Where do you go, my little rooster?" "I'm going home," answered the rooster, "begging did not bring me enough." "Take me with you," said the fox. "I do not have the strength to carry you," answered the cock, "but if you transform yourself into a flea and hide yourself under my wings, I will take you along with me." The fox turned himself into a flea and the cock put him under his wing. Then he wandered on for a while, and met a wolf. The wolf addressed the cock: "Where may you be going, my little rooster?" "Why, I'm going home," said the rooster. When the wolf heard this, he wanted to accompany him as well and said: "Take me with you." "You must change yourself into a flea and come sit under my wing, then I will take you," replied the cock. The wolf became a flea, and the cock stuck him under his side feathers.

959 Then, when he had moved on a little ways, he met a bear, who also wanted to be taken along. The rooster again said if he became a flea he could come along. The bear did just that, and the rooster slipped him under his leg plumage. So he walked on for a while and finally came to his old home. He turned into the courtyard and started to crow:

960 "Doodle-doo, doodle-doo!
The rooster has a gold helmet!
The master is just a poor knave,
who drove his rooster out!"

961 The lord of the castle fell into a huge rage and ordered his servant to kill the rooster. The servant felt sorry for the cock who could crow so beautifully, and refused to do the job that was so repugnant to him. "Well now, you take that cock into the stable and lock him up with the wild stallions, they will soon trample him to death," said the master. The cock was brought to the stable and closed up with the wild stallions. But he came to no harm there, because as the stallions began to stomp around, the rooster spoke, "Come out from under my leg, dear bear, and devour as many as you want and destroy the rest." Immediately the bear appeared and sitting as a flea on the leg of the cock, ate as many of the master's best breeding stallions as he could, and killed and butchered the rest. The next day the king himself came to convince himself that his rooster was crushed and flat as a pancake. But lo! The rooster was still alive and crowed as before:

962 "Doodle-doo, doodle-doo!
The rooster has a gold helmet!
The master is just a poor knave,
who drove his rooster out!"

963 Now in that castle were twelve strong, angry bulls; the king ordered his servant: "Arouse and set those bulls on that rooster so that they smash him to pieces. Finally his impudent crowing will come to an end." Good, the servant let the bulls loose on that irreverent rooster. But as soon as the bulls started to rush at him he reached under his side wing, and that flea changed back into the wolf and slew and ate all the bulls. Then the cock began to sing as before:

964 "Doodle-doo, doodle-doo!
The rooster has a gold helmet!
The master is just a poor knave,
who drove his rooster out!"

965 The King heard this and said in anger to his servants: "We've got twelve big billy-goats, lock that brassy cock up in their pen for the night. Then we will finally have peace from his irritating 'doodle-de-doo.'"

966 No sooner said than done: The servant brought the rooster to the billy-goats and locked him in the pen. Straightaway the goats went after that rooster. But the cock knew just what to do: he called the third flea out from his feathers. This one turned into the fox and tore and gutted the goats quite miserably. He ate as much as he could.

967 In the morning, you could see how the rooster had fared. He was still alive! As soon as the door to the pen opened, the fox slipped out and went his way, wherever that might have been. When the king heard of all that had happened, he began to quake in anger and said: "I will have to kill this preposterous animal myself, come what may!" Having made his royal decision, he went into the barn to strangle that rooster with his own hands. Soon he caught the bird and twisted his neck around, but as he was dying, the cock gasped out, "Even when I am dead, you will not hear the end of me. You will hear me crow once again, but then your own end will be near." When the lord of the castle heard that, he thought in his mind, "I must eat this outlandish troublemaker, and he will finally be silenced from this mad crowing." Then the king prepared a banquet and invited all the lords and ladies from the region. The dead rooster was cooked as a roast.

968 Well, the guests were all gathered together, they sat down at that banquet table and began to feast. Then the king of the castle grasped the roasted cock, cut off a bit of meat and put it to his mouth, saying: "You managed many things in your life, but your crowing doodle-doo will no more be heard." As soon as he had said this, the cock suddenly stuck his head out of the speaker's lips, and crowed as before:

969 "Doodle-doo, doodle-doo!
The rooster has a gold helmet!
The master is just a poor knave,
who drove his rooster out!"

970 When the good company heard this strange voice coming from the mouth of the king they all fell into the greatest consternation, stood up and left the banquet hall. Finally, when the lord recovered from his surprise, he called to his servants, "Go get an ax and when that rooster again comes out of my mouth, split his head!"

971 The servants did as they were commanded, and as soon as the cock again stuck its head out of the king's mouth, they raised the ax. With

the ax coming down, the cock quickly drew his head back, and the ax smashed the head of the lord of the castle. He sank back, dead; just as the rooster had predicted. And that is the way it is.[179]

972 In popular belief, the rooster is "first an oracular animal that especially with his crowing, but also foretells many things with his doings in general."[180] If the barnyard rooster dies, then the master must also die. As the announcer of the coming day, he drives away the demons of the night. Due to his vigilance, he is in general an animal that defends one from demons and protects one from carrying out devilish deeds. (Hence his crowing at the denial of Jesus by Simon Peter.) The crowing of the cock warns against disaster and announces the proximity of evil forces. People who cannot endure the crowing of the cock are suspected of being in league with the devil. Grünbaum mentions the idea of a heavenly cock in the Jewish and Arabian traditions.[181] This is the primal image of the praiser of God, reflected in the earthly cock. These are messengers of light, the cock is consecrated to Apollo, who is pictured with a cock on his hand.[182] On *Abraxasgemmen,*[183] the cock figured as a symbol of the sun. It can distinguish day from night and wakes people to work and prayer. The rooster wakes from sleep, laziness, and the night of sin. The rooster is a border guard on the threshold to the hereafter; this is why a rust-brown rooster stands at the threshold and greets new arrivals to the kingdom of the Germanic goddess of the underworld.[184] At the same time, the rooster, because he proclaims the appearance of the new sun, the new day, at the threshold to Hades, is a symbol of hope and resurrection and is often depicted in this role in ancient tombs.[185]

973 These connections show that the lord of the castle (also called the "king") rejects that voice of his soul that could lift him out of his mundane nature. It is his own Self, his inner immortal personality, that resists rebirth after death. The cock is as old as the lord of the castle himself, and if he wants to eliminate his rooster, he is relentlessly destroying his own aging, the natural rhythm of his life. In the verses of the cock, the lord of the castle is being made aware of the great value of his golden helmet, compared to which the limited mundane personality is a "poor knave."

---

179 [Translated from Löwis of Menar, *Finnische Volksmärchen*, Jena, 1922, pp. 148–152.]

180 See Bächtold-Stäubli under *Hahn* [rooster, cock] and *Hahnenkrähen* [cock crow].

181 See M. Grünbaum, *Aufsätze,* Berlin, 1901 pp. 37ff.

182 On the cock as an attribute animal, "of the all-knowing sun god and opponent of demons," see also Bächtold-Stäubli under *Alektryomantie* [alectryomancy, i.e., rooster divination].

183 [Amulets from late antiquity and the early Middle Ages (400 to 1000 AD) were considered to possess supernatural or magical powers and stemming from the Gnostic sect of Basilides around AD 130.]

184 See Führer, *Nordgermanische*, p. 82, and Mogk, *Germanische*, p. 117.

185 See Bachofen, *Die Unsterblichkeitslehre der orphischen Theologie auf den Grab- denkmälern des Alterthums. Nach Anleitung einer Vase aus Canosa im Besitz des Herrn Prosper Biardot in Paris,* dargestellt von Dr. J. J. Bachofen mit einer Tafel in Farbendruck, Basel, 1867, p. 21; see also Bachofen, *Das Lykische Volk und seine Bedeutung für die Entwicklung des Altertums*, Freiburg i. Br., 1862, p. 61f.

974 Yet this is only one aspect of the cock; in that he embodies the male principle, he is also a symbol of instinctual life. In our fairytale this is confirmed particularly through his association with the bear, wolf, and fox, here transformed into the "fleas" of the rooster. This shows that they belong very closely to his essence, as if they were other aspects of himself. It also says that all these drives, urges, instinctive impulses, and desires, which the bear, wolf, and fox represent are sources of inner turmoil within the lord of the castle and are capable of wreaking great destruction in parts of his being. They destroy useful domesticated animals. Psychologically, this means that the natural forces nourishing and supporting life are defeated by the wild instincts. And of all this, the contempt for the cock is the cause, because the cock is the secret center of life, which governs these powers, and also the lord of the castle's alter ego.

975 If a person does not voluntarily follow their inner voice, they will be forced to succumb to its wish as fate. The lord of the castle must "swallow" his shadow, that is, take it into himself. Since he does not do this humbly in the framework of a ritual sacrificial meal vis-á-vis his victim, but rather in anger and with evil intent, it becomes his ruin. Impressive is the image of how the rooster "himself speaks out of his mouth," that is, as his own voice. He governs his own unconscious, which, against his own will, proclaims the truth.[186] In that the lord of the castle "kills" his own unconscious, he kills himself in the truest sense of the word. In his senseless rage, he destroys himself because he has failed to recognize the divine core, which approached him in the figure of his animal shadow.

976 Displaying hubris towards the figures of the magical realm and its tragic consequences is a common fairytale motif. When a person presumes to possess abilities and attributes lying beyond their actual capabilities, such an inflation always lead to catastrophes.[187] These disasters are often represented as acts of revenge by the Supernaturals. This is aptly depicted in the Grimm's fairytale, "The Fisherman and His Wife":

[186] See the cock as proclaimer of truth and conscience in the Livonian fairytale, "The Money Mill," in which a poor man plants a bean instead of eating it. The bean grows to heaven and the poor man climbs it and finds an angel grinding money from a mill. He asks for the mill and returns home with it. A rich and envious farmer steals the mill, but the poor man's cock crows out who did the deed. The rooster then goes to the barn of the thief and sings out: "Little man, beggar man, give the mill back to the poor man." The cock is locked in the barn and then the stables and each time he opens the gate a wolf comes and eats the cows and then the horses. He sings his song again, and is thrown into the well. He drinks the well dry and sings again. He is put into an oven but the cock put out the fire and sang again. The rich farmer kills and eats the bird but the cock crows his song from the farmer's belly. However, now the rich farmer takes the money mill and the rooster back to the poor man who is still milling money even today. Löwis of Menar, *Finnische Volksmärchen*, pp. 290–293. See related motifs in other fairytales, such as "The Little Half-Cock" or "The Cock and the Hand Mill." Due to his truth- proclaiming crowing, an old married couple can retrieve their magic handmill from a thieving boyar. Similarly, in "The Daughter With a Sweet-Tooth," the rooster again betrays the truth.

[187] See C.G. Jung, "Relation between the ego and the unconscious," CW 7, ¶225–227, 233ff.

977 Once upon a time there were a fisherman and his wife who lived together in a pigsty[188] near the sea. Every day the fisherman went out fishing, and he fished, and he fished. Once he was sitting there fishing and looking into the clear water, and he sat, and he sat. Then his hook went to the bottom, deep down, and when he pulled it out, he had caught a large flounder. Then the flounder said to him, "Listen, fisherman, I beg you to let me live. I am not an ordinary flounder, but an enchanted prince. How will it help you to kill me? I would not taste good to you. Put me back into the water, and let me swim." "Well," said the man, "there's no need to say more. I can certainly let a fish swim away who knows how to talk."

978 With that he put it back into the clear water, and the flounder disappeared to the bottom, leaving a long trail of blood behind him. Then the fisherman got up and went home to his wife in the pigsty.

979 "Husband," said the woman, "didn't you catch anything today?"

980 "No," said the man. "I caught a flounder, but he told me that he was an enchanted prince, so I let him swim away."

981 "Didn't you ask for anything first?" said the woman.

982 "No," said the man. "What should I have asked for?"

983 "Oh," said the woman. "It is terrible living in this shack. It stinks and is filthy. You should have asked for a little cottage for us. Go back and call him. Tell him that we want to have a little cottage. He will surely give it to us."

984 The man did not want to go, but neither did he want to oppose his wife, so he went back to the sea. When he arrived there it was no longer clear, but yellow and green. He stood there and said:

985 *Mandje! Mandje! Timpe Te!*[189]
Flounder, flounder, in the sea!
My wife, my wife Ilsebill,
Wants not, wants not, what I will.

986 The flounder swam up and said, "What does she want then?"

---

188 [The couple's original place of residence, in the Grimm's Low German, is called a *Pissputt*, literally, a "piss hole."]

189 [D. L. Ashliman, the translator of many Grimm's fairytales, leaves untranslated the formulaic introduction to the fisherman's oft-repeated call to the fish, *Mandje! Mandje! Timpe Te!* From other sources it is evident that *Mandje* is a dialect word for "Little Man," as in High German *Männchen*. "Timpe Te" appears to be the fisherman's name – elsewhere he is called "Domine" or "Dudeldee." Thus the verse, as recorded by the original source, Philipp Otto Runge, and immortalized by the Grimm brothers, appears to be a corruption of a more logical version (not unusual in folklore). Logically the fish, not the fisherman, would call out the salutation, *Mandje! Mandje! Timpe Te!*. Remarks by Ashliman.]

987 "Oh," said the man, "I did catch you, and now my wife says that I really should have asked for something. She doesn't want to live in a pigsty any longer. She would like to have a cottage." "Go home," said the flounder. "She already has it."

988 The man went home, and his wife was standing in the door of a cottage, and she said to him, "Come in. See, now isn't this much better?" There was a little front yard, and a beautiful little parlor, and a bedroom where their bed was standing, and a kitchen, and a dining room. Everything was beautifully furnished and supplied with tin and brass utensils, just as it should be. And outside there was a little yard with chickens and ducks and a garden with vegetables and fruit.

989 "Look," said the woman. "Isn't this nice?"

990 "Yes," said the man. "This is quite enough. We can live here very well."

991 "We will think about that," said the woman.

992 Then they ate something and went to bed.

993 Everything went well for a week or two, and then the woman said, "Listen, husband. This cottage is too small. The yard and the garden are too little. The flounder could have given us a larger house. I would like to live in a large stone palace. Go back to the flounder and tell him to give us a palace."

994 The man's heart was heavy, and he did not want to go. He said to himself, "This is not right," but he went anyway. When he arrived at the sea the water was purple and dark blue and gray and dense, and no longer green and yellow.

995 [The man called again and the flounder appeared. The man sadly asked for a stone palace and the flounder said he should go home, she was already standing before the door.] Then the man went his way, thinking he was going home, but when he arrived, standing there was a large stone palace. His wife was standing on the stairway, about to enter. Taking him by the hand, she said, "Come inside."

996 [They entered a magnificent castle. But again the wife wanted to think about it, and in the morning demanded that her husband ask the flounder to make her the king! So the man, saddened because his wife wanted to be king, went back.] "This is not right, not right at all," thought the man. He did not want to go, but he went anyway. When he arrived at the sea it was dark gray, and the water heaved up from below and had a foul smell. He stood there and repeated the call.

997 [Again, the flounder granted the wish and when the man returned home the palace had become much larger, with a tall tower and

magnificent decorations. Sentries stood outside the door, and there were so many soldiers, and drums, and trumpets. When he went inside everything was of pure marble and gold with velvet covers and large golden tassels. Then the doors to the great hall opened up, and there was the entire court. His wife was sitting on a high throne of gold and diamonds. She was wearing a large golden crown, and in her hand was a scepter of pure gold and precious stones. On either side of her there stood a line of maids-in-waiting, each one a head shorter than the other.

998 [This time his wife wanted to become the emperor. Being the king, she demanded that the man ask the flounder again to grant her wish.] So the man had to go. As he went on his way the frightened man thought to himself, "This is not going to end well. To ask to be emperor is shameful. The flounder is going to get tired of this."

999 With that he arrived at the sea. The water was all black and dense and boiling up from within. A strong wind blew over him that curdled the water. He stood there and repeated his call [The flounder came and again granted the wish.] The man went home, and when he arrived there, the entire palace was made of polished marble with alabaster statues and golden decoration. Soldiers were marching outside the gate, blowing trumpets and beating timpani and drums. Inside the house, barons and counts and dukes were walking around like servants. They opened the doors for him, which were made of pure gold. He went inside where his wife was sitting on a throne made of one piece of gold a good two miles high, and she was wearing a large golden crown that was three yards high, all set with diamonds and carbuncles. In the one hand she had a scepter, and in the other the imperial orb. Bodyguards were standing in two rows at her sides: each one smaller than the other, beginning with the largest giant and ending with the littlest dwarf, who was no larger than my little finger. The man went and stood among them and said, "Wife, are you emperor now?" "Yes," she said, "I am emperor." He stood and looked at her, and after thus looking at her for a while, he said, "Wife, it is very nice that you are emperor."

1000 "Husband," she said. "Why are you standing there? Now that I am emperor, I want to become Pope."

1001 "Oh, wife!" said the man. "What do you not want? There is only one Pope in all Christendom. The flounder cannot make you Pope."

1002 "Husband," she said, "I want to become Pope. Go there immediately. I must become Pope this very day."

1003 "No, wife," he said, "I cannot tell him that. It will come to no good. That is too much. The flounder cannot make you Pope."

1004 "Husband, what nonsense!" said the woman. "If he can make me emperor, then he can make me Pope as well. Go there immediately. I am emperor, and you are my husband. Are you going?"

1005 Then the frightened man went. He felt sick all over, and his knees and legs were shaking, and the wind was blowing over the land, and clouds flew by as the darkness of evening fell. Leaves blew from the trees, and the water roared and boiled as it crashed onto the shore. In the distance he could see ships, shooting distress signals as they tossed and turned on the waves. There was a little blue in the middle of the sky, but on all sides it had turned red, as in a terrible lightning storm. Full of despair he stood there and called out again.

1006 *Mandje! Mandje! Timpe Te!*
Flounder, flounder, in the sea!
My wife, my wife Ilsebill,
Wants not, wants not, what I will.
"What does she want then?" said the flounder.
"Oh," said the man, "she wants to become Pope."
"Go home," said the flounder. "She is already Pope."

1007 Then he went home, and when he arrived there, there was a large church surrounded by nothing but palaces. He forced his way through the crowd. Inside everything was illuminated with thousands and thousands of lights, and his wife was clothed in pure gold and sitting on a much higher throne. She was wearing three large golden crowns. She was surrounded with church-like splendor, and at her sides there were two banks of candles. The largest was as thick and as tall as the largest tower, down to the smallest kitchen candle. And all the emperors and kings were kneeling before her kissing her slipper. ["You are the Pope said the man, surely this is enough!" The new Pope had to think about it.]

1008 The man slept well and soundly, for he had run about a lot during the day, but the woman could not sleep at all, but tossed and turned from one side to the other all night long, always thinking about what she could become, but she could not think of anything. Then the sun was about to rise, and when she saw the early light of dawn she sat up in bed and watched through the window as the sun came up. "Aha," she thought. "Could not I cause the sun and the moon to rise?"

1009 "Husband," she said, poking him in the ribs with her elbow, "wake up and go back to the flounder. I want to become like God."

1010 The man, who was still mostly asleep, was so startled that he fell out of bed. He thought that he had misunderstood her, so, rubbing his eyes, he said, "Wife, what did you say?"

1011 "Husband," she said, "I cannot stand it when I see the sun and the moon rising, and I cannot cause them to do so. I will not have a single hour of peace until I myself can cause them to rise."

1012 She looked at him so gruesomely that he shuddered.

1013 "Go there immediately. I want to become like God."

1014 "Oh, wife," said the man, falling on his knees before her, "the flounder cannot do that. He can make you emperor and Pope, but I beg you, be satisfied and remain Pope."

1015 Anger fell over her. Her hair flew wildly about her head. Tearing open her bodice she kicked him with her foot and shouted, "I cannot stand it! I cannot stand it any longer! Go there immediately!" He put on his trousers and ran off like a madman.

1016 Outside such a storm was raging that he could hardly stand on his feet. Houses and trees were blowing over. The mountains were shaking, and boulders were rolling from the cliffs into the sea. The sky was as black as pitch. There was thunder and lightning. In the sea there were great black waves as high as church towers and mountains, all capped with crowns of white foam.

1017 *Mandje! Mandje! Timpe Te!*
Flounder, flounder, in the sea!
My wife, my wife Ilsebill,
Wants not, wants not, what I will
"What does she want then?" said the flounder.
"Oh," he said, "she wants to become like God."
"Go home. She is sitting in her pigsty again."
And they are sitting there even today.[190]

1018 What strikes one in this tale is its rounded artistic form: the incorporation of nature into the action, the colors seen by the fishermen in the seas, and beginning with the long trail of red blood to the caps of white foam at the end, all colors of the rainbow reveal their diversity. Then the increase in the splendor of the pageantry until all the soldiers and courtiers in the imperial palace come into motion, and in the end this is topped off by the massive

---

[190] [The original is in "wonderfully simple yet poetic Low German" (Ashliman). For a standard version, see *Complete Grimm's*, pp. 103–112. The edited version followed here is the online translation by D. L. Ashliman.]

grandiosity of the Pope scene with its bright lights. Only the beauties of the cosmos and the natural powers of God are greater than this. In addition, the behavior of the two protagonists changes against the forever taciturn uniformity of the fish, which, however, has unimagined consequences ; one could speak of the tale's perfect artistic sense. According to Bolte-Polívka,[191] the source is the painter, Philipp Otto Runge, who recorded this fairytale in the Pomeranian dialect in 1806 and sent it to J. G. Zimmer, the Heidelberg publisher of the *Wunderhorn*. The Brothers Grimm received the fairytale in 1809 from Achim von Arnim. Here perhaps lies the reason for the very picturesque design of this story, whereas most other tales are terse. But Runge's embellished display is not unnatural, the rich detail is carried by the movement of events in artistic harmony with the form and content.

1019 The fisherman, who sits by the sea and fishes, is emblematic of those who, with silent and tenacious patience, take their nourishment from the unruly element. He also represents those who bring up spiritual values from the psychic realm.[192] Thus he is a figure of the culture bringer.[193] Popular imagination plays with the mutual relationship between the fisherman and fish.[194] The fish is a "fruit" of the sea and is a symbol of fertility and life. It can foretell the future and is a manifestation of the soul. Mythology depicts many demons in the shape of fish. Because the fish is considered sacred in some religions, it can only be eaten as a sacrificial animal. The fish's way of life eludes the eye, making it particularly suited to hiding mysterious secrets from people. In popular superstition, the success of the fisherman depends on his own magical power. To improve his catch, he observes – according to old German superstition – chastity and fasting. In other cultures, fishermen kept away from women; encountering a woman was even considered a bad omen for the next fishing.

1020 In that the fish signifies the inspirational and nurturing function of the unconscious,[195] it symbolizes the psychic power that fulfils every wish of the imagination. Wishful thinking is a common fairytale motif and was derived from the ideas of primitive peoples.[196] With regard to wishful thinking, Emma Jung[197] comments on the fairytale formula, "at the time, when wishing still

---

[191] See Bolte and Polívka, *Anmerkungen*, vol. 1, p. 138.
[192] See C.G. Jung, "Archetypes of the Collective Unconscious," CW 9i, ¶51.
[193] [Literally, culture creator.]
[194] See Bächtold-Stäubli under *Fischer, fischen* [fishermen, fishing], *Fisch* [fish], and *Ichthyomantie* (ichthyomancy – divination using behavior of fish or fish entrails).
[195] C.G. Jung, "Archetypes of the Collective Unconscious," CW 9i, ¶248.
[196] See the tale retold above, "Lasse, My Servant," for an example of this wish fulfilling power. Furthermore, "The Poor Man and the Rich Man," "The Wishing-Table, the Gold-Ass, and the Cudgel in the Sack," "The Tailor and His Three Sons," and "The Wild Man." In a Danish fairytale, "Lazy Lars Who Got the Princess," the useless and lazy hero receives from a frog, whose life he had spared, the magical gift to grant every wish. He is saved from becoming completely spoiled by a princess for whom he had wished. She convinced him to wish that he become an able man and good worker.
[197] See Emma Jung, "Beitrag zum Problem des Animus," Zürich, 1934, p. 320.

helped," which refers to this as a past time. Also Jacob Grimm, in his *Deutsche Mythologie*,[198] notes the connection between wishing, imagining, and thinking. Thus, catching the miracle fish reveals possibilities to the fishermen's imagination that, however, can never be realized in real life.

1021 The fulfiller of all desires cannot be just an ordinary fish. In this tale, the fish tells the fisherman that he is an enchanted prince. Thus a kind of higher human being is hidden in him. In their writings, medieval alchemists describe a spirit that resides in the primal depths of the water. This figure is often described as a round fish in the sea.[199] Elsewhere, it is described as a king's son who has lost his soul lying in the depth of the waters crying for deliverance.[200] The fish is, therefore, a divine spirit that is hidden in the unconscious and is the source of all imagination.[201]

1022 Thus, the fisherman encounters a manifestation of the primal spirit. The fish here corresponds to the white horse in "Ferdinand the Faithful and Ferdinand the Unfaithful," who is also an enchanted prince behind whom lay concealed a creative spirit.[202] But the fisherman in our tale is unable to recognize the opportunity that is offered him and fails to ask the fish how he could be redeemed. At its request, he lets the fish swim away again.[203] Alas, the encounter with the fish has neither good nor bad consequences, just like the thousands of unused inner possibilities that every person carelessly misses occasionally. But then his wife's greed becomes involved. As so often in life, the woman has more intuitive awareness of the realities of the magical realm than the man, and she recognizes, therefore, the tremendous opportunities that her husband let slip away. Although at first she appears to be independent, she clearly represents that side of him which is open to the unconscious, his prescience and intuitive capacities; but also his secret desires hidden in his soul, unacknowledged, harbouring powerful unconscious ambitions. He lives so closely with her, without defending himself against her aspirations to power,

---

[198] J. Grimm, *Deutsche Mythologie*, Göttingen, 1844.

[199] On the "round" fish endowed with "a wonder-working virtue" as the arcane substance, see C.G. Jung, *Psychology and Alchemy*, CW 12, ¶101.

[200] See C.G. Jung, *"Visions of Zosimos,"* CW 13, ¶101; *Psychology and Alchemy*, CW 12, ¶434; *Psychologie und Religion*, CW 11, ¶92.

[201] In "Ichthys," vol. 1 (1910, p. 115), Dölger points out that the Babylonian culture bringer, Oannes, emerged half man, half-fish from the sea. He is identical with Ea, the "God of the water house," i.e., a fish deity (as defined in this work: a god of the magical kingdom). See the description of the two-headed monster in Dölger, "Ichthys," vol. 2, 1922, pp. 230–231.

[202] A Chinese fairytale, "The Bird with the Nine Heads," tells how the hero touches a fish nailed with four nails (mandala!) to the wall that then transforms into a handsome youth. It later turns out that he is the son of the great sea dragon. See also H. Usener, *Sintfluthsagen*, Bonn, 1899, esp. pp. 138–154. Usener considers the divine fish (also as an attribute of a god or the mount of a mythical figure) in wider mythological context. He mentions the dolphin as a double of Hermes (pp. 166ff). This concept makes sense since the figure of the miracle fish is a kind of alter ego, just like Hermes is a soul guide.

[203] See the story of Manu, the first man in Indian myth of the Deluge. A small fish asks for mercy and care, which he receives from Manu. Later when it has grown up, he advises Manu and during the flood tows Manu's ship to the summit of a mountain and continues to stand by him (Usener, *Sintfluthsagen*, pp. 25–26).

that he also becomes responsible for her behavior (like Adam does with Eve in the biblical narrative).

1023 In this fairytale, the wife wants to successively climb to the highest levels. That she claims only male offices is a good indication that she is not an independent personality but a part of the fisherman. Deep inside, he wants to be king, Pope, and even God. Like many seemingly modest people, he does not openly admit his aspirations to power, which are even stronger as a result.

1024 One can see the whole story as an inner personal drama, in that the man presents a limited ego consciousness and subjugates himself to the inordinate desires of his unconscious feelings. Thus, despite some doubts about the legality of his deeds, he still lets himself be driven to do foolish acts. The fisherman ends up in a hurried, restless state. He is constantly going back and forth from the sea to his wife to fulfill her wishes, which he dare not question. At first, he and his wife are granted the great honor that they seek: corresponding to its nature, the fish fulfills its generative, giving function. Only the ever-wilder discoloration of waters indicates his growing dissatisfaction. According to the secret yet inexorably present "justice" of the unconscious, this gradually takes on a negative aspect. The fisherman becomes more and more possessed and governed by his imperious wife, that is, he is increasingly subjugated by his own lust for power. His resistance weakens, and he succumbs increasingly to the unconscious: on the one hand, to the fish and, on the other, to his wife. In his immoderacy and inflation, the fisherman is actually swallowed up by the unconscious. His wife takes on the polar position as the evil one against the gradual opposition of the fish, bestowing gifts beyond limit. The ending is sweet and short, like the stroke of fate: in the moment when the megalomania of the fisherman reaches its climax, namely, when his wife desires to become God, the pendulum swings back, and the fisherman is forced to realize the actual reality of his existence. The house of cards collapses, the source of power in the unconscious suddenly dries up, landing the fisherman back in the bitter and sobering situation of his prosaic, everyday life. The fish who, had the fisherman followed the right path, might have bestowed on him his inner values, thus lifting him out of his lower, inferior sphere, leaves him because he became overly conscious, so that he became the plaything of the unconscious forces.[204]

1025 Significantly, some variants of the same tale are told as a dream process, from which the dreamer eventually awakes disappointed.[205] Being trapped by

---

[204] See similar stories about gain and loss due to incorrect or correct behavior relative to the unconscious: "The Soldier who went from a General to a Goat Herder," "The Unsatisfied Son," "The Raven and the She-Fox," "Raven Stories," and "The Fool Who Became King."

[205] Cf. Bolte and Mackensen, *Handwörterbuch*, under *Fischer un syne Fru* [The Fisherman and His Wife], especially section 3 with the quote from Spiess: "How the man who takes delight in a happy dream in his sleep at his awakening is suddenly thrown into the harsh, sober reality and feels like the beautiful magical image that the unconscious conjured up before him, he cannot stop from sliding

illusionary images from the unconscious is here pictured as a dream and falling back into reality as an awakening. This formulation is both a metaphor and a reality. There are only a few fairytales that characterized this dangerous confusion with its negative results down to the last consequences as psychologically true and subtly as "The Fisherman and His Wife."

1026 A charming Japanese parallel is "Hanatarekozô-sama":

> There once lived a poor old man in the land of Higo in the high mountain village Mayumi. Every day he went out into the mountains and collected firewood, which he brought back and sold in the town of Seki. One day, he found no one to buy his firewood and disheartened, stopped on the bridge of the river that ran into Seki. Since he could not get rid of the wood in the market and he did not want to lug it all back home, he decided to throw it, bundle by bundle, into the river. He called out: "River god, Ryûjin-sama, I give you here an offering and ask for a counter-gift!" No sooner had he thrown the last bundle into the river, than there arose a young woman from the waves more beautiful than any woman he had ever seen. She cried out to the old man, who was already going away, to come back. When he returned to the riverside he saw that she carried a tiny baby in her arms. The woman turned to him and spoke: "Because thou worked diligently day by day and because thou hast brought us today such wonderful wood, the river god is very pleased and gives this little child to you as a reward. It goes by the name Hanatarekozô-sama and will fulfill your every wish. Only you must never forget to serve him a lobster salad three times a day, otherwise your wishes will be for nothing." The old man accepted the gift and took the baby home. The child really did fulfill every wish of the old man. If he wanted to have some rice or any other food, he just asked the child, and no sooner was the wish uttered, than he heard a sound like a very fine sneezing, and what he wanted lay there before him. He thought of his house, it was like a hovel, and he wished for a beautiful palace. The child sneezed only once and lo! There stood a palace, and a farm, and barns filled with everything he needed.
>
> 1027 Thus lived the old man month after month in fullness, he had everything he wished for. Naturally, he did not go out every day collecting firewood like in the days before, his only job was to go every day into the town and buy lobster for the lobster salad that he served Harantarekozô-sama. Since he had everything he wanted, he came to

away, thus the fisherman with his wife, who still has all the royal pomp and glory before her eyes, suddenly finds herself back in her miserable fishermen's hut." See also the other parallels, as well as "The Upright Citizen Misery and the Beanstalk."

> feel that it was superfluous to do this work of traveling into the town. So one day he lifted the child down from his altar and said: "Hanatarekozô-sama, since I have everything I ever wanted, I have no further wishes of you. Please go back to the Dragon Palace and give the river god my deepest gratitude for everything." No sooner had he said this, than Hantarekozô-sama stepped silently out of the house. Immediately afterwards the old man heard a sound like a fine sneezing. Hardly had the sound died away, than the house and palace disappeared, and with them the barn and storage rooms with all the treasures they contained. In their place stood his old hovel. The old firewood collector was as poor as he had been before.[206]

1028 Here, a small child comes from the water instead of the fish. This child – as the "round fish" of the alchemists – represents the self. It symbolizes eternal youth, that which is not entangled in the world, a being engaged in divine play, from whom issue all the forces that shape reality. It is therefore considered to be the lord over infinite wealth. But only the wise, who can in humility adjust to this wealth of the soul, are permitted to share in it, while those harboring self-inflated hubris, or, as here, indifferent laziness, draw to themselves the immediate loss of these values.[207] In a related fairytale, "The Freeloader," a good-for-nothing freeloader embarks on the following adventure:

> 1029 There once was a man who was lazy and stupid. He had nothing he called his own, he disliked all work. He would go around: to one person he begged for something to eat, to another for something to drink. Thus he went through life, knowing neither fame nor shame. His neighbors were generous and helped him when his begging brought nothing. When he came around, people would say: "Here comes the Sponger! Certainly he wants something from us." He went on doing the same thing, acting as if he did not hear. Eventually nobody wanted anything more to do with him. He decided, therefore, to take his case to the Creator. In order to get closer to God, he climbed up a high mountain. A wolf that passed by asked the freeloader where he was going. "To God." "Well, then if that is true can you ask him a question for me? I eat a lot of animal meat, but still do not get any fatter, what should I eat to get fat?" The freeloader agreed and went on. He met an oak tree who wanted him to ask God

---

[206] Translated from Hammitzsch et al., *Japanische*, pp. 139–141.

[207] See also "The Fairy Harp," where a farmer receives a gift from the fairies of a harp which, whenever heard, makes the listener get up and dance. But the farmer misuses the harp to wreak personal revenge, and the instrument is taken from him.

why one side of his trunk was dry; a fish who wanted to know why he was blind in one eye. With the help of a deer, the lazy good-for-nothing reached God, and shivering, said he had nothing to eat or drink. The Almighty answered that he could go home now, he would find everything he needed. The man then asked the questions from the wolf, the oak, and the fish. The All-Knowing answered him. The man thanked God, mounted the deer and returned down the mountain path.

1030 After thanking the deer, he met the fish anxiously awaiting his answer. The freeloader reported what God had told him: the fish was blind in one eye because a diamond was stuck in its gill. The fish pleaded with the man to take the diamond out, which he did. In gratitude the fish gave the man the diamond. But the freeloader threw it away, saying that when he got home he would have everything he wanted and therefore did not need the diamond. The fish said to himself: "Now that is really a stupid human being!" But the sponger went on. He next met the old oak tree, also waiting for his answer. The man told the oak tree what he had learned from the Highest One: that one side of the oak was dry because a wine barrel lay buried beneath that side. The oak tree asked the man to dig up the wine barrel, and the freeloader complied. The barrel was filled not with wine but gold and silver! The oak tree gave all the contents to the man who gave the barrel a kick and it rolled down the hill into an abyss. The tree shook its leaves in consternation: "More dumb you cannot get. He could have given the gold and silver to needy people!" Then the freeloader came upon the wolf and promptly related the answer he had heard from the One On High: "If you want to get fat, you should eat human flesh." "Oh," said the wolf, "I see that you are a human!" and he tore at the man's throat and promptly ate him up."[208]

1031 The last two fairytales describe an imbalance between consciousness and the unconscious in that consciousness behaves unbefittingly. That such a process, with its catastrophic consequences for the human being, is possible at all, must have more profound reasons. In "The Fisherman and His Wife," nothing further is explored. Apparently, the cause is only the wife's or both protagonists' blind greed. In contrast, the tale, "My Old Woman Must Be Paid," tells a different story,[209] where after a revealing prelude, the plot brings

---

[208] A. Dirr, *Kaukasische Märchen*, Jena, 1922, pp. 9–13 [translated from the German]. See also "The Enchanted Linden Tree" and Zimmer, *Weisheit Indiens*, p. 20f., who retells a parallel tale with commentary; see *ibid.*, pp. 38–39.

[209] There are many variations on this theme. See Bolte and Polívka, *Anmerkungen*, vol. 1, p. 147: ". . . among the French and Italians . . . in most cases the man goes up to Heaven on a beanstalk and the

a whole new process to light. The rest of the action runs fairly parallel to the tales related above:

1032 An old couple lived impoverished in a dilapidated hut. They had nothing of value except a golden button on the woman's sewing spindle. Every day, the man would go hunting or fishing to provide them with food. Near the hut there was a large hill; the people living in this region believed that an elf by the name of Kidhus lived inside, but they had only mistrust for this being. One day, as was often the case, the man was off hunting and the woman sat in the house spinning. Since there was nice weather, she decided to do her work outside. She went out and spun for awhile. Suddenly, the golden button on her spindle fell off and rolled away. The woman lost track of exactly where it went and looked for it, but all in vain. When her husband came home she told him what had happened. "Surely it was Kidhus who took it. That is just the kind of thing that he does."

1033 The husband set off for Kidhus's hill, telling his wife that he was going to ask for the button back, or to get something better in return. This sounded a little strange to her and she wondered what it meant. The man went to the hill where Kidhus lived and banged on the ground a long time with his club. Finally he heard a voice.

1034 "Who knocks at my house?"

1035 The farmer answered, "It is I, the old farmer, dear Kidhus. My wife wants something in return for her button!"

1036 Kidhus asked what she wanted to have. The farmer thought and said, "Dear Kidhus, she would like a cow that gave a quarter of a barrel of milk each time she was milked." This Kidhus granted straightway. The man returned to his wife with the cow. The next day when all her pails were full of milk, she thought she could cook up some groats. But first she would need some flour. She went to her husband and asked if he would go to Kidhus again and ask for some flour. The man went and pounded on the hill with his cane again. When Kidhus answered, the man repeated what he said earlier. When asked what he wanted, the man said some flour. Kidhus immediately produced a ton of flour. The man went back home with the flour and his wife cooked up the groats.

1037 After they had finished eating, there was still a large amount of groats left. The woman thought of what she could do with them and decided to bring them to the Virgin Mary in Heaven. She quickly

Lord God himself or the Porter at the Gateway to Heaven fulfills the man's requests." See also *ibid* Note 1: "Among the Russians, Lithuanians, and the Tatar, it is a tree stump, a cat, a fox, a bird, or a saint."

saw, however, that this was not such an easy undertaking. They decided to go again to Kidhus and ask for a ladder that would reach to Heaven. Again the man went to Kidhus, and proceeded as before. Kidhus answered, "Is that shoddy button not paid for yet?" But the farmer asked him, pleading from his heart, saying he would like to take the rest of the groats to the Virgin Mary in Heaven. At this, Kidhus let himself be moved and gave him the ladder.

1038 Happy, the man returned home. The husband and wife made ready for the trip, packed up the groats, and started to climb. Soon they reached such a height that they became dizzy. They lost their balance and fell to the ground, their heads splitting into two pieces. Pieces of brain and groats scattered all over. Where parts of their brains landed on stones, there arose white lichen. Where the groats fell on stones, there grew yellow lichen. Both kinds of lichen you can find today on rocks all over.[210]

1039 Here the tragedy is preceded by an encroachment from the magical realm, the abduction of Kidhus, the elf. From the outset, the unconscious, represented by Kidhus, is portrayed as threatening and powerful. Kidhus takes the golden button from the woman's spindle.[211] This inconspicuous little thing is obviously of paramount importance, as proven by the fact that it is golden. The button is round; it is "the round one" and means, therefore, the center of the unconscious, that which is of highest value to the innermost psyche. The destruction of personality that follows is already hinted at in this process: the essential core that holds the whole being together is lost to the shadows in the form of an elfish natural being, so that the outbreak of demonic forces is prepared in the unconscious. The loss of the button establishes a bond with the magical kingdom,[212] which only becomes dangerous when it is not the return of the ring that is sought, but the extortion of the magical. The couple tries to exchange something inner that is lost with worldly values and thus becomes entangled in an uncertain relationship to the unconscious. The interchange of inner against outer values, and the unclear blending of the

---

210 H. and I. Naumann (trans.), *Isländische*, pp. 124–126; translated from their German version with slight editing.

211 [Thus, Kidhus may have a parallel in Tolkein's Golum, a character in *The Hobbit* and *Lord of the Rings*, who finds the "ring of rings" in the water and keeps it greedily for himself.]

212 See "Lump Paradise" and "Wait, Lump!" In both tales, a lump or clod rolls into the magical kingdom. In the first tale, an old man, in the second, a woman, follow the lump and return with something valuable from the magical realm. Out of greed, their neighbors imitate them and push their own lumps along, but behave arrogantly towards the demons and, of course, fare poorly. The theme of loss to the magical kingdom and the inflated, ungracious attitude, which in the tale from Iceland is the fate of *one* pair, is here experienced by all the main figures and their shadows. See also the same idea of a bonding to the magical kingdom created through the loss of an object in a Samoan myth reported in L. Frobenius, *Zeitalter*, Berlin, 1904, p. 71f.

magical with the mundane sphere are crucial human errors that have the most tragic consequences.[213] The mixture of conscious and unconscious rests ultimately on a shift of the inner focus, expressed in the Icelandic fairytale in the loss of the button. Since the real essence is lost, people lose their inner balance when encountering the shadow; they "reach beyond themselves" and become overly presumptuous. This is portrayed quite literally in the fairytale by ascending up the ladder to Heaven. The couple becomes inflated with its unconscious fantasies, culminating in the fact that they think they can offer the Virgin Mary alms (food scraps)! Therein also lies a weak attempt to conciliate the unconscious, rendering it less threatening. They seem to sense that something was not in order, and apparently this is true. They also want to play the Christian divinity off against the pagan Kidhus elf, and save themselves from the destructive forces of nature in the unconscious by transferring them into religious imagery of an established collective structure. They do not want to sacrifice anything, only reap personal benefit: with gifts of Kidhus they try to win the grace of the Virgin Mary! Possibly in a pre-Christian version of the tale there stood instead of the Virgin Mary, a pagan mother goddess, such as Perhta to whom gifts of groats and fish were sacrificed.[214] This alters the meaning of the tale but little, since the presumptuous couple do not sacrifice the remains of an excessive but fulfilled demand from the unconscious in humility, rather they squander it in a feigned oblation to the divinity. Since Kidhus still retains the button, which represents the essence of the soul, no escaping this fact through cheap tricks can succeed. In fact, there would have been only one way: a serious confrontation (*auseinandersetzung*) with Kidhus over the return of the button. The pseudo-sacrifice to the Virgin Mary is, therefore, fruitless. Overcome by vertigo,[215] the couple crashes to the ground. Psychologically, it is brought harshly "down to earth" and perishes.

1040 Another tale that depicts the catastrophic consequences when a person usurps the rights and abilities of the spirit realm is the fairytale, "To the Devil with the Money, I know What I Know!":

---

[213] "But we must always remember that the finger pointing at the moon remains a finger, and under no circumstances can it be changed into the moon. Danger always lurks where the intellect creeps in and takes the index for the moon itself," Daisetz Teitaro Suzuki, *An Introduction to Zen Buddhism*, Grove Press, New York 1964 p. 78. An impressive story of such a transposition is told in India: a student had just returned from his teacher where he had experienced Maya as a figment of his own intellect. He then felt that he was above all that. "An immense feeling came over him, he felt like a big bright cloud growing inexorably that filled the whole sky. And like that cloud he went over all heavy things." Then he came upon an elephant, and although the elephant's guide warned him to get out of the way, he refused, saying, "I am God, and the elephant is God. Should God fear himself?" He was saved only by the elephant pushing him to the side with his trunk. Then the teacher said to the despondent student, "You are right: you are God, and the elephant is God - but why did you not listen to God's voice that spoke from up high on the elephant down to you?" See Zimmer, *Weisheit Indiens*, p. 25. See also his commentary on the story (pp. 40ff.).

[214] See Bächtold-Stäubli under *Frau Rose* [Mrs. Rose].

[215] [The German word *Vertigo* also means scam, hoax, fraud.]

1041 A man had three daughters who had married trolls. He went to visit them, one after the other, and observed that the trolls could take meat from their head, reach into the fire without burning their fingers, and find fish in the sea when their eyes were green. Out of carelessness, he lost the money that the troll husbands had given him and tried to soothe his indignant wife: "To the devil with the money! I know what I know!" He wanted to show off to her the magic arts that the troll husbands had showed him, but when he tried to do the same as they did, he only injured himself and finally drowned in his attempt to fish like the last troll husband.[216]

1042 The above four stories vividly depict that "wrong" behavior toward the magical calls forth its destructive aspect. Some fairytales try to elucidate the subtle process of the *auseinandersetzung* with the unconscious and the correct behavior that is so hard to find by setting one hero, who does it right or "has luck," against another, who does it "wrong."[217]

1043 A good example of how the unconscious depends on a person's behavior is "Lucky Andrew":

1044 There was once a rich peasant who had two sons named John Nicholas and Lucky Andrew. The older was one of those fellows of whom one never can quite make head or tail. He was a most unpleasant customer to deal with, and he was more grasping and greedy than the folk of the Northland are, as a rule, though it is only too rare to find them unblessed with these attractive qualities. The other, Lucky Andrew, was wild and high spirited, but always good natured, and no matter how badly off he might be, he would always insist that he had been born under a lucky star. When the eagle, in order to defend his nest, belabored his head and face till the blood ran, he would still maintain that he was born under a lucky star, if only he managed to bring home a single eaglet. Did his boat capsize, which occasionally happened, and did they discover him hanging to it, quite overcome with the water, cold, and exertion, and asked him how he felt, he would reply: "Oh, quite well. I have been saved. I surely am in luck!"

1045 When their father died, both of them were of age, and not long after, they both had to go out to the sandbanks to fetch some fishing nets, which had been left there since the summer fishing. It was late in the fall, after the time when most fishermen are busy with the summer

[216] See also "The Mill at the Bottom of the Sea."
[217] See, for example, "The Old Man Who Brought the Withered Trees Back to Bloom" (Rumpf, *Japanische Volksmärchen*, p. 82), "Father From the Upper Field and Father From the Lower Field" (*ibid.*, p. 92), "The Golden Rain" (*ibid.*, p. 131), and "Should We Keep It, Should We Drop It?" (*ibid.*, p. 132).

fishing. Andrew had his gun along, which he carried with him wherever he went. John Nicholas did not say much while they were underway; but he thought all the harder. They were not ready to set out for home again until near evening.

1046 "Hark, Lucky Andrew, do you know there will be a storm tonight?" said John Nicholas, and looked out across the sea. "I think it would be best if we stayed here until morning!"

1047 "There'll be no storm," said Andrew. "The Seven Sisters have not put on their fog-caps, so you may be quite at rest."

1048 But his brother complained of being weary, and at length they decided to remain there for the night. When Andrew awoke he found himself alone; and he saw neither brother nor boat. He climb up to the highest point of the island to have a look around. Then he discovered his brother far out at sea, darting for the mainland like a seagull. Andrew did not understand the whole affair. There were still provisions there, as well as a dish of curd, his gun, and various other things. So Andrew wasted but little time in thought. "He will come back this evening," said he. "Only a fool loses heart so long as he can eat." But in the evening there was no brother to be seen, and Andrew waited day after day, and week after week; until at last, he realized that his brother had marooned him on this barren island in order to be able to keep their inheritance for himself, and not have to divide it. And such was the case, for when John Nicholas came in sight of land on his homeward trip, he had capsized the boat, and declared that Lucky Andrew had been drowned.

1049 But the latter did not lose heart. He gathered driftwood along the strand, shot seabirds, and looked for mussels and roots. He built himself a raft of drift timber, and fished with a pole that had also been left behind. One day, while he was at work, he happened to notice a depression or hollow in the sand, as though made by the keel of a large Northland schooner, and he could plainly trace the braidings of the hawsers from the strand up to the top of the island. Then he thought to himself that he was in no danger, for he saw there was truth in the report he had often heard, that the sea-folk made the island their abode, and did much business with their ships.

1050 "God be praised for good company! That is just what I needed. Yes, it is true, as I have always said, that I was born under a lucky star," thought Andrew to himself; perhaps he said so too, for occasionally he really had to talk a little. So he lived through the fall. Once he saw a boat, and hung a rag on a pole and waved with it; but that very moment the sail dropped, and the crew took to the oars and rowed away at top speed, for they thought the sea-trolls were making signs and waving.

1051 On Christmas Eve, Andrew heard fiddles and music far out at sea; and when he came out, he saw a glow of light that came from a great Northland schooner, which was gliding toward the land, but such a ship he had never yet seen. It had a mainsail of uncommon size, which looked to him to be of silk, and the most delicate tackling, as thin as though woven of steel wire, and everything else was in proportion, as fine and handsome as any Northlander might wish to have. The whole schooner was filled with little people dressed in blue, but the girl who stood at the helm was adorned like a bride, and looked as splendid as a queen, for she wore a crown and costly garments. Anyone could see that she was a human being, for she was tall, and handsomer than the sea-folk. In fact, Lucky Andrew thought that she was more beautiful than any girl he had ever seen.

1052 The schooner headed for the land where Andrew stood; but with his usual presence of mind, he hurried to the fisherman's hut, pulled down his gun from the wall, and crept up into the large loft and hid himself, so that he could see all that passed in the hut. He soon noticed that the whole room was alive with people. They filled it completely and more, and still more of them came in. Then the walls began to crack, and the little hut spread out at all corners, and grew so splendid and magnificent that the wealthiest merchant could not have had its equal; it was almost like being in a royal castle. Tables were covered with the most exquisite silver and gold. When they had eaten they began to dance. Under cover of the noise, Andrew crept to the lookout at the side of the roof, and climbed down. Then he ran to the schooner, threw his flint stone into it, and in order to make certain, cut a cross into it with his sharp-cutting knife. When he came back again, the dance was in full swing. The tables were dancing and the benches and chairs and everything else in the room was dancing, too. The only one who did not dance was the bride; she only sat there and looked on, and when the bridegroom came to fetch her, she sent him away. For the moment there was no thought of stopping. The fiddler knew neither rest nor repose, and did not pass his cap, but played merrily on with his left hand, and beat time with his foot, until he was dripping with sweat, and the fiddle was hidden by the dust and smoke.

1053 When Andrew noticed that his own feet began to twitch where he was standing, he thought to himself: "Now I had better shoot away, or else he will play me right off the ground!" So he turned his gun, thrust it through the window, and shot it off over the bride's head; but upside down, otherwise the bullet would have hit him. The moment the shot crashed, all the troll-folk tumbled out of the door together; but when they saw that the schooner was banned on the shore, they wailed and crept into a hole in the hill. But all the gold and silver dishes were left behind, and the bride, too, was still sitting there. She told Lucky Andrew that she had been carried into the hill when she was only a small child. Once, when her mother had gone to the pen to attend to the milking, she had taken her along; but when she had to go home for a moment, she left the child sitting under a juniper-bush, and told her that she might eat the berries but only if she repeated three times:

1054 "I eat juniper-berries blue,
Wherein Jesu's cross I view.
I eat whortleberries red,
Since 'twas for my sake He bled!"

1055 But after her mother had gone, she found so many berries that she forgot to say her verse, and so she was enchanted and taken into the hill. And there no harm had been done her, save that she had lost the top joint of the little finger of her left hand, and the goblins had been kind to her; yet it had always seemed to her as though something were not as it should be, she felt as though something weighed upon her, and she had suffered greatly from the advances of the dwarf who had been chosen for her husband. When Andrew learned who her mother and her people were, he saw that they were related to him, and they became very good friends. So Andrew could truly say he had been born under a lucky star. Then they sailed home, and took along the schooner, and all the gold and silver, and all the treasure, which had been left in the hut, and then Andrew was far wealthier than his brother.

1056 But the latter, who suspected where all this wealth had come from, did not wish to be any poorer than Andrew. He knew that trolls and goblins walk mainly on Christmas Eve, and for that reason he sailed out to the sand banks at that time. And on Christmas Eve he did see a light or fire, but it seemed to be like will-o'-the-wisps fluttering about. When he came nearer he heard splashes, horrible howls, and cold, piercing cries, and there was a smell of slime and seaweed, as at ebb tide. Terrified, he ran up into the hut, from whence he could see the trolls on the shore. They were short and thick like hay-ricks, completely covered with fur, with kirtles of skins, fishing boots, and enormous fist-gloves. In place of head and hair they had bundles of seaweed. When they crawled up from the strand there was a gleam behind them like that of rotting wood, and when they shook themselves they showered sparks about them.

1057 When they drew nearer, John Nicholas crawled up into the loft as his brother had done. The goblins dragged a great stone into the hut, and began to beat their gloves dry against it, and meanwhile they screamed so that John Nicholas's blood turned to ice in his hiding place. Then one of them sneezed into the ashes on the hearth in order to make the fire burn again; while the others carried in heather grass and driftwood, as coarse and heavy as lead. The smoke and the heat nearly killed the eavesdropper in the loft, and in order to catch his breath and get some fresh air, he tried to crawl out of the lookout in the roof; yet he was of much heavier build than his brother, stuck fast and could move neither in nor out. Then he grew frightened and began to scream; but the goblins screamed much louder, and roared and howled, and thumped and clamored inside and outside the hut. When the cock crowed they disappeared, and John Nicholas freed himself, too. Yet when he returned home from his trip, he had lost his reason, and after that the same cold, sinister screams, which are the mark of the troll in the Northland, might often be heard sounding from storerooms and lofts where he happened to be. Before his death, however, his reason returned, and he was buried in consecrated ground, as they say. But after that time no human foot ever trod the sandbanks again. They sank, and the sea-folk, it is believed, went to the Lekang Islands. Andrew's luck held good; no ship made more successful trips than his own; but whenever he came to the Lekang Islands he lay becalmed – the goblins went aboard or ashore with their goods – but after a time he had fair winds, whether he happened to want to go to Bergen (Norway), or sail home. He had many children, and all of them were bright and vigorous, yet every one of them lacked the upper joint of the little finger of his left hand.[218]

1058 The plot of this tale reveals how the unconscious can be seen and experienced from two sides. Lucky Andrew has good fortune, which rests on support from the unconscious forces, embodied by the trolls, and not on chance; rather, it is due to his courage also in vital situations and his unerring instincts towards the enchanting treasures and the dance of the trolls, into which he does not let himself be drawn. He remains steadfast against the ghosts, which allows him to deploy a time-honored and popular counterspell at the right

[218] Stroebe, *Norwegian Fairy Book*, pp. 236–244.

moment.[219] He has not followed the "sea-folk" out of curiosity or greed, but encounters them in an emergency. On the contrary, the older brother sails to the island out of greed and envy of the younger brother. He is overwhelmed by the unconscious, that is, he becomes mentally ill. Lucky Andrew, however, manages to wrest some soulfulness, represented by the enchanted girl, from the unconscious sphere. Possibly, this soulfulness has expressed itself as presumptuousness, due to his adherence to the daemons of nature.

1059 The different consequences of such contrasting behaviors are depicted similarly in the Chinese fairytale, "Women's Words Part Flesh and Blood":

> 1060 Once upon a time there were two brothers who lived in the same house. The big brother listened to his wife's words, and because of them fell out with his younger brother. Summer had begun, and the time for sowing the high-growing millet had come. The little brother had no grain, and asked his big brother to loan him some. The older brother ordered his wife to give it to him. But she took the grain, put it in a large pot and cooked it until it was done. Then she dried it and put it in a normal grain sack and gave that to the little fellow. He did not know that it was cooked grain and went out and sowed his field with it. But since the grain had been cooked, it did not sprout. Only one single grain of seed that had not been cooked sprouted up. The little brother was hard-working and industrious by nature, and hence he watered and hoed the sprout all day long. And the sprout grew mightily, like a tree, and from its crown an ear of millet sprang out like a canopy, large enough to shade half an acre of ground. In the fall the ear became ripe. Then the little brother took his ax and chopped it down. But no sooner had the ear fallen to the ground, than an enormous Roc came rushing down, took the ear in its beak and flew away. The little brother ran after him as far as the shore of the sea.
>
> 1061 Then the bird turned and spoke to him like a human being, saying: "You should not seek to harm me! What is this one ear worth to you? East of the sea is the isle of gold and silver. I will carry you across. There you may take whatever you want, and become very rich." The little brother was satisfied, and climbed on the bird's back, and the latter told him to close his eyes. So he only heard the air whistling past his ears, as though he were driving through a strong wind. Beneath him he heard the roar and surge of flood and waves. Suddenly the bird settled on a rock: "Here we are!" he said.

[219] The fact that he shoots "upside down" over the head of the bride is a process that cannot be easily imagined. It could be based on a carry-over from a difficult but magical procedure from the times of the bow and arrow. In *Empire*, Carnochan and Adamson report on a certain magical ceremony of an African tribe in which they must hit their target with the wrong end of the arrow (pp. 115 and 120).

1062 The little brother opened his eyes and looked about him: and on all sides he saw nothing but the radiance and shimmer of all sorts of white and yellow objects. He took about a dozen of the little things and hid them in his breast.[220]

1063 "Have you enough?" asked the Roc.

1064 "Yes, I have enough," he replied.

1675 "That is well," answered the bird. "Moderation protects one from harm."

1066 Then he once more took the younger brother up in the air and carried him back again. When the little brother reached home, he bought himself a good piece of ground in the course of time, and became quite well to do. But his brother was jealous of him, and said to him, harshly: "Where did you manage to steal the money?"

1067 So the little one told him the whole truth of the matter. Then the big brother went home and took counsel with his wife. "Nothing easier," said his wife. "I will just cook grain again and keep back one seedling so that it is not done. Then you shall sow it, and we will see what happens."

1068 No sooner said than done. And sure enough, a single sprout shot up, and sure enough, the sprout bore a single ear of millet, and when harvest time came around, the Roc again appeared and carried it off in his beak. The big brother was pleased, and ran after him, and the Roc said the same thing he had said before, and carried the big brother to the island. There the big brother saw the gold and silver heaped up everywhere. The largest pieces were like hills, the small ones were like bricks, and the real tiny ones were like grains of sand. They blinded his eyes. He only regretted that he knew no way by which he could move mountains. So he bent down and picked up as many pieces as possible. The Roc said: "Now you have enough! You will overtax your strength."

1069 "Have patience, just a little while longer," said the big brother. "Do not be in such a hurry! I must get a few more pieces!" And thus time passed. The Roc again urged him to make haste: "The sun will appear in a moment," said he, "and the sun is so hot it burns human beings up."

---

220 The translator, Richard Wilhelm, notes: "This fairytale is traditionally narrated. The Roc is called *Pong* in Chinese, and the treasures on the island are spoken of as 'all sorts of yellow and white objects' because the little fellow does not know that they are gold and silver" (*The Chinese Fairy Book*, p. 3).

1070 "Wait but a little while longer," said the big brother. But that very moment a red disk broke through the clouds with tremendous power. The Roc flew into the sea, stretched out both his wings, and beat the water with them in order to escape the heat. But the big brother was shriveled up by the sun.[221]

1071 Here the nature of the evil brother is clearly entangled with his scheming wife who, as in the fairytale, "The Fisherman and His Wife," personifies his worldly greed and malice, and sets him against his younger brother. He is nearer to the profane greedy one than to the character of the bumpkin who is close to the animal world. The little brother has a more humble relationship to the magical sphere, and therefore devotedly nurtures the solitary grain, which, embryonically, contains his later, fortunate destiny, and thus could be considered a symbol of the Self. A similar idea is expressed in Matthew 13, 31–32: "The kingdom of heaven is like to a grain of mustard seed, which a man took, and sowed in his field: which indeed is the least of all seeds, but when it is grown, it is the greatest among the herbs and becometh a tree, so that the birds of the air come and lodge in branches thereof."[222] We find the same thought in India:

1072 This my soul (ātman) in the innermost part of the heart, smaller than a grain of rice, or a grain of barley, or a grain of mustard, or a grain of millet or a grain of the grain of millet; this is my soul in my innermost heart, greater than the earth, greater than the aerial space, greater than [all] these worlds.[223]

1073 The corn that grows into a tree is a symbol of spiritual development, which lures the bird who becomes a soul guide and escorts the little brother into the magical land of wealth. The bird – as a feathered being – signifies something

[221] Wilhelm, *The Chinese Fairy Book*, pp. 1–3.

[222] For the Gnostic docetists, the primary Being is symbolized as a seed of a fig tree, which is smaller than small, larger than large, and contains infinite possibilities within itself. See Mead, *Fragments*, p. 218.

[223] Chāndogya-Upanishad 14:3, Deussen, *Sixty Upanishads* Vol.1, 111. See also "The Mass of the Ghosts," where a poor young orphaned boy inherited from his mother only a tiny grain of millet and with it went off into the world. The first night he found shelter with a farmer. Timidly, he asked if anyone might steal his grain of millet, it was all the wealth he had. The farmer reassured him that his grain would come to no harm. But in the morning, the boy watched as a rooster ate his only corn. The farmer gave him the rooster, and said: "The rooster ate your grain, now the rooster is yours." He went on and slept the next night at another farm. Again, he asked the farmer if anybody would steal his rooster, it was all the wealth he had. The farmer reassured him, but in the morning a pig went after his rooster and killed it. The farmer gave him the pig, saying "Take the pig, it is yours since it killed your rooster." So it went on, day after day; he acquired a cow and then a stallion. Upon this stately new steed he performed numerous heroic acts, saved a princess, and became a king himself. See also Collum, "Schöpferische Mutter-Göttin," Zürich, 1939, p. 297 f., and Charles Picard, "Die Grosse Mutter von Kreta bis Eleusis," in: *Eranos-Jahrbuch 1938: Gestalt und Kult der 'Grossen Mutter,'* 1939, p. 115f.

spiritual, a thought. For this reason, the bird can be a guide to new areas, as in the "Kaboi," in which the cry of the Sereima bird lured the people to the hole that ascended up to the surface of the Earth. Also in "Hansel and Gretel," a bird enticed the children into the forest, and carried them back across the water. Therefore, miracle birds appear in fairytales as helpful pack animals. In European legends, the counterpart to the Chinese bird *Pong* is the griffin, eagle, or kite,[224] in India, the Garuda bird,[225] and the bird Simurg in legends from Turkestan.[226] In the appendix to that collection of fairytales from Turkestan and Tibet,[227] it is said that Simurg had silver feathers and was so huge that he hid the Sun when he unfolded his wings. According to popular belief, his feathers are colorful, only around his neck is there a white band. Several traditions describe him as having a human face and being able to talk like a human. Jung writes: "Birds are thought and the flight of thought. Generally it is fantasies and intuitive ideas that are represented thus (the winged Mercurius, Morpheus, genii, angels)."[228] The bird is often an image of desire, of longing, and of idealized wishful thinking. Thus, the "brave daughters" of Odin/Woden,[229] the Valkyries and Fylgies[230] in the form of birds.[231] Often, mythological birds are images of the soul. In the Babylonian underworld, for example, the souls of the dead are clothed in wings,[232] while in Greco-Roman antiquity, they fly to heaven as birds.[233] Insofar as birds symbolically denote intuitions and ideas, they proclaim the truth or give advice in fairytales.[234] Finally, the bird is in general a symbol of the spirit, the

---

[224] See Ninck, *Wodan*, p. 89 and Bachofen, *Orphische Theologie*, p. 20. See also Grimm's fairytale, "The Griffin." The griffin is a mount of Apollo, the sun god. See Leisegang, "Schlange," p. 248f. For the eagle see, for instance, "The Duck Maiden" and "The Story of the Emerald Anka Bird."

[225] See Zimmer, *Kunstform*, p. 112. See also Hertel, *Indische Märchen*, p. 5 (and the appendix for "The Vedic Sauparna, a Vedic Mystery"). For the role that Garuda plays in Malaysian fairytales, see "The Garuda Bird."

[226] Gustav Jungbauer (ed.), *Märchen aus Turkestan und Tibet*, (*MdW*), 1923.

[227] Ibid., p. 296.

[228] C.G. Jung, *Psychology and Alchemy*, CW 12,¶305. See also Jung, *Psychological Types*, CW 6, ¶458.

[229] [In German: *Wunschmädchen*, literally "wish girls".]

[230] ["In Norse mythology, a fylgja (Old Norse, literally 'someone who accompanies,' plural fylgjur) is a supernatural being or creature which accompanies a person in connection with their fate or fortune. Fylgjur usually appear in the form of an animal and commonly appear during sleep, but the sagas relate that they could appear while a person is awake as well, and that seeing one's fylgja is an omen of one's impending death. When fylgjur appear in the form of women, however, they are then supposedly guardian spirits for people or clans (ätter)."]

[231] [See, for instance, the Rune box of Auzon where the Valkyries or Fylgier are depicted as Christian angels at the birth of Jesus.]

[232] See Jung, *Symbols of Transformation*, CW 5, ¶315 fn. 11.

[233] See Dieterich, *Eine Mithrasliturgie*, 3, pp. 184, 193, and 205; see further Bachofen, *Orphische Theologie*, p. 20. Some primitive cultures also portray the souls of the dead as birds. See Lévy-Bruhl, *The "Soul" of the Primitive*, pp. 287ff.

[234] Like Odin/Woden's ravens, birds in Germanic tales often possess superior wisdom; see Führer, *Nordgermanische*, p. 30. In the ancient world, the direction of birds' flight was taken as prophecy, and the famous seers of antiquity were experts in the language of birds. In an Inca fairytale, "The Shepherd and the Princess of the Sun," a songbird that appeared in a dream helps the lovestruck princess of the Sun to win her lover.

pneuma in antiquity and the deity in India.[235] The same symbol appears in mythology as the phoenix. Like the swan, it symbolizes the sun.[236]

1074 While the miracle bird in the previous Chinese fairytale brings salvation to the hero, the evil brother is burned by the sun on the flight back. The miraculous bird is itself a sun symbol, and thus the burning is the impact of its negative aspect, which was itself constellated through the thoughtless and greedy attitude of the big brother.

1075 "The *Peaged Arsai* Bird" has a similar plot:

> Once upon a time two brothers lived at Ngariap on Peliliu. Both were very assiduous and strong; the older one cut palmwine, and the younger gathered firewood. One day as usual the younger brother went early in the morning into the forest to cut wood where the mango trees stood. But when he came back home around noon, he did not bring any firewood. His brother was very upset and scolded him angrily. The younger said: "I could not bring wood, I had to fight a large bird that was sitting on a mangrove tree and threw fruit down at me while I struggled against him with clubs." "Oh, go back there," cried the older brother grumpily, "see that you finally bring back some wood so that we can make a fire." Thoroughly chided, the younger brother went into the forest again and returned shortly with enough wood for a small fire over which they cooked and ate lunch. In the afternoon the younger brother went again into the woods and came to the mangroves. The big bird was still there. The boy cut three elbow-length sticks and threw them at the bird, but it did not move from its perch. He then grabbed an ax and threw it at the monster, but the bird caught it and toddled away, carrying the ax with it. The bird carried the ax to its house in the south of the Ngariap, which stood next to the magical *Bars ra kesau* tree. There it set the ax on top of a wall board.
>
> 1076 When the younger brother returned home without his ax, his older brother became really furious. He chased the younger out again to bring back the ax. Oh, he was so angry that he begrudged the boy a single bite to eat and did not even allow him a sip of water. Weeping, the poor young man went back to the mangrove bushes to find the one that had stolen his ax. But he found no bird, only its tracks. So he followed them and came right to the magic tree and the house where the *Peaged arsai* bird[237] was sitting inside. Weeping, he sat down in

[235] See Leisegang, *Die Gnosis*, p. 217; see also Zimmer, "Yoga und Maya," pp. 387ff.
[236] See Jung, *Symbols of Transformation*, CW 5, ¶538; see also Bachofen, *Mutterrecht*, pp. 23–24.
[237] [A kind of chicken – footnote by Hambruch.]

front of the door. The bird came out and asked him, "Why are you crying now?" The boy told the bird how his brother had scolded him and chased him away to find the ax, without which they could not cut wood to make their fires. He added that his brother begrudged him even a bite to eat or a sip of water, and that he was now very hungry and thirsty. The bird listened and then invited him to come inside and eat something. It fetched a piece of fish and some taro, put them on a wooden platter, and placed it before the boy. But the boy replied in anger: "What should I do with such paltry morsels of food when I am so hungry?" "Eat, just eat!" said the *Peaged arsai*. Lo and behold, when the boy had swallowed one piece, there immediately appeared a new one. He ate and ate until he could not put down a morsel more. He looked fearfully at the bird, because he did not eat any more and it was the custom in Palau that you ate all you were given or took the rest with you. The bird just said: "Done!" and the pieces of food stopped appearing.

1077 Then he asked the boy: "What do you want to say to me now?" The boy replied: "My brother and I are alone, we have no wives; he cuts palmwine, and I forage firewood. Together we cook our syrup, that is our only food. Now I have lost my ax, and we are really done for!" "Do not worry and take up courage," cried out the *Peaged arsai*, "Go inside my hut. it is full of hatchets and axes, one more beautiful than the other. Go, take your pick. Under the house and around the sides are even more." The boy soon found his own ax again, and that one was good enough. Overjoyed, he returned to the bird. It said: "I knew that you were poor and hard-working and I appreciated that. I called you out to fight with me so I could get your ax and lead you to my house and you could get it back! I want to show you something good now. Go now back to your brother, and remember exactly what I say: When you come to the piece of land, *Gataulukes*, you may hear snapping and hands clapping. Do not turn around, but continue. When you reach *Galeulukes*, there look carefully all around if you hear something." The boy did exactly as the bird told him. Going through *Gataulukes*, he heard snapping and hands clapping but he continued onwards. Once in *Galeulukes*, however, when he again heard snapping and clapping, he carefully looked all around. And behold! there stood a most beautiful woman, right on his path! She walked up to him and said that she wanted to be his wife. There were many other beautiful girls there, and all wanted a husband. But he said to them: "This is my wife!" and took the woman who had first come to him. Now he happily returned home with his ax and a beautiful woman.

1078 When his brother saw the newcomers, he asked in astonishment how this all had happened. The younger brother reported all he had experienced and how he had found the woman. A few days later, the older brother said to his younger brother: “Today you will cut the palmwine, I will go fetch firewood.” Then he took the ax and vanished. He had not paid good enough attention to all the words of his younger brother, however, especially the names of the pieces of land he would go through. So when he came to *Gataulukes* he stopped there and looked all around. But alas! There were no beautiful girls there, just a bunch of ugly, old, sick women who all flew behind him and followed him back to his house. The younger brother was not very pleased with all these new additions to the household. They did not volunteer to go away and he remained silent. Then his elder brother asked: “What shall we do to get rid of these females?” The younger brother consulted with his wife and then said: ”Bring a pot and relieve ourselves into it” And so it happened, and when the pot was half full, the three closed it up and left it standing. A short time later the older brother called out: “I cannot stand it any long with these women, keep the house for yourself and make the palmwine alone!” Having thus spoken, he left. “Fine,” said the younger and started to cut palmwine. When he was finished, he dined with his wife and then said to the old women, pointing to the pot. “Here is your syrup, you can eat it all up.” He and his wife went out the door. Soon the women eagerly opened up the pot, but when a terrible stench emerged, they rushed hurriedly out of the house and disappeared forever. Now the younger brother and his wife moved back into the house. The woman planted taro, and he cut palmwine, so they had plenty to eat and drink.

1079 The older brother never returned. He had fled to *Ngardololok* and became the little demon *Imok*. His wives turned into evil, ugly forest devils, called *Tengangoi le galid*. To appease them, people place stinking fish in the bushes as sacrifices.

1080 Due to his age, the younger brother must do the simpler work, which leads him into the woods. There he has more chances to meet the magical. The bird has it in for him and thus attacks him with fruit. This establishes the connection and is a kind of enticement. At first, the attacked boy defends himself against the bird. As winged beings that live in the air, birds are symbols of spiritual contents and intuitive hunches. But then the young hero succumbs to the supernatural size of the psychic image appearing before him. The unconscious approaches first as a shadow figure in the shape of an animal, and the boy is inferior to this being. The attack of the bird indicates a disturbance of human consciousness as a result of an invasion from the psychic realm. When the youth heaves his ax at the magical bird, he seeks to mentally cope with and overcome this disturbance. The ax, like all cutting devices, for instance, swords or knives, signifies the intellect, the "sharply" differentiating mind by which human beings came to govern a part of nature. Cutting something up with a weapon means dissecting, differentiating, and understanding with the intellect.[238]

1081 The bird *Peaged arsai* simply takes away the hero's ax and leaves him standing. That is, the bird robs the younger brother of his mind, his intellect, and leaves him helpless.[239] Thus, his older brother must force him to pursue the bird to get his ax back. This means that he must confront the daemonic contents of his own soul, and investigate them internally. The bird thus becomes the mediator of a journey into the magical realm. The hero must have the courage to follow his own ideas and hunches; he must acknowledge his dependence on the unconscious and acquiesce. Only then can he find the way to succeed.[240] By following the bird, the hero reaches its home or the magical tree in the south. The tree is, as mentioned, a maternal symbol, and thus is connected to the inexhaustible supply of food and nourishment that the hero finds there. Having followed his intuitions, the hero arrives at the maternal ground of his soul. The journey into the unconscious is, strangely enough, not initially portrayed as dangerous; the young man even recovers his ax. But the danger of the adventure is revealed on the way back. He must now counter the negative aspect with skill and obedience.

1082 For the return journey, the youth receives the counsel not to look backwards. This is the well-known Orpheus motif.[241] The back side is the side of the unconscious, from which its apparitions, ancestral spirits, gods, monsters, and other soul parts pursue us, shadow figures that threaten to overwhelm us.[242] By turning to magic, Orpheus loses his soul, embodied in Eurydice, to the world of the spirits of the dead.[243] Also Perseus must overcome

---

[238] For more on this theme, see C.G. Jung, *Children's Dreams,* p. 140.

[239] In general, spirits like to steal the hero's weapon, that is, his mind. See "The Ride in the Huldren Boat," in which a man one night by accident finds himself in a huldren boat. [Huldra are Scandinavian female forest creatures, stunningly beautiful, sometimes naked, having long hair; but from behind they can be seen to be hollow like an old tree trunk, and have an animal's tail.] He must get in and fish from it. He becomes aware of the situation and forces the wood nymph to give him back his knife, which she had stolen. Whereupon the Huldra says, "Be damned, lucky child that you are!" Thus the man succeeds in escaping undamaged.

[240] See Wilhelm/Baynes, *I Ching*, p. 119: "Human life is conditioned and unfree, and when man recognizes this limitation and makes himself dependent upon harmonious and beneficent forces of the cosmos, he achieves success. . . By cultivating in himself an attitude of compliance and voluntary dependence, man acquires clarity without sharpness and finds his place in the world."

[241] Other examples include "The Boy Who Was Afraid of Nothing" and "The King of the Ants," which is discussed in Volume II. [See also "Hansel and Gretel," of course, as well as many North American traditional tales and the biblical story of Lot's wife, the pillar of salt.]

[242] See C.G. Jung, *Psychology and Alchemy*, CW 12, ¶55ff.

[243] See also the superstition in Ireland, which warns not to turn over while sleeping when you hear footsteps, because these are the deceased, whose look would be lethal, see Róheim, *Spiegelzauber*, p. 215, fn. 1.

Medusa's averted head, as seeing it would have petrified him. Those who look behind themselves perceive their own dark side. According to Japanese belief, the god Izanagi looked back and his shadow Susanowo, the god of death, destruction, and storm, came into being.[244] Looking back usually results in falling into the powers of the unconscious, a relapse into being at its mercy.[245] The more undeveloped consciousness is, that is, the more unconscious a person is, the more the magical apparition dissolves into a multiplicity of forms.[246] When, therefore, the elder brother turns around he sees a multitude of ugly female demons, which then follow him and never let go. As soon as the younger brother has gained some distance from the unconscious, he can look around and finds a beautiful girl on his path whom he takes for his wife. The women following the older brother prove later to be forest demons, and he himself becomes a small demon. He thus falls prey to the shadow, the magical world, and perishes as a personality; this is the necessary consequence of defying the strict precepts of the inner voice; his soul adapts to the shadow world and becomes an evil and tormenting demon.

1083 The plot depicts a confrontation between man and his soul, which appears as a bird emerging from the magical realm. The hero is confronted with an inner condition. Now begins an *auseinandersetzung* in which the ego tries to maintain its position (the ax is the pivot of events)[247] while submitting to the instructions of the objective psyche (obedience as a test on the return journey).[248] To the hero, who behaves correctly, the unconscious now appears in a new aspect, in the image of the sought-after and beloved wife.

1084 In several of the tales considered so far, the hero's *auseinandersetzung* with, or obedience to, the shadow has led him to a blissful union with a particularly distinguished maiden, portrayed as a princess, or as standing out with special features, or whose fate particularly distinguishes her from other women. In

---

[244] See Róheim, *Spiegelzauber*, p. 114 f.

[245] See the Japanese fairytale, "Omutaro," where the whale god instructs the hero not to turn and look back on the way home from the magical island. Since he is obedient, he brings the gift of meat back home to his parents intact. A neighbor boy hears of this and imitates the adventure, but looks back at the island on the return journey and the meat turns into stinking rubbish. See also "The Woman and the Elves," a woman who is harassed by the elves tries to escape. When she looks around her at her adversaries, she dies on the spot. In other situations, however, it is essential to have the demons before one's face and to look them in the eye. See "The Bridegroom and the Revenant" (see page 122), and "The Rolling Skull" (see page 143), where the head becomes a demon only after the man drags it on a string behind him. Also relevant is the belief that evil spirits lose their power with the light of day (see "The Servant and the Seafolk").

[246] Cf. C.G. Jung, *Child*, CW 9i, ¶279, and *Psychological Types*, CW 6, ¶418ff.

[247] Cf. Wolff: "All these forms of soul-image have their own lives and their own intentions, which under some conditions may be quite opposite to the integrity of the ego and its position in the outer world. This confrontation with the different tendencies of the "Objective-Psychic" [see next footnote] force the ego into an *auseinandersetzung* with them. Depending on the outcome of this confrontation, the ego can take the standpoint of this 'non-ego' into account or strengthen its own standpoint. This process is no different than dealing in important matters with a real person" ("Grundlagen," pp. 111–114, esp. p. 115).

[248] [*Objectiv-Psychischen*: a term used by Jung to refer to all acts and manifestations of an objective psychic nature.]

"The Mass of the Ghosts," a rat appears as a shadow figure of the hero and steers his thoughts to the Princess of the Golden Mountain. In "The Knight With the Sinister Laugh," the dramatic confrontation with the shadow-brother figure was a precondition for gaining the princess. In principle, a "Bearskin" has the same theme; the hero must fulfill the task set by the demon before the maiden belonged to him. In "The Son of Kimanaueze and the Daughter of the Sun and Moon," the frog mediated quite clearly between the youth and the daughter of the sun and moon. Even the tailor in "The Two Travelers" would never have become the husband of the princess had he not met the shoemaker who drove him to perform his wonderful exploits. Similarly, the hero in "Lucky Andrew," thanks to his evil brother, encounters the magical beings and retrieves the virgin they stole. The demonic servant in "Lasse, My Servant," even carries the princess to the Duke in the castle! In "Ferdinand the Faithful and Ferdinand the Unfaithful," the experience with the various shadow figures is subtly interwoven with the appearance of the female. Before meeting the princess, Ferdinand the Unfaithful induces the hero to travel to her land from which he brings her back (like Lucky Andrew who carries the girl from the troll island back into the human realm). Ferdinand the Faithful met the girl in the tavern in the same image but as an expressionless figure, while Ferdinand the Faithful had previously picked up the quill (at the behest of the white horse!). The relationship between the quill and the princess is confirmed in some variations where she first appears in the form of a golden bird. It can be assumed, therefore, that also in "The *Peaged Arsai* Bird," there is a connection between the knowing bird and the young woman chosen for the hero.

1085 This wonderful woman, who stands "on the path" of human life, which moves between the unconscious and consciousness, often appears in fairytales, first as a bird or as a sister of birds, or as a winged human being. A particularly beautiful example is "The Story of the Blind King Who Lived in the Western Lands," where a son sets out to find a bird that will cure his blind father through its song. After he had a dead man buried out of pity, a black bird that was sitting on a fig tree advises him to go to a clearing where he would find a winged woman in a walled enclosure. This woman watches over the sought-after miracle bird. The black bird who had given the advice later turns into a man (the shadow! – even the dead man can be understood as one.) He saves the hero and helps him to marry the winged women. The addition of the wings characterizes this woman as a spirit-being, a supernatural phenomenon. This concept appears also in the pre-Christian religions from the Mediterranean region. In an ancient Egyptian hymn it is said of the goddess Isis: ". . . through her feathers she spreads the shadows and by her wings she makes the wind. . . "[249] According to some low cultures, the soul lives in humans in the shape of a bird.[250] As chieftess of the Valkyries, Freyja, goddess of love, also bears wings and a dress of feathers.[251] And in a Russian fairytale, "The Virgin Tsar," it is said of the beautiful virgin Tsarina that she gave her servants wings and flew after the hero. Nor is the woman in the Micronesian fairytale a concrete woman, but rather a miraculous being, that is, a psychic image, a part of the soul. The magical chicken in "The *Peaged Arsai* Bird" most likely represents something similar: on the one hand, a miraculous bird that leads the hero to his wife, and on the other hand, as the female figures who, in the case of disobedience, appear as a multitude of demons.

[249] Roeder, *Urkunden*, p. 24.

[250] See Josef Winthuis, *Das Zweigeschlechterwesen bei den Zentralaustraliern und anderen Völkern. Lösungsversuch der ethnologischen Hauptprobleme auf Grund primitiven Denkens*, vol. 5, 1928, p. 207. On the bird as an image of the soul, see C.G. Jung, *Symbols of Transformation*, CW 5, ¶315; Tegethoff, "Amor und Psyche," p. 94; Leeuw, *Religion in Essence*, vol. 1, p. 282. For a comprehensive overview of the concepts of the soul as a bird, see Bächtold-Stäubli under *Seelenvogel* [soul bird]; see also Weicker, *Seelenvogel*, *passim*, esp. pp. 21ff., on the *eidolon* deduced from dream phenomena; see further Tobler, *Epiphanie*, pp. 28ff.

[251] See Hertz, *Dichtung*, Stuttgart and Berlin, 1907, pp. 39ff. and 44–45.

Chapter 19

The Magical Daughter [the anima]

1086 The mysterious woman appears in fairytales with divine, demonic, or animal attributes.[1] Most of the stories point to the wonderful way in which this phenomenon – emerging from the *other side* – enters into a person's life, such as when the fairytale hero gains a human wife who was bound to the magical realm (as in "Lucky Andrew"), or is simply a "beautiful woman" who comes from the magical realm and follows into the human one (as in "The *Peaged Arsai* Bird"). Although her magical features transcend the human, and although her appearance can only be hinted at with words such as "beautiful," it is expressly clear that, despite her otherworldly origins, she is closely related to humans. She also corresponds to the female figure of the soul that tends to occur in a man's dreams and whom Jung gave the name "anima."[2] Psychologically, she embodies a man's irrational and often unconscious feelings, which sometimes can give rise to illogical affects.[3] At the same time, like the the shadow, this female figure personifies the unconscious with both its friendly and threatening content. She is to some extent the image of his unknown, unconscious psychic character, which is related to his conscious attitude in a complementary way.[4]

---

[1] See the unearthly apparition in "Help in Need" and "The Son of Kimanaueze and the Daughter of the Sun and Moon," the descent from the cayman in "Makonaura and Anuanaitu," the demanding nature of the royal princess in "The Knight With the Sinister Laugh" and "Ferdinand the Faithful and Ferdinand the Unfaithful."

[2] [We have chosen to keep to the original German, which refers to the anima with the subject pronoun "she."The anima is, of course, a psychological figure.]

[3] The word soul "comes from the Gothic *saiwala* and the old German *saiwalô*, and these can be connected etymologically with the Greek *aiolos*, 'quick-moving, twinkling, iridescent.' The Greek word *psyche* also means 'butterfly.' *Saiwalô* is related on the other hand to the Old Slavonic *sila*, 'strength.' These connections throw light on the original meaning of the word *soul*: it is a moving force, that is, life-force" (C.G. Jung, "Basic Postulates of Analytical Psychology," CW 8, ¶663). Latin *anima* is identical to Greek *anemos* ("wind"), while Greek *psyche* ("soul") is akin to *psycho* = breathe, *psychros* = cold, etc. Cf. "*Every man carries within him the eternal image of woman*, not the image of *this or that particular* woman, but a definite woman. This image is fundamentally unconscious, an hereditary factor of primordial origin engraved in the living organic system of the man, an imprint or "archetype" of all the ancestral experiences of the female, a deposit, as it were, of all the impressions ever made by woman – in short, an inherited system of psychic adaptation. Even if no women existed, it would still be possible, at any given time, to deduce from this unconscious image exactly how a woman would have to be constituted psychically" (C.G. Jung, "Marriage as a psychological relationship," CW 17, ¶338). See also C.G. Jung, "Mind and earth," CW 10, ¶71f., "Psychology and religion," CW 11, ¶45–49, and "Relation between the ego and the unconscious," CW 7, ¶296ff.

[4] See Jung for more on this, especially, "Interposed between the ego and the world, she acts like an ever-hanging Shakti, who weaves the veil of Maya and dances the illusion of existence. But, functioning

1087 This elfish appearance manifests in fairytales (as in the dreams of individuals) in the dual aspect typical of natural beings; sometimes positive, sometimes negative, old or young, mother or girl, fairy or witch. The anima has wonderful knowledge of the secrets of the magical world and confers a certain clairvoyance of unconscious realities.[5] She possesses the "medicine of immortality" and is immortal, since she stands outside of time.[6] The Chinese fairytale, "The Two Scholars," relates how two men lose their way picking flowers and find themselves in a cave with two beautiful virgins who seemed to be meant just for them. The scholars marry the women on the spot. After what seems to them to be a few days, they grow homesick and return home, only to discover that they had been gone for over seventy years. While celebrating their return, however, they discover that the women had given them the magic wine of rejuvenation.

1088 The Chinese fairytale, "The Flower Elves," illustrates the same basic theme:

> Once upon a time there was a scholar who lived retired from the world in order to gain hidden wisdom. He lived alone and in a secret place. And all about the little house in which he dwelt he had planted every kind of flower, bamboos, and other trees. There he lived, quite concealed in his thick grove of flowers. With him he had only a boy servant, who dwelt in a separate hut, and who carried out his orders. He was not allowed to appear before his master unless summoned. The scholar loved his flowers as he did himself. Never did he set his foot beyond the boundaries of his garden.
>
> 1089 It once chanced that there came a lovely spring evening. Flowers and trees stood in full bloom, a fresh breeze was blowing, and the moon shone clearly. The scholar sat over his goblet and was grateful for the gift of life.
>
> 1090 Suddenly he saw a maiden in dark garments come tripping up in the moonlight. She made a deep curtsy, greeted him and said: "I am your neighbor. We are a company of young maids who are on our way to

between the ego and the unconscious, the anima becomes the matrix of all the divine and semi-divine figures, from the pagan goddess to the Virgin, from the messenger of the Holy Grail to the saint" ("Psychology of the transference," CW 16, ¶504).

[5] In a Norwegian fairytale, she is called the master maiden (cf. "The Master Maiden"). When the hero found her in a chamber in the giant's castle, she revealed to him the secrets that allowed him to solve the tasks requested by the giant. She then rescued the hero and escaped with him. Once back into the profane world, however, he forgot her. She then warded off various courting suitors with sly humor, regained access to the hero, and with another cunning trick, and lifted the enchantment of his forgetfulness just as he was about to marry another woman. He finally recognized her and they lived together happily ever after.

[6] On this general form, see C.G. Jung, "Concerning the anima archetype," CW 9i, ¶111–147; "Archetypes of the Collective Unconscious," CW 9i, ¶52ff.; "Relation between the ego and the unconscious," CW 7, ¶296ff.; and "Psychological aspects of the Kore," CW 9i, ¶356ff.

visit the eighteen aunts. We should like to rest in this court for awhile, and therefore ask your permission to do so."

1091 The scholar saw that this was something quite out of the ordinary, and gladly gave his consent. The maiden thanked him and went away. In a short time she brought back a whole crowd of maids carrying flowers and willow branches. All greeted the scholar. They were charming, with delicate features, and slender, graceful figures. When they moved their sleeves, a delightful fragrance was exhaled. There is no fragrance known to the human world which could be compared with it.

1092 The scholar invited them to sit down for a time in his room and asked their names and why he was granted their company. A maiden in a green gown said with a smile, "My name is Salix. We are all sisters and we want to visit the eighteen Zephyr-Aunts today."[7]

1093 A soberly-clad servant suddenly announced: "The Zephyr-Aunts have already arrived!" At once the girls rose and went to the door to meet them. "We were just about to visit you, Aunts," they said, smiling. "This gentleman here had just invited us to sit for a moment. What a pleasant coincidence that you aunts have come here, too. This is such a lovely night that we must drink a goblet of nectar in honor of you, Aunts!" Thereupon they ordered the servant to bring what was needed.

1094 An enchanted feast then ensued with the aunts and the sisters who magically provided the most delicious food and most magnificent fruits. The moon shone brightly and the flowers exhaled intoxicating odors. After they had partaken of food and drink, the maidens rose, danced, and sang songs. The scholar did not know if he was on Earth or in Heaven. Then one of the rather cool aunts carelessly spilled some nectar on the dress of one of the sisters, Punica. Punica reacted angrily, uproar and insults followed ending when the aunts marched off and the sisters scattered themselves among the flowerbeds.

1095 On the following evening the maidens all came back again. "We all live in your garden," they told him. "Every year we are tormented by naughty winds, and therefore we have always asked the eighteen aunts to protect us. But yesterday Punica insulted them, and now we fear they will help us no more. But we know that you have always been

[7] Note by Wilhelm on *Salix*: "The names of the 'Flower Elves' are given in the Chinese as family names, whose sound suggests the flower-names without exactly using them. In the translation the play on words is indicated by the Latin names." *Zephyr-Aunts*: "In Chinese the name given the aunt is 'Fong,' which in another stylization means 'wind'" (Wilhelm, *The Chinese Fairy Book*, p. 123).

well disposed toward us, for which we are heartily grateful. And now we have a great favor to ask, that every New Year's day you make a small scarlet flag, paint the sun, moon and five planets on it, and set it up in the eastern part of the garden. Then we sisters will be left in peace and will be protected from all evil. But since New Year's day has passed for this year, we beg that you will set up the flag on the twenty-first of this month. For the East Wind is coming and the flag will protect us against him!" The scholar readily promised to do as they wished, and the maids all said with a single voice: "We thank you for your great kindness and will repay it!" Then they departed and a sweet fragrance filled the entire garden.

1096 The scholar made a scarlet flag as described, and when early in the morning of the day in question the East Wind really did begin to blow, he quickly set it up in the garden. Suddenly a wild storm broke out, one that caused the forests to bend, and broke the trees. The flowers in the garden alone did not move. Then the scholar noticed that Salix was the willow; Prunophora the plum; Persica the peach, and the saucy Punica the Pomegranate, whose powerful blossoms the wind cannot tear. The eighteen Zypher-Aunts, however, were the spirits of the winds. In the evening the flower elves all came and brought the scholar radiant flowers as a gift of thanks. "You have saved us," they said, "and we have nothing else we can give you. If you eat these flowers you will live long and avoid old age. And if you, in turn, will protect us every year, then we sisters, will also live long."

1097 The scholar did as they told him and ate the flowers. And his figure changed and he grew young again like a youth of twenty. And in the course of time he attained the hidden wisdom and was placed among the Immortals.[8]

1098 A meeting with the anima figure does not always result in such a positive experience, however, especially when the human form is thereby altered. A Romanian fairytale, "Youth Without Age and Life Without Death," describes such an encounter.

1099 It happened once upon a time, a long, long time ago – for had it not happened in times of old, this story would never have been told. It took place at the time when pears grew on poplar trees, and the willows gave forth their gilly-flowers, when beasts had tails to fight with, when wolf and lamb loved each other like brothers, when the

[8] Shortened from Wilhelm, *The Chinese Fairy Book*, pp. 119–123.

foot of the flea was shod with ninety-nine pounds of iron yet he could leap into the high heaven and bring back fairytales for us, and when the flies themselves wrote on the wall the craziest stories for big and small.

1100 In those days lived a great and mighty king together with his wife, both of them young and comely. Much did they long for a child, and much did they do that one should be born.[9]

1101 The King and Queen sought out a wise man who told them they would soon receive a child, "but only one child shall be born to you. He shall be the kindest, bravest and most handsome of princes, but he will not be for long your joy and comfort." The wise man gave the queen some herbs and soon she became with child. When her time came, the unborn baby could be heard crying. No one could be found to quiet him. His father, the King, promised him many things if he would stop crying but to no avail. This went on until the King promised the unborn boy *Youth without Age and Life without Death.* Then the unborn baby ceased to cry. Soon thereafter the Queen gave birth to a boy and rejoicing filled the kingdom.

1102 The boy was called Fât Frumos ("Beautiful Boy") and as he grew, he became ever wiser and braver. He learned in one month what it would take other children to learn in one year. The growing boy soon became, however, sad and taciturn. On his fifteenth birthday he said to his father, the King, "The day has come when you must keep the promise you made to me before my birth." The King remembered his promise but did not know how to give something that no one has ever attained, so the young Prince set out himself into the world seeking "that for which he was born." He went to the stables but could find no horse that suited him. He noticed a scraggy, "glandered rawboned beast. The prince went up to him and placed his hand on its tail whereupon the horse turned around and said: 'What are your orders, master?'" The prince told the horse what he intended and the horse advised him to get a sword and spear, bows, arrows, and quiver and the armor that belonged to his father when he was young. "And for six weeks you must tend me with your own hands and feed me on barley boiled in milk."

1103 The young Prince did as told and the horse shed his old looks and became a proud stallion. Together they left the court, followed by "wagons containing food and gold and some two-hundred men-at-arms whom the king had ordered to accompany him." The Prince did

[9] [The following is summarized.]

not, however, keep these provisions and men for long. At the border he said farewell and kept only the provisions that his horse could carry.

1104 They came first to the land of the Woodpecker Witch, she who was "so evil that no one who ever crossed the boundaries of her estate remained alive." With the help of the horse, the Prince vanquished the old witch but spared her life. She invited him to a feast and the Prince healed a wound in her leg. She offered one of her three daughters as a wife to the Prince but he refused and continued onward.

1105 The Prince and his stallion came to the land of the She-Dragon, the sister of the Woodpecker Witch. Again with the agility of the horse who jumped and flew in the air, Fât Frumos sliced off one of the She-Dragon's heads. The dragon pleaded for her life and this granted, offered the Prince and his steed an even greater feast than her sister did. The prince healed the head he had severed and three days later he again set off with his horse.

1106 They then came to "a flowery meadow, where everlasting springtime reigned. So fragrant was the scent of its blossoms that it made one's senses reel." The horse warned his master that there was one more danger before they reached the dwelling of *Youth without Age and Life without Death*: a woods filled with the wildest of beasts. With his flying horse, they took flight over the woods and beasts. The horse was so agile that this succeeded, but just almost. While descending to the castle, the horse brushed the top of a tree. This awakened all the beasts who howled so fearsomely that one's hair stood on end. Quickly, the Prince and his horse alighted. Outside the palace stood its lady, feeding the beasts, which she called her pets. Had it not been for her the Prince would surely have been devoured. So glad was she to see, for the first time, a human being in her own shape, that she saved them, calming the beasts, and sending the Prince and his steed to shelter."

1107 Having spoken of that which he sought, the lady said: "If it is *Youth without Age and Life without Death*, then here it is!" The maiden had two sisters and they pleaded with the Prince to stay with them, for they were lonely. He readily accepted for this was what he had sought. He remained there and married the youngest sister. They gave him the right to wander over the whole estate, except for one valley, the *Vale of Tears*. Many years passed, but the youth did not notice, for he remained as youthful as the day he arrived. He roamed the estate and lived in peace without cares. One day, while hunting a hare, he found himself in the *Vale of Tears*. He caught the hare, but returned to the sisters with a great longing to see his mother and father. 'You have entered the *Vale of Tears*, unhappy one," they exclaimed in deep distress. They told him that his parents had died hundreds of years earlier and a trip to visit them, no matter how short, would end in disaster.

1108 The youth insisted on visiting his parents, just once, and then he would return. His faithful steed also warned him but the Prince paid no heed. The horse then agreed to take him back if he promised to take responsibility for all that would befall him. "As soon as I set you down at your father's place, I wish to return, even if you only wish to stay for an hour." The prince agreed and they bade the maidens farewell and embarked, "leaving the women tearful and broken-hearted."

1109 On the way back, they passed through the land of the She-Dragon but now there were towns where forests once stood. When asked where the dragon was, the people laughed and said that was fairytale nonsense that only grandparents believed. Going through the land of the Woodpecker Witch, they asked the same questions and received the same answers. Coming to his father's kingdom, they found towns and cities, nothing was the same. At the steps of the old palace the horse said to Fât Frumos,"Farewell, master, I go back from whence I came. If you wish to come, leap on my back and we will depart." The prince replied: "Go, my dear horse, I too hope to return soon." The horse sped off.

1110 The sight of the ruined palace, now overgrown with weeds and brambles, made the Prince sigh. With tears in his eyes he recalled how bright it had been in the days of his childhood. He wandered around the palace two or three times, visited every room, every spot that reminded him of the days gone by. Then he went to the cellar, the entrance to which was hidden under crumbling ruins. Hardly able to stand, for his white beard was now down to his knees, and holding his eyelids open with his fingers, he sought right and left, but found only a frail old chest. He opened it, but it was empty. As he lifted the lid of a small box, a trembling voice said to him: 'Welcome to you; it is good that you did not come earlier, for I too would have perished.' And the hand of death – which itself had shrunk and withered, lying in its box – touched his face. Prince Fât Frumos fell to the ground and at once turned into dust. And that is the end of my tale.[10]

[10] Edited from R. Vianu, *Fairy Tales from Romania*, pp. 116–137; original retold by Petre Ispirescu, translated by Mary Lazarescu.

1111 A version from the Caucasus, "The Earth Wants to Have Hers," tells of the son of a widow who – because his father died – went off to find a place where there was no death. He encountered a stag with golden antlers who was to die when his antlers reached Heaven. He then met a raven who was to die when he had filled up one particular deep pit with his droppings. Dissatisfied, the youth eventually reached a glasshouse in the sea. Inside lived a girl more beautiful than the sun who asked him to stay with her. He refused, saying he was looking for a country with no death. She told him that his quest was in vain: "The Earth wants to have what is hers, you will never achieve immortality." He remained with the eternally young girl, but after a thousand years, he was irresistibly drawn back to his home. The maiden gave him three apples to take with him on the journey. On his way back, he found that the raven and the stag had died, at his home no one knew him, and his mother's house was overgrown with brambles. He ate the apples and immediately became an aged man and died.[11]

1112 In both tales, the anima embodies the whole magical kingdom. Both heroes are particularly bound to the maternal sphere from birth: Fât Frumos preferred not to be born, the hero in the version from the Caucasus is the son of a widow. The heroes are filled with the idea of something eternal and spiritual, and their lives are shaped by this thought. Fât Frumos has a magic horse, which – as the previous section on the shadow has shown – symbolizes his psychic energy and natural vitality, a kind of alter ego, which mediates the relationship with the anima figure. He must first confront the mother imago and deal with the two witches before the path to the soul is free. The wild animals belong to this figure. She feeds and at the same time tames them, because they represent the human instincts, to which the anima gives impetus and governs. Both heroes strives for eternal immersion and lose their conscious standpoint. Although they reawaken – Fât Frumos is lured by a rabbit into the *Vale of Tears* (the hare, as the witch's animal, leads him to experience the negative aspects of the magical kingdom) – it is too late for life in this world; the anima does not accompany them, the soul-image remains in the hereafter. In this life, there is only death.

1113 When dealing with the archetype of the anima, other fairytales describe different aspects of this incompatibility of the spheres. Perhaps the most intelligible form of the intention to realize an intimate relationship with this soul-image is the hero's attempt to appropriate this miraculous female being, to make her "his own." These attempts lead often to a "magical marriage." In "Youth Without Age and Life Without Death," and "The Earth Wants to Have Hers," this takes place in a distant realm, the unconscious, and does not

[11] See also the parallel story in "The Red Emperor and the Vampire." There the youth meets a boy – the wind (spirit) – instead of the anima figure.

involve any interaction with the secular world. The conscious person has aged without maturing. If the magical marriage is consummated in "this world," psychologically this means that the man endeavors to move this soul-image, revitalized by his feelings, and epitomizing as it were his emotional life, of which he was largely unconscious, into his consciousness. In this sense, his soul is practically identical to his – to a large extent unconscious – emotional life. But this attempt often ends negatively.[12] The direct unification of the figures from the two realms proves to be impossible, or else the human being cannot bear the separation, and succumbs to the attraction of the anima. The person becomes enthralled,[13] and follows her into her realm, implying psychologically that he or she has lost their conscious viewpoint and sinks into the unconscious. From the conscious standpoint, this enrapturement is synonymous with complete extinction, which is why, as in "Help in Need," the wonderful woman is represented as an allurement into the realm of the dead.

1114 Similarly, in "The Star," the attraction by the anima figure is portrayed as a mortal danger:

> 1115 There was once a youth who lived in a bachelor's lodge.[14] One night he gazed upwards at the scintillating, starry night sky. One star in particular appealed to him because of its quiet brilliance.
>
> 1116 "It is a shame that I cannot lock you up in my gourd flask and admire you whenever I wanted," he sighed, looking longingly up at the cold, feelingless star. After a long time, he went back to the bachelor's lodging where his brothers slept. He soon fell asleep and dreamt of a beautiful star. In the night he suddenly woke up and saw to his surprise a young maiden with bright shining eyes looking down at him. He thought, "This is just a temptation," and swore to immediately turn away. "Why?" asked the girl, "I am the bright star that you wanted to put in your gourd flask."
>
> 1117 At first sight, the youth was dumbfounded. Then he said, "But you cannot really mean in my gourd flask." "Yes, I really can come down into it." The youth opened his gourd flask and put the star maiden inside. She raised her eyes to him and her wonderful gaze lit

[12] The detours that must be undertaken to avoid a negative outcome of the magical marriage are discussed in a later volume.

[13] [German: *entrücken.*]

[14] Young men of the Cherente tribe (a people of the Rio Tocantins in central Bolivia) lived in a kind of cloister, *koaran*, the bachelors' lodge, where they were reared. They entered as boys and remained until they married. Custom required that the youths and maidens remained chaste until marriage. Those who disobeyed were allowed a simple marriage ceremony, those who remained virtuous were given a special wedding ceremony that lasted weeks (see Feliciano Oliveira, "The Cherentes of Central Brazil," in: *Proceedings of the XVIII. Session, London 1912*, International Congress of Americanists, 1912, p. 395.)

everything up. From now on the youth had no peace. During the day, when he went out in the forest, he could only think of his star. Since that one flash of folly he could only think of "his" star. Thoughts and wishes of her troubled every moment.

1118 In his absence from the lodge, his brothers went and played a trick on him: they stole the palm nuts that he usually kept in his gourd bottle. One of them climbed up and untied his gourd flask from the balcony where he had fixed it up and threw it down. Another boy caught it. But when he opened it, he dropped it with a cry, "An animal with fiery eyes!" he yelled. The two youths left the gourd on the ground where it had fallen and made off in panic. When the lad returned, his brothers told him what had happened and warned him not to touch his gourd flask. He was angry with them, but did not betray the truth.

1119 He hung the flask back up on the balcony rafters where it was before. The star maiden only came out of her hiding place at night, and the young man, although somewhat frightened, gazed upon her beauty. One day the star told the young man that they must go out hunting. They came to a Bacaba palm and the star maiden asked him to climb up and bring down a cluster of fruit. When the youth was at the top and had cut off the bundle, she called up to him, "Hold on tight!" and she jumped up on the palm herself. She hit the tree with a rod and the palm began to grow. It grew taller and taller, until it reached high into the sky. They tied the top of the tree with leaves onto a thick wall and they both jumped off into the sky. The youth was sorely afraid; he saw only a wide barren field and far away, a house. The star maiden left him and went to that house. Soon she returned with food for the young man. She told him to stay just where he was and not leave that spot, and she went off again. The young man remained where he was, sad and confused about all that had happened. After a short while, he heard not far away the sound of hunting horns and voices. It seemed that there was a party with song and dance taking place nearby. The star maiden came back and again implored him not to leave the place where he was and to resist the temptation to go and look at the dancing. Then she left him alone again. The youth was not able to resist his curiosity, however, and he left the spot to visit the dance. What he saw was horrible! It was a kind of death dance. A group of skeletons turned around, this way and that, dancing in chaotic confusion. Rotting flesh hung on their bones and their desiccated eyes lay sunken in the skulls. The air was filled with a sickening stench.

1120 The young man ran away appalled. He met the star maiden who thoroughly scolded him for his disobedience. Then she let him bathe and clean himself from the defilement. Then she again went away. But he could not stay in this place any longer. As soon as he saw that she had gone some steps, he ran to the place where they had bound up the palm. The star maiden turned and saw what he was doing, rightly guessing his intentions. She ran back to stop him. But the youth quickly jumped on the palm, which shriveled up and became as it was before. The star looked sadly down at the young man and said, "Your leaving is to no avail, you will soon return."

1121 And so it happened. When he reached the ground, the youth felt a great headache. He could only just tell his father and his brothers what had happened. All their healing potions were in vain. He soon died. And thus the people learned that up there in the heavens there was no bliss and salvation awaiting them, even if the stars shone down so enticingly.[15]

1122 Stars have been identified with the soul for thousands of years.[16]

1123 The fairytale, "The Story of the Lafaang," portrays the incompatibility of the world beyond the anima with earthly existence in a particularly charming way:

1124 The daughter of Palai[17] fell in love with a Long Kiput youth, Lafaang by name, and invited him to ascend to the Heavens, warning him at the same time that the customs in her celestial home were very different from those of Earth. The girl was very beautiful, and Lafaang was not slow to find his way to her father's house. Palai, surprised to see this mortal visitor, enquired of his daughter, "Who is this man, and why does he come here?" "It is the man I wish to wed" replied the girl. The kind-hearted father told her to give her lover food, and consented to the realization of her hopes. So Lafaang took up his abode in the house of Palai and was wedded to his daughter. But in spite of repeated instructions, Lafaang found it very difficult to conform to the customs of his adopted country. He put his food into his mouth with his fingers instead of using a needle for the purpose, and by doing so distressed his wife, who chided him for his disobedience to her instructions. On the morrow of his arrival he was invited to clear a patch of jungle for a padi field. His wife told him

[15] For the original, see Oliveira, "The Cherentes of Central Brazil," p. 395f; this version is translated from the German version collected in Koch-Grünberg, *Südamerika*, pp. 206–208.
[16] See Weicker, *Seelenvogel*, p. 57f., and Dieterich, *Eine Mithrasliturgie*, p. 65.
[17] [Palai = the constellation Pegasus.]

that, in order to fell a tree, he was merely to lay the axe she gave him at the foot of the tree, which would forthwith fall to the ground. But habit was too strong to be controlled, and, when Lafaang set his hand to the task, he fell to chopping at the tree. But though he chopped with all his might and main he made no impression, and his gentle spouse was horrified to see the crudeness of his methods.

1125 On the next day he was told to watch Palai at work felling the trees. Squatting in the jungle he saw how the great trees fell when Palai merely laid the blade of the axe at the foot of each one. This spectacle filled Lafaang with terror and he would have ran away, but his wife reproached him for cowardice. On the following day he set to work again; and once more forgetting his lesson, he began to chop at the stems of the trees. This gross breach of custom was punished by the fall of a tree from that patch of jungle on to Lafaang so hard that it cut off his left arm.

1126 Upset by these disagreeable incidents and by the awkward appearance of his wife, who was now far advanced in pregnancy, Lafaang made up his mind to return to his own people. His wife reproached him for his intention; but, when she could not alter his determination, she gave him sugarcane tops and banana roots, previously unknown to men, and let him return back down to Earth by means of a long creeper. Before he reached the ground he heard the cry of his newborn child, and begged to be allowed to go back to see him. But his entreaties were to no avail, and weeping bitterly, he alighted on Earth at *Tikan Orum* [a spot in the upper Baram district]. Still his disobedience was not overcome; for, although he had been told to plant the sugarcane and banana by merely throwing them on the ground, he planted them carefully in the soil; and to this day a tall coarse grass (*bru*) grows on the spot. Nevertheless some sugarcane and banana plants grew up; but they were of an inferior quality, and so have they remained wherever they have spread in this world.

1227 Lafaang died among his own people on Earth, but the bright constellation that bears his name and shape[18] still moves across the heavens, reminding men of his journey to the world above the sky and of the misfortunes he suffered there.[19]

---

[18] [I.e., the constellation Orion.]

[19] Adapted from Charles Hose and William McDougall, *The Pagan Tribes of Borneo: A Description of Their Physical, Moral, and Intellectual Condition With Some Discussion of Their Ethnic Relations*, London, 1912, pp. 140–141.

1128 In these two tales, the hero is again a dreamer who feels attracted to the heavenly home and the stars and succumbs helplessly to their allure. In "The Star," although he experiences the ghastly, fatal abyss, he cannot tear himself away and is pulled along. This fairytale describes, concisely and aptly, the uplifting magical attraction and also the deadly, hostile nature of the unconscious world in its dual aspect, life-nurturing and life-destroying. Initially, the hero manages, through his intense longing, to pull his anima down into his personal earthly world and to take her captive. The star maiden is invisible to daytime consciousness and sealed in a bottle. She thus "belongs" to the youth. At night, however, she shines in all her beauty and begins her demonic temptation. Because she personifies the magical world, her temptation is most effective in the night. Evidently, she cannot endure life with the youth in his secular world, and she succeeds, apparently without his being aware of what is happening, to entice him into the otherworld. If his retrospective, actually forbidden, longing had led the young man to believe in a paradisiascal afterlife, now the deadly aspect of the anima's world is revealed. He is forbidden to watch the dance of the dead spirits, and overstepping this ban, he glimpses the dark background behind the beautiful but feigned appearance. But then he cannot bear the truth, and must soon thereafter join the dead and the star maiden.

1129 In the Chinese tale, "The Lady of the Moon," (see page 32) however, the emperor returns enriched to his daily life. The meeting remains a one-night, one-time ecstatic experience and does not lead to any *auseinandersetzung*. The meeting with the anima problem was elaborated in even greater detail in "The Fire-Ball." In that tale, the fishermen lets himself be carried — by a man lying by the wayside, whose hands and face are black (he is obviously the hero's shadow), and whose eyes are closed — to the house of a beautiful woman, who gives him a talisman. It turns out that this woman was a "voice from above" who had earlier advised him to loosen the fetters of the ghost who had been following him. Here, then, the anima first appears as an inner voice. She personifies intimation and intuition; she knows about the connections to the spirit realm, the unconscious, and everything about the problem of redemption from the pursuing ghost. The hero, however, fails and succumbs to the unconscious. He could not become a shaman, but lost his power because he "thought only about the beautiful woman he had seen." He leaves his village and remains lost to all.

1130 If the hero succumbs completely to the anima, he is lost to the world. Then, no *auseinandersetzung* (confrontation) with the problem, in which the opposites, consciousness and the unconscious, as personified by the anima, reach a balance, happens. The possibility of recognizing the otherworldly figures through experience remains unexplored.

1131 If the hero faces and confronts the problems created or brought on by the anima, as in "The Witchdoctor Makanaholo," where she appears as a vulture, he will be forced into the most momentous struggles and *auseinandersetzungen* with the gods of the deep, who appear behind the anima as parental imagos (just as in "Makonaura and Anuanaitu").

1132 Related to "The Witchdoctor Makanaholo" is "The Visit to Heaven,"[20] which also vividly portrays what lies behind the anima experience:[21]

1133 Long ago there was a war between the Kuyalakog and Palawiyang. The war took place in the region of the Uraukaima Mountains.[22] The Palawiyang attacked the Kuyalakog when they were out planting in the fields and killed many people. The surviving Kuyalakog got together and set out to exterminate the Palawiyang. They came upon a settlement with five huts and set them on fire at night so that the enemy could not flee in the darkness and would burn bright. They killed many Palawiyang with their clubs as they tried to flee their burning huts.

1134 One man, Maitchaule, lay unscathed between many dead. He had painted his face in blood to deceive the enemy. The attacking Kuyalakog went away. They believed that all Palawiyangs were dead. Only Maitchaule survived. He got up, bathed, and went to another enclave not far away. He thought he would find somebody there, but they all had fled too. He found only manioc bread and old roasted meat. He thought of his father and mother, whom the Kuyalakog had killed, and that now he had no one. Then he said to himself, "I will go and lay down next to my companions who are now dead!"

1135 He returned to his burned village, full of fear. There he found many vultures. Maitchaule was a witch doctor and had once dreamt of a beautiful maiden. He shooed away all the vultures and lay down between his dead companions to rest. Again he smeared himself with their blood. One hand he put on a head, in case the vultures returned, so that he could immediately defend himself. The vultures came again and began to fight amongst themselves over the corpses. The daughter of the Vulture King came too and landed right on Maitchaule's breast! As she was about to tear at his flesh, he said to her, "Change yourself

[20] "The fairytale, 'The Visit to Heaven,' and the tests that the hero has to pass belongs to a special class of legends, which have very wide distribution in the Americas, from Chile to the extreme northwest. Their features match so strikingly that one is entitled to believe that they sprang from a common root" (Koch-Grünberg, *Südamerika*, p. 321).

[21] [Due to its significance, and because it is unavailable in English, we have translated this tale from the original almost in its entirety.]

[22] [Located in northern Brazil, south of Canaima National Park (Venezuela).]

into a human woman! I am so alone here and have no one who helps me!" She stopped just before she was about to peck into him. He went with her to the abandoned enclave he had visited earlier. He said to her, "I am now going fishing, when I come back, I want to find you transformed into a woman!" The people that had fled had left plants and bananas and things to eat.

1136 Maitchaule went out. He closed the door of the hut and left the daughter of the Vulture King and went fishing. She changed herself into a woman. There was much corn in the house. She husked the corn and put the grains in a mortar and pestle, set a pot on the fire, and did all the things a woman does. She made cassiri[23] and put it in a gourd flask. Then she changed back into a vulture, because she was ashamed in front of the man. Soon Maitchaule returned with fish and game.

1137 [He saw the daughter of the Vulture King as a vulture but many human footprints going into and out of his house. He became suspicious.] Early the next morning before Maitchaule awoke, the daughter of the Vulture King transformed herself into a human woman again and went to get water. She brought water back, made the fire, put up the pot, sprinkled in pepper, and added a piece of venison. She cooked this and let it simmer on the fire. When Maitchaule awoke in the morning, the food was ready. He saw manioc cakes all prepared. In the meantime the girl had transformed herself back into a vulture. She did not want to show herself to him. He was still mistrustful, especially when he saw the pot on the fire. "There are people here!" he thought. Then he went out with his bow and arrow, closed and locked up the house. This time he went only a little ways and then turned back. He wanted to see who was doing all these things. He hid himself near the house. He had purposely left his fishing rod in the house. Now he stayed hidden and waited.

1138 After a while, the girl opened the house and stepped outside. She was a very beautiful young woman with strings of pearls falling from her neck upon her breast, and other strings of pearls around her arms and legs. She was wearing a pretty skirt of pearls too. The girl went to the river. Maitchaule went into the house, took his fishing rod and hid himself behind the entrance. The girl came back to the house.

1139 She put the water down and lay in the hammock. Then Maitchaule came out from his hiding place with his fishing rod in his hand. He saw her and thought, "Now I have a woman!" She was very beautiful

---

[23] [Cassiri is an intoxicating liquor brewed from sweet potatoes.]

with her pearls on her arms and legs. Ashamed, she wrapped herself in the hammock. Maitchaule said to her, "Do not be ashamed!" and lay down next to her.

1140 Then he said to her, "Didn't I tell you that you should change yourself into a woman and live with me? I have no mother, I have no one. I am completely alone. Now do not go away, stay here as my wife! We have a plantation, I have not planted it yet, but we can take it over. All my relatives have left out of fear of war with the Kuyalakog. I am totally alone. My relatives will never return. When we need food, I will go fishing and hunting. I will bring you deer, tapir, and fish. I am here with you, you will never be hungry. Stay with me here in the house and make manioc cakes for us to eat! I will go hunting. Do not go away!"

1141 Thus they lived together for a long time in that house. Then one day she said to him, "Now I would like to see my family! Be patient!" Maitchaule did not want to let her go. He said to her that if she left him, he would take some rope and hang himself. Then she said, "I am not going away! I am only going quickly to visit my family. Stay here and wait for me. Do not go away. I cannot take you with me without my father seeing you. I will tell my father that I am married to you." Then she said, "Do not cry when you see me flying up into the sky." He went out of the house and said to her, "Do not go away, stay with me! She calmed him and said, "I will not leave you, I only want to tell my father he has a son-in-law." Maitchaule still would not let her go. Then she said, "Okay, shave my hair off." The man cut all of her hair off. Then she said, "Cut a section of bamboo and stuff my hair inside, blow tobacco smoke in there and stop it up with beeswax! If tomorrow I do not return, then pack it with pitch. Then I must die there." Then she left him saying, "If I do not come back early tomorrow morning, then I will come in the afternoon." And she went and he watched her go. She hopped up and down a few times and turned into a vulture and flew in circles higher and higher. He watched her get smaller and smaller and then she disappeared. He went into his house, lay in the hammock and thought about all that had happened. He did not sleep that night, he contemplated the whole night through.

1142 Morning came. Before the woman left, she had said to him, "Go early in the morning and wait for me! If I do not come, wait for me until evening." He rolled himself a cigar of tobacco leaves. Then he went outside and sat down. When he had finished smoking, he went in the house and lay down. This time he slept. He dreamt. In the dream she said to him, "I am on my way back to you with my two brothers-in-law." He woke up suddenly and went outside and looked high up in the sky. There he saw three vultures, just like he had dreamed. Two white ones and one black one. He was full of joy as he saw them. They came, circling down and down until they were very close to him. They alighted on the ground. His wife came up to him and said, "Here are my brothers! Do not be ashamed in front of mine, I do not shame myself in front of yours! You can be with them just like you can be with me."

1143 The brothers grew fond of him. Then she said, "We will stay two more days here and then we will take to the sky." The brothers asked that he kill a deer for them to eat. Maitchaule went hunting and killed a deer and brought it home. The brothers cut up the deer, cooked it, and ate it. The leftovers they roasted on the spit.

1144 So they stayed two more days in the house of their brother-in-law. Maitchaule showed them his plantation, his fields. When they came, they had brought a feather dress of the King Vultures. The woman now told her husband to put on the feather clothing. This he did and became a vulture too. The woman chewed Kumi[24] and blew it on her husband. She said, "Now we want to go! Have no fear, I will come behind you!" The vulture brothers were already in the sky circling above and waiting for them. She told him, "Now flap your wings! When you beat your wings you will see the ladder that is strapped up there." As the man flapped his wings he became lighter and lighter. He saw the ladder and climbed up behind his brothers-in-law. His wife flew behind him, to catch him if he fell. He climbed high up into the heavens. They came to the entrance and went in. The house of the Father of the King Vultures was close to the Entrance to Heaven. The brothers-in-law and the woman went on ahead. The man stayed behind. She said, "We want to call our father, so that he can see you!" They went into the house of the Father (King) of the King Vultures, Kasanpodole,[25] and announced that a man, his son-in-law, was standing there. The old one was very happy and went out with his sons to see the husband of his daughter. He found Maitchaule and said to him, "Let us go into my house!" He took him inside. He cared well for him. There were many people there. When the people arrive in

[24] "Kumi, the Brazilian *Bribrioca*, is a magic plant with long, grass-like leaves" (Koch-Grünberg, *Südamerika*, p. 321).

[25] "The 'Father of the King Vultures' belongs to the most important mythical figures of this folk. He lives with his tribe, the King Vultures (*Sarcorhamphus papa Sw.*) and common vultures (*Cathartes*) in heaven where they become people after taking off their vulture plumage. He is a great magician, has two heads, and eats people. These characteristics point to the moon character of this strange mythical figure" (Koch-Grünberg, *Südamerika*, p. 321).

heaven, King Vultures take off their feathered clothing and are then people.

1145 A few days passed and then his wife said to Maitchaule:, "If you are hungry, go into the house of Periquitos! They have corn cassiri. You do not need to drink what we drink here. Go into the house of the Parrots. There too you can find corn cassiri. Go into the house of the Macaws, they too have corn cassiri." All the Parrots, Periquitos, and Macaws had corn cassiri. In heaven they were all people. Maitchaule went into the house of the Parrots and drank corn cassiri. He carried on a good life with the Parrots, Macaws, and Periquitos. One day the Father of the King Vultures said to his daughter, "Tell your husband that he should dry out Lake Kapöpiakupö within two days!" It was a very large lake. When Maitchaule returned from the house of the Periquitos, his wife said to him, "My father said that you should dry out Lake Kapöpiakupö in just two days." If you fail, the King Vultures will kill you and eat you. Maithcaule said to his wife, "I do not know how I can dry this huge lake out!"

1146 Maitchaule went up to the lake. He began by damming up the tributaries to the lake and scooping out the waters, so that the lake would flow into the river. [Along came a damselfly[26] and an Uoimeg bird and asked what he was doing and if they could help. The damselflies scooped water out and the Uoimeg bird held watch. After two days the lake was dry.] All the animals that had been in the lake waters now appeared on the desiccated bottom of the lake. There were many large water snakes, alligators, fish, turtles, and so on. The damselflies said, "It is finished, Brother-in-Law! Now you can tell your father! We will go away! Go, call your father." And they went away.

1147 Maitchaule went away with Uoimeg. They came to the house of Kasanapodole. Uoimeg remained outside, close by. Maitchaule said to his father-in-law, "The lake is finished!" Now the old man was delighted. Maitchaule said, "There are plenty of fish, water snakes, and alligators!" Kasanapodole sent one of his sons out to see if perhaps his son-in-law was lying. The son of the Father of the King Vultures went to look and found a lot of fish, alligators, and snakes. This was because the lake had been a very large lake. He returned to his father and Maitchaule and said, "Maitchaule was not lying, my Father. The lake is dry. There are very many fish, water snakes, alligators, turtles, and

[26] An insect similar to the dragonfly, having a hindwing almost identical to the forewing. "The great damselflies hover over the water surface on sunny days and splash the water surface with their abdomens" (Koch-Grünberg, *Südamerika*, p. 321).

other animals." The old one said, "Tomorrow we will invite all the other people to go and get the fish!"

1148 Kasanapodole then ordered Maitchaule to build a house on a cliff. If he did not complete the task, he would kill him and eat him.

1149 [This time the Earthworms and Weaver Bird helped Maitchaule to build the house.] Then Weaver Bird said, "You can now go to your father-in-law and tell him that the house is finished. I'm leaving! Do not tell him that I built the house!" The Weaver Bird went away. The Earthworms also went away. Maitchaule went to the house of his father-in-law and told him that his house was finished. The old man was delighted, and went to the house to see for himself. He found the house beautiful and returned home.

1150 Then he said to his son-in-law, "Now make me a stone bench with two heads just like my head!" Then he went away. The old man wanted the bench for his new house. Near the house there was a round rock. Maitchaule struck upon it. A piece flew off, but that was not enough. Then the White Termites came along. They asked him, "What are you making there, Brother-in-Law?" He replied, "I am making a bench for Kasanapodole. He ordered that I chisel out two heads on it, just like his two heads." Then the Termites ordered him to tie up his hammock in the house and said to him, "Do not watch us! We all want to help you! We want to make a bench but a bench that goes along, like people do!" Maitchaule went into the house, tied up his hammock, and climbed into it. The Termites were outside and made the bench. It was morning when he met them. They made the bench in no time. At noon they were done. Then they shouted, "The bench is ready, Brother-in-Law!" Then he went out and the Termites said to him, "Do not be frightened, Brother-in-Law! We want to let the bench walk into the house!" Then they said to the bench, "Go into the house." The bench had two heads just like Kasanapodole. The bench went inside, going like a turtle goes. Maitchaule was frightened. The Termites said to him, "Do not be afraid, the bench will not eat you! If you say to the bench, 'Go there, change your place, my bench!' then it will move. If you say to the bench, 'Stay there, my bench!' then it will stay there." Then they told him to tell the bench that it should move. "I want that you go outside, my bench! Stay just opposite the entrance!" The bench went out and stayed just opposite the entrance to the house. Then the Termites said, "Now you can say to your father-in-law, that his bench is ready. But do not tell him about us! We are going away now!" The Termites left. Maitchaule went and spoke to the Wasps. He told them, "When Kasanapodole sits on the bench, then sting him!"

1151 Then Maitchaule went to the house of his father-in-law. Kasanapodole gave him cassiri to drink. There were all rotten carcasses from the lake lying around: fish, alligators, snakes, all full of worms. This was Payua for the King Vultures.[27] Maitchaule drank nothing, he gave everything to his wife. She drank the Payua. Maitchaule drank corn cassiri in the house of the Perikitos, Parrots, and Macaws. He also drank manioc cassiri in the house of Ducks. They had manioc plants. Maitchaule then secretly hid a grain of corn in his mouth to take with him when he went back down to Earth. (In those days people did not have corn on Earth.)

1152 Maitchaule reported to his father-in-law that the bench was finished and said to him, "Do not be alarmed at the bench!" Kasanapodole spoke to Maitchaule, "Come with me!" He also invited his sons to come along and see the bench. They all went to the new house. Maitchaule now invited his father-in-law to sit on the bench and said to him, "Do not be afraid!" When Kasanapodole sat on the bench, the wasps stung him and the bench ran off with him. The old man was so terrified that he jumped up and ran away, all stung by the wasps. He banged his head against a tree and fell to the ground. All his sons also ran away. The old one turned around and around, he rolled on the ground, quite confused in his head, and he could not walk. Then Maitchaule ordered the bench to go close to the old man. When the bench arrived, the old man pushed it back. But the bench kept coming after him. Maitchaule told the bench to follow and to keep chasing after Kasanapodole. He said to the bench, "If the old man goes to his house, you come up behind him and stand at the entrance! The old man ran like crazy into his house, the bench chasing him right behind. The old man ran into his house and locked the doors behind him. The bench stopped and remained at the entrance. Then Maitchaule wondered how he could now return again to the Earth. Then the Murumuruta Bird, the Nightingale, came up to him. She asked him, "What are you doing, Brother-in-Law?" Maitchaule replied, "I'm wondering how can I get back down to the Earth!" Then Murumuruta said, "Wait, I'll go get Kumi!" She went away to fetch Kumi. Maitchaule stayed where he was and waited. In a short time, Murumuruta returned with Kumi. Murumuruta chewed Kumi and blew her breath on to Miatchaule. He became very light weight. Then Murumuruta told him to put on her feathered clothes. Maitchaule put on Murumuruta's clothes. Then the bird said, "Now beat your wings!"

[27] "Payuau is a dark, intoxicating drink made from fermented manioc, in contrast to the light cassiri" (Koch-Grünberg, *Südamerika*, p. 321).

Then Maitchaule flew. They flew away. They came to the Entrance to Heaven. Then the bird said, "Now bend over!" Maitchaule bent down and flew through the Entrance to Heaven. They flew away, downwards. Murumuruta knew where Maitchaule's relatives were. Near the house, by the river, there was a harbor. The bird left him there at the harbor and said to him, "Now go there to the house of thy kin! I'm leaving!" Murumuruta flew away.

1153 Maitchaule came into the house of his relatives. They recognized him and asked him, "From where do you come? Where have you been?" He replied, "I was in heaven at the house of the King Vultures." He said that he had captured the daughter of the king of all King Vultures and she carried him to Heaven. "Her father, Kasanapodole, wanted to eat me. So I left. Murumuruta brought me back here."

1154 He stayed there with his relatives. They had a new plantation. They planted the corn seed that Maitchaule had brought back. From this seed there grew a corn stalk with two ears of corn. His relatives wanted to eat the corn, but Maitchaule said, "No! Save the seeds, we can make many more corn plants from them!" The corn dried. Then they slashed and burned and prepared another plantation. They planted the corn seeds there. Other relatives learned that he had corn. They came and asked him for corn. He gave them not an ear of corn, but only one grain. He sold it for a hammock. He said to them, "I brought just one grain back from heaven, and I paid for it there. Down here, you would never have found corn. I had to go to Heaven to bring it down here." Thus he spread corn among the people. They planted more corn, and it has come down to all of us. This is the corn that we have today.

1155 Maitchaule put the Wasp next to the Weaver Bird. Since that time, the Weaver Bird is always together with the Wasps. The Weaver Birds make nests near the house of Wasps.[28] They are friends to this day. This is the end of the story.[29]

1156 Characteristically, the hero first dreams of a beautiful girl – the unknown woman, the image of his soul. Her appearance heralds his momentous destiny. Then occurs a great external disaster, the murderous invasion of an enemy tribe, which destroys everything in Maitchaule's life that had previously existed. The collapse of his previous worldly relationships is a symptom or

[28] "The weaver bird (*Oriolus sp.*) builds very artistically designed hanging nests, very often in the neighborhood of big wasps' nests – a natural protection" (Koch-Grünberg, *Südamerika*, p. 321).
[29] Koch-Grünberg, *Südamerika*, pp. 109–122.

condition for this turning inward; only then do the internal images begin to speak up more loudly. This inner turning point is like dying, Maitchaule lies in utter desperation among his dead relatives. This corresponds to his inner psychic situation. The daughter of the father of the king vultures now chooses to attack and eat him. But he "grasps" this threat and turns things around; he makes her his prisoner. Because the hero is a magical doctor, a shaman, he intuitively understands that the attack of the vulture-woman stands in relation to his dream and the girl of his dreams. The beautiful maiden that he is looking for must, therefore, be hidden behind this bird. Besides, the king vultures of that region belong to be gods, whose nature especially the shaman knows about. As so often, the anima first appears covered in feather, that is, as an intuition, as a fleeting spirit-being. The magician's great desolation gives him the energy to focus on this inner manifestation: he holds the bird. He sees his own secret human-female nature and takes this girl as his wife. With his conscious mind, he thus obtains a piece of his hitherto unconscious inner life.

1157 At first, the "magical marriage" between the man called to be a shaman and the anima-bird succeeds. But the anima is, in the hierarchy of the unconscious, only one level. "Winning" her – psychologically, this means making this psychic entity conscious – just activates another archetypal figure, which takes over its effect. The daemonic father draws to himself the anima and the psychic energy that radiates from her.[30]

1158 The figure of a hidden masculine divinity was discussed above in Chapter 2.1 and is represented by the "father" of the soul-figure in almost every fairytale we have so far discussed. For example, we saw this in "The Boy Who Was Afraid of Nothing," where Balor's daughter Eithne gave birth to the future hero in a tower, and "Makonaura and Anuanaitu," which reflects a strong parallel with the present fairytale. In the latter tale, the anima also desires to return "to the parents" and forces the hero into an *auseinandersetzung* with her father, the mysterious two-headed god of the depths.[31]

---

[30] Commenting on the *auseinandersetzung* between the ego and the anima (in this fairytale, the hero represents the ego), Jung writes: ". . . the conscious mind has not become master of the unconscious, and the anima has forfeited her tyrannical power only to the extent that the ego was able to come to terms with the unconscious. This accommodation was not a victory of the conscious over the unconscious, however, but the establishment of a balance of power between the two worlds. Hence the 'magician' could take possession of the ego only because the ego dreamed of victory over the anima. That dream was an encroachment, and every encroachment of the ego is followed by an encroachment from the unconscious:

"Changing shape from hour to hour
I employ my savage power."

Consequently, if the ego drops its claim to victory, possession by the magician ceases automatically ("Relation between the ego and the unconscious," CW 7, ¶381). [The Goethe passage is from *Goethe's Faust, Parts I and II* (abridged version translated by Louis MacNeice), Faber & Faber, London, 1951, p. 282, Part II, Act V, modified.]

[31] This reminds us of the *auseinandersetzung* that the hero has with the evil smith of Pont-de-Pîle in the "Golden Feet" (see above, page 192). There, however, the anima is represented by two figures. The daughter of the blacksmith portrays only the negative aspect, the daughter of the Marquis embodies

1159 Since each figure of the unconscious can represent all the unconscious, a solitary figure attracts others figures or contents who personify the content where an *auseinandersetzung* is necessary. Therefore, when the relationship with the anima is seriously engaged in, it must be followed by a journey into the beyond. In the "The Visit to Heaven," this is expressed by the daughter of the father of the king vultures longing to return to her own people, so that the hero can either give up the magical connection (like many fairytale heroes) or embark on the path to the gods.

Because the man is afraid that the woman will not return, she cuts off her hair and gives it to him as a pledge through which he holds her life in his hands. Hair contains the entire being and is often regarded as the seat of the secret life force (as in the story of Samson and Delilah). Primitive peoples are often convinced that there is a *participation mystique* between a person and their bodily growths, secretions, and excretions (which Lévy-Bruhl calls "accessories").[32] Maitschaule need not really make use of the hair, however, because his wife soon returns with two of her brothers. Thus Maitschaule, his wife, and her two brothers make up a foursome, three men and one woman, for the journey to the otherworld. A tetrad always points to a mandala structure and inner wholeness.[33] The hero is dressed in feathers, and thus is assimilated with the magical sphere. He thus makes the journey as a bird, that is, he uses his intuition, which arises from his connection with the anima. She flies behind him to the realm of the gods. Supported and borne by his inner female side, he rises to the heights. The flight is at the same time an ascent on a previously unseen ladder. As in "A Legend of Flowers" (see page 83), it represents a connection to the unconscious. Like any sublimation, it can be interpreted as a gradual development.

1160 In this way, he reaches the king vulture, who, however, is a human being in heaven. The king vulture is an archetype of the whole species, or, as Lévy-Bruhl formulates it, a symbol, the genius, the epitome of the life substance of all individual beings. As a totem, he is partly a magician, partly an animal, since he often appears on the earthly world as an animal. In the *alcheringa*, the timeless-eternal land of the ancestors, he is a magical doctor.[34] In the following, we will repeatedly refer to the difference in these two realms. It is

---

only the positive aspect. See also the fairytale, "Tsetlwalakame," in which the hero Gyii, son of the first man, must take the woman he loves away from her father, Tsawatalalis, a sorcerer. The old man is sometimes designated the Heavenly Father-in-Law, or directly, the Sun. Krickeberg relates this to the myth of the birth of the Raven, and that Gyii is the eastwards waning crescent moon that follows the sun. Significant here is that the chthonic god uses hinged doors and cracks in trees, which are otherwise maternal symbols. He obviously combines aspects of both these demons of the depths in himself.

[32] On the mystical relationship of people to their "accessories" (i.e. appurtenances and footprints), see Lévy-Bruhl, *The "Soul" of the Primitive*, p. 115f.

[33] On the number four and the female element as the fourth element within the Trinity, see C.G. Jung, *Psychology and Alchemy*, CW 12, ¶192, ¶201, ¶319ff., and especially, *"Psychologie und Religion,"* CW 11, ¶107.

[34] See Lévy-Bruhl, *The "Soul" of the Primitive*, pp. 49–50, 186.

obviously important to the storyteller that the foreign invader drink different beverages than the vultures. Because the hero, Maitchaule, is a shaman and clearly aware of these laws, he neither loses his discerning consciousness nor identifies with the divine figures of the unconscious, which would have fatal consequences for him. Equating himself with the unconscious would put him in danger of being "poisoned." The initially friendly father godhead suddenly reveals his man-eating side to his son-in-law, and assigns him "impossible tasks" to prove his abilities. The hero accomplishes his tasks with the support of helpful animals, that is, with the help of his instincts. The image of the godhead on the bench is identical to the task given to the hero of "Makonaura and Anuanaitu" by the caiman god Kaikutschi.

1161 By successfully completing his tasks, the hero can escape from being destroyed by the dark spirit. But he cannot transform its darkness, which would be psychologically equivalent to conscious realization. Maitchaule must flee, therefore, and also leave behind "his" beautiful woman. She never really committed herself to him, but always lived according to her father's purposes. In other fairytales, which we will discuss later, the anima figure turns toward the man.[35] That he does not complete all his tasks may be related to the fact that he proceeds *only* instinctively (i.e. aided by the animals). This clearly shows the primitive stage of this fairytale. A really conscious *auseinandersetzung* is not possible for the hero. (This situation is also similar to the tragic ending of "Makonaura and Anuanaitu.") Maitchaule returns down to Earth with the help of another bird, the nightingale, meaning again by his intuition. He brings back a special prize, however, a grain of corn, which enabled cultivating this invaluable plant for the first time. The acquisition of a plant suitable for cultivation through a passage into the otherworld is a fundamental subject of many tales of primitive peoples because cultural development is the most important task. Achieving a spiritual goal or developing in that direction, such as overcoming the obstacles which hinder forming a permanent connection with the anima in this world, is rarely mentioned. Mostly, as in this tale, the marriage is brief, magical, and soon dissolved.

1162 One parallel tale to this "visit to Heaven" is "The Daughter of the King Vultures," which is so similar to the previous one that we will only provide an outline here:

1163 The King Vultures were accustomed to fly down to a lake to bathe. There they took off their feather dress and went swimming in the form

[35] This is also shown in the Norwegian fairytale mentioned above, "The Master Maiden." There, the girl of the tale's title helps the youth solve his tasks and escapes with him from the realm of the giants. In return the hero asks that she help him overcome the demons. Characteristically, in some variants of "Ferdinand the Faithful and Ferdinand the Unfaithful," the king who requires the successful completion of the impossible tasks is the father of the princess. See Bolte and Polívka, *Anmerkungen*, vol. 3, pp. 21, 23, 25.

of young girls. A young man once stole the feather dress of one of the maidens and demanded that she stay with him. Since they liked each other, she agreed and he stowed her vulture dress away in a chest. Soon she gave birth to a son who quickly grew up. One day the wife suggested that they make a visit her father. The man agreed and the woman bound *Janiparana* leaves to the arms of the father and their son. She donned her plumage and fanned the men with her wings. His arms became feathered. The men tried out flying; the son flew up on a tree branch, but the husband fell back to the ground. The woman announced she would help him and flew behind him up to Heaven's Gate. The son had no problem, but the father arrived totally exhausted from his flight. They removed their plumage and took on their human forms again. In Heaven it was the same as on Earth, the King Vultures also took off their plumage and went around in the shape of humans. The family continued on their way and came to the house of the Sun, the Moon, and the Wind; all of which welcomed the family and asked where they were going. "To my father," the woman answered, and they continued onward. Finally they came to the house of the old King of the King Vultures.

1164 [They were formally welcomed but the King was incensed that a man was there and planned to kill him. He gave him a series of tasks: to build a dugout canoe, to dam up a river, and to cut down a forest. None of these could the man do himself; he was helped by the Woodpeckers and the Dragonflies. Exasperated that the man had survived all his tasks, the old King of the King Vultures invited the man to set the forest on fire with him. Of course it was a trick to burn the man, but this time the Spider came to his aid: he let himself be changed into a spider and survived again. When the old one found the man sitting there completely unharmed, he angrily smashed his gourd with tapioca flour to the ground in frustration and infuriated, returned home.]

1165 The man's wife now said that they should leave the house of her father, otherwise the old one would now surely kill him. They went back to the house of the Vulture King and packed up their belongings and made manioc flour. Then they set off on their return back down to Earth. The Old One commanded his warriors, the Urubus (black vultures), to go and find the man. But the wife had prepared for this turn and had packed a long knife, just in case. When the Urubus came upon them, she bravely flayed her knife and sliced off the head of one, the wings of another, and chased the rest away. The family fled and came again to Heaven's Gate and prepared their descent. The son took right off and flew down without hesitation. His father panicked that he would fall and crash to the ground as soon as he would try to fly. But the woman comforted him and told him she would help. She flew beneath him and supported him so that he did not fall. Totally exhausted and out of breath the man landed on the ground. He had to sit down and lean on her when they arrived, he was so tired.[36]

1166 Here, the hero succeeds in gaining permanent possession of his anima. The female element is consistently well-disposed toward the man, whereas in the previous fairytale, as soon as the woman arrived in Heaven, she distanced herself from her husband and aligned herself with her father. In the second version (see above), the wife even fights against other vultures to protect her husband and ensures his safe return flight. The fact that the man is closer and connected more strongly to the feminine element of his soul [than the hero of the previously discussed tale] is evident from him transforming himself into a spider.[37] He assimilates himself to the Mother Goddess and returns to Earth, reborn, through the hole in heaven. The fact that the woman returns with him also corresponds to this stronger, instinctive assimilation of the feminine side in the unconscious.

1167 The initial appropriation of the anima was accomplished by stealing her plumage. This represents the widespread motif of the "swan maiden" in its pure form. The temporary or partly animal-like nature of the anima is the subject of many fairytales. Her chthonic side associates itself with the man's affects and his dark shadow while conferring an animal-like intuition, an affinity with nature, and an unerring instinct. She provides orientation in the dark side of life, for unconscious processes, and mediates the encounter with the mysterious primal spirit hidden in nature. An important example of this function of the anima figure is related in the Inuit tale, "Ititaujang":

1168 A long, long time ago, a young man, whose name was Ititaujang, lived in a village with many of his friends. When he grew up he wished to take a wife and went to a hut in which he knew that an orphan girl lived. As he was bashful and afraid to speak to the young girl himself, however, he called her little brother, who was playing before the hut, and said, "Go to your sister and ask her if she will marry me." The boy ran to his sister and delivered the message. The young girl sent her younger brother back and bade him ask the name of her suitor. When

[36] Koch-Grünberg, *Südamerika*, Jena 1921 pp. 180–186 [in German, here shortened].
[37] The Great Mother [here personified by the Spider] often helps the hero against the demons of the darkness. Consider how Wau-uta helped protect the baby against the Tiger-Man, in "The Story of Haburi." In many fairytales, the devil's grandmother is also a helpful figure; see, for instance, Grimm's "The Devil with the Three Golden Hairs."

she heard that his name was Ititaujang she told him to go away and look for another wife, as she was not willing to marry a man with such an ugly name.[38] But Ititaujang did not capitulate and sent the boy once more to his sister.

1169 "Tell her that Nettirsuaqdjung[39] is my other name," said he. The boy, however, said upon entering: "Ititaujang is standing before the doorway and wants to marry you." Again his sister said "I will not have a man with that ugly name." When the boy returned to Ititaujang and repeated his sister's words, Ititaujang sent him back once more and said, "Tell her that Nettirsuaqdjung is my other name." Again the boy entered and said. "Ititaujang is standing before the doorway and wants to marry you." The sister answered, "I will not have a man with that ugly name." When the boy returned to Ititaujang and told him to go away, he was sent in the third time on the same commission, but to no better effect." Again the young girl declined his offer, and upon that Ititaujang went away in great anger. He did not care for any other girl of his tribe, but left the country altogether and wandered many days and nights over hills and through valleys, up and down the country.

1170 After many travels he finally arrived in the land of the birds and saw a small lake in which many geese were swimming. On the shore he saw there were a great number of boots. Cautiously, he crept nearer and stole as many boots as he could get hold of. A short time afterward the birds left the water and found many of their boots were missing. They became greatly alarmed and flew away. Only one of the flock remained behind, crying, "I want to have my boots back, I want to have my boots!" Ititaujang then came forth now, and answered, "I will give you your boots if you will become my wife." She objected, but when Ititaujang turned around to go away with the boots she agreed, although rather reluctantly.

1171 Ititaujang now allowed her to put on her boots and immediately she was transformed into a beautiful woman. They wandered down to the seaside where they settled in a large village. Here they lived together for some years and had a son. In time Ititaujang became a highly respected man as he was by far the best whaler among the Eskimo. One day the Eskimo killed a whale and were busy cutting it up and carrying the meat and blubber to their huts. Though Ititaujang was hard at work, his wife stood lazily by. When he called her and asked her to help as the other women did she objected crying, "My food is

[38] *Ititaujang* means "anus-like" – note by Boas.
[39] "Single little sea otter."

not from the sea, my food is from the land; I will not eat the meat of a whale; I will not help."

1172 Ititaujang answered. "You must eat of the whale; that will fill your stomach." Then she began crying and exclaimed, "I will not eat it; I will not soil my nice white clothing." She went down to the beach, eagerly looking for birds' feathers. Having found a few she put them between her fingers and between those of her child; both were transformed into geese and flew away.

1173 When the Eskimo saw this they called out, "Ititataujang, your wife is flying away!" Ititaujang became very sad; he cried for his wife and did not care for the abundance of meat and blubber, nor for the whales spouting near the shore. He followed his wife and traversed across the land in search of her. As he wandered he sang a song: "There, up there, I carry my desire to go, up there in the land of the birds, I-ja-ja-ja."

1174 After having traveled for many weary months he came to a river. There he saw a man who was busy chopping chips from a piece of wood with a large hatchet. As soon as the chips fell off he polished them with his penis and they were transformed into salmon, becoming so slippery that they glided from his hands and fell into the river, down which they descended to a large lake near by. The name of the man was Exaluqdjung (the little salmon).[40]

1175 On approaching the man, Ititataujang was almost frightened to death for he saw that the back of this man was altogether hollow. He could look from behind right through to the man's mouth. Cautiously he crept back and by a circuitous way approached this mysterious person from the opposite direction.

1176 When Exaluqdjung saw him coming, he stopped chopping and asked, "Which way did you approach me?" Ititaujang, pointing in the direction he had last come from and from which he could not see the hollow back of Exaluqdung, answered, "It is from there I have come." Exaluqdjung on hearing this, said, "That is lucky for you. If you had come from the other side and had seen my back, I should have immediately killed you with my hatchet." Ititaujang was very glad that he had turned back and thus deceived the salmon-maker. He asked him, "Have you seen my wife, who came this way?" Indeed, Exaluqdjung had seen her and said, "Do you see yonder the little island in that large lake? There she lives now, she has taken another husband."

[40] Krickeberg, the editor of a German collection of fairytales from North America, notes that "the story of the man who made fish from wood chippings is known in all Eskimo tribes from Alaska to Greenland and is also found along the Northwest Pacific coast"; see Krickeberg, *Nordamerika*, p. 370, especially "The Man Who Makes Salmon For Human Beings" (mentioned below).

1177 When Ititaujang heard this, he greatly despaired as he did not know how to reach the island. But Exaluqdjung kindly promised to help him. They descended to the beach. Exaluqdjung gave him the backbone of a salmon and said, "Now shut your eyes. The backbone will turn into a kayak and carry you safely to the island. But mind that you do not open your eyes, that will upset the boat.

1178 Ititaujang promised to obey. He shut his eyes, the backbone became a kayak and he went over the lake. As he did not hear any splashing of water, he was anxious to see whether the boat was moving. He opened his eyes just a little bit. But had he scarcely taken a short glimpse when the kayak began to swing violently and become a backbone again. He quickly shut his eyes and it returned to being a boat and continued steadily onwards. In a short time he landed on the island.

1179 There he saw the hut and his son playing on the beach nearby. On looking up and seeing Ititaujang, the boy ran to his mother crying, "Mother, father is here and is coming to our hut." The mother answered, "Go and play, your father is far away and cannot find us." The child obeyed, but as he saw Ititaujang approaching he ran back to the hut and said, "Mother, father is here and is coming towards our hut." Again the mother sent him away, but he returned very soon, saying that Ititaujang was now quite near.

1180 Scarcely had the boy said so when Ititaujang opened the door. When the new husband saw him he told his wife to open a box that was in a corner of the hut. She did so, and many feathers flew out of it and stuck to them. The woman, her new husband, and the child were thus again transformed into geese. The hut disappeared; but when Ititaujang saw them about to fly away he got furious and cut open the belly of his wife before she could escape. Then many eggs fell out.[41]

1181 The man's name was a terrible curse, constantly reminding him of his ugliness and ridiculousness. It prevented him from finding a normal way in the world and acquiring a wife. A curse may, however, also be a calling. The accursed is then the chosen one, from the side of the unconscious, that is, from behind — hence his name. His wretchedness drives him into the land of birds, souls, and dreams. In the land of intuitions and dreams, he finds the pond of the wild geese. Here, we encounter the motif of the swan maiden, albeit in an altered form. As a rule, the animal garb is stolen, whereas in this tale the opposite happens: a part of the *human* garb is stolen and the magical being is deprived of its greater possibilities. These come to depend on the grace of the

[41] F. Boas, "The Central Eskimo," 1888, pp. 615–618. [Readers are advised to consult the original version for particular phrasings.]

profane world. This may have to do with an intervention in an otherwise rhythmically occurring process. The wild geese live as women, sometimes as birds. In other words, the anima manifests sometimes in a tangible form closer to consciousness, and sometimes as a winged fleeting feeling, an idea, or a thought. The theft of the women's boots may have an erotic significance.[42]

1182 Through the robbery, one of the women fell into the hero's hands. This, of course, happens to the one who under no circumstances wants to accept losing the chance to become a woman. So there is a longing on the part of the anima to become human and to be redeemed from her animal nature.[43] The animal aspect is imposed upon her by ego consciousness, whose bright light represses the anima and banishes her to the unconscious. It is the task of humans to redeem her from this state. Thus, in "The Farmer and the Golden Sun," a Russian farmer lifts a duck out of the water (at her request!), which then turns into a beautiful maiden, the sister of the sun. The duck was created from crackling fat (*Griebenschmalz*), which the farmer had brought with him from hell and which represents the sinners roasted there! This reveals the secret identity of the anima with the shadow, the dark, inferior human being. In a parallel version to the Grimm's "The Three Feathers" (see future volume) from the Hessian region of Germany, the Simpleton finds an ugly toad in a jewel-studded underground chamber. The toad calls out to him, "Embrace me and lose yourself!" The Simpleton refuses and the toad calls out a second and then a third time, "Embrace me and lose yourself!" Then the Simpleton grabs the toad and carries it up to a pond and they jump in together. No sooner do they touch the water than the Simpleton finds a most beautiful maiden in his arms.[44] In another Hessian version, the hero must jump into the pond at the toad's command and wrestle with her, through which she regains her beautiful human form.

1183 These tales clearly illustrate the task of redeeming the soul. The motif of the swan maiden symbolizes an effort to become conscious, to pull the higher being that is hidden behind the feral up into higher awareness. This motif is connected to the frequently occurring test of *staying awake*, as is portrayed in the Norwegian fairytale, "Farther South Than South and Farther North Than North and in the Great Hill of Gold." In this tale, the hero, a boy, must find out who is trampling the wheat fields at night. He must stay awake and watchful through the night, and in this way discovers that the culprits are three pigeons. When confronted, they turn into beautiful young women. They were cursed by a troll to carry out their destructive work. This troll hated

---

[42] On the erotic significance of the shoe, see Dr. Aigremont, Fuss- und Schuh-Symbolik und -Erotik: Folkloristische und sexualwissenschaftliche Untersuchungen, Leipzig, 1909.

[43] This longing is formulated particularly poetically in "The Little Mermaid" (Hans Christian Andersen). Lüthi (p. 114) calls the animal-like fairytale princess who seeks redemption the "human soul" par excellence, that part of the soul that actively longs for union with the spiritual realm.

[44] Bolte and Polívka, *Anmerkungen*, vol. 2, p. 31.

"Christian blood" and is, therefore, related to the devil-like figure of the dark god. The boy redeems the three maidens from the troll and marries the middle one.

1184 Another form of making the anima conscious, seen figuratively as her deliverance from animal form, is the motif of dismembering, or chopping off her head. A German fairytale collected after the Grimm Brothers is called, "How the Fool Rescued the Princess":

> 1185 As an exception, a simpleton was given permission to guard the skinny family cow. As soon as he took on his task, then the cow took off. He held tight on her reins as she pulled him across the fields and over a large body of running water. On the other side of the river she pulled him into a barn where there was a golden manger with silver fodder racks full of the most beautiful hay. The cow proceeded to eat her fill there. Then she towed the simpleton back home and his people praised him for the cow's beautiful appearance and for his taking such good care of her. As he was towed a second time over the water, he met a black dog who pleaded with the simpleton not to beat it, but the next day to bring an ax and cut off its head. The simpleton fulfills this request exactly, he comes the next day with an ax and courageously follows the dog on its request on a long path to a tree stump where he chops off the dog's head. Suddenly a most beautiful princess stands in front of the simpleton. All around her are many redeemed counts and countesses, lords and ladies. The simpleton is chosen as the husband of the princess. "If you want to know whether the simpleton ever returned the cow, you will have to ask his father in the village."[45]

1186 The cow, which leads the hero to the anima figure, is an image of the Great Mother. In the psychology of Jung, the Mother-Imago is a precursor to the anima image,[46] especially when the consciousness is childlike and immature, like the Simpleton in fairytales. The cow, as an image of the nurturing nature of the unconscious, knows the springs of life, the land beyond the waters from which arises the spiritual wealth of the individual.

1187 The anima appears here – as the black dog – in animal form, because her essence has not been experienced by consciousness. She is only a dark, instinctive entity; and it requires a violent intervention to bring her nature to light. Like being vigilant or observing, or lifting the bird out of the water, dismemberment is an image of making a specific content conscious, in particular through spiritual work. This appears to be an act of violence against

---

[45] Zaunert (ed.), *Deutsche Märchen seit Grimm*, pp. 187–189.

[46] See C.G. Jung, "Relation between the ego and the unconscious," CW 7, ¶314.

the unconscious, but it leads to salvation from an inner dullness. Another image of this act is the theft of the animal robes or shoes, which represents a less profound awareness and, therefore, usually only temporarily confers a human guise on the anima.

1188 The Inuit tale "Ititaujang" is concerned at least initially with the reverse process: the hero takes the anima's human garments (in this case, her boots) and does not force her into this world, but instead he invades her realm. After he conquers her, they go to live together. But he does not take her to his former home. Rather, he seems to live in the magical realm or at least in the borderland (seashore!), meaning that he partially submits himself to her. Evidently, living with her makes him a famous whale hunter. Since the anima represents the voice of the unconscious, of nature, and of the instincts, becoming conscious of her means makes him more aware of the workings of nature. In primitive tales, it often leads to hunting success. Due to her half-animal, half-human nature, she creates a bond with the animal world. Only the hunter who can empathize with animals and instinctively understand them can have luck in bringing down game. Living together with the woman from the land of the birds, from the soul, makes the man, for better or for worse, unconscious. But at least in this tale, this state is not permanent. Because the man does not really recognize the essential nature of this woman, with time life with him becomes unbearable for the bird woman. Forcibly cut off from her realm, she refuses to accept the man's food. Separation is inevitable, either permanently or as a prelude to the further journey of the man into the realm of the unconscious. Like the magician Maitschaule in "The Visit to Heaven," the man in the present tale gains access to the dark god, driven by his desire for the lost woman.[47] In "Ititaujang," the woman sticks bird feathers between her fingers and those of her son – who represents the pledge of the relationship and the future continuation of the father – and takes him back to the land of wild geese, into the unconscious.

1189 Now Ititaujang comes upon the mysterious "Maker of Salmon," whose back is hollow. Although he makes fish out of wood flakes by magic and thus continually creatively generates life,[48] he is also clearly a god of death. So once again behind the anima stands the figure of the Hidden God in his dual aspect (remember the two heads of the king vulture in "The Visit to Heaven" and in "Makonaura and Anuanaitu," and Balor's deadly back side in "Balor and the Birth of Lugh"). Fish symbolize, as already stated, the nurturing and inspiring contents of the unconscious. The man sends them upstream to the lake, that is, he constantly creates this life-sustaining, upwards-striving basal current of

[47] See "The Shepherd and the Three Samoviles," which also begins with the motif of the swan maiden, and where the shepherd must also journey to the magical realm to win back his wife for a second time.
[48] See the image of the Salmon-Maker in "The Man Who Makes Salmon For Human Beings."

the unconscious. Although Ititaujang thus discovers the source of the nourishing life stream of the unconscious, he also notices that he is facing death. He arrives at the center, where life and death flow as one, to the mysterious primal essence and creative godhead. This one is called "the little salmon." He is also the totem ancestor of the salmon, from which all the individual fish (wood chips) splinter off. Ititaujang conceals his knowledge of this god's deadly aspect. Had he admitted as much, he would have attested to his superiority and his shamanic vocation, and thus engendered a serious confrontation with this god (remember Maitchaule's difficult test in "The Visit to Heaven"). He prefers to play ignorant and ignore the difficulties. Consequently, the plot peters out undramatically. He lets himself be carried upstream in an enchanted boat, made of salmon bones, to the island where the wild goose lives, in other words, back to the origin. In the kayak, he opens his eyes against the orders of Exaluqdjung and finds himself in the face of this imminent danger so he quickly closes them again. Thus he slips deep into unconsciousness and reaches the anima. She has married another wild goose, and thus has become reconnected to the animal side in the unconscious.

1190 To begin with, the anima is often accompanied by the "shadow" of the man as her male companion. The cayman in "Makonaura and Anuanaitu" was also such a shadow brother of the anima. In that tale, Makonaura, the hero, killed this brother and this act set off the string of tragic consequences. A particularly good example of the anima's connection to the shadow is the tale mentioned above, "The Story of the Blind King Who Lived in the Western Lands," in which a black bird sitting on a fig tree shows the hero the way to the desired "winged woman," who possesses the healing bird. The dark bird later becomes a man and, as a reward for his services, desires half of the hero's entire estate. The hero is even willing to divide his winged wife with the sword for his sake. But the dark one is satisfied with the proof of love and disappears. Here, too, the shadow and anima appear as a pair of birds. In the fairytale about Ititaujang, the anima returns to her former state, bound to her animal shadow side. This signifies that she has become completely unconscious again. When Ititaujang spies the anima and her second husband, they try to escape under a cloud of feathers sticking on them. The sought-after figures evaporate under the conscious gaze. The hut also disappears with their human form. Circumspectly, Ititaujang intervenes at the last second with a violent step to stop the anima from flying away. He slashes open her stomach, out of which a large number of eggs fall to the ground. Eggs as seeds signify the primeval elements that contain the future. Through his conscious engagement, Ititaujang comes to realize the creative seeds hidden in the anima. He recognizes the intrinsic value of the anima experience, the character and substance of the anima. With this reference to the seeds that symbolize what is to come the story ends in a remarkably undetermined, unformed, and dreamlike way. This course of events is characteristic: although the fairytales of natural peoples often indicate deep relationships and suggest possible developments, these do not crystallize into a clear and coherent shape.

1191 The Icelandic tale "The Sealskin" is equally tragic and unfolds without attaining a goal.

> 1192 One time long ago a man from Myrdal in the East was walking early one morning before people had arisen for the day. He came to some cliffs and saw an entrance to a cave. He could hear noises, there was merrymaking and dancing going on inside. Outside the cave he noticed a large number of sealskins. He picked up one of them, took it home, and locked it in his trunk. A little later, in the course of the day, he returned to the cave's entrance. There sat a beautiful young girl, completely naked and crying bitterly. She was the seal to whom the skin belonged that he had taken. The man gave the girl some clothing, comforted her, and took her back home with him.
>
> 1193 As time went on, she came to accept him, but she never got along very well with other people. Mostly she would just sit and look out to sea. After some time the man took her as his wife. They lived happily together and had many children.
>
> 1194 The peasant fisherman had securely hidden the sealskin, locking it up in his trunk, and he carried the key with him everywhere he went.
>
> 1195 Many years later, he rowed out fishing as usual, but on that day he had forgotten the key at home under his pillow. Others say that the peasant went to a Christmas service with his people, but that his wife had been sick and was unable to go with them. They say that he had forgotten to take the key out of the pocket of his everyday working clothes. In any case, when he arrived back home that evening the trunk was open, and his wife had disappeared with the skin. She had found the key and out of curiosity looked through the trunk. There she had discovered her sealskin. She could not resist the temptation, said farewell to her children, donned the sealskin, and jumped into the sea. People say that before she sprang into the sea, she called out:
>
> 1196 "I want and yet I want not,
Seven children have I at the bottom of the sea,
Seven children have I as well here above."
>
> 1197 It is said that this touched the peasant's heart. After this when he rowed out fishing a certain seal would often swim around his boat, and it seemed that tears were running from its eyes. From this time

on he was always successful in catching fish, and luck often came to his harbor.

1198 When people of the town saw this couple's children walking on the beach, there was often a seal swimming along out in the sea as if it was accompanying them. It would throw colorful fish and pretty shells up on the beach to them. But the mother never again returned to land.[49]

1199 Essentially, this tale begins similarly to the previous one. Again, the anima has sometimes an animal form, sometimes a human one. It is forced to take on a human existence but feels uncomfortable in it.[50] Only this time, when she returns to her animal nature, she does not take the children with her and, therefore, remains in tragic conflict; she has "seven children in the sea and seven children on the land."

1200 The number seven is often associated with the image of the soul. It is the sacred number of Athena, virgin and "permeated with light nature," who sprang from the head of Zeus, and is "above all that is material."[51] According to Plato, the world soul revolves in seven inner circles and an undivided outer circle, and the whole is a loop circulating within itself.[52] (This speculation refers to the orbits of the planets.) According to Neopythagorean number theory, the number seven is the only prime number between one and ten that does not generate [i.e., beget, produce] other numbers and is itself not generated by (is not itself a product of) other numbers.[53]

1201 It corresponds, therefore, to the motherless Nike, or Parthenos, or the one who steers the universe.[54] According to one Hellenistic cosmogony, the soul arises from the seventh laugh of the primeval godhead.[55] The sacred number seven generally plays an important role: there are seven days of the week (a seven-day week is approximately a quarter of the average lunar cycle), seven planets, seven colors, seven metals, seven vowels, seven tones, etc.[56] The number seven is in this context connected to the idea of hierarchy, revolution, return, or rebirth. It is a symbol of development and movement as opposed to the static four and eight that epitomize a fullness attained. "The seven steps

---

[49] [This version translated from Avenstrup and Treitel, *Isländische*, pp. 258–259. The online English translation of Ashliman was also consulted.]

[50] See the concept of the animal and human form of soul in Tobler, *Epiphanie* and in Bächtold-Stäubli under *Tier* and *Tiergestalt* [animals and animal figures].

[51] See Bachofen, *Mutterrecht*, p. 60.

[52] See Plato, *Republic*, pp. 300–01, Stephanus, pp. 616–617, and Plato, *Timaeus*.

[53] [In Jung and von Franz (see *Number and Time* and Jung's *Note on Number*), the term *generate* = *beget* when applied to numbers refers to "be produced by multiplication of other numbers" and to "increase itself by self-multiplication." The source of the reference to Neopythagorean theory has not yet been found.]

[54] See Leisegang, *Die Gnosis*, pp. 42–43.

[55] See Reitzenstein, *Hellenistic*, pp. 269–70.

[56] See Dieterich, *Eine Mithrasliturgie*, p. 186.

symbolize the transformation."[57] In that seven always indicates passage and transformation to eight, it also signifies rebirth.[58]

1202 We consider the connection of the female figure, the seal mother, with her seven children to be significant. The heroine in "Little Snow White," lives with seven dwarfs. In "The Seven Ravens," a sister is delivered to the seven brothers, making eight.[59] Seen from the psychology of the man, an eighth figure in female form points to a part of the soul farthest removed from consciousness who sits unredeemed in the depths – this precisely describes the anima. The tragic end of the fairytale about the sealskin means that here the anima could not be redeemed, and slips back again into the unconscious, into the sea, and returns to her animal aspect.

1203 Here, the seven children are doubled, seven on land and seven in the sea. That is, the future, the goal, is half conscious, half unconscious – only a vague hint of the possibility of change. The realm of consciousness and the unconscious separate again, the melancholic words of the seal-woman as she parts and the touching picture of the weeping seal, of mourning her husband, and the children accompanied by their seal siblings show the tragedy of this division and the longing for redemption of the unknown soul figure, which is ambivalent about striving towards the light.[60]

---

[57] C.G. Jung, *Psychology and Alchemy*, CW 12, ¶99, Fig. 28; see also *I Ching* Hexagram 24, *Fu, Return, The Turning Point*, "All movements are accomplished in six stages, and the seventh brings return" (Wilhelm & Baynes, *I Ching*, p. 98). See also "The Creation of the World," in which the godhead creates a world seven times, each one of which his blundering brother destroys. With the eighth try, he succeeds because he has locked up his brother behind four crossed superimposed iron rods where each of the eight ends pointed to one of the eight heavenly directions (a mandala). See Mead, *Fragments*, pp. 370–71, esp. p. 379. In Gnostic speculation, while the Ogdoads (four male-female pairs) represent the Pleroma, the Fullness, the seven planetary spheres signify the soul's path of ascent or descent. This idea was also expressed in the image of Sophia, the mother of all living things, and her seven sons; with them she represents the perfected eight. See also Mead, *Fragments*, pp. 323, 526ff. and Leisegang, *Die Gnosis*, pp. 176f., 179f., 334. See also the seven bull-headed young men (along with Mithras, they again make eight) in the Mithras Liturgy: on this, see Dieterich, *Eine Mithrasliturgie*, p. 72f.

[58] In Christian theology, the "Seven Sleepers of Ephesus," refers to a group of Christian youths who hid inside a cave outside the city of Ephesus around 250 AD to escape the persecution of Christians being conducted during the reign of the Roman emperor Decius. Having fallen asleep inside the cave, they purportedly awoke approximately 150–200 years later during the reign of Theodosius II. The same story reaches its highest prominence in the 18th sura of the Quran. In this version a dog is also a part of the seven, making an eighth. See Jung, *Symbols of Transformation*, CW 5, ¶282 and "Rebirth," CW 9i, ¶240ff, esp. ¶242 fn. 6, ¶246 fn. 16. See also Goethe's *West- Eastern Divan, XII. Book of Paradise: The Seven Sleepers*:

> Neither to the king nor people
> E'er returns that chosen mortal;
> For the Seven, who for ages–
> Eight was, with the dog, their number–
> Had from all the world been sunder'd. . .

Even with the Aztecs, there is a land of birth and country of origin called the "Seven Caves." See Krickeberg, *Azteken and Inka*, pp. 325 and 332.

[59] On Rama, the seventh son of Devaki, see Zimmer, Maya, p. 327. According to Ninck, Wodan, p. 261, multiple births indicate connections to the elves, especially to an origin in water, as in the present Icelandic fairytale.

[60] See the legend cited in Laistner, *Das Rätsel*, vol. 1, p. 134f., of a shepherd who lived with a mermaid in her home in a lake.

1204 The following variant comes from the Faroe Islands, "The Swan Woman:"""

> Seals descend from people who drowned themselves. During the Twelfthtide nights (between Christmas and Epiphany) they become humans again. On one of these nights, a young man stole the sealskin of a beautiful girl, and forced her to marry him. They lived happily together, but one day he forgot the key to the chest where he kept her seal coat at home. His wife found the skin and by the time her husband returned, she had disappeared. His children, however, remained quietly at home. Back in the sea, the seal-woman met up with the male seal whom she had earlier known and loved. Years later, when the men of the island were out hunting the seals at their breeding place at night, the female seal appeared to the young man in a dream and asked him to spare her husband and their two young seal children. She showed him their place on the beach and the patterns of their sealskins. The young farmer disregarded the warning and all the seals were killed. By chance, he received seal meat of the husband and parts of two young seals as his share of the kill. For supper the seal hunters boiled up the head, front, and hind legs. When the meat was set before them, there was a great crash and a terrible noise. The seal wife entered the smokehouse as the ugliest troll that had ever been seen. She sniffed at the trough and shouted angrily: "Here is the old man with the turned-up nose, Harek's hand, and Fridrik's foot! This will be avenged on all the men of Mikladal. So many of them will fall down or be drowned until there is enough to all hold hands and encircle the entire island of Kallsöy." Her curse was fulfilled.

1205 The opening sentences of this tale tell us that the seals embody drowned human beings. They are thus the dead souls, which, as indicated, for many

---

> They had a child together. As a result of his homesickness, they visited the upper world. But when he refused to return to the lake, they divided the child. They threw the bottom half into the lake; it became a fish. The man buried the upper half by the lakeside from which a lily grew. It lay over the water and in the twilight the fish swam around the floating flower.

Here the experience of the anima remains a reminder of the tender contents of the unconscious. The aquatic origin of the anima is also clearly depicted in the Russian fairytale, "The Wise Wife" (N. Guterman, (trans.), *Russian Fairy Tales*, p. 521), where

> ...the Simpleton found the wife he desired by following the advice of an angel. The angel told him to go to a certain river, sit on a certain bridge, and look into the water. "All kinds of fish will pass you by, big and small. Among these fish there will be a perch with a little ring. Snatch this fish and throw it behind you on the damp earth." The Simpleton does this and the perch turned into a lovely maiden.

Behind the thrower is the magical place, it is there that he sees the beautiful maiden. In *front* of him, in consciousness, he saw only a fish. In "The Fisherman and His Wife," there appears the figure of the higher inner personality of the fisherman as a fish. The fact that both anima and the shadow occur in this form publicizes their close relationship, just like Anuanaitu and her brother in "Makonaura and Anuanaitu," siblings and children of the old cayman. See also Frobenius, *Zeitalter*, pp. 42ff, 304ff.

primitive cultures assume animal form. These animals are thus marked as *special* animals, in that people "behold" them with part of their own psychic energy, which is sacred to them.[61] In psychological terms, they have become bearers of a projection of parts of the soul and thus taboo.

1206 Winning the anima through the theft of animal's garb shows how an individual can regain a part of this projection and integrate it – or at least – affiliate it to [her or] his human life. In this tale, the man's insensitivity prevented him from permanently holding that prize, which was given to him like the spontaneous occurrence of a happy thought. In a moment of carelessness, his soul-image slips back away into the animal realm (i.e., his unconscious). The male seal is a picture of his shadow, whom the anima now joins in indissoluble union. Because the man is spiritually connected with these animals, he cannot behave impersonally towards them, as the other hunters, without injuring himself. The appearance of the anima in a dream shows the *psychological* [62] quality of this phenomenon in a characteristic manner. What others could do without being punished, was not permitted to this fellow with his greater psychological knowledge. Whether he liked it or not, he was obliged to carry out the instructions of his soul. Disregarding those instructions, he suffers the appropriate punishment: his anima becomes an evil troll. She reveals to him her demonic and overwhelming character. Her curse, that the sea will now claim as many victims as she lost, could also be interpreted symbolically as meaning that the unconscious will engulf and seize ever more lives.[63]

1207 More significant and richer in detail is "The Mermaid and the Great Dubhdach,"[64] an Irish tale in which the mysterious cause of the animal aspect of the anima is explained:

1208 In ancient times before St. Patric came, heathen Gentiles lived in Ireland. They had many daughters, whom their fathers loved above all else. That was the way it was. When gossip ran around that a certain holy man was gaining power over the heathen kings, the Gentiles did not relish the supremacy of this "wonders-producing Patric." This little "swineherd Patric" was regarded as a stranger and the pagans feared him. They heard rumors that if he were to gain the upper hand in Ireland, he would flood the country with foreigners. The fathers did not want their daughters marrying any intruders and so they took them to Inis Eisgir Abhann in Sligo (now Enniscrone). Underway,

[61] [In German, the word *betrachte* (behold) comes from *trächtig machen* (make an animal pregnant).]
[62] [In German, *seelisch*; other translations: mental, spiritual.]
[63] [In other words, the victims will go insane.]
[64] The meaning of the name Dubhdach is not clear: it may refer to *dubhach* = sad, grief-stricken, or to *Dubhthach*, a converted Druid.

they cast an enchantment over the maidens and drove them out into the sea. There they lived on as a tribe under the waves. The story of their fate was passed on from father to son and handed down from one century to another up to the present day. The old people in the country are as sure as the fact that they have hair on their heads that these maidens still today live under the sea.[65]

1209 Even the supreme king of the heathens, Culfogach,[66] had a daughter who was among those who were to go beneath the waves. When it came time to say farewell to his daughter, he was deeply sad and troubled. When all the other girls were already in the sea, he hurried in haste to cast his enchanting robe over her. But the robe was torn as she sprang into the sea. Now, because the hood of the garment was torn, not as much magic clung to her as to the other young women. She could not reach down to the sea floor, therefore, but tarried among the waves. Now and then she would come up on the beach and comb her hair.

1210 Times were good and times were not bad. Long after the heathens had been buried in the ground, the people would tell of the beautiful maidens who lived under the sea. When they would occasionally catch sight of the mermaid daughter of Culfogach on the rocks at ebb tide, they thought she must be a queen in comparison with other women. Now there lived in Inis Eisgir Abhann a noble old family with the name Dubhdach, whose sons tried in vain to catch sight of the beautiful mermaid. This continued for many years until two of the brothers died, but the youngest survived. It so happened that one day as he was wandering on the cliff edge he saw far on the waves something swaying that looked like a woman. He watched closely as this figure came closer and closer to the coast. He hid behind a cliff and watched as this strange jetsam wafted onto the rocks. Then he saw her as she rose out of the waves and climbed onto the rocks. She shook off her shroud, drew her comb out from between her breasts and began to comb her hair. The great Dubhdach had never before seen a more beautiful maiden with his own eyes. He crept down to the rocks without being seen by the girl, snuck up behind her and stole away her magic garment. When she heard the footsteps behind her, she quickly jumped up to dive into the sea. But since she did not have her magic mantle, she could not return to the waters. Without her enchanted covering, she had no magic.

[65] [From here, von Franz and von Beit's summary is translated with slight amendments from the German translation by Müller-Lisowski.]

[66] According to a note by the German collector and translator, the name means "cunning pirate."

1211 When the mermaid took cognizance of her situation, she turned to Dubhadach, reached out her hand, winked at him, and beckoning with her pointing finger, she indicated that he was to return her clothing. But he was determined by his life not to let go of what he now possessed. He ran with the force of love, because he knew that she would have to follow him. And by God, as she saw Dubhdach going away with her garment, she was forced to follow since there was no one there to help her. So she ran as fast as the soles of her feet could carry her all the way to his house. Dubhdach hesitated to destroy her magical garments fearing that their magic would bring disaster, and so he hid them. All the pleading and admonishing of the girl to return what was hers fell onto deaf ears. Dubhdach gave her a female servant who instructed her in the ways of women. The mermaid proved herself magnificently, there was no woman in the whole region who was as pleasant and well-behaved as she. They were married and lived happily together for fourteen years. God gave them three sons. When the oldest was already thirteen, Dubhdach went out into the garden and all his children followed behind. They watched as he drew three or four stones from the garden wall, stuck his hand in the hole and took out his wife's garment to see if it was rotten. When he saw that he was being observed, he quickly put the clothing back and closed up the wall, thinking that his children had been playing and noticed nothing.

1212 But by God, the oldest son later that same day told his mother what they had observed. She immediately thought that this might be her enchanting dress. She feigned a serious illness, and because Dubhdach was so devoted and would do anything she wanted, she sent him on a long journey to go by foot to get some healing Ox-Tongue herbs. No sooner he was en route, than she went into the garden, drew the stones from the wall, and pulled out her magic garment. It was as perfect as the day she last removed it, how long had she yearned for it! With her children she rushed to the beach but because they had no hoods, she put her cap on them and one after the other turned them into three large rocks, some twenty arms-reach from the land.

1213 When her husband returned, he immediately noticed the desolate state and inquired of the servant what had happened. She told him all and he rushed down to the sea. He arrived just in time to see her swimming out in the waves and he called out, pleading for her to return.

1214 "Live well," she said "You have lost me forever. Do you see those three rock standing about the sea, those are your three sons. I have

> enchanted them. As long as Ireland remains under the power of foreigners from other lands, these three rocks shall be clearly visible. And when the people of Ireland will regain sovereignty over their own land, those cliffs will recede day by day until the sharpest eye of a living person will no longer see them." Dubhdach returned home broken-hearted and soon died of loneliness and grief. For a quarter of a year thereafter one could hear for miles around the wailings of hundreds of people every night.[67]

1215 In the pagan world, the anima had a human form, which is here regarded as a kind of heroic antiquity like the *Alcheringa* of the Australian native peoples. The introduction of Christianity forced the "cunning pirates" to enchant their daughters, the old nature gods were devalued to demons and with them beliefs about the bearers of soul-images were also demonized. In the popular imagination, however, these long-familiar figures survived. These partly nature-deities were more tangible to the primitive mentality and more akin to natural instincts than the spiritually-shaped ideas of Christianity.[68] Probably the effect of the conversion and dark memories of the pre- and early history of Ireland mixed themselves into the presentation of this tale. Irish history is replete with successive invasions of the island, each bringing a "foreign" rule and a change of religion. This fairytale describes the separation of the naturalistic anima image that sinks back into the unconscious, as a safeguard against "foreigners." Their own fathers executed this separation. They knew that the "marriage" of their daughter to a stranger would bring no harmony, because the new mentality (here Christianity) bore no relationship to pagan nature. The pirate threw animal garments over their daughters so that they could live in the sea, in the magical kingdom, and thus be free. In the introductory lines, the cultural-historical facts merge with the archetypal zoomorphic image of the anima, a well-known motif found in fairytales of all peoples.

1216 The father of the mermaid is called "cunning pirate," a name clearly meant honorably, indicating boldness, audacity, and artfulness. The pirate is at the same time even more, a wizard, a king of old, in whom the magical is revived; a demon, a parallel figure to Odin/Woden, also the owner of a wishing mantle.[69] He turns out to be that hidden God, that spirit living in the depths of creation, the primordial father of the soul, a character like Balor (in "Balor

[67] Müller-Lisowski, *Irische Volksmärchen*, pp. 243–48. [The tale ends: "This story is still today in the mouths of the living, of Dubhdach and the people of the sea with which he was so closely connected. Two of the cliffs have long disappeared and I have heard that the third is also now gone. I wish our Ireland was free and we could be happy and again blossom as long ago with: 'Strongholds without roofs, and fortresses without towers, despite the fact that the Dubhdachs have lost their powers.'"]

[68] See C.G. Jung, *Psychological Types*, CW 6, ¶422–425.

[69] Or "camouflage jacket"; see Ninck, *Wodan*, pp. 88, 124.

and the Birth of Lugh,"), Kasanapodole, Father of the King Vultures in "The Visit to Heaven"), and Kaikutschi (in "Makonaura and Anuanaitu"). Thus, a *spiritual* power imposes the animal aspect upon the anima. Those who endeavor to re-humanize their enchanted souls must come to grips with this side of paganism or the attempt is doomed to fail. For those who fail to recognize the spiritual side of anima, the experience of the anima will remain a fleeting encounter, condemned to a tragic end. The animal aspect is thus only a garment, an outer shell, which beckons to an inner experience, and exerts a mysterious fascination. Human beings experience this fascination as the magical animal's yearning for redemption, as a part of their soul, which wants to come to them.

1217 A simple example from the numerous existing tales about the anima as an animal needing redemption is "The Tailor and the Treasure":

> 1218 One time a fun-loving tailor got lost in the woods, drunk after a party. There he came across a treasure cave in the center of which stood a beautiful maiden. She said that he could own everything there if he could kiss her without flinching. The tailor agreed, but with the first kiss, she turned into a hideous crocodile, the second time into a ghastly toad. When at the third kiss she changed into a coal black, hairy, and bleating billy goat, the tailor became possessed with fear. Dread overcame him and he took flight with great leaps out of the hall and out of the cave. A hurricane drove after him, roaring and crashing down with such might that he could no longer hear or see. He fell down deadly tired at the foot of a cliff. When he roused himself again, he could not find the opening in the rock face. He crept sadly away and from then on never could he bear talk of billy goats without getting angry.[70]

1219 The anima's manifestation as a billy goat reveals its devilish side. With the introduction of Christianity, the chthonic father deity took the form of the devil. The anima then also assumed a similar form as his daughter. In particular, her natural-daemonical being instills fear in the man. Her animal aspect means psychologically that the anima first appeals to the animalistic side of the man. He must lovingly accept and embrace this side in order to win the human values from the experience, for concealed behind the animal shape or garment are the higher manifestations of the anima.

1220 The garment is often an expression of "external form" and, therefore, also of "bodily, physical appearance." But the outer form also expresses the inner being. In this sense, the robe is a component of ancient mystery rites. Almost every initiation was accompanied by a baptismal rite in which an old animal

[70] Zaunert, *Deutsche Märchen seit Grimm*, p. 81.

robe was removed and a light or sky dress was donned. This event signified a mystical change in the sense of purification.[71] The fairytale about the pirate's daughter reports the reverse situation: a return to the animal level. Seen from a Christian perspective, this is the work of the devil, as in "Bearskin," where the devil himself forces the soldiers to become animals. In pagan terms, transformation into an animal meant an increase in power, as in the phrase "to fly into a berserker rage," which was also synonymous with "changed skin" or "changed clothes.[72]

1221 As a result of the devaluation of the naturalistic image of the anima, she now haunts him as an elfin water being, and lures people to destroy him, or rather to get him to redeem her,[73] to free her from her animal clothing and let her participate in his life.[74] Thus, in our story, the mermaid, yearning to meet her redeemer, from time to time appears in human form on the shore. This might explain why Dubhdach has the name meaning, "the sorrowful one, or the concerned one," because he is secretly attracted by these inner forces and "suffers with" them. Unlike the other girls of her tribe, the mermaid cannot completely disappear in the sea because her magic robe is torn. That is, she represents that piece of Dubhdach's soul that is not completely satisfied with being an animal. She remains on the surface, close to conscious mind and almost graspable, that is, almost comprehensible.[75]

1222 The great Dubhdach comes from an old family whose sons are committed to finding the girls from the other world, and thus to preserving the connection with their own roots and history, when the tribe of maidens still lived on Earth. He is the "youngest," the last of his race, and at the same time the last endeavor after many fruitless efforts to reconnect to the past through a soul-image. He succeeds in catching her, but his knowledge of magical things does not spare him from the great grief that is perhaps expressed in his name. The lonely man hides on the coast with many cliffs (the border region of the unconscious) and fetters the maiden to his mundane life by intentionally stealing her coverings. The assimilation made possible by the theft and splitting off of the magical veil of the soul is an outer one since it leaves behind only a sober adaption to the profane. The girl must learn all the arts of human culture - in contrast to parallel figures in fairytales of more natural peoples (e.g., "The Visit to Heaven" or "Ititaujang"). Already this shows the greater distance from the unconscious. But the secret is suppressed; the depths are

---

[71] Cf. Reitzenstein, *Hellenistic*, pp. 280, 42, 46, 54, 58ff, 175, 208, 285f., 445ff.; Leisegang, "Schlange," p. 214f.; Puech, "The Concept of Redemption in Manichaeism," p. 312f.

[72] See Ninck, *Wodan*, p. 42. Changing back into a sacred totem animal often takes place by putting on the mask or costume symbolizing that animal. See Lévy-Bruhl, *The "Soul" of the Primitive*, pp. 166, 171. Or the totem animals shed their animal skins and appear as human beings (*ibid.*, pp. 50ff).

[73] [Meaning: to change his attitude towards this female aspect of his unconscious.]

[74] On Melusina in the speculation of Paracelsus, see Jung, *Paracelsus*, CW 13, ¶179ff., 215ff.

[75] [In German, *fassbar*, literally "graspable," comes from *anfassen*, to grasp, to grab hold of, and means "to comprehend."]

only bridged when the emotional relationship must content itself with secular forms. Male consciousness tries to "master" its feelings. But those otherworldly values that he "immures" are his connection to the divine-natural. The great Dubhdach does not dare destroy the magic skin because he fears its power. He suspects the magical significance of the repressed animal aspect and is, in spite of his conquest, not really the master of the situation. He hopes that the garment will decay with time in its seclusion, apparently not realizing that he is striving to destroy something that is actually timeless! After a long and happy marriage, a secret inner tension drives him into the garden to look again at the magical robe. He underestimates the relationship of children to the magical; they reveal the truth. In "The Sealskin," the man forgets the key to the chest, which means that he leaves the opportunity to gain access to the unconscious in the hands of the anima. Separating the animal aspect off from the anima is a conscious intervention in a natural situation, and, therefore, can be perceived by the unconscious as an act of violence. Thus, there is often an unconscious resistance or tendency to undo what has happened. If the human does not make this trend entirely clear. Especially when his first knowledge of the sublime mystery of the anima was accidental (i.e., the theft of the garment), like an intuitive flash, then it only takes a moment of weakness for the unconscious to regain the upper hand.[76] Thus, the mermaid takes back her magic veil and disappears again into the sea.[77] It is noteworthy that here, too, the failure of the relationship occurs in conjunction with the number seven. The mermaid leaves her husband after twice seven years (in "The Sealskin," the couple had twice seven children, seven on land and seven in the sea). Seven years represent a complete time cycle, after which there is a return. At the same time, seven is the precursor for eight, the symbol of complete fulfillment that stands in a similar relationship to seven as three stands to four. Three is directed movement, four is, however, a static number and signifies achieved wholeness.[78] So the three children and twice seven years point to the incompleteness of the relationship. The last important step is missing, namely, confronting the magical covering and the one who threw it over the girls. Had Dubhdach taken this *auseinandersetzung* upon himself, he could have learned a lot about the cultural history of his country and about the foundation of his soul.

---

[76] In "The Griffin," a parallel Arawak tale, the hero, in contrast, permanently gains the anima figure, because he did not hide the skin of a female dog but rather burned it. That is, he had the courage to transform and purify the magic dress. In other cases, such as "Story of the Fish-Woman," the burning leads to the wife's melting away into water from which she had emerged. In this latter case, such an attempt to make conscious was obviously too premature and, therefore, too violent so that the unconscious eludes him.

[77] See also the Russian fairytale, "The Frog Princess," where the frog-princess vanishes after the hero burns her frog skin. On the burning of animal skin, see von Franz, *Redemption Motifs*, p. 62f.]

[78] See C.G. Jung, *Trinity*, CW 11, ¶179ff, ¶243ff.

1223 Thus, the mysterious anima vanishes again into the unconscious. The three children, who as half-profane creatures cannot follow their mother into the sea but remain in the border region, on the shore, turned into rocky cliffs, as symbols of the subjugation of Ireland, the split between the former magical past and the new culture, between dreamy ancestors and alert thinking. They embody that part of soul that cannot live in the new world of consciousness and becomes a "stumbling block," an inner hardening that expresses the great sterile grief of Dubhdach, from which he soon perishes. This is because by losing the anima he loses the animating connection to the land beyond, to the ancestral land, which he can recover only through dying.

1224 A Chinese fairytale, "The Disowned Princess," expressly emphasizes that the anima figure confers long life. Here, too, she belongs to the watery realm, which is portrayed with lush palette, and whose inhabitants are depicted with the characteristic features of beings from the unconscious psyche:

> 1225 In the time of the Tang dynasty there lived a man named Liu I, who had failed to pass his examinations for the doctorate. So he traveled home again. He had gone six or seven miles when a bird flew up in a field, and his horse shied and ran ten miles before he could stop him. There he saw a woman who was herding sheep on a hillside. He looked at her and she was lovely to look upon, yet her face bore traces of hidden grief. Astonished, he asked her what was the matter.
>
> 1226 The woman began to sob and said: "Fortune has forsaken me, and I am in need and ashamed. Since you are kind enough to ask I will tell you all. I am the youngest daughter of the Dragon-King of the Sea of Dungting, and was married to the second son of the Dragon-King of Ging Dschou. Yet my husband ill-treated and disowned me. I complained to my stepparents, but they loved their son blindly and did nothing. And when I grew insistent, they both became angry, and I was sent out here to herd sheep." When she had finished speaking, the woman burst into tears and lost all control of herself. Then she continued: "The Sea of Dungting is far from here; yet I know that you will have to pass it by on your homeward journey. I should like to give you a letter to my father, but I do not know whether you would take it."
>
> 1227 Liu I answered: "Your words have moved my heart. Would that I had wings and could fly away with you. I will be glad to deliver the letter to your father. Yet the Sea of Dungting is long and broad, how am I to find your father there?"
>
> 1228 "On the southern shore of the Sea stands an orange tree," answered the woman. "The people there call it the tree of sacrifice. When you find that tree you must loosen your girdle and strike the tree with it

three times in succession. Then some one will appear whom you must follow. When you see my father, tell him in what need you found me, and that I long greatly for his help."

1229 Then she fetched out a letter from her breast and gave it to Liu I. She bowed to him, looked toward the east and sighed. Unexpectedly, sudden tears rolled from the eyes of Liu I as well. He took the letter and thrust it in his bag. Then he asked her: "I cannot understand why you have to herd sheep. Do the gods slaughter animals like men do?" "These are not ordinary sheep," answered the woman; "these are rain sheep."[79] "But what are rain sheep?" "They are the thunder rams," replied the woman.

1230 And when he looked more closely, he noticed that these sheep walked around in proud, savage fashion, quite different from ordinary sheep. Liu I added: "But if I deliver the letter for you, and you succeed in getting back to the Sea of Dungting in safety, then you must not treat me like a stranger."

1231 The woman answered: "How could I use you as a stranger? You shall be my dearest friend." And with these words they parted.

1232 In the course of a month Liu I reached the Sea of Dungting. He asked for the orange tree and, sure enough, found it. He loosened his girdle, and struck the tree three times. At once a warrior emerged from the waves of the sea, and asked: "Whence do you come, honored guest?" Liu I said: "I have come on an important mission and wish to see the King."

1233 The warrior made a gesture in the direction of the water, and the waves turned into a solid street along which he led Liu I. The dragon castle rose before them with its thousand gates; magic flowers and rare grasses bloomed in luxurious profusion. The warrior bade him wait at the side of a great hall. Liu I asked: "What is this place called?" "It is the Hall of the Spirits," came the reply.

1234 Liu I looked about him: all the jewels known to earth were there in abundance. The columns were of white quartz inlaid with green jade; the seats were made of coral, the curtains of mountain crystal as clear as water...

1235 [He was told he had to wait, the warrior explained that his master, a dragon was in a conversation with a priest of the sun. "Dragons are powerful by the power of water. They can cover hill and dale with a

[79] The outcast princess is represented as "herding sheep." In Chinese, the word sheep is often used as an image of clouds. Sheep and goats are designated by the same word in Chinese (note by Wilhelm).

single wave. The priest is a human being. Human beings are powerful through fire. They can burn the greatest palaces by means of a torch. Fire and water fight each other, being different in their nature. For that reason our master is now talking with the priest, in order to find a way in which fire and water may complete each other." When the conversation was finished, a man in a purple robe with a scepter of jade appeared, the dragon king. He asked what brought Liu I, a human being, to his presence. Liu I told his story and the king wept. It was true, he had made a mistake and married his daughter to the wrong husband. It turned out that the king had the duty to watch over his brother, Tsian Tang, a rather wild and uncouth dragon being. Tsian Tang heard the king weeping and learned of the story. He disappeared in a moment when the court was weeping and soon returned, telling that he had eaten the bad husband, destroyed his fields, and brought the princess back. He carelessly offered her in marriage to Liu I, but the latter refused, saying ""I served as a messenger, because I felt sorry for the princess, but not in order to gain an advantage for myself. To kill a husband and carry off a wife is something an honest man does not do. And since I am only an ordinary man, I prefer to die rather than do as you say."]

1236 On the following day Liu I took his leave, and the Queen of the Dungting Sea gave a farewell banquet in his honor. With tears the queen said to Liu I: "My daughter owes you a great debt of gratitude, and we have not had an opportunity to make it up to you. Now you are going away and we see you go with heavy hearts!" Then she ordered the princess to thank Liu I.

1237 The princess stood there, blushing, bowed to him and said: "We will probably never see each other again!" Then tears choked her voice. Now it is true that Liu I had resisted the stormy urging of her uncle, but when he saw the princess standing before him in all the charm of her loveliness, he felt sad at heart; yet he controlled himself and went on his way. The treasures which he took with him were incalculable. The king and his brother themselves escorted him as far as the river. When, on his return home, he sold no more than a hundredth part of what he had received, his fortune already ran into the millions, and he was wealthier than all his neighbors. He decided to take a wife, and heard of a widow who lived in the North with her daughter. Her father had become a Taoist in his later years and had vanished in the clouds without ever returning. The mother lived in poverty with the daughter; yet since the girl was beautiful beyond measure she was seeking a distinguished husband for her.

1238 Liu I was content to take her, and the day of the wedding was set. And when he saw his bride unveiled on the evening of her wedding day, she looked just like the dragon-princess. He asked her about it, but she merely smiled and said nothing.

1239 After a time heaven sent them a son. Then she told her husband: "Today I will confess to you that I am truly the Princess of Dungting Sea. When you had rejected my uncle's proposal and gone away, I fell ill of longing, and was near death. My parents wanted to send for you, but they feared you might take exception to my family. And so it was that I married you disguised as a human maiden. I had not ventured to tell you until now, but since heaven has sent us a son, I hope that you will love his mother as well." Then Liu I awoke as though from a deep sleep, and from that time on both were very fond of each other. One day his wife said: "If you wish to stay with me eternally, then we cannot continue to dwell in the world of men. We dragons live ten thousand years, and you shall share our longevity. Come back with me to the Sea of Dungting!" Ten years passed and no one knew where Liu I, who had disappeared, could be. Then, by accident, a relative went sailing across the Sea of Dungting. Suddenly a blue mountain rose up out of the water.

1240 The seamen cried in alarm: "There is no mountain on this spot! It must be a water-demon!"

1241 While they were still pointing to it and talking, the mountain drew near the ship, and a gaily-colored boat slid from its summit into the water. A man sat in the middle, and fairies stood at either side of him. The man was Liu I. He beckoned to his cousin, and the latter drew up his garments and stepped into the boat with him. But when he had entered the boat it turned into a mountain. On the mountain stood a splendid castle, and in the castle stood Liu I, surrounded with radiance, and with the music of stringed instruments floating about him.

1242 They greeted each other, and Liu I said to his cousin: "We have been parted no more than a moment, and your hair is already gray!" His cousin answered: "You are a god and blessed: I have only a mortal body. Thus fate has decreed." Then Liu I gave him fifty pills and said: "Each pill will extend your life for the space of a year. When you have lived the tale of these years, come to me and dwell no longer in the earthly world of dust, where there is nothing but toil and trouble." Then he took him back across the sea and disappeared. His cousin retired from the world, however, and fifty years later when he had taken all the pills, he disappeared and was never seen again.[80]

[80] Slightly edited from Wilhelm, *The Chinese Fairy Book*, pp. 151–161.

1243 What is so appealing about this tale is the interrelation between the two worlds, where the secular world also comes to the fore, as well as how the problem of a *permanent* relationship and the hero's back-and-forth between the two worlds are considered.

1244 At the beginning, we hear that Liu I failed his exam. As a result, he is cut off from his normal progress in the secular world and his conscious goals. Maybe the reason for his failure is already expressed in the fact that a significant experience of the unconscious from the psychic realm is approaching. All his instinctive life force draws him to this, even against his will. The will of these forces is expressed, for instance, by the shyness of his horse when confronted with the bird. Birds signify sudden ideas, intuitions that make him "head-shy" and drive him into the unconscious. Thus he comes to the slope of a mountain, where he meets a woman hitherto unbeknownst to him who tends the cloud sheep. These cloud sheep aptly express the unreal, ghostly world into which he has fallen, and whose content is still "nebulous" to him. The dragon princess is his guide and mediator in this new world. But she needs redemption, because she has been abandoned by her husband. While Liu I continues to strive for his goal in the profane world, "her words moved his heart," and he becomes seized with an unaccountable sadness that forces him to turn inward. His soul is completely isolated and displaced into an unworthy state.[81]

1245 The dragon princess is an image of the anima and this represents – psychologically, according to Jung – the inward-oriented attitude of the personality. Jung calls that part of the personality whose concerns are directed towards its effect on the outer world, the "persona," which originally meant "the mask once worn by actors to indicate the role they played."[82] The moment of encounter is here characteristic in that an attitude opposed to the persona appears just at the moment of failure in the outer world. Only in an emergency situation does the inner world become so charged that the soul can be discovered as an entity desperately "wanting something else."[83] Through the encounter with the dragon princess, Liu I is induced to immerse himself in his own depths, where he discovers the root of the conflict.

---

[81] [The soul (*Seele*) is feminine in German, and translated here as in the original to emphasize the implication that the soul is identical to the anima.]

[82] C.G. Jung, "Relation between the ego and the unconscious," CW 7, ¶243ff.

[83] C.G. Jung, *Spiritual Problem*, CW 10, ¶160. Consider also this quote from Jung's *Paracelsus*: "The anima belongs to those borderline phenomena which chiefly occur in special psychic situations. They are characterized by the more or less sudden collapse of a form or style of life which till then seemed the indispensable foundation of the individual's whole career. When such a catastrophe occurs, not only are all bridges back into the past broken, but there seems to be no way forward into the future. One is confronted with a hopeless and impenetrable darkness, an abysmal void that is now suddenly filled with an alluring vision, the palpably real presence of a strange yet helpful being, in the same way that, when one lives for a long time in great solitude, the silence or the darkness becomes visibly, audibly, and tangibly alive, and the unknown in oneself steps up in an unknown guise. . ." (CW 13, ¶216).

1246 The princess directs Liu I immediately to her father. Already the first contact with the anima leads the hero into the depths of the unconscious and to the deity prevailing there. This ruler unveils the conflicts that are ultimately the cause of the suffering of his soul, and that force him to become aware of the tensions hidden in the depths.

1247 The palace is at the bottom of a lake, but all the observations described by the waiting Liu I apply to the seabed: the crystal clarity, the "Palace of Frozen Radiance" with the white and green colors of the water, to yellow tones and corals, strange smell, and dark endless outlines. This blending of lake and sea in the description merely seeks to express the impression of infinite water. The princess herself appears (after she had been herding sheep clouds) on the lake bottom in a robe of "misty fragrance." Water is dominant in her dress and actions: she is nebulous, a vision, and yet —like all dream images — she is real and takes effect. Her home, her origin, her nature is water; but this element is also the basic building material of the world.[84]

1248 Liu I must wait because the dragon king is conferring with a Sun priest, a human, about the union of water and fire. The dragon, which is great "by the power of water," has a different meaning in China than in the Near East and Europe. He belongs not to the hostile demons, but is a symbol of creative life force. "The dragons of the seas are the guardians of the pearls, which fulfill all wishes, the true treasure of divine wisdom . . . At the same time, the dragons fertilize the Earth, because in spring they ascend from the flood to high heaven and send, with thunder and lightning from their clouds, the longed-for water down to the parched earth."[85] In Taoist and Buddhist esoterism, ". . . the dragon signifies the secret activity of the luminous force within us which unites the upper and lower cycles . . ."[86] According to the *I Ging*, the dragon is the electrical force, which manifests itself in lightning and thunderstorms,[87] and is the water when it is enclosed in a gorge or abyss, as in Hexagram No. 29, *Kan – the Abysmal (Water)*.[88] This side of the dragon symbol is shown in

[84] According to the Chinese tale, "Help in Need," Lake Dungting also means "Lake of the Maidens." In the Chinese imagination, which is decisive for us in understanding this fairytale, the earth is a four-sided square island in the middle of a circular pond, the world sea. Once again it is clearly a mandala image. Dragons and their kings rule in each of the four ocean quadrants. (See Rousselle, "Das Wasser als mythisches Ereignis chinesischen Lebens," p. 210. Lake Dungting with its dragon palace also stands for the four-part ocean. The relationship of the dragon princess to the water is also indicated by the fact that she herds the cloud sheep, the rain servants. She is the embodiment of the Yin principle of Chinese philosophy, the female primal principal of the world. In its original meaning Yin signified "the cloudy," "the overcast," and her opposite, Yang, meant "banners waving in the Sun," the illuminated, bright. Yin is also just the dark, southern or northern side of a river or mountain. (See Wilhelm/Baynes, *I Ching*, p. *lvi*.) Liu I meets the princess on the side of a mountain! We also find images in Western concepts that are similar; thus Heraclitus says: "Souls are vaporized from what is moist" (Fragment 44; see Heraclitus, *The Complete Fragments*, trans. William Harris).

[85] Rousselle, "Wasser," p. 211.

[86] Ibid., *Dragon and Mare*, p. 111.

[87] See Wilhelm/Baynes, *I Ching*, 1967 p. 7; Hexagram 1, *Chien - the creative element*.

[88] Ibid., p. 114f.

"The Disowned Princess," in Tsian Tang, who guards the treasure of wisdom through the King. This is why the king wears a purple robe and a scepter of jade. His wild brother wears, however, a scarlet red, thousand foot long dragon with a fiery beard that appears amid lightning and thunder and is at enmity with the heavenly rulers. The image of the fire concealed in the water (Tsian Tang) expresses the idea of a hidden, that is, unconscious spirit.[89] Fiery water is a symbol of the spirit. This inner polarity of fire in water, of spirit in matter, of consciousness in the unconscious, is differentiated into two figures, which otherwise together form a pair of opposites united within one divinity. Liu I must dive into this world of polarities if he wants to recognize them as moving elemental forces.

1249 The contents of the Princess's letter of complaint, which Liu I transfers to the king dragon, cause the royal brother to fall into a dreadful fury. In other words, an immense fiery passion and unconscious emotion hitherto "fettered" threatens to engulf everything. The evil, destructive force lives there just as does its opposite, the giving and nourishing healing power. This raging force now gains the upper hand and deeply frightens Lui I. This wild outbreak serves, however, to "rehabilitate" the abandoned princess. Nevertheless, under the influence of the domineering, drunken Tsian Tang, Liu I cannot accept the offer to marry the dragon princess; he still fears the dominance of the unconscious and will not give himself completely over to its guidance. This resistance to the union corresponds to the sense that the anima figure is connected intimately with those tendencies and contents of one's being that were not previously recognized by consciousness, as shown in Tsian Tang's unruly behavior.[90] The magical powers are still alien to everyday life. Tsian Tang says to Liu I: "But if you were not willing to marry her, you may go your way, and should we ever meet again we will not know each other." Liu I does not want to bind himself to the princess, and thus remain permanently in the magical kingdom. He decides to return home, therefore, with only the treasures he has received thus far. With his knowing and proud rejection, Liu I overcomes the magical-demonic and gains the respect of the magical figures. But for the sake of his freedom he sacrifices the best of the whole inner experience, the burgeoning love for the divine woman whom he met at the beginning. The unconscious avenges this act most bitterly: two of his wives die on him. Free, but lonely, and robbed of any human relationship, he is forced a third time in a different form to accept that which was despised by his secular sensibilities. He marries a beautiful but poor girl. After the birth of their son, this woman reveals herself as the dragon princess, and admits she sought him out of love. The divine world refuses to let go of the connection

[89] See C.G. Jung, "Archetypes of the Collective Unconscious," CW 9i, ¶40.

[90] See C.G. Jung, *Psychologie und Religion*, CW 11, ¶129.

once it is established – even if Liu I apparently still behaves as if he were superior – and offers him, at first unrecognized, the possibility of the relationship anew.

1250 Yet this coming together of the two kingdoms is not permanent. The dragon princess will lose her immortality if she remains in the profane world. For her sake, Liu I must now sacrifice his profane existence. She removes him completely from the earthly world and in return gives him immortality in the other world. He sinks into the sphere of eternal youth and happiness and is absorbed by the world of dreams and feelings. He is enchanted[91] by the world of archetypal images; having become a spirit, he is immortal. He appears to mortals in a colorful boat and then in a splendid castle on the top of a mountain rising out from the water in magical similarity to a god. Liu I has become an appealing nature spirit for humans, a resident of the Dragon Empire. In an Eastern view, this ending is a most satisfactory solution because the occidental mind ". . . based as it is on the standpoint of the unconscious, sees consciousness as an effect of the anima."[92] Thus, this tale depicts immersion in the timeless world of archetypes as a participation in an eternal life, as blissful immortality.

1251 In assessing the end of this fairytale, we note that it deviates from that of "Youth Without Age and Life Without Death," and "The Earth Wants to Have Hers," according to the different cultural environments. In Western Europe, the definitive and complete link to the realm of anima is felt as tragic; it has a reputation of being a fateful inner voice, as is evident from the Irish fairytale "Connla and the Fairy Maiden":[93]

> 1252 Connla, the Red with the Fiery Hair, was the son of Conn of the Hundred Fights.[94] One day as he stood by the side of his father on the hill of Usna (Uisneach), he saw a maiden clad in wonderful attire coming towards him. "Whence comest thou, o woman?" asked Connla. "I come from the Plains of the Ever Living," she said, "there where there is neither death nor sin. There we always keep holidays and celebrate festive banquets that do not require any preparation. Cheerful conviviality without any quarrel reigns with us. We live in deep peace; and because we have our homes in the round green hills,

---

[91] [German: *entrücken*.]

[92] C.G. Jung, *Golden Flower*, CW 13, ¶62.

[93] [The collector, Joseph Jacobs, notes that "Part of the original is in metrical form, so that the whole is of the *cante-fable* species which I believe to be the original form of the folk-tale. . . The tale of Connla is the earliest fairy tale of modern Europe. Besides this interest it contains an early account of one of the most characteristic Celtic conceptions, that of the earthly Paradise, the Isle of Youth, *Tir-na n-Og*. This has impressed itself on the European imagination; in the *Arthuriad* it is represented by the Vale of Avalon, and as represented in the various Celtic visions of the future life, it forms one of the main sources of Dante's *Divina Commedia*"; see Jacobs, *Celtic*, pp. 243–244.]

[94] ["Conn the hundred-fighter had the head-kingship of Ireland from 123–157 A.D., according to the *Annals of the Four Masters*, i. 105"; see Jacobs, *Celtic*, p. 243.]

men call us the Hill Folk (the Sidh people)." The king and all with him wondered much to hear such a voice as they saw no one. For save Connla alone, none saw the Fairy Maiden. "To whom art thou talking, my son?" said Conn the king. Then the maiden answered for him, "Connla speaks to a young, fair maid, whom neither death nor old age awaits."

> 1253 "I love Connla the Red, and now I call him away to the Plain of Pleasure, Moy Mell, where Boadag (Buadhach) is eternally king.
>
> 1254 A king whose land knows neither lament nor woe since he came to power.
>
> 1255 Oh, come with me, Connla of the Fiery Hair, with your neck like milk, ruddy as the dawn with thy tawny skin.
>
> 1256 A fairy crown awaits thee to grace thy comely face and royal form.
>
> 1257 Come, and never shall thy comeliness fade, nor thy youth, till the last awful day of judgment."

1258 The king in fear at what the maiden said, which he heard though he could not see her, called aloud to his Druid, Corann by name. "Oh, Coran of the many spells," he said, "and of the cunning magic, I call upon thy aid. A task is upon me too great for all my skill and wit, greater than any laid upon me since I seized the kingship. A maiden unseen has met us, and by her power would take from me my dear, my comely son. If thou help not, thy king will be taken by woman's wiles and witchery."

1259 Then Coran the Druid stood forth and chanted his spells towards the spot where the maiden's voice had been heard. And none heard her voice again, nor could Connla see her longer. Only as she vanished before the Druid's mighty spell, she threw an apple to Connla. For a whole month from that day Connla would take nothing, either to eat or to drink, save only from that apple. But as he ate it grew again and always kept whole. And all the while there grew within him a mighty yearning and longing after the maiden he had seen. But when the last day of the month of waiting came, Connla stood by the side of the king his father on the Plain of Arcomin, and again he saw the maiden come towards him, and again she spoke to him.

1260 [She lured him with her verses telling him this time about the gruesome death of the warriors among which he was destined to die.

> When Conn immediately called for the druid Coran, she turned against Conn (Connla's father) and warned him of the druid's arts. Since Connla remained silent about everything, his father asked him in astonishment whether the woman's words went to his heart. Connla answered uncertainly; he loved his own, but the longing for that woman left him with no peace. Then the woman sang a song of his futile struggle against the waves of his longing that urged him to sail with her in her "curragh, the gleaming, straight-gliding crystal canoe" to the Sidh of Buadhach. Before nightfall they could be in that land of joy to all who sought it. Only girls and women lived there. Then Connla jumped away from his own people into the crystal canoe. The king and court watched as it glided away over the bright sea towards the setting sun.]

1261 Away and away, till eye could see it no longer, and Connla and the Fairy Maiden went their way on the sea, and were never seen again... Now when Conn saw his second son, Art, coming towards him, he said: "Now Art will be very lonely. That is why he is called 'Art the Lonely.'"[95]

1262 Connla, the "Red" with the "fiery hair," is characterized by this property as a sun hero, who is hastening towards his demise [i.e., the sunset]. His handsomeness is a distinction that attracts the demons. In addition, red is, as already mentioned, the color of the underworld, which means that Connla has been marked by the magical from his birth. His first encounter with the magical woman, when he hears her fateful boding voice, occurs on a hill overlooking the bustle of the world. This experience corresponds to the pagan Norse notion of the hero's encounter with the Fylgia, a supernatural being who accompanies a person in connection to his or her fate or fortune. She is similar to a valkyrie who calls a man to acts of heroism, who leads a warrior to battle, victory, or death, and who conveys secret wisdom.[96] For the man, experiencing the anima always has a fateful significance, and heralds a turning point in life. The fairy maiden appears to Connla in "a strange attire." The others who are present cannot see her, but they can hear her alluring voice. Thus, Connla's unconscious experience is so intense and stems from such deep layers of the soul that even people around him participate, at least in part, and are moved by the vibrating energy.

1263 The call and promises of the magical maiden are like the songs of the sirens, enticing the hero and then killing him. Also Connla's father

[95] [Edited from Jacobs, *Celtic*, pp. 1–4 (English), Müller-Lisowski, *Irische Volksmärchen*, pp. 10–14, and Thurneysen, *Sagen*, p. 73f (both in German).]

[96] See Ninck, *Wodan*, pp. 202f., 226f., 237.

immediately notices that the voice of the beautiful woman signals a call into the land of the dead, in spite of all her promises of eternal bliss. His subsequent efforts to hold his son back are to no avail, however, since the maiden threatens to bring about a horrible death at the hands of the war god if he does not follow her. His fate lies on the side of doom. [From the point of view of the son] the father symbolizes his conflict between the spirit of rational reason and tradition and a conscious stance against the feminine, alluring voice of the unconscious. But the father's power is too weak so he has to turn to Corann, the Druid, to protect his son through religious rites. The priest has the task of holding the eerie, invisible, and dark element of magic at bay. With his enchanting song, which – as all music – is an immediate expression of feeling, he succeeds in temporarily banishing and driving off the anima. But the ritual chant is not enough; the enticing soul-image remains stronger. The woman disappears, but throws an apple back to Connla, which is his exclusive source of nourishment.

1264 This apple from a virgin of the Westlands[97] reminds us of the golden apples of the Hesperides from their garden in the distant West that confer immortality. In Germanic belief, the goddess of apples Idhunn (Idun) the "ever young," "the rejuvenator," "the rejuvenating one," grants eternal youth with a bite of her apples from the world ash tree Yggdrasil.[98] This image lives on in many Germanic fairytales, including "The White Snake," "The King's Son, Who Feared Nothing," and "The Golden Bird." In some Chinese fairytales, the "Queen Mother of the West" appears, who bears the peaches of immortality.[99]

1265 Because the image of the apple is connected with the idea of enlightenment, the apple is also sometimes identified with the sun.[100] At the same time, the apple is a symbol of love, and the throwing of an apple a token of affection. It is also a symbol of sex and fertility.[101] As a spherically shaped fruit, the apple symbolizes the unification of opposites (hence the love spell), and the likeness of God (see the apple from the Tree of Knowledge), because roundness has

---

[97] On the Irish concepts of afterlife, see Müller-Lisowski, *Irische Volksmärchen*: "Islands in the west, hills, bottom of the ocean, Island of the Women, Mountain of the Women, Land of Youth, Land of the Living, Land Beneath the Waves" (p. 320).

[98] See Führer, *Nordgermanische*, p. 84; Mogk, *Germanische*, p. 75; Bolte and Mackensen, *Handwörterbuch* under *Apfel* [apple]. See also "The Master Maiden," in which the true bride has a golden apple. See also "The Golden Castle that Hung in the Air," in which a child of the princess recognizes its father by handing over a golden apple. According to "Silverwhite and Lillwacker," two girls become pregnant by eating a magic apple. In "The Princess and the Glass Mountain," the prince first throws an apple to the "wild man" in the cage and thus frees him. Later he finds the princess on the glass mountain holding a golden apple in her hand.

[99] See, for instance, "King Mu of Dschou," and the note in Wilhelm, *The Chinese Fairy Book*, pp. 98–99.

[100] See C.G. Jung, *Symbols of Transformation*, CW 5, ¶327f., fn. 2.

[101] See Wikipedia, *The Judgment of Paris*, also Bächtold-Stäubli under *Apfel* [apple]; Ninck, *Wodan*, pp. 10, 262; Aigremont, *Volkserotik und Pflanzenwelt*, vol. 1, pp. 59–68; Silberer, *Problems of Mysticism*, p. 77.

always symbolized completion, inviolability, and self-sufficient bliss.[102] Plato declared the spherical to be the most perfect shape, an idea that influenced the medieval alchemists, who sought to make the round stone of wisdom.[103] According to Plato's *Timaeus*, roundness signifies an image of the soul. In some ways, the female soul-image is identical with the ball that she possesses.

1266 The identity of fruit with the anima is evident from an oriental motif that is found in the tales of various countries. One example is "The Three Lemons," a Norwegian tale:

> 1267 Once there were three brothers who served a king. The youngest brother was called "Mike by the Stove" because he always sat behind the stove. In the king's service, Mike by the Stove proved to be the most hard-working and efficient, and his brothers became jealous. Now the king's wife had died and he was a widow. Mike's brothers went and declared to the king that Mike the Stove had claimed he could obtain the most beautiful princess in twelve kingdoms as a new wife for him. When the king heard this, he told Mike by the Stove he had better do as he had said, else he would have him brought to the block, and have his head chopped off.
>
> 1268 Mike by the Stove replied that he had neither said nor thought anything of the kind; but that seeing the king was so severe, he would try it. So he took a knapsack full of food and set out. But he had only pushed a little way into the wood before he grew hungry, and thought he would sample the provisions they had given him at the king's castle. When he had sat down in all peace and comfort under a pine-tree by the side of the road, an old woman came limping along, and asked him what he had in his knapsack. "Meat and bacon, granny," said the youth. "If you are hungry, come and share with me!" She thanked him, satisfied her hunger, told him she would do him a favor in turn, and limped off into the wood. When Mike by the Stove had eaten his fill, he slung his knapsack across his shoulder once more, and went his

---

[102] On the role of Sphäira [ball] in Orphic symbolism, see Bachofen, Gräbersymbolik, pp. 124–25 and Ibid., Orphische Theologie, pp. 15ff. See also the motif of throwing a ball in Rilke's Late Poems:

> As long as you can catch that which you throw yourself,
> all is merely skill and but meaningless gain;
> only when you suddenly become the catcher of the ball
> thrown to you by an eternal playmate,
> who aims into your very center, with a precise knowing swing,
> in one of those curves of God's great bridgework:
> only then does catching become a power
> not yours, but the world's . . .

[Translated from the German based on an online translation by "Volker"; accessed May 2003.]

[103] See C.G. Jung, *Psychology and Alchemy*, CW 12, ¶109 fn. 41, ¶433; *Pychology and Religion*, CW 11, ¶92f.

way; but he had only gone a short distance before he found a whistle. That would be fine, thought he, to have a whistle, and be able to whistle himself a tune while he traveled, and before long he even succeeded in making a pleasant sound. That very moment the wood was alive with dwarfs, all of them asking with one voice: "What are my lord's commands? What are my lord's commands?" Mike by the Stove said he did not know he was their lord; but if he had any command to give, he would ask them to bring him the fairest princess in twelve kingdoms. That would be easy enough, said the dwarfs; they knew exactly who she was, and they could show him the way; then he himself could go and fetch her, since the dwarfs were powerless to touch her.

1269 [It turned out that the princess was in the troll's castle with two sisters. Mike by the Stove went there and when they saw him enter, they turned into three lemons. Mike took the lemons and went on his way. He became thirsty and bit into the first lemon. There was a princess, visible up to her arms, crying out for water or she would die. Mike looked around, found no water, and so this princess died. The same thing happened further on. Then the land became exceedingly hot and dry and Mike was forced to bite into the third lemon.] When he had bitten into this lemon, the third princess looked out: she was the most beautiful in twelve kingdoms, and she cried that if she could have no water, she must die on the spot. Mike by the Stove ran about and looked for water, and this time he met the king's miller, who showed him the way to the millpond. When he had come with her to the millpond, and had given her water, she came completely out of the lemon. But she had nothing to wear, and Mike by the Stove had to give her his smock. She put it on, and hid in a tree; while he was to go to the castle and bring her clothes, and tell the king he had found her, and how it had all happened.[104]

1270 The Spanish version, "Three Oranges With One Leap" (summarized here), is as follows:

1271 A young man searched for the most beautiful woman in the world and was directed by an old woman to a long hike on which he reached a castle garden. Among the many trees there was an orange tree with only one single branch from which three fruits hung. One had to pluck all three fruits at once with one single jump. (If he climbed up

[104] See Stroebe, *Norwegian Fairy Book*, pp. 15–22.

> the tree, he could not climb back down!) The hero succeeded, and on the way back he cut into the first orange. Inside was a princess who asked for bread. Since he had none, she disappeared back into her orange and onto the tree. With the second orange he succeeded in giving her bread, but she required in addition water and then disappeared. With the third orange he managed to provide both bread and water and she then joined him happily on his way.[105]

1272 In all these versions, in which the hero regards the anima figure as something simply to "eat," or, "drink," and thus to acquire her as belonging to the ego, she then requires the sacrifice of a life-sustaining substance, water as a psychic element and bread as a symbol of matter. Otherwise, she cannot live in this world.

1273 The figure of the anima is thus one with the symbol of spiritual wholeness, the Self, which Jung calls "the totality of the conscious and unconscious psyche." It is superordinate to the anima, a figure that represents only the unconscious. Unlike the shadow and anima, the Self is not a natural phenomenon; rather it usually carries the character of a result, a goal attained, a personification of the whole fate and is, therefore, more comprehensive than the ego.[106] Therefore, the Self can only be expressed by a symbol. The most important symbols of the Self are: the child and the mandala in its various forms, such as the sphere, circle, flower, square, egg, rose, star, sun, ball, and wheel.[107]

1274 Because the round shape symbolizes indivisibility, invulnerability, and immiscibility with the outer exterior, after receiving the apple Connla eats nothing more, and assimilates nothing else from the outside.[108] Moreover, he who has ingested food from the underworld cannot return to the living.[109] Although Connla is nourished only by the apple, the image of spiritual totality that includes the unconscious and, therefore, he loses no weight because he

---

Summarized from Meier, *Spanische*, pp. 24–30. In "Goldapple's Daughter" (Christensen, *Iran*, pp. 60–68), six girls request bread and water, only the seventh remains alive. See also "The Dragon's Bitter Orange Trees" and "The Cedar Lemons" (J. G. v. Hahn (trans.), *Griechische Märchen*, vol. 1, no. 49). See also *ibid.*, vol II, pp. 249–250, notes and variants. Cf. Goethe's *Dichtung und Wahrheit* [*Poetry and Truth*], Book 2, especially the boy's tale, "*Die neue Paris* (The New Paris)," in which three "nice little wenches" arise from three apples. According to Laistner, *Das Rätsel*, vol 1, p. 133, the *Mahrte* [an Old German word for a supernatural being in human, usually female, form (the English word "nightmare" comes from the German *Nachtmahr* based on the same root)] transforms into an apple when the dreamer catches her..

[106] See C.G. Jung, *Psychology and Alchemy*; CW 12, ¶247, "Relation between the ego and the unconscious," CW 7, ¶274 ¶398f ¶404f.; *Golden Flower*, CW 13, ¶67; *Psychology and Religion*, CW 11, ¶140; *Forward to Suzik's "Zen Buddhism,"* CW 11, ¶885.

[107] See Jung, *Child*, CW 9i, ¶278f ¶299; *Psychology and Religion*, CW 11, ¶112f ¶123 ¶157.

[108] See Marcus Aurelius, *Meditations*, Book 8, no. 41: "The things which are proper to the understanding, however, no other man is used to impede, for neither fire, nor iron, nor tyrant, nor abuse, touches it in any way. When it has been made a sphere, it continues a sphere."

[109] See Róheim, *Spiegelzauber*, p. 107, fn. 1.

has assimilated its inexhaustible character that represent the eternal energy flow of the unconscious.[110]

1275 Connla is fulfilled by the vision and when the mysterious woman reappears after a month, he jumps onto the crystal ship and sails with her to the realm of Buadhach, where he disappears forever. This describes his complete and definitive union with the anima and his enchantment[111] into the unconscious. Connla thus shares the fate of Liu I in "The Disowned Princess," who retreats with the dragon princesses into Lake Dungting. Except that in the Irish fairytale, the melancholy of those left behind, and the painful, deadly aspect of experience, are more prominent in the father's words about "Art, the Lonesome One."

1276 The psychic union of consciousness with the soul-image is an experience of the second half of life, in which human life draws closer to the world of the hereafter. In Iranian belief, the anima comes toward the righteous man after his death as a beautiful virgin and reveals itself as his "religious knowledge," or as his "personality."[112] Ecstatic enchantment[113] is often represented in Germanic concepts as transport on a ship, called the death ship. The ancient people of Iceland even buried their dead on a ship in the earth. Just as human beings [i.e., consciousness] originally arise out of the water [i.e., the unconscious], so do they return back there again [at death]. The death ship on which Connla sails out to sea corresponds to the life boat in which the newborn hero is so often driven ashore.[114] The crystal ship, in which Connla retreats with the wonderful woman, is like a vessel in which the alchemical union takes place. The Old German word *scaff* [ship] is related to *scef* = vessel (cf. Latin *scapha* = boat).[115] And as a vessel this ship is yet again (like the other attributes of the anima) identical to the anima herself and an image of the female, the receptive principle.[116]

1277 In the image of the baptismal font, in which the transformation of the inner personality of the natural person into a child of God takes place, the vessel is also connected to the idea of rebirth. In alchemy, the vessel in which the transformation of the substances takes place, has a mystical significance. It is here that the opposing male and female principles are united.[117] The anima appears, therefore, in fairytales often associated with the glasshouse or glass

---

110 See C.G. Jung, CW 9i, "Rebirth" ¶248.

111 [German: *entrücken.*]

112 See Reitzenstein, *Hellenistic*, pp. 199, 356, 518f.

113 [German: *entrücken.*]

114 See Ninck, *Wodan*, pp. 13, 210ff, 218, 265–66; Mogk, *Germanische*, p. 60; Niedner, "Islands Kultur zur Wikingerzeit," p. 73; Bächtold-Stäubli under *Schiff, Schiffer* [boat, skipper]; Usener, *Sintfluthsagen*, *passim*.

115 [Also in English, boat = vessel, meaning both a ship and a receptacle.]

116 See Rank, *Myth of the Birth*, p. 66; C.G. Jung, *Symbols of Transformation*, CW 5, ¶311f; Abraham, "Traum and Mythus,"p. 16.

117 See C.G. Jung, *Psychology and Religion*, CW 11, ¶166. See the *Vision of Arisleus*, in which the dead Thabritius and his sister Beya, with whom he committed incest, are sunk in a glass house in the sea; Jung, *Psychology and Alchemy*, CW 12, ¶437f ¶449.

coffin, such as in "Little Snow White," or in "The Glass Coffin." In a Russian fairytale, "The Frog Tsar Daughter," [not to be confused with "The Frog Princess"], this is a glass house with golden doors. Also, in a Siberian tale, "The Girl in the Stone Chest," the anima sits out of reach of all her suitors in a stone chest. She is thus enclosed within stone, hidden in dark matter. This suggests a glass house,[118] since it has to do with transfigured matter, giving the spirit an envelope, a sheath, and serving as a transfigured body. In "The Lady of the Moon," it is said that "The whole moon world seemed to be made of glass," the palace was made of liquid crystal, and crystal clear music floated through the air.[119] The crystal itself is a symbol of the Self, the sought-after treasure, the Philosopher's Stone.[120] In a Turkish fairytale, "The Story of the Crystal Palace and the Diamond Ship," the anima is described as follows: first, she grows up in an underground mine with a glass roof. Later, she has a glass palace with golden furniture built on the sea(!). "Its radiance filled the world." A love story unfolds with the Prince of Yemen, who visits her on her ship. To follow him, she orders a ship of diamonds to be built with a mast of rubies and cabins made from other precious stones. Out of revenge – because he initially left her – she tortures the prince with her demanding whims. Among different tasks, she requires him to build her a golden bridge decorated with real roses on which she will await him at the other end. Later she even wants him to bury himself there. In the end, they reconcile with each other. These genuine oriental decorations of large amounts of precious stones and gems are also a reflection of the high esteem placed on the anima: it is supposed to appear as the most precious thing in the world. The underground mine and the glass palace on the sea describe her inaccessibility. (In an Irish fairytale, "The Cat and the Fool," the virgin lives in a castle surrounded by constantly rotating magic wheels so that no one can get to her.) The anima's unapproachability is represented here as a castle difficult to capture, as a glass mountain, or as a glass or crystal palace.

1278 Entering into the realm of anima, as Connla experienced it, is similar to the process that the Hindus call the Union with Being. But it is an unconscious state, as shown in the *Chandogya-Upanishad*, Part 6, Chapter 8, Verse 1: "Uddalaka the son of Aruna said to his son Svetaketu: 'Learn from me, my dear, the true nature of sleep. When a person has entered into deep sleep, as it is called, then, my dear, he becomes united with Pure Being (*sat*), he has

[118] See the glass house in "The Earth Wants to Have Hers." There the anima has apples and gives three of them to the hero. These lead him to his delivery i.e., completion, in this life, to his death.
[119] See also the crystal-like action of water kingdom in "The Disowned Princess."
[120] See C.G. Jung, *Psychology and Alchemy*, CW 12, ¶221ff; Wilhelm, *Secret of the Golden Flower*, p. 143. See also the *Quran*, Sura 24, "The Light," verse 35: "Allah is the *light* of Heaven and of the Earth. His Light is like a niche and within it a lamp, the lamp is in glass, the glass as like brilliant star," One of Confucius' names is "Son of the Watercrystal" (see the fairytale, "A Legend of Confucius"). Wilhelm notes that "The 'Watercrystal' is the dark Lord of the North, whose element is water and wisdom, for which last reason Confucius is termed his son" (*The Chinese Fairy Book*, p. 65). In "The Two Travelers," the horse stamps a piece of earth into the sky, upon which a jet of "water as pure as crystal" rises up.

gone to his own Self. That is why they say he is in deep sleep (*svapiti*); it is because he has gone (*apita*) to his own (*svam*).'" And Carus emphasizes: "As far as the mystery of the eternity of the being-in-itself in this sense and at this depth encompasses the human soul, another important finding arises of itself and confronts us, namely, *that this eternal being*, if it again puts on the clothing of temporal life, must be in its very pure being-in-itself considered not as a *conscious*, but rather as an *unconscious* being."[121] It signifies a merging with the universe, with nature. Thus the anima is called "the Beauty of the Earth" (as in "The Beautiful One of the Earth"), or in an Uzbekistan fairytale, "The Beautiful Dunye," where *Dunya* = treasure, outer space,[122] which refers again to wholeness, the world soul.

1279 This theme concerns just that "journey into the universe," about which the Chinese sage Yü Tsing (according to Master Lü Dsu) says:

1280 "Four words crystallize the spirit in the space of energy.
In the sixth month white snow is suddenly seen to fly.
At the third watch, the sun's disk sends out blinding rays.
In the water, blows the wind of Gentle.
Wandering in heaven, on seats the spirit-energy of the Receptive.[123]
And the still deeper secret of the secret.
The land that is nowhere, that is the true home. . ."[124]

1281 A related story that is in many respects an ecstatic rapture[125] into the afterlife by the anima is the Japanese fairytale, "Aitaka Myôyin:"

1282 [An old couple were once splitting bamboo and found inside a tiny human child, a girl of supernatural beauty. The girl grew up very fast and radiated a supernatural glow. The messengers of the emperor came to invite her to the imperial palace, but she refused to go. Then the emperor came himself.]

1283 As soon as the emissaries of the Emperor had left the house of the old couple, the daughter turned to her foster parents in tears and said, "I will never forget the love and care you have given me all this time. But

---

[121] Carus, *Psyche*, p. 488 [Combination of free and literal translation.]. See also Silesius, *The Cherubinic Wanderer*, p. 140, no. 139, *The Blissful Drowning*:
"If thou bring thy boat on the sea to the Godhead, Thou art so blessed, as to drown in it."
See also the self-sacrifice of the great wizard Merlin, who gives himself up into the hands of the Elfin Viviana and reveals his secrets to her. He vanishes from the world, and one hears only his plaintive farewell; Zimmer, "Merlin," pp. 151ff. See also Guest, *Mabinogion*, pp. 383–385. On behalf of Arthur, Gawain goes off to find Merlin, hears a moan, and sees only a kind of smoke like air. From that misty cloud, Merlin speaks to him and explains his misfortune and how he came to be imprisoned, that Gawain would never see again, and that he, Merlin, would then never talk to anybody save his mistress.
[122] See *Märchen aus Turkestan und Tibet*, p. 63, fn. 1.
[123] Cf. Connla's apple!
[124] "A magic spell for the far journey"; see Wilhelm, *Secret of the Golden Flower*, p. 53.
[125] [German: *entrücken*.]

now the time has come when I must leave you and return to the peak of Mount Fuji, from where I once came to you. Think not ill of me that I leave you, and do not hold me ungrateful." The two old people begged her to stay, without her they did not want to live any longer. She replied: "Do not mourn over my inevitable fate above. From time to time I will come and visit your cabin and inquire after your well-being, but here I can now no longer live among people."

1284 With these words, she left their abode and ascended to the summit of Mount Fuji. When the emperor came to Suruga at the foot of Mount Fuji, he was told by the two elders that their foster daughter had left to climbed up the mountain. Upon hearing this news, a deep depression took possession of the emperor. He asked the old man to lead him to the summit of the mountain, and they immediately departed. As the two of them reached the fifth station on the way to the top and rested there, the emperor took the crown from his head, and they lay down. After they had rested, they continued their ascent to the summit. When they reached the top, the one they sought emerged from out of a cave. She took the Emperor's hand and led him saying, "If it is really your only desire to live with me, then follow me." They entered her cave and were never seen again.[126]

1285 Another version of the same story, called "The Story of the Old Man Who Found a Tiny Girl and Brought Her Up," relates towards the end:

1286 The emperor asked the girl: "Will you not come with me to my palace, and be my wife?" Then the maiden answered him: "With great pleasure I would be your Empress, but unfortunately I am not a human being." Dismayed, the emperor asked, "What are you then? Are you a god or a demon?" The maiden answered: "I am neither god nor demon, but I cannot stay here in this world. Soon someone will come and take me up to Heaven. Abandon your intention, dear Emperor, and return back to your court."

1287 The emperor thought to himself, as he heard those words, "What does she mean by her speech? That certainly cannot be the truth! Surely the only reason she said all that about Heaven coming to take her was only an excuse to turn down my proposal to her." But just as he was engaged in his musings, many heavenly beings came down with a palanquin for the girl. They let the maiden mount and then carried her to heaven. But the form of these heavenly emissaries was not

[126] Translated from Rumpf, *Japanische Volksmärchen*, pp. 78–85.

> anything like that of people of this world. Having witnessed all that transpired with his own eyes, the emperor thought to himself, "Yes, indeed, that woman was certainly not of this world!" He returned to his palace, but he later often remembered the maiden. Every time he thought of her, she appeared in his memory more beautiful than all the children of this world. Then he longed to see the woman he could not forget. But since he saw that is was to no avail, his power was limited, he could do nothing but accept the painful sacrifice. No one knew who this woman was. No one found an explanation of why she had come into the house of the old couple, to grow up as their daughter. For all the people of this world it remained a mystery. And since it is such a strange story, I have retold it here.[127]

1288 Both stories impressively describe the strange, "otherworldly" character of the anima, whose essence is foreign and incomprehensible to the people of this world. Those who fall in love with her often are then drawn by her into the other world.[128]

1289 The beautiful ghostly girl comes from a bamboo cane and grows as fast as a bamboo shoot; she is like the *spiritus vegetativus*, which lives in this plant. This is similar to many European myths where the anima appears as a tree nymph or as the reed or laurel that was transformed into a woman.[129]

1290 Since the psychic principle of life represented by the anima reaches down to the plant kingdom, the anima is sometimes represented as a flower. This is also a motif and a well-known song in Germany: Sah ein Knab' ein Röslein steh'n [A boy saw a rose standing]. Two parallel fairytales, "A Soldier Redeems the Princess from a Curse" and "The Vampire," tell of a beautiful girl who was killed by a dead lover or a demon and then grew as a flower on her own grave to be later picked by a prince. In the night, she once again becomes a maiden; in one story, she secretly steals his food; in the other, she takes him into her arms, until he recognizes that the woman is the flower in human form. From that moment of awareness, she remains permanently human and marries him. In the Roma tale, she later defeats her murderer, who tried to kill her a second time. The anima appears here as a flower after a state of complete separation (being dead and buried).[130] In other words, it exists as a living thing, but in a

---

127 Hammitzsch et al., *Japanische*, pp. 20–23.

128 [In the fairytale mentioned above, "The Beautiful One of the Earth," the hero falls hopelessly in love with the woman who ruthlessly mistreats him. However, he does not give up, and with the help of objects that he finds in the cellar of his parent's house and some magical grapes, he eventually manages to win her over and to bring her to his world, where they live happily ever after. In that tale, she is called "of the Earth," perhaps a clue as to why in this particular tale it turned out the way it did.]

129 See the myth of Daphne and its discussion in Mannhardt, *Wald- und Feldkulte*, vol. 1, *passim*, esp. p. 38 fn. 1.

130 On this motif, see Köhler, "Kleinere Schriften," vol. 3, pp. 274ff, no. 38: *Vom Fortleben der Seelen in der Pflanzenwelt* [On the continued existence of the soul in the plant world].

purely vegetative state, far removed from human consciousness.[131] As something round, the flower is also a symbol of the Self, as in "Connla and the Fairy Maiden," where the symbol of the anima was also associated with the image of the Self. To this extent, the flower shows the aspect of the Self as an emotional experience in a preliminary stage of conscious understanding.[132] In the East, the lotus flower is the seat and origin of the gods and also the place of rebirth. That is why in the tales mentioned above ("A Soldier Redeems the Princess from a Curse" and "The Vampire"), the flower is a symbol of the reborn anima. In general, flowers symbolize new life,[133] and are therefore probably also planted on graves.

1291 The above-mentioned fairytales show that the "beloved woman" is non-human and does not characterize something physically real. It is clear that she represents an experience beyond the boundaries and laws of this world. She comes from a world in which the dead can be resurrected and people can become flowers and then humans again. Therein lies a danger, however, which is more or less strongly hinted at in every encounter with the anima: contact with the realm of the dead. She either comes from or belongs to the other world, or she maintains a strong, and, therefore, dangerous relationship to that world. Since the anima is not from the world of consciousness but comes from the unconscious, she tries to pull the hero there. If the hour has not come for him to follow her into her own realm, a tragic separation is usually inevitable. This is mirrored in the famous English legend "Thomas the Rhymer and the Queen of Elfland," in which the hero visits the kingdom of the elves and receives the gift of poetry and prophecy. He then takes leave of the Fairy Queen and returns again to this life. Only when his death draws nigh do a white stag and a female dog appear that lead him back into the other world. In this legend, the hero can resist the attraction of the world of the dead by his unusual strength and the grace of the Fairy Queen and also because he refuses to partake of food from the other side. Thus, his enchantment[134] is postponed until the natural end of his life. In many other tales, the anima breaks into the life of the hero as a tragic fate.

1292 The painful incompatibility of the spheres is described in a tale from the South Sea Islands, "Tapairu, the Beauty from the Land of the Fairies," as follows:[135]

---

131 See Jung, "Zum psychologischen Aspekt der Korefigur," CW 9/1, ¶315.

132 See the various forms of anima in "The Beautiful Princess in the Garden," where the princess asks each newcomer what he likes most. The older brothers answer: most beautiful are the flowers or the fruits of the garden, and are forthwith punished. The youngest answers that she herself is the most beautiful being in the garden, which is the simple answer that she wanted.

133 See, for example, the tale from a native tribe of Australia, "Sturt's Desert Pea, the Flower of Blood," recorded in Parker, *Australian*, pp. 31–38.

134 [German: *entrücken*.]

135 The word "fairy" is likely an artifact of the translation and does not reflect the original word.

1293 In Rarotonga, at the pretty village of Aorrangi, is the small fountain of Vaitipi. On the night after full moon, a woman and a man of dazzling white complexion rose up out of the crystal water. When the inhabitants of this world were supposed to be asleep, they came up from the shades to steal taro, plantains, bananas, and cocoa-nuts. All these good things they took back to the netherworld to devour raw.

1294 Little did the fairies suspect that they had been seen by mortals and that a plan was being devised to catch them. A large scoop net of strong *cinet* was made for this purpose, and constant watch set at the fountain by night. On the first appearance of the new moon they again came up and, as usual, went off to pillage the plantations. The great net was now carefully spread out at the bottom of the spring, and then they gave chase to the fair beings from the spirit-world. The fairy girl was the first to reach the spring, and dived down. She was at once caught in the net, and carried off in triumph. But in replacing the net after the struggle, a small space remained uncovered and through this tiny aperture the male fairy contrived to escape.

1295 The lovely captive became the cherished wife of the chief Ati, who now carefully filled up the spring with great stones, lest his fairy spouse should return to netherworld. They lived very happily together. She was known all over Rarotonga as the "incomparable one (*Tapairu*) of Ati." She reconciled herself to the ways of mortals, and grew content with her novel position. In the course of time she became pregnant, and when the period for her delivery had come, she said to her husband, "Perform on me the Caesarean operation, and then bury my dead body. But cherish tenderly our child." Ati refused to accede to this proposition, but allowed Nature to take her course, so that the fairy became the living mother of a fair boy.

1296 When at length the child had become strong, the mother one day wept bitterly in the presence of her husband. She told him that she was sorely grieved at the destruction of all mothers in the shades upon the birth of the first-born. Would he consent to her returning thither to put an end to so cruel a custom, and that Ati should accompany her. This was agreed upon, and accordingly the great stones were dragged up from the bottom of the spring. All kinds of vegetable gums were now collected, and the fairy carefully besmeared the entire person of Ati, so as to facilitate his descent to the lower world.

1297 Holding firmly the hand of her human husband, the fairy dived to the bottom of the fountain, and nearly reached the entrance to the invisible world. But Ati was so dreadfully exhausted, that out of pity for him she returned. Five times was this process repeated – in vain! The fair one from spirit-land wept because her husband was not permitted to accompany her; for only the spirits of the dead and immortals can enter.

1298 Sorrowfully embracing each other, the "incomparable one" said, "I alone will go to the spirit-world to teach what I have learnt from you." At this she again dove down into the clear waters, and was never again seen on Earth. Ati went sorrowfully back to his old habitation; and thenceforth their boy was called "Ati-ve'e" (the forsaken, in memory of his lost fairy mother). He was surpassingly fair, like his mother from spirit-land; but strangely enough, his descendants are dark, like ordinary mortals.

1299 It is to this lovely fairy woman the old song of the Ati clan alludes:

1300 *Kua ve'eia te pou enua* She has descended again to spirit-world!
Ka paa 'i te rau atua o Ati e i Vaitipie! Men praised the divine being first seen by Ati at the fountain,
Akana tu a kino te inangaro! But his heart is now filled with grief.
Hence the origin of the common name "Tapairu" (the peerless one, in memory of their fairy ancestress).[136]

1301 The beautiful woman that Ati captures on a night of a full moon, when the spirits appear, comes from the water like nixies and mermaids. She is a character from the unconscious, a spirit-being, a typical personification of the anima. The spring from which she emerges has a maternal meaning and is a general image, a symbol of the living essence of the soul.[137] The mermaid used to steal fruit with her male companion, who embodies the shadow originally always associated with the anima, in order to feed themselves. She was thus connected with the upper world and even depended on this connection to survive. This stealing contains a longing for redemption (as it does with the daughter of the wily pirate in "The Mermaid and the Great Dubhdach"). Seen from the upper world, losing the fruit means losing the soul. It is a disturbance, which, like the loss of the ax in "The *Peaged Arsai* Bird," also ushered in the experience of the anima. This theft is a quiet impingement of the unconscious into the world of consciousness that foretells the imminent emergence of the anima problem.

1302 The white color of the figures is most likely a sign of special beauty. Moreover, white is very often the color of the magical kingdom. The snow kingdom of Frau Holle is white; as is the silvery moon of the fairy realm in "The Lady of the Moon." Also Aztlan, the ancestral land of the dead for the Aztecs in "How Motecuzhoma Sought the Seven Caves," is called "the white

[136] Slightly edited from William Wyatt Gill, Myths and Songs from the South Pacific, pp. 294–296 (titled there as "The fairy of the fountain"); for a German version, see Danzel, Südsee, pp. 47–49.
[137] See C.G. Jung, *Psychology and Alchemy*, CW 12, ¶94; see also the Germanic belief in elf-like beings who live in the water, as reported in Führer, *Nordgermanische*, p. 15f.

land."[138] At the same time, white is the color of the purest light and transfiguration[139] and is considered the color of virginity and innocence.[140]

1303 In the vision of the sun in the *Mithras Liturgy*, the godhead wears a white robe and Helios' chariot is drawn by four white horses.[141] In the East, for instance in Tibet, white is the attribute of the highest world of the god's angels.[142] In China, Po, one of the parallel forms of the anima, is described with the characters for white and demon. Thus, she is a white ghost and signifies the female, chthonic body-soul.[143] A similar idea occurs in alchemical speculation where the white woman is almost always associated with the red man. The woman is called the shining white dove or Beya, from Arabic *albeida* (the white one).[144] A Koryak tale, "Big Raven and the Evil Spirits," tells of an anima figure, the daughter of evil spirits, who is so "dazzingly beautiful," that she only needs to stretch her hand out of her hut to illumine the whole landscape.

1304 In the Polynesian tale "Tapairu, the Beauty from the Land of the Fairies," the anima is described typically as a white night and spring spirit, like a demon emerging from the unconscious. As the hunter in "Ititaujang" and "The Sealskin," Ati tries to bind the beautiful woman to him by pulling her into his

---

[138] See Ninck, *Wodan*, p. 180. The swan is often a transformed nixie. Similar figures are the white stag or the white deer. See here *ibid.*, p. 283. See also the magical role of the white snake in "The White Snake." According to Carnochan und Adamson, *Empire*, pp. 106–07, the white snake indicates death and the ancestral land. In a Warau (Bolivia) fairytale, "Why the Boa Constrictor Does Not Eat People," one of the people that the boa eats reappears completely hairless and white.

[139] See Bächtold-Stäubli under *weiss* [white]: "... the word white comes from the Indo-European root *kwid* or *kwit*, Sanskrit *śkr*, meaning "white," "shinning" ... and also old Slavic, *svêtu*, "light" and literally *szvaityti*, "to make bright." It is ultimately connected to the ancient Greek *λημκωσ*, (leucos) " light word," that has generally become the word for color ... White is the color of the gods of light... In particular there is a close relationship between white light, the lightening flash, and then the light of enlightenment, and therefore also to the deities and demons of the storm... White objects can give their owners the service of the will of gods, demons and people. Those who partake of the meat of a white snake can understand all languages, the sound of animals, and receive the gift of prophecy... The magical power of the color white is associated also to witchcraft. On their meetings in the Avers mountains (Switzerland), the witches appear as white goats... White clothes offer their bearer a particularly strong protection. Contact with the gods and demons can be dangerous and only those with divine power or in a state of purity can avoid harm, it is understandable that people who are responsible for dealing with the supernatural powers, like priests and magicians, try to protect themselves by wearing white robes to ward off the evil effects... As the apotropaic character of the colorwhite fell into oblivion, clothing of pure light became popular as party dress... The white color of sacrificial animals has in most cases an apotropaic character... In Pomerania white signifies the color of dwarf-like creatures who live underground, called *Undererdschken* ["Subterraneans"] by Bolt. Some demons take on the color white, for instance, the deathly pallor of the corpse... This connection of white and death (ghosts, spirits of the dead, etc.) is also the cause of the bad omen often attributed to white." See also Bachofen, *Die Sage von Tanaquil, Eine Untersuchung über den Orientalismus in Rom und Italien*, p. 316; Ninck, *Wodan*, p. 294; Jung, *Symbols of Transformation*, CW 5, ¶233.

[140] See Collum, "Schöpferische Mutter-Göttin," pp. 247–249.

[141] See Dieterich, *Eine Mithrasliturgie*, p. 11; Leisegang, "Schlange," p. 188, fn. 2. See also the white light elves and the light horse of the Dag in Führer, *Nordgermanische*, p. 9f.

[142] Cf. Evans-Wentz, *Tibetan*, p. 107f.

[143] See C.G. Jung, *Golden Flower*, CW 13, ¶57. See the "white lady," the spook who haunts medieval castles.

[144] See C.G. Jung, *Psychology and Alchemy*, CW 12, ¶435 fn. 37, ¶443; "Die Visionen des Zosimos," ¶124.

sphere by force. At first, he succeeds: they were very happy, the nixie becomes human, and the man experiences the blissful presence of the beautiful spirit-being. But the birth of their child seals the woman's fate. She falls prey to death and must therefore return to the hereafter. From the precepts of her origin in the fairy kingdom, she must preserve her virginity and may not completely unite with the other world.

1305 The idea of virginity is intimately bound up with the image of the anima. Philo of Alexandria writes that in the human sphere the union for the purpose of procreation makes women out of virgins, but when the *soul* begins to commune with God, he turns the women into virgins again.[145] Athena, who sprang from the head of Zeus, and who therefore also represents an anima figure, is an eternal virgin, like Artemis. This virginity means purity, that is, a not-being-mixed-with-worldly-affairs, because the image of the anima blossoms into its full significance only if it is not mixed with the outer world. Thus, in fairytales fairies and mermaids are forbidden to bear children because the anima is intended to be a pure spirit-being. The commandment of the land of the fairies that forbids any real connection with a mortal is based on the knowledge that the arresting power of the ghost-like anima will expire and that she must slide back into the unconscious as soon as she has let her life flow into that which is in itself most significant. That is, the child as a symbol of the Self, which really connects the two worlds.[146]

1306 The only way out that is now open is the same as that taken by Connla in "Connla's Sea-Journey:" to follow the anima into her own kingdom. Like Orpheus, Ati must also take the step of entering the land of the dead, hoping he can prove that his fervent feelings are authentic and thereby beg the dark royal ruling couple to release his beloved wife. Since Ati, despite his great efforts, cannot master the journey into the underworld, separation is the only possibility; the "Incomparable One" returns forever into the well.

1307 The problem of the anima being transported, enraptured, into the afterlife and of having magical effects is also evident in "The Seven Maidens":

---

[145] See Reitzenstein, *Hellenistic*, pp. 118–119, 311–312.

[146] For the modern Greek myth, see Laistner, *Das Rätsel*, pp. 121–122

> A young farmer plays the lyre so beautifully that the Nereids take him into their silvery cave, to listen to his music. He falls in love with one and succeeds, with the instructions of an old woman, to bring her under his power to silence her. She follows him and gives him a son and does not break her silence. The man cannot bear this and seeks advice from the old woman again. He returns to his fairy wife and pretends to throw their child into the oven. The woman screams and tears the child unto herself. "And since the other Nereids never took her back into their circle because she was a mother, she built a new house near the cave of the Nereids. One sees her occasionally with her baby in her arms."

Here the same law is described in reverse image. Through her motherhood and the birth of the child, this Nereid loses her ghostly, virgin anima figure, and no longer fits into the magical realm. Her silence indicates, on the other hand, her "otherness," and so she remains in limbo close to the profane world. The inflated cruelty of the man ultimately destroyed their spiritual harmony. The silence of the anima figure indicates the fact that in the happy vision of the young man, she does not "say" everything for him. Her dreamlike quality cannot mean everything, despite the birth of the child, the Self symbol. The secular hardness of man's attitude devalues the relationship and is the cause of the tragic unresolved end.

1308 Two Forest Nenets[147] lived together in a desolate place, they hunted fox, sable, and bear. It once happened that one of them went on a journey, and the other stayed home. The traveling one met an old woman who was cutting birch trees. "You are cutting around, in a circle! You should cut from two sides, I will show you how." And he took an ax and cut many birches and brought them on a sled to the tent of the old woman. She was his father's sister. He put the wood on the ground. The old woman spoke: "Hide yourself so that no one sees you." He hid himself. The old woman remained standing on the hill. Seven maidens came to her. "Who cut down this tree? This is not the way you cut down trees. Who is here with you?" The old one: "No one is here with me. I have cut this tree down myself!" The girls went away without entering the tent.

1309 The Nenets man came out of his hiding place and went to his father's sister. The old woman spoke: "In the dark forest is a lake, a long lake, go there! When you arrive, the seven maidens will be swimming. They leave their clothes on the shore. Creep up quietly and take one of the girls' clothes and hide them."

1310 The man went forth and came to the lake, it happened as the old woman had said. He took the most beautiful clothes and hid them. The seven girls swam to the shore. They began to get dressed, but the clothes of one of the maidens had disappeared. She ran back into the water, the other girls went away. The one left behind cried into the lake, she did not know who took her clothes. She spoke: "Whoever took my clothes, I will become his wife if he gives me my clothes back." The Nenets man did not trust the woman and kept himself back.

1311 The woman in the lake thought and spoke to herself. "Our old one had an even older sister, she had a son. If it was he who stole my clothes, I will become his wife." Now the man arose from his hiding place and the girl saw him. "It is true! You are the sister-son of our old woman! Give me back my clothes and I will become your wife." "If I give you back your clothes, you will rise up to the sky, how can I have you for my wife?"

1312 "You can believe me that I will be your wife; give me my clothes, I am freezing!" The man replied: "Not far from here are seven brothers who all live together in a secluded place. They come and go. When they come back to their tent, they take their hearts out and hang them on the tent posts. If you can bring these seven hearts to me, I will give

[147] [The Forest Nenets are a Siberian people living in the Taiga. In the original, the story is told in the present tense, here changed into the past to be consistent with other tales in this book.]

you your clothes, otherwise you will not get them, even if you die on this spot."

1313 "I will take these hearts. Now give me my clothes!"

1314 "I will not give them to you until you tell me how you are going to get the hearts of the seven sons."

1315 "I will go in the night and take them."

1316 "Not that way, many have tried that already, and none has ever succeeded. Come closer to me and I will tell you how you can get them into your power."

1317 She swam to the shore. The Nenets man spoke: "These seven men took my sister from me, you have to get her to help you. Go to this sister, she holds watch over all the hearts and from her you must request them."

1318 They agreed and he gave the clothes to the woman. She put on the clothes and forthwith demanded an extension of time in which she would get the hearts. "Within five days I will come with my herd of reindeer and my tent."

1319 The man went back to his companion. "Where have you been, what did you see?"

1320 "I have been nowhere, I have seen nothing." His comrade said: "You have obviously been to our father's sister! The seven brothers without hearts killed our mother, they will also kill you if you go there! Never go to that old woman!"

1321 They lived there five days. On the fifth day, the girl came out of the air with her reindeer herd and her tent, and became his wife. "Let us now go to the seven brothers [to seek revenge for their killing of your mother]," said the woman.

1322 "We will see if we can get hold of their hearts." They went to the tent of the seven brothers. The man and his wife went into the tent, no one could see the woman. The man was visible and he spoke to the sister: "Where do the seven brothers put their hearts when they come back to their tent?"

1323 "There on the tent rods they put them, and then they lay down directly and always sleep without hearts." The sister continued, "They trust me and when they come back to the tent I take a bowl and go around from one brother to the next. Each one lays his heart in the bowl. I then hang the hearts up on the rods."

1324 Then the man spoke: "Take the bowl, take all the hearts down from the rods and put them in the bowl. In the morning, when they ask for their hearts, throw the hearts of the six younger brothers away, wherever you want. They can die. But then take the heart of the eldest brother, go to him and say: 'When my mother comes back to life, I will give you your heart back, otherwise not.'"

1325 The couple succeeded in seizing the hearts of the seven Samoyeds and after they blackmailed the eldest to revive the mother, they kill them all by throwing their hearts to the ground. On the advice of the father's sister, the man, back home, gives his new wife a knife and tells her to do whatever she wants with it. The woman took all the hearts that were in the tent, also that of her husband and her own, and threw them all in the air. The father's sister came and saw that all of them were without hearts and said, "All here are without hearts, they are not alive, they are not dead, what should I do? I will go to the long lake, maybe I will find someone there."

1326 At the lake the old father's sister took the clothes of the remaining six bathing maidens and hid them. The six sisters cried and lamented, "We do not know where our sister has gone!" They swam to the shore and one of them was missing her clothes. She jumped back in the lake and the others went away. The one left in the lake cried, "Whoever has taken my clothes, I will become that person's wife and every dead person I will make living again, if only I could have my clothes back. In the air we catch many hearts and with these I can help those who are dead." The old woman [the father's sister] came out of hiding, "See, here are your clothes!"

1327 "Give me my clothes, I will fulfill everything that I have promised." "Give me all the hearts that you have found and then I will give you the clothes," said the woman. "You live in the air, your sister is now on the ground, when she asks for something, can't you help her?" "If she lives, we will do everything she wants."

1328 The maiden gave her all the hearts, and the old woman gave her back her clothes. The old one now went to the tent where the people without hearts lived, that all had gone up into heaven. All of the hearts were now *pure* and *sacred*. "Now," said the woman, "Let us go up to heaven, to our sisters." They gathered reindeer together, made ready for the journey, and rode into the air. For seven days they went through a thick fog, where they could see nothing, and then they came to a warm, a very warm and good place. There they live still today.[148]

[148] The original is untitled. Translated from Castren, *Ethnologische*, pp. 172–176.

1329 We have already encountered the motif of the seven anima figures and the swan maiden. That the anima magically helps in taking revenge against powerful opponents is a characteristic notion of natural peoples. The anima bestows psychic clairvoyance and superiority. The most impressive account is, however, where the anima conjures away everyone's hearts, so that they are "neither dead nor alive." This is the primitive expression for "anima possession," in which the man lives in an inhuman state (i.e., without a human heart), when every spontaneous relations to other people, every living response, is suppressed. Instead of opening up to life, such a man spends his life in a kind of floating, not-quite-present state: dazzled, fascinated, and spellbound by his anima's trickery. In our fairytale, when the old woman brings the hearts back, this signifies a balancing, an equalization mediated by the natural wisdom of the unconscious. People come to themselves again, and it is important that their hearts are pure and sacred. Every phase of enchantment results also, in the positive sense, in a detachment from all worldly concupiscence and enmeshment in everyday life. In the end, the anima experience leads to a definite ecstatic retreat into the afterlife, a detachment from the world and life. This is a strange paradox, which is perceived simultaneously as a blessed deliverance and as a tragic departure from the world.

1330 A lively description of the nature of the anima, which merits no comment, is "The Girl Who Was Faster Than Horses":

1331 There was once a girl who was of no father begotten and of given birth by no mother born. She was not formed by any parent, but by *Vilen*[149] from snow taken from the bottomless gorge at the time of the summer solstice. The Wind had revived the girl with its breath, she was breastfed by the dew, the mountains clothed her with their fallen leaves, and the fields adorned her with their flowers and garlands. She was white as snow, more red than a rose, brighter than the sun, in short, such a girl had never been born to the world before and no one like her will ever grace the world in the future. She issued a call throughout the whole world that she was organizing a race on such-and-such a day and such-and-such a place, whatever young man on horseback could outrace her, she would make him her own. When

[149] [The Vila are Slavic versions of nymphs, who have power over storms, which they delight in sending down on lonely travelers. They live in meadows, ponds, oceans, trees, and clouds. They can appear as swans, horses, wolves, or beautiful women. In South-Slavic mythology the vila are believed to be female fairy-like spirits who live in the wilderness and sometimes in the clouds. They were believed to be the spirits of women who had been frivolous in their lifetimes and now floated between here and the afterlife. They sometimes appear as swans, snakes, horses, falcons, or wolves that they can shapeshift into, but usually they appear as beautiful maidens, naked or dressed in white with long flowing hair.]

the day of the race arrived young men from the world over converged by the thousands on their horses. It was going to be very difficult to decide which one of them was the best.

1332 The girl stood on the starting line, on both sides stood all the suitors high on horseback all lined up. The maiden was alone on foot without a horse. She said unto them, "At the goal I have placed a golden apple. Whoever first arrives there and takes the apple, I will belong to him, but if I get there first and grab that apple before any of you, then ye shalt know that you will never leave the place alive. Therefore think well before you decide to start!" The riders looked at each other and each entertained the hope that they would succeed in reaching the apple first and to have the girl for their own. They said to each other, "One thing we know for sure: she is running on foot and will never be able to overtake us, so that surely one of us will get the apple first, and none of us will die from someone on foot and she will surely not pass by. But from our midst one of us will get to the apple first. May God and luck be favorably disposed today!"

1333 Now when the girl clapped her hands to signal the start, all rushed full gallop, leaning forward in the saddle. In middle of the way, by God, the girl seemed to grow weary and she began to slow down. Suddenly, a little pair of wings appeared at her armpits to help her go faster and she began to take the lead. The riders urged their steeds onwards, spurs were set, whips whistled constantly in the air above the horsed heads, and indeed they began to overtake the girl. When she saw this, she pulled her hair out from her head and threw it behind her. In no time a terrible mountain range sprang up. The suitors on horseback were at a loss to know what to do: should they ride to the right or to the left? But that did not prevent them from furiously riding onwards. Again, the girl took the lead, but the riders spurred their horses forwards and caught up to her. When the girl noticed that the mountains did not do the trick, she let a tear fall, and out poured an immense river. The riders flung themselves in and almost all foundered and found their deaths. Only one rider, the emperor's son, made it across the wild currents and relentlessly pursued the girl. But when he saw that the girl was gaining ground on him, he implored her three times in the name of God to stand still. Suddenly she remained standing, right in the place where she was, just as if spellbound. Then he overtook her, lifted her up, and placed her behind him on his horse. Together they swam onwards to dry land and continued through the high mountains homewards. When they arrived at the highest crest of the mountain range, the prince looked

> behind him, but the girl was nowhere to be seen, she had disappeared![150]

1334 The deceptive game of this unreal nature being, chased by a horde of young men, driven by their instincts, seems to find its end when the emperor's son calls in divine help. But then he believes that he can just ride on with her into the secular world, and becomes the fool beside this mighty soul-image.

1335 Less poetic, but all the more gruesome and spooky, is the Slavic fairytale "Stanko and the Vila." This describes another anima experience:

1336 There once was a shepherd who knew how to play on the single and double shepherd's flute better than anybody near and far. One day early in the morning, just when dawn broke, he went out of his hut ahead of his flock. He played the flute so pure and mild, the notes seemed to flow out from his instrument. Only a swallow in the sun at the time of Lent can sing so sweetly. Indeed, just then the bells of the town church began to ring the *Ave Maria*. But Stanko – that was the name of the poor man – forgot to pray and instead played the *Ave Maria* prayer on his flute. Just as he finished, he reached the fence at the entrance to the village, and lo and behold! What sat there, but a wench all in white, a real *vila!* Stanko neared the woman on the fence post, when she let out a piercing cry that shot through his bones, and just like *vila* do, she flew up into the air. A hot breeze wafted over Stanko, he sank down on the ground, the footboard on the wood bridge split in two. He pulled himself together and rushed home, all the way with the *vila* close on his heels. He sat down at his table to eat dinner, the *vila* sat herself down at his side by his knee. When he went to bed, the *vila* went to bed with him. When he got up to work, the *vila* got up too, she followed him at every turn. When the people noticed that the *vila* did not part from Stanko's side they appealed to magicians and conjurers – but all in vain. Stanko's mind began to run riot, he was found beaten and tied up, or bound to the crown of trees that were impossible to climb. After years of torment he was found drowned in a manure pit.[151]

[150] Translated from Krauss, *Sagen und Märchen der Südslaven*, vol. 1, pp. 462–464.

[151] Translated from Krauss, *Darstellungen aus dem Gebiete der nichtchristlichen Religionsgeschichte*, vol. 2: *Volksglaube und religiöser Brauch der Südslaven*, no. 108. For a commentary, see Leskien (ed.), *Balkanmärchen aus Albanien, Bulgarien, Serbien und Kroatien*, (*MdW*), p. 324, especially the note to tale no. 12, "The Girl and the Vampire:" "*Samovila* is the Bulgarian name for nymph-like creatures that are called *Vila* by the Serbs. They are described as beautiful women who live in forests, mountains, and especially in lakes. See, in general, Krauß, *Darstellungen aus dem Gebiete der nichtchristlichen Religionsgeschichte*, vol. 2: *Volksglaube und religiöser Brauch der Südslaven*. On the mental powers of nymphs and their damaging effect on men, see Mannhardt, *Wald- und Feldkulte*, vol. 2, pp. 36ff.

1337 Some fairytales reflect the idea of the anima as a sinister spook, a haunting figure whose character is similar to images of the unconscious. One example is the Icelandic tale "Una, the Elfen Girl":

> 1338 The young man with the name of Geir had a good farm, but had recently lost his wife. Once, when people were making hay, he saw how a pretty young woman joined them and without a word helped them work. This repeated itself day after day throughout the summer. The hard work was always accomplished easy as pie. No one knew from whence she came and whither she went. Finally, the farmer thanked her and took her on as housekeeper. She brought a great chest with her to the women's quarters. She proved herself with her diligent work and all the peasants came to like her, especially the pious peasant man, Geir. But despite invitations and persuasive gestures she never joined them in the church. That was the only thing that the pious man did not like about her. At Christmas time when the people went out singing carols in the evening, Una (for that was the name Geir gave her) remained alone at home. She was twice seen about, but then she was ready in the morning and again at work.
>
> 1339 Once, during the carol singing, a young boy – he was a servant of the farmer – felt ill and went to his home. On the way, he saw Una at work. He hid himself and watched her. He saw how she donned a festive dress from her trunk and became an unusually beautiful woman. Then she took out a red blanket and went over to the common meadows where there was a small marsh. The boy secretly followed her. There she spread out the blanket, and to see exactly what she was doing, the boy crept right up to the blanket. Suddenly the girl, the blanket, and the boy sank as if by smoke into the ground and they landed on a green meadow.
>
> 1340 Una took the blanket under her arm and went to a grand homestead. She was greeted warmly and sat down with the people to a sumptuous meal. The boy managed to steal a piece of rib meat and dried sheep meat that appeared more savory and juicy than he had ever seen. The festivities lasted with games until early morning, all very artful and beautiful. Then as the day approached, Una made her farewells, explaining that the farmer would soon be coming back from the church. They all said goodbye in a most friendly way and Una left. The boy followed secretly behind. They returned again to the upper world on the blanket. Una went home and packed the blanket in the trunk in her room, the boy always observing unseen. Now the farmer came out of the church. He saw the boy there and asked how his stomachache was. The boy reported that he felt much better. They went together back to the farmer's home. Una greeted them and at

> table they had, as was the local custom, dried meat. The farmer took a large piece of lamb and said: "Has anyone ever seen such a fine piece of lamb jerky?" "Could be!" said the servant boy and showed them the piece of lamb rib that he had brought back. When Una saw this, she flushed red and left the table, never to be seen again.[152]

1341 Here the image of the anima is clearly separated from the farmer's wife; the anima figure appears only after the wife's death. Typically, the anima appears to the lonely and those rejected by the world. Through the death of the farmer's wife, there is a vacuum in his life into which images from the unconscious can flow. An aspect of the otherworld approaches him as a ghostly woman. Una is a kind of marginal figure, a being who haunts between this world and the hereafter, consciousness and the unconscious. As often in Norse fairytales, the world of the spirits is a remnant of the pagan era and stands in hostile opposition to Christianity. In this resistance, Una reveals her essence as a part of nature, or of the farmer's soul, which could not find a place within the Church.

1342 Once a human enters into the secrets of Una's world and threatens her with the danger of being discovered, she flees and never appears again. Apparently, she knows that strict boundaries exist between the spheres. She also knows the adverse resistance of consciousness to the spirit-world and its dangers. She escapes before the secular environment with its lack of understanding can take a stand against her being, her origin, and her longing for human existence. After all, is she not a dangerous spook, which, in its unrecognized natural condition, could behave mischievously, perhaps even harmfully? Indeed, she is a piece of the Land of the Dead, and could threaten the very lives of the farmers.[153] The farmer makes no attempt, as Ati did in "Tapairu, the Beauty from the Land of the Fairies" (see page 449), to follow her and preserve the relationship, since his horror of the spirit-world seems to prevail.[154]

---

[152] Translated from H. and I. Naumann (trans.), *Isländische*, pp. 54–56. See many similar stories in L. Laistner, *Das Rätsel*, Berlin 1889 *passim*.

[153] In a related story, "The Elfin Queen Hilda," the lethal effect of the young elfin woman is attributed to a curse thrown by her mother-in-law, an old troll queen. The spell by the Great Mother, i.e., nature as inescapable fate, is removed when a man – the hero of the fairytale – has fathomed the secret. His knowledge puts an end to the fatal effect of the curse, but in this case does not prevent the separation of the spheres. A bridge is hardly to be expected, coming from the level of consciousness that these kinds of fairytales reflect.

[154] A Chinese tale, "The Transformed Woman," tells of an anima figure who relentlessly agitates as a dangerous spook. A scholar took frequent walks in the mountains. One day he visited a small mountain village and stopped in at the village inn. The host had a pretty daughter who impressed the scholar so much that he took her home as his mistress. After a few years, the scholar was appointed to an administrative position and left for his district job with his mistress. The woman, who at the beginning had been gentle and kind, suddenly began to act wild, willful, opinionated, and headstrong. In her outbreaks of anger, she even took to beating and biting the servants and housemaids. Her husband only then began to take serious notice of her behavior and became suspicious. One day he went out hunting

1343 A similar tale is "The Forest Woman":

> One day a lonely young woodcutter rested for a moment in the forest. Suddenly, a ball of yarn rolled right up to his feet. He looked up and saw a beautiful maiden shimmering in the sun atop a nearby mountain. She asked him to bring her the ball of yarn. He did just that and promptly fell in love with the wondrous appearance. He stood long entranced, and then remembered his work, got his ax and went on with his job. But he could only think of what he had seen and experienced. He did not know what to do. In the evening when he and his comrades lay down to sleep, he wanted to be in the middle, but that did not help much. In the night she came and took him and he had to go with her, whether he liked it or not. They went inside the mountain, and all was so splendorous, such as he had never seen before. He could not find the words to praise what he saw, it was all so wonderful. He remained there for three days. When he woke up after the third night's end, he was back among his comrades. They thought he had gone home to get more provisions and he said that was so. But after that, he was no longer as he was before: no sooner had he sat down, but he would jump up and run away. It was as if the forest nymph had taken away his senses.

1344 Some time later, he was again working in the forest, splitting wood. He had just driven a wedge into a felled trunk and a long split was opening up. He heard a noise and looked around. There came his beautiful woman bringing him a silver bowl with his noon meal. It was groats and cream and smelled delicious in a bowl as fine as silver. She sat down on a felled trunk and the young man put aside his ax and sat on a nearby stump. He then noticed something strange and looked carefully at the woman. She had a long cow tail that had fallen into a split in the log that was kept open with a wedge. He could hardly contain himself and began to think. He eased over to the trunk and

---

with a friend and brought back a large number of foxes and rabbits. A servant told him that she had witnessed how his mistress had gone and devoured some of the game raw! Now the man noticed that the legs of the woman were no longer human legs. He avoided contact with her and slept in another room. One day a servant brought home a deer he had killed. The scholar announced he had to make a trip to an outlying village, but actually stayed around the house and hid to see what the woman would do. Indeed, in due time, he saw her with flowing hair and naked breasts, her eyes bulging out, completely transformed with the dead deer in her left hand. With her right hand she ripped the fur off, tore the carcass open, and ravaged the meat. He could hear the bones crunch as she devoured the remains. The terrified man ran and brought back people from the village with swords and clubs to help. When the woman saw them coming, she tore off her clothes and stood there, she had turned into an ogre with flashing eyes and teeth like swords, and a blue body. The people stood shivering in fear and no one could approach the monster. The man fainted in terror. The woman-ogre looked shyly around all sides, grabbed half of the deer, climbed the wall, and ran away. She was in such haste that she left a thick cloud of dust behind her. No one ever discovered where she had fled.

> worked the wedge until he could pull it out. The split closed and the tail was caught! Then he wrote the name of Jesus on the bowl. The woman got to her feet and tried to flee. She was in such haste, that she ran, tearing off the tail, which remained in the trunk. Gone she was, leaving a bowl with a piece of meat and cow dung.
>
> 1345 From that time on, he never could venture into the forest again, he was afraid she would wreak revenge upon him. But four or five years later, one of his horses ran away and he was forced to follow it into the forest. He came upon a hut with people, neither the hut nor the people had he ever seen before, and could not understand where they came from. At the door was an ugly woman and in the corner a small child who could have been four or five years old. The woman took a mug of beer and brought it to the child, "Take this, go out and bring your father a drink of beer." He was so terrified that he ran away. Since then he heard nothing more from the woman or the child, but strange he remained throughout his life.[155]

1346 The anima figure wants to "ensnare"[156] the boy with the ball of yarn; the spherical shape of the ball pretends to be something of the highest value, which turns out to be an illusion. The yarn symbolizes a kind of thread of fate that ties him to her, thus indicating the fatal and inescapable relationship that any genuine anima image involves. The cow's tail, which deters the young man, is basically a harmless reference to the animal-like background of the anima.[157] But the Christian (as opposed to primitive) attitude attaches something abominable, almost devilish, to this feature. This is why the wood-cutter turns to the old spiritual practices of the Christian Church that were used for exorcising and banning demons. By this he devalues, however, the experience of the anima, since she appears to him like some kind of spook.[158]

---

[155] Translated from Stroebe, *Nordische*, vol. 1, pp. 194–97; for the original, see Asbjörnsen and Møe, *Huldreeventyr*, vol. 1, p. 46, from the "medicine woman" in Hadeland, Norway. "[This version] could have provided the impetus for 'Per Gynt with the Green Ones in the Dovre Mountains,' and 'The Ugly Boy with the Beer Mug'" (Stroebe, *Nordische*, vol. 1, p. 197).

[156] [German *garn* = yarn; *umgarnen* = ensnare.]

[157] On demons with cow and goat tails, see Mannhardt, *Wald- und Feldkulte*, vol. 2, pp. 140, 146f.

[158] See Peuckert, *Volksglaube*, p. 78 for a parallel Finnish tale (summarized below):

> A young man once went looking for his horse that had run away. He found himself going deeper and deeper into the woods and came upon a maiden who invited him to her house "in the most distant corner of the forest." He stayed there and married the girl. But after some time the boy asked to see his mother . . . He was finally allowed to go. He should go at the next Sunday to the village church and walk up to the altar and put his head under the mantle of the priest. He would thereby become visible again because ever since his marriage he had become invisible. This he did. But it so happened that the priest recognized him and then gave him the Holy Communion. Then the boy stayed with his parents. But a restlessness overcame the boy, he took to wandering everywhere, ceaseless without stopping. Every day he would go into the woods looking for the way to his forest wife, but despite all his efforts, he never found her.

1347 An Icelandic example, which also describes the destruction caused by a cult practice, is "The Knight and the Forest Woman":

1348 In Germany there once lived a knight. He lived carelessly and lost all the inheritance that his rich father had bequeathed him. . . He then married a beautiful forest woman,[159] whom he had met alone by a stream, because she promised to give him money whenever he needed it and as much as he wanted. He lived happily with her for many years. They had two daughters and two sons. She fulfilled her promise and gave him as much money as he wanted whenever he wanted. She was also friendly and generous, and everyone liked her. She would attend the church services like everyone else, but never stayed for the Mass or took the communion wafer. She always found an excuse to leave at that moment. The people took to wondering about this and finally told the deacon, who was the husband's brother. The deacon had heard the gossip and quickly made off to his brother's house. There he found the woman alone with her children. He was welcomed kindly and they got along splendidly together. He remained there overnight and on the next day, prepared a service. He called the woman to attend. She came and the deacon read the Mass. When it came time for the Consecration, she said that she had to leave. "What for?" asked the Deacon. "I have an errand to attend to." The woman said. He bade her to remain, and stand still. She agreed. She stayed there into the quiet singing of the choral. Again, she said she had to leave, and the deacon again urged her to stay. She agreed, but soon became agitated again. She really had to take care of something. This time, the deacon threw a shawl around her shoulders and held her fast on the spot. Above

---

In the same reference, Peuckert retells yet another parallel:

> A lonely collier in the forest one day thought how nice it would be if someone would come to him in the evening and help him with his charcoal kiln. And as he was thinking this, a young woman came to him. She offered to help him clean up his charcoal pile if he would afterwards become her lover. He wanted to promise her this, and thought that it could actually end up that way, but it might be wise to first see how she worked. To this she agreed but then stipulated that he not look out the window of the hut in which he slept at that place where he made his charcoal. He slept for an hour, but then he quietly stood up, and very still he peeked out the window to see his beauty. There she was, working hard at the kiln. But she had fingers like the prongs of a pitchfork! She would shift the coals about with her fingers and quench the fire with her tail. When he saw all of her beauties, he began to curse: "Get out of here, go back to where you came from! I do not want you!" She walked away and behind her followed a great storm. (Peuckert, *Volksglaube*, p. 76.)

[159] For a definition of this figure, see Peuckert, *Volksglaube*, p. 79: "For in those earlier times when we first heard details of these wild women – even before the documents of the eleventh century – with names like "wild woman huts" or *ad domum wilderô wibô* [at the house of the wild woman] writes Burchard of Worms of the wild women, usually called the Forest Women . . . They would appear corporeally and showed themselves as their wont to men whom they had chosen to be their lovers. They would take their pleasure, and when satisfied, they would disappear and become completely invisible again."

> them was a chimney that drew out the smoke from the room. When the eucharist bread was raised high to be blessed, she took hold of her two daughters and they flew up and out the chimney. No one ever saw or heard of the woman or her daughters again. Her two sons, who had been brought up Christian, remained with her husband. They became rich and respected men. Their father later took another wife. No one has ever mentioned that the man encountered any kind of misfortune. And thus ends this strange story.[160]

1349 The Mass symbolizes Christ's becoming human and his sacrificial act to redeem mankind: that act of salvation in which, however, matter, and the spirit-world that resides within matter, do not partake. The Christian mystery reaches into the depths of humanity but does not descend into the darkness of nature and matter. It is often depicted as the ghostly anima, who longs for a human soul in order to partake of redemption and immortality,[161] or how she hates the Christian sacrament, because this builds an insurmountable barrier between her and the people. Psychologically, this barrier is a barrier to consciousness, which does not want to let certain dark regions of the soul belonging to nature break in.

1350 This motif of the demonic anima figure is especially widespread in Nordic tales from the time when Christianity did not completely prevail.[162] We meet this also in the fairytale, "Charcoal, Nils, and the Troll-Woman":

1351
> In the old days there lived on a headland that juts out into the northwestern corner of Lake Basval, in the neighborhood of the Limde mining district, a charcoal-burner named Nils, generally

[160] Translated in summary from H. and I. Naumann (trans.), *Isländische*, pp. 157–60.

[161] See Paracelsus, as quoted in Peuckert, *Volksglaube*, pp. 156–157: "But now they [the forest wenches] *are* people, but alone like animals without souls. Now it follows from this that they can be married, so that a water woman takes a man from Adam, and they make a home together and bear [children] . . . But now further it is also well known that such women also receive a soul, in that they are so conjoined that they like other women are before God and through God are redeemed. It follows now, that they vie for the man, bind themselves diligently, and secretly make themselves familiar, the same way a heathen, who asks and vies for baptism and courting so that he can attain a soul. Thus after such a love they set themselves against the people, that they are in the same covenant with them. For all understanding and wisdom is with them except the soul."

[162] For an example of the happy outcome of the conflict, see "The Troll Woman":

> A spook haunted the mountain hut of a certain family. It was told that there was a very beautiful girl among the mountain folk [i.e., trolls] who went about there. The son of the family, a dragoon, took up his arms and rode up to the haunted hut. Even from afar he saw a great fire burning in the hut, an old couple, and a beautiful girl. When he arrived at the hut, he saw that they all had cow's tails. In spite of this he fell directly in love with the girl. But when he raised his pistol over the girl's head and fired a shot, she became as ugly as she had been beautiful, and had a long nose pointing out from her face. By the shot, however, he had won her as a wife. For their marriage ceremony he asked that all the bridesmaids stand behind so that no one would notice their tails. As was their custom whenever they entertained guests, at the wedding the mountain folk left generous gifts of money behind for the newlyweds. Since he found her so hideous, the dragoon had, at first, handled his new wife with disrespect. Only when he watched her bend a horseshoe with her bare hands did he realize how strong she was and then he feared and respected her.

known as Charcoal Nils. He let a farmhand attend to his little plot of land, and he himself made his home in the forest, where he chopped wood in the summer and burned it to charcoal in the winter. Yet no matter how hard he struggled, his work was unblessed with reward, and no one ever spoke of him save as "Poor Charcoal Nils." One day, when he was on the opposite shore of the lake, near the gloomy Harsberg, a strange woman came up to him, and asked whether he needed someone to help him with his charcoal burning.

1352 "Yes, indeed," said he, "help would be very welcome." So she began to gather blocks of wood and tree trunks, more than Charcoal Nils could have dragged together with his horse, and by noon there was enough wood for a new kiln. When evening came, she asked the charcoal-burner whether he was satisfied with the day's work she had done, and if she should come back the next day. That suited the charcoal-burner perfectly, and she came back the next day and the following ones also. And when the kiln had been burned out she helped Nils clear it, and never before had he had such a quantity of charcoal, nor with charcoal of such fine quality.

1353 So she became his wife and lived with him in the wood for three years. He would occasionally return alone to his home in the village. The woman did not mind this, but had him promise that whenever he returned to the kiln, he should rap three times with his ax against an old pine tree near the entrance. They had three children, and this worried Nils but little, seeing that she looked after them and they gave him no trouble. But when the fourth year came, she grew more exacting, and insisted on going back to his home with him, and living with him there. Nils wished to hear nothing about this; yet since she was so useful to him in his charcoal-burning, he did not betray his feelings, and said he would think it over.

1354 It happened one Sunday that he went to church where he had not been for many years, and what he heard there brought up thoughts he had not known since the innocent days of his childhood. He began to wonder whether there were not some hocus-pocus about the charcoal-burning, and whether his success was due in part to the forest woman, who aided him so willingly.

1355 Preoccupied with this and other thoughts, he forgot while returning to his kiln, that he had promised to rap three times with his ax against the old pine tree before entering the kiln area. On this occasion, he forgot to make the sign, and as a result he saw something that nearly robbed him of his wits. As he drew near the kiln, he saw it all aflame, and around it stood the three children and their mother, and they were clearing out the kiln. They were pulling down and putting out so that flames, smoke and ashes whirled sky-high, but instead of the spruce-branches that were generally used to put out the fire, they had bushy tails which they dipped in the snow!

1356 When Charcoal Nils had watched this scene for a while, he slunk back to the old pine tree, and made its trunk echo to the sound of his three ax-strokes till one could hear them on the Harsberg. Then he went to the kiln, as though he had seen nothing, and all went on as before. The kiln was glowing with a handsome, even glow, and the tall woman was about and working as usual.

1357 As soon as she saw Charcoal Nils, she came back with her pressing demand that he take her home to his little house, and that they live there. "Yes, that shall come about," said Nils to console her, and turned back home saying that he was going to fetch a horse. But instead he went out on the headline of Kallernas, on the eastern shore of Lake Kasval, where a wise man lived, and asked the latter what he should do. The old man advised him to go home and hitch his horse to his charcoal-wagon, but to hitch the horse in such wise that there would be not a single loop either in the harness or the traces. Then he was to mount the horse and ride back to the kiln without stopping, have the troll-woman and her children get into the wagon, and at once drive out on the ice with them.

1358 The charcoal-burner did as the old man told him, saddled his horse, paying strict attention that there were no loops in the saddle or bridle, rode across the ice through the wood to his kiln, and told the troll-woman and her children to get in. Then he quickly turned back through the wood, out onto the ice, and there let his horse run as fast as he could. When he reached the middle of the lake, he saw a pack of wolves running along in the direction of Abodaland, at the northern end of the lake, and heading for the ice. Then he tore the saddle-harness from the traces so that the wagon with the troll-folk was left standing on the bare ice, and he rode as fast as his horse could carry him for the opposite shore. When the trolls saw the wolves they began to scream.

1359 "Turn back, turn back!" cried the mother. "And if you will not for my sake, then at least do so for the sake of Vipa (Peewee), your youngest daughter!" But Charcoal Nils rode for the shore without looking back. Then he heard the troll-woman calling on others for aid.

1360 "Brother in the Hars Mountains, Sister in Stripa, Cousin in Ring Rocks; Take the loop and pull!" "There is no loop to pull!" came the answer from deep within the Harsberg. "Then catch him at

> Harkallarn." "He is not riding in that direction." The reply came from Ringfels.

> 1361 And indeed Charcoal Nils did not ride in that direction; but over stick and stone straight to his own home. Yet when he reached his own courtyard, the horse fell, and a shot from the trolls tore away a corner of the stable. Nils shortly after fell sick, and had to lie abed for a number of weeks. When he was well again he sold his forest land, and worked the little farm by the cottage until his death. So that was one occasion when the troll-folk came off second best.[163]

1362 In this tale, the troll woman wants to finagle the man into a human marriage, out of a similar desire as the woman in "The Mermaid and the Great Dubhdach." But the anima's dark and dangerous nature aspect lurks in the background as the troll-woman's "Brother in Hars Mountain," "Sister Stripa," and "Cousin in the Ring Rocks." The bushy tails of the woman and the little half-trolls indicate their animal nature. Going to church enlivens the Christian-cult consciousness and the critical attitude towards the connection. This saves the collier from his uncomfortable situation. But since he does not fulfill his obligations to this soul figure, and instead flees from her, he loses his horse and becomes ill. His body and instincts suffer from part of the soul being split off. Evidently, he never again dared to go into the forest, which symbolizes the unconscious, but became a tiller of the soil.[164]

1363 In a number of Nordic fairytales, the spirit-world of the trolls is portrayed as dangerous and in strong opposition to Christianity due to the relatively primitive mentality of the storyteller, for whom the unconscious world, which evidently could overpower him, presents a great danger. For him or her, Christianity leads to a more conscious state. The anima experience is dismissed as being a spook.

1364 Only a few fairytales within Christian culture attempt to incorporate the anima figure into the doctrinal scheme. These allow her to appear as a "daughter of God" (as in "The Good Lord's Godchild" and "God's Son-In-Law and the Judge"). In most other fairytales where the anima is positive, she is the daughter of a dark father figure, a chthonic deity. It appears that fairytales are relatively untouched by Christianity. It is mainly a peculiarity of Norse tales that raise the question of the relationship between the fairytale characters and Christianity. In general, the Norse tales depict these figures as destructive elements, because they devalue the nature deities and the anima.

---

163 [Slightly edited from Stroebe, *The Swedish Fairy Book*, pp. 162–66. Stroebe (p. 166) notes: "Malicious as the troll-folk are, when a marriage takes place between a troll-woman and a human being, the woman is beyond reproach, good and kind, the only reproach that can be made her is that she is not a Christian."]

164 For a variation on this tale and other material, see Mannhardt, *Wald- und Feldkulte*, vol. 1, pp. 134ff.

1365 Returning to the monster-like quality of the magical woman described in the tale of Charcoal Nils, we should add that sometimes even with non-Christian people the anima figure is devalued out of fear, because she makes the man strange and can prevent him from performing his daily tasks, that is, his struggles with nature. Different Japanese fairytales describe pretty girls who, however, belong to the tribe of forest devils, approach men who live alone, and seek to lure them into ruin. Such a maiden (as for instance "The Woman Who Ate Nothing,") tried to carry the man in a *sake* barrel into the woods where he just managed to escape her devilish relations. A similar tale is "The Woman Who Ate No Rice":

1366 A forest witch, a *Jamababa*, offered an old cooper to be his wife, saying that he need not provide food for her, she needed nothing to eat. He secretly observed that she had a mouth under her hair in the middle of her head, with which she covertly ate everything that he had when he was not at home. When he tried with the help of a friend to get rid of her, she ate his friend, packed the man, who was frozen in fear, like a kitten in her hands, put him on her head, and ran off into the forest. The man managed to jump onto a passing branch and learned that two plants just nearby caused her decay: mugwort (*Artemisia vulgaris*) and iris. Having now lost his fear, he jumped down, grabbed the plants, and threw them on the she-demon who perished on the spot.

1367 Also related is another tale from Japan, "The Witch's Daughter":

Once when a man was bathing in a washtub in front of his house, the *Yamaonna*[165] carried him away. He escaped up into a tree. When the she-demon had left, he came down from the tree and followed the *Yamaonna* unnoticed until she came to her cave. When the *Yamaonna* had disappeared into the cave, the man secretly listened in at the entrance and heard the following conversation between the old witch and her daughter. "Mother, I have brought with me today a handsome man to be my bridegroom," said the daughter, and laid the tub on the ground. When she saw that the man had escaped, she became very angry and began to swear. Then said the old witch, her mother, "I always have told you that you will never find a husband, now you can see for yourself this is true!" The witch's daughter then said, "The next time I will turn myself into a spider and catch him in my web, then he will certainly not get away and I will bring him here." "O, my daughter, the people in the village are dreadfully clever and cunning,

165 [Mountain woman.]

look well after yourself. If you turn yourself into a spider and the man gives you a blow with his right hand, then that is not bad. But if he smashes you with his left hand, then it can cost you your life." Now when the man had heard this, he returned home. In the middle of the next night he saw a large spider who let itself down from the ceiling above his bed. He remembered what he had heard outside the cave and dealt the spider a blow with his left hand. The spider let out a cry of pain and suddenly disappeared before his eyes. Since that time he was never bothered by the pursuits of the witch's daughter.[166]

1368 Here the anima appears as a second figure next to the evil Great Mother. This shows how closely its image is related to that of the mother archetype,[167] and how the Great Mother represents the deadly, devouring power of the unconscious. The mother is the first bearer of the anima image in men.[168] This is the reason why many myths and fairytales portray the anima character as a kind of mother-mistress. A good example of this is "The Adventures of Matandua, the One-Eyed," in which the hero's drowned mother takes on a ghostly anima role towards her son and becomes his spiritual guide. The moon fairy in the Chinese tale "The Lady of the Moon" is also a half-anima, half-mother image.

1369 Occasionally, the anima's negative aspect is mixed with the image of the devouring mother. A Yukaghir fairytale, "Tale About Three Storks," tells about a man who did not know where he was born. The Yukaghir thought that they were all born of this man. He was rich in everything. One time, a She-Monster came to him and wanted to be his wife. The She-Monster said, "You must take me for your wife. Otherwise I shall devour you." To save his life, the man married the She-Monster, but later freed himself from this devouring mother-anima. "He found and won a new girl. This one belonged to the other side, the stork tribe, and became his new wife."[169] Here, the hero gains a positive anima relationship, through which he overcomes the She-Monster, who is turned into a sea-worm by the stork helpers. Thus, she embodies the anima's chthonic aspect, the unconscious, as an animal soul. This aspect of the anima is almost always described as dangerous and, therefore, the separation from her is often regarded as liberating.[170]

166 Rumpf, *Japanische Volksmärchen*, pp. 180–181.

167 On the psychologically related connection between the two figures in Gnosticism, see Bousset, *Hauptprobleme der Gnosis*, chapters 1 and 2.

168 See C.G. Jung, "Relation between the ego and the unconscious," CW 7, ¶314. See also the fairytale, "Youth Without Age and Life Without Death," in which the hero has first to overcome two witches before he reaches the forever-young anima figure.

169 Bogoras, *Tales of the Yukaghir*, pp. 35–38. [Her helpful relatives, the storks, also freed the new wife from a destructive two-headed eagle, "the mightiest of all creatures," before she and her husband got back to his home and lived happily ever after.]

170 See also the fairytale, "How a Girl as a Witch Tortured Many Young Men to Death," which we merely summarize here:

1370 In a Chinese fairytale, "The Poison Mixer," the anima is represented as a wild woman, who gives her unfaithful husband a poison that rises in him as a golden serpent:

1371 Once upon a time, a traveling salesman from the north, was on a long tour in the south of China. He took a woman to wife who came from a wild tribe in those lands. They lived together in the southern lands for some time and had children together. Then one day he told her that he had to go back to his home for a while. But his wife did not trust him and put a bit of her magical poison in a glass of wine. After he had drunk it, she told him that if he forgot her and their children, the poison would work. He left and after two years, he thought to himself, "Surely there is no poison that works after such a long time," and he indeed forgot all about his wife in the south. One day, after he had drunk a bit of wine, he got an awful feeling in his throat and suddenly a golden snake stuck its head out, leaving its tail still in his stomach. He realized that this was the poison and quickly packed up and went back to the woman in the south. Once there, he apologized sincerely and she forgave him. With a nod she made the snake disappear. From then on, the man traveled only short distances and never broke his promise to return back to her soon.[171]

1372 Another Yukaghir tale, "Smallpox (version 2)," tells of the anima as a red, disease-producing demoness that destroyed people. A powerful shaman from one village managed to subdue her through his magical arts so that his village was spared and only the neighboring tribes suffered. Once more, the anima is depicted entirely negatively, just as splitting off, through consciously drawing boundaries, is perceived as an act of redemption. Another possibility is that the hero defeats the initially hostile anima through his power or trickery and

---

Every night a girl killed young boys who were sleeping at her house. (See the same motif in *The Book of Tobit* 7-8.) She changed herself into a horse and trampled the boys to death until a young man, upon the advice of an old woman, threw a bridle over her, and she turned into a mare. He then rode upon her for two nights whereupon she died. Her father demanded that he bury her. The old woman gave him a candle, with which he sat on the edge of the stove, reading and speaking prayers and drew a protective circle around himself. In the night the girl rose out of her coffin and asked a lot of devils to torture him. But they could not find him and the rooster crowed. This was repeated a second night in which the young man had to protect himself with two circles. In the third night, the primordial mother advised one of the devils to set the cornice on fire to get through the three circles and reach the young man. This time the protective circles held out until the cock crowed. In the end and with much effort, the boy succeeded in following the last piece of advice from the old woman. He went to the graveyard where the witch-woman was and drove a stake into her chest. Since then she stirred no more and the father gave the lad the money he had agreed upon.

See also the term *Alpdruck* [German for "mountain pressure, pushing"], as caused by the anima and her "pressure-walk," in Laistner, *Das Rätsel*, pp. 42f., 105; see also "Big Raven and the Evil Spirits," where the hero wins over the anima from the realm of evil spirits.

[171] Wilhelm, *The Chinese Fairy Book*, pp. 227–229.

wins her to be a loving wife. There is a very different type of fairytale, compiled by Aarne,[172] in which the anima steals the hero's magic objects and treats him ignominiously until he overcomes her. One such tale is "The Beautiful One of the Earth" (summarized below) :

1373 A certain youth once sacrificed his whole fortune to win the Beautiful One of the Earth. The Beautiful One accepted all his gifts, promised her love, and then ruthlessly tortured him. He offered even more gifts and was then promptly punished for every further gift. In his frenzy of love he plundered his family's cellar for still more valuables to give her. In doing this, he came across a cloak that made the bearer invisible. With this cloak he got into her castle again and even to her presence. But again she foiled him and got him to give her the cloak. With each failure he became even more determined to get the Beautiful One. He found a pot that when rubbed would conjure up an army of magical warriors. With this impressive army, she let him into her castle again. But then she promptly fooled him into giving her his magical pot and chased him away again. Next he came across some special red and white grapes. If someone ate the red grapes, little horns would appear all over their body, if they then eat the white ones, the little horns would all disappear. Now the Beautiful One loved grapes and so she gratefully accepted his gift of the red ones. When she ate them, little horns sprung up all over her body, which horrified her no end. Then the hero arrived at her castle disguised as a doctor. He promised to cure her, but only if she told him, on her word, the truth and all of the truth. She agreed and confessed to all she had done. The doctor then asked for all the objects she received through her ruthless behavior. Naturally, she had not told the whole the truth, but the doctor-hero knew what was true and what not, and demanded that she tell him everything. Only when she gave him all the objects, did he give her the white grapes. She was immediately healed. Now he rubbed his pot and the magical army appeared. This time he was in charge and demanded she return to his home with him as his wife. He commanded the army to raise her whole palace and bring it to his family. This they did, and the couple, with the hero's parents, lived happily together for the rest of their lives.[173]

---

[172] Aarne, *Types*, 1961, and Ashliman (ed.), *A Guide to Folktales in the English Language: Based on the Aarne-Thompson Classification System*, 1987. See also "Donkey Cabbages," "The Purse, the Whistle, and the Hat," "The Magic Ring," and "Peter's Three Gifts."

[173] Leskien, *Balkanmärchen*, pp. 244–251.

1374 The anima proves here to be an irrepressible and unpredictable demon who truly harms and torments the man. She misuses his passion for her and ruthlessly strips from him, one-by-one, all his conscious values and masculine advantages. We see here the basis of the fairytale motif of the hero being transformed, by a curse, or by a Nereid, or a similar anima figure.[174] It is a typical effect of the anima on a man that expresses itself when he appears "effeminate" and "moody" and his characteristic level is lowered. He can only redress this situation if he manages to recognize the paradoxical nature and double aspect of all unconscious phenomena, and to be able to deal with this. He must know that the anima can cuckold him, make him look ridiculous, laughable, absurd, or even make him act like an animal.[175] She can also, however, redeem him from this state. The magic of the fruits symbolizes the anima's effect. When the hero gives her the red and white grapes and lets those work, he reveals her dual nature, as an evil animal and as a beautiful woman. She loses her negative power through this characterization. But only the superior and the chosen or called heroes are up to this task.

1375 In fairytales, the anima's dual aspect is often also represented by the juxtaposition of two women, a black and a white bride, or a true and a false bride. In all the examples of this duality, the two women are one and the same and the theme is her twofold impact.[176]

1376 A fairytale in which the anima is portrayed solely in a negative and dangerous role, and in which the hero fails to elicit her positive side, is "The Strange Boy":

> 1377 At a village far away in the north there once lived a man with his wife and one child, a son. This boy was very different from others, and while the village children ran about and shouted and took part in sports with one another, he would sit silent and thoughtful on the roof of the *kashim*. He would never eat any food or take any drink but that given him by his mother.
>
> 1378 The years passed by until he grew to manhood, but his manner was always the same. Then his mother began to make him a pair of skin boots with soles of many thicknesses, a waterproof coat of double thickness, and a fine coat of yearling reindeer skins. Every day he sat on the roof of the *kashim*, going home at twilight for food and to sleep until early the next morning; then he would go back to his place on the roof and wait for daybreak.

---

174 See, for example, "The Man Who was Changed into a Woman and then Back to a Man," "The Story of Cefa and Sefa"; on the *Secret of King Oddur*, see Bolte and Polívka, *Anmerkungen*, vol. 3, p. 80.

175 In one variant, the hero becomes a donkey; see Aarne, *Vergleichende Märchenforschungen. Akademische Abhandlung*, p. 91.

176 For more details, see vol. 2 (*Archetypal Symbols in Fairytales: Antitheses and Renewal*), Book IIb.

1379 One morning he went home just after sunrise and found his new clothing ready. He took some food and put on the clothing and told his mother that he was going on a journey to the north. His mother cried bitterly and begged him not to go, for no one ever went to the far northland and returned again. He did not mind this, but taking his bear spear and saying farewell, he started out, leaving his parents weeping and without hope of ever seeing him again.

1380 The young man traveled far that day, and as evening came on he reached a hut with smoke rolling up through the hole in the roof. Taking off his waterproof coat, he laid it down near the door and crept carefully upon the roof and looked through the smoke hole. In the middle of the room burned a fire, and an old woman was sitting on the farther side, while just under him was an old man making arrows. As the young man lay on the roof, the man on the inside cried out, without even raising his head, "Why do you lie there on the outside? Come in." Surprised at being noticed by the old man without the latter even looking up, he arose and went in. When he entered the house the man greeted him and asked why he was going to the north in search of a wife. The old man continued, "There are many dangers there and you had better turn back. I am your father's brother and mean well by you. Beyond here people are very bad, and if you go on you may never return."

1381 The young man was very much surprised to be told the goal of his journey when he had not revealed it even to his parents. After taking some food he slept until morning, then he prepared to go on his way. The old man gave him a small black object filled with a yellow substance like the yolk of an egg, saying, as he did so, "Perhaps you will have little to eat on your way, and this will give you strength." The traveler swallowed it at once and found it very strong to the taste, so that it made him draw a deep breath, saying, as he did so, "Ah, I feel strong." The young man took up his spear and went on. He came again to a solitary hut and experienced the same as before. The old man also warned him about going north but saw that it was no use. This time the old man gave him a small, clear, white object, telling the traveler that he would not get much to eat on the road, and the object would help him. The young man at once swallowed the clear white thing, but did not find it as strong as the object he had swallowed the day before. The old man said that if he heard anything on the way which frightened him, then he must do the first thing that came into his mind.

1382 "I will have no one to weep for me should anything happen," said the traveler, and he journeyed on, spear in hand. Toward the middle of the day, he came to a large pond lying near the seashore, so he turned off to go around it on the inland side. When he had passed part of the way around the lake, he heard a frightful roar like a clap of thunder. It was so loud that it made him dizzy and for a moment he lost all sense of his surroundings. He hurried forward, but every few moments the terrible noise was repeated, each time making him reel and feel giddy, even to the point of fainting, but still he kept on. The noise became even louder and it seemed to come nearer at every roar, until it sounded like it was on one side very close to him. Looking in the direction whence it came, he saw a large basket made of woven willow roots floating towards him in the air, and from it came the fearful noise.

1383 Seeing a hole in the ground close by, the traveler jumped into it just as a terrible crash shook the earth and rendered him unconscious. He lay as if dead for some time, while the basket kept moving about as if searching for him and continuously giving out the fearful sounds. When the young man's senses returned, he listened for a short time, and, everything having become quiet, went outside of his shelter and looked about. Close by, the basket was resting on the ground with a man's head and shoulders poking out of its top. The moment he saw them, the young man cried out, "What are you waiting for? Go ahead, don't stop! Let me hear one of those good loud noises from you!" Then he sprang back into the hole again and was instantly struck senseless by the fearful noise made by the basket. When he had recovered sufficiently he went out again, but he could no longer find the basket. Then he raised both of his hands and called upon the thunder and lightning to come to his aid. Just then the basket came near again, with only the man's head sticking out from the top. The young man called the thunder and lightning to roar and lash out at the basket. Thunder and lightning obeyed and roared and crashed with such force that the basket shaman began to tremble with fear and fell to the ground.

1384 As soon as the thunder stopped, the basket began to retreat, the shaman being almost dead from fear. The young man cried out, "Thunder, pursue him; go in front of him and behind him, and terrify him!" Thunder did so, and the basket floated away slowly, falling to the ground now and then. Then the traveler went on and arrived at a village just at twilight. As he drew near, a boy came out from the village to meet him, saying, "How do you come here from that direction? No one has ever come here from that side before, for the basket shaman allows no living thing to pass by the lake! Nothing, not even a mouse! He always knows when anything comes that way and goes out to meet and destroy them."

1385 "I did not see anything," said the traveler. "Well, you have not escaped yet," said the boy, "for there is the basket man now, and he will kill you unless you go back." When the young man looked he saw a great eagle rise and fly toward him, and the boy from the village quickly ran away. As the eagle neared him, it rose a short distance and then turned down to seize him with its claws. As it dove down, the young man struck himself on the breast with one hand and a gerfalcon darted forth from his mouth straight toward the eagle, flying directly into its abdomen and passing out of its mouth and away into the air.

1386 This gerfalcon was from the strong substance that the young man had been given by the first old man on the road. When the gerfalcon flew out from the mouth of the eagle, the eagle closed its eyes, gasping for breath. This gave the young man the chance to jump to one side so that the eagle's claws struck only the earth where he had been standing. Again the eagle flew up and then dove back down, and again the young man struck his breast with his hand. This time an ermine sprang from his mouth and darted like a flash of light at the eagle. It lodged itself under the bird's wings, and in a few moments had eaten its way twice back and forth through the bird's side. The eagle fell to the ground, dead, whereupon the ermine jumped off and vanished. This ermine came from the gift of the second man at whose hut the traveler had stopped.

1387 When the eagle fell, the young man started towards the shaman's house, and the boy cried out to him, "Don't go there, for you will be killed!" To this the traveler replied, "I don't care, I wish to see the women there. I will go now, for I am angry, and if I wait till morning my anger will be gone and I will not be as strong as I am at present." "You had better wait till morning," said the boy, "for there are two bears guarding the door and they will surely kill you. But if you will go, then go and be destroyed. I have tried to save you and I will have nothing more to do with you." And the boy went angrily back to the *kashim*. The young man then went on to the house and looked into the entrance passage. He saw a very large white bear lying there asleep. He called out, "Ah, White Bear!" at which the bear sprang up and ran at him. The young man leaped up to the top of the passageway and, as the bear ran out at him, he drove the point of his spear into its brain, so that it fell dead. Then he drew the body to one side, looked in again, and saw a red bear lying there. Again he called out, "Ah, Red Bear!" The red bear ran out at him and he sprang up to his former place. The red bear struck at him with one of its forepaws as it passed, and the young man caught the paw in his hand and, swinging the bear about his head, threw it to the ground, swung it up and threw it down again. This he repeated until there was nothing but the paw left, and this he threw away. Then entered the house without any further trouble.

1388 Sitting at the side of the room were an old man and woman, and on the other side there was a beautiful young woman whose image he had seen in his dreams that had caused him to make his long journey. She was crying when he went in, and he went and sat beside her, saying, "What are you crying for; who do you love so much that you cry for them?" To which she replied, "You have killed my husband, but I am not sorry for that, for he was an evil man. But then you killed the two bears. They were my brothers, and I feel badly and cry for them." "Do not cry," he said, "for I will be your husband." Here he remained for a time, taking this woman for his wife and living in the house with her parents. After he had lived there for a while, he saw that his wife and her parents became more and more gloomy, and they cried very often. Then he saw things done that made him think they intended to do him evil. Becoming sure of this, he went to his wife and put his hand on her forehead. He turned her face to him, and said: "You are planning to kill me, you unfaithful woman, and as a punishment you shall die." Then taking his knife, he cut his wife's throat, and went gloomily back to his village, where he lived with his parents as before. When the memory of his unfaithful wife had become faint, he took a wife from among the maidens of the village and lived happily with her the rest of his days.[177]

1389 Here the anima lives far to the north in the land of darkness.[178] According to ancient Germanic belief, the north is the land of the dead and the abode of giants, which are hostile to the gods.[179] Also, the "wild hunt" comes from the north.[180] In Mediterranean belief, the north is the area of the bear, a dark

---

[177] Nelson, *Eskimo - Bering Strait*, pp. 491–94.

[178] See the tale of an anima figure as an odd bear character in "The Man Who Visited the Polar Bears."

[179] See Mogk, *Germanische*, pp. 60, 117: an iron forest separates the empire of giants from the kingdom of the gods.

[180] See Ninck, *Wodan*, p. 81. See also Goethe:

> [The spirits] drive impetuous from the frozen north,
> With fangs sharp-piercing, and keen arrowy tongues.

(*Faust*, Part I [line 1130 in the German original]). Ancient heathen Germans prayed towards the North. See Ninck, *Wodan*, p. 98. Also in China, the north is the region of darkness and death. See Pelliot, "Die Jenseitsvorstellung der Chinesen," p. 71f. According to the Menomini, "In the direction of the north wind live the *manabai'wok* (giants), of whom we have heard our old people tell. The *manabai'wok* are our friends, but we do not see them any more. They are great hunters and fishermen, and whenever they are out with their torches to spear fish we know it, because then the sky is bright over the place where they are." (Hoffman, "The Menomini Indians," p. 210.)

circle of fire, from which the north wind blows as an enemy of the Sun.[181] In Scandinavian fairytales, the deserted wondrous realm of the trolls lies in the North.

1390 The north is thus a symbol of the unconscious; on his way there, the hero meets his ancestors at two places. Thus, the north is also the land of the dead and the spirit-world among the Inuit. As ghosts and spirits, the ancestors are supposed to know all thoughts. In another Inuit fairytale, "The Story of Wolf," the hero is helped by a dead elderly couple on his journey to the beyond because they will receive their grandchild through him. "When dead folk are afoot on Earth, their graves become houses." They spoke to the wolf as if he was their grandchild. Rasmussen's storyteller, *Apákag*, said, "Now Wolf had won the ghosts's friendship and obtained their power and protection, and later this was to be of great gain to him."[182] In the regeneration rites of certain indigenous cultures, the ancestors from the *Alcheringa* time play an important role. This refers to a confrontation with ancestral elements in the unconscious. The ancestors are superior to the living since they represent that ideal prehistory. In rites with the heroes of the past who dwell at the source of life, or with animal ancestors, the people sit together with these ancestral in a kind of renewal bath.[183] In *Kalevala*, the Finnish epic, "the hero Wäinämöinen learns three magic words in the belly of a monster, his dead ancestor. . ."[184]

1391 The hero of our tale increases his "strangeness," in that he only wants to go to the North, that land of origin steeped in the deepest mystery, where the world soul lives hidden in darkness. Microcosmically, this is where the soul resides in the deepest unconsciousness. Before he embarks on this perilous journey, his more conscious forces and the images of his ancestors warn him, yet in vain.

1392 The fact that he is "strange" from the beginning " is already evident in him only eating those foods that his mother gives him; also, he lives quietly absorbed in his own thoughts at home. This attachment to the mother is a bond with the unconscious, because the mother is the first image of women in the man's soul, and embodies for him the unconscious, which is why the separation from her, and in general the right relationship with her, is often

---

[181] See Leisegang, *Die Gnosis*, p. 23.

[182] Rasmussen, *Eagle's Gift*, p. 142.

[183] See C.G. Jung, *Psychology and Alchemy*, CW 12, ¶170ff; see further Rousselle, "Lau Dsi's Gang durch Seele, Geschichte und Welt. Versuch einer Deutung," p. 188. In China, the unconscious therefore means the land of the ancestors; see Wilhelm, *Secret of the Golden Flower*, p. 112, and C.G. Jung, "Rebirth," CW 9i, ¶224f. Daudet supposes that the structure of the personality contains ancestral elements, which under certain conditions may suddenly come to the fore. The individual is then precipitously thrust into an ancestral role. Now we know that ancestral roles play a very important part in primitive psychology. Not only are the ancestral spirits supposed to be reincarnated in children, but an attempt is made to implant them into the child by naming after an ancestor. So, too, primitives try to change themselves back into their ancestors by means of certain rites, I would mention especially the Australian conception of the *alcheringa mijina*. (See Lévy-Bruhl *La Mythologie primitive*, [who writes] on ancestral souls, half-man and half-animal, whose reactivation through religious rites is of the greatest functional significance for the life of the tribe.)

[184] Silberer, *Problems of Mysticism*, p. 314.

essential for his whole life.[185] It even seems that "the image of the 'soul' [anima] somehow coincides with the mother-imago."[186] The anima is actually a rejuvenation of the mother herself.[187] For this reason, the figures of a mother and a daughter are often found together in mythology. The most well-known pair is probably Demeter and Persephone, the two main figures of the Eleusinian mysteries. In the Inuit tale, "Giviok (Kiviok)" (retold above on page 217), a daughter always stood next to the mother-witch. Thus, the overwhelming power of the anima is already contained in the supremacy of the mother. In our present tale, "The Strange Boy," this power of the feminine possesses the boy and makes him "different" from the beginning and also binds him to her.[188] The youth is thus partly called to heroism by his attachment to the unconscious, and partly beholden to the unconscious in a negative sense. This situation is present throughout the whole story. Jung writes on this problem:

1393 > . . . at the root of the regressive longing. . . [lies] a specific value and a specific need which are made explicit in myths. It is precisely the strongest and best among men, the heroes, who give way to their regressive longing and purposely expose themselves to the danger of being devoured by the monster of the maternal abyss. But if a man is a hero, he is a hero because, in the final reckoning, he did not let the monster devour him, but subdued it, not once but many times.[189]

1394 The "strange" youth does not, however, succeed.

1395 At first, the hero gains the power of his ancestral souls, and with them defeats the dark powers of the depths and finds the woman he sought. Yet the whole journey ends in profound tragedy: in the end, he returns home, disillusioned, turns completely away from the unconscious, and barely finds a connection to ordinary life.

1396 The ancestors impart the knowledge of the dangers and give the youth the necessary help. They convey strength, just like the white horse in "Ferdinand the Faithful and Ferdinand the Unfaithful," who in some versions warns the hero and in others advises him to ride onwards; it both inhibits and promotes. A divine father figure stands hidden behind this horse. The ancestors give the hero a small black object, filled with a yellow substance like the yolk of an egg, that transforms into a helpful gerfalcon and the white thing that turns into a

---

[185] See C.G. Jung, "Relation between the ego and the unconscious," CW 7, ¶314.
[186] Ibid., *Symbols of Transformation*, CW 5, ¶406, ¶514.
[187] Ibid., *"Mother Archetype,"* CW 9i, ¶156.
[188] Ibid., "Archetypes of the Collective Unconscious," CW 9i, ¶61: "For the son, the anima is hidden in the dominating power of the mother, and sometimes she leaves him with a sentimental attachment that lasts throughout life and seriously impairs the fate of the adult."
[189] Ibid., *Relation*, CW 7, ¶260, ¶477.

helpful ermine. These animal allies bestow magical opposing forces for the upcoming battle against the anima's demonic husband. These gifts maintain the hero's protection by the ancestors, in a similar way as, according to some Australian tribes the *tjurunga* (or *churinga*) connects the individual to the ancestors. It represents the individual's second ego or "second self."[190] The ancestors advise the strange boy in an even more significant way to act in the magical realm: according to his instincts, without conscious deliberation or inhibitions. Also, the helpful animals that emerge from the gifts most likely symbolize spontaneous helpful reactions. The egg also means being whole in the germ. By a pond, the wandering youth is halted by the appearance of a basket shaman. He is presented with the choice, either to drown in the waters of the pond (the unconscious) or to vie himself with the dark demon. In the first half of the struggle, he manages due to his own skill, while in the second half he must rely on the powers received from the ancestors.

1397 Like the container, the basket is a female symbol. Here, however, it contains a male demon. The basket shaman is thus a combination of witch and giant, an embodiment of the power of the unconscious in its primal hermaphroditic form as an undifferentiated, totally unconscious being, in which the divine powers of shadow and anima are merged into one. Since the young woman calls the figure of the basket shaman and the great eagle her husband, we can consider the basket shaman as a primitive shape of the anima herself, which later emerges as representing the dark, negative side of the magical. In "Tapairu, the Beauty from the Land of the Fairies" and "Ititaujang," a shadow companion or nature demon also appeared next to the anima figure. In a Norwegian tale, "Farther South Than South and Farther North Than North and in the Great Hill of Gold" (see page 72),

> 1398 [A] young farm lad wants to discover why his father's wheat fields are being trampled every night. After his two older brothers fell asleep at the task he went to a lower field and managed to stay awake. He observed how three doves flew to the field, took off their feather dresses and turned into "the most beautiful maidens one would want to see." The young man first asks them why they dance and trample the wheat fields.
>
> 1399 "Alas, it is not our fault," said the maidens. "The troll who has enchanted us sends us here every Saturday night to trample the field. But now give us our feathers, for morning is near." And they begged for them in the sweetest way. "I do not know about that," said the young fellow, "you have trampled down the field very badly; perhaps if I might choose and have one of you?" "That would please us,"

[190] See Lévy-Bruhl, *The "Soul" of the Primitive*, pp. 189 and 191.

returned the maidens, "but it would not be possible; for three trolls guard us: one with three, one with six and one with nine heads, and they kill all who come to the mountain."...

1400 [The boy later defeats the trolls and frees the princesses.][191]

1401 But here the primitive man fails. He overcomes the last danger – the negative anima – not with consciousness but in anger, in a frenzy, and semi-aware of the trouble. He lets his affect take over despite the warnings from a boy from the village, who appears to represent a better, more reasonable ego. (Since the hero lives out exclusively his strange side, this shadow characterizes his unknown, compensatory "reasonable" side.) The entrance to the hut is guarded by two bears, of red and white color. Red and white – as mentioned earlier – are colors of the underworld. The bears appear here, with respect to their fierce power, as guardians. They represent affects and emotions, and their two colors perhaps hint at a latent conflict between them. But whereas the shaman in "Flight to the Moon" entrusts his bear-spirit to protect his passage by the walruses standing on guard – and so does not involve his consciousness in the conflict,[192] the hero in "The Strange Boy" succumbs to his own affects and emotions and slays the anima's bear brothers. Like the alligator brother in "Makonaura and Anuanaitu," they represent the shadow. To brutally eliminate the anima's companions instead of accepting them forebodes disaster. Similarly, the basket shaman was a shadow figure, but even the anima herself says he was a bad man. The bear brothers, on the other hand, are animal forces of nature, the morally neutral and more positive side of the shadow.

1402 The anima mourns and, seeking revenge, decides to kill the hero. The hero realizes this, anticipates her plan, and returns, disappointed, to secular life. Killing the anima means that he turns completely away from this figure, devalues her, forcefully, with his rational mind, and pushes her back into the unconscious. He thus frees himself from his strangeness and his obsession, can marry in the profane world and, what is important, can lead a normal life. But he has passed by all those special possibilities that experiencing the unconscious offers. He could have become a great shaman had he experienced his journey more knowingly.

1403 For the primitive mind, the danger of being overwhelmed by the unconscious is, however, so great that it often views this only as destructive. The Inuit fairytale, "The False Woman who Became a Night Owl," tells of a purely negative anima experience:

---

[191] Stroebe, *Norwegian Fairy Book*, pp. 228–35.

[192] Compare the tailor in "The Two Travelers," who lets the animals act against the cobbler and does not let himself get directly involved in retaliation.

1404 There was once a caribou hunter who went hunting by the sea. He walked and walked and continued walking until he came to the banks of a big and foaming river. There he heard a voice – a lovely voice singing a song – and he listened and listened, until he could distinguish the words.

1405 Come, come
Lonely hunter,
In twilight stillness.
Come, come,
Long have I missed thee – missed thee,
Now will I Kiss thee – kiss thee!
Come! Come!
Near is my nest.
Come! come!
Lonely hunter Even now,
In twilight stillness!

1406 The hunter was overwhelmed by an irresistible longing. With all his might, he ran after the sound, along the bank of the river, running like a man who had lost all his senses, until he saw a lovely young woman sitting on a cliff on the opposite river bank and beckoning to him. But the river was big and broad and foaming, and the hunter stopped irresolute until the woman again took up her song:

1407 Come! come!
Lonely Hunter
Even now,
In twilight stillness!

1408 Immediately he threw off all his clothes and sprang out into the river. As he swam on and on in the cold stream, he became caught by the current. He battled and battled desperately, sometimes above and sometimes under the water, until half dead, numb with cold and exhausted he reached the other bank and ran up to the woman, who sat upon the cliffs beckoning and smiling. But at the very moment that he reached her, she burst into scornful laughter, changed into a night owl, and flew away laughing. Half dead with cold, the hunter staggered down again to the river. His clothes lay on the other bank – he again took to the freezing waters. He swam on and on, battled again against the currents, and he finally reached the other shore. But when his foot touched the ground, he sank down prostrated. He lost consciousness and froze to death.

1409 That was where his comrades found him. And no one understood what had happened to the great and famous caribou hunter. For he lay there naked and frozen to death, and just beside him lay his warm clothing. All thought he had lost his reason. No one knew the nature of the quarry that he had hunted.[193]

1410 Here, the anima appears as an evil nocturnal spirit who lures the hero to ruin.

1411 Of course, even among primitive peoples, the relationship to the anima and remaining in the magical sphere was not always considered negatively. In "Rakian," for instance, the hero, after a tragic separation, succeeds in following the anima figure into the otherworld. In contrast to Ati, the hero of the tale, "Tapairu, the Beauty from the Land of the Fairies," Rakian manages to carry the anima's redemption from the animal aspect into the spirit-world. Like Connla (in "Connla and the Fairy Maiden"), Rakian remains trapped in the otherworld and loses his connection to the profane world. The anima appears first as a white bee, and thus initially once again bears the anima aspect in need of redemption. Not only Christian consciousness, but all human culture seems to impose this aspect on her. Among indigenous peoples, however, the cleft between humans and animals is significantly reduced, making the possibility of transforming from one form to another greater.[194]

---

[193] Told by Apákag. Slightly edited from Rasmussen, *Eagle's Gift*, pp. 133–135.

[194] See Lévy-Bruhl, *The "Soul" of the Primitive*, pp. 36ff. Van der Leeuw writes:

> See Lévy-Bruhl, *The "Soul" of the Primitive*, pp. 36ff. Van der Leeuw writes: "Whoever allows himself to be duly impressed by the stories of the Indians of North and South American, must feel that to their minds there was no distinction between the animal and the human being. Marriage and childbirth, war and treaty bind them together; and hardly any metamorphism is necessary to make an animal out of a human, or conversely. This transposition becomes more imperative as the contrast between the two is more clearly grasped, and then the so-called *Lycanthropy* comes into existence. Although this is best known under the form of man moving about in the guise of a wolf, the fusion of the animal and man is by no means pure lycanthropy in the proper sense. In Indonesia, the crocodile, the dog, the cat, and above all the tiger are "werewolves," while in ancient Germanic times we find the *berserker*, the "bear-skinned man" who can transform himself into the bear's shape. . . Behind it there lies an ecstatic experience; the animal is the completely "Other" to which man flees for refuge when he is satiated with humanity. The women of the Dionysian cult sought the divine in the animal. They lived themselves, as it were, entirely into the animal, not from love of the "animalism" in any modern sense, since the idea was not then in existence! But only in order to gain freedom from themselves. . . In the cult of Dionysus the animal was precisely the god with who man sought to unite himself" (*Religion in Essence*, vol. 1, pp. 80–81.)

There are many stories of the transformation of animals into humans, for example, in the Inuit tale, "Wander-Hawk Meets a Woodpecker in a Man's Shape":

> One evening Wander-hawk chose a place to pitch his camp. He felled trees, built a shelter of small pines, spread a layer of branches on the ground, gathered wood, and lighted a big fire. Then he hunted ptarmigan for his supper and cooked them over the fire on a spit, sitting beside the fire. But what was that? Suddenly there stood a man just outside! And he cried to him: "I thought I should be alone this evening! Hi! Come in and we will eat together." A strange, unfriendly man it was who now came in. His eyes seemed always to be looking past things, and he did not look Wander-hawk in the face. But he was offered food, and they ate

Correspondingly, the fissure between the conscious and the unconscious is less deep.[195]

1412 "Rakian," a fairytale from the Malay islands, provides the following account:

> in silence. Wander-hawk became more and more angry with all this unfriendliness until, beside himself because of the other's taciturnity, he jumped over the fire, seized the silent fellow by the nape of the neck, and held him over the blaze so that the fringes of his furs were scorched. Thereupon he threw him high over the wind shelter, out on the snow beyond the camp fire. He listened for angry words, but all that he heard was a tapping sound, like someone knocking on a tree trunk. Shortly after, a woodpecker flitted up and flew off. A woodpecker in a man's shape had been his guest (Rasmussen, *Eagle's Gift*, p. 190.)

From the same *Wander-Hawk* cycle (*ibid*), see also "The Wolverine That Had Broken a Tooth," "The Frightened Lynx, or 'What Does Your Big Toe Eat?'," "Wander-Hawk Weds a Night Owl," and "All the Woodland Creatures Build a Birch-Bark Canoe for Wander-Hawk."

[195] Many Siberian fairytales provide particularly clear examples in which animals occur as human beings and human beings as animals. Thus in the Yukaghir tale, "Sea-Jumper," the anima sometimes changed herself into a she-wolf. When the man gets upset about this, his father says, "Your mother was like that, but when I brought her here, all this vanished quite soon." (!) Another example of the sliding interface between human and animal is the Ainu tale, "Poi-Yaumbe," where the hero, Poi-Yaumbe, telling his own story, relates [summarized]:

> One night I [Poi-Yuambe] was unable to sleep, but whether what I now relate was seen, a dream, or whether it really took place, I do not know. I saw upon the tops of the mountains a great herd of bucks feeding by themselves. At the head of this great herd there was a very large speckled buck and a speckled doe. I set out with my elder brother and younger sister. We succeeded in killing numerous deer with our bow and arrows but then realized that the deer were human beings who had come to pick a fight with us. We fought violently and much blood spurted. The spotted doe turned into a woman and also fought against us. My younger sister was slain and the enemy ("the bad, malignant man") threatened to avenge my brothers in the event that we killed him. I was hit hard and fainted. When I awakened I decided to go to *Samatuye* ["to be cut in two"], where our opponents lived. To get there I flew the air until I came to a hut on top of a mountain amidst the clouds. Through a tiny crack I saw a tiny man and a tiny woman who was very beautiful. I fell in love with her on the spot. The little man felt uneasy and asked sister, the beautiful woman, to prophesy. She fell into a trance and told of the battle that their elder brother had instigated against the fierce warriors of the Ainu. She said that the clouds darkened and she could not prophesy any more. Now I hero the hut and battled with the tiny man and all his relatives. During this battle, the beautiful little woman said that she could not agree with her elder brother for having caused a needless battle and then sided with me, she fell in love with me. Together we slew all opponents and afterwards got married, settled down, and had many brave sons and daughters (Batchelor, pp. 313–25.)

We summarize here another variation on this theme, "The Boy and the Bakurao," a tale from the Tembé of South America:

> While his mother plants manioc roots, a boy follows a Bukurao bird who leads him farther and farther into the jungle. The boy went on and found a woodpecker and alligator and then a family of wild boars that took him in. He lived there for many years. The wild boar changed into humans when they left their boar skins at home. Soon the boy too got his wild boar skin so he could change back and forth. One day the wild boar decided to go to the human plantings and steal mania roots. The boy went along and soon realized this was the very place where his mother had left him and a basket many years earlier. He took off his boar skin, and hid while the boar went about their business. Soon his mother came by and put her basket down. She saw the boy and recognized her son. She cried and wanted to embrace him; but he said, 'Don't touch me, mother, stay there and weep! Then his mother asked him to go home, and he followed her from afar. But at home he always kept himself separate from the people, slept in a corner, and sang all night about his adventures, as well as the songs he had learned from the boars. He had already become a wild boar himself. (T. Koch-Grünberg, *Südamerika*, Jena 1921 pp. 188–191.)

See also the fairytales from Europe, "The Tale of the Pig" and "Cadwalader and All His Goats," as well as Hertz, *Werwolf, passim*.

1413 Once there was a *mangis* tree in which there were large bees' nests, and when there was sufficient honey in the nests a man named Rakian went to the tree and began to drive bamboo pegs into it so that he could climb up. There were many bees' nests in the tree and Rakian, seeing that the bees of the nest right at the top of the tree were white, decided to climb there and take it. He thought, "I have never yet seen white bees before." Then he climbed up the steps he had made in the tree to take the white bees' nest and drew his *parang* to cut it down. But the bees did not swarm out from the nest and while he was sawing away at the branch from which it hung he heard the bees say, "That hurts." Then Rakian, wondering, sheathed his *parang* and heard the bees talking to him, "If you wish to take the nest take it gently and do not cut it down." He listened and cut the nest carefully and put it into his *bareit*. Then he descended and went home, placed the *bareit* with the bees into his room. The next day he went to work and when he returned he found rice and fish ready cooked on his *paha* (shelf) above the fire. He thought somebody has come here and cooked and taken away my bees' nest." So he went to his *bareit* and found the bees' nest still there. The next few days the incident repeats itself. Each time he checks to see if anyone has stolen the bees, but they are still there.

1414 One day he determined to return early and see who was cooking his food for him. So early in the morning he set out as if for his *kabun*, but when he had gone a little way he went straight home again and hid himself near the house. For a long time he waited and nothing happened, but at last the door of his house creaked and a beautiful woman came out of his room, and, taking his bamboo water vessel went out of the house to the river to get water. Then when she had gone down to the river Rakian entered his room without the woman seeing him and went to look at his bees. But when he opened his *bareit* he found that there were no bees in it, only the nest. So he took the nest from the *bareit* and hid it and concealed himself in the house. After a time the woman came back from the river and went to the *bareit* to look for the bees' nest. "Oh," said she, "who has taken my box (sarong) [i.e., garments, clothes]?"

1415 She hunted for the nest and at last began to weep, saying, "Who can have taken it? It cannot be Rakian for he has gone to work at his *kabun*. I am afraid that he will come back and find me." When it was nearly dark Rakian came out from his hiding-place as if he had just come back from his *kabun*; but the woman sat there without speaking. "Why are you here?" said Rakian, "perhaps you want to steal my bees."

"I do not know anything about your bees," said the woman. So he went to the *bareit* to look for his bees but of course they were not there for Rakian himself had hidden the nest. "Oh," said he, "My bees' nest is not here, perhaps you have taken it." "How should I know anything about your bees' nest?" said she. "Well, it does not matter," said Rakian, "will you cook for me, for I am very hungry?" "I do not want to cook," said the woman, "for I am vexed." So Rakian kept on telling her to cook for him, but the woman refused and at last she said, "Where is my *saron*?" "I have not taken it," said Rakian. "I believe you have hidden it," said the woman, "and all my clothes and goods are in it." At last Rakian said, "I will not give it to you for I am afraid you will get into it again." "I will not get into it," said the woman. "if you like, you can take me for your wife. My mother wished to give me to you in this way because you have no wife here and I have no husband either in my country." Then Rakian took the bees' nest and gave it to the woman. "What is it?" said he. "It is my *kawal*," replied the woman. "But," said she, "if you take me as your wife do not ever call me a bee woman, for if you do I shall be much ashamed." So they married and had a child.

1416 Now one day there was a feast at a neighboring house and Rakian went there. The people asked where his beautiful wife came from. At first he was steadfast, but then he drank a lot and in his intoxication the truth slipped out. When he returned home his wife was at first silent, than she reproached him for breaking his promise and declared that she wanted to go home, but the child she would leave with him. In seven days her father would walk upstream, then she would go away with him. Rakian wept but could not dissuade her.

1417 At the end of seven days Rakian saw a white bee flying to the ulu of his house. His wife came down the steps from his house and saying, "There is my father." She became a bee again and flew off after her father. Rakian rushed into the house and seized the child, for it was in his heart to follow his wife and her father. At the end of seven days he lost sight of them and still he had not come to any kampong. On the eighth day he came to a bathing-place at a river. Then both he and the child, being hungry and weary, lay down by the side of the river and slept. At last a woman came from the kampong and woke Rakian and said, "Rakian, why don't you go to your wife's house instead of sleeping here with your child, for the house is not far off?" After he had bathed, the woman took them to a nearby village. "That is her house," said his guide, pointing to a long-house, "but her room is right in the middle of it. There are eleven rooms in the house and if you enter it you must not be afraid, for the roof beams are full of bees, but they do not attack men." So Rakian climbed up into the house and found it full of bees, both large and small, but in the middle room there were none. Then the child began to cry and Rakian sat down. "Otun," [an expression of endearment] said a voice in the middle room, "Why do you not come out? Have you no pity on your child who is weeping here?" After a time Rakian's wife appeared in the room and the child ran to her at once, and Rakian's heart became light; but his wife said to him, "What did I tell you at first that you were not to tell whence I came? If you had not been able to follow me here, certainly there would have been distress for you." When she had finished speaking all the bees dropped down from the roof beams to the floor and became men. As for Rakian and his child they stayed in the kampong and did not go back any more.[196]

1418 The bee that Rakian meets is white and therefore unusual. (The color white characterizes her as a magical being.) According to many native peoples, if an animal looks extraordinary, it is considered to be a "doctor animal" because a magical spirit, a magical soul, inhabits it. Thus – psychologically speaking – a projection has happened: that animal has become a symbol of an unconscious psychic content. As becomes evident in this fairytale, it is the projection of the anima image. She represents the queen and subsequently the bee woman symbolizes the whole bee colony. The number is not important; Rakian meets the bee, that is the life principle, his genius,[197] his totem archetype.[198] When the woman appears, all the bees, the whole nest, disappear, since she embodies their original principle, which previously appeared in multiple ways. (If the anima image is split into a multiplicity, psychologically this indicates that it still adheres to the collective and non-individual, to the psychic layers farthest from consciousness.)

1419 The bee's nest corresponds – as the woman's words clearly establish – to the animal garb in other fairytales. Thus, the splitting into a plurality, and the animal mask – as far as both forms indicate unconsciousness – mean the same thing. In both cases, the original image lies concealed behind these manifestations. The bee as a winged being denotes the anima's spiritual

[196] Slightly shortened from Evans, "Folk Stories of the Tempassuk and Tuaran Districts, British North Borneo," pp. 457–459.
[197] [See footnote on page 163.]
[198] On the personification of the mystic principle of life as it relates to bees, see Lévy-Bruhl, *The "Soul" of the Primitive*, pp. 21–26: "What interests the Chaga [a Bantu-speaking tribe of Africa] especially is not any particular specimen of these insects, or their number: it is the bees, that wonderful race that can produce wax and honey. It is certainly seen in a mass, but it is essentially a principle, genius, mystic power of which it is natural to speak in the singular"; see also Ibid., p. 67.

nature.[199] After Rakian hides away the bee's nest ("my saron, clothes," as the bee-woman called it), the anima appears in her true form as the unknown woman. The distrust is mutual. At first, Rakian is stronger because he possesses the "garments"; thus, consciousness has again succeeded in usurping the anima's mystery by a forceful intervention. It soon becomes apparent, however, that the whole situation springs from a magical intention, from the "Great Mother." Namely, the mother of the bee woman had decided that the lonely man should get a wife and that the anima, who in the Magical had now found a husband, should find each other. (See the abandonment of the dragon princess in "The Disowned Princess.") The bee lady "forfeited" her magical clothing under the condition that her husband keeps the secret of her true identity. The soul thus reveals itself to a certain extent to consciousness, and thereby participates in human life. (Hence the common motif that she, as an elfish beings, long for a human soul.) But the relationship is only possible when consciousness has not exposed the insight it has received into the mystery of the bee being too secular and uncomprehending fellow human beings.[200]

1420 The bee woman demands a certain subtle consideration of her origin and her former animal self. This animal, that is, subhuman and yet divine aspect of her being[201]cannot be accommodated within the sphere of secular human consciousness and, therefore, must be kept hidden from the world in order not to expose the bee woman to the profane contempt of animals or the religious fear of spirit-beings.[202] Moreover, the loneliness, the non-mixing with

---

[199] On bees as a manifestation of the soul, see Weicker, *Seelenvogel*, p. 29. See further Tobler, *Epiphanie*, p. 36f., and Bächtold-Stäubli under *Insekt* [insect]. Mythologically, bees are connected to the idea of chastity and virginity. See Bachofen, *Mutterrecht*, p. 234, and Bächtold-Stäubli under *Biene* [bee]. See also "The Tale of Sänämâ," in which the anima initially appears as a bee. Bees are also ritually significant because they produce honey, which is regarded as an inspiring divine substance. In India it is the food of the immortals, in ancient times it played a role in the various mysteries. See Zimmer, *Maya*, p. 150; Güntert, *Weltkönig*, p. 256, and Bächtold-Stäubli under *Honig* [honey]. In "Rakian," the anima is possessed by the mysterious substance of life.

[200] See the *Wisdom of Sirach* (*Ecclesiasticus*), 27:17-24: "He that discloseth the secret of a friend loseth his credit, and shall never find a friend to his mind. Love thy neighbor, and be joined to him with fidelity. But if thou discover his secrets, follow no more after him. For as a man that destroyeth his friend, so is he that destroyeth the friendship of his neighbor. And as one that letteth a bird go out of his hand, so hast thou let thy neighbor go, and thou shalt not get him again. Follow after him no more, for he is gone afar off, he is fled, as a roe escaped out of the snare because his soul is wounded. Thou canst no more bind him up. And of a curse there is reconciliation: but to disclose the secrets of a friend, leaveth no hope to an unhappy soul."

[201] See Waitz, *Anthropologie*, Part 2, p. 177: In the opinion of many Africans, "The human being is in no way at the pinnacle of nature and above the animals. The animals are enigmatic creatures whose lives and activities are dark and mysterious and therefore sometimes under and sometimes over humans."

[202] That even a praising and admiring mention of the nature of the anima can be destructive is illustrated by the fairytale, "Wila Remain Wila," in which the anima, a Wila (a wild female nymph/spirit-being and often the daughter of a vampire) marries the hero of the fairytale and protects their property from hailstorms. As he exclaims joyfully, "Wila remain Wila," she immediately leaves him and has to search the realm of the stars and bring back from there. On this motif, see also Thimme, *Märchen*, pp. 49–50.
In other cases, the same occurs when the man asks about her origin. Once a farmer took a "salige" woman to wife (a white, holy, pure woman), a shy but helpful and wise female spirit

the collectivity, is the basic requirement for a connection to the anima, which can only be recognized as a piece of one's own inner being.

1421 Revealing the mystery of her origin means revealing one's own personal secret, through which the individual is differentiated from the others. Rakian breaks his promise in his drunken state, that is, in a state in which he has lost clear consciousness and fallen in with the collective. At that moment, he betrays his most personal secret and simultaneously a taboo–protected extra-human relationship into which he was awarded insight. He thus commits a double offense: first, the breach of trust of his (unkept) promise; and second, his treason shows that he did not really understand the divine-animal background of the anima experience. In contrast to Rakian, the hero of a Russian fairytale, "The Farmer and the Golden Sun," takes the right action: he protects his anima, the sun's sister, from the people's envy by transforming her

---

> who lived in caves or river banks and helped farmers, mostly in the Alpine regions of Europe). He vowed never to ask about her origins. The couple was blessed with wonderful children and grew happily old together. One day he asked her, in jest or curiosity, "Did you really come out of the baby's well?" (Meaning: were you born like a normal human?) Immediately the woman vanished, taking their children with her right before his eyes. Her partings words rang forever painfully in his ears, "If you ask, then you complain!" . . . Other legends tell of how the husband once eavesdropped on his wife while she was bathing and saw that she had changed into a snake or a frog. He quickly went to the priest for help who tried to banish the enchantment with holy water. But then the woman disappeared forever . . . Sometimes it is only the outcry of the man when he surprises his wife in her elvish form, or as a *Mahrte* or *Trute* [beings like Wila mentioned above], and frightens her. This is what is related in the Greek legend of Peleus. One day he eavesdrops on his wife Thetis, a sea nymph, and observes how she burns away the mortality of their son Achilles with fire. Seeing this, Peleus lets out a cry. "Thetis heard him, and catching up the child threw him screaming to the ground, and she like a breath of wind passed swiftly from the hall as a dream and leapt into the sea, exceeding angry, and thereafter returned never again." [One source of is Apollonius Rhodius, *Argonautica*, 4. 757ff (translated by Rieu).]

Another fairytale in which even the hero may not discover the mystery of the animal-anima is the Yukaghir tale, "Story of the Fish-Woman":

> A lonely fisherman pulls up *Shérkala*, the fish-girl from the sea, and takes her home, and lays her in the corner of his house. When he came back from fishing the next day, he had caught nothing, but his house was cleaned and festively decorated, and a good meal prepared. One day he pretended to depart; but, instead of going away, he lay down on the earth bench close to the window. He lay there very quietly; but after a while he lifted his head and looked through the window. The Shérkala-Fish arose as far as her tail, and then turned into a young pretty girl. She ripped up her own belly and took out fish-roe, which she put into the kettle. Then she swept the floor and put everything in good order. The man suddenly rushed in and caught the fish skin of Shérkala, which lay on the floor. He threw it into the fire, and it was burned. "What have you done," said the girl. "We lived so happily, and now I must go away." She fell down and melted away into sea water. (Bogoras, *Tales of the Yukaghir*, pp. 153–54.)

Like the Fish Prince in "The Fisherman and His Wife," the anima figure is here lifted out of the water, the unconscious, on a hook. Also, similar to "Ititaujang," she harbors seeds (fish roe) that in this case she donates to the man. When the man through an intervention of consciousness tries to dispose of her animal nature by purifying it in fire (in other fairytales, burning redeems the animal aspect). This is here portrayed as a violent act. The anima is so frightened that she dissolves, leaving only the empty aspect of the unconscious in the form of seawater, that all-sheltering and concealing-element. Apparently the man is not ready for the incarnation of the anima in human form. In this case the act of the observation and conscious recognition are like a betrayal of the environment, like a secularization that destroys the magical mystery of life. Such stories illuminate in what subtle conditions the redemption of the anima is tied for the man.

(on her advice) for the duration of his journey into a small stone in the corner of his living room.

1422 Discussing the imperative to keep the anima experience secret, Jung writes: "The experience of the unconscious is a personal secret communicable only to very few, and that with difficulty; hence the isolating effect. . . But isolation brings about a compensatory animation of the psychic atmosphere. . ."[203] Beholding the anima means the unconscious intrudes into consciousness. Such intrusions, so Jung,

> 1423 . . . bring about a momentous alteration of his personality since they immediately constitute a painful personal secret which alienates and isolates him from his surroundings. It is something that we 'cannot tell anybody.' We are afraid of being accused of mental abnormality–not without reason.[204]

1424 At the same time, however,

> 1425 [The possession of a secret is] an essential precondition of any individual differentiation, so much so that even on a primitive level man feels an irresistible need *actually to invent secrets*: their possession safeguards him from dissolving in the featureless flow of unconscious community life and thus from deadly peril to his soul. It is a well-known fact that the widespread and very ancient rites of initiation with their mystery cults sub served this instinct for differentiation. Even the Christian sacraments were looked upon as "mysteries" in the Early Church, and, as in the case of baptism, were celebrated in secluded spots and only mentioned under the veil of allegory.[205]

1426 These are real secrets about things that can only be hinted at with symbols and images. Also Carus emphasizes that "some of the most important processes of our lives remain shrouded in impenetrable darkness."[206] Every

---

[203] C.G. Jung, *Psychology and Alchemy*, CW 12, ¶61.

[204] Ibid., ¶57, ¶118.

[205] Von Franz and von Beit's emphasis. See C.G. Jung, *Problems of Modern Psychotherapy*, CW 16, ¶124, and *Symbols of Transformation*, CW 5, ¶300. On keeping secrets in Gnostic cult communities, see Leisegang, *Die Gnosis*, pp. 28, 198. Alchemy struggled to remain a hidden science. See Jung, *Psychology and Alchemy*, CW 12, ¶423. See also Silberer, *Problems of Mysticism*, p. 389, who cites Leade, *Fountain*, 1696. On the secrecy of tribal teachings among the primitive, see Thurnwald, "Primitive Initiations-riten,"pp. 333–34, 365, and Winthuis, *Zweigeschlechterwesen*, p. 97.

[206] Carus, *Psyche*, p. 96; see also *ibid.*, p. 256:

> The poet is to the scientist as the feminine to the masculine, and precisely because he grasps the Mystery as such, that is, more unconsciously, he often comes closer to it than the latter, when the latter proceeds everywhere from the basic principle that the goal is to bring everything and everyone into perfectly clear conscious. Of course, we are convinced that this latter view is erroneous, and that each [individual] has the right and [choice of] their own

betrayal of the secret threatens the protective boundaries of the personality. Either the unconscious-spiritual is lost or the person loses themselves to the unconscious.[207] In Rakian's case, both happens.

1427 The loss of the magical partner due to uncovering his or her underlying mystery is the underlying motif of the *Lohengrin* saga. It is prefigured in many legends and tales, especially in the fairytales of indigenous peoples. Another example, which is also closely parallels Rakian's story, is the tale "Why Honey is So Scarce Now":

1428 In the olden times bees' nests and honey were very plentiful in the bush, and there was one man in particular who earned quite a reputation for discovering their whereabouts. He would find a nest where no one else could. One day, while chopping into a hollow tree where he had located some honey, he suddenly heard a voice from the inside calling, "Take care! You are cutting me." On opening the tree very carefully, he discovered a beautiful woman, who told him she was Maba [lit. 'honey'], the Honey-Mother, that is, the Spirit of the Honey. As she was quite naked, he collected some cotton that she made into a cloth, and he asked her to be his wife. She consented on the condition that he never mention her name, and they lived very happily together for many years. And just in the same way that he became universally acknowledged as the best man for finding bees' nests, so she made a name for herself in the way of brewing excellent/ecassiri and *paiwarri*. She had to make only one jugful, and it would prove quite sufficient, no matter the number of visitors. More than this, the one jugful would make them all drunk! She thus proved herself to be a splendid wife. One day when the drink was finished, however, he went around as housemaster, in the usual manner, to his many guests and expressed regret that even the last dregs of the liquor had now been drained. He promised them, however, that the next time they came, the liquor would be provided by Maba – yes, he made a mistake and thus spoke of his wife by her intimate name. And no sooner had be mentioned the name than she flew away to her bees' nest. He put up his hands to stop her, but she had already flown. And

path to higher knowledge. The real task of consciousness in so far as it is to bring things into the utmost clarity, means to acknowledge and receive the unconscious in its darkness and mystery. In terms of a pictorial representation this means not simply accepting light in the light, but rather true clarity is achieved by artistically combining both light and dark.

[207] Cf. Jung, "Relation between the ego and the unconscious," CW 7, ¶243 fn. 1.

with her, his luck flew, and since that time honey has always been more or less scarce.[208]

1429 In this fairytale, we see once again how the so-called genius of the animal species[209] is associated with the mystical primeval image or archetype in the figure of the beautiful woman, who represents the spirit of the honeybee. She embodies the unconscious principle that had already bestowed on the man his special ability to find nests of honey. Through his anima, he had a secret relationship with bees. That is, he has a bee soul, whom he meets in the flesh one day. But in his pride, he cannot keep silent and trust in the deeper meaning. Instead, he reveals his secret by mentioning her name, so that she vanishes and slips away into the unconscious.[210]

1430 In contrast, Rakian managed to follow his bee-wife. First, she tells him that she is heading upstream (back to the origin!) with her father, who is going to collect her. After seven days, a white bee buzzes around their house. Then the woman became a bee again and traveled back to her home. Again, the number seven appears in conjunction with the anima, once more as a hint of something unfinished, uncompleted. Here the woman transforms back to her former shape without the recovery of her animal garb, this time brought about by the appearance of her father who, as in "The Mermaid and the Great Dubhdach," turns out to be the origin of the daemonic aspect of his daughter. Rakian follows the woman with their child for seven days and they sleep on the eighth day. Eight is the number of completion! Then, a woman advises him to search for the queen bee in the central chamber of a house full of bees. On his path into the magical sphere, he enters a beehive as a human being, the mystical, archetypal beehive, from which the queen comes. By trespassing on this center, he regains the connection to the queen and the bees become humans. There is a unification of consciousness and unconscious in the center of the personality through which some aspects of human consciousness are carried into the animal world (into the unconscious). Mutual assimilation takes place and dissolves the opposites. Rakian never returns home. Like

---

208 Roth, *Inquiry into Animism*, pp. 204–205.

209 [See above, page 163.]

210 On the betrayal of the secret that destroys good luck in hunting, see also, a tale from the Warao people in South America, "Black-Tiger, Wau-uta, and the Broken Arrow." There, the hero receives from the female frog Wau-uta a wonderful arrow under the condition that he never divulged to anyone that it was she who had taught him to be so good a marksman. For a while he remained most successful in the hunt and refused to answer all the entreaties of his relatives as to the secret of his good hunting luck. But "[T]he same old story, drink proved his undoing; he let loose his tongue, and divulged what had happened." The next morning he wakes up with his old arrows and his old bad luck in hunting. [From Roth, *Inquiry into Animism*, pp. 213–14.] We find a similar meaning in the Inuit fairytale, "The Man in the Moon," in which the wife of a hunter is mistreated and she went up to the Man in the Moon. He treated her well and sent her back down to earth and continued to provide her with oil for her lamps and special caribou meat. When one day she ate of the seal meat brought back by her hunter husband, she no longer received the magical gifts from the Man in the Moon. See also Goethe's poem *Der getreue Eckart* [Faithful Eckart].

Connla (in "Connla's Sea-Journey"), he has forever entered the eternal world of anima, the realm of the archetypes.

1431 More frequently among the primitives, stories about encountering the anima (like the tale about Maba, the honey-mother) end in absolute separation after the betrayal (i.e., the *Lohengrin* motif). We also see this in the Arawak fairytale, "The Tiger Changed into a Woman":

> 1432 There was a man justly noted for his skill in hunting bush-hog. Though his friends might be more than a match for him in hunting other game, with bush-hog he had hardly an equal, certainly no superior. He would always succeed in killing five or six, when the tiger who invariably followed on the heels of the pack would catch only one or two. The tiger could not help noticing his success, and on the next occasion that our friend went into the bush, the tiger changed itself into a woman and spoke to him. She asked him how he managed to kill so many bush-hog, but all he could tell her was that he had been trained to do this ever since the days of his early boyhood. She next expressed her desire to have him for a husband, but he, knowing her origin, was not too anxious to give a firm answer. She overcame his scruples, however, by convincing him that if they lived together, they could kill even more bush-hog than it was possible to do singly. And then he agreed. He lived with her for a long, long time, and she turned out to be an exceedingly good wife, for besides looking after the cooking and grilling, she made an excellent huntress. One day she asked him whether he had a father and a mother. Learning that his parents and other relatives were still alive, she inquired whether he would not like to pay them a visit. She felt sure that from not having seen him for so long, the old people would think him dead. And when he said, "All right! I would like to go home," she offered to show him the road and to accompany him, but only on the condition that he never told his folk from what nation she was sprung.
>
> 1433 When they arrived, they were welcomed warmly. The first question his old mother asked him was, "Where did you get that beautiful woman?" Naturally, he told her that he had found her when out hunting one day in the bush, taking great care to omit all mention of the fact that she was really a tiger. While at his old home, the couple went out hunting again and again, invariably returning with an extraordinarily large bag. This, unfortunately, proved to be their undoing. All his friends and, family became suspicious of his luck, and made up their minds to discover to what nation his beautiful wife

> belonged. He was often asked, but always refused to divulge the secret. His mother, however, became so worried and upset that he at last did make a clean breast of it to her, strictly warning her not to tell anyone else, as his wife might leave him altogether. Now trouble soon came. One day the husband's people made plenty of cassiri, to get the old woman drunk, but when asked about her daughter-in-law she wouldn't tell: they gave her more drink and still she held her tongue: at last they gave her so much drink, that out came the secret and all the friends now knew that the beautiful creature whom they had so envied was after all only a tiger. The woman, however, who had heard her mother-in-law exposing her origin, felt so ashamed that she fled into the bush, growling, and that was the last that was ever seen or heard of her. Her husband, of course, upbraided his mother roundly for betraying him, but she said she really could not help herself; they had made her so drunk. And the poor husband would often go into the bush and call his wife, but there never, never came a reply.[211]

1434 As in "Rakian," yet more emphatically here, the animal woman takes the initiative and appeals to the hero. At first, he is frightened of her twofold nature, especially as she previously represented the unconscious "other side," which male conscious resists.[212] He lets himself be seduced by the anima's promise of greater hunting success, because therein lies the positive side of the encounter with his inner animal side. It gives him control over the world of instincts, as well as a connection with nature and a sensitivity to the habits of animals. Only through *participation mystique* with the animal can you hunt it,[213] as the story of Maba, the queen bee, shows. The tigress is like this man's

---

211 Slightly edited from Roth, *Inquiry into Animism*, pp. 203–04.

212 See Jung, *Psychologie und Religion*, CW 11, ¶129, and *Psychology and Alchemy*, CW 12, ¶192f.

213 See also the Hawaiian tale "Pikoi the Rat-Killer":

> To a family on Kauai six girl-gods were born and only one real girl and one real boy. These "gods" were guardians of the family, or, perhaps it should be said, they watched carefully over some especial brother or sister, doing all sorts of marvelous things such as witches and fairies like to do for those whom they love. The "god-sisters" of this family were all rats and were named "Kikoo," which was the name of the bow used with an arrow for rat-shooting. The boy became a most skillful rat killer, who could foil hidden and far-off rats with his bow and arrows. With the help of his rat sisters, to whom he says an incantation prayer, he wins a rat-hunting bet, in which he killed a rat which no one else could see, since only its whiskers were sticking out from a far-away bush. His arrow traverses forty rats at one shot. He went on to win many honors, was a skillful surfer, and friend of the low-class people of Hawaii.

Father Le Jeune, who observed the Native Americans in Canada in the 1600s, writes that these people say that all animals of every kind have an elder brother who is as it were the source and origin of all individuals, and that this elder brother is wondrously great and powerful. . . If during sleep this eldest animals or principle of animal life is seen, the hunting will be successful; if the dreamer sees the senior of the beavers, he will trap beavers. . . (quoted in Lévy-Bruhl, *The "Soul" of the Primitive*, pp. 63-64.) See Bächtold-Stäubli under *Jagd, Jäger* [hunting, hunter]: "It is proven that for the primitive hunter, hunting is considered actually to be a mystical confirmation. For success the hunter must master "hunting soul." Apparently, he has lived alone in the forest, far away from his clan, ever since his marriage. This signifies isolation, which has been caused by the invasion of the unconscious. The tigress compels him to visit his family, because she is also the voice of instinct, which warns against any damaging one-sidedness. She imposes a rule of silence, however, as the condition under which he can establish an outer connection with his clan. For most primitive peoples, marriage is a matter of kinship, and individual choice is almost impossible.[214] Therefore, the connection with such a mystical beast-anima has such an isolating effect, just as the consequences of betraying the clan are so severe.[215]

1435 Another South American tale, "The Man With the Howler Monkey Wife," is similar fashion, although here the secret is betrayed to the animal clan and not to the husband's family group:

> 1436 One time long ago, an Arawak hunter had been far out into the bush in search of game, and it almost seemed as if he were to find no use for his bow and arrows. Late in the afternoon, however, he shot a baboon [Howler Monkey, *Mycetes*], which proved to be a female. It was too late to bring it home, so he built himself a banab with a view to making himself comfortable for the night. This done, he cut off the animal's tail, roasted and ate it, putting the remainder of the carcass on the grill spit to get smoke-dried during the night. Next morning he was up early, entered the bush again, was very successful, and returned in the evening laden with game. As he approached the banab, you can imagine his surprise on seeing a woman lying in his

objective conditions of course but foremost he must be, as it were, clothed in a mystical power." See also Lévy-Bruhl, *How Natives Think*, p. 38f.

214 See Lévy-Bruhl, *The "Soul" of the Primitive*, pp. 77ff.

215 A similar tale is "Why Black Tiger Kills People":

> The hero manages to escape being cooked by a family of black tigers because the daughter takes a liking to him. They marry and have two cubs who can growl like thunder. When the hero visits his family, his mother asks to meet his wife and her grandchildren. Upon discovering that her son has married a black tigress, the man's mother kills them both in a drunken fury. The two cub-sons escape and return to their grandfather tiger, who promptly wreaks revenge on the people.

In a tale from the Donau region, "Stepmother,"

> The stepson had to herd the pigs in the forest. They wander into a dark hole and come to a bright world, where they feed on tasty grain. Encouraged by an old mother, the boy follows and meets three maidens there who dress him, feed him, and present him with gifts. They tell him that if he can hold their secret for ten years, they will be redeemed. Back home, he managed to remain silent for a long time despite the pressure and cajoling of his stepmother. Until she brought him to a court of justice. There he betrayed the secret and since then whenever he went to the hole in the forest the entrance was closed tight and he heard the sound of women weeping.

This fairytale is from a higher level of culture and differentiates both aspects of the mother and the need for salvation of the maidens who represent the anima in a trinity.

hammock, and no baboon on the spit. Not understanding whence she could have come, he asked her what she was doing there, and she told him that, on account of his loneliness, she had come to help look after the meat and keep him company. After further questioning, she assured him that there was no baboon on the spit when she had arrived. He had his suspicions as to her origin aroused on noticing that her fingers were naturally clenched, and that with the one hand she was continually trying to keep extended the fingers of the other.[216] He accordingly asked her straight whether she herself was not the baboon that had so mysteriously disappeared, but she denied it. She was a good-looking wench, however, and he took her as wife, with the result that they lived happily together, so happily that they kept no secrets from each other.

1437 One day her husband asked her again about the baboon, and what had become of it. She now admitted that she was the baboon transformed into her present shape, but that he must not speak about it to anyone. A few days later they took their departure from the banab, and made their way to the husband's house, bringing plenty of game with them. And here they lived a very long time – still quite happily together. It is true that he would frequently be asked by his relatives as to what tribe his wife belonged, but he never told them.

1438 One morning early, hearing the baboons calling, she informed her husband that her uncles were drinking cassiri, and suggested that they should both go and join the party. The uncle Baboon was howling on the topmost branches of an immense cashew tree, the trunk of which was so big that one could make a proper foot-path upwards. The couple made their way to the tree, and followed the track. Up and up they went, until they found themselves in real Baboon country, and arrived at the threshold of a big house. And what a lot of drink there was! And so many Baboons to drink it! Everyone got drunk and then each began to chatter, the one asking all kinds of questions from the other. Our friend was again asked what nation his wife came from and, being now in his cups, let out the secret, and told them she was really a Baboon. But no sooner had he uttered the forbidden word, than everything – his wife, drinks, house, and baboons – all suddenly vanished, and he found himself desolate and alone at the top of the cashew tree. But how to get down was the puzzle: he was at too great

[216] [When a monkey is barbecued, its digits [fingers], owing to muscular contraction, invariably become strongly flexed (note by Roth).]

> a height to jump to the ground, and the trunk was too huge for him to encircle and scale. He knew not what to do, and he felt very miserable. A *bunia* bird helped him to get down from the tree but then he did not know where he was and a hummingbird offered to lead him home. But it flew far too swiftly, and the man could not keep up with it: so it came back and made a second start, this time following the course of a straight line before it disappeared. The man followed the line, and came to a path, where the bird met him again and said, "Follow the path." The man did so, and got home.[217]

1439 The hunter is "lonely" and it is "late," that is, night, when the unconscious arises, is approaching. Semi-conscious, the man meets the magical animal, which he kills with brute force and whose tail he cuts off to eat. The tail is the part of the monkey that differentiates it significantly from people and brands it an animal. The man's actions correspond to the theft of the animal garment and, therefore, to the motif of the swan maiden. He cuts off the animal side, and thus appropriates it. By doing this, he becomes more "ape-like," and thus more unconscious, more instinctual. And corresponding to his consciousness approaching the unconscious, it reciprocates and the female baboon becomes a woman, a human being. Once the man takes his wife from the forest to his home, however, the longing arises in her to return to the magical sphere. Not taking into account the origins of the anima seems to create a compensating urge to return there and thus his baboon wife entices her husband to a drinking party among the apes. The anima experience is a liminal experience, simultaneously real and unreal, a dream *and* a real experience. The anima is, after all, a "liminal" figure: she acts as bridge to the contents of the unconscious. As soon as someone attempts to drag the experience too much into consciousness, a compensatory movement occurs: the anima disappears into the unconscious or entices that person to follow her there.

1440 In his intoxication, the husband betrays the origin of his wife. This time not to his secular family, but to his magical clan. This also means non-differentiation and unconsciousness, slipping away into the collective, like betraying the profand world. The man makes a fool [ape] of himself among other fools [apes] ! He loses his personal conscious distinction, and thus loses his experience. He boasts of the acquired animal nature in a way that is hurtful to the human sense of tact. He loses himself downward to the shadow figures; strangely enough, the unconscious avenges this by cutting him off from itself. The human awakes sobered, the magical adventure of the night is gone, he is

217 Slightly edited from Roth, *Inquiry into Animism*, pp. 209–10.

lost, disoriented, and only one bird, a lucky intuition, helps him back down to the human world by the tree that he had presumptuously climbed up.[218]

1441 For the primitives, falling back into one's animal nature is an obvious danger, because the borders are still fluid and permeable, as shown in the previous examples. The vow of silence is an artificial barrier, therefore, erected to safeguard individual differentiation, towards the inside as much as towards outside, from above and below, that is, against the inner, unconscious instinctual world, as against outer society. It also protects humankind against animals and the divine.[219]

1442 Japan also knows of such tragic anima experiences with the motif of betrayal. One example is the fairytale "The Bells of Mii Temple":

> 1443 Many years ago, there somewhere lived a young man. One day as he was walking on the beach, he came upon some children who were trying to kill a snake. He asked them to let the snake live and so saved its life. A few days later, a beautiful woman came knocking where he lived and asked if she could stay there overnight. He received her in a friendly way and she stayed the night. Then she stayed the next night and the next night and soon they became intimate friends and then one day she became pregnant. When the time came to give birth, she asked that he build her a birth hut in a corner of the yard behind their house. But then she asked him never to look inside, no matter what might happen. The young man thought this was a bit strange but he built the hut for her and when her time came, she went in. As such things go, the husband became very curious and thought just a peek could do no harm. He was surprised to see a large snake that was hugging a baby child. At that same moment the snake disappeared

---

[218] [A pun is lost here in translation: the German word *sich versteigen* (to be presumptuous) is almost identical to the word *ersteigen* (ascended).]

[219] See also "The Man With a Bad Temper," where the human by his arrogance towards his animal wife created an insurmountable separation of spheres. He chided her scornfully as being an "ape," and thus haughtily exposed her origins. He sees only the animal in her and not the magical being that distinguishes her from the ordinary monkey and furnishes her the opportunity to be human. Humiliating the soul-image to the ordinary animal drives her away. The monkey woman hurriedly flees into the magical, which the anima finds "above" in the tree tops, the man remains "below," down on the ground and cannot follow, as if this "reversal" is a punishment for his arrogance. The family clan of the monkey woman conjure up a wind that binds tree tops on either side of the river together so that she can cross the border waters, while not a ghost's breath helps him. Angrily he returns home and destroys his household property (Roth, *Inquiry into Animism*, pp. 150–151.) [Translated into German by von Franz and von Beit, and translated here in English.] With regard to becoming poor after the loss of the anima, see the Russian fairytale, "Danilo the Luckless," in which the swan maiden conjured up the most glorious landscape, mansions, and feasts, but after Danilo the Luckless had betrayed her name after getting drunk, she set up a special celebration and when all had drunk themselves into a stupor, transformed everything back and left her guests sitting in the mud and flew away (Guterman, trans., *Russian Fairy Tales*, pp. 255–261.) In the figure of strange "animal people" or "human animals," natural people saw their ancestral spirits, a magical power, which contained a soul; see Lévy-Bruhl, *The "Soul" of the Primitive*, pp. 36–49.

and when he went into the hut, he found only a note. There it was written: "I am the snake whose life you once saved at the beach. To pay you my gratitude, I came to you. But since you saw me in my real form, it is no longer granted to me that I may continue to live with you. But this child of ours I leave behind for you as a keepsake. Take good care of the precious stone which lies in the baby's hands. As long as it holds the precious stone, it will not cry. If it still continues to cry come to the beach and clap your hands three times, then I will be immediately there."

1444 The man looked at the child and saw that indeed it held a precious stone in its hands. As written in the note, the man brought up the child. The prince of the land heard of this wonderful story and ordered the man to deliver the precious stone over to him. Against his will, the father had to obey. But from this moment on, the child began to cry and could not be quieted. Then the man remembered what his snake-wife had written in her note. He went to the beach and clapped three times. Immediately a large snake appeared. He asked the snake to take on the form of his one-time wife. The snake transformed into the beautiful woman.

1445 The man now told the story of what happened with the child and the stone. The snake-woman said, "This precious stone was one of my eyes, I have only the other one. When I give my one remaining eye to you, I will then be blind. But for the sake of our child I will take on this blindness. But then I ask that you donate a bell in the Mii Temple and every time when I hear the bell, I will know that another day or night has transpired."

1446 Then she gave him the other precious stone. The man donated a large bell to the Mii Temple that is still there today."[220]

1447 The beginning of this tale requires no explanation. Once more, the violation of secrecy brings a happy relationship to a joyless end. Separation makes the anima lose her gemstones, that is her eyes, and thus her value and, what amounts to the same, her vision. The anima, after all, is a function that could make the unconscious see more clearly. Her values are not passed on to the man but to the child, but eventually to the regional prince and to the indigenous cult. This is significant because the state government and the cult worship of the gods are simultaneously the collective regulation of inner and outer relations. The collective bodies appear here in place of an individual psychological function since the anima mediates the relationship, on the one

[220] Translated from Hammitzsch et al., *Japanische*, pp. 131–32.

hand, between the individual and the outer world and, on the other hand, between the individual and his unconscious. By violating his psychic secret, his true being, the man squanders the possibility of shaping his own individual destiny, and must now immerse himself in collective life, which is dull and devoid of any special individual meaning.

1448 In a short English tale, "Cadwalader and All His Goats," the motif of the animal anima has survived in quite a primitive form:

> 1449 The shepherd Cadwalader had a particularly beloved goat named Jenny. Although she usually behaved most reasonably, one evening she just would not let herself get caught and lured the shepherd Cadwalader far away into the mountains. When she at last fled to an inaccessible ledge high on a cliff, the shepherd in frustration and anger threw a rock at her that caused her to fall.
>
> 1450 Now Cadwalader was very sad and went to the place of the disaster where the goat lay dying. He knelt beside her and she licked his hand. This touched him so much that he wept buckets of tears. He took the head of the animal in his arms and suddenly the dying goat transformed into a beautiful young woman. She looked at him in a very friendly way with her big brown eyes and spoke: "Have I finally found you, Cadwalader? Come with me." He lay his hand in hers and let her lead him away. Her hand felt exactly like a goat's hoof, but when Cadwalader looked at it, it appeared to be a normal human hand, although it was whiter and more delicate than any hand he had ever seen. The maiden led him on and on, never before had Cadwalader heard such a pleasant chatter.
>
> 1451 She took him to a high mountain peak where in the moonlight he found himself suddenly surrounded by countless goats. They all rushed at him in a furious frenzy and butted him into an abyss. He lost conscious and returned to his senses first when the sun was rising and birdsong awoke him in the morning. But from that day on until his death, he never again cast his eyes either on his goat Jenny, or on the fairy maiden who had helped her wreak revenge on him.[221]

1452 This tale provides a rare and vivid example of the primitive psychological level in which the image of the anima is projected onto an animal. In this case, the shepherd cannot win the human side of his anima, because he cannot patiently accept her unpredictable and petulant goatish nature. He lacks a genuine

---

[221] [Translated from Ehrentreich, *Englische Volksmärchen*, p. 178f. For an English version, see Jones, *Tales for Wales*, pp. 220–23.]

empathetic attitude towards the at first elfish, checkered, and obscure nature of his unconscious, which reacts so waywardly inside him. As a result of his impatience and lack of understanding, he is forever cut off from these psychic forces, which could otherwise grant him great value and could have endowed him with an exceptional individual destiny.

1453 Other European fairytales also contain the motif of the expulsion of the supernatural wife through uncomprehending and contemptuous treatment. The resistance of the Christian world of consciousness often plays a role in these tales. One example is "The Player on the Jew's Harp":

> 1454 The son of a farmer set off to look for an ox that had mysteriously disappeared... He searched in every direction, far and near, until he thought he could smell the ox; yet in spite of this, he could see no sign of a living being anywhere, all day long. Finally he grew angry, and swore that for his part, the bewitched beast might go to the end of the world; if he did not want to join the rest of the herd, he could please himself. With that he turned around, and went to the herdsman's hut as fast as he could. And there, at the fence of the herdsman's hut, stood the great ox licking salt. One of his horns had been broken off. Where he had been knocking about so long he himself probably knew, the young fellow did not. [It being so late, he decided to stay in the hut, and made a warm, bright fire.] When he had eaten his supper, he threw himself down on the bed of planks, pulled his Jew's-harp out of his waistcoat pocket, and began to play the "Bells of St. Thomas" round. But he had not been playing long before he fell asleep, with the instrument in his mouth. Suddenly he woke again, and it seemed to him that he could hear something rustling softly at the other end of the hut. He turned his head slightly, and saw a beautiful young girl standing by the table, braiding her hair. It was so long that it fell down over her hips, and as lovely and shiny as though it had been gilded. At first the young fellow could not see her face, but once, when she happened to turn in his direction, it seemed to him that she was the fairest and finest-looking maiden he had ever laid eyes on. The young fellow did not dare address her, for she thought herself alone, and looked so dear and trustful that he dreaded frightening her away. So he lay there as still as a mouse, and did not venture to move so much as a foot.
>
> 1455 Suddenly in came another girl; but she appeared to be coarser, and had a large mouth and dark complexion, not as clear and fresh as that of the first girl; and she did not please him as well. Both were dressed alike, in green jackets and bodices of red satin, blue stockings, and with bright silver buckles on their shoes. The younger maiden had

white sleeves, that were so fresh and clean they fairly shone. Her bodice was cut low, and showed a handsome round clasp, which tinkled delicately whenever the maiden made the slightest move. And now the young fellow realized what sort of maidens these were, and could not get over his astonishment that there were such beautiful women among the underground folk. It was Saturday evening, and this was probably the reason they were dressing and adorning themselves so busily: no doubt they were expecting company or suitors. The young fellow could not make out what they said to each other, for they whispered so softly that he only caught a word now and then. Once they spoke of a little white lamb that had gone lame that day. "Yes, it is the fault of that young fellow who has been rushing around in all the empty huts among the hills, looking for his fire-red ox. I saw him throw a stone at the little lamb," said the older girl, the one with the large mouth and dark skin." He really should be punished for that!" said she.

1456 "Yes, but he never knew it was a lamb," replied the younger one, the beauty with the red cheeks. "And it was not right of grandmother to hide his ox, and make him hunt for it far and near."

1457 "He might have taken his ox, for it was standing just beside the hut, and he ran right past it," said the other girl.

1458 "Yes, but you know he took it to be a rat," the younger one answered. "Oh, how stupid those people are," said the older one again, and laughed until she shook. "They pretend to be wiser than wise, and cannot even tell a fire-red ox from a rat! Ha, ha, ha!" and she laughed so heartily that her sister was also carried away, and the young fellow himself could not help but smile a bit.

1459 [The young man played his mouth harp and the girls ran helter-skelter in fright, but then poked their heads back in the hut and saw him. The three of them had a light fanciful conversation about music, dance, and licorice.] Toward evening the girls wanted to leave. Yet that drove the young man to despair, and he begged them to stay for a little while. But the girls simply would not. Their mother would not allow it, said they. When the young fellow saw that they were really going, he went quite out of his mind. He had grown so very fond of the younger huldra[222] maiden, and now he was never to see her again. Without knowing what he was doing, he threw the jew's-harp at her, and hit her on the head, just as she was passing through the door. And with that she turned and came in again.

[222] [In Scandinavian folklore, the huldra (derived from the root meaning "secret" or "covered") is a seductive forest creature, the "Lady of the Forest."]

1460 "Mother, mother! A Christian has won sister Sireld!" cried the other, out in front of the hut. Soon after, a very ancient woman came hobbling and shuffiing into the hut. Her face was so wrinkled and dark that her yellow teeth shone out from it, for teeth she had, in spite of her age. "Now you may keep her, since you have won her, for now she is no longer bewitched," said the old woman to the young fellow. "And if you are kind to her, you shall never lack food or clothing, and you shall have all that you need, both Sundays and workdays. But if you treat her unkindly, you shall pay for it!" said the old woman, and raised her cane as though she were about to use it on the young fellow. Then she hobbled out again.

1461 It seemed to him that he had won a wife very quickly, after all, in this manner, and he asked her how it all came to be. "The jew's-harp struck my head with such force, that a drop of blood flowed," said the girl, "and it was the best thing you could have done, for I would much rather live with Christians than with the underground folk," said she. [They were married and all were happy.] But after the wedding he gradually began to ill-treat her. For you must know that he could never forget she was not a Christian. He sulked, and was always angry and ill-natured, and never gave her a kind word. And he refused to grant her least request. Though it might be the merest trifle, he never had more than a short "No," for anything she asked. And in spite of this she was kind and friendly, and acted as though she did not hear his angry words, and was always helpful and amiable. But it made no difference, he grew worse from day to day. And they began to go downhill, for strife in the home drives luck away. One day there was not even a crust of bread in the house. And then she grew sad, for all might have been different for them had he but treated her better. He was standing in the smithy at the moment, about to shoe a horse, and she went out to him.

1462 "Won't you build me the pen now, the one I have so often asked you for?" she begged. "Do it now, and I will shoe the horse!" And she tore the red-hot horseshoe from the anvil, and bent it in shape with her bare hands. When he saw that she was mistress of such arts, he grew frightened, and actually built her a fine, big pen back of the stable, set in a post, and drove a hook into it, just as she had said. The following morning the pen filled with fire-red cattle, big, fat, handsome beasts, that gave a great deal of milk. Such fine cows had never been seen anywhere. And on the hook hung a copper milk-pail, and a pair of horns of salt, with a silver ring from which to hang them. And now it was not long, as you may imagine, before they were more than prosperous at the farmstead again. For a time everything went well. He let her work and command in the house, and she had unfailing luck in all she undertook, so that wealth flowed in to them from every side. But at length he once more began to ill-treat her. Wherever he went he remembered that she was no Christian, no matter how kind and amiable and obedient she might be, and just like any one else, save that she was far, far more beautiful. Once he reached down the poker from the wall, and was about to beat her. She jumped up and begged him insistently not to touch her: "For else both of us will be unhappy!" But he would not listen to her, and beat her about the head, until the blood ran over the poker and fell on his hand. And then she suddenly disappeared from his sight. It seemed as though she had floated through the wall, or sunk into the ground. He saw nothing, but he heard a woman sob and weep, very quietly and softly, and painfully, and with a deadly sadness. After a little while all was silent and then he heard no more. He searched day in, day out, here and there, hither and yon. His neighbors, too, went along and helped him search; but to no avail. He never did find her, and could not even discover a trace of her. When he was in the hill pastures during the summer, and the rest of the folk were up there as well, and even after they had gone, he would sit night after night, and play "The Blue Melody," yet he never saw her again, nor any of her folk.

1463 In the summer his little girl was old enough to begin going to school. And one day she said to her father, when he came up to the hills: "I am to bring you a kind greeting from mother!"

1464 "Ah, no, my little girl, is that really the truth? Where did you speak to her!" he asked.

1465 "She and two others came here the day that Guro fetched the sheep, and since then she often comes here," answered the little one, "and they gave me their clasps, too," said she, and showed him three handsome round clasps.

1466 "Won't she come back home to us?" he asked, as well you may imagine.

1467 "She said that she really could not do that, and that she had to protect you continually against folk who wanted to harm you!" said the little one. Sadness had been his portion before this, and now it did not grow any less. And it was a blessing that before many years had passed the earth closed over him.[223]

---

[223] Edited and summarized from Stroebe, *Norwegian Fairy Book*, pp. 293–303.

1468 As in the fairytale, "The *Peaged Arsai* Bird," the magical sphere approaches the human world by stealing something from people. Psychologically, this means losing energy to the unconscious. Behind the theft stands the grandmother of the subterranean sphere, the Great Mother, the unconscious. Cursed, the young herdsman opens himself up to the underworld. The fact that two maidens appear to him, one coarser and darker, implies a splitting of the anima into a beneficial aspect and into a dark and shadowy one. This dual aspect is also revealed in the conversation of the two female spirit-beings. They mock the young man as being stupid, rob him, and let him find things and make unexpected discoveries. Corresponding to the double aspect of the anima, the boy becomes deeply fascinated and at the same time feels a certain resistance. When the girl is about to disappear, he falls into a sudden fit of rage and injures her. He thus wins over the girl since she is no longer "bewitched." The anima stirred the man's feeling function, a part of his own nature whose function is relatively unknown to him. The anima experience is identical to the unconscious experience mediated through his own feeling. Her ghost- or witch-like effect removes her completely beyond his control. Through his outburst of rage, the boy becomes aware of his feeling, he "attains" his soul-image and sees the anima in her human aspect, so that he can recognize his feelings [and claim them as being his own]. The blood is red like fire and is considered the seat of the emotional life of the soul. The appearance of blood thus symbolizes the process of becoming conscious in the heat of the moment (i.e., affect). The statement of the huldra maiden, that this injury was the best thing that could have happened to her (expressing her desire not to remain with the underground folk), again points to that desire that we recognize from so many fairytales, for redemption of the spirit nature-beings, the desire to share in human consciousness and life. Although the spirit maiden brings only blessings to the man, he despises her because she is not a Christian. This is a profane and actually unchristian attitude, with which he justifies his lack of control over himself relative to his wife. Corresponding to his wrong attitude towards the unconscious, he then has some bad times, until he has a second fit of anger, in which he again injures the woman and this time draws even more blood. Now he loses her forever. The conscious recognition of his emotions did not have the purpose of granting the freedom to degenerate into intemperance; rather it makes the man conscious of the demonic background of his affects. In that he whimsically lives out his feelings, he once again loses the psychological meaning, and the anima's secret is hidden from him again. This is embedded in her round clasp, which their daughter shows him, a symbol of the Self. The man's loss of the soul is so serious that he is soon drawn into the land of the spirits and the dead.[224]

[224] For another example see the Japanese tale, "Bentgen and the Horse Driver." There, a well-known singer and horse driver passed by the temple of the goddess Benzaïten every night, singing in his

1469 Only those specially called succeed in bringing back the anima who has vanished into the magical kingdom, such as a wizard or medicine man, who must mediate between two worlds, without falling prey to one side or the other. (Only those like Maitschaule in "The Visit to Heaven," or the hero of the parallel tale, "The Daughter of the King Vultures," who accept the magical competition with the demonic lords of the magical kingdom are reassured enough to take on this task.)

1470 In the tale "Old Man Coyote, the Man, the Buffalo Cow, and the Elk Cow," the hero succeeds with the help of magical power to compete with the male companions of his animal wife and to regain his lost anima.

> 1471 One day Old Man Coyote met a man carrying a bow and a quiver of arrows, roaming all over the world. Old Man Coyote said to him, "Come here, and I will show you something you will like." He took the man to the buffalo cow, stuck fast in the mud. Then Old Man Coyote told him to make connection [i.e., copulate] with this buffalo, which the man did. Afterwards, Old Man Coyote took the man to another place where a cow elk was mired, and the man was told to do as he had done with the buffalo cow, which he did, and the Old Man Coyote laughed at him. In the course of several weeks the buffalo cow and elk cow each gave birth to a boy.
>
> 1472 Shortly after his meeting with Old Man Coyote, the wandering man returned to his people. One day he was playing a game of ring and arrows. While playing, he was approached by a little boy with a short neck and curly hair, and who wore a buffalo-calf robe. The little boy said to him, "Father, if you win anything, give me some." The man looked about him and said, "I will." Shortly afterward another little boy, with lighter hair and longer neck, approached and asked him the same question. When the man had finished playing he called the two boys to him and asked, "How is it you call me father?" Each of the

---

beautiful voice. In this temple there was a miraculous object, "a living image of the goddess." Many worshippers saw in this figure a very beautiful woman. One night as the horse driver passed by singing, a woman of unearthly beauty stood outside the temple. He immediately recognized her as being the goddess herself. She told him that she always listened with delight to his voice and his songs and, therefore, decided to spend the night with him. But he must keep silent about their relationship, otherwise she will kill him. If he keeps their secret, however, she will provide him with protection from disease and distress. The pack driver enjoyed her love evening after evening. But then after awhile he yearned to share his secret relationship. He could no longer keep it to himself and a few days later he began to tell a friend about their secret relationship. But even before he could finish, he dropped dead, right to the ground (Rumpf, *Japanische Volksmärchen*, p. 275, first version). [The available edition of Rumpf 's translations – H. Hammitzsch et al., *Japanische*, p. 267 – includes another version.])
Another example of the fatal outcome of betraying a secret, is given by "The Snake's Comb." Here, a hunter kills and cooks up the meat of a large snake because he remembered that eating snake meat will give one the gift of understanding the speech of animals. When he, however, reveals the secret of his special knowledge, he falls down dead.

boys said, "Don't you remember the time when our mothers were stuck in the mud?" The man said he did. He told each of the boys to go and bring his mother to him, which they did, but in the form of women.

1473 After looking carefully at each, the man did not care for the elk woman, but lived with the buffalo woman, who said: "I will live with you only under the condition that you do not call me harsh names." The man promised, and lived with her for some time, but one day he was vexed at something she did, and he broke his promise, and pronounced a forbidden word. She quickly transformed herself into a buffalo cow and her child turned into a buffalo calf.

1474 The man tried to catch them. After many days of chasing them he came upon a big herd of buffalo, and as he was sitting on a hill looking at them, a little buffalo calf came silently up to him and said: "Father, my uncles are going to try you by placing all the calves of my age in a circle facing the center, and you are to be in the center, and you are to pick me out of the number. If you fail, my uncles are going to gore you to death; but I will give you a signal when you approach me by twitching my left ear. They also want you to find my mother by picking her out of a circle. I will go and lick some white clay and will act as though I were going to nurse, and will rub the white clay on her left shoulder, so that you may know her when you come to her." The buffalo made a big dance, and then told the man if he were unable to point out his wife and child they would gore him to death. After forming the circles of cows and calves, the man picked out his wife and child, which angered the buffalo uncles of the child, and they prepared to gore him to death.

1475 Now it had happened that while the man was on his way trying to find his wife and child, he had met Old Man Coyote, who instructed him to place a long thin piece of buffalo sinew and a breath feather of the eagle on the top of his head, that it might revolve when dancing. Now when the buffalo closed in to gore him, the feather rose in the air. Since his being was in the feather, there was no one in the center of the circle; the buffalo gored each other, breaking legs and shoulders; and they did this repeatedly, until at last they abandoned it, saying that his medicine was stronger than theirs, and they let him have his wife and child to take back to his camp.[225]

[225] Slightly revised from Simms, *Traditions of the Crows*, pp. 289–290. [There are many tales of a woman who marries a male animal; see also *ibid.*, pp. 301–303, "Bones-Together."]

1476 This story is similar to the South American tales about animal marriages discussed above, but has a larger format. Here the hero is a roving archer lacking connection to the earth.[226] The counsel of Old Man Coyote to mate with the cow and elk, who are stuck in the mud, arises from a higher wisdom, because through this a unification with the opposite takes place, a connection with the maternal principle, that is, with what is "stuck in the mud," with unmovable, stagnating nature. Old Man Coyote is an ideal image,[227] and in this tale a part of the hero's future, his primordial image, which he must realize. He can only individuate through the connection to the cows because true wisdom belongs to the principle of the earth, the feminine, which gives a sense of reality and fertile ground to the restless, roving spirit of the man. The fact that two cows appear first, and that the whole plot takes place twice, is based on the fact that very often unconscious images that approach the border to consciousness appear in dual form. Sometimes, the two appear as if they were opposites, since only as such, as a duality, can the approaching (initial unconscious) be grasped by the conscious mind. (Here, the pair is a dark buffalo cow and a light elk cow). As soon as the action progresses, the double phenomenon disappears and the problem continues as a unity. The boy, who as a half-breed stands closer to the father, mediates the connection with the cow mothers so that they can appear in human form, and the man chooses the buffalo woman to be his wife. Thus, he recognizes in retrospect – after the first connection had taken place half in the unconscious state (in the mud!) – the human nature of the anima and tries to integrate her into his life.

1477 After violating the ban to mention her origin, the woman flees with the child. Now the man faces the task of the great journey into the unconscious, the confrontation with all its conditions. He must compete with the woman's brothers, that is, with her male companions (as in other fairytales, like "The Visit to Heaven" and "The Daughter of the King Vultures," where it was the anima' father). In this tale, there is no fight with the father of the buffalo woman, the dark demon of the Earth, but with a more shadowy multiplicity of buffalos, the family of the woman. The primordial image of the buffalo that stands behind her is completely split, indicating that this aspect is still unknown (unconscious) to the hero. Nevertheless, this concerns a central decision, because the many buffalo circling close together around form a figurative wholeness. The hero is completely surrounded by, and thus taken prisoner by the buffalos; the anima's animal aspect, from which he had first detached them, binds him and inevitably forces him into a confrontation

---

226 See the rambling wanderer in "The Legend of K'anigyilak.

227 The German collector, Krickeberg, writes of this figure: "The 'white man' (*Vihuk*, the Arapaho *Nihanschan*) is, as the 'Old Man' (*Napiw* of the Blackfoot, 'Old Man Coyote' for the Crow, the common fairytale hero of the Plains tribes, half world-creator ["Maker of all things" – Crow], half trickster, resembling Mänäbusch of the Algonquian and Coyote/Hare/Rabbit of the plateau tribes, always given an animal name but considered to be pure human; see Krickeberg, *Nordamerika*, p. 388.

(*auseinandersetzung*). He must first recognize his wife and son – those with whom he is personally related – in this sphere and discriminate them from the animals, thus proving that he has not lost himself (i.e., in his being undifferentiated from them). The boy helps him attain the goal, whereas the mother remains passive. The son is closer to the man, because he is part of his [human] nature. As an intermediate between man and buffalo, he embodies the idea of a possible connection of the spheres. This is similar to "The Visit to Heaven," in which the successful tests of knowledge are of little help. The magical forces now attack him even more ferociously and threaten to crush the hero in the center of the circle. By standing in the center, he has challenged the principle of the buffalos to engage in the definitive test (*auseinandersetzung*) and risks suffering the full brunt of their onslaught. He has – in psychological terms – confronted the conflict head on. But just as the unconscious threatens to completely overrun him, that mysterious spirit who initiated the whole experience – Old Man Coyote - comes to his aid. He signals the arrival of a saving idea: to pass his soul over into the magical feather on his head.

1478 As a pars pro toto, the feather also stands for the bird,[228] and as such personifies the psychic-spiritual nature. The bird, and particularly the eagle, frequently symbolizes the spirit[229] (in oriental fairytales, the feather therefore plays an important role standing for the miraculous phoenix or the Simurgh bird. As a magical talisman, they help the heroes).[230] As a result, feathers, especially those worn on the head, take on the significance of thoughts. This is demonstrated particularly clearly by certain beliefs, such as those of the Huichol (Wixáritari people, Mexico), according to which a large variety of meaningful objects are called "feathers," from which follows that the term "feather" denotes the psychic force of that object. This is why feathers and plumage are so valuable for the Native Americans. Feathers have intrinsic mystical powers and serve the shaman as magical media.[231] When symbols are adorned with feathers, their spiritual-psychic qualities are implied.[232]

---

[228] On the *participation mystique* between "appurtenances" (e.g., feathers and hair), and the whole person, see Lévy-Bruhl, *The "Soul" of the Primitive*, pp. 123ff.

[229] In ancient times, the eagle was the image of the soul soaring to God. See Dieterich, *Eine Mithrasliturgie*, pp. 54, 184, and Bachofen, *Orphische Theologie*, p. 20.

[230] See Bolte and Mackensen, *Handwörterbuch* under *Feder* [feather]. See also "The Griffin."

[231] See Lévy-Bruhl, *How Natives Think*, pp. 24 and 100–101. See also the feathers of life in "The Brothers Visit Their Father," especially in Matthews, *Navajo Legends*, pp. 231–32: "By life-feather or breath-feather (*hyiná biltsós*) is meant a feather taken from a live bird, especially one taken from a live eagle. Such feathers are supposed to preserve life and possess other magic powers."

[232] On the divine images of the Egyptians decorated with feathers that are described in *The Egyptian Book of the Dead*, see Roeder, *Urkunden*, pp. 292–93. See also "The Pirarukus," in which the primordial image of the catfish appears not as a catfish but as its feathered mask (see Koch-Grünberg, *Südamerika*, pp. 32–29; see also the plumed sun symbol of the Hopi in "The Coming of the Hopi from the Underworld," especially in Krickeberg, *Nordamerika*, p. 330, where the collector notes that feathers correspond to sun rays. In this respect, a hero adorned with feathers signals an acceptance of the power of the sun. In "Akalapischeima and the Sun," Wei, the sun, wears feather plumage (esp. Koch-Grünberg,

1479 In that his true nature takes refuge in the eagle feathers on his head, the hero assumes part of the eagle's nature, refines it, and elevates it to a spirit-being. The buffalo demons are powerless against this because he is thus hidden from them. As the buffalo said, the man's medicine was stronger; and they are forced to recognize his psychic superiority, a superiority that was granted to him through an idea of Old Man Coyote.[233] Now the man can take his animal wife and their child "to his camp" in their human form. That is, he can incorporate his instinctive soul and his new form of existence into his previous life.

1480 Despite its primitive features, this fairytale expresses much more clearly, through its far-reaching images, than the previous ones about animal marriages the task of the appointed hero, who must connect with the earth in order to become a real shaman. As a rambler and wanderer, he is a masculine, enterprising, conquering spirit; by turning to a cow stuck in the mud, and by confronting the overpowering buffalo, he regains his roots to the earth and thus real wisdom.

1481 Whereas in this fairytale the hero, who pursues the lost anima, is forced to confront the entire herd of buffalo, in the following tale, "The Jack-of-all-trades of the Plains," the mysterious companion of the woman is portrayed as a single mystical being, a totem ancestor, upon whom the existence of the tribe depends. This fairytale portrays the tragic destruction of this divine ancestor by the conscious intervention of a man foreign to the tribe:

1482 A man and a woman first had a boy child and then a girl. When they grew up, the daughter was first to marry and receive her dowry. With this, the parents said to the boy: "We will now find you a girl to marry from a respected family." But the boy spurned the offer, "I cannot endure the girls from around here!" So he decided to leave that land. His parents accepted his decision, but said if he ran into misfortune, that that was not their fault. So he went away very far into an unknown region. In one village, he saw many girls, some were mashing grain, others were cooking. They pleased him and so he went to the men of the village. "Fathers," he said, after greetings were finished, "I like your daughters, I would like to marry one of them." The men were pleased and showed their daughters and he chose one. The man agreed to a

Südamerika, p. 94, where the sun wears a headdress of parrot feathers and then beetle elytra (forewings). See also "The Twins" (Koch- Grünberg, *Südamerika*, pp. 213–15): "The father of the twins has the job here, according to its attributes, a crown of red *arara* and tucan feathers and fiery eyes, to judge, an undoubtable color character, whereas the sons later themselves become the sun and moon" (Koch-Grünberg, *Südamerika*, p. 220).

[233] On this figure, see also the helpful ancestors with their good advice in the Inuit tale, "The Strange Boy."

marriage and said, "Of course your parents will come soon to arrange the dowry with us." "No, the man said, "they will not come. I have the dowry right here with me. Here it is, take it" "Surely you will come later to take home your bride." "Do not make yourself ill with your hard exhortations, just let me take my bride with me."

1483 They considered and accepted the man's conditions. Then they took the girl aside to a hut and explained to her how she should behave as a wife. "Be good to your parents-in-law and take good care of your husband." They offered the pair a younger girl to go with them to help in their new household. But the bride refused. Then the man offered her two, ten, twenty girls to help that she could chose herself. All the girls were brought before her, but she refused them all, saying, "You can give me the buffalo from this land, our buffalo, the jack-of-all-trades from the plains, they can serve me." "Why the buffalo? You know that our life depends in many ways on the buffalo, they are well cared for here with us. What do you want to do with them in a foreign land, they will starve and die and then we will all die with them!"

1484 "But of course I will care for them well," the bride said. Before she left her parents, she took with her a pot and a small package of medicinal roots, a horn for cupping and a small knife to cut and a gourd full of oil. Then she brought these with her to her husband. The buffalo followed them, but it was only visible to the woman; the man had no idea that the jack-of-all-trades from the plains was the servant that accompanied her.

1485 When they arrived at the groom's home they were received with cries of joy, "Hoyo, hoyo, hoyo!" When his parents saw them, they said, "Now, see, indeed you have found a wife. You did not want any from those we recommended but that does not matter, it is good the way it is. You had to have your way. When you get enemies, you cannot complain to us."

1486 The man accompanied his wife to the fields and showed her which one were his and which one belonged to his mother. She took careful notice of everything and went back with him to the village. When they were underway, she said to him, "I have lost my pearls in the fields and must go back to find them." Actually she wanted to see how her buffalo was doing. She told the buffalo, "Here are the boundaries of the fields, stay here! There is a forest nearby in which you can hide." "It is good" said the buffalo to her.

1487 Whenever the woman wanted water, she would go to her fields and set the empty bucket in front of the buffalo. The buffalo would take it to the lake, fill it and bring it back to his mistress. When she wanted firewood, he would go into the thicket, bring down trees with his horns and return with as much wood as she wanted. The people in the village began to wonder, "What kind of powers does that woman have?" Scarcely has she gone to get water and she brings a full can back. If she wants wood, she goes and comes right back with her bag stuffed full of dry wood!" But no one suspected that she had a buffalo who was at her beck and call like a faithful servant. But she never brought him anything to eat because there was only one plate for her and her husband to share. Back at her home, they had a special plate for their Jack-of-all-trades from the plains and they made sure he was well-nourished. She kept taking her water cans to him and he would faithfully go to the lake, but the agonizing pain of hunger now went with him.

1488 The woman then showed the buffalo a piece of brush land that he could clear to make a field. That night, the buffalo took a hoe and spade and cleared a large field. "How skillful she is," said the people, "and how fast she works!" In the evenings, the buffalo spoke to his mistress: "I am hungry and you give me nothing to eat, I will soon not be able to work for you!" "Oh dear," she said, "but what can I do? We have only one plate in the whole house. The people were right when they said you must begin to steal, yes, then go out and steal! Go here in my field and take a bean here and there. Then go to the next field, do not rob all from one field, but from several. Then the owners might not notice and not get upset."

1489 In the night the buffalo came and ate a bean here and a bean there, he jumped from one field into the other and went back to his hiding place. Next morning when the women went to their fields, they could not believe what they saw, "Hey, what has happened here? This we have never seen before! A wild animal has destroyed our crops and fields." They could not find any tracks. "Oh, our poor land!" they cried, and went back to tell the other villagers of their plight.

1490 That evening the foreign woman said to the buffalo, "The people noticed, but they did not get all that upset. Go ahead and steal again tonight." And so it happened. The owners of the ransacked fields now became very angry and called on the watchmen of the village to get their guns. Now it happened that the husband of the young woman was a sharpshooter, and went to watch over his own field. That night the buffalo thought it best not to go to the fields of the other women, and so he went to the field of his mistress. The man saw him and said, "Wait! That is a buffalo, a foreign being here. He aimed and shot. The bullet went in one side and out the other and the "Miracle animal of the plains" fell down dead. "That was a good shot," said the man, and went to tell the people of the village.

1491 Now his wife began complaining and bent over in pain, "Oh, I have great pains all over my body, oh, oh!" He told her to calm down, but she only looked like she was sick, she wanted to explain why she was crying so hard since she heard of the death of the buffalo. She was given medicine, but she threw it away when nobody was watching.

1492 Everyone in the village now went with baskets and knives to butcher the buffalo. The woman remained back in the village, then followed the people, she was holding her stomach and crying. When the man saw her he said, "You are sick, go back and stay in our home." "No, I do not want to stay alone in the village." Her mother-in-law went to her, and comforted her saying, "You are ill, you do not know that death could come and take you away." When the big basket was filled with meat, the woman said, "Let me carry the head." "No, it is heavy and you are sick." But she persisted and took the head of the buffalo and carried it back to the village. But instead of going into her home, she went into the shed where her cooking pots were and put the head of the buffalo down. She stubbornly remained there, no one could get her to move. Her husband came and told her to come to their home, she would be much better off there. But she angrily refused, "Do not disturb me!" Her step-mother came and the man again, entreating her to come into the house, but she obstinately refused.

1493 Then they finally left her alone and went back to his hut, but that night he could not sleep. He listened. The woman made a fire, took the head, and put it in one of her cooking pots with water on the fire. Then she took down the bag of medicine that she had brought with her. She made a small cut with the knife behind the ear, just where the bullet entered. There she put the horn and sucked and sucked with all of her bodily might. At first came only a piece of clotted blood, but then liquid blood. She then began to treat the head with the medicine she had brought from her home. When the water was boiling, she filtered the clotted blood from the wound through the cupping horn, then she warmed the wound with steam from the cooking pot and rubbed in the fat from the gourd. All this soothed her. Then she sang:

1494 Oh, my father, Jack-of-all-trades from the plains,
Well they told me so, they told me so,
Jack-of-all-trades from the plains.
They told me: You will go through deep darkness
In all directions you will go on lost and confused in the night,
Jack-of-all-trades from the plains,

You taste the young miracle tree plants,
you wake up from your ruins, that have died before their time,
chewed by a knawing worm. . .
You let flowers and fruit fall on your way,
Jack-of-all-trades from the plains!

1495 When she had ended her incantation, the head began to move, the limbs grew back and the buffalo felt himself alive again. He shook his ears and horns, stood up and stretched his legs.

1496 Her husband had not been able to sleep that night. He got up and said to himself, "Why has my wife been crying so hard? I have to see how she utters these sobs!" He went to the shed where she was, but she burst out enraged, "Leave me alone!" And then the head of the buffalo fell to the ground, bored through by the bullet, dead, as before.

1497 The man turned and left the shed, he had not understood nor seen a thing from all that had happened. The woman again took the cooking pot, filled it with water and fresh medicine, encased the cuts, sucked out blood with the cupping horn, let steam on the wounds, and sang again her magic incantation.

1498 Once again the head of the buffalo turned upwards, his limbs grew, he felt himself coming to life. He stood up on his feet, shook his ears and horns. Then the husband came again, untroubled and distraught. What was his wife doing now? Again she became irate. This time the man decided to stay in the shed and observe what was going on. The woman picked up all her utensils, the cooking pot, the fire, and went outside. She pulled up grass to fire up the coals and began a third time to wake the buffalo up from death.

1499 It was becoming light, day was approaching, and along came the mother-in-law. Again the head of the buffalo fell dead to the ground as before. The sun came up and the wounds worsened. The woman said to them, "I would like to go totally alone to the lake to bathe. Her husband answered her, "But how will you go there, you are sick!" The woman went anyway on her way. She soon returned, "On the way I met someone from my village who told me my mother was very, very ill. I told him that he should come to the village here, but he refused saying, 'One would offer me food and that would only make it more difficult for me.' He turned to go and then said that I should hurry, out of fear that my mother could die before I arrive. Live well! I will go now." All these words were naturally lies, she had the idea of going to the lake and thought up this story to have a reason to go tell her people that the buffalo had died.

1500 She left and on her way with her basket on her head, sang the incantation to the buffalo. Wherever she went, the people followed behind her and accompanied her to her village. The woman told them that the buffalo was no longer alive.

1501 Then messengers were sent out all over the land to call together all the people. They reproached the young woman with heavy accusations.

1502 "Don't you see? We told you so! You refused to take with you the girls and wanted only the buffalo! Now you have killed us all!" They were going on this way when her husband arrived. He had followed his wife from his village. He laid his rifle against a tree trunk and sat down. They greeted him, saying, "Greetings, criminal, greetings! You have killed us all!" He did not understand and asked himself, how could one call me a criminal and murderer? I killed a buffalo, yes, but that is all. The people answered him, "Yes, but this buffalo was the helper and advisor of your wife. He scooped water for her, he cut wood for her, he worked in the fields for her." Completely amazed, the man said, "Why did no one tell me this? Had I known all this, I certainly would not have killed him." "Yes but it is now so, our whole lives, our existence depended on him." Then the people began to speak the incantation and with each verse, they cut open their necks; first that of the young woman.

1503 "Oh, my father, Jack-of-all-trades from the plains."

1504 Then her parents, her brothers, her sisters came, one after the other,
"You will go through the deep darkness,"
The other: "You will go lost and confused through the night,"
And another, "You have bitten from the magical tree plant that died before its time!"
Still another, "You let the flowers and fruit fall on your way."

1505 All the people sliced open their necks and executed the small children that they carried in cribs on their backs. They spoke, "Then why should we let you live, that you would only lose your mind?" The man turned away and returned to his own village. He told his people how, in that he had killed the buffalo, he had killed all the people of his wife's village. His parents said to him, "Now do you see? Didn't we tell you that you would bring misfortune. When we offered to find an appropriate wife for you, you just wanted to follow your own head. Now you have lost all your valuables. Who will give it back to you now that they are all dead, all those relatives of the woman to whom you gave your money!"

1506 And that is the end.[234]

[234] Translated from Meinhof's *Afrikanische Märchen*, pp. 100–08, who translated this tale from Junod's French edition (*Ba-Ronga*, pp. 353–62).

1507 Similar to "Makonaura and Anuanaitu," this fairytale depicts the momentous destruction of the paternal totem animal that stands behind the anima. In this case, the hero is able to rescue himself, though not without losing some of his possessions, into secular life. Whereas Makonaura first kills the brother of the beautiful stranger at the water's edge, and only later takes on the battle with the father of all alligators, Kaikutschi, here the figure of the anima's servient and dark companion is the father himself. In her magical incantations, the woman addresses the buffalo's spirit as "my father." Psychologically speaking, he appears, on the one hand, as a lesser shadowy part of the personality and simultaneously, on the other hand, as a superior divinity, as his name reveals.[235] He unites animal nature and the divine magical powers.

1508 Unlike Ititaujang, who is spurned by all and forced by necessity to look for an extraordinary woman, the hero here takes leave of his community without the prerequisite of loneliness and rejection. He only wants to take a wife of his own choice. Herein lies a certain arrogance towards his clan, a claim to distinctiveness, to which he, however, cannot do justice. Possibly here lies the root of the tragic course of this tale, as his parents' final words make clear. The hero chooses a "stranger," an "unknown woman," to be his wife. He follows a psychic attraction and joins himself to his anima, but at the same time to a world with a different kind of mysterious background of which he does not take cognizance. By taking a woman from a foreign clan, he runs into difficulty with its totem principle, which must be kept secret, and about which those not belonging to the clan are not allowed to know anything.

1509 The woman conceals, probably realizing that her husband is not capable of initiation into her totem, her father's existence, who follows her as a servant. Despite her family's warnings, she takes him with her. The fact that both his family and hers is reluctant shows that the rightly existing barriers between consciousness and the unconscious should not have been crossed, because the hero has no calling, and the woman does not long for redemption. As a result, the man's desire for the unknown woman appears here to be unconsciously driven rather than by an inner justification, and this may also be why the woman concealed the existence of her mystical father.

1510 The clan and the totem ancestor of the girl are first described in a secular manner because the primitives believe that the matters of the afterlife reflect the real world.[236] The description as a real situation, with no features of an inwardly experienced event, can be explained by the primitive's mentality, who experiences the wonderful (only) outwardly, projected onto animals and strangers; for them the outside world is psychically permeated, so that the

---

235 [The "original" French name given to this figure is *Gambadeur-de-la-Plaine*, whereby *Gambade* means "jump, skip, frolic."]

236 See "Flight to the Moon," the Inuit house in the moon or in "Blue-Jay Visits his Sister Io'i in the Land of the Dead," the world, that Blue Jay encounters.

realms are not separated, as civilized peoples believe. This is why the fairytales of primitive peoples seem so real and their reports of the real seem to be like fairytales.

1511 While the anima, as so often, appears to be easily integrated into conscious life, problems arise with her secret companion (in other fairytales, expressed as the anima's longing to return to her father). The male spirit-being, which stands behind her, cannot simply integrated.

1512 The buffalo represents the miraculous power of the strange woman that the man naively ascribes to her. But the fascination emanating from the anima-image is based precisely on her connection with the dark god. Just as any significant content of the unconscious consumes substance, the buffalo-god needs nourishment. And because the man does not even suspect his existence, and does not consciously sacrifice food, the buffalo is forced to steal it. Unconsciously, the man suffers a continuous loss of soul, which none of the woman's efforts can make up for. The god becomes an autonomous and destructive demon. The anima, who responds to him more than to the secular man, supports his thievery and thus secretly stands by his side; the man more and more loses contact with the anima and only lives in the illusion that he possesses a real woman. He overlooks her magical aspect. The unconscious "starves" because it receives no attention. Finally, it steps out of its invisibility and confronts the man as a real, visible buffalo. What for the man had been previously an invisible, unheeded spiritual principle, now becomes an actual threat. Against this new kind of danger the man is perplexed and does not know how to react except to use the "miracle weapon" of the white man, the rifle. Guns represent the intellect that invented them; it does "not believe in spirits"[237] and destroys the buffalo deity.

1513 The anima, who had brought her god with her, has the ability to revive him by magic. Here her own magical skills appear for the first time, proving that she is not only an ordinary woman, but a miraculous being. But the man's and his mother's destructive, profane interference[238] prevent the revival of the god.

1514 The head contains the seed of revival, the whole being.[239] With this head, the woman secretly performs the magic ritual of revival. Her incantation reveals that she considers the buffalo her father and a great magician. It also

---

[237] If a version should ever turn up that is less influenced by "the whites" and where the weapon is a bow and arrow instead of a flint, this would not alter the above interpretation, since the meaning of "piercing through" is the same.

[238] Cf. the negative role of the mother in "The Tiger Changed into a Woman" and "The Adventures of Mrile."

[239] See "The Moon," "The Rolling Skull," "Skull Acts as Food-Getter," and "Hitchinna." See also Frazer, *The Golden Bough*, p. 523: "The Baganda greatly fear the ghosts of buffaloes which they have killed, and they always appease these dangerous spirits. On no account will they bring the head of a slain buffalo into a village or into a garden of plantains: they always eat the flesh of the head in the open country. Afterwards they place the skull in a small hut built for the purpose, where they pour out beer as an offering and pray to the ghost to stay where he is and not to harm them."

shows what her clan predicted, that the way of the buffalo in the secular world would be a mistaken path in the dark night.

1515 One can see in the destructive path that a person travels who does not recognize, acknowledge, and realize the spirit-world, the totem godhead can be viewed in two ways: from the standpoint of consciousness, it seems as if human beings perish when confronting the archetype and lose themselves in the unconscious, as in "Makonaura and Anuanaitu." From the point of view of the unconscious, the divine image might be said loses itself in the world and dies when humans do not accord it a reality (hence the starvation of the buffalo!). This is also portrayed in "Makonaura and Anuanaitu," where both ways of viewing are connected. In the African tale, the fate of the totem god is depicted only from the point of view of the unconscious; indeed the incantation is that of an anima figure. She also says of the buffalo father that he is a young gourd plant that "dies before its time," consumed by a gnawing worm. She thus implies that the image of her secret father could be the germ of future possibilities of spiritual development that are prematurely devoured by a blindly consuming creature (a worm). Here the tragic development of the male is outlined, who as one uncalled and unchosen blindly and greedily usurps magical powers.

1516 The song about "Jack-of-all-trades" also states that he still drops flowers and fruits on his way. This reveals that he, like Byamee (in "A Legend of Flowers"), is heralded as the primordial father and creator of all the beautiful things of the Earth, as his name implies.

1517 The man disturbs the woman's resurrection spell. From the beginning, she continues to hide the buffalo from him. Her magical rites to revive the deity are a mystery that he may not behold since he has no real relationship to the realm of the psyche and the secrets hidden there. The woman assumes that neither can he recognize her true origin nor is he mature enough to value the insight into her real nature. She believes that he would not honor or comprehend the secret if revealed. The anima, as a purely natural being, cannot inhibit the man's negative attitude. She completes her task unconcerned by his wrong attitude. Through his and his mother's disturbing presence, her magic fails. According to the typical scheme seen so far, the magical partner withdraws following the betrayal to the secular.

1518 The death of the totem animal leads to the extinction of the entire clan[240]; nothing else is possible following the *participation mystique* with the life principle that it embodied. The totem was also the guiding spiritual primordial image of the tribe; it is said the children would "lose their minds" after its death. It is what gave meaning to their life.[241] This dissolution and destruction

---

240 See G. v. d. Leeuw, *Religion in Essence*, vol. 1 p. 78ff. On this theme, see "The One-Sided Old Man," where the whole tribe falls dead when the One-Sided Old Man is killed.

241 See Lévy-Bruhl, *The "Soul" of the Primitive*, pp. 71–72: "This intimate dependence on [the headman] is expressed by the Thonga, not in abstract terms, but in striking images. 'The chief is the Earth. He is

of the magical sphere, that is, the world that belongs to the anima, and her own death, signifies for the man the complete and final loss of his psychic inner life. He remains as a dead part of his total personality, a despised part of his own clan, and is separated from that world for which he had longed in his youth. The reproaches by his parents, prejudiced by their one-sided, worldly, practical thinking, stamp him as a proud and rightly punished fool.

1519 At the same time, as so often in the fairytales of primitive peoples, the attempt to penetrate the magical sphere is portrayed as a hopeless venture, which can only end badly, and against which the laws of the clan provide the best protection. The primitive experiences the proximity of the unconscious as overpowering, divine, and dangerous. As in a reflection, the clan also objects to the anima taking the buffalo; when she returns home, she is accused of betraying him to the profane world. The man's reproach, "Why did you not tell me?," once again reveals his ignorance of the secrets of the magical world, which follows transpersonal laws and is uninterested in the outcome, whether good or bad. Thus, the people just shrug their shoulders, indicating "That is just how it is."

1520 This tale shows that the anima stands on the border between the two spheres, and is a part of both. She does not let herself be carried by the hero into his secular world, nor does he let himself be enthralled[242] into her world. If the fairytale hero violates certain prohibitions, whose observance the magical sphere requires, then the spheres are separated, which can be perceived either as a tragic loss or as a liberation from the spook. More sophisticated fairytales are not content with just this separation, but describe a subtle and dangerous confrontation with the unconscious, through which the hero can win the anima and her hidden values, without having to fear being devoured by her realm. The difficulties in dealing with the anima, the threats faced by the man who encounters her, and the fulfillment of all desires that possessing her promises, confer upon a distinctly dual aspect. The following Serbian fairytale, "The Wonderful Hair," describes this with unsurpassable finesse:

1521 > There once lived a man who was poor and had many children. He could not feed them and even one morning he was close to killing all of them in order not to see them suffer from starvation. It was only his wife who kept him from carrying out this horrible deed. One night while he slept, a lovely child appeared to him and said, "Man, I see

---

the cock . . . he is the bull; without him the cows cannot bring forth. He is the husband; the country without him is like a woman without a husband. He is the man of the village . . . A clan without chief has lost its reason. It is dead. . . The chief is our great warrior; he is our forest where we hide ourselves, and from whom we ask for laws . . . The chief is a magical being. He possesses special medicines with which he rubs himself or which he swallows, so that his body is taboo,' etc." (Quote taken from Junod, *Life*, Neuchatel, pp. 356–357.

242 [German: *entrücken*.]

you are on the point of sacrificing your soul by killing all your poor children. I know that you are in misery and, therefore, have come to help you. Early tomorrow morning you will find under your pillow a mirror, a red handkerchief, and an embroidered scarf. Take these three things with you and do not say a word to anyone. Go out into the forest where you will find a stream. Now travel upriver until you come to its source. There you will meet a girl, shining like the sun, with long hair flowing over her shoulder, but wearing no clothes, just as she was born from the mother. But beware and do not speak a word to her lest bad things happen to you! At the first sound that you make she will bewitch you into a fish or something else edible and eat you right up. If she should ask you, however, to run your hand through her hair, then do not refuse her request. Now when you rummage through her hair, you just might find one hair that is red as blood. Quickly pluck it out and hurry back. When the maiden notices and starts to run after you, you should drop first the embroidered scarf, then the red handkerchief, and lastly let the mirror fall. She will stop each time to pick them up and tarry a bit, but you must run on and look for some rich person who will purchase that hair. Do not let yourself be cheated because the hair is of immense value! With the proceeds you will be rich and can then feed your children."

1522 When the poor man awoke in the morning, he indeed found under his pillow all that the child had told him in the dream. Without delay, he got up and made his way into the woods. When he had found the stream, he went along upstream until he reached its source. He looked around and saw the maiden sitting on the edge of the water catching sunbeams that she threaded through a needle to embroider a cloth that was woven from the hair of heroes. Just when caught she sight of him, he went and joined her. The girl stood up, however, and asked him, "Where are you, unknown hero?" But he was silent. She asked him again, "Who are you and why have you come here?" And many more questions. But the man remained silent as a stone. With his hands he motioned as if to say that he had no voice and was looking for help. Then she told him to sit at her feet. Delighted by this gesture, he immediately complied. She bowed her head down to him so that he could ruffie through her hair. He carefully ran his hands through her hair, eagerly seeking the red strand. No sooner had he found it, then he gently separated it from the neighboring hairs, plucked it out, sprang up, and ran away as fast as he could.

1523 The girl noticed this of course and, no less nimble than he, ran after him. Soon she was upon his heels, and looking around and seeing that she had almost caught up, he threw down the embroidered cloth, as he had been told in the dream. When she saw it, she stopped running and studied the cloth from all sides, admiring the beautiful embroidery. Meanwhile, the man gained a significant lead. Then the maiden hid the cloth in her bosom and hurried after him. Since she was faster than he, she soon almost reached him and he threw down the red handkerchief. Again, she stopped to pick it up and contemplated it in wonder. The poor man again gained a distance from her. But this time she grew angry at being distracted, threw the embroidery and handkerchief away, and hastened after the man. Hot in pursuit, she again caught up to him and in dire straights, he threw down the mirror. The maiden had in her whole life never seen a mirror and full of curiosity, she stopped to pick it up. She looked at herself in the mirror and thought she was seeing a second look-alike girl. Deeply sunk in her new discovery, the man was able to rush far, far ahead. So far that she could never catch up to him. When the maiden finally looked up, she realized what had happened and turned back to the spring.

1524 The man reached his house happy and healthy, showed the hair to his wife and his children and told them all that had happened. His wife only laughed and made fun of him because of the red hair, but he paid no attention, and forthwith made off to the nearest town to sell the hair there. Soon after arriving at the marketplace, a crowd of curious onlookers and merchants gathered around him. Offers for the hair were soon raised, first a gold coin, then two, then three, and so on until at last someone offered one hundred pieces of gold. Now the Emperor heard of the red hair and called the man to his palace. The man could not refuse the offer of one thousand pieces of gold and sold the red hair to the emperor. Now what was so special about this one red hair? The emperor carefully split it in half and found there exceedingly valuable knowledge and facts recorded since the creation of the world.

1525 Thus the man became rich and went on to live a carefree and happy life with his wife and children. The child that had appeared to him in a dream was, however, an angel sent by the Lord God, who wanted to help the man. This angel-child of God also wanted to bring to light the many concealed and mysterious things that had never been revealed to mankind up to that time.[243]

[243] [Translated from Karadzic, *Volksmärchen der Serben*, a collection of Serbian fairytales translated into German by Wilhelmine Karadzic, with a preface by Jakob Grimm, pp. 182–186.]

1526 Outer distress as a precondition for encountering one's inner figures is a familiar theme. First, the poor man meets not the anima, but the dream image of a child who foretells the future and bestows advice and help to overcome the dangers of the encounter with the anima. Probably as a result of later Christian revision, the child is called an angel sent from God, that is, a messenger from the otherworld. Psychologically, the child symbolizes the "individuality that is not yet conscious."[244] This future-oriented meaning makes stories about child deities widespread. The child is thus a symbol of the highest value. It unites the opposites and is

1527 [A] ll that is abandoned and exposed and at the same time divinely powerful; the insignificant, dubious beginning, and the triumphant end. The "eternal child" in man is an indescribable experience, an incongruity, a handicap and a divine prerogative; an imponderable that determines the ultimate worth or worthlessness of a personality."[245]

1528 As is evident from the last fairytale, the child symbol appears in an

> . . . agonizing situation of conflict from which there seems no way out – at least for the conscious mind. A meaningful but unknown content always carries a secret fascination for the conscious mind. The new configuration is a nascent whole; it is on the way to wholeness, at least in so far as it excels in "wholeness" the conscious mind when [it is] torn by opposites and [the new configuration] surpasses it in completeness. Nothing in all the world welcomes this new birth, although it is the most precious fruit of Mother Nature herself, the most pregnant with the future, signifying a higher stage of self-realization.[246]

1529 And,

> [The child] is a personification of vital forces quite outside the limited range of our conscious mind; of ways and possibilities of which our one-sided conscious mind knows nothing; a wholeness which embraces the very depths of Nature. It represents the strongest, the most ineluctable urge in every being, namely the urge to realize itself.[247]

---

244 See C.G. Jung, *Psychological Types*, CW 6, ¶808.
245 C.G. Jung, *Child*, CW 9i, ¶300.
246 Ibid., ¶285-86.
247 Ibid., ¶289; see also "The Adventures of Mrile."

1530 That is why the child in our story knows and can give advice to the man on how he can wrest the saving wisdom from the anima, whom he meets as an ambivalent dazzling force of nature, without succumbing to her. Thus, the image of the child "anticipates the figure that comes from the synthesis of conscious and unconscious elements in the personality."[248] The child also symbolizes the spiritual attitude of humility and obedience, a prerequisite for entering the Christian kingdom of God, a symbol of salvation.[249] Not without reason is the child in this story accorded such great importance that it appears as God's messenger. The cause of its appearance is the immense danger that threatens the man in his encounter with the anima. In this fairytale, the problematic and threatening side of the anima is not kept hidden, but vividly depicted. Here, however, she is not a scary ghost, but rather a dazzling naked beauty who holds the deepest secrets of our own world, which God wants to reveal to the world. Insofar as this tale depicts the ambiguous nature of the anima figure in its full weight and significance, it surpasses all the previous descriptions of this archetype.

1531 The man may not speak to the goddess of the spring, because otherwise she would turn him into a fish or another animal to eat. This is reminiscent of the magical abilities of the goddess Circe in Homer's *Odyssey*, half-mother goddess, half-anima, who also provides the hero with secret knowledge. The ability of the Great Mother or anima to transform the man into an animal means psychologically (as explained above) that she emanates such a fascinating effect that the man is swallowed up entirely by the unconscious and sinks to an animal level. He becomes like a fish, that is, something living that moves only in the realm of the unconscious. To protect oneself against such magic, according to the fairytale, it is best not to speak at all, which is equivalent to not making contact. As long as someone is not really conscious, they are unable to confront the anima in terms of an I-Thou relationship; in this case, they should avoid closer contact, through which they could be devoured.

1532 After snatching the sought-after treasure from the head of the spring goddess, the hero must immediately flee and protect himself by throwing objects behind himself. While these objects hold off the pursuer without changing their shape, there are similar flight scenes in which the objects thrown behind become large obstacles. This kind of flight motif is very common and based on an archetype that Franz Boas calls "magic flight."[250] In

---

[248] Ibid., ¶289.
[249] See Jung, *Psychological Types*, CW 6, ¶364f., and Silesius, *The Cherubinic Wanderer*, p. 60, no. 50, *God becomes a little child*:

> Divine immensity is in a child enclosed
> Oh, how I wish to be a child within this child!

[250] See Frobenius, *Zeitalter*, pp. 408ff, esp. p. 409.

some fairytales, such scenes even become the main motif.[251] As observed,[252] this motif recalls a popular type of anxiety dream. Psychologically, it indicates an unconscious threat. The magic flight symbolizes escaping from one's inner demons,[253] which consciousness is unable to master. Under some circumstances, such an escape should be regarded not only as cowardice, but as the only possible protective action.

1533 This happens when consciousness lacks the strength to withstand the unconscious content, but would be devoured or dispersed by it (equivalent to inducing a dissociation or even an outbreak of insanity). If the conscious mind succeeds in asserting itself, however, then it defeats or reconciles (in psychological terms, assimilates) the dangerous contents of the unconscious. This is especially true since, as experience shows, the demons lose their threatening aspects when the person overcomes his or her fear. Once again, we see how the unconscious loses its menacing countenance depending on the person's attitude.[254] The threat is a part of the Self; whoever splits it off from themselves, loses something.

1534 Throwing objects behind oneself (as Bolte and Mackensen's *Handwörterbuch* shows) is an ancient magical tradition. "Behind" is the unconscious, and throwing something behind therefore means sacrificing, donating, or offering something to the unconscious. This sacrifice creates a barrier that inhibits the pursuer. The discarded objects usually have symbolic importance. Thus, this is a primitive ritual. Every ritual serves the purpose of protection against "the uncanny things that live in the depths of the psyche."[255] This "uncannily alive" is characterized by the fact that the objects thrown

---

[251] Thus, for example, "The Girl and the Evil Spirit," "Ču'mo," "The Young Man and the Bears," "Skull Acts as Food-Getter," "The Nixie of the Mill-Pond." See further "The Mother and her Dead Son," "The Magical Escape," and "A Tale of Two Girls"; see also Krickeberg, *Nordamerika*, p. 371, as well as "Black Arts," "The Magic Horse," "The Mass of the Dead," and "Reindeer Born." For even more examples, see Hertz, *Werwolf*, pp. 81 and 121f. For a general theory, other material and further references, see Wesselski, *Versuch*, pp. 30f., 69f., 176f. In "Die Magische Flucht," Aarne examines the prototype of the magic flight and attempts to trace the original motif to the escape from the fairytale Otherworld or from the realm of the dead.

[252] See Bolte and Mackensen, *Handwörterbuch*, under *Flucht, magisches* [flight, magical].

[253] [In *Projection and Re-Collection* (1995, p. 99f.), von Franz substantiates this further as an escape from *being possessed* by inner demons.]

[254] On the strength and weakness of the conscious standpoint, see C.G. Jung, "Psychology of the transference," CW 16, ¶381 and *Children's Dreams*, p. 209: "A persecutory dream always means: this wants to come to me. When you dream of a savage bull, or a lion, or a wolf pursuing you, this means: it wants to come to you. You would like to split it off, you experience it as something alien – but it just becomes all the more dangerous. The urge of what had been split off to unite with you becomes all the stronger. The best stance would be [to say]: 'Please, come and devour me!' Working with such a dream in analysis means to familiarize people with the thought that they should by no means resist when this element faces them. The Other within us becomes a bear, a lion, because we made it into that. Once we accept this, it becomes something else."

[255] C.G. Jung, *Archetypes of the Collective Unconscious*, CW 9i, ¶21. Also, words and concepts serve the same purpose (cf. Carus, *Psyche, zur Entwicklungsgeschichte der Seele*, p. 14, fn.), of giving form to the unconscious so that it can be assimilated.

behind are sometimes animated[256] or otherwise transformed; often they were magnified, for example, a brush becomes a brush mountain and salt transforms into a salt sea, etc. The sacrificed object is thus empowered by energy flowing from the unconscious and its meaning amplified. It is as if fear opens the locks with this energy flow so that the sacrificed object is enlarged by this fear, just as previously the pursuer became larger or ever more threatening through the fear. The sacrifice activates a kind of mechanical process through which the evil forces of the unconscious are defeated and continue to take effect without further action by the fugitives. An old alchemistic proverb says: "Nature rejoices in nature, nature subdues nature, nature rules over nature"[257]; this law of reversal of the opposites within the unconscious is enlivened by this magical rite. The widespread occurrence and meaning of the motif of the magic flight is based on this fundamental psychological truth.

1535 In the present tale, the objects thrown behind are not transformed, but hold the attention of the pursuing demon-maiden. The head scarf and the handkerchief are products of human artistry and effort and are, therefore, likely to fascinate a natural being. In addition, they are products of female labor; when belonging to a man, they thus differentiate his feminine nature, which helps him to ward off the undomesticated anima forces. The third item is a mirror, an object used in many magic practices as a means of acquiring secret knowledge. In China, mirrors are carried on the back to ban evil demons.[258] Also, one can kill a basilisk by holding up a mirror to his deadly gaze so that it strikes the beast itself.[259] A mirror doubles the image of the reflected objects and as a copy makes visible and indicates the psyche in its function of generating images and awareness. The symbol of the mirror is, therefore, the appropriate remedy to becoming entangled in the unconscious. This situation is shown in the lively scene where the pursuer, amazed, fascinated, and bewildered stops to observe her own image. The dawning awareness, "this is you," brings her destructive, unrestrained onslaught to a halt by drawing a boundary between the conscious ego and the unconscious.[260]

---

[256] See, for example, "The Fire-Ball" and the motif of Deucalion and Pyrrha. [After Deucalion and his wife Pyrrha had survived the Flood, they consulted an oracle of Themis about how to repopulate the Earth. Deucalion was told to cover his head and throw the bones of his mother behind his shoulder. Deucalion and Pyrrha understood "mother" to be Gaia, the mother of all living things, and the "bones" to be rocks. They threw rocks behind their shoulders and these became people. Pyrrha's stones became women, Deucalion's became men.]

[257] [Democritus in Berthelot, *Alchemistes Grecs*, vol.II, p. i, 3.]

[258] See Róheim, *Spiegelzauber*, *passim*.

[259] See Bächtold-Stäubli under *Basilisk*.

[260] See the curious "back-to-front" magic flight of three magical girls (anima figures) in "The Emperor's Son and the Monster (Ogre)." The maidens fled from the hero into the Magical and by leaving behind a comb, a stone, and a mirror, first a forest rose up, then a castle, and finally a river. But the hero's club shattered the castle, his dagger cut down the forest and divided the river so that he caught up to the girls. They told him that they had created the obstacles because they had feared that he would kill them.

1536 After this successful attempt at separation, at least the psychological situation is not the same as before: the man has succeeded in retrieving a great prize: the red hair, which he had wrested from the magical woman. Of the anima it is said that she could be found at one particular spring, as in "Tapairu, the Beauty from the Land of the Fairies," that is, at the source of life, which she herself embodies. She shines like the sun, thus the power of light and illumination are attributed to this figure.[261] She is characterized as a source of consciousness because the dark body of the unconscious radiates the light of consciousness. Obviously, she possesses hidden divine wisdom, which the man later steals. This enlightening knowledge is concealed in one red hair of the goddess of the spring. Red hair indicates the solar quality of the bearer.[262] Since it emerges from the head, hair symbolizes thoughts and intellectual knowledge. Thus deep secrets of the world are hidden in her magical hair. The hero, however, does not share in the wisdom, but passes the precious content on to his sovereign. This indicates that this is something the hero cannot integrate alone; having such great collective value, it belongs to the general public. Only a superior person, someone appointed – here represented by the emperor – can divide the hair. This latter refers not to "splitting hairs" as being choosy or finicky in the negative sense, but positively as the application of a subtle, precise ability to differentiate. Only someone with such a capacity can make the wisdom coming from the anima, that is, the unconscious, fruitful for the conscious mind. The hero of the tale finds a material gain, symbolizing a more vital than spiritual salvation and renewal of life flowing from the unconscious out of inner necessity. Just as he could not speak with the anima,

---

Here the anima tried to escape the aggressive hero by fleeing into the unconscious, but with an earthy vitality (the club that shatters barriers) and reason (the dagger that cleaves), the conscious mind is strong enough to capture the soul-image.

[261] See Jung:

> The *solificato* is consummated on the person of the anima. The process would seem to correspond to the *illuminatio*, or enlightenment. This "mystical" idea contrasts strongly with the rationalist attitude of the conscious mind, which recognizes only intellectual development as the highest form of understanding and insight. . . It is clear, therefore, that a "lightening up" of the unconscious is being prepared, which has far more the character of an *illuminatio* than of rational "elucidation." The *solificatio* is infinitely far removed from the conscious mind and seems to it almost chimerical (*Psychology and Alchemy,* CW 12, ¶68.)

See also the relation anima-sun in the fairytale, "The Boy Who Married the Sun," in which the only remaining son of a poor widow with the help of Raven, cures the daughter of the Sun and brings her back to his home. In this tale the sun and the golden egg are symbols of the newly acquired consciousness. See also, "How Ememqut Wooed the Daughter of the Sun-Man."

[262] On "the sun-hero, 'young, comely, with golden locks and fiery crown,'" see Jung, *Symbols of Transformation*, CW 5, ¶164; on the connection between sun and the color red, see Jung, *Mysterium Coniunctionis*, CW 14, ¶110. On the identification of hair with life, see Dölger, "Ichthys," vol. 2, p. 298f. See also same reference on cutting off the hair as a death consecration and as sacrificial element in Bächtold-Stäubli under *Haar* [hair]. Red hair arouses suspicion, but is also desirable and beautiful. Often one single hair contains both life and strength. The people of Serbia, Croatia, and Bosnia believe that "if the *vila* loses even one single hair from her head, she must lose her life." See also Bächtold-Stäubli about cutting the hair of a man possessed or of a witch, as exorcism. These amplifications show that a stronger hero than the one in the above Balkan tale would not have had to flee, he could have carried the redemption [lit. "ex-demonizing"] of the anima out to the end.

nor overcome her, he cannot exploit the spiritual benefit and projects it onto the figure of the superior person.

1537 In the anima's hair, the emperor finds all the important things, "about everything and what was done at the creation of the world." The soul contains the whole past of mankind, all the earlier stages of development from mineral to plant to animal. Thus, the anima is often considered to have superior wisdom. In the Arawak fairytale, "Arawanili, the First Medicine Man," a beautiful mermaid teaches the hero how to use a magic rattle against all diseases. In this sense, the anima embodies the natural sciences; thus the hero of "The Old Man of Cury" gained his medical and magical knowledge from a grateful mermaid. Such wise female figures are also known outside the realm of fairytales, such as the female personification, Sapientia Dei, as she is represented in the Wisdom of Solomon and was worshipped in some Gnostic schools, whose veneration was continued by the later alchemists. She helped God create the world.[263] This is why she knows all his ways. She corresponds to the Ennoia of Simon Magus, Barbelo, the Gnostic Sophia, etc. She is the reflection of God, and also the instrument through which God transforms his knowledge into creative acts.[264] This corresponds exactly to the fundamental concept of our story: through this mysterious female figure, God "wanted to help the poor man that secrets hitherto concealed would be revealed." Thus, the soul is the instrument through which God reveals his secrets to man. Carus expresses the same thought:

1538 It is certain, however, that where we are allowed to use the predicate of wisdom to such an extent, it is in any case in the innermost deepest meaning to think of a kind of highest consciousness there at the same time, of which only we are unable to form an idea, and whose concept, therefore, as an unknown, coincides with the concept of a supreme unconscious. In short, only from this point of view do we understand that what we have called the divinity of the unconscious is given only in the immensity and incomprehensibility of a supreme divine consciousness.[265]

1539 The idea of a mystical union of the soul with the Wisdom of God is an archetype. And this explains the appearance of the anima in fairytales from around the world, represented as a mysterious-wonderful woman. The above selection of tales may give some idea of the highs and lows of the anima experience that leads and drives a man. In addition, they give an inkling of

---

263 See *Wisdom of Solomon* (*Book of Wisdom*) 8.4: "For it is she that teacheth the knowledge of God, and is the chooser of his works" (Douay-Rheims version). See also *ibid* 7, 21, and 25.

264 See Mead, *Fragments*, pp. 330ff. In India, the goddess Parvati has a similar function; see Zimmer, *Mother*, pp. 73, 76–77.

265 Carus, *Psyche*, p. 400f.

what a difficult task the encounter with this figure of his own unconscious presents. This encounter, or search for the anima, is rarely presented in short, episodic encounter scenes, but rather as part of a chain of events and adventures, which can best be grouped as the "great journey/quest" or the "night sea journey" of the hero. This lengthy, subtle, and adventurous journey constitutes the process of a profound confrontation with the previously introduced and explained phenomena, through which an individual is gradually led to the secret goal of inner wholeness.[266]

[266] Of course, the same laws apply to the female psyche. The same archetypes appear there, but with a different sign and another sense. A female shadow accompanies the feminine psyche. The animus of the woman corresponds to the anima of the man. Since the number and variations of fairytales in which these figures appear in the foreground is smaller than those that reflect the figures of the male psyche, and because only a brief consideration would also be inadequate and at the same time distracting, they will be summarized in Book 2 in the section on the maiden's quest.

Bibliography

Aarne, Antti, *Vergleichende Märchenforschungen. Akademische Abhandlung*, Druckerei der Finnischen Literaturgesellschaft, Helsingfors 1908.

– "Die magische Flucht, eine Märchenstudie", in: *Folklore Fellow Communications*, Nr. 92, 1930.

– *The Types of the Folktale: A Classification and Bibliography*, The Finnish Academy of Science and Letters, Helsinki 1961.

Abegg, Emil, "Krishnas Geburt und das indische Weihnachtsfest", in: *Mitteilungen der Geogr.-Ethnogr.-Gesellschaft*, Vol. 38, 1937/1938, pp. 29–57.

– *Indische Psychologie*, Rascher Verlag, Zürich 1945.

Abraham, Karl, "Traum und Mythus", eine Studie zur Völkerpsychologie, in: *Schriften zur angewandten Seelenkunde*, no. 4, ed. by Sigmund Freud, Franz Deuticke, Leipzig and Wien 1909, Verlags-Nr. 1517.

Abt, Regina and Bosch, Irmgard/Mackrel, Vivienne, *Traum und Schwangerschaft. Eine Untersuchung von Träumen schwangerer Frauen*, Daimon Verlag, Einsiedeln 1996.

Afanaßjew, Alexander N., *Russische Volksmärchen*. Deutsch von Anna Meyer, C.W. Stern (Buchhandlung L. Rosner) Verlag, Wien 1906.

Ahlqvist, August, Über die Sprache der Nord-Ostjaken. Sprachtexte, Wörtersammlung und Grammatik, in: *Edlund in Commun. (Forschungen auf dem Gebiet der Ural-Altaischen Sprachen III. 1)*, VI 1880, p. 194.

Aichele, Walther (editor), *Zigeunermärchen, (MdW)*, ed. by Fr. v. d. Leyen and P. Zaunert, Eugen Diederichs, Jena 1926.

Aigremont, Dr., *Volkserotik und Pflanzenwelt. Eine Darstellung alter wie moderner erotischer und sexueller Gebräuche, Vergleiche, Benennungen, Sprichwörter, Redewendungen, Rätsel, Volkslieder, erotischen Zaubers und Aberglaubens, sexueller Heilkunde, die sich auf Pflanzen beziehen*, Erster Band, Hallescher Verlag für Literatur und Musik, Gebr. Trensinger, Halle a. S. 1909.

Aigremont, Dr., *Fuss- und Schuh-Symbolik und -Erotik: Folkloristische und sexualwissenschaftliche Untersuchungen*. Mit einem Geleitwort von Dr. Friedrich S. Krauß, Deutsche Verlags-Aktien-Gesellschaft, Leipzig 1909. 9, 502 Alexander, Hartley Burr, "Latin-American Mythologies", in: Gray, Herbert Louis (ed.): *Mythology of All Races*, Vol. 2, Marshall Jones Company, Boston 1920.

Altmann, Christine (editor), *Kleine Märchenzeitung Schweizerischen Märchen-Gesellschaft SMG*, 3. Jahrgang, Mai 1998.

Anonymous, Historia de los mexicanos por sus pinturas, in: Icazbalceta, Joaquín García (ed.): *Nueva colección de documentos para la historia de Mexćo*, Volume 5, Díaz de León, Mexico 1888–92.

Árnason, J and Jórgen, *Íslenzkar þjóðsögur og Æfintýri (Icelandic Folktales and Legends)*, Volume arnason1862, (in Icelandic), J.C. Hinrichs, Leipzig 1862.

Ashliman, D. L. (ed.), *A Guide to Folktales in the English Language: Based on the Aarne-Thompson Classification System*, Greenwood Press, New York 1987.

– *The Grimm Brothers' Children's and Household Tales (Grimm's Fairy Tales)*, Princeton University Press, Princeton NJ 1998-2009.

Astrup, Eivind, *Unter den Nachbarn des Nordpols*, H. Haessel Verlag, Leipzig 1905, autorisierte Übersetzung aus dem Norwegischen von Margarethe Langseldt. Aurelius, Marcus; George Long, Translated by (ed.), *The Meditations*, The Peter Pauper Press Inc., Mount Vernon 1957.

Avenstrup, Age and Treitel, Elisabeth, *Isländische Märchen und Volksagen*, Axel Juncker Verlag, Berlin 1919.

Bachofen, Johannn Jakob, "An Essay on Ancient Mortuary Symbolism," in: *Myth, Religion, & Mother Right, Selected Writings of J. J. Bachofen*. Transl. by Ralph Manheim. Bollingen Series LXXXIV, Bollingen, Princeton University Press, Princeton, NJ 1973, pp. 19–65.

Bachofen, Johann Jakob, *Versuch über die Gräbersymbolik der Alten*, Bahnmaier's Buchhandlung (C. Detloff), Basel 1859.

– *Das Mutterrecht: Eine Untersuchung über die Gynaikokratie der alten Welt nach ihrer religiösen und rechtlichen Natur*, Krais & Hoffmann, Stuttgart 1861.

– *Das Lykische Volk und seine Bedeutung für die Entwicklung des Altertums*, Herder'sche Verlagsbuchhandlung, Freiburg i. Br. 1862.

– *Der Bær in den Religionen des Alterthums*, Ch. Meyri, Basel 1863.

– *Die Unsterblichkeitslehre der orphischen Theologie auf den Grabdenkmälern des Alterthums. Nach Anleitung einer Vase aus Canosa im Besitz des Herrn Prosper Biardot in Paris*, dargestellt von Dr. J. J. Bachofen mit einer Tafel in Farbendruck, Felix Schneider's Buchhandlung, Basel 1867.

– *Die Sage von Tanaquil, Eine Untersuchung über den Orientalismus in Rom und Italien*, J. C. B. Mohr, Heidelberg 1870.

Bächtold-Stäubli, Hanns, *Handwörterbuch des deutschen Aberglaubens*. W. de Gruyter & Co. Bd. I–VII, Berlin and Leipzig 1927–1936. Vol. VIII–X, Berlin 1936–1942. editor unter bes. Mitwirkung von E. Hoffmann-Krayer and Mitarbeit zahlreicher Fachgenossen.

Bargheer, Ernst, *Eingeweide. Lebens- und Seelenkräfte des Leibesinneren im deutschen Glauben und Brauch*, Walter de Gruyter & Co., Berlin and Leipzig 1931.

Bastian, Adolf, *Beiträge zur vergleichenden Psychologie. Die Seele und ihre Erscheingungsweisen in der Ethnographie*, Ferd. Dümmler's Verlagsbuchhandlung (Harrwitz und Grossmann), Berlin 1868.

- *Die Verbleibs-Orte der abgeschiedenen Seele, Ein Vortrag in erweiterter Umarbeitung*, Weidmannsche Buchhandlung, Berlin 1893.

Batchelor, John, Specimens of Ainu Folk-Lore, in: *Transactions of the Asiatic Society of Japan*, R. Meiklejohn & Company, Yokahama 1880.

- *The Ainu of Japan. The Religion, Superstitions, and General History of the Hairy Aborigines of Japüan*, The Religious Tract Society, London 1892.

- *The Ainu and Their Folk-Lore*, Religious Tract Society, London 1901.

Baumann, Dieter, "Individuation in the Spirit of Love", in: *The Fountain of the Love of Wisdom: an Homage to Marie-Louise von Franz*, ed. by Emmanuel Kennedy-Xypolitas, Chiron Publications, Wilmette, Illinois 2006, pp. 167–176.

Baynes, Charlotte, "Der Erlösungsgedanke in der christlichen Gnosis", in: *Eranos-Jahrbuch 1937: Gestaltung der Erlösungsidee in Ost und West II*, hrsg. von Olga Fröbe-Kapteyn, Rhein-Verlag, Zürich 1938, p. 155–209.

Beit, Hedwig von, *Das Märchen. Sein Ort in der geistigen Entwicklung* [The Fairytale. Its place in Spiritual Development], Francke Verlag, Bern and München 1965.

- *Symbolik des Märchens*, Band I, 8. Auflage, Francke Verlag, Tübingen 1997. viii

Berthelot, Marcellin, *Collection des ancien alchimistes grecs.* Volume 2, Georges Steinheil Éditeur, Paris 1888.

Boas, Franz, "The Central Eskimo," in: *Sixth Annual Report of the Smithsonian Institution*, Smithsonian Institution, Bureau of Ethnology, Washington D.C. 1888.

- Sagen der Kootenay, in: *Verhandlungen der Berliner Gesellschaft für Anthropologie, Ethnologie und Urgeschichte, 1891* [1891].

- *Chinook Texts*, U.S. Bureau of American Ethnology, Bulletin no. 20 U.S. Bureau of American Ethnology 1894, Bulletin no. 20.

- *Indianische Sagen von der Nord-Pacifischen Küste Amerikas.* Verlag von A. Asher & Co., Berlin 1895.

- *The Mythology of the Bella Coola Indians*, Memoirs of the American Museum of Natural History, New York 1898.

- *Tsimshian Mythology*, U.S. Bureau of American Ethnology, Government Printing Office, Washington, D. C. 1916.

Boehm, Max and Specht, Franz (ed.), *Lettisch-litauische Volksmärchen*, (*MdW*), ed. by Fr. von der Leyen and P. Zaunert, Eugen Diederichs, Jena 1924.

Bogoras, Waldemar, *Tales of the Yukaghir, Lamut, and Russianized Natives of Eastern Siberia*, Anthropological Papers of the American Museum of Natural History, New York 1918.

Bolte, Johannes, "Das Märchen vom Gevatter Tod", in: *Zeitschrift des Vereins für Volkskunde*, ed. by Karl Weinhold, 4. Jahrg. 1894, Nr. 4, pp. 34–40.

– and Polívka, Georg, *Anmerkungen zu den Kinder- and Hausmärchen der Brüder Grimm*, Vol. 1, Dieterich'sche Verlagsbuchhandlung, Th. Weicher, Leipzig 1913.

– *Anmerkungen zu den Kinder- and Hausmärchen der Brüder Grimm*, Vol. 2, Dieterich'sche Verlagsbuchhandlung, Th. Weicher, Leipzig 1915.

– *Anmerkungen zu den Kinder- and Hausmärchen der Brüder Grimm*, Vol. 3, Dieterich'sche Verlagsbuchhandlung, Leipzig 1918.

– *Anmerkungen zu den Kinder- and Hausmärchen der Brüder Grimm*, Vol. 4, Dieterich'sche Verlagsbuchhandlung, Leipzig 1930.

– *Anmerkungen zu den Kinder- and Hausmärchen der Brüder Grimm*, Vol. 5, Dieterich'sche Verlagsbuchhandlung, Th. Weicher, Leipzig 1932.

Bolte, Johannes and Mackensen, Lutz, *Handwörterbuch des deutschen Märchens*, Volume 1–2, W. de Gruyter & Co., Berlin and Leipzig 1930/1934.

Bousset, Wilhelm, *Die Himmelsreise der Seele*, Archiv für Religionswissenschaft, Band IV, Tübingen and Leipzig 1901.

– *Hauptprobleme der Gnosis*, Vandenhoeck & Ruprecht, Göttingen 1907.

Brie, Maria, *Das Märchen im Lichte der Geisteswissenschaft*, Preuß and Jünger (Inh. Kropff and Weinberger), Breslau 1922.

Brett, William Henry, *Legends and Myths of the Aboriginal Indians of British Guiana*, William Wells Gardner, London 1880.

Brinton, Daniel G., *Nagualism. A Study in Native American Folk-lore and History*, Macmillon & Company, Philedelphia 1894.

Carnochan, F. G. and Adamson, Hans Christian, *The Empire of Snakes*, Frederick Stokes & Co., New York 1935.

Carus, Carl Gustav, *Psyche, zur Entwicklungsgeschichte der Seele*, Flammer und Hoffmann, Pforzheim 1846.

– *Psyche, zur Entwicklungsgeschichte der Seele*, Kröners Taschenausgabe, Nr. 98, mit einem Nachwort, ed. by R. Marx, Alfred Kröner Verlag, Leipzig 1931.

– *Psyche Part One: The Unconscious*, Spring Publications, New York 1970, Trans. by R. Welch.

Castrén, A., *Ethnologische Vorlesungen über die altaischen Völker*, A. Schiefner, St. Petersburg 1857.

Chamberlain, Basil Hall, *Aino Folk-Tales*, The Folk-Lore Society edition. London 1988.

Chatelain, Heli, *Folk-Tales of Angola: Fifty Tales, with Ki-Mbundu text, Literal English Translation, Introduction, and Notes*, Houghton Miffiin and Company, Boston and New York 1894, Memoirs of the American Folklore Society Vol. 1.

Christensen, Arthur (ed.), *Märchen aus Iran, (MdW)*, ed. by Fr. v. d. Leyen, Eugen Diederichs Verlag, Jena 1939.

Collum, V. C. C., "Die schöpferische Mutter-Göttin der Völker keltischer Sprache, ihr Werkzeug, das mystische 'Wort', ihr Kult und ihre Kult-Symbole", in: *Eranos-Jahrbuch 1938: Gestalt und Kult der "Grossen Mutter"*, hrsg. von Olga Fröbe-Kapteyn, Rhein-Verlag, Zürich 1939, p. 221– 324.

Couch, Mabel Quiller, *Cornwall's Wonderland*, J. M. Dent & Sons Ltd., London & Toronto 1914.

Croker, Thomas Crofton, *Fairy Legends and Traditions of the South of Ireland*, Part III, John Murray, London 1828.

Cumont, Franz, *The Oriental Religions in Roman Paganism*, Open Court, Chicago 1911.

Curtin, Jeremiah, *Creation Myths of Primitive America: in relation to the religious history and mental development of mankind*, Little, Brown and Company, Boston 1898.

Danzel, Hedwig and Theodor-Wilhelm, Danzel, *Sagen und Legenden der Südsee-Insulaner (Polynesien)*, Folkwang-Verlag, Hagen i.W. und Darmstadt 1923.

Danzel, Theodor-Wilhelm, "The Psychology of Ancient Mexican Symbolism", in: *Spiritual Disciplines: Papers form the Eranos Yearbooks*, Princeton University Press, Princeton NJ 1960, Bollingen XXX-4, pp. 102–114.

Meister Eckhart, *Meister Eckhart, Selected Writings*, Penguin Books, London 1994, Trans. by Oliver Davies.

Deursen, Arie van, *Der Heilbringer. Eine ethnologische Studie über den Heilbringer bei den Nordamerikanischen Indianern*, J. B. Wolters Uitgevers-Maatschappij, Groningen-Den Haag-Batavia 1931.

Deussen, Paul (trans.), *Die Geheimlehre des Veda*, 5th edition. F. A. Brockhaus, Leipzig 1919.

Deussen, Paul, *Sixty Upanishads of the Veda, two volumes*, Motilal Banarsidass, Delhi 1980/1997, translated by V.M. Bedekar and G.B. Palsule.

Uther, Hans-Jörg (ed.), *Diederichs Märchen der Weltliteratur*, Rowohlt Taschenbuch Verlag, Reinbek 1992.

Dieterich, Albrecht, *Abraxas. Studien zur Religionsgeschichte des späten Altertums*, B. G. Teubner, Leipzig 1891.

- *Nekyia. Beiträge zur Erklärung der neuentdeckten Petrusapokalypse*, 2nd edition. B. G. Teubner, Leipzig 1893.

- *Eine Mithrasliturgie,* ed. by Otto Weinreich, B. G. Teubner, Leipzig and Berlin 1923.

Dirr, Adolf (ed.), *Kaukasische Märchen,* (*MdW*), ed. by Fr. v. d. Leyen and P. Zaunert, Eugen Diederichs, Jena 1922.

Dixon, Roland, Some Coyote Stories from the Maidu Indians, in: *The Journal of American Folk-Lore*, 13 [1900], pp. 267–269.

Dölger, Franz Joseph, *"Ichthys". Das Fischsymbol in frühchristlicher Zeit,* Vol. 1, in Kommission der Herder'sche Verlagsbuchhandlung zu Freiburg i. Br. and d. Buchhandlung Spithover zu Rom, Freiburg i. Br. 1910.

Dölger, Franz Joseph, *"Ichthys". Der Heilige Fisch, in den antiken Religionen und im Christentum,* Vol. 2, Verlag der Aschendorffschen Verlagsbuchhandlung, Münster i. W. 1922, p. 454–507.

- "Antike Parallelen zum leidenden Dinocrates in der Passio Perpetuae"vol. 2, in: *Antike und Christentum. Kultur- und religionsgeschichtliche Studien*, 1930, p. 1–40.

Dorsey, George A. and Kroeber, Alfred L., *Traditions of the Arapaho collected under the Auspices of the Field Columbian Museum of the American Museum of Natural History*, Volume Anthropological Series, Vol. 5, Publication 8i, Field Columbian Museum, Chicago 1903.

Dorsey, George A., *Traditions of the Skidi Pawnee*, Houghton, Miffiin and Company, Boston and New York 1904a, Memoirs of the American Folk-Lore Society, 8.

- *The Mythology of the Wichita*, Volume Publication No. 21, Carnegie Institution of Washington, Washington DC 1904.

Dottin, Georges, *Manuel pour servir à l'Etude de l'Antiquité Celtique*, 2nd edition. Librairie ancienne Honoré Champion, Édouard Champion, Paris 1915.

Durán, Fray Diego, *The History of the Indies of New Spain*, University of Oklahoma Press, Norman 1994, Translated, Annotated, and with an Introduction by Doris Heyden.

Ebersold, Walter, *Unsere Märchen*, Roter Reiter-Verlag, Zürich 1946. 6 Ehrenreich, Paul, "Beiträge zur Völkerkunde Brasiliens", in: *Veröffentlichungen aus dem Kgl. Museum für Völkerkunde*, Volume 2, Museum für Völkerkunde, Berlin 1891.

Ehrentreich, Alfred (ed.), *Englische Volksmärchen,* (*MdW*), ed. by Fr. v. d. Leyen, Eugen Diederichs Verlag, Jena 1938.

Enzyklopädie des Märchens. Handwörterbuch zur historischen und vergleichenden Erzählforschung, Walter de Gruyter, Berlin 1979.

Erman, Adolf, *Die Religion der Ägypter. Ihr Werden und Vergehen in vier Jahrtausenden*, Walter de Gruyter, Berlin and Leipzig 1934.

Ernst, Paul (ed.), *Tausend und ein Tag / Orientalische Erzählungen*. Erster Band, ausgew. and eingel. v. Paul Ernst. Übertr. v. Felix Paul Greve, Insel-Verlag, Leipzig 1909.

Evans, Ivor H.N., "Folk Stories of the Tempassuk and Tuaran Districts, British North Borneo". in: *Journal of the Royal Anthropological Institute* 43 1913. 596

Evans-Wentz, W. Y., *The Tibetan Book of the Dead*, 2nd edition. Oxford University Press, Oxford 2000.

Fison, Lorimer, *Tales from Old Fiji*, Alexander Moring Ltd, London 1904.

Franz, Marie-Louise von, *Aurora Consurgens, A Document Attributed to Thomas Aquinas on the Problem of Opposites in Alchemy*. A Companion Work to C. G. Jung's *Mysterium Coniunctionis*. translated by R. F. C. Hull and A. S. B. Glover, Princeton University Press, Princeton NJ 1977, Bollingen Series, LXXVII.

- *The Feminine in Fairy Tales*, Shambala, New York 2001.

- *The Interpretation of Fairy Tales (An Introduction to the Psychology of Fairy Tales)*, Spring Publications Inc, New York 1970.

- *Number and Time, Reflections Leading Towards a Unification of Depth Psychology and Physics*, translated by Andrea Dykes, Rider & Company, London 1974.

- *Projection and Re-Collection in Jungian Psychology: Reflections of the Soul*, Inner City, Toronto 1995.

- *The Psychological Meaning of Redemption Motifs in Fairytales*, Inner City, Toronto 1980.

- *Psychologische Märcheninterpretation*, Verlag Stiftung für Jung'sche Psychologie, Küsnacht 2012.

- *Symbolik des Märchens*, Verlag Stifting für Jung'sche Psychologie, Küsnacht 2015.

Franz, Marie-Louise von, "Marie-Louise von Franz im Film von Françoise Selhofer" in: *Jungiana*, Reihe A Band 2, 1989.

Frazer, James George Sir, *Golden Bough, a Study in Magic and Religion*, Macmillan & Co., New York 1922.

Frobenius, Leo, *Das Zeitalter des Sonnengottes*. Erster Band, Georg Reimer, Berlin 1904.

Führer, Maria, *Nordgermanische Götterüberlieferung und deutsches Volksmärchen. 80 Märchen der Brüder Grimm vom Mythus her beleuchtet*, Neuer Filser-Verlag, München 1938.

Gardner, John and Maier, John/Henshaw, Robert, *Gilgamesh (translated from the Sin-Leq-Unninnt version)*, Alfred A. Knopf, Inc., New York 1984.

Gautz, Jeffrey, *The Mabinogion*, Penguin Books, London 1976.

Gerber, Irene, "Yonec. Zu einer Märchendichtung der Marie de France", in: *Jungiana,* Reihe A, Band 9, 2000, pp. 53–96.

Gill, William Wyatt, *Myths and Songs from the South Pacific*, Henry S. King & Co, London 1876.

Goethe, Johann Wolfgang von, *Goethe's Theory of colors*, John Murray, London 1840, translated by Charles Lock Eastlake.

- *Goethe's Faust, Parts I and II* (an abridged version translated by Louis MacNeice), Faber & Faber, London 1951.

- *Faust, A Tragedy*, 2nd edition. Norton & Company, New York 1976/2001, translated by Walter Arndt, edited by Cyrus Hamlin.

Graulich, Michael, *Myths of Ancient Mexico*, University of Oklahoma Press, Norman 1997, translated by Bernard R. Ortiz de Montellano and Thelma Ortiz de Montellano.

Gregg, Josiah, *Commerce of the Prairies: or, The journal of a Santa Fé trader, during eight expeditions across the great western prairies, and a residence of nearly nine years in northern Mexico*, Volume 2, J. W. Moore, Philadelphia 1855.

Gregory, Lady Augusta, *Gods and Fighting Men: The Story of the Tuatha De Danaan and of the Fianna of Ireland, arranged and put into English*, John Murray, London 1904.

Grierson, Elizabeth W., *The Scottish Fairy Book*, J. B. Lippincott Company, Philadelphia and New York 1910.

Grimm, Brothers, *Irische Elfenmärchen*, Friedrich Fleischer, Leipzig 1826. 333 Jakob Grimm, Wilhelm Grimm, *The Complete Grimm's Fairy Tales*, Routledge and Kegan Paul, London 1975.

Grimm, Wilhelm and Jacob (ed.), *Kinder- und Hausmärchen, gesammelt durch die Brüder Grimm, (MdW)*, Band 3, ed. by Fr. v. d. Leyen, Verlag der Dieterich'schen Buchhandlung, Göttingen 1856.

Grimm, Jacob, *Deutsche Mythologie*, Volume 1, 2nd edition. Dieterische Buchhandlung, Göttingen 1844.

Grimm, Jacob Ludwig Karl, *Grimm's household tales with the author's notes by Jacob Grimm*, G. Bell & Sons, London 1884, 1910, Translated by Margaret Hunt.

The Complete Grimm's Fairy Tales, introduction by Padraic Colum, folkloristic commentary by Joseph Campbell, Routledge and Kegan Paul, London 1975. Grünbaum, Max, *Gesammelte Aufsätze zur Sprach- und Sagenkunde*, ed. by Felix Perles, S. Calvari & Co., Berlin 1901.

Guest, Charlotte, *The Mabinogion.* Translated by Charlotte Guest, Introduction by Rev. R. Williams. M. A. Everyman's Library, Ed. by Ernest Rhys, J. M. Dent & Sons Ltd. / E.P. Dutton & Co. Inc., London / New York (1906) 1937.

Güntert, Hermann, *Der arische Weltkönig und Heiland. Bedeutungs-geschichtliche Untersuchungen zur indo-iranischen Religionsgeschichte und Altertumskunde*, Max Niemeyer, Halle a. S. 1923.

Guterman, Norbert, (trans.), *Russian Fairy Tales*, Folkloristic commentary by Roman Jakobson, Pantheon Books, New York 2006.

Hahn, Johann Georg von (Übers.), *Griechische und albanesische Märchen*, Vol. 1, Verlag v. Wilhelm Engelmann, Leipzig 1864. 538 – *Griechische und albanesische Märchen*, Vol. 2, Verlag v. Wilhelm Engelmann, Leipzig 1864.

Hamann, Hermann, "Die literarischen Vorlagen der Kinder- und Hausmärchen und ihre Bearbeitung durch die Brüder Grimm", in: *Palaestra XLVII, Untersuchungen und Texte aus der deutschen und englischen Philologie*, Band 47, ed. by Alois Brandl, Gustav Roethe und Erich Schmidt, Mayer & Müller, Berlin 1906.

Hambruch, Paul (ed.), *Südseemärchen aus Australien, Neu-Guinea, Fidji, Karolinen, Samoa, Tonga, Hawaii, Neu-Seeland and a., (MdW)*, ed. by Fr. v. d. Leyen and P. Zaunert, Eugen Diederichs, Jena 1921.

– *Malaiische Märchen aus Madagaskar und Insulinde, (MdW)*, ed. by Fr. v. d. Leyen and P. Zaunert, Eugen Diederichs, Jena 1922.

Hammitzsch, Horst/Schuster, Ingrid (eds.), *Japanische Volksmärchen, (MdW,)* übers. v. Fritz Rumpf, ed. by Fr. v. d. Leyen and P. Zaunert, Eugen Diederichs, Jena 1964.

Hastings, James, *Encyclopaedia of Religion and Ethics*, T. &. T. Clark und Charles Scribner's Sons, Edinburgh and New York 1910.

Heraclitus, *Heraclitus, The Complete Fragments, Translation and Commentary and The Greek text*, Middlebury College, Internet 1994, Trans. by William Harris. Herder, Johann Gottfried von; Suphan, Bernhard (ed.), *Herders Sämmtliche Werke*, Volume 1–33, Weidmann'sche Buchhandlung, Berlin 1877–1913. 2 Hertel, Johannes (ed.), *Indische Märchen, (MdW)*, ed. by Fr. v. d. Leyen and P. Zaunert, Eugen Diederichs, Jena 1925.

Hertz, Wilhelm, *Aus Dichtung und Sage. Vorträge und Aufsätze*, Karl Vollmöller (editor), J. G. Cotta'sche Buchhandlung, Stuttgart and Berlin 1907.

– *Der Werwolf. Beitrag zur Sagengeschichte*, A. Kröner, Stuttgart 1862.

Hoffman, Walter James, The Menomini Indians, in: *Fourteenth Annual Report of the Bureau of Ethnology*, Government Printing Office, Washington DC 1896. Hoffmeister, Johannes (ed.), *Wörterbuch der philosophischen Begriffe*, Vol. 225, Der Philosophischen Bibliothek, Felix Meiner Verlag GmbH, Leipzig 1944.

Hose, Charles and McDougall, William, *The Pagan Tribes of Borneo: A Description of Their Physical, Moral, and Intellectual Condition With Some Discussion of Their Ethnic Relations*, Macmillon & Company, London 1912.

Isler, Gotthilf, "Jung, Carl Gustav", in: *Enzyklopädie des Märchens*, Band 7, Lieferung 2/3.

- "Franz, Marie-Louise von", in: *Enzyklopädie des Märchens*, vol. 5, installment 1.
- "Franz, Marie-Louise von", in: *Enzyklopädie des Märchens*, vol. 5, installment 1. Jacob, Georg, "Märchen und Traum. Mit besonderer Berücksichtigung des Orients", in: *Beitr. z. Märchenforschung d. Morgenlandes*, Band 1, ed. by Georg Jacob and Theodor Menzel, Orient-Buchhandlung Heinz Lafaire, Hannover 1923.

Jacobi, Jolande, *Die Psychologie von C. G. Jung. Eine Einführung mit Illustrationen*, Rascher Verlag, Zürich 1939.

Jacobs, Joseph (ed.), *Celtic Fairy Tales*, David Nutt, London 1892 (URL: www.sacred-texts.com).

James, Montagne Rhodes, *Tales from Lectoure*, Rosemary Pardoe, Chester, UK 2006.

Jegerlehner, Johannes, *Am Herdfeuer der Sennen, Neue Märchen aus dem Wallis*, aus dem Volksmund gesammelt, A. Francke, Bern 1929.

Jochelson, Waldemar, "The Koryak", in: Boas, Franz (ed.): *The Jesup North Pacific Expedition*, Volume VI, AMS Press, Inc., New York 1975.

Jones, Ernest, *Der Alptraum in seiner Beziehung zu gewissen Formen des mittelalterlichen Aberglaubens*, Psychoanalytischer Verlag, Leipzig 1912.

Jones, Gwyn, *Tales from Wales (Welsh Legends and Folk-Tales)*, Oxford University Press, Oxford 1955.

Jung, Carl Gustav, *Alchemy Vol. 1 and 2: The Process of Individuation. Notes on Lectures given at the Eidgenössische Technische Hochschule, Zürich November 1940–July 1941*, compiled by Barbara Hannah, Printed privately, *Zürich* 1960.

- "Über den Archetypus. Mit besonderer Berücksichtigung des Animabegriffs" in: *Zentralblatt für Psychotherapie* Vol. 9, Nr. 5 1936.
- *Bericht über das Deutsche Seminar von Dr. C. G. Jung, 5.–10. Oktober 1931 in Küsnacht-Zürich*, compiled by Olga von Koenig-Fachsenfeld, Printed privately, Stuttgart 1932.
- *Children's Dreams, Notes from the Seminar Given in 1936–1940*, Lorenz Jung and Maria Meyer-Grass (editors), translated by Ernst Falzeder and Tony Woolfson, Princeton University Press, Princeton 2008.
- *Memories, Dreams, Reflections*, Aniela Jaffe (editor), translated by Clara and Richard Winston, Vintage Books, New York 1963.
- *Seminar über Kinderträume und ältere Literatur über Traum-Interpretation*, a. d. ETH Zürich, edited by Hans H. Baumann, Printed privately, Zürich 1936/37.

Jung, Carl Gustav, *Collected Works (= CW)*, Volume 1-20.

- "Address on the Occasion of the Founding of the C. G. Jung Institute, Zurich, 24 April 1948" in: *The Symbolic Life,* CW18, 2nd edition, Princeton University Press, Princeton 1969.
- "Basic Postulates of Analytical Psychology" in: *The Structure and Dynamics of the Psyche,* CW8, 2nd edition, Princeton University Press, Princeton, 1970.
- "Commentary on 'The Secret of the Golden Flower'" in: *Psychology and Religion: West and East,* CW11, 2nd edition, Routledge & Kegan Paul, London, 1975.
- "Concerning the Archetypes, with Special Reference to the Anima Concept" in: *The Archetypes and the Collective Unconscious,* CW9i, 2nd edition, Routledge and Kegan Paul, London, 1969.
- "Concerning Rebirth" in: *The Archetypes and the Collective Unconscious,* CW9i, 2nd edition, Princeton University Press, Princeton, 1969.
- "The Development of Personality" in: *The Development of Personality,* CW17, 2nd edition, Princeton University Press, Princeton 1971.
- "Foreword to Suzuki's 'Introduction to Zen Buddhism'" in: *Psychology and Religion: West and East,* CW11, 2nd edition, Princeton University Press, Princeton 1975.
- "General Aspects of Dream Psychology" in: *The Structure and Dynamics of the Psyche,* CW8, 2nd edition, Princeton University Press, Princeton, 1970.
- "Marriage as a Psychological Relationship" in: *The Development of Personality,* CW17, 2nd edition, Princeton University Press, Princeton, 1971.
- "The Meaning of Psychology for Modern Man" in: *Civilization in Transition,* CW10, 2nd edition, Princeton University Press, Princeton, 1970.
- "Mind and Earth" in: *Civilization in Transition,* CW10, 2nd edition, Princeton University Press, Princeton, 1970.
- *Mysterium Coniunctionis,* CW14, 2nd edition, Princeton University Press, Princeton, 1970.
- "On the Nature of the Psyche" in: *The Structure and Dynamics of the Psyche,* CW8, 2nd edition, Princeton University Press, Princeton, 1970.
- "On the Nature of Dreams" in: *The Structure and Dynamics of the Psyche,* CW8, 2nd edition, Princeton University Press, Princeton, 1970.
- "On Psychic Energy" in: *The Structure and Dynamics of the Psyche,* CW8, 2nd edition, Princeton University Press, Princeton, 1970.
- "On the Psychology of the Unconscious" in: *Two Essays on Analytical Psychology,* CW7, 2nd edition, Princeton University Press, Princeton, 1971.
- "Paracelsus as a Spiritual Phenomenon" in: *Alchemical Studies,* CW13, 2nd edition, Routledge & Kegan Paul, London, 1967.
- "The Phenomenology of the Spirit in Fairy Tales" in: *The Archetypes and the Collective Unconscious,* CW9i, 2nd edition, Princeton University Press, Princeton, 1969.

- "The Philosophical Tree" in: *Psychology and Alchemy*, CW13, 2nd edition, Routledge & Kegan Paul, London, 1967.
- "The Practical Use of Dream Analysis" in: *The Practice of Psychotherapy*, CW16, 2nd edition, Princeton University Press, Princeton, 1985.
- "A Psychological Approach to the Dogma of the Trinity" in: *Psychology East and West*, CW11, 2nd edition, Princeton University Press, Princeton, 1975.
- "The Psychological Aspects of the Kore" in: *The Archetypes and the Collective Unconscious*, CW9i, 2nd edition, Princeton University Press, Princeton, 1969.
- "Psychological Aspects of the Mother Archetype" in: *The Archetypes of the Collective Unconscious*, CW9i, 2nd edition, Princeton University Press, Princeton, 1969.
- "Psychological Commentary on 'The Golden Flower'" in: *Alchemical Studies*, CW13, 2nd edition, Routledge & Kegan Paul, London, 1967.
- "Psychological Commentary on 'The Tibetan Book of the Dead'" in: *Psychology East and West*, CW11, 2nd edition, Princeton University Press, Princeton, 1975.
- "The Psychological Foundation of Belief in Spirits" in: *The Structure and Dynamics of the Psyche*, CW8, 2nd Edition, Princeton University Press, Princeton, 1970.
- *Psychological Types*, CW6, 2nd edition, Princeton University Press, Princeton, 1970.
- "The Psychology of the Child Archetype" in: *The Archetypes and the Collective Unconscious*, CW9i, 2nd edition, Princeton University Press, Princeton, 1969.
- "The Psychology of the Transference" in: *The Practice of Psychotherapy*, CW16, 2nd edition, Princeton University Press, Princeton, 1985.
- The Relation between the Ego and the Unconscious in: *Two Essays on Analytical Psychology*, CW7, 2nd edition, Princeton University Press, Princeton, 1971.
- "A Review of the Complex Theory" in: *The Structure and Dynamics of the Psyche*, CW8, 2nd Edition Princeton University Press, Princeton, 1970.
- "Spirit and Life" in: *The Structure and Dynamics of the Psyche*, CW8, 2nd Edition, Princeton University Press, Princeton, 1970.

"The Spiritual Problem of Modern Man" in: *Civilization in Transition*, CW10, 2nd edition, Princeton University Press, Princeton, 1970.

- "The Structure of the Psyche" in: *The Structure and Dynamics of the Psyche*, CW8, 2nd Edition, Princeton University Press, Princeton, 1970.
- *Symbols of Transformation*, CW5, 2nd edition, Princeton University Press, Princeton, 1967.
- "Transformation Symbolism in the Mass" in: *Psychology and Religion: West and East*, CW11, 2nd edition, Princeton University Press, Princeton, 1975.

- "The Visions of Zosimos" in: *Alchemical Studies*, CW13, 2nd edition, Routledge & Kegan Paul, London, 1967.

- "Wotan" in: *Civilization in Transition*, Princeton University Press, Princeton CW10, 1970.

Jung, Carl Gustav and Kerényi, Carl, *Essays on a Science of Mythology: The Myth of the Divine Child and the Mysteries of Eleusis*, Princeton University Press, Princeton, NJ 1969.

Jung, Emma, "Ein Beitrag zum Problem des Animus" in: *Wirklichkeit der Seele: Anwendungen und Fortschritte der neueren Psychologie,* ed. by C. G. Jung, Rascher & Cie. A.G. Verlag, Zürich 1934, p. 296–354.

Jungbauer, Gustav (ed.), *Märchen aus Turkestan und Tibet, (MdW)*, ed. by Fr. v. d. Leyen and P. Zaunert, Eugen Diederichs, Jena 1923.

Junod, Henri A., *Bulletin de la Societe Neuchateloise de Geographic*, Volume 10, Les Ba-Ronga. Etude ethnographique sur les indigenes de la Baie de Delagoa, Attinger Fréres, Neuchatel 1898.

- *The Life of a South African Tribe*, Volume 1: The Social Life, Attinger Fréres, Neuchatel 1912.

Kappes, Alison, "Bibliographie von Marie-Louise von Franz", in: *Jungiana,* Reihe A Band 2, 1989, pp. 33–46.

Karadzic, Vuk Stefanovic, *Volksmärchen der Serben.* trans. into German by Wilhelmine Karadzic with a preface by Jacob Grimm, Druck und Verlag von G. Reimer, Berlin 1854.

Kennedy-Xypolitas, Emmanuel (ed.), *The Fountain of the Love of Wisdom: an Homage to Marie-Louise von Franz*, Chiron Publications, Wilmette, Illinois 2006.

Kerényi, Karl, "Das göttliche Mädchen. Die Hauptgestalten der Mysterien von Eleusis in mythologischer und psychologischer Beleuchtung", in: *Albae Vigiliae,* no. VIII/IX 1941.

- "Mensch und Maske"[Humans and Masks], in: *Eranos-Jahrbuch 1948 - Der Mensch (2),* ed. by Olga Fröbe-Kapteyn, Rhein-Verlag, Zürich 1949.

Kerényi, Karl, "Kore", in: *Essays on a Science of Mythology: The Myth of the Divine Child and the Mysteries of Eleusis*, Princeton University Press, Princeton 1969, pp. 101–155.

Koch-Grünberg, Theodor (ed.), *Indianermärchen aus Südamerika, (MdW),* ed. by Fr. v. d. Leyen and P. Zaunert, Eugen Diederichs, Jena 1921.

Köhler, Reinhold, "Kleinere Schriften", in: *Kleinere Schriften zur Neueren Litteraturgeschichte Volkskunde und Wortforschung,* Band 3, ed. by Johannes Bolte, Verlag von Emil Felber, Berlin 1900.

Köpping, Klaus-Peter, *Adolf Bastian and the Psychic Unity of Mankind*, Lit Verlag, Münster 2005.

Kovács, Betty, "Journey of the Mothers", in: Castle, Leila (ed.): *Earthwalking Sky Dancers: Women's Pilgrimages to Sacred Places*, Frog, Ltd., Berkely 1996, pp. 199–201.

Krauss, Friedrich Salomon, *Sagen und Märchen der Südslaven, in ihrem Verhältnis zu den Sagen und Märchen der übrigen indogermanischen Völker-gruppen*, Volume 1, Verlag von Wilhelm Friedrich, Leipzig 1883.

Krauß, Friedrich Salomon, *Darstellungen aus dem Gebiete der nichtchristlichen Religionsgeschichte*, Vol. 2: *Volksglaube und religiöser Brauch der Südslaven*, Vorwiegend nach eigenen Ermittlungen, Verlag der Aschendorffschen Buchhandlung, Münster i. W. 1890.

Krauss, Friedrich Salomon, *Darstellungen aus dem Gebiete der nichtchristlichen Religionsgeschichte*, Vol. 2: *Volksglaube und religiöser Brauch der Südslaven*, Vorwiegend nach eigenen Ermittlungen, Verlag der Aschendorffschen Buchhandlung, Münster i. W. 1890.

Kremnitz, Mite, *Romanian Fairy Tales*, Henry Holt and Company, New York 1885, Adadpted and Arranged by J. M. Percival.

Kretschmer, Paul (ed.), *Neugriechische Märchen*, (*MdW*), ed. by Fr. v. d. Leyen and P. Zaunert, Eugen Diederichs, Jena 1917.

Krickeberg, Walter (ed.), *Indianermärchen aus Nordamerika*, (*MdW*), ed. by Fr. v. d. Leyen and P. Zaunert, Eugen Diederichs, Jena 1924.

– *Märchen der Azteken und Inkaperuaner, Maya und Muisca*, (*MdW*), ed. by Fr. v. d. Leyen, Eugen Diederichs, Jena 1928.

Kroeber, Alfred L., Cheyenne Tales, in: *The Journal of American Folk-Lore*, 13 1900, p. 161–191.

Kunike, Hugo (ed.), *Märchen aus Sibirien*, (*MdW*), ed. by Fr. v. d. Leyen, Eugen Diederichs, Jena 1940.

Laiblin, Wilhelm, "Urbild der Mutter", in: Laiblin, Wilhelm (ed.): *Märchenforschung und Tiefenpsychologie*, Wissenschaftliche Buchgesellschaft, Darmstadt 1936, pp. 100–150.

Laistner, Ludwig, *Das Rätsel der Sphinx. Grundzüge einer Mythengeschichte*, Verlag Wilhelm Hertz, Berlin 1889.

– *Psyche, zur Entwicklungsgeschichte der Seele*, Flammer und Hoffmann, Pforzheim 1900.

Lang, Andrew, *Custom and Myth*, 2nd edition. Longmans, Green, and Co., London 1885.

– *Myth, Ritual, and Religion*, Longmans, Green, and Co., London 1887.

– *The Blue Fairy Book*, Dover, New York 1965.

Layard, John, "Der Mythos der Totenfahrt auf Malekula"[The Myth of the Death Journey on Malekula], in: *Eranos-Jahrbuch 1937: Gestaltung der Erlösungsidee in Ost und West (2)*, ed. by Olga Fröbe-Kapteyn, Rhein-Verlag, Zürich 1938, p. 241–291.

- "The Making of Man in Malekula", in: *Eranos-Jahrbuch 1948: Der Mensch (2)*, hrsg. von Olga Fröbe-Kapteyn, Rhein-Verlag, Zürich 1949, p. 209–283.

Leade, Jane, *A Fountain of Gardens*, J. Bradford, London 1696.

Leeuw, Gerardus van der, *Religion in Essence and Manifestation: A Study in Phenomenology*, Vol.1, Harper & Row Publishers, New York 1963, Trans. by J. T. Turner.

Leisegang, Hans, *Die Gnosis*, Kröners Taschenausgabe Vol. 32, Alfred Kröner Verlag, Leipzig 1924.

- "Das Mysterium der Schlange. Ein Beitrag zur Erforschung des griechischen Mysterienkultes und seines Fortlebens in der christlichen Welt", in: *Eranos-Jahrbuch 1939: Die Symbolik der Wiedergeburt in der religiösen Vorstellung der Zeiten und Völker*, ed. by Olga Fröbe-Kapteyn, Rhein-Verlag, Zürich 1940, p. 151–250.

- The Mystery of the Serpent, in: *The Mysteries: Papers from the Eranos Year-books 2*, Routledge & Kegan Paul, London 1955, Book ordered from Colibris 23 January 2014, pp. 194–260.

Le Jeune, Paul, *Relation of what occurred in New France in the year 1633*. Volume 6 (1634), Compiled and edited by Reuben Gold Thwaites, The Burrows Brothers Company, Cleveland 1634.

Leskien, August (ed.), *Balkanmärchen aus Albanien / Bulgarien, Serbien und Kroatien, (MdW)*, ed. by Fr. v. d. Leyen and P. Zaunert, Eugen Diederichs, Jena 1919.

Leyen, Freiderich Von der (ed.), *Julspuk, Nordische Volksmärchen aus Schweden*, Buchverlag König, Greiz 2009.

Lévy-Bruhl, Lucien, *The "Soul" of the Primitive*, Macmillan, New York 1928.

Lévy-Bruhl, Lucien, *How Natives Think*, authorized translation by Lilian A. Clare (1926), Washington Square Press, Inc., New York 1966.

Lincke, Werner, *Das Stiefmuttermotiv im Märchen der germanischen Völker*, Verlag Dr. Emil Ebering, Berlin 1933, German. Studien, no. 142.

Littmann, Enno (ed.), *Die Erzählungen aus den Tausendundein Nächten*, Deutsche Ausgabe in sechs Bänden. Original translation after the original Arabic publication of the Calcutta edition of 1839, Insel-Verlag, Leipzig 1923.

Loepfe, Alfred, *Russische Märchen*, Otto Walter, Olten 1941.

Löwis of Menar, August von (ed.), *Finnische und estnische Volksmärchen*, (*MdW*), ed. by Fr. v. d. Leyen and P. Zaunert, Eugen Diederichs, Jena 1922.

- *Russische Volksmärchen*, (*MdW*), ed. by Fr. v. d. Leyen and P. Zaunert, Eugen Diederichs, Jena 1927.

Löwis of Menar, August von, *Russian Folktales,* translated by E. C. Elstob and Richard Barber, Bell & Sons, London 1971.

Loidl, Sonja, *Das Märchen von der Unkel (KHM 105) unter spezieller Berücksichtigung des Seelentier-Motivs*, München 2006.

Lüthi, Max, *Die Gabe im Märchen und in der Sage. Ein Beitrag zur Wesenserfassung und Wesensscheidung der beiden Formen,* Inaugural-Dissertation der Philosophischen Fakultät, Universität Bern, Bern 1943.

– "Psychologie des Märchens. Märchendeutung. Zu einem Buche Hedwig von Beits", in: *Neue Zürcher Zeitung, Literatur und Kunst,* Sonntag, 12. April, Blatt 4, 1953.

– "Besprechung von Band II. Gegensatz und Erneuerung", in: *Neue Zürcher Zeitung,* Nr 2806/7, 1957.

– *The European Folktale: Form and Nature*, Indiana University Press, Bloomington & Indianapolis 1982, trans. John D. Niles.

– *The European Folktale: Form and Nature* (trans. by John D. Niles), Indiana University Press, Bloomington & Indianapolis 1982.

– "Hedwig von Beit", in: *Enzyklopädie des Märchens* 2. x Mannhardt, Wilhelm, *Wald- und Feldkulte,* Vol. 1: *Der Baumkultus der Germanen und ihrer Nachbarstämme. Mythologische Untersuchungen*, Gebrüder Borntraeger (Ed. Eggers), Berlin 1875.

Mannhardt, Wilhelm, *Wald- und Feldkulte,* Vol. 2: *Antike Wald- und Feldkulte aus nordeuropäischer Überlieferung*, Gebrüder Borntraeger (Ed. Eggers), Berlin 1877.

Manning-Sanders, Ruth, *Damian and the Dragon: Modern Greek Folk-Tales,* Oxford University Press, Oxford 1965.

Marett, Robert Ranulph, *The Threshold of Religion*, Methuen & Co. Ltd., London 1909.

Matthews, Washington, *Navajo Legends*, Houghton, Miffiin and Company, Boston and New York 1897, Memoires of the American Folk-Lore Society.

Mead, G. R. S., *Fragments of a Faith Forgotten,* 2nd. Ed. John M. Watkins, London 1931.

Meier, Harri; Leyen, Fr. von (ed.), *Spanische und Portugiesische Märchen*, Eugen Diederichs, Jena 1940.

– *Spanische und portugiesische Märchen,* (*MdW*), übertr. and eingel. v. Harri Meier, ed. by Fr. v. d. Leyen, Eugen Diederichs Verlag, Jena 1940.

Meier, P. Jos., Mythen und Erzählungen der Kustenbewohner der Gazelle-Halbinsel (Neu-Pomern), in: *Anthropos, Internationale Sammlung Ethnologischer Monographien, Vol. 1*, Druck und Verlag der Aschnedorffschen Buchhandlung, Münster i. W. 1909.

Meinhof, Carl (ed.), *Afrikanische Märchen, (MdW)*, ed. by Fr. v. d. Leyen and P. Zaunert, Eugen Diederichs, Jena 1921.

Meister Eckhart, *Deutsche Mystiker des vierzehnten Jahrhunderts. 2. Vol.: Meister Eckhart,* Teil 1, ed. by Franz Pfeiffer, Vandenhoeck & Ruprecht, Göttingen 1906.

Meyer, Elard Hugo, "Germanische Mythologie", in: *Lehrbücher d. germ. Philologie* Vol. 1, Mayer & Müller, Berlin 1891.

Meyer, Rudolf, *Die Weisheit der deutschen Volksmärchen*, Verlag der Christengemeinschaft, Stuttgart 1935.

- *Die Weisheit der Schweizer Märchen*, Columban-Verlag, Schaffhausen 1944.

Mogk, Eugen, *Germanische Religionsgeschichte und Mythologie*, 2nd edition. W. de Gruyter & Co., Berlin and Leipzig 1927, Sammlung Göschen.

Müller, F. Max, *The Upanishads, Sacred Books of the East, Vol. 15*, Clarendon Press, Oxford 1884.

Müller-Lisowski, Käte (ed.), *Irische Volksmärchen, (MdW)*, ed. by Fr. v. d. Leyen and P. Zaunert, Eugen Diedrichs, Jena 1923.

Murphy, John, *Primitive Man: his Essential Quest*, Humphrey Milford, London 1927.

Musset, Alfred de, *Poésies Nouvelles*, 1836–1852, G. Charpentier, Paris 1883.

Nansen, Fridtjof , *Eskimo Life*, Longmans, Green and Co., London and New York 1893.

Naumann, Hans and Naumann, Ida (trans.), *Isländische Volksmärchen*, (*MdW*), ed. by Fr. v. d. Leyen and P. Zaunert, Eugen Diederichs, Jena 1923.

Neihardt, John G., *Black Elk Speaks, as told by Nicholas Black Elk through John G. Neihardt (Flaming Rainbow)*, University of Nebraska Press, Lincoln & London 2000.

Nelson, William Edward, *The Eskimo About Bering Strait*, Washington DC 1900 - Annual Report.

Neumann, Karl Eugen (Übers.), *Die Reden Gotamo Buddhos. Aus der mittleren Sammlung Majjhimanikayo des Pali-Kanons*, Volume 2, R. Piper & Co., München 1921.

Niedner, Felix, "Die Edda" Erster Band - Heldendichtung, in: *Thule: Altnordische Dichtung und Prosa,*Vol. 1. editor v. Felix Niedener and übertr. v. Felix Genzmer, Eugen Diederichs, Jena 1914.

"Islands Kultur zur Wikingerzeit", in: *Thule: Altnordische Dichtung und Prosa*, Eugen Diederichs, Jena 1920.

Nimuendajú-Unkel, Eurt, Sagen der Tembe-Indianer, in: *Zeitschrift für Ethnologie*, [1915], p. 290–291.

Ninck, Martin, *Wodan und germanischer Schicksalsglaube*, Eugen Diederichs, Jena 1935.

- "Älteste Märchen von Europa", in: *Sammlung Klosterberg, Europ. Reihe,* ed. by H. U. von Balhasar, Benno Schwabe, Basel 1945.

Novalis, *Fragmente,* Erste vollständige, geordnete Ausgabe, ed. by Ernst Kamnitzer, Wolfgang Jess Verlag, Dresden 1929.

O'Donovan, John, translator, *Annála Rioghachta Eireann. Annals of the Kingdom of Ireland by the Four Masters, from the earliest period to the year 1616*, 2nd edition. Royal Irish Academy, Dublin 1856.

Oliveira, Feliciano, The Cherentes of Central Brazil, in: *Proceedings of the XVIII. Session, London 1912*, International Congress of Americanists 1912.

Otto, Walter F., "Der Sinn der eleusinischen Mysterien", in: *Eranos-Jahrbuch 1939: Die Symbolik der Wiedergeburt in der religiösen Vorstellung der Zeiten und Völker,* ed. by Olga Fröbe-Kapteyn, Rhein-Verlag, Zürich 1940, p. 83–112.

Parker, Langloh Katie, *Australian Legendary Tales, Folk-Lore of the Noongahurrahs as told to the Piccaninnies*, David Nutt, London 1896.

- *More Australian Legendary Tales*, David Nutt, London 1898.

Pelliot, Paul, "Die Jenseitsvorstellung der Chinesen", in: *Eranos-Jahrbuch 1939: Die Symbolik der Wiedergeburt in der religiösen Vorstellung der Zeiten und Völker,* ed. by Olga Fröbe-Kapteyn, Rhein-Verlag, Zürich 1940, p. 61–82.

Peuckert, Will-Erich, *Deutscher Volksglaube des Spätmittelalters,* Sammlung Voelkerglaube, ed. by Claus Schrempf, W. Spemann Verlag, Stuttgart 1942.

Picard, Charles, "Die Grosse Mutter von Kreta bis Eleusis", in: *Eranos-Jahrbuch 1938: Gestalt und Kult der 'Grossen Mutter',* ed. by Olga Fröbe-Kapteyn, Rhein- Verlag, Zürich 1939, p. 91–119.

Plato, *The Republic,* 2nd edition. BasicBooks, London 1968, Translated with notes by Allan Bloom.

Powell, J. W., Sketch of the Mythology of the North American Indians, in: Powell, J. W. (ed.): *First Annual Report of the Bureau of Ethnology to the Smithsonian Institution 1878-1880*, Government Printing Office, Washington, Washington, DC 1881, pp. 19–72.

Price, Raymond M., *The Pre-Nicene New Testament*, Signature Books, New York 2006.

Przyluski, Jean, "Ursprünge und Entwicklung des Kultes der Mutter-Göttin", in: *Eranos-Jahrbuch 1938: Gestalt und Kult der "Grossen Mutter"*, ed. by Olga Fröbe-Kapteyn, Rhein-Verlag, Zürich 1939, p. 11–34.

- "Die Mutter-Göttin als Verbindung zwischen den Lokal-Göttern und dem Universal-Gott", in: *Eranos-Jahrbuch 1938: Gestalt und Kult der "Grossen Mutter"*, ed. by Olga Fröbe-Kapteyn, Rhein-Verlag, Zürich 1939, p. 35–57.

Puech, Henri-Charles, The Concept of Redemption in Manichaeism, in: *The Mystic Vision: Papers from the Eranos Yearbook 1936 – The Shaping of the Idea of Redemption in the East and the West*, Joseph Campbell (Ed.), Bollingen Series XXX, Princeton NJ 1970, pp. 247–314.

Radin, Paul, *Primitive Man As Philosopher*, D. Appleton Co., New York 1927.

- *The Trickster: A Study in American Indian Mythology*, Greenwood Press, New York 1956.

Rank, Otto, "Der Mythus von der Geburt des Helden. Versuch einer psychologischen Mythendeutung", in: *Schriften zur angewandten Seelenkunde*, No. 5, ed. by Sigmund Freud, Franz Deuticke, Leipzig and Wien 1922.

- *Seelenglaube und Psychologie. Eine prinzipielle Untersuchung über Ursprung, Entwicklung und Wesen des Seelischen, Franz Deuticke, Leipzig and Wien 1930, Verlags-Nr. 3345.*

- *The Double. A Psychoanalytic Study*, University of North Carolina Press, Chapel HIll 1971, Translated and edited, with an Introduction by Harry Tucker, Jr.

- *Psychology and the Soul*, John Hopkins University Press, Baltimore MD 2003.

- *The Myth of the Birth of the Hero*, trans. Gregory C. Richter and E. James Lieberman, John Hopkins University Press, Baltimore MD 2004.

Rasmussen, Knud, *The Eagle's Gift, Alaska Eskimo Tales*, Doubleday, Doran & Company, Inc., New York 1932, Trans. by Isobel Hutchinson.

- *Die Gabe des Adlers, Eskimoische Märchen aus Alaska*, Societäts-Verlag, Frankfurt a. M. 1937, übers. and bearb. v. Aenne Schmücker.

Reitzenstein, Richard, *Das iranische Erlösungsmysterium. Religionsgeschichtliche Untersuchungen*, A. Marcus & E. Weber's Verlag, Bonn a. Rh. 1921.

- *Hellenistic mystery-religions their basic ideas and significance*, Pickwick Press, Pittsburgh 1978, translated by John E. Steely.

Rhys, John, *The Hibbert Lectures*, Williams and Norgate, London 1898.

Riklin, Franz, "Wunscherfüllung und Symbolik im Märchen", in: *Schriften zur angewandten Seelenkunde*, no. 2, ed. by Sigmund Freud, Franz Deuticke, Leipzig and Wien 1908, Verlags-Nr. 1457.

Rink, Henry, *Tales and Traditions of the Eskimo, with a sketch of their habits, religion, language and other peculiarities*, William Blackwood & Sons, Edinburgh & London 1875.

Robinson, James M. (ed.), *The Nag Hammadi Library in English*, Harper & Row Publishers, San Francisco 1981.

Roeder, Günther, *Urkunden zur Religion des alten Ägypten*, Religiöse Stimmen der Völker, ed. by Walter Otto, Eugen Diederichs, Jena 1923.

Rohde, Erwin, *"Psyche". Seelencult und Unsterblichkeitsglaube der Griechen*, J. C. B. Mohr (Paul Siebeck), Tübingen 1910.

- *Psyche: the cult of souls and the belief in immortality among the Greeks*, Transl. W. B. Hillis, Volume 2, Routledge & Kegan Paul, Oxon 1925.

Psyche: the cult of souls and the belief in immortality among the Greeks, Transl. W. B. Hillis, Kegan Paul, Trubenr & Co., Ltd., London 1925 (reprinted 2019 Martino Fine Books).

Róheim, Géza, *Spiegelzauber*, Vol. 6, Internationaler Psychonalytischer Verlag, Leipzig and Wien 1919, Internat. Psychoanalytische Bibliothek.

Rosen, Georg, *Tuti-Nameh. Das Papageienbuch. Eine Sammlung orientalischer Erzählungen. Nach der türkischen Fassung übersetzt von Georg Rosen*, Volume 17, Bibliothek der Romane, Insel-Verlag, Leipzig 1912.

Roth, Walter E., "An Inquiry into the Animism and Folk-Lore of the Guiana Indians", in: *Thirtieth Annual Report of the Bureau of American Ethnology, 1908-1909*, Bureau of American Ethnology, Washington D.C. 1915, p. 103–386.

Rousselle, Erwin, "Lau Dsi's Gang durch Seele, Geschichte und Welt. Versuch einer Deutung", in: *Eranos-Jahrbuch 1935: Westöstliche Seelenführung*, ed. by Olga Fröbe-Kapteyn, Rhein-Verlag, Zürich 1936, p. 179–205.

– "Dragon and Mare, Figures of Primordial Chinese Mythology", in: *Mystic Vision, Papers from the Eranos Yearbooks*, Volume 6, Princeton University Press, Princeton 1970, pp. 103–119.

– "Das Wasser als mythisches Ereignis chinesischen Lebens", in: *Die kulturelle Bedeutung der komplexen Psychologie*, ed. by Psychologischer Club Zürich, J. Springer, Berlin 1935, p. 209–213.

– "Drache und Stute, Gestalten der mythischen Welt chinesischer Urzeit", in: *Eranos-Jahrbuch 1934: Ostwestliche Symbolik und Seelenführung*, ed. by Olga Fröbe-Kapteyn, Rhein-Verlag, Zürich 1935, p. 11–33.

– "Spiritual Guidance in Contemporary Taoism", in: *Spiritual Disciplines: Papers form the Eranos Yearbooks*, Princeton University Press, Princeton NJ 1960, Bollingen XXX-4, pp. 59–101.

Ruben, Walter, *Die Philosophen der Upanishaden*, A. Francke AG, Bern 1947.

Rumpf, Fritz (ed.), *Japanische Volksmärchen, (MdW)*, ed. by Fr. v. d. Leyen, Eugen Diederichs Verlag, Jena 1938.

Russell, Frank, *The Pima Indians*, Smithsonian Institution, Bureau of Ethnology, Washington DC 1908, 26th Annual Report of the Bureau of American Ethnology.

Sahagún, Bernardino de, *Historia General de las Cosas de Nueva España* (General History of the Things of New Spain), ed. Angel María Garibay, Porrúa, Mexico 1956.

Scheftelowitz, Isidor, *Das Schlingen- und Netzmotiv im Glauben und Brauch der Völker* [The Snare and Net Belief among Folk Culture] (Religionsgeschichtliche Versuche und Vorarbeiten), Wünsch-Deubner, Gießen 1912.

Schmitt, Paul, “Archetypisches bei Augustin und Goethe”, in: *Eranos-Jahrbuch 12: Studien zum Problem des Archetypischen*, ed. by Olga Fröbe-Kapteyn, Rhein-Verlag, Zürich 1945, Festgabe, p. 95–115.

Schopenhauer, Arthur, “Versuch über das Geistersehn und was damit zusammenhängt”, in: *Parerga und Paralipomena, Kleine philosophische Schriften*, F. A. Brockhaus, Leipzig 1877.

- “Essay on Spirit Seeing and Everything Connected Therewith”, in: *Parerga and Paralipomena: short philosophical Essays*, Oxford University Press, Oxford 1974, translated by E. F. Payne, pp. 225–310.

Schweitzer, Bernhard, *Herakles: Aufsätze zur griechischen Religions- und Sagengeschichte*, J. C. B. Mohr (Paul Siebeck), Tübingen 1922.

Seligman, C. G. and Barton, C. M. G./Giblin, E. L., *The Melanesians of British New Guinea*, Cambridge University Press, Cambridge, UK 1910.

Schoolcraft, Henry R., *The Myth of Hiawatha, and other oral legends, Mythologic and Allegoric, of the North American Indians*, J. B. Lippincott Company, Philadelphia 1856.

Silberer, Herbert, “Über die Symbolbildung”, in: *Jahrbuch für psychoanalytische und psychopathologische Forschungen*, Vol. 3, ed. by Ernst Bleuler and Sigmund Freud, Franz Deuticke, Leipzig and Wien 1912, p. 663–682.

- *Problems of Mysticism and Its Symbolism*, Moffat, Yard and Company, New York 1917, Trans. Smith Ely Jelliffe.

Silesius, Angelus [Johann Scheffier], *The Cherubinic Wanderer*, Paulist Press, New Jersey 1986, trans. by Maria Shrady.

Simms, Stephan Charles, *Traditions of the Crows*, Field Columbian Museum, Chicago 1903.

Simpson, Jacqueline and Árnason, Jón, *Icelandic Folktales and Legends*, Tempus, Stroud, Gloucestershire 2004, Originally published in 1972.

Steinen, Karl von den, *Die Bakairi-Sprache* [The Bakairi Language], K.F. Koehlers Antiquarium, Leipzig 1892.

Steiner, Rudolf, *Märchendeutungen*. Vortrag gehalten zu Berlin, 26. Dezember, Berlin 1908.

- “Märchendichtungen im Lichte der Geistesforschung”, in: *Ergebnisse der Geistesforschung*, Band 11, ed. by Marie Steiner, Zbinden und Hügin, Basel 1942.

Stroebe, Klara (ed.), *The Swedish Fairy Book*, Frederick A. Stokes Company, New York 1921, Trans. Frederick H. Martens.

- *The Danish Fairy Book*, Frederick A. Stokes Company, New York 1922, Trans. Frederick H. Martens.

Stroebe, Klara (Übers.), Nordische Volksmärchen, Vol. 1 - Dänemark und Schweden, ed. by Fr. v. d. Leyen and P. Zaunert, Eugen Diederichs, Jena 1922.

Stroebe, Clara (ed.), The Norwegian Fairy Book, Frederick A. Stokes Company, New York 1922, Trans. Frederick H. Martens.

Suzuki, Daisetz Teitaro, An Introduction to Zen Buddhism, Grove Press, New York 1964.

Tegethoff, Ernst, "Studien zum Märchentypus von Amor und Psyche", in: *Rhein. Beitr. and Hülfsbücher z. germ. Philologie and Volkskunde*, Band 4, ed. by Th. Frings, R. Meissner, J. Müller, Kurt Schroeder, Bonn and Leipzig 1922.

Tegethoff, Ernst (ed.), *Französische Volksmärchen 2: Aus neueren Sammlungen, (MdW)*, ed. by Fr. v. d. Leyen and P. Zaunert, Eugen Diederichs, Jena 1923.

TENT, *The Adventures of Mrile*, Texts and Explorations of Narrative Tradition – at enargea.org retrieved June 2011 (URL: http://enargea.org/tales/black_African/Mrile.html).

Thimme, Adolf, *Das Märchen. Handbücher zur Volkskunde*, Verlag von Wilhelm Heims, Leipzig 1909.

Thomas, W. Jenkyn, *The Welsh Fairy Book*, F. A. Stokes, New York 1908. 116 Thurneysen, Rudolf (ed.), *Sagen aus dem alten Irland*, Wiegandt & Grieben, Berlin 1901.

Thurnwald, Richard, "Primitive Initiations- und Wiedergeburtsriten", in: *Eranos-Jahrbuch 1939: Die Symbolik der Wiedergeburt in der religiösen Vorstellung der Zeiten und Völker*, ed. by Olga Fröbe-Kapteyn, Rhein-Verlag, Zürich 1940, pp. 321–328.

Tobler, Otto, *Die Epiphanie der Seele in deutscher Volkssage*, Christian-Albrechts-Universität zu Kiel, Kiel 1911, Inaugural-Dissertation.

Tylor, Edward B., *Primitive Culture: Researches into the Development of Mythology, Philosphy, Religion, Art and Custom* (two volumes), John Murray, London 1871. Uhlenbeck, Christianus C., Original Blackfoot Texts from the Southern Piegans Blackfoot Reservation, Teton County, Montana. in: *Verhandelingen, Nieuwe reeks*, Verhandelingen der Koninklijke Nederlandse Akademie van Wetenschappen, Afd. Letterkunde. Nieuwe reeks, Amsterdam 1911, pp. 91ff.

Usener, Hermann, *Die Sintfluthsagen*, Religionsgeschichtliche Untersuchungen, dritter Theil, Friedrich Cohen, Bonn 1899.

Vianu, Raymond, *Fairy Tales and Legends from Romania*, Twayne Publishers, New York 1972, Translated Ioana Sturdza, Raymond Vianu [and] Mary Lazarescu. Vico, Giambattista, *Principi di Scienza Nuova (The New Science of Giambattista Vico)*, Cornell University Press, Ithaca 1968.

Virolleaud, Charles, "Die Grosse Göttin in Babylonien, Ägypten und Phönikien.

I. Ischtar, Isis, Astartes", in: *Eranos-Jahrbuch 1938: Gestalt und Kult der "Grossen Mutter"*, ed. by Olga Fröbe-Kapteyn, Rhein-Verlag, Zürich 1939, p. 121–160. Voth, H. R., *The Traditions of the Hopi*, Volume 8, Anthropological Papers, Publication 96, Field Columbian Museum, New York 1905.

Waitz, Theodor, *Anthropologie der Naturvölker,* Teil 1 and 2, Friedrich Fleischer, Leipzig 1859.

- *Anthropologie der Naturvölker,* 2. Teil, Friedrich Fleischer, Leipzig 1860. 598 Weicker, Georg, *Der Seelenvogel. In der alten Literatur und Kunst. Eine mythologisch-archaeologische Untersuchung,* B. G. Teubner, Leipzig 1902.

Wells, Roger and Kelly, John W., *English-Eskimo and Eskimo-English Vocabularies,* Government Printing Office, Washington D.C. 1890.

Wesselski, Albert, Versuch einer Theorie des Märchens, Prager Deutsche Studien, No. 45, E. Gierach and H. Cysarz eds. Sudetendeutscher Verlag Franz Kraus, Reichenberg i. B. 1931.

- *Deutsche Märchen vor Grimm,* Rudolf M. Rohrer Verlag, Brünn-Leipzig 1938. Wilhelm, Richard (ed.), *The Chinese Fairy Book,* Frederick A. Stokes Company, New York 1921, Trans. Frederick H. Martens.

- *The Secret of the Golden Flower, a Chinese Book of Life,* Routledge & Kegan Paul, London 1962, trans. from German by Cary F. Baynes.

- *The I Ching or Book of Changes, Princeton University Press, Princeton, NJ 1967, trans. Cary F. Baynes.*

Winthuis, Josef, "Das Zweigeschlechterwesen bei den Zentralaustraliern und anderen Völkern. Lösungsversuch der ethnologischen Hauptprobleme auf Grund primitiven Denkens", Volume 5, *Forschungen zur Völkerpsychologie und Soziologie,* Verlag von C. L. Hirschfeld, Leipzig 1928.

Wolff, Antonia (Toni), "Einführung in die Grundlagen der komplexen Psychologie", in: *Die kulturelle Bedeutung der komplexen Psychologie. Festschrift zum 60. Geburtstag von C. G. Jung,* ed. by Julius Springer, Psychologischer Club Zürich, Berlin 1935, p. 3–168.

Wolfram von Eschenbach, *Parzival,* new edition by Wilhelm Hertz, J. G. Cotta'sche Buchhandlung Nachfolger, Stuttgart and Berlin 1923.

Wünsche, August, *Die Sagen vom Lebensbaum und Lebenswasser. Altorientalische Mythen,* Verlag von Eduard Pfeiffer, Leipzig 1905.

- *Der Sagenkreis vom geprellten Teufel, Akademischer Verlag, Leipzig and Wien 1905.*

Wundt, Wilhelm, Völkerpsychologie. Eine Untersuchung der Entwicklungsgesetze von Sprache, Mythus und Sitte, Wilhelm Engelmann, Leipzig 1910–15.

Zaunert, Paul (ed.), *Deutsche Märchen seit Grimm,* (*MdW*), ed. by Fr. v. d. Leyen, Eugen Diederichs, Jena 1919.

- *Deutsche Märchen aus dem Donaulande,* (*MdW*), ed. by Fr. v. d. Leyen and P. Zaunert, Eugen Diederichs, Jena 1926.

Zihlmann, Josef, *Heilige Bäume und Orte,* Comenius Verlag, Hitzkirch 1985.

Zimmer, Heinrich, *Kunstform und Yoga im indischen Kultbild,* Frankfurter Verlags-Anstalt A.G., Berlin 1926.

– "Yoga und Maya", in: *Corona,* 4. Jahr, 4. no., ed. by Martin Bodmer, Verlag der Corona, Zürich. R. Oldenbourg, München and Berlin 1934.
– "Zur Bedeutung des indischen Tantra-Yoga", in: *Eranos-Jahrbuch 1933: Yoga und Meditation im Osten und im Westen,* ed. by Olga Fröbe-Kapteyn, Rhein-Verlag, Zürich 1934, p. 9–94.
"Indische Mythen als Symbole", in: *Eranos-Jahrbuch 1934: Ostwestliche Symbolik und Seelenführung,* ed. by Olga Fröbe-Kapteyn, Rhein-Verlag, Zürich 1935, p. 97–151.
– *"Maya" der indische Mythos*, Deutsche Verlags-Anstalt, Stuttgart and Berlin 1936.
– *Weisheit Indiens. Märchen und Sinnbilder,* L. C. Wittich Verlag, Darmstadt 1938.
– "Merlin", in: *Corona,* 9. Jahr, no. 2, ed. by Martin Bodmer, Verlag der Corona, Zürich. R. Oldenbourg, München and Berlin 1939, p. 265–279.
– "On the Significance of Indian Tantric Yoga", in: *Spiritual Disciplines: Papers form the Eranos Yearbooks*, Princeton University Press, Princeton NJ 1960, Bollingen XXX-4, pp. 3–58.
– "Death and Rebirth in the Light of India", in: Campbell, Joseph (ed.): *Man and Transformation: Papers from the Eranos Yearbooks*, Volume 5, Pantheon Books, Bollingen Foundation, New York 1964, pp. 326–352.
– "The Indian World Mother", in: – (ed.): *The Mystic Vision: Papers form the Eranos Yearbooks*, Princeton University Press, Princeton NJ 1968, Bollingen XXX-6, pp. 70–102.
– *The King and the Corpse, Tales of the Soul's Conquest of Evil.* Princeton University Press, Princeton NJ 1972.
– "Merlin as wise old man", in: Goodrich, Peter H./Thompson, Raymond H. (eds.): *Merlin: A Casebook*, Routledge, New York 2003, translated by Friedhelm Riuckert, pp. 258–272.

Index of Authors

Index of Fairytales

Subject Index

waters, 19, 24, 36, 41, 50, 73, 91–93, 100, 106, 148, 162, 166–169, 175, 199, 210, 217, 241, 266, 294, 320, 321, 323, 325, 329, 361, 362, 402, 415, 423, 450, 479, 481, 497
waves, 53, 54, 57, 71, 106, 159, 213, 219, 220, 358, 359, 363, 374, 423, 424, 430, 438
Wayland, 196
Wayland the Smith, 195
weather, 21, 33, 57, 185, 243, 302, 366
weaving, 203, 204, 222
web, 130, 193, 204, 319, 468

www.ingramcontent.com/pod-product-compliance
Lightning Source LLC
LaVergne TN
LVHW091514200926
848483LV00008B/462/J